New Perspectives on Cahokia

Views from the Periphery

Contributors

Jeffrey P. Brain
29 Ridgeway
Needham, MA 02192

John Claflin
Diachronic Research Associates
1930 South 4th St.
Springfield, IL 62703

Clark A. Dobbs
The Institute for Minnesota Archaeology
3300 University Ave. S.E., Suite 202
Minneapolis, MN 55414

Fred A. Finney
c/o Office of the State Archaeologist
Univeristy of Iowa
East Lawn Building
Iowa City, IA 52242

Melvin L. Fowler
Department of Anthropology
University of Wisconsin-Milwaukee
Milwaukee, WI 53201

Guy E. Gibbon
Department of Anthropology
215 Ford Hall
University of Minnesota
Minneapolis, MN 55455

Lynne Goldstein
Department of Anthropology
University of Wisconsin-Milwaukee
Milwaukee, WI 53201

Alan D. Harn
Box 185
Rural Route 1
Lewistown, IL 61542

Elden Johnson
Institute for Minnesota Archeology
620 Sullivan Drive
Minneapolis, MN 55421

John E. Kelly
502 Dianne
Columbia, IL 62236

Charles W. Markman
824 North Biltmore Drive
St. Louis, MO 63105

Mark A. McConaughy
Section of Archaeology
State Museum of Pennsylvania
Box 1026
Harrisburg, PA 17108-1026

George R. Milner
Department of Anthropology
409 Carpenter Building
The Pennsylvania State University
University Park, PA 16802

Roland L. Rodell
Mississippi Valley Archaeology Center
1725 State Street
La Crosse, WI 54601

James B. Stoltman
Department of Anthropology
5240 Social Science Building
University of Wisconsin-Madison
Madison, WI 53706

Joseph A. Tiffany
California State Polytechnic University
3801 West Temple Ave.
Pomona, CA 91768-4051

Richard W. Yerkes
Department of Anthropology
The Ohio State University
245 Lord Hall
124 West 17th Avenue
Columbus, OH 43210-1364

New Perspectives on Cahokia

Views from the Periphery

Edited by James B. Stoltman

Monographs in World Archaeology No. 2

 PREHISTORY PRESS

Madison Wisconsin

Copyright © 1991 by the Individual Authors

Prehistory Press
7530 Westward Way
Madison, Wisconsin 53717-2009

James A. Knight, Publisher
Carol J. Bracewell, Managing Editor

ISBN 0-9629110-2-X
ISSN 1055-2316

Library of Congress Cataloging-in-Publication Data

New Perspectives on Cahokia : views from the periphery / edited by
    James B. Stoltman
            p.   cm. - - (Monographs in world archaeology ; no. 2)
    Includes bibliographical references.
    ISBN 0-9629110-2-X (pbk.)
    1. Cahokia Site (East Saint Louis, Ill.) 2. Mississippian
culture--Illinois. 3. Indians of North America--Illinois-
-Antiquities. I. Stoltman, James B., 1935- . II. Series.
E99.M6815N49 1991
977.3'89--dc20   91-62444

Table of Contents

Introduction
James B. Stoltman.. *vii*

Part I: Cahokia and the American Bottom

1. Mound 72 and Early Mississippian at Cahokia
   Melvin L. Fowler 1

2. American Bottom Mississippian Cultures: Internal Developments and External Relations
   George R. Milner 29

3. Specialization in Shell Artifact Production at Cahokia
   Richard W. Yerkes 49

4. The Evidence for Prehistoric Exchange and Its Implications for the Development of Cahokia
   John E. Kelly 65

Part II: Beyond the American Bottom

5. Cahokia from the Southern Periphery
   Jeffrey P. Brain 93

6. The Rench Site Late Late Woodland/Mississippian Farming Hamlet from the Central Illinois River Valley: Food for Thought
   Mark A. McConaughy 101

7. The Eveland Site: Inroad to Spoon River Mississippian Society
   Alan D. Harn...129

8. The Shire Site: Mississippian Outpost in the Central Illinois Prairie
   John Claflin 155

9. Above the American Bottom: The Late Woodland-Mississippian Transition in Northeast Illinois
   Charles W. Markman..177

10. The Implications of Aztalan's Location
   Lynne Goldstein **209**

11. The Fred Edwards Site: A Case of Stirling Phase Culture Contact in
   Southwestern Wisconsin
   Fred A. Finney and James B. Stoltman **229**

12. The Diamond Bluff Site Complex and Cahokia Influence
   in the Red Wing Locality
   Roland L. Rodell **253**

13. The Mississippian Presence in the Red Wing Area, Minnesota
   Guy E. Gibbon and Clark A. Dobbs **281**

14. Cambria and Cahokia's Northwestern Periphery
   Elden Johnson **307**

15. Modeling Mill Creek-Mississippian Interaction
   Joseph A. Tiffany **319**

Part III: Synthesis and Conclusions

   Cahokia as Seen from the Peripheries
   James B. Stoltman **349**

Introduction

James B. Stoltman
University of Wisconsin-Madison

As is well known, the American Bottom region of southern Illinois was the scene of the rise and fall of the largest and most complex polity in all of North America prior to European contact. The focus of this cultural fluorescence was the site of Cahokia, which reached its zenith between ca. A.D. 1000 to A.D. 1200. During this period, the time of the Lohmann, Stirling, and early Moorehead phases in the American Bottom, evidence of Cahokia-inspired cultural interaction can be seen in the archaeological record of the midcontinental United States from Mississippi to upper Michigan and from southern Indiana to South Dakota. The primary objective of this volume is to shed light upon this period of inter-cultural interaction, the most extensive such episode in the Eastern United States since the demise of the Hopewellian Interaction Sphere.

In order to address this issue, a series of scholars who had first-hand knowledge of sites or regions known to have experienced cultural interaction with the Cahokia cultural province, whether directly or indirectly, were requested to write papers. Initially, this "package" of papers was assembled as a full-day symposium that was presented at the Society for American Archaeology meetings in New Orleans on 26 April 1986. Since that time, there has been a protracted gestation period for this volume as various contributors refined, polished, and, in some cases, substantially rewrote their papers. In the interregnum since the symposium, prior commitments and various unpredictable factors prevented some of the original participants from contributing papers to this volume, while a number of additional contributors were added. The net result is a volume that is somewhat different from the SAA symposium, but which still retains the focus and flavor of that symposium. The strong point of the symposium, and of this volume, I believe, is that the contributors generally have not simply reiterated old data and ideas, but have presented, analyzed, and/or synthesized many new data that have not been published before. While there are some notable omissions (e.g. the Collins and Audrey sites and the Apple River region, all in Illinois, and Steed-Kisker in western Missouri), the reader should find this to be a reasonably comprehensive and unusually rich series of papers concerning the major known examples of cultural interaction between the American Bottom region and its neighbors.

The volume is organized into three parts. The first, consisting of Chapters 1 through 4, focuses upon the American Bottom region in general, and upon Cahokia in particular. The goal of this part is to summarize the relevant information about Cahokia and its immediate environs that is especially pertinent to the theme of cultural interaction between the American Bottom and its peripheries. While each of the chapters in Part I is multi-faceted, each has a primary objective of presenting the relevant information concerning one of the processes that has commonly been identified, whether alone or in combination with others, as contributing to the emergence and maintenance of a system of inter-regional interaction like that widely identified with Cahokia.

Thus, a particular concern of Fowler in Chapter 1 is to present the relevant data, mostly from his excavations of Mound 72, that pertain to the issue of social organization and complexity at Cahokia. This topic is important to the theme of the volume because the emergence of hierarchical social organization is widely viewed as a causal factor in the development of prestige goods economies in which high social statuses are validated and maintained by the acquisition, consumption, distribution, and/or redistribution of preciosities, i.e. exotic goods. As is amply demonstrated in Fowler's paper, a markedly hierarchical social organization was well established at Cahokia by the Lohmann phase (i.e. at least by A.D. 1000), an important consideration for any analysis of Cahokia-hinterland cultural interaction.

Chapter 2, by George Milner, summarizes a variety of data derived principally from the FAI-270 project, of which he was a major participant, but its special concern is with the role of population growth and concomitant environmental degradation as possible contributing factors to the rise and fall of Cahokia. If the American Bottom region was subjected to increasing social and environmental stress during the mature stages of Cahokia society, perhaps the widespread appearance of Cahokia influences in the hinterlands could be associated with movements of people forced outward from the American Bottom, i.e. population pressure.

In Chapter 3 Richard Yerkes reviews the evidence for craft specialization, especially of marine shell beads, in the American Bottom. The possibility of the centralized control over production and distribution of crafts like shell (ceramics, salt, and stone hoes are other products often discussed in this context) is especially germane to the theme of this volume. Not only does this bear upon the topic of social complexity, but it also provides a basis for formulating a series of test implications for evaluating the nature of culture contact situations in the hinterlands. For example, if such centralized control existed, it seems reasonable that centrally-controlled resource procurement stations ought to exist in the hinterlands or that products of presumed Cahokia derivation ought to be not just stylistically but also materially identical from widely dispersed sites in the hinterlands.

In the final chapter of Part I, John Kelly meticulously compiles and summarizes the evidence for exotic goods in the American Bottom from the Late Woodland through the Mississippian periods. His main goal is to provide the requisite background for evaluating the relative importance of commodity exchange as a factor contributing to the rise of a complex, hierarchical society at Cahokia. This is especially relevant to the thesis that hierarchical societies sometimes arise in resource-poor regions as a result of the emergence of a "managerial elite" under whose control a widespread exchange network was established.

In all four chapters of Part I it should be explicitly understood that the authors were not asked to defend, nor do any espouse, a mono-causal explanation for the rise or fall of Cahokia. Each was asked to emphasize one process—hierarchical social organization, population pressure, craft specialization, and exchange—not because any of these alone adequately explains the nature of Cahokia, but because all of these considerations combined provide an especially rich context within which to evaluate the nature of cultural interaction between Cahokia and its peripheries.

Part II of this volume is comprised of eleven chapters, each of which can be considered a "case study" of a site or region that appears to have experienced culture contact with Cahokia, either directly or indirectly. In all of these instances, the primary, though not necessarily sole, evidence for cultural contact with the Cahokia cultural province is the presence of Powell Plain and/or Ramey Incised pottery types in contexts well beyond the American Bottom. On the basis of both visual stylistic inspection and preliminary comparative petrographic analyses, it is apparent that Powell Plain and Ramey Incised ceramic types occur in the hinterlands of Cahokia both as trade vessels and as indigenous imitations. Thus, the mere identification of these types in hinterland contexts does not adequately account for their presence, but, rather, raises a number of issues in need of further investigation.

In order to investigate more effectively the nature of cultural interaction between a hinterland site and the Cahokia cultural province, much more information is needed than a mere assertion of the presence of the Cahokia marker types. We need also to know the relative proportions of the various ceramic types in the local assemblages, as well as other features of the total cultural inventories that could be intrusive as opposed to local, not to mention the nature of the indigenous cultural complexes present immediately prior to the appearance of Cahokia contact. In other words each author was encouraged to consider the total cultural context immediately before and during the time of Cahokia contact in order to facilitate the construction of the fullest possible picture of the overall pattern of cultural interaction that occurred between the American Bottom and its peripheries. An additional point was stressed, to which a number of authors responded. Namely, since cultural interaction is inherently a two-way phenomenon, it could be anticipated that archaeological evidence existed *in the hinterlands* suggesting the production of local commodities for exchange within the Cahokia cultural sphere. It was hoped that explicit consideration of this dimension would significantly enhance our understanding of the overall exchange system that almost certainly centered ultimately upon the Cahokia site during the period A.D. 1000 to A.D. 1200. Ultimately, then, a primary goal of the case studies in Part II was collectively to shed new light on the network of exchange that connected Cahokia to its peripheries under the supposition that this information would in turn shed important new light on the overall character of the Cahokia polity.

Part III constitutes an attempt by the editor to synthesize the highlights of the combined papers and to refocus them upon the main theme of the volume, namely, what can be inferred of the nature of Cahokia through observing the effects of its interaction with its peripheries.

PART I

Cahokia and the American Bottom

1

Mound 72 and Early Mississippian at Cahokia

Melvin L. Fowler
Department of Anthropology
University of Wisconsin-Milwaukee

The Cahokia site (Figure 1.1) is not only the largest precolumbian site within the confines of the United States but is often considered to be the source of many developments in the late prehistoric period in the East. This symposium is organized to discuss, among other things, the extent and nature of the Cahokian interaction.

The discoverer of the Cahokia site, Henry Marie Brackenridge, held the same opinion of the site as recent investigators. As representative of its ancient greatness he compared its population to that of the city of Philadelphia in the early 19th century (ca. 50,000). He had the following to say about the area when he first saw it in 1811:

> As the sward was burnt, the earth was perfectly naked, and I could trace with ease any unevenness of surface, so as to discover whether it was artificial or accidental. I everywhere observed a great number of elevations of earth, to the height of a few feet, at regular distances from each other, and which appeared to observe some order; near them I also observed pieces of flint, and fragments of earthen vessels. I concluded that a very populous town had once existed here. . . . The mounds were the sites of temples, or monuments to the great men. It is evident, this could not have been the work of thinly scattered tribes (Brackenridge 1814:188. Emphasis added).

Few, if any, now question Brackenridge's assessment of the size and significance of Cahokia. The questions of the origins of this great site, its complexity of organization, and the nature of its interaction with other societies are being dealt with in contemporary research. The origins, or even the evolution of Cahokia as a unique community are not the concerns of the present report. The complexity of social organization and Cahokia's interaction with other communities are. The former has sometimes been assumed while the latter has been dealt with largely through distributional studies of artifact types, particularly ceramics.

For example, one idea about the origin of the Oneota Tradition has been that Oneota is a outgrowth of Cahokia Mississippian influence to the north (Griffin 1960). Many Oneota motifs, it has been argued, are derived from those on Ramey Incised pottery. This ceramic type is associated with the period at Cahokia dating after 1050 A.D. currently referred to as the Stirling phase. In fact most models of Cahokia interaction focus on Ramey ceramics. Furthermore, many of us over the years have considered Ramey Incised and the Stirling phase as representing the era when Cahokia became fully developed and went through its "Classic" period.

Robert Hall has summarized both the nature of Cahokia's community complexity and its interactions with other areas as follows:

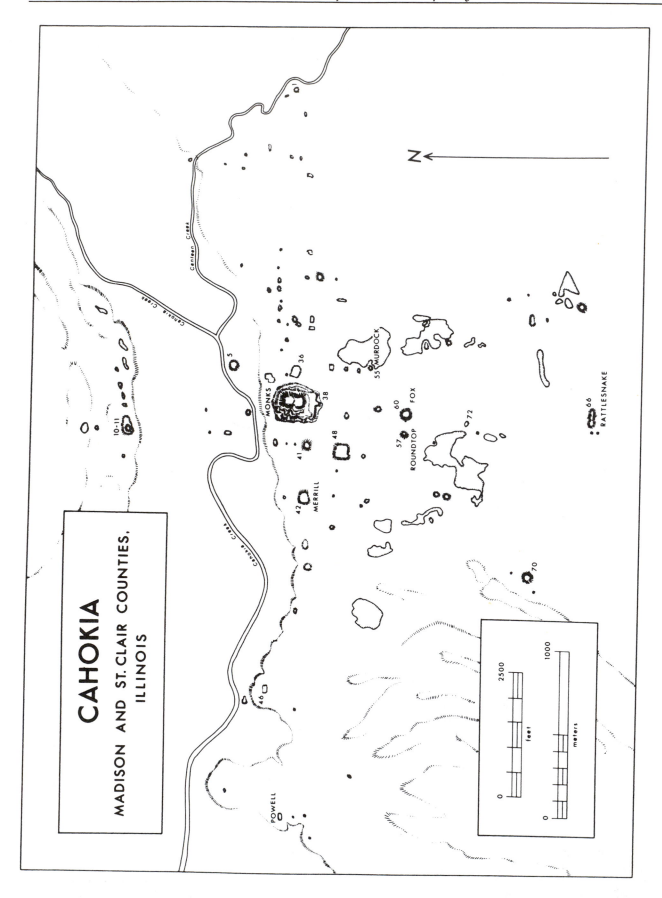

Figure 1.1. A map of the Cahokia site showing locations of mounds. Major mounds such as Monks Mound (38) and Mound 72 are identified by number. Source: Michelle Patin.

. . .[F]rom sometime after A.D. 900 until around A.D. 1300 . . . Cahokia was the seat of the largest political chiefdom and probably the most complex ranked society in North America, a city state in the process of formation. . . . Cahokia is seen as having had several changing faces, each reflecting an episode of interaction with other cultures. The first of these which may be called Mississippian [Emergent and Early Mississippian before 1050 A.D.?] saw interaction to the south and in particular the lower alluvial Mississippi Valley. This was followed by the period of the Cahokia Interaction [Stirling-Moorehead Phases after 1050 A.D.], which saw the development of the distinctive Cahokia Mississippian tradition and the spread of its influence through a broad area to the north and west of Cahokia (Hall n.d.:90-91, brackets added).

In the following pages I will present data on the social complexity of Early Mississippian Cahokia based upon the excavation of Mound 72. This will be followed by an assessment of the implications of this for an examination of the nature and extent of Cahokian interaction.

Mound 72

Mound 72 (Fowler 1969, 1974, 1975) is, in terms of most mounds at Cahokia, a *small* ridged-top mound in the south central portion of the site (about 860 meters south of Monks Mound). It is unique in that the ridged top of the final mound stage is oriented on an azimuth of 120 degrees if viewed from the NW to the SE, or, at about the angle of the winter solstice sunrise—if the observer is at the southeast, the azimuth would be about 300 degrees or the summer solstice sunset (Figure 1.2).

Observations of its relationships to other mounds lead us to believe that Mound 72 was a "marker" mound (Fowler 1969:19-26). We predicted that there would have been a post at the southeast end of the

mound on a north-south community center line. At the spot predicted we found a deep post pit (Figure 1.3, F1) now labeled Post Pit (PP) 1 (Fowler 1969: Fig. 15). Remnants of the post were long since gone, but cribbing logs were still in place.

A primary mound, 72Sub1, was directly associated with PP1 (Figure 1.3). In fact the post pit had been dug and the post in it replaced at least three times during the use of 72Sub1. In this mound and directly associated with PP1 was a status burial on a platform of shell beads (Figures 1.3 and 1.7). Associated with this burial were retainers with rich grave offerings of hundreds of projectile points, shell beads, a copper tube, chunky stones and other exotic items.

There is evidence of one other post pit under Mound 72 (Figure 1.3, F 204). This post was extracted and the pit modified for a group of burials. A mound, 72Sub2, was built over this feature. The northwest post pit (PP2) was also associated with a wall trench structure and a small midden area (the North Midden, Feature 206) containing potsherds, animal bones and some flint debris. A C-14 assay of material from the North Midden was 935 RCYAD, statistically the same date as the PP1 assay average of 955 RCYAD (see Table 1.1).

Woodhenges and Sun Circles

The orientation of Mound 72 and the spacing of the post pits in the mound are of particular interest in terms of discoveries made at Cahokia prior to our digging into Mound 72.

In the early 1960s extensive excavations had been conducted in portions of the Cahokia site because of the proposed construction of interstate highways in the area (Fowler, ed. 1962, 1963, 1969). One of the localities is Tract 15A about 1000 meters west of Monks Mound. Among the archaeological features discovered in Tract 15A were large pits, referred to as "bath tubs" because of their shape, where large posts had been placed in the ground. A similar pit with the bottom portion of a large post in it was found at the center of the Mitchell site (Porter 1969: Figs. 59 and 60; 1974). The Mitchell site find clarified the function of the "bathtubs" by demonstrating that they were post

Table 1.1 Uncalibrated Radiocarbon Assays from Mound 72, Cahokia Mounds Historic Site.

Feature No.	Feature Type	Radiocarbon Yrs.	Years A.D.	Range Yrs. A.D.	Lab No.
1	Post Pit	970 ± 50	980	930-1020	W293
1	Post Pit	1020 ± 55	930	875-980	W298
206	North Midden	1015 ± 60	935	875-995	W447
227	Central Midden	900 ± 45	1050	1005-1095	W492
229	Litter Burial	920 ± 60	1030	970-1090	W575
	Averages	965 ± 54	985	931-1019	

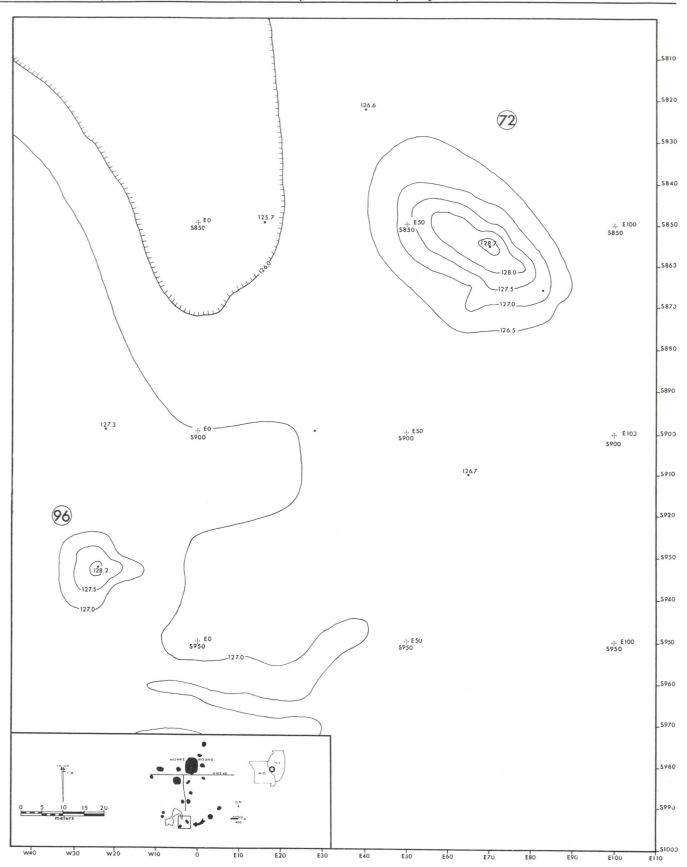

Figure 1.2. Contour map of the Mound 72 area of the Cahokia Mounds historic site based upon the 1966 UWM map and a 1979 resurvey of the area. North on this map and all maps in this report is Grid North which is 1°18′ east of true north.

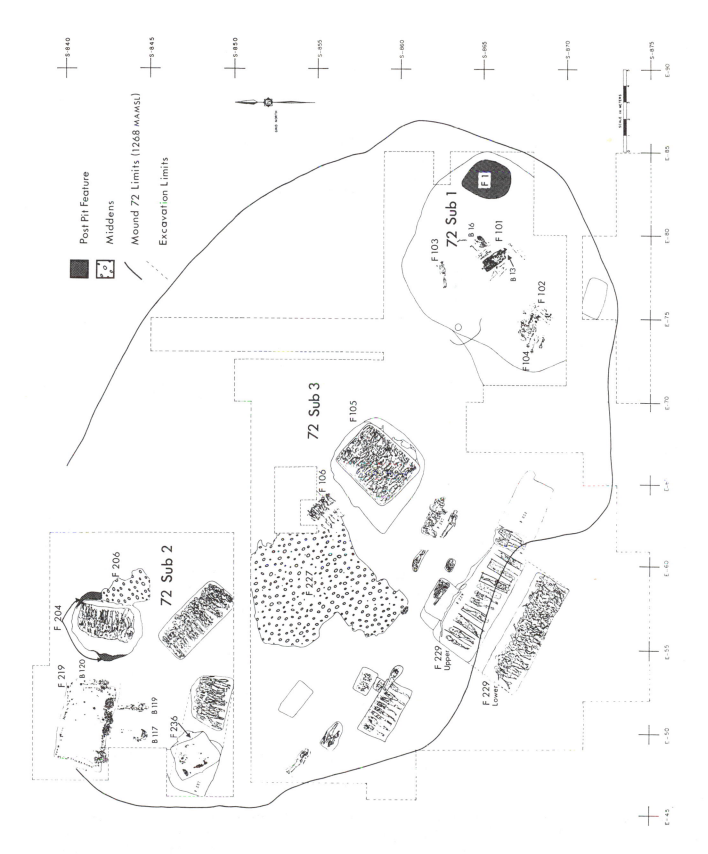

Figure 1.3. Map showing the extent of excavation in Mound 72 and the distribution of the burials and other features.

pits for the installation of marker monuments at important spots in the community.

Warren Wittry plotted the distribution of the post pits at Tract 15A and discovered that they were in arcs or portions of circles. He proposed that at least five of these arcs were present and that they probably had been portions of complete circles (Wittry 1964, 1969). A hypothesis proposed by Wittry was that some of the posts were aligned at angles from the center of the circle where it might be expected to observe the sunrise at the solstices and equinoxes (Wittry 1969: Fig. 26). Because of this, he applied the name Woodhenge to these circles.

For example, one of the poles is aligned to summer solstice sunrise at an azimuth of about 60°. This angle only approximates the solstice sunrise point. Detailed calculations, considering the angle of the ecliptic and the latitude, come out to an azimuth of 59.3° or an angle of 30.7° north of equinox. Taking into consideration parallax, refraction due to atmospheric conditions, and the altitude of the horizon, 30° north of east (Azimuth 60°) is about the maximum angle at which one could expect to observe the sunrise on the horizon at summer solstice.

Woodhenge 2, the most completely explored of the arcs of posts, was dated as having been constructed about 1000 A.D. or probably in the Early Mississippian Period. It was 125 m (410 ft) in diameter. The posts placed in the ground were about 60 cm. (2 ft) in diameter and were set in the ground 1.2 m (4 ft). Although the complete extent of Woodhenge 2 has not been confirmed by excavation, there were probably 48 posts in the circle with a radial displacement between posts of 7.5°.

A previously unrecorded mound, now numbered 96, is located about 125 m southwest of Mound 72 (Figures 1.2 and 1.4). It is very low, about 1.5 m high, and apparently was T-shaped with the stem pointing due east. The distance between PP1 and the highest point of Mound 96 is 126.7 m (415 ft). This line is at an azimuth of 59.2° or 30.8° north of east—very near the calculated summer solstice sunrise angle!

A point exactly halfway between Mound 96 and PP1 is the center of a circle which passes through PP1, PP2, and Mound 96 (Figure 1.4). In other words all of these points are on a circle with a radius of 63.3 meters. On this circle PP1 is at the summer solstice sunrise (SSR) angle and mound 96 is at the winter solstice sunset (WSS) position. The radial displacement between PP1 and PP2 is slightly more than 15° or twice the radial displacement of 7.5° proposed by Wittry for posts in Woodhenge 2. Thus circa 1000 A.D., in the Mound 72 area of the Cahokia site, there was a woodhenge nearly identical to Woodhenge 2 in radius and positioning of posts.

No investigations have been carried out near the center point, but if Woodhenge 72 is similar to Woodhenge 2 there is in all probability another post pit in this area. In Woodhenge 2 the observation post was about 1.5 m (5 ft) east of the geometric center of the circle.

In effect, then, I have proposed two hypotheses about PP 1: (a) it was a marker post for a north-south center line of the Cahokia Community and (b) it was a marker post for the summer solstice sunrise position on Woodhenge 72 (Figures 1.4 and 1.5). I do not have any problems with PP 1 being *both* a solstice post and a centerline marker for Cahokia. One can assume that the solstice position would be a very important locus in a woodhenge which might make it more important as a marker post for other purposes than, for example, a central or observation post. By a line of sight along the WSS and SSR positions a true north-south line would have been established. This is precisely the same center line previously proposed.

I am also proposing two functions for woodhenges. They may have served not only as solar calendrical observatories but also as "surveyor's" instruments or aligners. Sherrod and Rolingson (1987) have recently published a study of late period archaeological sites in the lower Mississippi valley area. They started their project as an examination of astronomical orientations of the Toltec site mounds but soon expanded to the study of the layout of the sites and engineering ideas utilized by Mississippian peoples. Their study includes a detailed examination of the Cahokia site.

One of the most controversial of Sherrod and Rolingson's proposals is that, downplaying the role of Woodhenges as astronomical observatories, the Woodhenges were in-the-ground alidades or surveying instruments. They refer to this as the Cahokia Aligner. The Cahokia Aligner was used in determining the placement of critical features in the site both in angular alignments from the observation points (woodhenges) and in distance measurements. Sherrod and Rolingson propose that Woodhenge 2 was only one of the aligners. They suggest another east of Mound 27 as well as one in the general location of the proposed Woodhenge 72.

Woodhenges as Public Monuments

Woodhenges have often been referred to as observatories. There is little doubt that they could have been used to observe the passage of the sun throughout the year. In effect they could have served as mnemonic calendars keeping track of the passage of the solar year. The posts which would have been most important for this purpose would be the three on the east marking the extreme points where the sun could

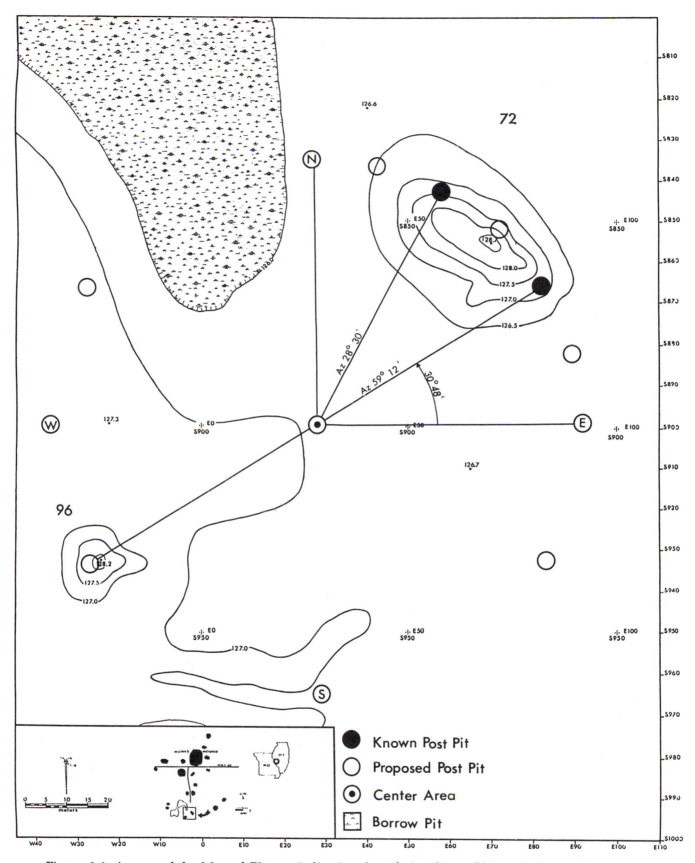

Figure 1.4. A map of the Mound 72 area indicating the relationships of Mounds 72 and 96, the known post pits and proposing the location of other features.

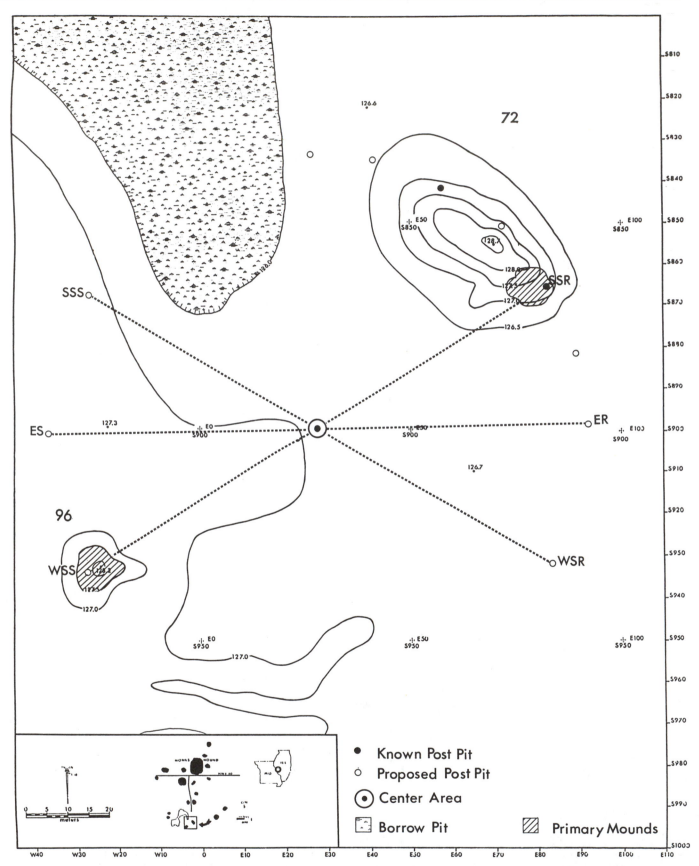

Figure 1.5. Woodhenge 72. The locations of PP1, PP2,Mound 96 and other features of proposed woodhenge are shown. SSR: Summer Solstice Sunrise, ER: Equinox Sunrise, WSR: Winter Solstice Sunrise, WSS: Winter Solstice Sunset, ES: Equinox Sunset, SSS: Summer Solstice Sunset.

have been observed on the horizon from the shortest day of the year, approximately December 21, to the longest day of the year, about June 21. The post on the east would mark the days of the year, March 21 and September 21, of equal hours of daylight and dark. Similar posts to the west would have marked sunset directions.

The time from the appearance of the sunrise over the winter solstice location, for example, until its return to the same location 365 days later could calibrate the passage of one year. The observation of sunrise over other posts could have been used to signal propitious times for seasonal activities such as planting around the time of the spring equinox and harvest after the autumnal equinox.

If these woodhenges were simply solar observatories, then only the east and west solstitial and equinoctial posts would have been necessary. Yet Wittry proposes on good grounds that Woodhenge 2 had 48 posts. Based upon the virtual identity in size and spacing of posts between Woodhenge 2 and the proposed Woodhenge 72, it is probable that the latter also had 48 posts.

Many cultures divide the world into four quadrants based upon the cardinal points. This appears to have been symbolized by Mississippian peoples, as with many other cultures of the Americas, by a circle, or concentric circles, with a cross in the center. This circle and cross motif probably can be considered as calendric as well.

Such a symbol was found on a ceramic vessel recovered from a pit near the winter solstice sunrise post pit of Woodhenge 2 (Figure 1.6). While it is of a vessel form generally considered to be later than the Early Mississippian date suggested for Woodhenge 2, the sun circle inscribed on its surface and its context indicate that it must have been a commemorative offering, dedicated to the WSR position.

The woodhenges are but the circle and cross implanted in the ground as an architectural manifestation of the world view as well as an observatory of the annual solar pilgrimage. Although east, west, and solstice positions are the only "necessary" positions, a complete circle would represent the fullness of the annual cycle and the completeness of the world view.

It does not seem probable that these circles were just places where "scientific" observations were made of astronomical phenomena, but also were architectural codifications of hundreds, if not thousands, of years of practical observations. The points on the horizon where the sun would rise on solstices and equinoxes must have been well known. The many generations of observing these phenomena had made this knowledge very precise. By early Mississippian times these observations had been standardized and

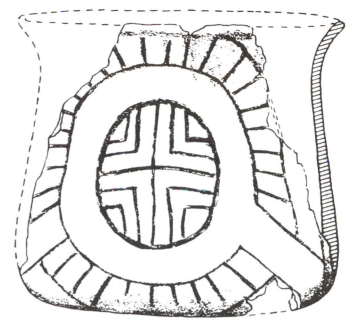

Figure 1.6. Beaker found in offertory pit near Winter Solstice Sunrise position of Woodhenge 2. This vessel is approximately 14 cm in diameter at the orifice. Adapted from Vogel 1975 Figure 68 i.

became part of the religious and practical knowledge of the society. This knowledge is represented in Early Mississippian culture by woodhenges. They must be considered as forms of monumental public architecture incorporating within their form and monumentality many social and sacred values. As such they would have been locations of extreme importance in the communities.

The importance of calendrically related public monuments, the rituals conducted in them, and their interrelationship to the community and social hierarchy is indicated by ceremonies observed by the among the Natchez:

> The sun is the principal object of veneration to [the Natchez]. . . . It is for [this] reason that the great chief of this nation. . . takes the title of brother of the Sun. . . . To enable. . . [the Chief and the Sun] to better converse together they raise a mound of artificial soil on which they build his cabin ....The door fronts east, and every morning the great chief honors by his presence the rising of his elder brother, and salutes him with many howlings *as soon as he appears above the horizon*. Then he orders that they shall light his calumet; he makes him an offering of the first three puffs he draws; afterwards raising his hand above his head and turning from the east to the west, *he shows* [the

Sun] *the direction he must take in his course* (LePetit as quoted in Swanton 1911:174. Emphasis and brackets added).

Burials and Submounds

We uncovered more in Mound 72 than post pits and woodhenges. Included in these discoveries were more than 260 individuals buried in a minimum of three primary or sub-mounds as well as in the final mound stage (see Figure 1.3). Associated with these burials, either directly or in commemorative pits, were pottery vessels, hundreds of projectile points, shell beads, copper and bone artifacts, chunky stones, and some burials which were also commemorative offerings.

One of the primary mounds, 72Sub1, was built over the position of PP1 or the solstice post (Figure 1.3). The preserved portions of 72Sub1 indicate that it was a low, flat-topped, square mound with a small platform extension on the center of the west side. The large post in PP 1 was at the center of the east end of this mound. There were at least three different posts put in this same locality, one before 72Sub1 was built and two afterwards. The pit discovered in our excavations was actually the extraction pit for the removal of the second post and the insertion of the third. There is a small platform on the east end of 72Sub1 which is probably the result of the post installation and replacement activity.

The form of 72Sub1 is similar to Mound 96 both in shape and dimension. Mound 96, however, was never buried by later mound construction and "...the gnawing tooth of time..." (Snyder 1911:301) has blurred its contours. Originally it must have appeared similar to 72Sub1. The major difference between these two T-shaped mounds is that Mound 96 faces with the stem of the T due east and 72Sub1 due west.

The central personage in 72Sub1, often referred to as the Beaded Burial, was placed about 5 m due west of PP 1 on a platform of shell beads (Figure 1.3, B 13 and Figure 1.7). This individual was oriented with his feet to the NW, not toward either PP 1 or 2 but to an intermediate position. Directly associated with the Beaded Burial were the remains of at least four other individuals (Figure 1.3, F 101).

To the SW of the central figure was another burial group (Figure 1.3, F 102). These individuals were put in place with a quantity of grave goods (see discussion of artifacts below). None of these burials or the central burials was in a pit, but they were laid out on the surface of the ground, or on a low platform, before the mound was built. The SW burials of 72Sub1 appear to be "retainers," or offerings along with their grave goods, to the central Beaded Burial. These grave offer-

ings were obviously sumptuary and suggest a particularly high status for the central figure.

At the opposite end of Mound 72 was another important burial. This was an extended burial placed over the traces of a charnel house, Feature 219 (Figure 1.3, B119). Associated with this individual were other primary burials and a large number of bundles. Three large dedicatory pits, which included both burials and artifact offerings, were placed around this area and covered over with primary mound 72Sub2 (Figure 1.3).

A third primary mound, 72Sub3, was built midway between PP1 and PP2. This was in the geometric center of the total mound. Its peak is apparent in the contours of the final Mound 72 as the highest point mapped. This mound was built over an offertory burial pit containing over 50 young women between the ages of 18-25 (Figure 1.3, F105 and Figure 1.8). Nearby were four males whose heads and hands had been removed and presumably stored or buried elsewhere (Figure 1.3, F106 and Figure 1.9). Clearly all of these individuals were sacrifices dedicated to the overall significance of Mound 72.

A post between Post pits 1 and 2 in Woodhenge 72 would have indicated precisely the alignment of the female burial pit and the peak of 72Sub3 observed from the central area of Woodhenge 72. This post would also have been at 7.5° radial displacement north of PP1, or the same spacing found in Woodhenge 2 (Figures 1.4 and 1.7). No excavations were carried out to the subsoil at the proposed location so that the presence of this postpit remains to be confirmed.

The burials in Mound 72 indicate that an elaborate social hierarchy had developed at Cahokia. Of importance to consideration of the nature of the status differentiations represented by Mound 72 is the fact that the major burials are near the large post pits. Another factor is that the major individuals in both sub-mounds 1 and 2 have indications of strong ties to areas far from Cahokia.

Sequence of Construction, Planning, and Engineering

There was a sequence to the buildup of Mound 72. The first features in place were the post pits. The next phase was the construction of two primary mounds, one over each of the post locations. The next stage was the construction of several modifications and extensions of 72Sub2 in the direction of 72Sub1. This culminated in mound 72Sub3 over the headless males and the female burial pit.

The final stage of Mound 72 was building and shaping the ridge-topped mound. The final mound was essentially ridge-shaped with a peak in the center

Figure 1.7. The central burial from 72Sub1 (see Figure 1.3, B 13). The arrow points to grid north. The strings are on the grid lines at 50 cm intervals.

Figure 1.8. The Female burial pit in the center of primary mound 72Sub3 (see Figure 1.3, F105). The grid lines are at 50 cm intervals. Grid north is to the upper left and is indicated by the grid line running diagonally from upper left to lower right of the burial pit.

Figure 1.9. The decapitated and handless male burials from primary mound 72Sub3 (see Figure 1.3, F106).

—the top of 72Sub3. By this time the solstice post in PP1, toward which all of the earlier sub-mounds and burials had been focussed, had been removed and the overall mound was oriented to the solstice angle.

Along the southwest margins of the final mound were a series of rectangular pits with burials in them. The most elaborate of these was a large pit with two layers of burials. The lower layer was a jumble of many individuals (Figure 1.3, F229 and Figure 1.10). Over these were ten individuals who had been transported to their final resting place on litters (Figure 1.11). The poles of these stretchers were made of cedar that were still preserved. A radiocarbon assay from one of these poles dated to approximately 1030 RCYAD or about 100 years after the age estimates for PP1 (see Table 1.1). Assays from the central midden (Feature 227) of ca. 1050 RCYAD and the litter burials are essentially the same age. These are the last features placed under the mound as it was being shaped into its final ridge-top and they probably date no later than 1050 A.D.

Final pits were dug into the mound and late period burials were placed in them. The data are not clear on this but some of the burials just mentioned may have been included in the fill during the construction of the last stage of Mound 72. No diagnostic artifacts nor organic materials were found with these late burials, so their dating is unknown. They must have been after 1050 A.D. at a minimum. They undoubtedly signify the continuing importance of Mound 72 and can be considered as late dedicatory offerings.

There is evidence of careful planning of this whole sequence. Woodhenge 72 may well have served as a Sun Calendar, but it also was a surveying instrument, or Aligner, for Mound 72. Specifically, this involved the layout of the burial precinct between PP 1, the SSR post, and PP 2. The burials, and indeed the final extent of the mound, are largely restricted to the space between these two posts. The three sub-mounds were built over post positions in Woodhenge 72. These sub-mounds and the burials within them were dedicated to the posts within Woodhenge 72 which they covered.

Non-Ceramic Artifacts

Ceramics, chipped stone artifacts, and debris were recovered from the midden areas and mound fill contexts. More exotic artifacts were recovered with the burials and as offering caches (Figure 1.12). With one group of offering burials in 72Sub1 were some astonishing grave goods. Several large chunkey stones were found piled together (Figures 1.12 and 1.13). These were well-made discoids with concave sides. Nearby was a large pile of mica (Figure 1.12). This had not been formed into artifacts and must have been buried

as a cache of raw material. In this same group of offerings was a rolled sheet of copper about a meter in length and 3 cm in diameter (Figures 1.12 and 1.14). Associated with this copper were strings of shell beads. These were very large, some 3 cm in diameter. The shell beads were in rows along the side of the copper cylinder (Figure 1.12).

There were large numbers of projectile points found both in the retainer burials in 72Sub1 (Figures 1.12 and 1.15) and in an offertory pit dug into 72Sub2 (Figure 1.3, F 236). In 72Sub1 they appear to have been in groups of hafted points, while in 72Sub2 they must have been unhafted and in a bag placed in the offering pit. There are several significant characteristics of these projectile points. One is the general high quality of the workmanship on all of them. There is no evidence that they were ever used. Another characteristic is that, especially in 72Sub1, they were neatly sorted into distinct groupings. It is probable that they represent materials from different regions brought to Cahokia specifically for use in the burial program.

There is one group of points that in both material and form can be traced to northeast Oklahoma. Another small group was made of Hixton silicified sediment from Wisconsin. Others appear to be of heat-treated Kaolin flint from southern Illinois. A large number were made of Crescent quarry chert (the regional source) and are primarily the typical Cahokia tri-notched triangular form.

Although significant because of their exotic qualities, these are not typical day to day living artifacts. The real importance of the Mound 72 artifacts is in their indications of the far flung interaction of the Early Mississippian Cahokians. In the caches and burial offerings are representations of both the extent of the economic interactions of Cahokia and the status of the individuals buried with these grave goods.

Ceramics

Within Mound 72, there are at least three contexts from which ceramics were recovered (Appendix 1.1). One context is the middens below the mound (Figure 1.3, F206 and F227). These middens seem to have been related to the mound building activities. Some burial pits were dug through the earlier portions of the middens and mixed materials from the two midden areas.

The ceramics from the midden areas show a variety of vessel forms and tempering materials including shell and grog (Figures 1.16 and 1.17). First, Feature 227, the central or south midden, has the widest variety of vessel forms. This includes bowls, seed jars, jars, and bottles (Figure 1.16). The other midden, Feature 206, contained only bowl forms (Figure 1.17 c-h). Sherds of a crock-like vessel and a stump ware vessel (Figure 1.17 g and h) were found in both middens,

Figure 1.10. The lower level of burials in Feature 229 viewed from the southeast. The arrow indicates grid north and is divided into 10 cm units.

probably as a result of the disturbance of this area by the digging of more recent burial or offering pits. Feature 206 was directly associated with PP2, and the limited range of vessel forms may indicate that these vessels were offerings dedicated to this post; whereas, the wider range of vessel forms and sizes from Feature 227 suggest a more general usage.

A second context for ceramics was associated with burial activities. These were of two types—pots placed with individuals and those placed in separate offertory pits. The pots placed with individuals came primarily from Feature 219, the charnel house in 72Sub2 (Figure 1.17). One grog tempered vessel (Figure 1.17 m) was very thin-walled and badly broken. However,

Figure 1.11. The upper level or Litter Burials in Feature 229 viewed from the southeast. The arrow indicates grid north and is divided into 10 cm units.

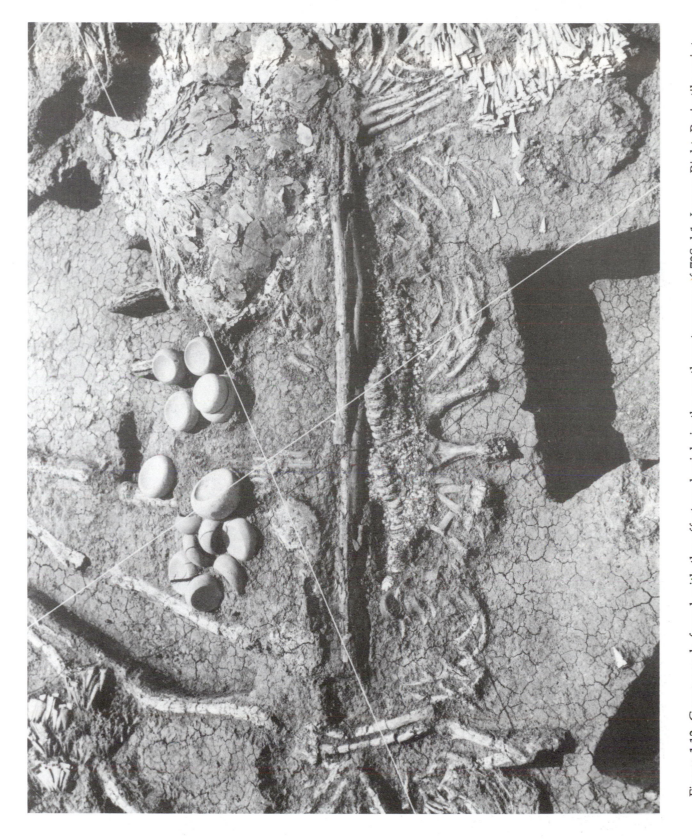

Figure 1.12. Grave goods found with the offertory burials in the southwest corner of 72Sub1. Lower Right: Projectile point cache. Upper Right: Mica pile. Center: Roll of sheet copper and large conch shell beads. Upper Center: Chunkey Stones.

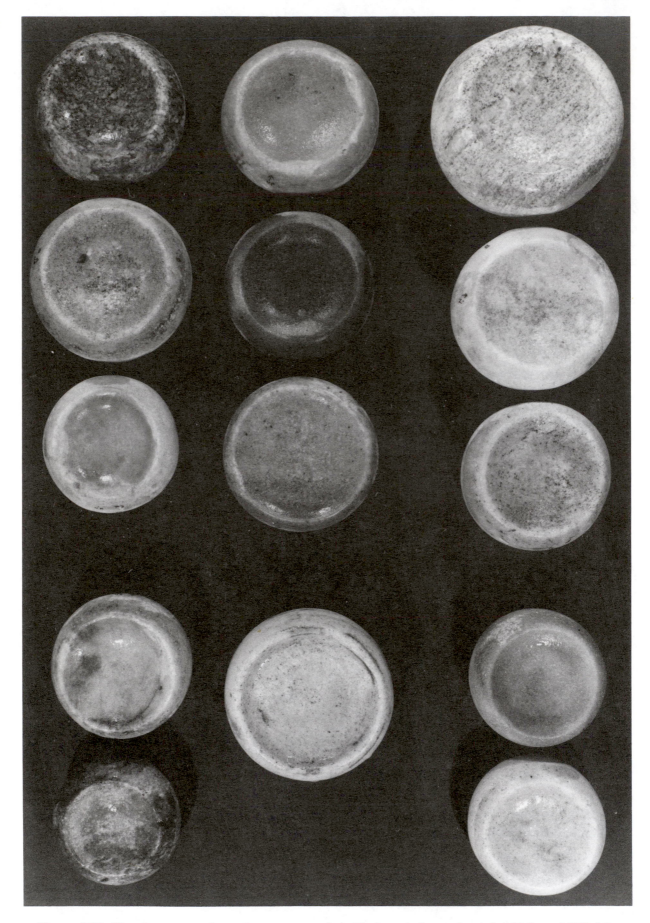

Figure 1.13. Chunkey stones from the grave goods with the southwest burials of Mound 72Sub1. Scale: diameter of upper right stone = 10 cm.

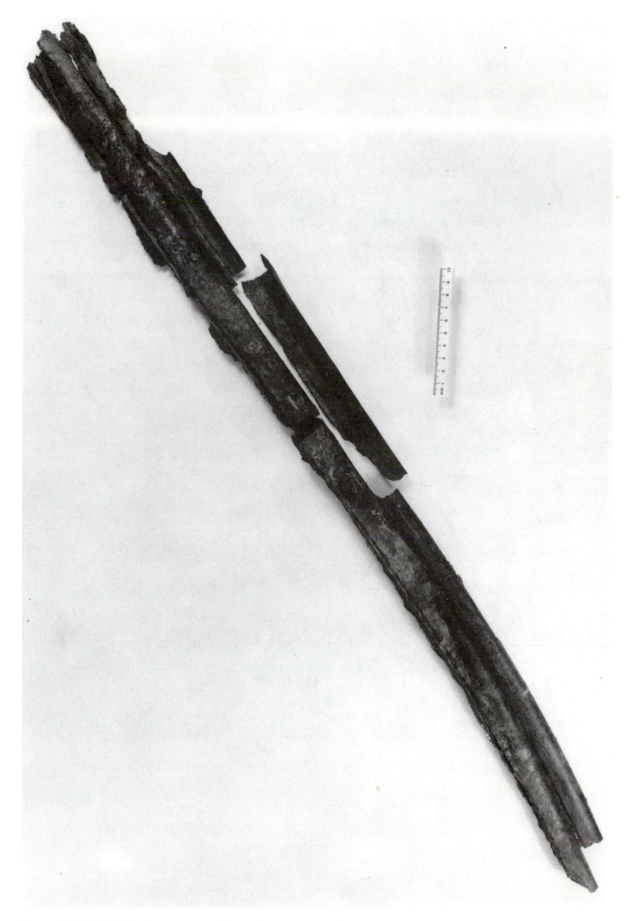

Figure 1.14. Rolled sheet copper from the grave goods associated with the southwest burials in Mound 72Sub1. Scale is 10 cm.

Figure 1.15. Projectile point cache from 72Sub1. This was associated with a separate burial from the artifacts shown in Figure 1.12. Lower Center: Black stemmed points from the Caddo area. Upper Center: Stemmed points of Lower Mississippi Valley origin. Center: Serrated triangular points made of Illinois Kaolin chert. The string at the right is the E75 N-S grid line.

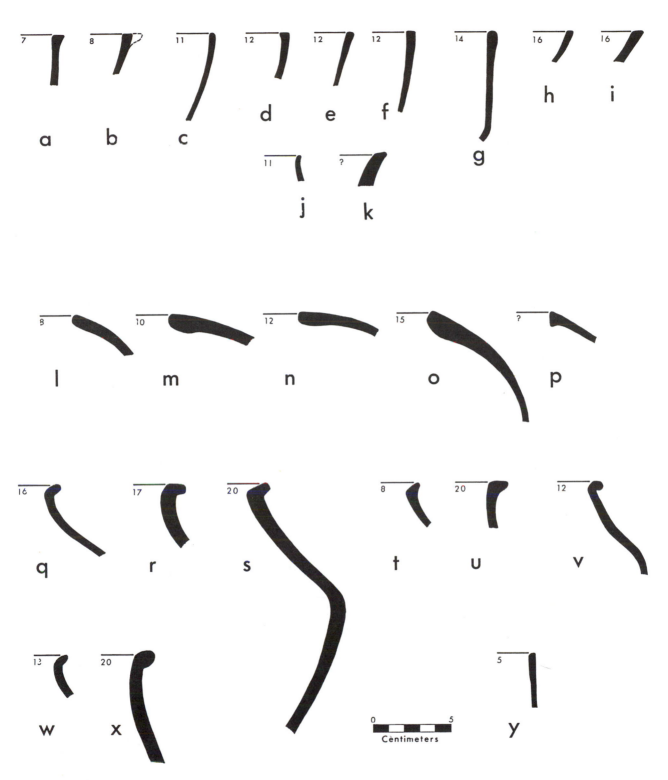

Figure 1.16. Rim profiles of ceramics from the central midden, Feature 227, under Mound 72. The numbers under the lines to the left of the profiles indicate the orifice diameter in centimeters. Bowls: a through k; Seed jars: l through p; Jars: q through x; Bottle: y. Following is correlation of the rim profiles with the catalog numbers listed in Appendix 1.1. a. 70 66 11; b. 70 69 5; c. 70 63 42; d. 70 66 8; e. 70 63 107; f. 70 87 54; g. 70 58 19; h. 70 59 5; i. 70 85 9; j. 70 83 2; k. 70 23 9; l. 68 1414 1; m. 70 58 14; n. 70 62 19; o. 70 65 16; p. 70 63 41; q. 70 69 12; r. 70 64 12; s. 70 62 12; t. 70 61 3; u. 70 162 1; v. 70 303 1; w. 70 158 1; x. 70 158 2; y. 70 63 101.

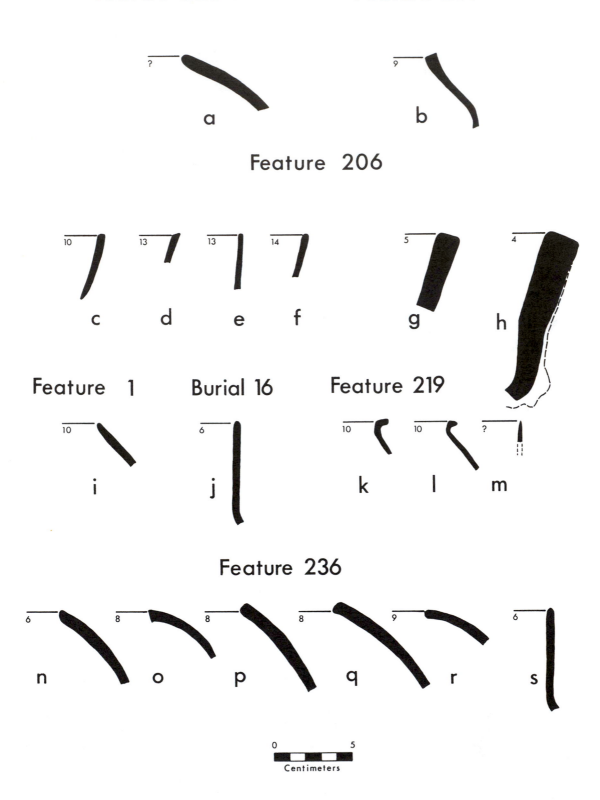

Feature 228   Feature 230

a   b

Feature 206

c   d   e   f   g   h

Feature 1   Burial 16   Feature 219

i   j   k   l   m

Feature 236

n   o   p   q   r   s

0   5
Centimeters

Figure 1.17. Rim profiles of pottery from dedicatory features and status burials in Mound 72. The numbers under the lines to the left of the profiles indicate orifice diameter in centimeters. Following is correlation of the rim profiles with the catalog numbers listed in Appendix 1.1. a. 70 41 4; b.70 70 1; c. 69 997 1; d. 69 980 2; e. 69 922 1; f. 69 767 1; g. 69 881 0 (Fea. 206) and 70 87 62 (Fea` 227); h. 69 997 206 (Fea. 206) and 70 60 227 (Fea 227); i. 67 1602 6; j. 67 1770 2; k. 70 232 0; l. 70 242 0; m. 70 244 0; n. 70 92 2; o. 70 98 2; p. 70 98 5; q. 70 98 2; r. 70 98 2; s. 70 98 2.

the incised decoration on it of parallel lines and its form are indicative of a Lower Mississippi Valley association. Also associated with the charnel house burials were two Powell Plain jars (Figure 1.17k and l). They are very uniform in dimension. The exteriors have the classic polished black slip. These are typical of the Powell Plain found in the burial contexts as opposed to those in the midden, which have thicker walls and are less carefully slipped and polished.

Associated with a burial near the primary burial in 72Sub1 was a polished, black-slipped water bottle nearly identical to the one found in Feature 236 (Figure 1.17s). This also had the yellow sandwich cross-section and was very thin-walled.

Several vessels (Figure 1.17n-s) were found in the offering pit in 72Sub2 (Figure 1.3 F236). Of these vessels two were plain-rim seed jars, three were punctated-rim seed jars, and one was a water bottle identical to the one just described.

A fragment of a red-slipped, plain-rimmed seed jar found in the bottom of the post pit in 72Sub1 (Figure 1.17 i) was probably a dedicatory offering placed in the pit next to the post.

A third context is mound fill. This of course is disturbed and redeposited material. Indeed, it appears to be a mixture of the ceramics from both the other contexts. The largest concentration of mound fill sherds is just above the central midden (Feature 227). It is from this mound fill deposit that we recovered the only examples of resist decoration.

All of the ceramics found in the various contexts described above fit within the range of the Lohmann phase (Vanderleest n.d.) as defined by the archaeologists of the FAI 270 Project dating to ca. 1000 A.D. Characteristic of both the Mound 72 and Lohmann ceramics are seed jars, Powell Plain jars and bottles with a significant percentage of shell tempering. Absent in both these assemblages is Ramey Incised which is characteristic of the later Stirling phase.

There are some interesting differences in the types of ceramics associated with different features. The vessel forms found with different features have been mentioned in preceding paragraphs.

There were several rimsherds (16 out of total of 77) that had an unoxidized core which I have referred to as "Yellow Sandwich" since the oxidized outside layer or layers had a yellowish color. Table 1.2 shows the distribution of these sherds in terms of their associations. Whereas they have been found in all contexts, they predominate in the special features. This is particularly true of Feature 236 where five of the six vessels in this offertory pit had this characteristic. Feature 227, the only non-offertory feature listed in this table, had a proportion of the unoxidized core similar to the mound fill and the overall assemblage. Whereas those

Table 1.2 Association of Vessels with Unoxidized Core--Yellow Sandwich: Mound 72

Feature or Association	Number of Vessels (Rims)	Yellow Sandwich	% YS
Feature 1	1	1	-
Burial 16	1	1	-
Feature 219	4	1	25%
Feature 236	6	5	83%
Feature 227	27	3	11%
Mound Fill	38	5	13%
TOTALS	77	16	20%

contexts, such as Burial 16 and Feature 1, which had only a single associated vessel can not be considered statistically significant, it is of interest that these vessels manifested this trait. It seems to me that the unoxidized core vessels represent a distinct category intended primarily as status markers and offerings. They may well have been manufactured from special clays or by a process slightly different from the other pots. Thin section or other examinations will have to be made of these to compare them with the more "common" ceramics in the assemblage.

An exception is Feature 219, the charnel house, where only one vessel of the four showed the yellow sandwich. This was a Powell Plain jar associated with Burial 122. This was a small highly polished black or smudged vessel with very thin walls. It shows every indication of being a special vessel. Feature 206, not shown in Table 1.2, is an exception also in that it does not have any rimsherds with the yellow sandwich. The unique character of the ceramics from Feature 206 is in the limitation of its vessel forms to open bowls.

While there appears to have been a time difference between the earliest stages of Mound 72, the post pits and the north midden (Feature 206), and the central midden (Feature 227) and the Litter Burial pit (Feature 229), the associated ceramics indicate functional but not temporal contrasts. In general, the ceramics from the mound fill, presumably the last stages of the total sequence, are similar in range of variation to the ceramics recovered from specific contexts below the mound. It is probable that this mound fill was collected from a nearby area which had been occupied during the Lohmann phase. What may be later Mississippian intrusive burials in the mound had no associated ceramics so that they cannot be temporally fixed. Both the ceramics from the three contexts in Mound 72 and the radiocarbon assays suggest a relatively short time period for all the activities of Mound 72 and that Mound 72 is well within the range described for the Lohmann phase at Cahokia.

Early Mississippian at Cahokia

Presently Mound 72 is the only Early Mississippian marker and burial mound excavated at Cahokia. Data on the extent and nature of the early Cahokia community come from the various excavations at the Cahokia site. Almost everywhere that excavations have been undertaken, evidence of Early Mississippian habitation has been found, indicating that the extent of the site was much the same as in later times. Furthermore, in many cases the density of residential structures is nearly as great as later times.

The most recent of these is in the Interpretive Center Tract (ICT) excavated by archaeologists from Southern Illinois University at Edwardsville. Here the first major occupation of the area was Early Mississippian (Lohmann phase). A large number of houses were found which were all oriented toward the Cahokia grid (Collins 1987). This indicates a strong sense of community planning and organization in Early Mississippian times. Also associated with the Lohmann phase in the ICT were small quantities of artifacts, such as projectile points and lithic debris, similar to those recovered from Mound 72. Chips of Hixton silicified sediment were found associated with the Lohmann ICT occupation but not with later phases (De Mott 1987). The recovery of the Hixton chips and artifacts from Mound 72 and the ICT indicates an interaction to the north for Early Mississippian Cahokians. Both the Hixton and copper materials came from Wisconsin and the Great Lakes region.

Although there have been questions raised about previous population estimates in the order of tens of thousands of inhabitants at Cahokia (Gregg 1971, Griffin and Jones 1978, Ford 1974) it is probable that Early Mississippian Cahokia was of the same order of magnitude as in the Stirling phase and later Mississippian. It may have been larger since recent discoveries of Early Mississippian residences in the ICT is below the elevation that was considered limiting in earlier population estimates.

Recent archaeological studies at Cahokia, including those at Mound 72, have greatly changed our concepts of the nature and influence of Early Mississippian at Cahokia. Cahokia was a formally organized, large central community with a defined social hierarchy and economic ties with most of central North America by the latter half of the tenth century.

This large early community must have been controlled by a well-defined social hierarchy to have achieved the organization and extent it did. Evidence for this comes from the only Early Mississippian burial mound to have been excavated, viz., Mound 72. Among the more than 260 burials observed in Mound 72 a few were placed in such positions as to indicate their importance and social status. The rich offerings buried with them, including the bulk of the burials, are further indications of their status in the community.

In all probability the important burials in Mound 72 represent a sequence. The first of these were the most impressive burials with quantities of offerings and commemorative mounds built over them. The later ones are all oriented toward or along the axis of the early mounds and might well be considered further commemorations of the original high status persons. Whether this sequence represents burials of important persons in a single lineage has not been determinable to date. An alternative hypothesis would be that the two sub-mound personages were the most important persons. The others may be offerings from other communities whose important persons were buried here to commemorate the connection of these other communities to Cahokia.

The nature of the importance of the few status individuals in Mound 72 in relationship to the overall community can be deduced from several factors. First, the two most important individuals, the primary interments in 72Sub1 and 72Sub2, were buried in obvious relationship to the two major post pits. Both of these individuals were located about 5 meters to the west of the respective post pits.

Were the individuals buried near the Solstice Post and within the confines of Woodhenge 72 the keepers of esoteric knowledge, i. e. knowledge "designed for or understood by the specially initiated alone...or relating to knowledge that is restricted to a small group" (Webster's Collegiate Dictionary)? Were they of a group of people who controlled the physical organization of the community?

Cahokia and its Early Mississippian Frontiers

Most past discussion of Cahokia's interaction with other areas has been based upon Stirling and later phases at Cahokia or "Classic" Mississippian. As Robert Hall (Unpublished Manuscript) has pointed out, the Early Mississippian interactions at Cahokia have been generally considered to have been to the south, or the Lower Mississippi Valley, and the fully developed Mississippian interactions were to the north.

The primary factor in the discussions of these later northern interactions has been Ramey Incised pottery. This elegant type of pottery appears at Cahokia in the latter part of the 11th century. Its undecorated variant, Powell Plain, appears at Cahokia in Early Mississippian. The variation in this latter type in Early Mississippian indicates that it is a developing ware that in a sense became more formalized in the Stirling phase.

A ceramic form not often considered for this type of discussion are the red-slipped, punctated-rim seed jars. These types are either shell or grog-tempered. One variant of this type, with limestone temper, is referred to as Monks Mound Red. These forms are common to the south of Cahokia in Emergent Mississippian times and may be the source from which they came northward to Cahokia and beyond. To the north of Cahokia, however, these are rare and might be considered more important indicators of contact with Cahokia. A shell-tempered variant of this type is found at Aztalan (J. D. Richards, Personal Communication), for example, but the context is not well defined.

The implication of utilizing any types of ceramics for discussing Cahokian interaction is that the presence of specific types, or variants thereof, are usually interpreted to signify some sort of direct contact. The models relating to such stylistic imports or diffusions have not been well defined.

Since the data we now have from Cahokia on Early Mississippian interaction is on sumptuary goods connected to the elite segments of society, the reciprocals, that is Cahokia artifacts on the frontiers might be found only in similar contexts. This implies a model of areal interaction being carried out by persons of high status within the interacting communities. These special variations of more common forms would be found only in elite situations as statements regarding the social position of the individuals involved. In this regard, then, the ceramics need to be looked at in more detail. In Mound 72, as described previously, there were limited forms and varieties used in the burial offerings. These special forms of seed jars and Powell Plain—thinner walled, more highly polished and with the unoxidized core or sandwich cross-section—found in elite contexts on the frontiers would indicate special kinds of contacts and interactions.

It may be, however, that Early Mississippian Cahokia was such a precocious center that homage to important persons was a one-way street. The indicators of strong Early Mississippian Cahokian interaction may be found only at Cahokia! This would imply a quite different model for Cahokian interaction with other areas in early Mississippian times.

A further range of data to be considered in looking at Cahokia's interaction with its far flung hinterland are the woodhenges and the implications they have for site organization and world views. Woodhenges have not been found outside of Cahokia. However posts have been found at critical points in some sites, such as the Mitchell Site (Porter 1969, 1974) and the Collins Site (Douglas 1974) in north central Illinois, and these may well be indications of the principles of site organization and planning such as those indicated by Sherrod and Rolingson (1987) and postulated in this paper as well as world view concepts.

To my knowledge there has not been an association of the sun circle symbolism with Early Mississippian except in the monumental architecture of the woodhenges (the beaker from the vicinity of Woodhenge 2 is surely of a later period). Delineation of this "characteristic" Early Mississippian cosmology, engineering principles, and site organization in a context distinguishable from the resident cultural matrix should be an indicator of Early Mississippian interaction.

Conclusions

By Early Mississippian times, the 10th century A.D., Cahokia was already a large complex planned community. The finding of post pits and woodhenges at critical points in the overall site indicate careful planning. This community was controlled by well-defined social hierarchy. The Early Mississippian Cahokians had extensive trade networks throughout the Mississippi Valley and peripheral areas. There is little room for doubt that Cahokia was probably the premiere community, not only in the American Bottom, but in the Mississippi Valley in Early Mississippian times.

Many fascinating and interesting models of Cahokia interaction throughout the Mississippi Valley area have been proposed using fully developed (later) Cahokian Mississippian data. However some data, such as Mound 72, indicate that such networks were extant and powerful in Early Mississippian times, i.e. prior to 1050 A.D. Investigations of the interactions of Cahokia Mississippian in either time frame should consider models of sociopolitical organization at Cahokia to indicate the kinds of data and contexts of such data which might indicate the nature and extent of the interaction.

References Cited

Brackenridge, Henry Marie
    1814 *Views of Louisiana Together with a Journal of a Voyage up the Mississippi River in 1811.* Quadrangle
      Books (1962) Chicago.
Collins, James M.
    1987 The ICT II: An Evolutionary Model of Micro-Cahokia Residence. Paper Presented at IAS
      Workshop. Edwardsville, Illinois.

De Mott, Rodney C.
  1987 A Brief Descriptive Summary of the Chipped Lithic Material from the ICT-II. Paper Presented at IAS Workshop. Edwardsville, Illinois.
Douglas, John
  1976 Collins: A Late Woodland Ceremonial Complex in the Woodfordian Northeast. PhD Dissertation, Department of Anthropology. University of Illinois, Urbana.
Ford, Richard I.
  1974 Northeastern archaeology: past and future directions. *Annual Review of Archaeology* 3:385-413.
Fowler, Melvin L.
  1969 The Cahokia Site. In *Explorations into Cahokia Archaeology*, edited by Melvin L. Fowler, pp. 1-30. Illinois Archaeological Survey, Bulletin 7.
  1974 *Cahokia: Ancient Capital of the Midwest.* Addison – Wesley Module in Anthropology No. 48. Addison– Wesley Publishing Co. New York.
  1975 A Precolumbian Urban Center on the Mississippi. *Scientific American* 233(2):92-101
Fowler, Melvin L., and Robert Hall
  1972 Archaeological phases at Cahokia. *Illinois State Museum Research Series: Papers in Anthropology* No. 1. Illinois State Museum, Springfield.
Fowler, Melvin L., Editor
  1969 *Explorations into Cahokia Archaeology.* Illinois Archaeological Survey. Bulletin 7.
Gregg, Michael L.
  1975 A Population Estimate for Cahokia. In *Perspectives in Cahokia Archaeology*, edited by J. Brown, pp. 126-136. Illinois Archaeological Survey, Bulletin 10.
Griffin, James B.
  1960 A Hypothesis for the Prehistory of the Winnebago. In *Culture in History: Essays in Honor of Paul Radin*, edited by S. Diamond, pp. 809-865. Columbia University Press, New York.
Griffin, James B. and Volney Jones
  1978 The University of Michigan Excavations at the Pulcher Site in 1950. *American Antiquity* 42:462-488.
Hall, Robert L.
  n.d. Cahokia Identity and Interaction Models of Cahokia Mississippian. Unpublished Manuscript.
Hall, Robert L.
  1962 *The Archaeology of Carcajou Point.* The University of Wisconsin Press, Madison.
Porter, James W.
  1969 The Mitchell Site and Prehistoric Exchange Systems at Cahokia. In *Explorations into Cahokia Archaeology*, edited by Melvin L. Fowler, pp. 137-164. Illinois Archaeological Survey, Bulletin 7.
  1974 *Cahokia Archaeology as viewed from the Mitchell site: A Satellite Community at A.D. 1150-1200.* PhD Dissertation, Department of Anthropology, University of Wisconsin-Madison. University Microfilms, Ann Arbor.
Sherrod, P. Clay, and Martha Ann Rolingson
  1987 *Surveyors of the Ancient Mississippi Valley.* Arkansas Archaeological Survey Research Series No. 28. Arkansas Archaeological Survey, Fayetteville.
Skele, Mikels
  1988 *The Great Knob: Interpretations of Monks Mound.* Studies in Illinois Archaeology No. 4. Illinois Historic Preservation Agency, Springfield.
Snyder, John Francis
  1914 Prehistoric Illinois–The Great Cahokia Mound. *Journal of the Illinois State Historical Society* 6:506-508.
Swanton, John R.
  1911 *The Indians of the Southeastern United States.* Bureau of American Ethnology, Bulletin 137. U. S. Government Printing Office, Washington D.C.
Vanderleest, Barbara
  n.d. Mound 72 Ceramics. Unpublished research paper on file at the Archaeological Research Laboratory, University of Wisconsin-Milwaukee.
Wittry, Warren
  1969 The American Woodhenge. In *Explorations into Cahokia Archaeology*, edited by Melvin L. Fowler, pp. 43-48. Illinois Archaeological Survey, Bulletin 7.

Appendix 1.1. Rimsherds from Burials, Features and Mound Fill of Mound 72.

Catalog			Context		Md. Fill			Form	Temper				Slip&Polish			Yellow	TypeName
Yr.	Bag	No	Bur.	Fea.	SW	CN	SE		Sh.	Grg	Lmst	Grt	Ext.	Int.	Rim	Sandwich	
67	1770	1		1				Seed Jar	1	2			x		x	x	Cahokia Red Film
67	1770	2	16					Bottle	1	2			x			x	Powell Plain
69	92	1		206				Jar	1	2			x	x	x		Powell Plain
69	607	1		206				Seed Jar	3	2		1					Loyd Plain
69	767	1		206				Bowl	3	2		1	x	x			Merrell Red Film
69	881	0		206				Stumpware	2			1					Crock ?
69	902	1		206				Seed Jar		1			x		x		Monks Mound Red
69	922	1		206				Bowl		2	1						MonksMoundPlain
69	977	0		206				Stumpware	2	1							Cahokia Boot
69	977	1															
69	980	2		206				Bowl	1	2			x	x			Cahokia RedFilm
70	272	1		214				Jar	1	2			x	x	x		PowellPlainVar.?
70	232	0	122	219				Jar	1				x		x	x	Powell Plain Everted Rim
70	234	1	123	219				Juice Press	1	2							Crock ?
70	242	0	122	219				Jar	1				x				Powell Plain Ext. Lip
70	244	0	117	219				Bowl		1							L. Miss. Valley type?
68	1414	1		227	x			Seed Jar	1				x	x			Cahokia RedFilm
70	23	9		227				Bowl	1	2							St. Clair Plain ?
70	56	10		227	x			Bowl	1			2					Cahokia RedFilm
70	58	14		227				Seed Jar	1	2				x	x	x	Cahokia RedFilm
70	60	0		227	x			Stumpware	2	1							Cahokia Boot
70	61	0		227				Bowl, Lobed	1				x	x			Cahokia RedFilm
70	61	3		227				Jar			1		x	x			PowellPlainTemp. Var.
70	62	10		227	x			Jar									Powell Plain Extruded Lip
70	62	19		227				Seed Jar	1	2			x				Cahokia RedFilm
70	63	41		227				Seed Jar		2	1		x	x			Monks Mound Red
70	63	42		227				Bowl	1				x	x			Cahokia RedFilm
70	63	102		227				Bowl	1			2	x	x			Cahokia RedFilm
70	63	107		227				Bowl	1	2			x	x			Cahokia RedFilm
70	64	12		227				Jar	1							x	Powell Plain Extruded Lip
70	65	16		227				Seed jar	1	2			x	x			Cahokia RedFilm
70	66	8		227				Bowl	1			2	x	x			Cahokia RedFilm
70	66	11		227				Bowl	1				x		x		Cahokia RedFilm
70	69	12		227	x			Jar	1				x	x	x		Powell Plain Extruded Lip
70	83	47	227					Bottle	1	2			x	x			
70	83	54		227				Bowl			1		x	x			Monks Mound Red
70	85	9		227				Bowl	1	2			x	x			Cahokia RedFilm
70	87	57		227				Bowl	1	2			x	x			Cahokia RedFilm
70	303	1		227	x			Jar	1				x	x	x		Powell Plain Ext. Lip
70	1572	1		227				Seed Jar		2	1		x			x	Merrell Red Film
70	158	1		227	x			Jar	1			2	x	x	x		Powell Plain Ext. Lip ?
70	158	2		227	x			Jar	1				x	x	x		Powell Plain

Appendix 1.1 Continued

Yr	Bag	No	Bur. Fea.	SW	CN	SE	Form	Sh.	Grg	Lmst	Grt	Ext.	Int.	Rim	Yellow Sandwich	TypeName
70	162	1	227	x			Jar	1				x	x	x		Powell Plain Ext. Lip
70	70	1	230	x			Jar			1						
70	92	2	236				Bottle	1				x			x	Powell Plain
70	97	2	236				Seed Jar	2		1	3	x	x		x	Monks Mound Red
70	98	2	236				Seed Jar	2		1		x	x		x	Monks Mound Red
70	98	3	236				Seed Jar	1				x	x			Cahokia RedFilm
70	98	5	236				Seed Jar	2		1		x	x		x	Monks Mound Red
70	98	6	236				Seed Jar	1				x	x	x		Cahokia RedFilm
68	545	5			x		Bowl	1	2			x	x			Cahokia RedFilm
68	789	1			x		Bowl	1								
68	789	12		x			Jar	1								Powell Plain Rolled Lip
68	803	1			x		Seed Jar	1				x			x	Cahokia RedFilm
68	1179	1			x		Jar	1				x	x			Powell Plain Ext. Lip
68	1196	2			x		Bowl			1		x	x			Monks Mound Red
69	924	1		x			Bowl/Press	1	2							
69	545	4					Bowl	1	2			x	x			Cahokia RedFilm
70	20	3			x		Seed Jar	1	2			x			x	Cahokia RedFilm
70	21	1			x		Jar ?	1	2				x			
70	26	1			x		Bowl	1	2	3		x				Merrell Red Filmed?
70	61	51			x		Bowl	1				x	x	x		Cahokia RedFilm
70	111	1		x			Bottle	2	1			x			x	
70	111	3		x			Bowl			1		x	x	x		Monks Mound Red
70	115	1		x			Bowl			1		x	x	x		Monks Mound Red
70	142	1		x			Jar	1								Powell Plain Var.?
70	147	6			x		Jar/Press	1	2							
70	149	1			x		Seed Jar	1	2			x	x?			Cahokia RedFilm
70	149	3			x		Bowl			1		x	x		x	Monks Mound Red
70	153	1			x		Jar	1								Powell Plain Ext. Lip ?
70	158	3			x		Jar			1		x	x			Powell Plain Ext. Lip
70	158	6			x		Jar/Bottle	1	2							
70	167	3			x		Seed Jar	1				x	x		x	Cahokia RedFilm
70	170	1			x		Press?			1						Crock
70	357	1			x		Bowl			1		x				Monks Mound Red
71	1541	1			x		Jar	1								Powell Plain

2

American Bottom Mississippian Culture: Internal Developments and External Relations

George R. Milner
Department of Anthropology
The Pennsylvania State University

The Mississippian cultural tradition includes the most organizationally complex Precolumbian societies to develop within the borders of the United States (see Griffin [1985] for a historical review of this cultural category). Several of these societies were encountered by Europeans during their first incursions into the Southeast (e.g., Hally et al. 1990; Hudson et al. 1985; Smith 1987; Swanton 1939), and the hierarchically organized Natchez of the lower Mississippi River valley survived until the early eighteenth century (DuPratz 1972; Neitzel 1965, 1983). Others had disintegrated earlier in either the prehistoric or protohistoric periods (reviews in Smith 1986; Steponaitis 1986; Stoltman 1978). One such cultural system was situated in the part of the Mississippi River valley known as the American Bottom. This area is the wide expanse of fertile floodplain in the vicinity of present-day East St. Louis, Illinois. Cahokia, the largest prehistoric site in eastern North America, was located within this region, as were many other nearby sites. At its peak of development during the eleventh and twelfth centuries, Cahokia-area society had some form of as yet ill-defined contact with peoples far beyond the American Bottom. By the fifteenth century, however, Cahokia's florescence had long since passed. The site was largely abandoned (Fowler and Hall 1972, 1978), and the immediately surrounding floodplain was depopulated (Milner 1986).

Numerous archaeologists have focused on the late prehistoric cultural transformations that occurred at Cahokia and in the immediately surrounding area. Selected aspects of this voluminous work are summarized here with an emphasis on two topics: the development and eventual dissolution of an organizationally complex Cahokia-area Mississippian cultural system, and the evidence for some form of contact between the American Bottom and other parts of the midcontinent. These issues bear some relationship to each other, especially when archaeologists look to Cahokia to explain particular manifestations of cultural sequences elsewhere. Some currently popular models of interregional interaction fail to address temporal incongruities in supposed contact situations or how Cahokia could have possibly projected its power broadly enough to have been responsible for distant events, including those transpiring hundreds of kilometers away from the American Bottom. The interregional contact issue is only covered briefly in this paper because other contributors to this volume consider such interaction in considerably more detail, particularly as they identify Cahokia-style artifacts in their respective study areas.

The Cahokia-Area System

The amount of information laboriously gathered by many researchers on Cahokia-area sites coupled with recent refinements in chronological controls make it now possible to address the foundation, florescence, and eventual demise of the late prehistoric cultural system centered on sites in the American Bottom and the adjoining uplands in Illinois and Missouri. The late prehistoric period in this region spanned a time of comparatively rapid alterations in artifact inventories and styles, architectural construction techniques, and patterns of settlement, among other archaeologically visible signs of cultural change (Emerson and Jackson 1987b; Fowler and Hall 1972, 1978; Kelly 1987; Kelly et al. 1984; Milner 1987a, 1987b, 1990b; Milner et al. 1984). A hierarchically organized society was in existence by the early Mississippian Lohmann (A.D. 1000-1050) and Stirling (A.D. 1050-1150) phases, having undergone an extended period of development in the preceding Emergent Mississippian period (A.D. 800-1000).

The Mississippian settlements consisted of Cahokia, the region's paramount center, as well as many other sites that varied in size and in their internal configuration (Fowler 1974, 1975, 1978; Milner 1987b, 1990b; Milner et al. 1984). Subsidiary sites included locally important centers with one or more mounds encompassed by extensive habitation areas as well as numerous low-density outlying settlements. The latter consisted largely of dispersed farmsteads, and they lacked associated mounds.

Over the long run, this was an unstable cultural system. Within several hundred years it had disintegrated and the region was all but abandoned. The collapse of an organizationally complex Cahokia-centered cultural system seems to have been underway in the Moorehead phase (A.D. 1150-1250). It certainly continued throughout the Sand Prairie phase (A.D. 1250-1400), the end of the Mississippian sequence as it is presently recognized in the American Bottom. While the terminal date for this sequence is to some extent arbitrarily placed at A.D. 1400, the three centuries prior to the initial late seventeenth century European incursion into the region are poorly represented by archaeological materials, despite considerable fieldwork.

Alternative Sociopolitical Models

Most archaeologists classify Mississippian societies in the American Bottom and elsewhere as chiefdoms (Anderson 1990; Ford 1974; Griffin 1983; Hines 1977; Milner 1990b; Peebles and Kus 1977; Smith 1978, 1986; Steponaitis 1978, 1986; Stoltman 1978). Although Cahokia has been occasionally called a state (Conrad 1989; Gibbon 1974; Hall 1986; O'Brien 1972b; Sears 1968), available evidence is not consistent with the interpretation that the American Bottom Mississippian cultural system featured the scale of structural organization implied by the use of the term "state." As outlined below, however, archaeologists concerned with this region are only beginning to address alternative models of the sociopolitical landscape, various measures of cultural complexity, their interrelationships, and the ways these indices changed over time. This process will require considerable additional fieldwork and museum-based studies, and it is a more fruitful avenue of research than the selective invocation of a few criteria for classification purposes alone. Archaeologists are just starting to identify the complicated ways in which various indices of societal scale changed over the hundreds of years leading to and following Cahokia's ascendancy over the region.

Over the past three decades there has been a general, but by no means universal, acceptance of Cahokia and its satellite sites as an example of a highly elaborated, centralized, and populous cultural system. As far as interregional relations are concerned, such interpretations serve as the basis for often unrestrained speculation about the efficacy of Cahokia's influence on or control over distant peoples.

Characterizations of Cahokia and affiliated Mississippian sites typically refer to Fowler's (1974, 1975, 1978) deservedly influential settlement model that features a hierarchy of sites consisting of four distinct levels. Cahokia was the primary center, judging from its great size, numerous mounds accompanied by other forms of public architecture, extensive areas of dense habitation debris, and complex intrasite organization. It dominated social and economic relations among three levels of lower ranked sites. The subsidiary sites included two kinds of mound centers that were often strategically situated along key waterways. These second- and third-level sites encompassed either multiple or single mounds, respectively. The bottommost, or fourth, tier in the hierarchy consisted of low-density occupation sites lacking mounds. In the context of this paper, it is significant that the multitiered settlement system has been cited as one of Cahokia's state-like characteristics (Kelly 1980:171).

Judging from physical remains alone, the Cahokia cultural system certainly ranked among the most elaborated of the Mississippian period societies in the Eastern Woodlands. Nevertheless, there are several good reasons to question the highly centralized, greatly differentiated, heavily populated, and reasonably stable interpretation that is presented in much of the current literature on the region.

The town-and-mound centers distributed throughout the region were not all contemporaneous, nor were peak periods of occupancy of equal duration. This is evident from previous archaeological assessments of several mound centers (e.g., Gregg 1975b; Griffin 1977; Harn 1971; Porter 1974), as well as an examination of ceramic vessel fragments from major sites (University of Illinois, Illinois State Museum, University of Michigan, University of Missouri, and St. Louis Science Center collections were examined during a project supported by a Penn State Research Initiation Grant for 1987-1988).

Problems also arise with viewing the second and third-level sites as representing distinct intermediate positions within a settlement hierarchy. Mounds within Mississippian period centers were certainly integral parts of site plans, and they were typically associated with the superordinate social stratum, although used for various purposes. To date, however, advocates of the organizationally complex, tightly knit, and four-tiered Cahokia system have not marshalled clear evidence for economic or decision-making differentiation among the second and third-ranked sites, i.e., the mound centers other than Cahokia. Instead, the number and size of mounds probably reflect, at least in part, the varied histories of chiefly lineages, each of which made their mark on a site by the initiation or enlargement of highly visible earthworks and associated features. The amount of earth moved in mound construction at intermediate-level sites is just as likely to be a result of the length of time a particular site was a politically important center and the elite group's ability to mobilize labor as it is indicative of multiple ranked nodes in a tightly integrated hierarchy of functionally differentiated sites.

An alternative model, presented elsewhere (Milner 1990a, 1990b), is more consistent with existing information, much of it collected during the past two decades. In contrast to the conventional view of Cahokia, this model more closely approximates the general characteristics of what archaeologists are increasingly calling middle-range societies.

The most salient characteristic of the Mississippian sociopolitical landscape seems to have been the repetitive nature of its constituent elements. Multiple organizationally similar outlying communities were dominated by locally important centers marked by mounds associated with an elite social stratum. The mound center dominated territories, in turn, were linked through elite-mediated ties to a similarly structured, but more elaborate, sociopolitical unit centered on the Cahokia site.

The town-and-mound complexes yielding Cahokia-like Emergent Mississippian and Mississippian period materials are located primarily, but not exclusively, along the Mississippi River corridor from Madison County, through St. Clair and Monroe counties, and into Randolph County (Kelly 1980:193-194, 1990b; Milner 1990b; Porter 1974:23-31). Unfortunately, there is considerable uncertainty about the nature of the occupations at the sites with mounds, especially the timing of their ascendancy as politically dominant places within their respective areas. Porter (1974) has argued that mound construction at Mitchell, a multi-mound Mississippian center north of Cahokia, spanned a reasonably short period of time, lasting on

the order of a few generations, not hundreds of years. If correct, his results indicate that the site was a prominent element of the sociopolitical landscape for a correspondingly short period of time, underscoring the inherent instability of the chiefdom level of sociopolitical organization (e.g., Anderson 1990). Archaeologists working in the American Bottom must direct much more attention toward teasing apart a series of superimposed settlement systems consisting of both large and small sites. The conflation of sites with different histories—a result of our current temporal controls—produces a composite settlement pattern that is more dense and complex than the arrangement of sites at any single point in the past.

Leading figures in their respective mound centers would have exercised control over territories that differed in size and encompassed a number of the outlying, low-density occupation sites that lacked mounds. The spatially discrete Mississippian period sociopolitical units centered on locally prominent town-and-mound centers were probably quasi-autonomous politically, especially with regard to purely local affairs. Given the abundance and distribution of basic resources along the valley, there is no reason why these sociopolitical units would not have been self-sufficient economically in terms of life-sustaining necessities, at least during all but disastrous years.

The self-sufficient, quasi-autonomous, and similarly structured sociopolitical units were presumably linked with Cahokia by as yet unknown means through the superordinate social groups ensconced in their respective town-and-mound complexes. These linkages would have been bolstered through social conventions and more powerful incentives stemming from the material benefits of formal affiliation with a strong paramountcy and the threat posed by its numerical advantage. Exchanges of materials were probably used by key members of the elite stratum to reinforce and expand their basis of support. Therefore, these transactions had more political and social significance than economic importance (see the recent discussion in Brown et al. [1990]). The establishment of elite-mediated avenues of communication would have also served to buffer localized and irregularly occurring shortfalls in resource productivity caused by unpredictable environmental perturbations, such as abnormally wet or dry years (see the description of the American Bottom environment in Chmurny [1973]). Access to the labor needed to build the disproportionately numerous and often monumentally proportioned public architecture at Cahokia was presumably facilitated by linkages maintained among the elite groups at the various mound centers.

The strength of the ties among the elite social strata at the different mound centers presumably varied over time, and they would have become increasingly attenuated with distance from the paramount center. Thus the potential for decomposition into a series of individual territorially based and similarly structured sociopolitical units, each with a functioning decision-making body already in place, would have been a continual threat to the internal cohesion of the Cahokia-dominated system. The integrity of the regional system (i.e., the complex chiefdom) was maintained only to the extent that the divisive interests of separate, elite-dominated sociopolitical units, each fully capable of independent existence, were dampened by a powerful Cahokia.

This was quite likely a volatile sociopolitical landscape, particularly from an archaeological perspective spanning hundreds of years. Rival chiefly lineages jockeyed for advantageous positions; factions squabbled over the proper succession to positions of authority, among other concerns; and leading social groups fissioned along kin-based cleavage planes. Varied histories of elite group ascendency and, presumably, the spatial extent of their dominion would have resulted from shifting cooperative and competitive social relations extending across the many generations encompassed by the Mississippian period.

Elite Groups and Major Centers

By the early Mississippian period Lohmann phase, if not before, there had developed an elite social stratum who resided, along with other people, in the mound centers. The presence of a superordinate social stratum is clearly indicated by segregated burial areas in mound centers, the form of mortuary facilities, and differential access to items fashioned from nonlocal materials, with many artifacts interpreted as symbols of superordinate rank (Fowler 1974, 1975; Milner 1984a; Winters 1974). Another form of conspicuous display was the sacrifice of large numbers of people on important occasions, which occurred at Cahokia's Mound 72 (Fowler 1974, 1975, 1989:144-150). Archaeologists, however, should not overemphasize the significance of these victims (e.g., Conrad's [1989] use of sacrifices as a diagnostic signature of a state-level sociopolitical system). Many middle-range societies sacrifice people, often captives, and the origin(s) of the Mound 72 victims is not known. Poorly understood variation in the location, form, and content of elite mortuary facilities indicates the differentiation of rank positions within the superordinate stratum.

Precise temporal controls are lacking for most of the American Bottom cemeteries. Nevertheless, it is clear that spatial and artifactual distinctions between elite and nonelite burial areas were present early in the Mississippian period, and they were maintained for a long time thereafter (Milner 1984a).

The differential use of space, which is so integral a part of Mississippian mortuary practices in the American Bottom and elsewhere (Goldstein 1980; Hatch 1976; Milner 1984a; Peebles and Kus 1977), is also reflected by the internal configuration of the region's paramount town-and-mound center, which is known largely through Fowler's (1974, 1975, 1978, 1989) work. Inferences about the nature of Cahokia's organization are necessarily limited by the lack of basic information, including a comprehensive map that combines archaeological excavations, mounds, and significant features. Nevertheless, it is clear that there was some degree of organized structure to the site plan as indicated by the presence of a central palisaded precinct, the arrangements of mounds, and the existence of cemeteries and special-function areas featuring large, public architecture (Fowler 1974, 1975, 1978, 1989; Fowler and Hall 1972; Holley et al. 1989; Wittry and Vogel 1962). The site as a whole, however, appears to have been a complex amalgamation of habitation, public, and ritually significant areas rather than a carefully laid out series of secular and sacred spaces conforming to an overarching site plan. These mounds, plazas, and residential areas have been aptly characterized as "subcommunities" by Fowler (1975:100, 1978:466, 1989:202). This intrasite organization suggests that a segmentation into quasi-distinct and presumably kin-based social groups permeated all of American Bottom society, including the occupants of the largest sites.

Furthermore, it is not surprising that there were significant changes in the ways particular parts of Cahokia were used during an occupation spanning hundreds of years. The problems posed by a lengthy occupation have plagued assessments of Cahokia's organizational structure and its resident population since the early nineteenth century (see Griffin's [1985] discussion).

The internal configurations of the other town-and-mound complexes were not nearly so complex. Nevertheless, certain characteristics, most particularly mounds surrounding plazas, are evident at some other major sites (Bushnell 1904; Porter 1969, 1974).

Outlying Communities

One of the most significant developments documented for the Emergent Mississippian to Mississippian period transition was a shift in the internal organization of the outlying, low-density occupation settlements. Emergent Mississippian settlements were often small villages consisting of groups of structures. Residential structures were aligned along the banks of sloughs or were arranged around open areas often containing a central post, a few sizable storage pits, or a large, presumably public, building (Emerson and Jackson 1984, 1987b; Kelly 1987, 1990a, 1990b; Kelly et al. 1984, 1990; McElrath et al. 1987). Structures that were either isolated or associated with only a few other irregularly distributed buildings also occur (Emerson and Jackson 1987a; Fortier 1985; Jackson 1988; McElrath and Finney 1987; Milner 1984c; Stahl 1985).

By the beginning of the Mississippian period, the outlying settlements in the Mississippi River floodplain had undergone a profound transformation in the prevailing mode of intrasite organization. Small nucleated villages were replaced by widely spaced farmsteads. Each Mississippian farmstead consisted of one or sometimes more structures and associated features, including sizable pits employed for storage purposes (Emerson et al. 1983; Finney 1985; Fortier 1985; Hanenberger 1990b; Jackson 1990a, 1990b, 1990c; Mehrer 1982, 1988; Milner 1983, 1984b; Milner et al. 1984; Pauketat and Woods 1986; Szuter 1979; Yerkes 1987).

A few special-function buildings, including several excavated sweat lodges and a large public building, were interspersed among the residential structures. They probably played a part in various community activities, and they might have been associated with nearby domestic structures perhaps occupied by leading community figures (Emerson and Milner 1981; Milner 1990b; Milner et al. 1984). The groups of features that included special-function buildings were occasionally placed in areas that have remained locally prominent to the present day. For example, these features were situated at a slightly higher point along the ridge at the Range site (Mehrer 1982, 1988) and at the intersection of two of the Julien site ridges (Milner 1984b). In the immediate vicinity of Cahokia, these feature complexes tended to have a more elaborate set of associated artifacts and functions than they did elsewhere. Finely crafted figurines with fertility connotations fashioned from a nonlocal material were found in excavations at the BBB Motor and Sponemann sites, and an unusual mortuary component was associated with the former feature complex (Emerson 1982, 1989; Emerson and Jackson 1984; Prentice 1986; Fortier, 1988).

Taken together, these Mississippian period features seem to represent the remains of a series of separate communities, each consisting of a number of dispersed farmsteads accompanied by the infrequently occurring special-function feature complexes (Emerson and Milner 1981; Mehrer 1988; Milner 1983, 1984b, 1990b; Milner et al. 1984). The boundaries of individual communities possibly approximated the limits of some topographic features such as ridge-and-swale complexes that, along with the marshes and sloughs that filled abandoned river channels, gave the valley its distinctive appearance.

Food production through a diversified subsistence strategy was a principal activity of the widely spaced farmstead residents (Johannessen 1984; Kelly and Cross 1984). The floodplain orientation of the society as a whole is consistent with an adaptive stance focused on the presence of rich valley soils suitable for horticulture with a simple hoe technology. Plentiful food resources were derived from a floodplain terrain consisting of often narrow ridges adjacent to marshes and open-water habitats, such as creeks and sloughs. Bottomland food resources obtained through localized production and collection strategies were supplemented on occasion by those from the neighboring uplands, such as hickory nuts (Johannessen 1984). Although the valleys of tributary creeks and the heavily dissected uplands that border the main valley supported additional farmsteads (Hanenberger 1990a; McElrath and Finney 1987; Prentice and Mehrer 1981), the Mississippi River floodplain was clearly the focus of occupation and food procurement activities. The overall occupation and resource foci are consistent with Mississippian adaptive strategies elsewhere (e.g., Smith 1978, 1985).

A replacement of outlying nucleated villages by communities consisting of dispersed farmsteads probably followed the development of increasingly sophisticated and inclusive means of regional social integration that dampened outright conflict. The threat of conflict presumably was reduced once Cahokia established its hegemony over the region.

An occupational pattern featuring widely distributed farmsteads would have yielded obvious benefits to the inhabitants of the outlying communities, since the dispersal of single-family residences was an effective way to maximize access to well-drained bottomlands. These areas typically occur as narrow strips of ridge crest bounded by swales, many of which would have been filled with water on a seasonal or permanent basis. The land-water relationship was an important element of day-to-day life because much of the floodplain would not have been useful for habitation or cultivation purposes. For example, less than half (37%) of the 15 km long segment of floodplain immediately south of Cahokia was habitable, an estimate based on modern topography and the location of Mississippian period structures at eleven sites with a combined excavation area totaling 21.2 ha (Milner 1986). An additional 10.1 ha at fifteen other nearby sites have been cleared of plowzone and examined for evidence of subsurface cultural remains, resulting in a combined total of 31.3 ha in the short segment of floodplain where the distribution of securely dated features is known.

The basic organizational structure of the outlying sites, which featured the dispersal of people in widely separated single-family farmsteads, persisted for hundreds of years during the Mississippian period. Once established, it proved to be remarkably resistant to change, despite the varying occupational histories and presumed influence of mound centers throughout the region.

Population Estimates

The conventional portrayal of American Bottom Mississippian society is associated with high population estimates for the peak period of Cahokia's development. Frequently cited figures for Cahokia range from 10,000 (Thomas 1907; Reed et al. 1968) to between 25,500 and 43,000 (Gregg 1975a), with the high end of the range favored by most archaeologists (e.g., Benchley 1976:23; Fowler 1974, 1975, 1978, 1989:192; O'Brien 1972b). Many more people would have lived in nearby mound centers and outlying communities. Taken together, the occupants of these sites would have formed an enormous population in this segment of the river bottoms.

Numerous archaeological projects conducted in various environmental settings have shown that people were indeed concentrated in the main valley. Nevertheless, some archaeologists doubt that teeming multitudes populated the bottoms (e.g., Ford 1974; Griffin 1983; Milner 1990b).

Unfortunately, there have been few attempts to grapple with the problems associated with estimating population size, which is as intractable an issue in the American Bottom as it is elsewhere. The commonly cited high figures for the peak period of Cahokia site occupancy are derived from Gregg's (1975a) count of excavated structures and an estimate of the usable land within the traditionally employed site boundaries (the excavation data are not published). Gregg's (1975:132, 134) calculation, the only one based on buildings, resulted in an estimate of 25,500 people for the Stirling phase, thought to be a conservative figure, that is raised to 42,780 in an editorial note. The estimating procedure apparently incorporates the assumption that individual structures or rebuilding sequences were occupied for the entire Stirling phase, which is assigned a duration of 100 years (the current chronology [Milner et al. 1984] does not differ in this respect from the one used when the estimate was made [Fowler and Hall 1972]). It is unlikely, however, that all such buildings, or reconstruction sequences, lasted that long. Therefore, the estimates for the peak occupation at the Cahokia site should be revised downward.

The only currently available population estimates for the surrounding area pertain to a 15 km long segment of the floodplain south of Cahokia. The occupants of settlements lacking mounds in this part of the

bottoms have been estimated as numbering somewhere in the low thousands (Milner 1986). At this point, there is no reason to suspect that the basic peripheral settlement pattern was markedly different elsewhere in the East St. Louis area, including the immediate vicinity of Cahokia.

The putative tens of thousands of Cahokia site residents packed into a ca. 13 km² area, only half of which was usable land, could not have produced or acquired the basic resources needed to ensure their survival without rapidly declining returns (for consistency, Gregg's [1975a] areal information is cited here). The occupants of nearby town-and-mound centers, which like Cahokia were presumably numerous, would have exacerbated the problems associated with heavy resource exploitation. It is unlikely that the resource deficit could have been filled by the efforts of widely scattered households in the surrounding floodplain who managed to consistently generate great surpluses that were transported to major centers. These people only possessed a generalized, hoe-based agricultural technology, and they pursued a mixed subsistence strategy that focused on an array of cultivated plants, including maize, and wild plant and animal species (Johannessen 1984; Kelly and Cross 1984).

The American Bottom Mississippian period population apparently reached its peak during the Stirling phase (Gregg 1975a; Milner 1986). Thereafter it declined. This is shown in Figure 2.1 where the number of dated structures at eleven peripheral floodplain sites located south of Cahokia are expressed as percentages of the total excavated, with figures standardized for different phase lengths. The procedure used for deriving the residential structure total (N=98) was based on the number of field-documented structures (N=86). It incorporated adjustments to the latter figure in order to accommodate archaeological evidence for rebuilding episodes, shallow structures destroyed in the plowzone, and paired structures where one building might have been used for non-residential purposes (the counting procedure and references to relevant site reports can be found elsewhere [Milner 1986]). The overall pattern is similar when internal floor area is used, instead of the number of structures. Differences in the two distributions reflect an increase in the average size of Mississippian residential structures from the Lohmann through the Sand Prairie phases (Milner 1986; Milner et al. 1984). The peak of occupation at Cahokia is also reported as having occurred during the Stirling phase (Gregg 1975a), although few of the many excavations at the site, some of which are extensive, have been analyzed in any detail.

The demographic pattern for the river valley contrasts with that of the tributary drainages in the uplands. There appears to have been an uneven spatial

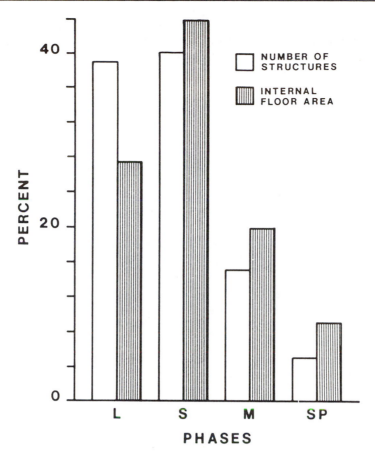

Figure 2.1. The number of residential structures at eleven outlying sites and the combined floor area of completely excavated structures are presented according to phase affiliation (figures are expressed as percentages and are standardized by estimated phase duration): (L) Lohmann, (S) Stirling, (M) Moorehead, and (SP) Sand Prairie.

as well as temporal distribution of late prehistoric sites in drainages east of the American Bottom, with most dating either to the beginning or to the end of the period encompassing the development and dissolution of a Cahokia-dominated cultural system (Bareis 1976; Woods 1986:72; Woods and Holley n.d.). The temporal and geographical patterning of sites to the west of the valley in Missouri is, at present, unclear because of limited research. The available evidence, however, suggests that the late Mississippian depopulation of the floodplain was linked to the short-distance movement of people to settings in the uplands flanking the main valley.

Pattern of Change

There appears to have been a gradual increase in population size and cultural complexity during the Emergent Mississippian period that occurred in tandem with developments elsewhere in the central Mississippi River valley (e.g., Kelly 1990b; Kelly et al.

1984; Milner 1990b). As discussed previously, at the beginning of the Mississippian period there was a seemingly sudden alteration in the prevailing organization of small outlying communities. This was a time of active mound construction at major sites coupled with the separation of habitation areas and specialized precincts at Cahokia. Social stratification, evident primarily in mortuary practices, made its appearance early in the Mississippian period, if not before. One town-and-mound complex, Cahokia, became the superordinate center, dominating all others in the region. By then the American Bottom settlements were linked together as part of a system that is archaeologically apparent as different-sized sites. The elite groups at contemporaneous mound centers, although they were subordinate to Cahokia, probably exercised control over their own support populations, which would have varied in size. The regional sociopolitical system probably was forged from uneasy alliances among similarly structured, self-supporting, and contentious peer polities, which for a time were dominated by Cahokia.

The peak in Mississippian cultural development in the region appears to have been relatively short lived, at least considering the long periods of time that fall into the realm of archaeological study. Although difficult to measure and date, Cahokia's florescence seems to have been a Stirling phase phenomenon that may well have begun in the preceding Lohmann phase and extended into the subsequent Moorehead phase. The fragmentation and eventual collapse of the Cahokia-dominated system was apparently a protracted affair. It is first recognized archaeologically as a decrease in the floodplain population with a concomitant increase in upland occupation, and only later as alterations in intrasite organization and intersite relationships.

The dissolution of the Cahokia cultural system was underway in the Moorehead phase, to the extent that available population estimates serve as a reliable indicator of social conditions in the main valley. The reasons behind a suspected dispersal of people to the surrounding uplands and its centrifugal effects on this prehistoric society represent important areas for future research. In this context, it is important to note that Fowler (1975) has raised the issue of resource depletion, which has been broadened to outright environmental degradation by Brown and co-workers (1988).

Only in the Sand Prairie phase, however, is there abundant unambiguous archaeological evidence for major structural changes in American Bottom society. This process is archaeologically apparent at Cahokia as a time of continuing depopulation and a restructuring of the site's internal configuration (Fowler 1974, 1975; Fowler and Hall 1972, 1978; Gregg 1975a; Milner 1984a). Residential structures were built to the west of Monks Mound where sizable and unusually shaped architecture, marking some form of specialized precinct, had once been located (Fowler 1974, 1975; Fowler and Hall 1972; Wittry and Vogel 1962). Nonelite burials were placed in at least one mound in the central portion of the site, indicating an alteration in that earthwork's function (Milner 1984a). A palisade screening Cahokia's central precinct was not present during the terminal Mississippian phase, although it had been rebuilt on several occasions during the preceding Stirling and Moorehead phases (Fowler 1974, 1975, 1989:195-197). A less structured settlement organization is indicated by Sand Prairie phase graves, which often occur either alone or in groups consisting of only a few burials situated near residential structures rather than in formally defined cemeteries (Milner 1984a; excavation summary in Wittry and Vogel 1962). Overall, it seems that by the Sand Prairie phase the elite stratum of Cahokia had lost much of their earlier ability to enforce adherence to a site plan in the core of the town-and-mound complex.

The Sand Prairie phase also appears to have been a time of increasing autonomy for local communities. Further societal segmentation is suggested by a shift from large cemeteries on prominent bluff-edges to the small, single-community, floodplain cemeteries that are characteristic of the Sand Prairie phase (Milner 1984a). An increased emphasis on the primary social and economic elements of this society, the communities of dispersed farmsteads, presumably accompanied the failure of regularly effective mechanisms for regional social integration. Expedient associations forged on the local level may account for the presence of an anomalous, short-duration, and small Oneota occupation at the Sponemann site (Jackson, personal communication 1988). This component and the similar Bold Counselor occupations of the central Illinois River valley to the north are both interpreted as intrusions into these two river valleys (Esarey and Santure 1990).

The nonsynchronous nature of changes in different measures of cultural scale and complexity is not unexpected. As far as Cahokia is concerned, it would be surprising indeed if the elite had not attempted to maintain their deteriorating position by extracting as much as possible from a failing system in order to furnish themselves with at least the outward trappings of high office and, hence, the appearance of authority. This might appear in the archaeological record as a continuation of mound building, the maintenance of Cahokia's center as an inviolable area screened by a palisade, and the presence of high-status artifacts buried with members of the elite social stratum. The last vestiges of social inequality may have been evident for some time, continuing through much or all of the Sand Prairie phase. Cahokia's collapse, about which little is known, clearly represents a research problem every bit as complicated as its origin (e.g., Fowler 1975; Moberg 1983).

Interregional Contact

People in the Cahokia area participated in the wide circulation of nonlocal raw materials and finished artifacts during the Emergent Mississippian and Mississippian periods. Unfortunately, the form and intensity of this interaction are poorly understood, like so many other aspects of the late prehistoric era (e.g., Brown et al. 1990). While far from clear, the mechanisms underlying such interaction remain important issues in the study of regional cultural trajectories because the specific course of change and the success of individual human populations are influenced by cooperative and antagonistic contact with other peoples. Thus the development of a major center such as Cahokia and the nature of its external relations are important aspects of the study of eastern North American prehistory.

Archaeological Evidence

Atypical vessels from Emergent Mississippian assemblages that have been likened to ceramic types known from farther south along the Mississippi River valley, including Varney Red Filmed and Coles Creek Incised, have been found at Cahokia and neighboring sites (Emerson and Jackson 1984:73-77, 1987b; Kelly 1980:157-159, 332-333, 365-367, 1987, 1990b; Kelly et al. 1979:32; Milner 1984c:77; O'Brien 1972a:31). Other nonlocal ceramics, including Yankeetown and Dillinger vessels from southwestern Indiana and southern Illinois, respectively, also occur occasionally at Emergent Mississippian American Bottom sites (Emerson and Jackson 1984:73-77, 1987b; Kelly 1980:368-370, 1987, 1990b, this volume). Not surprisingly, unusual vessels interpreted as coming from other regions or fashioned after nonlocal pottery have been found in Mississippian period contexts as well, including Cahokia and outlying smaller sites (Bareis and Porter 1965; Hall 1967; Milner 1984b:143-144, Figure 59b; O'Brien 1972a:31).

Cahokia's interaction with other regions appears to have broadened early in the Mississippian period, presumably building on earlier contacts. Ceramics that originated in the Cahokia area or were fashioned after these vessel forms occur at a number of midcontinental sites. Ramey Incised jars, a distinctive Stirling and Moorehead phase vessel form, are particularly widely distributed (e.g., Kelly 1980:205-206), presumably in part because they are easy to recognize in archaeological assemblages.

Examples of Ramey Incised jars or the similar but undecorated Powell Plain type have been found at Illinois sites north and east of the American Bottom (Bennett 1945:153-158, Plates 23, 24; Conner 1985; Goldstein 1980:170-172, 175, 177, 182; Hargrave 1983; Harn 1975, 1980:21). These vessels also occur at sites in northeastern Iowa (Tiffany 1982), in the Diamond Bluff-Red Wing area of Wisconsin and Minnesota (Gibbon 1974), and in southern Wisconsin, especially at Aztalan (Barrett 1933:322-335, Plates 79, 90; Bleed 1970; Freeman 1986; Hall 1967). A few specimens that approximate the Ramey Incised type have been found at sites as distant as northern Michigan (Dorothy 1980; McPherron 1967:116-118, Plate 23a-c). Connections between Cahokia and areas to the west and northwest, including the Steed-Kisker and Mill Creek sites of northwestern Missouri and Iowa, respectively, have been recognized for many years, particularly with regard to the presence of vessels resembling Ramey Incised jars (Anderson 1981:112-118, Figure 17j,l-n; Anderson 1987; Chapman 1980:156-161; Griffin 1946, 1967; Hall 1967; Henning 1967; O'Brien 1969, 1981; Tiffany 1983; Wedel 1943:208-214). Vessels similar to those from Cahokia-area sites, including specimens conforming to Ramey Incised jars, among others, have been found in northeastern Arkansas (Morse and Morse 1983:239), at the Angel site in southwestern Indiana (Kellar 1967), at the Kincaid site in southern Illinois along the Ohio River (Cole 1951:150, Plate 27), at Annis Mound and Village in western Kentucky along the Green River (University of Kentucky Museum of Anthropology collections), and as far south as several Yazoo Basin sites in northwestern Mississippi (Phillips 1970:256-260, Figure 73h; Williams and Brain 1983:200-203).

Some form of later interaction with the Cahokia area during the Moorehead and Sand Prairie phases is indicated by vessel forms such as the Cahokia Cordmarked jar and the Wells Incised plate. For example, assemblages from sites elsewhere in the midcontinent include examples of Cahokia Cordmarked jars or similar pottery, especially those from sites located in other parts of Illinois (Bennett 1945:153-158, Plate 27; Brown 1967:36; Cole 1951:151, Plate 27; Conner 1985:215-219; Conrad et al. 1981; Hargrave 1983; Harn 1975, 1980:21).

It is apparent that Cahokia-like ceramics were widely distributed among distant peoples, although there are problems with the differentiation of tradewares from locally produced copies. Clearly much additional work is needed to develop the means of sourcing putatively nonlocal pottery and, especially, documenting the ways in which these objects were used in remote areas.

Artifacts fashioned from exotic raw materials also indicate contact with distant places. Nonlocal raw materials including distinctive cherts, hematite, galena, whelk shell, mica, copper, a reddish material that has been likened to bauxite and the fireclay of east-central Missouri, among others, have been found at large and small late prehistoric sites in the American Bottom. Some items, such as copper, mica, and whelk shell, originated in distant regions. Nearby southeastern Missouri was probably the source of much of the galena and hematite (Walthall 1981). Most of the objects were undoubtedly acquired through some form of exchange network, but it is possible that a few such items were obtained locally. Hematite occurs in the beds of creeks that drain the uplands (Kelly et al. 1987:313, 1990:188), and the glacial till east of the valley has been reported to contain pieces of galena and copper (Schoolcraft 1819:198; Walthall 1981:33).

Many nonlocal materials were available to the Mississippian period elite social stratum of the major town-and-mound centers. Their cemeteries frequently yield large amounts of often sizable and elaborately crafted objects, including those made of nonlocal materials, that apparently symbolized social positions of high rank (Fowler 1974, 1975; Milner 1984a; Winters

1974). The large quantities of such items in burial facilities associated with the superordinate social stratum is one of several criteria differentiating these mortuary areas from the cemeteries associated with the nonelite segment of society.

The occupants of the lowest tier in the Mississippian period settlement hierarchy—the farmsteads—also enjoyed some degree of access to nonlocal materials. Some items were fashioned into ornaments and utilitarian items, whereas others were ground to produce red (hematite and the fireclay-like material) and white (galena) pigments. Nonlocal cherts were usually used to make the distinctive large hoes that are frequently found at American Bottom Mississippian sites. The preferred material came from quarries near the town of Mill Creek in Union County, Illinois (Phillips 1900; Winters 1981). Other hoes were made from Kaolin chert, also from southern Illinois, as well as locally occurring stone. Apparently the Mill Creek and Kaolin chert hoes were exchanged as completely formed bifaces (e.g., Brown et al. 1990; Winters 1981). Not surprisingly, they were highly valued in the American Bottom. Broken hoes were often reworked, and caches of the tools, including large fragments, occur at both farmsteads and mound centers (Milner 1983:158, 1984b:172; Pauketat and Woods 1986; Snyder 1877). These caches include a remarkable group of over 70 hoes uncovered in the nineteenth century at the East St. Louis Mound Group (Rau 1869). Several of these specimens still exist, and they have been identified by Kelly as Mill Creek chert (Kelly and Gums 1987).

Intraregional Circulation of Nonlocal Goods

Limited archaeological samples and the lack of published data from diverse contexts that include the mound complexes prohibit rigorous investigations of either diachronic patterns of access to nonlocal materials or the mechanisms of exchange. Nevertheless, the items found in elite mortuary facilities indicate that the superordinate social stratum was able to obtain valued objects from distant sources for use in socially important contexts. The differential distribution of high-quality items, especially elaborate artifacts fashioned from exotic raw materials that served as symbols of exalted status, is well documented. Available evidence, primarily from mortuary contexts, indicates that these items tended to be retained by members of the superordinate stratum, and they circulated among the most socially important groups at the various mound centers.

Nonlocal items that were typically less ostentatious and often used for utilitarian purposes found their way into the hands of lower ranked people. Some of these items were probably acquired through elite-mediated exchange networks, and they subsequently percolated down to all levels of American Bottom society, including the farmstead residents. The broad distribution of exotic goods would reflect the continual need of leaders to solidify and expand their constituencies through a combination of both rewards and largesse fostering indebtedness. There appears to have been an uneven distribution of exotic items even among the nonelite segment of society. Special-function feature complexes in the vicinity of Cahokia yield finely crafted figurines made from a nonlocal material (Emerson 1982, 1989; Emerson and Jackson 1984; Prentice 1986; Fortier 1988), and a few skeletons in nonelite cemeteries were interred with disproportionately rich burial accouterments (Milner 1990b). The composition of Mississippian period farmstead assemblages probably also reflects individual-to-individual transactions involving small quantities of nonlocal objects that were used for various purposes, particularly to seal interpersonal relationships through the exchange of gifts. Given sufficient time, these items could have crossed considerable distances.

It is quite possible that the observed archaeological pattern resulted from the combined effects of these processes (see Fried [1967], among others, on the complementary nature of different modes of exchange in organizationally complex societies). Down-the-line exchange accommodates the finding that nonlocal materials continued to be available to the residents of Sand Prairie phase farmsteads during the period of Cahokia's decline as a major center. Although patterns of farmstead-level access to exotic materials are far from clear because of insufficient data, there is no apparent diminishment of nonlocal materials in Sand Prairie assemblages, especially with regard to Mill Creek hoes (e.g., Milner 1987a). Opportunities for common people to acquire nonlocal goods survived the dissolution of the regional organization that supported an elaborated elite social stratum responsible for the construction of monumental architecture on a massive scale at major centers.

Nature of Interregional Contact

Documenting the mere presence of distinctive nonlocal objects, including tradewares or locally produced imitations, does not by itself indicate the nature and significance of connections between peoples of different regions (Brown et al. [1990] recently called attention to the need for further work on interregional exchange). Many explanations have been proposed over the years for the occurrence of Mississippian components upstream from the American Bottom as well as the wide circulation of Cahokia-style artifacts.

Particular phenomena have been attributed to wandering migrants, proselytizing missionaries, or long-distance traders; inspiration from or reaction to more organizationally complex societies; the long reach of a rapacious elite group; and down-the-line exchange. There is a smorgasbord of opinion regarding several key dimensions of these scenarios. Debates focus on the nature and intensity of contact, either direct or indirect; whether such connections played a causal role in cultural change or were essentially ephemeral phenomena; and the general classes and amount of materials exchanged between distant groups.

Models of intergroup contact must at the very least address the organizational scale of the societies involved and the physical distance separating them. In order for Cahokia to have been the guiding force behind long-distance, tightly controlled, regularly effective, and long-lasting exploitative relationships, American Bottom society would have had to have been highly centralized, and it must have possessed the means of consistently imposing its will on distant peoples. This would have been facilitated by a large and organized population that could be drawn upon in times of need. Several positions taken in recent years that cast Cahokia as a domineering, exploitative, and expansionist polity require that it was indeed a populous and highly centralized sociopolitical system.

As discussed previously, however, there are good reasons to question the accuracy of much of the conventional wisdom concerning American Bottom Mississippian society. The standard interpretation is especially problematic because population figures and the degree of societal centralization have tended to become exaggerated with frequent repetition, particularly when used to buttress arguments that rest on Cahokia's firm grip on a far-flung "periphery," "hinterland," or "frontier."

A few examples from the existing literature, all lacking supporting evidence, illustrate these points. American Bottom Mississippian society has been said to have had a market economy with rulers that acted as a "merchant class" (Porter 1969; 1974:28-29, 35-37, 176). They managed to hold sway over a vast hinterland where Ramey Incised pottery was presented to visiting dignitaries who traveled extensively to pursue their self-serving economic ends. It has been suggested that Cahokia was able to wrest enough food from people living 200 km away in the central Illinois River valley to have had a noticeable affect on the health of the outlying population (Goodman and Armelagos 1985). This exploitative relationship would have required sustained, strong force coupled with a high level of transportation efficiency and administrative organization. In addition, the cultural chronologies for the two areas indicate that the postulated interaction occurred

after Cahokia's peak of development. Southern Ontario has been included within Cahokia's economic orbit simply because canoes can be paddled along interconnected rivers and lakes (Little 1987). Cahokia's insatiable demand for bulk commodities through affiliated sites is invoked as the impetus behind the particular trajectory taken by Iroquoian culture in western New York (Dincauze and Hasenstab 1989; Hasenstab 1987). Raw materials were shipped toward the American Bottom, characterized as a "population and energy sink," through "bulk-breaking facilities" in the Ohio River valley and elsewhere (Dincauze and Hasenstab 1989:74-75). Cahokia's periphery received manufactured goods in return.

There is no doubt that nonlocal materials were exchanged through one means or another among widely distributed peoples throughout the late prehistoric time horizon. This is hardly surprising, as it had been happening for thousands of years. During the late prehistoric era, these items presumably passed from one social group to another in various ways, including down-the-line exchanges. The movement of some of these materials, judging from their archaeological contexts, must have been mediated by members of the elite social stratum in the Mississippian societies of the Southeast and Midwest, including Cahokia.

Nevertheless, the long-distance movement of limited amounts of often small and socially significant materials, frequently taking many years to pass from one hand to another, is simply not the same as the regular transportation of large quantities of bulk commodities, such as foodstuffs, through a vast intersociety nexus of coordinated economic transactions. From the perspective of the American Bottom, it is difficult to see Cahokia as an exploitative polity that had the need or the capacity to organize massive shipments of goods that were transported frequently and safely over distances totaling hundreds of kilometers.

Conclusion

Changes in the organizational character of the late prehistoric Cahokia-area sociopolitical system correspond rather closely to the waxing and waning of its interaction with other midcontinental societies, although both processes are poorly understood. While there is no consensus regarding the scale of the Cahokia-dominated regional system, there are reasons to doubt that it was as centralized, populous, and stable as customarily portrayed. Although impressive, the Cahokia system bore many similarities to societies elsewhere in the Mississippian world. It is hard to reconcile available information with archaeological scenarios featuring an expansionistic, exploitative Cahokia that dominated relations among cultures distributed throughout much of the midcontinent. Nevertheless, people in the American Bottom did participate in the wide circulation of nonlocal materials, and many of the items that have survived seem to have been used in prestige-enhancing displays and transactions.

This region's connections with societies elsewhere seemingly broadened early in the Mississippian period. The heyday of outwardly oriented interaction, however, had a limited duration, at least as it is imperfectly monitored by the wide distribution of diagnostic ceramics. Such an interpretation is for the most part compatible with developmental trajectories as they are presently understood for the upper Midwest (Anderson 1987; Gibbon 1974; Stoltman 1986), the central Illinois River valley (Harn 1975), and the northwestern Mississippi Yazoo Basin (Griffin 1986; Williams and Brain 1983:375-376, 410-412).

In terms of the broad sweep of eastern North American cultural evolution, Cahokia's impact was a pulse that once felt was soon gone. Moreover, its influence would have become rapidly attenuated with distance from the American Bottom. Given the scale of the societies involved, it is unlikely that there were once fleets of well-protected canoes regularly plying midcontinental waterways and transporting vast quantities of bulk goods across long distances from an exploited and distant periphery (or frontier) to enrich a core (or heartland), despite the recent arguments of several archaeologists. More realistic evaluations of the nature of interregional contact require additional research directed toward establishing finer controls over local cultural sequences and documenting the specific nature of changes over time in artifact inventories, modes of adaptation, the contexts of nonlocal material use, and social organization (e.g., Smith 1984). Only then can archaeologists clearly identify the nature of interaction among widely distributed cultures and reasonably evaluate the impact of Cahokia on local cultural sequences elsewhere in the midcontinent.

Acknowledgments

This paper was originally presented at the annual meeting of the Society for American Archaeology in 1986. The amount of information on American Bottom prehistory has increased dramatically since the late 1970s, largely as a result of large-scale contract archaeology projects mostly supported by the Illinois Department of Transportation. I would especially like to acknowledge Thomas E. Emerson's contributions to our present understanding of the principal elements and internal structure of Mississippian period outlying communities. We have worked intermittently on these topics, often together, for over a decade since we were both in the field. The comments of Virginia G. Smith, John E. Kelly, Claire McHale Milner, Sissel Schroeder, and James B. Stoltman on this paper are gratefully appreciated.

References Cited

Anderson, David G.
  1990 *Political Change in Chiefdom Societies: Cycling in the Late Prehistoric Southeastern United States.* Unpublished Ph.D. Dissertation. Department of Anthropology, University of Michigan, Ann Arbor, Michigan.
Anderson, Duane C.
  1981 *Mill Creek Ceramics: The Complex from the Brewster Site.* Report 14. Office of the State Archaeologist, University of Iowa, Iowa City, Iowa.
  1987 Toward a Processual Understanding the of Initial Variant of the Middle Missouri Tradition: The Case of the Mill Creek Culture of Iowa. *American Antiquity* 52:522-537.
Bareis, Charles J.
  1976 *The Knoebel Site, St. Clair County, Illinois.* Circular 1. Illinois Archaeological Survey, Urbana.
Bareis, Charles J., and James W. Porter
  1965 Megascopic and Petrographic Analyses of a Foreign Pottery Vessel from the Cahokia Site. *American Antiquity* 31:95-101.
Barrett, Samuel A.
  1933 *Ancient Aztalan.* Bulletin of the Public Museum of the City of Milwaukee 13. Milwaukee, Wisconsin.
Benchley, Elizabeth
  1976 *An Overview of the Prehistoric Resources of the Metropolitan St. Louis Area.* Cultural Resource Management Studies. National Park Service, U.S. Department of the Interior, Washington, D.C.

Bennett, John W.
  1945 *Archaeological Explorations in Jo Daviess County, Illinois.* University of Chicago Press, Chicago, Illinois.
Bleed, Peter
  1970 Notes on Aztalan Shell-Tempered Pottery. *The Wisconsin Archeologist* 51:1-20.
Brown, James A.
  1967 *The Gentleman Farm Site.* Reports of Investigations 12. Illinois State Museum, Springfield, Illinois.
Brown, Alan J., George R. Holley, Neal H. Lopinot, and William I. Woods
  1988 Cultural and Natural Explanations for Buried Late Prehistoric Sites in the American Bottom. Paper presented at the annual meeting of the Society for American Archaeology, Phoenix, Arizona.
Brown, James A., Richard A. Kerber, and Howard D. Winters
  1990 Trade and the Evolution of Exchange Relations at the Beginning of the Mississippian Period. In *The Mississippian Emergence*, edited by Bruce D. Smith, pp. 251-280. Smithsonian Institution Press, Washington, D.C.
Bushnell, David I.
  1904 *The Cahokia and Surrounding Mound Groups.* Papers of the Peabody Museum of American Archaeology and Ethnology 3(1). Harvard University, Cambridge, Massachusetts.
Chapman, Carl H.
  1980 *The Archaeology of Missouri, II.* University of Missouri Press, Columbia.
Chmurny, William W.
  1973 *The Ecology of the Middle Mississippian Occupation of the American Bottom.* Unpublished Ph.D. Dissertation, Department of Anthropology, University of Illinois, Urbana, Illinois.
Cole, Fay-Cooper
  1951 *Kincaid: A Prehistoric Illinois Metropolis.* University of Chicago Press, Chicago, Illinois.
Conner, Michael D.
  1985 Site Structure and Function. In *The Hill Creek Homestead and the Late Mississippian Settlement in the Lower Illinois Valley*, edited by Michael D. Conner, pp. 193-220. Research Series 1. Center for American Archeology, Kampsville, Illinois.
Conrad, Lawrence A.
  1989 The Southeastern Ceremonial Complex on the Northern Middle Mississippian Frontier: Late Prehistoric Politico-Religious Systems in the Central Illinois River Valley. In *The Southeastern Ceremonial Complex: Artifacts and Analysis*, edited by Patricia Galloway, pp. 93-113. University of Nebraska Press, Lincoln.
Conrad, Lawrence A., Timothy W. Good, and Susan Jelly
  1981 Analysis of Cordmarked Ceramics from Settlement C. In *The Orendorf Site: Preliminary Working Papers 1981* (3 vols.), compiled by Duane Esarey and Lawrence A. Conrad, pp. 117-159. Archaeological Research Laboratory, Western Illinois University, Macomb, Illinois.
Dincauze, Dena F., and Robert J. Hasenstab
  1989 Explaining the Iroquois: Tribalization on a Prehistoric Periphery. In *Centre and Periphery: Comparative Studies in Archaeology*, edited by Timothy C. Champion, pp. 67-87. Unwin Hyman, London.
Dorothy, Lawrence G.
  1980 The Ceramics of the Sand Point Site (20BG14) Baraga County, Michigan: A Preliminary Description. *The Michigan Archaeologist* 26:39-86.
DuPratz, Le Page
  1972 *The History of Louisiana.* Claitor's, Baton Rouge, Louisiana. Originally published 1774, London.
Emerson, Thomas E.
  1982 *Mississippian Stone Images in Illinois.* Circular 6. Illinois Archaeological Survey, Urbana, Illinois.
  1989 Water, Serpents, and the Underworld: An Exploration into Cahokian Symbolism. In *The Southeastern Ceremonial Complex: Artifacts and Analysis*, edited by P. Galloway, pp. 45-92. University of Nebraska Press, Lincoln, Nebraska.
Emerson, Thomas E., and Douglas K. Jackson
  1984 *The BBB Motor Site.* University of Illinois Press, Urbana, Illinois.

1987a Emergent Mississippian and Early Mississippian Homesteads at the Marcus Site (11-S-631). In *The Radic Site and The Marcus Site*, pp. 305-391. University of Illinois Press, Urbana, Illinois.

1987b The Edelhardt and Lindeman Phases: Setting the Stage for the Final Transition to Mississippian in the American Bottom. In *The Emergent Mississippian: Proceedings of the Sixth Mid-South Archaeological Conference, June 6-9, 1985*, edited by Richard A. Marshall, pp. 172-193. Occasional Papers 87-01. Cobb Institute of Archaeology, Mississippi State University, Mississippi State, Mississippi.

Emerson, Thomas E., and George R. Milner

1981 The Mississippian Occupation of the American Bottom: the Communities. Paper presented at the 26th Meeting of the Midwest Archaeological Conference, Madison, Wisconsin.

Emerson, Thomas E., George R. Milner, and Douglas K. Jackson

1983 *The Florence Street Site*. University of Illinois Press, Urbana, Illinois.

Esarey, Duane, and Sharron K. Santure

1990 The Morton Site Oneota Component and the Bold Counselor Phase. In *Archaeological Investigations at the Morton Village and Norris Farms 36 Cemetery*, edited by Sharron K. Santure, Alan D. Harn, and Duane Esarey, pp. 162-166. Reports of Investigations No. 45. Illinois State Museum, Springfield.

Finney, Fred A.

1985 The Carbon Dioxide Site. In *The Carbon Dioxide and Robert Schneider Sites*, pp. 3-167. University of Illinois Press, Urbana, Illinois.

Ford, Richard I.

1974 Northeastern Archeology: Past and Future Directions. *Annual Review of Anthropology* 3:385-413.

Fortier, Andrew C.

1985 The Robert Schneider Site. In *The Carbon Dioxide and Robert Schneider Sites*, pp. 171-313. University of Illinois Press, Urbana, Illinois.

1988 A Mississippian "Busk" Ceremonial Complex at the Sponemann Site. Paper presented at the 33rd Meeting of the Midwest Archaeological Conference, Urbana, Illinois.

Fowler, Melvin L.

1974 *Cahokia: Ancient Capital of the Midwest*. An Addison-Wesley Module in Anthropology 48:3-38.

1975 Pre-Columbian Urban Center on the Mississippi. *Scientific American* 233:92-101.

1978 Cahokia and the American Bottom: Settlement Archeology. In *Mississippian Settlement Patterns*, edited by Bruce D. Smith, pp. 455-478. Academic Press, New York.

1989 *The Cahokia Atlas*. Studies in Illinois Archaeology 6. Illinois Historic Preservation Agency, Springfield.

Fowler, Melvin L., and Robert L. Hall

1972 *Archaeological Phases at Cahokia*. Papers in Anthropology 1. Illinois State Museum, Springfield, Illinois.

1978 Late Prehistory of the Illinois Area. In *Northeast*, edited by Bruce G. Trigger, pp. 560-568. Handbook of North American Indians vol. 15, William G. Sturtevant, general editor. Smithsonian Institution, Washington, D.C.

Freeman, Joan E.

1986 Aztalan: a Middle Mississippian Village. *The Wisconsin Archeologist* 67:339-364.

Fried, Morton H.

1967 *The Evolution of Political Society: An Essay in Political Anthropology*. Random House, New York.

Gibbon, Guy E.

1974 A Model of Mississippian Development and its Implications for the Red Wing Area. In *Aspects of Upper Great Lakes Anthropology*, edited by Elden Johnson, pp. 129-137. Minnesota Historical Society, St. Paul, Minnesota.

Goldstein, Lynne G.

1980 *Mississippian Mortuary Practices: A Case Study of Two Cemeteries in the Lower Illinois Valley*. Scientific Papers 4. Northwestern University Archaeological Program, Evanston, Illinois.

Goodman, Alan H., and George J. Armelagos

1985 Disease and Death at Dr. Dickson's Mounds. *Natural History* 94:12-18.

Gregg, Michael L.

1975a A Population Estimate for Cahokia. In *Perspectives in Cahokia Archaeology*, pp. 126-136. Bulletin 10. Illinois Archaeological Survey, Urbana, Illinois.

1975b *Settlement Morphology and Production Specialization: the Horseshoe Lake Site, a Case Study.* Unpublished Ph.D. Dissertation. Department of Anthropology, University of Wisconsin, Milwaukee, Wisconsin.

Griffin, James B.

1946 Cultural Change and Continuity in Eastern United States Archaeology. In *Man in Northeastern North America*, edited by Frederick Johnson, pp. 37-95. Papers of the Robert S. Peabody Foundation for Archaeology 3. Phillips Academy, Andover, Massachusetts.

1967 Eastern North American Archaeology: A Summary. *Science* 156:175-191.

1977 The University of Michigan Excavations at the Pulcher Site in 1950. *American Antiquity* 42:462-490.

1983 The Midlands. In *Ancient North Americans*, edited by Jesse D. Jennings, pp. 243-301. W. H. Freeman, New York.

1985 Changing Concepts of the Prehistoric Mississippian Cultures of the Eastern United States. In *Alabama and the Borderlands*, edited by R. Reid Badger and Lawrence A. Clayton, pp. 40-63. University of Alabama Press, Tuscaloosa, Alabama.

1986 Review of *Excavations at the Lake George Site, Yazoo County, Mississippi*, by Stephen Williams and Jeffrey P. Brain. *Southeastern Archaeology* 5:71-73.

Hall, Robert L.

1967 The Mississippian Heartland and its Plains Relationship. *Plains Anthropologist* 12:175-183.

1986 Upper Mississippi and Middle Mississippi Relationships. *The Wisconsin Archeologist* 67:365-369.

Hally, David J., Marvin T. Smith, and James B. Langford

1990 The Archaeological Reality of De Soto's Coosa. In *Columbian Consequences*, vol. 2, edited by David H. Thomas, pp. 121-138. Smithsonian Institution Press, Washington, DC.

Hanenberger, Ned H.

1990a The Karol Rekas Site (11-Ms-1255). In *Selected Early Mississippian Household Sites in the American Bottom*, pp. 425-509. University of Illinois Press, Urbana, Illinois.

1990b The Olszewski Site (11-S-465). In *Selected Early Mississippian Household Sites in the American Bottom*, pp. 253-423. University of Illinois Press, Urbana, Illinois.

Hargrave, Michael L.

1983 Ceramic Vessel Form, Decoration, and Chronology. In *The Bridges Site (11-Mr-11) A Late Prehistoric Settlement in the Central Kaskaskia Valley*, by Michael L. Hargrave, Gerald A. Oetelaar, Neal H. Lopinot, Brian M. Butler, and Deborah A. Billings, pp. 176-216. Research Paper 38. Center for Archaeological Investigations, Southern Illinois University, Carbondale, Illinois.

Harn, Alan D.

1971 An Archaeological Survey of the American Bottoms in Madison and St. Clair Counties, Illinois. In *An Archaeological Survey of the American Bottoms and Wood River Terrace*, by Patrick J. Munson and Alan D. Harn, pp. 19-39. Reports of Investigations 21. Illinois State Museum, Springfield, Illinois.

1975 Cahokia and the Mississippian Emergence in the Spoon River Area of Illinois. *Transactions of the Illinois State Academy of Science* 68:414-434.

1980 *The Prehistory of Dickson Mounds: The Dickson Excavation* 2nd ed. Reports of Investigations 35. Illinois State Museum, Springfield, Illinois.

Hasenstab, Robert J.

1987 Canoes, Caches, and Carrying Places: Territorial Boundaries and Tribalization in Late Woodland Western New York. *Journal of the New York State Archaeological Association* 95:39-49.

Hatch, James W.

1976 *Status in Death: Principles of Ranking in Dallas Culture Mortuary Remains.* Unpublished Ph.D. Dissertation. Department of Anthropology, Pennsylvania State University, University Park, Pennsylvania.

Henning, Dale R.

1967 Mississippian Influences on the Eastern Plains Border: An Evaluation. *Plains Anthropologist* 12:184-221.

Hines, Philip
   1977 On Social Organization in the Middle Mississippian: States or Chiefdoms? *Current Anthropology* 18:337-338.
Holley, George R., Neil H. Lopinot, William I. Woods, and John E. Kelly
   1989 Dynamics of Community Organization at Prehistoric Cahokia. In *Households and Communities*, edited by Scott MacEachern, David J. W. Archer, and Richard D. Garvin, pp. 339-349. Archaeology Association, University of Calgary, Calgary.
Hudson, Charles, Marvin Smith, David Hally, Richard Polhemus, and Chester DePratter
   1985 Coosa: A Chiefdom in the Sixteenth-Century Southeastern United States. *American Antiquity* 50:723-737.
Jackson, Douglas K.
   1988 Investigations at the Keller-Samson Borrow Pit: Early Emergent Mississippian Occupations in Madison County, Illinois. Paper presented at the 33rd Meeting of the Midwest Archaeological Conference, Urbana, Illinois.
   1990a The Esterlein Site (11-Ms-598). In *Selected Early Mississippian Household Sites in the American Bottom*, pp. 91-216. University of Illinois Press, Urbana, Illinois.
   1990b The Sandy Ridge Farm Site (11-S-660). In *Selected Early Mississippian Household Sites in the American Bottom*, pp. 217-252. University of Illinois Press, Urbana, Illinois.
   1990c The Willoughby Site (11-Ms-610). In *Selected Early Mississippian Household Sites in the American Bottom*, pp. 17-89. University of Illinois Press, Urbana, Illinois.
Johannessen, Sissel
   1984 Paleoethnobotany. In *American Bottom Archaeology*, edited by Charles J. Bareis and James W. Porter, pp. 197-214. University of Illinois Press, Urbana, Illinois.
Kellar, James H.
   1967 Material Remains. In *Angel Site* (2 vols.), by Glenn A. Black, pp. 431-487. Indiana Historical Society, Indianapolis, Indiana.
Kelly, John E.
   1980 *FormativeDevelopments at Cahokia and the Adjacent American Bottom: A Merrell Tract Perspective.* Unpublished Ph.D. dissertation. Department of Anthropology, University of Wisconsin-Madison.
   1987 Emergent Mississippian and the Transition from Late Woodland to Mississippian: The American Bottom Case for a New Concept. In *The Emergent Mississippian: Proceedings of the Sixth Mid-South Archaeological Conference, June 6-9, 1985*, edited by Richard A. Marshall, pp. 212-226. Occasional Papers 87-01. Cobb Institute of Archaeology, Mississippi State University, Mississippi State, Mississippi.
   1990a Range Site Community Patterns and the Mississippian Emergence. In *The Mississippian Emergence*, edited by Bruce D. Smith, pp. 67-112. Smithsonian Institution Press, Washington, D.C.
   1990b The Emergence of Mississippian Culture in the American Bottom Region. In *The Mississippian Emergence*, edited by Bruce D. Smith, pp. 113-152. Smithsonian Institution Press, Washington, D.C.
Kelly, John E., Andrew C. Fortier, Stephen J. Ozuk, and Joyce A. Williams
   1987 *The Range Site: Archaic through Late Woodland Occupations.* University of Illinois Press, Urbana, Illinois.
Kelly, John E., and Bonnie L. Gums
   1987 *Phase I Cultural Resource Investigations of the I-55/70 Expressway, East St. Louis, St. Clair County, Illinois.* Contract Archaeology Program, Southern Illinois University, Edwardsville, Illinois.
Kelly, John E., Jean R. Linder, and Theresa J. Cartmell
   1979 *The Archaeological Intensive Survey of the Proposed FAI-270 Alignment in the American Bottom Region of Southern Illinois.* Archaeology Scientific Reports 1, Illinois Department of Transportation, Springfield, Illinois.
Kelly, John E., Steven J. Ozuk, Douglas K. Jackson, Dale L. McElrath, Fred A. Finney, and Duane Esarey
   1984 Emergent Mississippian Period. In *American Bottom Archaeology*, edited by Charles J. Bareis and James W. Porter, pp. 128-157. University of Illinois Press, Urbana, Illinois.
Kelly, John E., Stephen J. Ozuk, and Joyce A. Williams
   1990 *The Range Site 2: The Emergent Mississippian Dohack and Range Phase Occupations.* University of Illinois Press, Urbana.

Kelly, Lucretia S., and Paula G. Cross
  1984 Zooarchaeology. In *American Bottom Archaeology*, edited by Charles J. Bareis and James W. Porter, pp. 215-232. University of Illinois Press, Urbana, Illinois.
Little, Elizabeth A.
  1987 Inland Waterways in the Northeast. *Midcontinental Journal of Archaeology* 12:55-76.
McElrath, Dale L., and Fred A. Finney
  1987 *The George Reeves Site*. University of Illinois Press, Urbana, Illinois.
McElrath, Dale L., Joyce A. Williams, Thomas O. Maher, and Michael C. Meinkoth
  1987 Emergent Mississippian and Mississippian Communities at the Radic Site. In *The Radic Site and the Marcus Site*, pp. 1-304. University of Illinois Press, Urbana, Illinois.
McPherron, Alan
  1967 *The Juntunen Site and the Late Woodland Prehistory of the Upper Great Lakes Area*. Anthropological Papers 30. Museum of Anthropology, University of Michigan, Ann Arbor, Michigan.
Mehrer, Mark W.
  1982 *A Mississippian Community at the Range Site (11-S-47), St. Clair County, Illinois*. FAI-270 Archaeological Mitigation Project Report 52. Department of Anthropology, University of Illinois, Urbana, Illinois.
  1988 *The Settlement Patterns and Social Power of Cahokia's Hinterland Households*. Unpublished Ph.D. Dissertation. Department of Anthropology, University of Illinois, Urbana, Illinois.
Milner, George R.
  1983 *The Turner and DeMange Sites*. University of Illinois Press, Urbana, Illinois.
  1984a Social and Temporal Implications of Variation among American Bottom Mississippian Cemeteries. *American Antiquity* 49:468-488.
  1984b *The Julien Site*. University of Illinois Press, Urbana, Illinois.
  1984c *The Robinson's Lake Site*. University of Illinois Press, Urbana, Illinois.
  1986 Mississippian Period Population Density in a Segment of the Central Mississippi River Valley. *American Antiquity* 51:468-488.
  1987a Cultures in Transition: The Late Emergent Mississippian and Mississippian Periods in the American Bottom, Illinois. In *The Emergent Mississippian: Proceedings of the Sixth Mid-South Archaeological Conference, June 6-9, 1985*, edited by Richard A. Marshall, pp. 194-211. Occasional Papers 87-01. Cobb Institute of Archaeology, Mississippi State University, Mississippi State, Mississippi.
  1987b The Development and Dissolution of an Organizationally Complex Mississippian Period Culture in the American Bottom, Illinois. Paper presented at the Southeastern Archaeological Conference, Charleston, South Carolina.
  1990a Cultural Dynamics, Data, and Debate: Perspectives from Late Prehistoric Western Illinois. Paper presented at Mississippian Transformations: Social Change in the Late Prehistoric Midwest. Purdue University, West Lafayette, Indiana.
  1990b The Late Prehistoric Cahokia Cultural System of the Mississippi River Valley: Foundations, Florescence, and Fragmentation. *Journal of World Prehistory* 4:1-43.
Milner, George R., Thomas E. Emerson, Mark W. Mehrer, Joyce A. Williams, and Duane Esarey
  1984 Mississippian and Oneota. In *American Bottom Archaeology*, edited by Charles J. Bareis and James W. Porter, pp. 158-186. University of Illinois Press, Urbana, Illinois.
Moberg, Carl-Axel
  1983 Mississippian Seen from La Tène: On Comparisons of Prehistoric Social Disorganizations. In *Lulu Linear Punctated: Essays in Honor of George Irving Quimby*, edited by Robert C. Dunnell and Donald K Grayson, pp. 167-184. Anthropological Papers 72. Museum of Anthropology, University of Michigan, Ann Arbor, Michigan.
Morse, Dan F., and Phyllis A. Morse
  1983 *Archaeology of the Central Mississippi Valley*. Academic Press, New York.
Neitzel, Robert S.
  1965 *Archeology of the Fatherland Site: The Grand Village of the Natchez*. Anthropological Papers Vol. 51(1). American Museum of Natural History, New York.
  1983 *The Grand Village of the Natchez Revisited*. Archaeological Report 12. Mississippi Department of Archives and History, Jackson, Mississippi.

O'Brien, Patricia J.

1969 The Chronological Position of the Cambered Jar at Cahokia and its Implications. *American Antiquity* 34:411-416.

1972a *A Formal Analysis of Cahokia Ceramics from the Powell Tract*. Monograph 3. Illinois Archaeological Survey, Urbana, Illinois.

1972b Urbanism, Cahokia and Middle Mississippian. *Archaeology* 25:189-197.

1981 Steed-Kisker: a Cultural Interpretation. *The Missouri Archaeologist* 42:97-108.

Pauketat, Timothy R., and William I. Woods

1986 Middle Mississippian Structure Analysis: The Lawrence Primas Site (11-Ms-895) in the American Bottom. *The Wisconsin Archeologist* 67:104-127.

Peebles, Christopher S., and Susan M. Kus

1977 Some Archaeological Correlates of Ranked Societies. *American Antiquity* 42:421-448.

Phillips, Phillip

1970 *Archaeological Survey in the Lower Yazoo Basin, Mississippi, 1949-1955* (2 vols.). Papers of the Peabody Museum of Archaeology and Ethnology 60. Harvard University, Cambridge, MA.

Phillips, W. A.

1900 Aboriginal Quarries and Shops at Mill Creek, Illinois. *American Anthropologist* 2:37-52.

Porter, James W.

1969 The Mitchell Site and Prehistoric Exchange Systems at Cahokia: AD 1000±300. In *Explorations into Cahokia Archaeology*, edited by Melvin L. Fowler, pp. 137-164. Bulletin 7. Illinois Archaeological Survey, Urbana, Illinois.

1974 *Cahokia Archaeology as Viewed from the Mitchell Site: A Satellite Community at A.D. 1150-1200*. Unpublished Ph.D. Dissertation. University of Wisconsin, Madison, Wisconsin.

Prentice, Guy

1986 An Analysis of the Symbolism Expressed by the Birger Figurine. *American Antiquity* 51:239-266.

Prentice, Guy, and Mark Mehrer

1981 The Lab Woofie Site (11-S-346): An Unplowed Mississippian Site in the American Bottom Region of Illinois. *Midcontinental Journal of Archaeology* 6:33-53.

Rau, Charles

1869 A Deposit of Agricultural Flint Implements in Southern Illinois. In *Annual Report of the Board of Regents of the Smithsonian Institution for the Year 1868*, pp. 401-407. Washington, D.C.

Reed, Nelson A., John W. Bennett, and James W. Porter

1968 Solid Core Drilling of Monks Mound: Technique and Findings. *American Antiquity* 33:137-148.

Schoolcraft, Henry R.

1819 *A View of the Lead Mines of Missouri*. Charles Wiley and Co., New York.

Sears, William

1968 The State and Settlement Patterns in the New World. In *Settlement Archaeology*, edited by K. C. Chang, pp. 134-153. National Press Books, Palo Alto, California.

Smith, Bruce D.

1978 Variation in Mississippian Settlement Patterns. In *Mississippian Settlement Patterns*, edited by Bruce D. Smith, pp. 479-503. Academic Press, New York.

1984 Mississippian Expansion: Tracing the Historical Development of an Explanatory Model. *Southeastern Archaeology* 3:13-32.

1985 Mississippian Patterns of Subsistence and Settlement. In *Alabama and the Borderlands*, edited by R. Reid Badger and Lawrence A. Clayton, pp. 64-79. University of Alabama Press, Tuscaloosa, Alabama.

1986 The Archaeology of the Southeastern United States: From Dalton to De Soto, 10,500-500 B.P. *Advances in World Archaeology*, Vol. 5, edited by Fred Wendorf and Angela E. Close, pp. 1-92. Academic Press, Orlando, Florida.

Smith, Marvin T.

1987 *Archaeology of Aboriginal Culture Change in the Interior Southeast*. University of Florida Press, Gainesville, Florida.

Snyder, John F.

1877 Deposits of Flint Implements. In *Annual Report of the Smithsonian Institution for 1876*, pp. 433-441. Smithsonian Institution, Washington, D.C.

Stahl, Ann B.
    1985 *The Dohack Site*. University of Illinois Press, Urbana, Illinois.
Steponaitis, Vincas P.
    1978 Location Theory and Complex Chiefdoms: A Mississippian Example. In *Mississippian Settlement Patterns*, edited by Bruce D. Smith, pp. 417-453. Academic Press, New York.
    1986 Prehistoric Archaeology in the Southeastern United States, 1970-1985. *Annual Review of Anthropology* 15:363-404.
Stoltman, James B.
    1978 Temporal Models in Prehistory: An Example from Eastern North America. *Current Anthropology* 19:703-729.
    1986 The Appearance of the Mississippian Cultural Tradition in the Upper Mississippi Valley. In *Prehistoric Mound Builders of the Mississippi Valley*, edited by James B. Stoltman, pp. 26-34. Putnam Museum, Davenport, Iowa.
Swanton, John R. (editor)
    1939 *Final Report of the United States De Soto Commission*. House Document 71. 76th Congress, 1st Session, Washington, D.C.
Szuter, Christine R.
    1979 *The Schlemmer Site: a Late Woodland-Mississippian Site in the American Bottom*. Unpublished M.A. Thesis, Department of Anthropology, Loyola University, Chicago, Illinois.
Thomas, Cyrus
    1907 Cahokia or Monk's Mound. *American Anthropologist* 9:362-365.
Tiffany, Joseph A.
    1982 Hartley Fort Ceramics. *Proceedings of the Iowa Academy of Science* 89:133-150.
    1983 An Overview of the Middle Missouri Tradition. In *Prairie Archaeology: Papers in Honor of David A. Baerreis*, edited by Guy E. Gibbon, pp. 87-108. Publications in Anthropology 3. University of Minnesota, Minneapolis, Minnesota.
Walthall, John A.
    1981 *Galena and Aboriginal Trade in Eastern North America*. Scientific Papers 17. Illinois State Museum, Springfield, Illinois.
Wedel, Waldo R.
    1943 *Archeological Investigations in Platte and Clay Counties, Missouri*. Bulletin 183. United States National Museum, Washington, D.C.
Williams, Stephen, and Jeffrey P. Brain
    1983 *Excavations at the Lake George Site, Yazoo County, Mississippi, 1958-1960*. Papers of the Peabody Museum of Archaeology and Ethnology 74. Harvard University, Cambridge, Massachusetts.
Winters, Howard D.
    1974 Some Unusual Grave Goods from a Mississippian Burial Mound. *Indian Notes* 10:34-46.
    1981 Excavating in Museums: Notes on Mississippian Hoes and Middle Woodland Copper Gouges and Celts. In *The Research Potential of Anthropological Museum Collections*, edited by Anne-Marie E. Cantwell, James B. Griffin, and Nan A. Rothschild, pp. 17-34. Annals of the New York Academy of Sciences 376. New York.
Wittry, Warren L., and Joseph O. Vogel
    1962 Illinois State Museum Projects. In *First Annual Report: American Bottoms Archaeology*, edited by Melvin L. Fowler, pp. 14-30. Illinois Archaeological Survey, Urbana, Illinois.
Woods, William I.
    1986 *Prehistoric Settlement and Subsistence in the Upland Cahokia Creek Drainage*. Unpublished Ph.D. Dissertation. Department of Geography, University of Wisconsin, Milwaukee, Wisconsin.
Woods, William I., and George R. Holley
    n.d. Upland Mississippian Settlement in the American Bottom Region. In *Cahokia and the Hinterlands: Middle Mississippian Cultures of the Midwest*, edited by Thomas E. Emerson and R. Barry Lewis. University of Illinois Press, Urbana, Illinois, in press.
Yerkes, Richard W.
    1987 *Prehistoric Life on the Mississippi Floodplain*. University of Chicago Press, Chicago, Illinois.

3

Specialization in Shell Artifact Production at Cahokia

Richard W. Yerkes
Department of Anthropology
The Ohio State University

The American Bottom of the Mississippi River Valley was probably the most densely populated area in Eastern North America between A.D. 900 and 1400. This region is dominated by the Cahokia site, the largest Precolumbian site north of Mexico, which covered nearly 16 km², and grew to include nearly 120 earthen mounds arranged in 11 possible mound and plaza groupings (Fowler 1978, 1989). However, there are at least 10 other town-and-mound centers within 25 km of Cahokia, and hundreds of smaller Mississippian sites can be found on the floodplain and in the uplands between the Illinois-Missouri-Mississippi confluences and the mouth of the Kaskaskia River. Archaeological investigations have been conducted on only about one quarter of one percent of the Cahokia site (Hall 1975:30), but large quantities of exotic materials and finely made craft objects have been recovered, as well as evidence for numerous civic-ceremonial structures, a large palisade, and "woodhenges" for solar observations. Numerous houses and dense deposits of domestic debris have also been encountered in the small excavated portion of the Cahokia site (Fowler 1978; Milner 1990).

The materials found at outlying Mississippian sites in the American Bottom region are usually classified as domestic tools and debris. However, exotic materials including mica, galena, marine shell, and nonlocal chert have been recovered from several small sites. Finely-made articles such as bauxite figurines, Ramey Incised pottery, effigy ceramic vessels, spatulate celts (or spuds), Ramey Knives, and marine shell beads have also been found in Mississippian "domestic" contexts and in cemeteries located outside of the Cahokia site limits (Emerson 1989; Milner 1990).

The archaeology of the American Bottom is impressive, but it has become fashionable to scale down estimates of the size of the prehistoric population at Cahokia and its hinterland, and to understate the complexity of the political and economic organization of Cahokia society. Middle Mississippian populations are usually described as ranked societies with varying degrees of political and economic complexity, or groups that had reached the chiefdom level in the evolutionary scheme popularized by Elman Service (Drennan and Uribe 1987; Griffin 1983:280; Peebles and Kus 1977). Several archaeologists and ethnohistorians have suggested that large Mississippian polities like Cahokia may have formed primitive states (Gibbon 1974; Hall 1986:368; Hudson 1976:203-206; O'Brien 1972; Sears 1968), but others have claimed that the idea of a Mississippian state at Cahokia is based on inflated population estimates, an overstatement of the integrated nature of the site hierarchy implied by the four-tiered settlement model developed by Fowler (1974, 1978), and an exaggerated picture of the authority of the ruling elite (Griffin 1983;:283; Milner 1990; Muller 1987).

The debate about Mississippian political and economic organization has included the concepts and definitions found in the band-tribe-chiefdom-state evolutionary scheme elaborated by Service (1962, 1963, 1975) but the debaters have not been consistent or critical in their use of these terms. However, Lawrence Conrad (1989:93-98) has attempted to clarify the issue by providing a valuable review of Service's definitions of "primitive states" and "chiefdoms," and applying the terms in a discussion of Mississippian social organization. Conrad's study provides the theoretical foundation for my examination of craft specialization and socioeconomic organization at Cahokia.

The Primitive State at Cahokia

Conrad noted that in Service's scheme, both chiefdoms and states were characterized by social classes, but the determinant characteristic of a primitive state was,

> ...the use of force and constant threat of force from an institutionalized body of persons who wield force. A state constitutes itself legally: it makes explicit the manner and circumstances of its use of force, and it outlaws all other uses of force as it intervenes in the disputes between individuals and groups (Service 1963:xxvi).

Conrad concluded that in a primitive state, the role of the kin group in resolving disputes between individuals is diminished. "The state redresses grievances against individuals, and the family is powerless to help individuals with grievances against the state" (Conrad 1989:94).

Service's second characteristic of primitive states involves politico-economic classes:

> Thus the aristocracy are the state bureaucrats, the military leaders, and the upper priesthood. Other people are the producers. Full-time professionalism in the arts and crafts developed also, and the artisans can be regarded as still another socioeconomic group (Service 1963:xxvii).

The development of full-time professionalism marks an important change in economic systems. It represents new relationships between people and elements of production, as well as changes in the power of individuals to control resources, distribute products, and produce surplus goods. Following Service, Arnold (1987b:1) believes that the development of craft specialization is a key factor in the rise of cultural complexity, but she found that it is very difficult to define and identify professionalism or economic specialization. Arnold noted that expert artisans that are capable of producing finely made materials are not necessarily "professional" craft specialists. She used archaeological indicators that reflect organizational qualities to define craft specialization as:

> ...conditions of organized production and distribution of large volumes of manufactured goods (...in excess of local needs) by groups of individuals who are freed at least part time from subsistence pursuits (1987b:2).

Arnold concludes that prehistoric craft specialization can be recognized when there is evidence for: (1) very high volume of production materials, (2) identifiable workshops separated from domestic areas, (3) distinct patterning in regional artifact distribution reflecting organized and controlled production and exportation activities, (4) high degree of technological standardization and high success rates in production, (5) control over critical resources, (6) presence of distinctive arrays of specialists' tools with burials (1987b:30). But are these indicators for craft specialization (and state-level organization) documented in the archaeological record for the Cahokia settlement system?

Service suggests that archaeological deposits reveal the hierarchical nature of chiefdoms through the presence of status burials, subsidized specialists in the fine arts, public monuments, storage facilities, and foreign trade items, but he noted that, "...there seems to be no way to discriminate the state from the chiefdom stage..." in these kinds of archaeological data (Service 1975:304). Conrad (1989:95) points out that many archaeologists ignore this difficulty and conclude that while there is evidence for chiefdoms at Mississippian sites, there is none for states.

The question of Mississippian statehood is further clouded by the fact that Service did not believe that there were any primitive states in Southeastern North America at the time of European contact, even though the Natchez, Taensas (?), Timucua, and Calusa societies of the early Historic period meet his criteria for this form of socioeconomic organization (Conrad 1989). This is not really surprising, if we consider that most cultural evolutionists since the time of Lewis Henry Morgan have argued that cultural complexity declines as one moves from the lower latitudes to the temperate woodlands. For example, Carl-Axel Moberg (1983:168) observed that culture contact situations in "Temperate Forest" societies in Europe and North America have been described from the perspective of "Mediterranean" groups that were bent on conquering the "heathen" and "barbarian" forest-dwellers (Hudson 1976:98). This "southern perspective" in accounts of northern European Iron-age societies led to the characterization of La Tène or Hallstadt groups as "barbarian stratified societies" rather than primitive states (Moberg 1983:175-176). The "state" designation was reserved for the "civilized" societies found to the south of the Woodland groups.

The popular view that Southeastern societies were not as politically sophisticated nor militarily or economically structured as their Mesoamerican counterparts may have originated with the accounts of the first Europeans in the New World, but it is interesting to remember that a veteran of the Inka conquest, Hernando De Soto, dealt with the Southeastern rulers in the same fashion that the Spanish had dealt with the Mesoamerican and Andean lords. The accounts of De Soto's invasion include descriptions of powerful rulers, aristocrats, retainers, temples, and other elaborate structures found in impressive Indian societies such as Cofitachequi, Coosa, and Alibamu (Hudson 1976:107-116).

The Spanish battles with the Southeastern warriors forced the treasure-seekers to conclude that these Woodland people were "bellicose and free" (like the Gauls encountered by Caesar?), and would not be dominated as easily as the Mexican and Peruvian Indians (Hudson 1976:114). There were times when even the most aggressive members of De Soto's expedition were forced to back down and seek peace with the lords of "provinces" like Quizquiz and Quigualtam (Brain 1978:356-357).

Jeffrey Brain remarked that the power and confidence of the rulers of the Southeastern societies that opposed the European invaders is revealed in the response that the Cacique of Quigualtam sent to De Soto after the Spaniard had demanded his subservience:

> It is not my custom to visit anyone, but rather all, of whom I have ever heard, have come to visit me, to serve and obey me, and pay me tribute, either voluntarily or by force: if you desire to see me, come where I am; if for peace, I will receive you with special goodwill; if for war, I will await you in my town; but neither for you, nor for any man, will I step back one foot (Bourne 1922, I:154-155; cited in Brain 1978:357).

Quigualtam was never visited by the Spanish, but it has been associated with the proto-Natchez Emerald phase in the Lower Mississippi Valley (Brain 1978), and the Cacique may have been the ancestor of the Natchez "Great Suns" described by the French between A.D. 1682 and 1730 (Swanton 1911). The Natchez are the best known of the primitive states that survived into the Historic period in the Southeast, and Conrad (1989:95-98) cites several ethnohistoric

accounts that demonstrate that their government had a monopoly on the use of force in both domestic and external affairs. Natchez aristocrats could have a commoner killed without any complaint from the victim's kin group. Natchez people (not slaves or war captives) were also killed as part of the burial program for aristocrats (the best documented example of this practice was the account of the death of Tattooed-Serpent in A.D. 1725; see Hudson 1976:328-334).

These elaborate ceremonies are also recorded in the prehistoric record. Archaeologists view the mass graves and retainer sacrifices in Mound 72 at Cahokia as a prehistoric example of the elaborate burial rituals that were conducted after the death of a Mississippian aristocrat, and ethnohistorians see the Natchez ceremonies as the last survival (in a reduced form) of the full Mississippian mortuary ritual (Hudson 1976:334). However, Conrad (1989:98) suggests that the Mound 72 burial data also demonstrate the life-and-death power of one Mississippian class over another, a power that is only found in primitive states.

Social Classes and Professionalism in the Arts and Crafts

The French accounts describe a number of individuals in Natchez society whose full-time job was to serve the Great Sun or other aristocrats, and several state offices such as full-time war chiefs and temple attendants are mentioned as well (Conrad 1989:97; Oswalt 1988:444-455). However, the French made no mention of professionalism in the arts and crafts among the Natchez. Conrad (1989:97) argues that the large quantities of finely made craft goods at prehistoric Mississippian sites, including the "politico-religious" materials in the Southeastern Ceremonial Complex, indicate that, "specialized artisans under state control did exist, along with efficient procurement systems for the needed raw materials." In the classification of specialists recently proposed by Brumfiel and Earle (1987:5), these individuals would be called *attached specialists*, who produce goods or provide services to patrons. The archaeological data on the organization and production of politico-religious materials at Cahokia seem to meet most of Arnold's (1987) criteria for prehistoric craft specialization.

It is possible that by the eighteenth century the decline in aboriginal population and the introduction of European goods into the Natchez economy had reduced the demand for professionally produced craft goods, and that full-time craft specialists were no longer supported by the Natchez elite (it should be noted that the Chumash microblade industry that Arnold [1985, 1987a, 1987b] has associated with the production of marine shell bead money in California declined rapidly after the introduction of iron needles in the eighteenth century as the microblade manufacturing specialists were no longer needed).

Some have suggested that the accounts of De Soto's invasion provide us with hints that earlier contacts with Europeans had disrupted the aboriginal societies and that the power of Southeastern rulers had begun to erode by the sixteenth century (Brose 1989; Hudson 1976). Others have argued that native Southeastern societies were never more than low-level chiefdoms, and that the "state-like" features of the Natchez and other historic groups were adopted only after contact with "civilized" Europeans (Muller 1987:11). Regardless of the slant that one gives to these ethnohistorical accounts, it must be remembered that they all refer to Southeastern societies *after* they had some direct or indirect contact with Europeans (Brose 1989:28). We have no ethnographic or ethnohistoric account of precontact societies in the Mississippi Valley, thus our interpretation of Mississippian religious, political, and economic systems must be based solely on the analysis of archaeological data. While we may find analogies for some of the prehistoric systems we describe in ethnohistorical accounts, we must not limit ourselves by assuming that *all* of the forms of socioeconomic organization that existed in prehistoric Mississippian societies were documented by the "military adventurers, Counter-Reformation missionaries, and unlicensed low-venture capitalists" (Brose 1989:note 6) that compiled this ethnohistoric record.

Mississippian Craft Specialization

Lawrence Conrad (1989) examined the ethnohistoric record, and found documentary evidence for the institutionalized use of force and the cross-cutting of society into politico-economic classes among several historic Southeastern societies (most notably the Natchez), but he found no mention of full-time professionalism in the arts and crafts. Still he concluded that examples of what Service called primitive states did exist among some historic and prehistoric Middle Mississippian groups, because the combination of archaeological and ethnohistorical data supports such a conclusion. Conrad argues that, "even without ethnographic analogy, occupational specialization would be assumed at Cahokia from the existence of very large quantities of exotic materials, fine craft objects, tremendous and well-planned earthworks and fortifications, large numbers of people living and working together in a naturally constricted area, and the localization of certain work areas" (Conrad 1989:98).

My own studies of the Cahokia "Microlithic Industry" and Mississippian shell craft production have supported the case for craft specialization at

Cahokia and at other Mississippian sites in the American Bottom region (Yerkes 1983, 1986, 1989a, 1989b, 1989c), but a number of colleagues have challenged this position. Muller (1984, 1986, 1987), Pauketat (1987), and Milner (1990) have argued that evidence for the production of fine craft objects such as Ramey Incised pottery, bauxite statues and pipes, and marine shell beads is not enough to demonstrate occupational specialization. There must be evidence that these items were manufactured only by a small group of "specialists" and that the goods were not produced for "local" consumption, before professionalism in the arts and crafts can be established. These authors believe that a simple socioeconomic system (typical of low-level chiefdoms) of casual production and exchange by artistically inclined farmers would account for the manufacture and distribution of the quantities of craft goods recovered from Mississippian sites in the American Bottom region. While they concede that some form of task specialization *may* have existed in Cahokia Mississippian society, they believe that the available evidence is, "...insufficient for discriminating among different levels in the incidental to full-time work continuum" (Milner 1990:14).

Milner has concluded that there is absolutely no evidence for any occupational specialization at the outlying Mississippian communities in Cahokia's hinterland, but his conclusion is presented without any supporting evidence. In response to these critics, I will present a summary of the evidence for craft specialization in the Cahokia "Microlithic Industry" and in marine shell bead production.

The Cahokia Microlithic Industry

Analysis of the Cahokia "microlithic" technology has revealed that the microdrills, microblades, and microblade cores that are included in the Cahokia Microlithic Industry represent a lithic production trajectory that was designed to produce long, thick, prismatic microblades that served as blanks for microdrills that were used to perforate shell material (Koldehoff 1987; Mason and Perino 1961; Morse 1964; O'Brien 1972; Yerkes 1983; 1989a, 1989b). The microblade cores were produced by breaking up nodules or tabular blocks of white Burlington chert using the bipolar technique. Platforms were prepared, and burin blows were struck to remove the microblades (which resemble burin spalls more than "true" microblades). The "classic" Cahokia microblade cores look like large burins, although bipolar and amorphous cores are also present in the microlithic assemblages. The microblades were then finely retouched to form rod-shaped microdrills which were then hafted and used to drill shell (Figure 3.1).

Very few microblade cores have been found at Mississippian sites outside of Cahokia in the American Bottom, and concentrations of microcores and unretouched microblades (or microdrill blanks) have only been documented at four locations within the site proper (Figure 3.2). The largest microdrill workshop covered at least two hectares near Mound 12 in the Kunneman Group at the northern limit of the Cahokia site. Dan Morse, Gregory Perino, and Ronald Mason were all impressed by the abundance of microlithic artifacts that "literally covered the ground" (Morse 1974) at the Kunneman Tract, and they

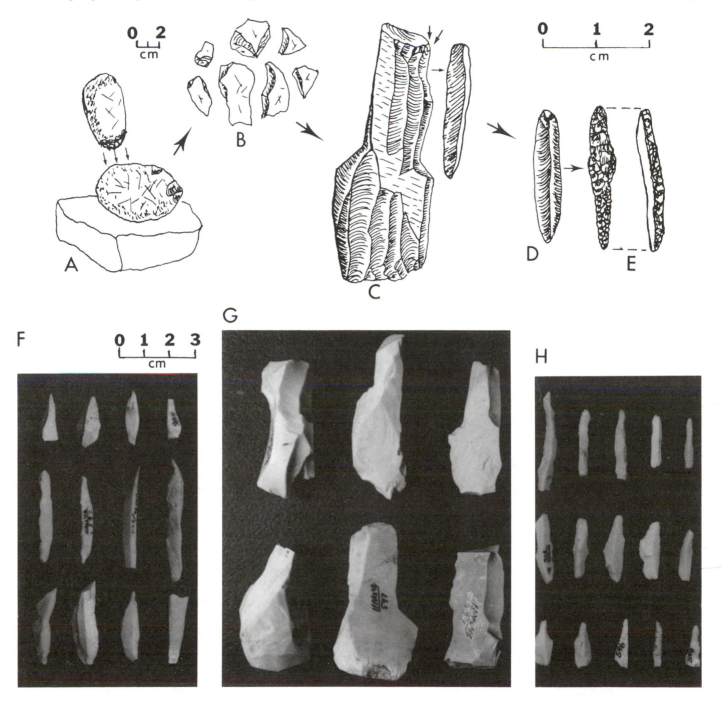

Figure 3.1 The production sequence for Cahokia microdrills (note scale differences). (A) Bipolar technique used to reduce large blocks of Burlington chert. (B) Blocky fragments of Burlington chert used as microcore blanks. (C) Cahokia microcore showing removal of "microblade" with burin blow. (D) Unmodified burin spall (microblade). (E) Retouched microdrill. (F) Cahokia microblades from the Powell Mound. (G) Cahokia microcores from the Powell Mound. (H) Cahokia microdrills from the Powell Mound.

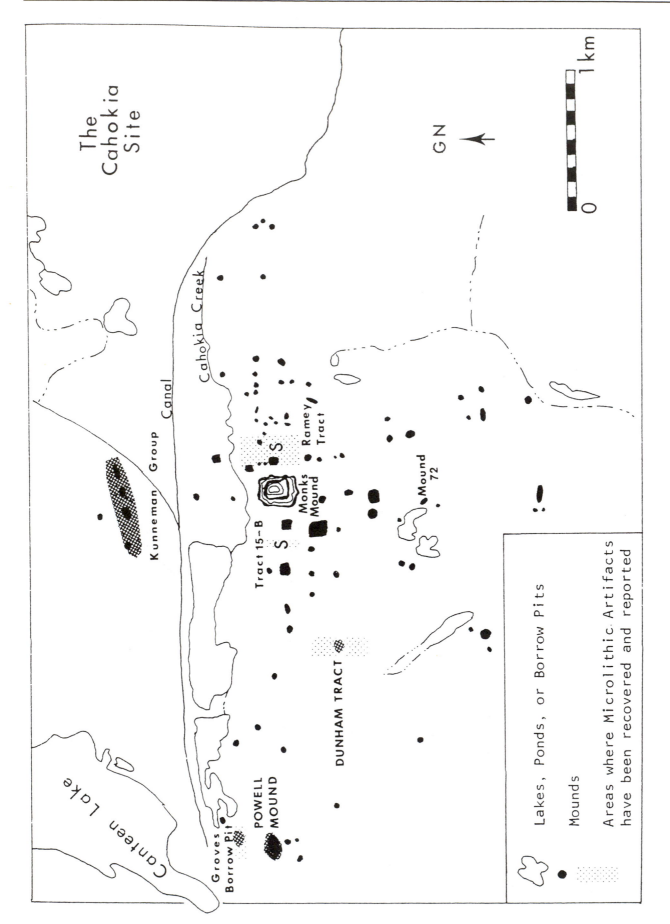

Figure 3.2 The location of microdrill workshops (crosshatched shading) and shell bead manufacturing areas (S) at the Cahokia site.

remarked that debitage related to the manufacture of other types of flint tools such as projectile points, bifacial knives, or hoes was absent (Mason and Perino 1961:554). Alan Harn (1971:37) mentioned that no microdrills were recovered at most of the sites that he surveyed on the southern American Bottom, but he did find "great quantities" of microliths within an 80 m² area at the Kunneman locality (1.1 km north and west of Monks Mound on a ridge bordering Cahokia Creek). Harn (1971) also noted that no other types of artifacts were associated with the microdrill workshops at the Kunneman Tract.

Analyses of small samples of microcores, microblades, and microdrills collected from the surface in this area led to the definition of the Cahokia Microlithic Industry by Mason and Perino (1961) and Morse (1974), but no systematic investigations were carried out at the Kunneman Tract until 1984, because the chicken farmer that owned the land "dislikes State and Federal Employees" and carried a ball peen hammer with him to run off archaeologists (Morse 1974:17). The chickens that roamed the site were known to have used the microliths as gizzard stones (Mason and Perino 1961:555), further complicating the study of microdrill production at the Kunneman workshop.

The Kunneman Tract and Santa Cruz Island

The forms of the Cahokia microliths are quite similar to the microcores, microblades, and microdrills in the Chumash microlithic industry of California. Both "industries" were designed to produce large quantities of standardized microdrills that were hafted and used to drill marine shell beads (Arnold 1987b:Appendix 1). The microblade industry that developed on Santa Cruz Island was an integral part of a system of seafaring trade that was based on a true shell bead money during the Late Period (A.D. 1150-1785) of Chumash cultural development (Arnold 1987a, 1987b). Arnold's analysis of the Chumash microblade industry revealed that microdrills and shell beads were produced by craft specialists at "centralized" locations on the Santa Barbara Channel Islands. She argues that the sophisticated organization of the microdrill and shell bead production and distribution system indicate that the Chumash were among the more complex North American aboriginal societies (1987a). She also notes that the volume of microlithic artifacts at workshop sites such as China Harbor (SCrI-306) suggests that the Chumash industry was the most intensive bladelet manufacturing industry in aboriginal North America (1985:51).

When the grab samples of microlithic artifacts from the Kunneman Tract were compared with controlled surface collections and excavated samples of micro-cores, microblades, and microdrills from sites on Santa Cruz Island, California, the density at Kunneman seemed to be well below the concentrations found at the Proto-Historic Chumash quarries and workshops (Arnold 1985:51). However, Arnold (1987b:120) noted that this may partly be due to the pattern of collection and excavation practices at Cahokia, where the densities of microblade materials may prove to be much greater than are currently recorded. This pattern of collection was improved when archaeologists from Southern Illinois University at Edwardsville conducted controlled surface collections at the Kunneman Tract (Brown et al. 1986). Preliminary results of their survey (provided by George R. Holley) can be compared with the Santa Cruz Island data (Table 3.1) to find how the Cahokia microlithic industry stacks up against the Chumash industry.

It should be noted that data on the surface density of microcores, microblades, and microdrills at Cahokia are only available from a one hectare area of the Kunneman workshop. The total extent of the Kunneman workshop has been estimated to be twice that size (2 ha.), or slightly more than the total area of *all* of the quarries, workshops, and villages associated with the Chumash microlithic industry on Santa Cruz Island. On the Island, the raw material for microdrill production was available at the quarries (within 9 km of all of the workshops and villages), and the marine shell that was used to make beads could be obtained from local beaches. At the Kunneman tract, chert had to be obtained from the Crescent Hills quarries (located 45 km away across the Mississippi River in the Meramec Valley, although "minor amounts" of Burlington chert may have been available in local alluvial contexts, see Williams 1989:323-324). Marine shell had to be imported from the Gulf or Atlantic coasts, between 1,070 and 1,340 km away (Table 3.1:A). Comparisons of microdrill and shell bead production at the two locations must consider that the Channel Island industries used local materials, while the Cahokia artisans had to import their raw materials.

The length of occupation at the quarry and workshop sites on Santa Cruz Island was between 500 and 900 years, while the Kunneman workshop was occupied for a maximum of 400 years (A.D. 1000-1400), although the bulk of the microdrill and shell bead production may have taken place during the Stirling and Moorehead phases (A.D. 1050-1250). While the surface density of microcores and microblades at the Santa Cruz Island Quarry site (SCrI-93) and at the northeast slope area of the China Harbor workshop are between 4 times and 29 times greater than the Kunneman Tract densities, the density of microdrills at Kunneman was 29 times greater than the density of finished drills at the Santa Cruz Island sites (Table 3.1:B).

Table 3.1. Microblade Production at the Kunnemann Tract Workshop, Cahokia and at Prehistoric and Historic Chumash Quarries, Villages, and Workshops on Santa Cruz Island, California.

A. Site Area, Distance to Chert and Shell Sources, and Length of Occupation

	Total Area (m²)	Distance to Chert Source	Distance to Marine Shell	Length of Occupation
Santa Cruz Island [a]				
Quarries	11,616	0	local beaches	900 years
Villages	7,054	2-9 km	on the	500 years
Small Worshops	969	0-3 km	Island	900 years
ALL SITES	*19,638 (1.96 ha)*	*0-9 km*		*500-900 yrs*
Kunneman Tract	**20,000 (2.0 ha)** [b]	**45 km**	**1,070-1,340 km**	**400 yrs**

B. Surface Density of Microlithic Artifacts (number per square meter)

Surface Density of:	Micoblade Cores	Microblades	Microdrills	Surface Area	Ratio of Microblades to Cores
Santa Cruz Island					
SCrI-93 Quarry	0.81 (1,527) [c]	0.80 (1500) [c]	0	1,875 sq. m	0.98: 1
China Harbor Village [d]					
Northeast Slope	0.96	5.76	0.02	estimated	6.00: 1
Outside House	0.08	0.29	0.02	from	4.50: 1
Inside House	0.01	0.15	0.01	test units	9.75: 1
Site Average	*0.09*	*0.51*	*0.02*	*566 sq. m*	*5.49: 1*
Kunneman Tract [e]	**0.12 (1,205)** [c]	**0.19 (1,916)** [c]	**0.57 (574)** [c]	**1 ha.**	**2.07: 1**

C. Number of Microlithic artifacts on surface per hectare per year of occupation

SITE	Microcores	Microblades	Microdrills
SCrI-93 Quarry	9.00	8.89	0
China Harbor	1.80	10.20	0.4
Kunneman	3.01 (6.02) [f]	4.79 (9.58) [f]	1.44 (2.87) [f]

D. Estimated Production Per Year

SITE	Microcores	Microblades	Microdrills
SCrI-93 Quarry	16,850	16,647	
China Harbor	3,370	19,100	749
Kunneman	5,635(11,271) [f]	8,970 (17,939) [f]	2,696 (5,374) [f]

[a] Data on Santa Cruz Island sites from Arnold (1987b).

[b] Total area of Kunneman workshop estimated from U.S.G.S.   Monks Mound quadrangle, and descriptions in Mason and Perino (1962), Morse (1974), and George Holley (pers. com.).

[c] Number of artifacts recovered during controlled surface collections.

[d] Surface density at the China Harbor site calculated by dividing the artifact density per 10 x 10 x 10 cm level in test units by 10.

[e] Results of controlled surface collection of 1 ha. of Kunneman Tract provided by Dr. George Holley of SIU-Edwardsville (a report is forthcoming in June, 1990).

[f] Number in parentheses is based on a 200 year occupation of the Kunneman Tract.

The disparity in microcore, microblade, and microdrill densities at the two areas may be the result of the Chumash exchange system, where substantial numbers of finished microdrills were exported from Santa Cruz Island (Arnold 1987b). Many of the microcores and microblades found on the Island were waste products associated with core preparation activities at or near quarry sites. Microcores may have arrived at the Kunneman workshop in a more "finished" or "prepared" state, and less core preparation waste may be present there (but it should be noted that no evidence for preliminary microcore preparation has been *reported* from the Cresent Hills quarries). When the density of microlithic artifacts at the two areas are adjusted for length of occupation (Table 3.1:C), we find that the level of microdrill production at Santa Cruz Island and at the Kunneman workshop are quite comparable, particularly if we estimate that the Kunneman workshop was occupied for 200 years.

This comparison is not meant to detract from the intensity of microblade production by the Chumash, but to show that similar levels of production are represented by the microlithic artifacts at the Kunneman workshop. If the estimated annual production rate of microliths is proportional to the density of microlithic artifacts on the surface, then we can use Arnold's figures to estimate annual production at Kunneman. That is, if the surface density of microcores at Kunneman is 1.67 times (or 3.34 times, if Kunneman was only occupied 200 years) the density of cores at the China Harbor site, then the estimated annual production of microcores was 1.67 (or 3.34) times greater at Kunneman than at China Harbor, where Arnold estimated that an average of 3,370 microcores were being produced each year (see Table 3.1:C, D). When we calculate annual production, we find that an average of 5,635 (or 11,271) microcores were being produced per year at the Kunneman workshop, while 8,970 (or 17,939) microblades were manufactured, and 2,697 (or 5,374) microdrills were produced. Remember, these calculations are based on a one hectare area of the Kunneman workshop (one half of the total site area). If we estimate that about half as many microdrills were produced annually at all of the other microdrill workshops at Cahokia (see below) and take the low estimates from Kunneman (based on 400 years of occupation), we can project a minimum production of 4,000 microdrills per year. This would allow the Mississippian artisans at the site to manufacture at least 40,000 shell beads per year (if each drill was used to drill only 10 beads), or a bare minimum of 16,000,000 beads during the 400 year span of occupation.

Arnold (1987b:233) found several indicators of economic specialization in the Chumash microlithic industry, including control of resources, economic reorganization, technological improvements, and the establishment of microdrill manufacturing centers designed to handle high production demands. These indicators are also present at the Kunneman workshop, along with evidence for a large volume of production and for standardization in the manufacturing procedure for microdrills. The evidence for craft specialization in lithic *and* shell production at Cahokia is quite compelling.

Other Microdrill Workshops at Cahokia

The Kunneman group was undoubtedly the center of microdrill manufacturing at Cahokia, since the other microdrill workshops are smaller. Some 48 microcores, 49 microblades, and 44 microdrills were found in or near three pits beneath the base of the Powell Mound at the western edge of the Cahokia site limits (Ahler and DePuydt 1987; Yerkes 1983, 1989b), while 199 microblades, 91 microdrills, and an unspecified number of microcores were recovered during excavations at the Groves Borrow Pit, 180 m northeast of the Powell Mound (Winston 1963). George Holley (personal communication) informed the author that another workshop may be present south of the Powell Mound area on the western end of Cahokia, and 9 microcores, 10 microblades, and 8 microdrills were found in small clusters on the surface of the Dunham Tract, which is located about 1 km southwest of Monks Mound (Yerkes 1983:502).

Shell Bead Manufacturing Areas at Cahokia

It appears that microdrill production locations were separate from shell bead manufacturing areas at Cahokia, since no shell beads or shell refuse have been found at the microdrill workshops (Harn 1971; Mason and Perino 1961; O'Brien 1972; Yerkes 1983, 1989a). Microwear analysis of microcores, microblades, and microdrills from the Powell Mound and Dunham Tract revealed that the "burin-like" microcores, amorphous microblade cores, and unretouched microblades (or burin spalls) were not utilized, but many of the microdrills had wear traces on their edges that indicated that they had been used to drill shell (Yerkes 1983). This may be taken as evidence that some shell bead manufacturing *did* take place at the microdrill production areas, but it is also possible that the utilized microdrills were discarded at the microlithic workshops when they were removed from their hafts and replaced by new chert microdrills (Keeley 1982; Yerkes 1983, 1989b).

In either case, the production of microdrills was not an "incidental activity" carried out by the average Mississippian farmer, but a task that was restricted to a few special locations within Cahokia and probably conducted by a small portion of the population. Most of the microdrill production took place at the Kunneman workshop. The smaller concentrations of microlithic artifacts may represent special locations were microdrills were produced and some shell bead manufacturing also took place, or they may be areas where microdrills were "retooled." The microdrill production activities at the three areas have not been dated, but associated "Old Village" ceramics suggest a time range of A.D. 1000-1200.

Bead Making or Shell-Working Workshops at Cahokia

The Powell and Dunham Tract localities may have served as shell-working areas as well as microlithic workshops, but there are two other areas of the Cahokia site where concentrations of microdrills have been found *without* associated microcores or microblades, but in close proximity to substantial amounts of shell beads and shell refuse. One of these areas is located on Tract 15-B within a public compound or "marketplace" just west of Monks Mound in the central precinct (Benchley 1981:4; Harn 1971:36; Vogel 1975).

The other is the Ramey Field east of Monks Mound in the central precinct where 97 microdrills and an unspecified amount of shell were found in surface collections (Benchley 1981:44-46). Moorehead (1928:28) reported finding *Busycon* shell during his test excavations at the "village site" in the Ramey Field, and Titterington (1938) noted that 147 microdrills were found here along with "salt-water shells from the Gulf of Mexico" that were used in the manufacture of ornaments. Titterington (1938:3) also reported that a refuse pit that was exposed in the Ramey Field in 1937 contained four drilled marine conch shell pendants, two grooved conch shell pendants, two partially worked conch shells, and nine unworked conch shells. He also reported a cache of 1,960 drilled marine shell beads found 1.5 km west of Monks Mound between the central precinct and the Powell Mound.

While freshwater mussels were used in the manufacture of drilled shell hoes at Cahokia, marine conch, clam, and snail shells imported from the Gulf and Atlantic coasts were used to make shell beads and other ornaments (Baker 1928). Parmalee (1958) noted that Cahokia probably had the greatest concentration of marine conch shells found at any inland site in eastern North America. It is unlikely that the accumulation of marine shell at the site was the result of "incidental activities," but rather reflects the regular use of exotic raw material in the production of craft items. Like the microdrill workshops, the location of the shell craft areas is restricted to a few localities, and they are found in the central precinct, or "elite area" of Cahokia. Virtually no microdrills or shell materials were recovered during the investigation of residential or domestic areas of Cahokia such as Tract 15-A, the Merrill Tract, the Collinsville Airport, Master Feed and Seed property, or the Interpretative Center Tract.

Microdrills and Shell Craft Activities Outside of Cahokia

Large concentrations of microlithic artifacts, marine shell beads, and shell refuse are not common outside of Cahokia. Microcores, microblades and 79 microdrills were found in two houses and a single pit in the Fill site area south of Long Lake at the Mitchell town-and-mound center north of Cahokia. Very little shell material was recovered (Porter 1974:941), and this area may represent a microdrill production area.

Microdrills have been found at 10% (n=12) of the 114 Mississippian sites recorded on the American Bottom, and Koldehoff (1989) recovered microdrills from 21% (n=5) of the 24 Mississippian sites he investigated in the uplands of the Douglas Creek watershed 23 km southeast of Cahokia (Table 3.2). A study of the temporal and spatial distribution of microdrills and shell artifacts at these outlying Mississippian sites revealed that during the Lohmann phase (A.D. 1000-1050) large numbers of microdrills were concentrated in one or two households at a few sites outside of Cahokia. During the Stirling phase (A.D. 1050-1150), a few microdrills and cores were found in some of the household units at several outlying "farmstead" sites, but large assemblages of these artifacts are only present at two large mound centers, Cahokia and Mitchell (Table 3.3). After A.D. 1200, the only households with microdrills are found at Cahokia and in three sites located in the Douglas Creek watershed (Yerkes 1989b).

The distribution pattern during the Lohmann phase resembles the *household specializations* described by Flannery and Winter (1976), where craft production was limited to a few households at certain settlements in a region. Household specialization in shell bead production continues during the Stirling phase, but there is a shift to a *regional specialization* with most of the shell-working going on at the larger temple mound centers. Even at the outlying sites, bead production may have been under the control of local leaders. Northeast of Cahokia at the Robert Schneider site, five of the six micro-drills in the lithic assemblage were found in the largest of four Stirling phase structures (Fortier 1985). On the southern American Bottom at the Labras Lake site, microdrills were found only in the central household cluster, which included the largest house at the site. The size, orientation, storage capacity, and contents of the large structure indicate that it may have been the residence of a local leader

Table 3.2. Distribution of Microdrills at Mississippian sites outside of Cahokia on the American Bottom and in the Douglas Creek Watershed (A.D. 900-1400).

Area Phase Type	Sites with Microdrills Present	Sites with Microdrills Absent	Sites with Worked Shell	TOTAL SITES
I. American Bottom [a]				
Fairmount/Lohmann (A.D. 900-1050)				
Second Line Sites	0	1	0	1
Third Line Sites	2	3	0	5
Fourth Line Sites	1	42	0	43
ALL TYPES	3 (6%)	46 (94%)	0	49
Stirling/Moorehead (A.D. 1050-1250)				
Second Line Sites	1	3	0	4
Third Line Sites	0	4	1	4
Fourth Line Sites	7	43	2	50
ALL TYPES	8 (14%)	50 (86%)	3	58
Sand Prairie Phase (A.D. 1250-1400)	1	6	0	7
ALL PHASES	12 (10%)	102 (90%)	3	114
II. Douglas Creek (surface collections) [b]				
Lohmann/Lindhorst (AD 1000-1050)	1[c]	7	0	8
Lohmann/Lindhorst and Stirling (AD 1000-1150)	1	0	0	1
Sand Prairie (AD 1250-1400)	3	5	2	8
Indeterminate	0	7	0	7
ALL PHASES	5 (21%)	19 (79%)	2	24

[a] Site types and distribution data from Fowler (1974), Harn (1971), and Yerkes (1989a,1989b). Phases from Bareis and Porter (1984) and Folwer and Hall (1972).

[b] Site distribution data and phases from Koldehoff (1989). This is a revision, based on updated information, of the "Richland Creek" section of Table 1 in Yerkes (1989b).

[c] Microwear analysis of this microdrill (from the Beil site, S-547) revealed that it was used on stone.

(Yerkes 1989c). Microdrills are present at more sites on the American Bottom during the Stirling phase, but this is in line with the increase in Mississippian sites in the region that has been noted for the period following A.D. 1050 (Milner 1990).

The critics have claimed that the distribution of microdrills and shell refuse at outlying Mississippian sites represents the normal variation in activities conducted at farmsteads (Milner 1990) or that the concentration of microdrills and shell craft artifacts in certain household units at these sites is the result of "site formation processes" (Pauketat 1987). However, these claims are weakened by the lack of data on activity patterns or site formation and deposition processes at Mississippian sites on the American Bottom. In fact, the only site where these issues have been addressed

Table 3.3. Number of Microdrills Recovered from Household Units (Clusters) at Mississippian sites on the American Bottom.

Phase	Site Name	Household Unit(Cluster)	Number of Microdrills	Total Number of Tools [a]
Lohmann (A.D. 1000-1050)	Lohmann	Feature 1	0	15
		Feature 5	11	25
		Feature 9	0	14
		Feature 11	0	14
		Feature 13	0	17
	Turner	Cluster 1	33	72
		Cluster 6	0	N/A
Stirling (A.D. 1050-1150)	Labras Lake	Household 1	1*	26*
		Household 2	2*	33*
		Household 3	2*	23*
		Household 4	0	11*
		Household 5	0	12*
		Household 6	0	14*
	Turner	Cluster 2	3	45
		Cluster 3	17	93
		Cluster 4	2	95
		Cluster 7	0	N/A
	Julien	Feature 36	1	13
		Feature 115	0	12
	Robert Schneider	Cluster 1A	5	71
		Cluster 1B	1	20
		Cluster 2	0	14
		Cluster 3	0	17

Mitchell   only two households at this 100-acre site contained microdrills (77 in one, 79 in the other).

BBB Motor   10 microdrills were found in 4 pits in the southern temple area a single microdrill was found in the northern temple area.

Phase	Site Name	Household Unit(Cluster)	Number of Microdrills	Total Number of Tools [a]
Moorehead (A.D. 1150-1250)	Turner	Cluster 5	0	22
	Julien	Feature 3	0	22
		Feature 5	0	20
		Feature 7	0	38
		Feature 208	0	17
		Feature 241	0	60
Sand Prairie (A.D. 1250-1400)	Julien	Feature 2	0	53
		Feature 17	0	29
		Feature 82	0	10

[a] Represents "diagnostic" tools as tabulated by Prentice (1985) and Yerkes (1987).
* Labras Lake totals include only those artifacts that had recognizable microwear traces.

through refitting studies and functional analysis is Labras Lake (Yerkes 1987, 1989c), and the results of those studies supported the case for specialized production of shell beads and other craft items in the household of a local leader.

The scale of craft specialization outside of Cahokia certainly did not approach the level found in the large microlithic workshops and shell bead making areas in that impressive site. Indeed, the patterning in regional artifact distribution reflects the centralized control of microdrill and shell bead production by the Cahokia elite (cf. Arnold 1987:30; Brumfiel and Earle 1987). However, the available archaeological data do support the case for part-time or limited specialization in shell-bead production at outlying sites. The pattern of shell craft activities in rural Mississippian society may resemble the flexible system of production Spence (1985) described for rural Aztec groups, where production was not controlled or dependent on the state bureaucracy, and all of the craftspeople were not concentrated in the large centers.

In a recent review of prehistoric archaeology in the Southeastern United States, Steponaitis remarked that:

> [I]t may not be coincidence that microlithic tools, abraders, and other possible signs of shellbead manufacture are most prevalent in many regions between A.D. 800 and 1300, precisely when Mississippian polities emerged and consolidated. Beads, beaded garments, and other valued craft items probably served as tokens in social transactions. Displayed as possessions, these tokens enhanced personal prestige; presented as gifts, they could be used to build alliances and inflict social debts. Exchanges of such items, especially among budding elites, were instruments of political strategy as much as, if not more than, purely economic activities (Steponaitis 1986:392).

David Brose (1989:29) noted that there was little clear distinction between politics, religion, and economy in Mississippian society, and interpretations of craft activities and economic practices must consider the political and religious context of those practices. We should not be surprised if we cannot find an analog for Mississippian craft specialization in western colonial economic history or in native Southeastern societies during the contact period, since a different religious and political context existed for each of those cases. If we apply the criteria developed by Service, then Cahokia was the center of a primitive state, but it is our task to learn what kind of state it was, and how certain individuals were able to gain so much power over the lives of their contemporaries. Did the production of "prestige items" such as marine shell beads contribute to the rise of the elite, or did the rise of the elite increase the demand for prestige items? I believe that as we learn more about the nature of Mississippian craft specialization we will also learn more about the religious and political character of that complex society.

Acknowledgments

I would like to thank James B. Stoltman for the opportunity to contribute a paper to this volume. The article is a revision of an invited paper presented in the symposium, *Craft Specialization in Complex Societies: Evidence from Functional Analyses of Stone Tools*, organized by April K. Sievert, at the 55th Annual Meeting of the Society for American Archaeology, April 18-22, 1990, Las Vegas, Nevada. Brian Hayden and Thomas Hester made constructive comments on an earlier draft, and Brad Koldehoff and George R. Holley provided unpublished data that were used in the study. I am especially grateful to George Holley for providing counts of microlithic artifacts recovered from the microdrill workshop at the Kunneman Tract of the Cahokia site during the 1985-86 survey conducted by SIU-Edwardsville. The final report of the SIU-E investigations at the Kunneman Tract will be available in June, 1990.

References Cited

Ahler, Steven R., and Peter J. DePuydt
  1987 A Report on the 1931 Powell Mound Excavations, Madison County, Illinois. Report of Investigations 43. Illinois State Museum, Springfield.
Arnold, Jeanne E.
  1985 Economic Specialization and Prehistory: Methods of Documenting the Rise of Lithic Craft Specialization. In *Lithic Resource Procurement: Proceedings from the Second Conference on Prehistoric Chert Exploitation*, edited by S.C. Vehik, pp. 37-58. Occasional paper 4. Southern Illinois University at Carbondale, Center for Archaeological Investigations.
  1987a Technology and Economy: Microblade Core Production from the Channel Islands. In *The Organization of Core Technology*, edited by J. K. Johnson and C. A. Morrow, pp. 207-238. Westview Press, Boulder.

1987b *Craft Specialization in the Prehistoric Channel Islands, California.* University of California Publications in Anthropology 18, Berkeley and Los Angeles.

Baker, Frank C.
1928 The Use of Molluscan Shells by the Cahokia Mound Builders. In *The Cahokia Mounds,* by W. K. Moorehead, pp. 147-154. University of Illinois Bulletin 26(4), Urbana.

Bareis, C. J., and J. W. Porter (editors)
1984 *American Bottom Archaeology.* University of Illinois Press, Urbana and Chicago.

Benchley, Elizabeth D.
1981 Summary Report on Controlled Surface Collections of the Ramey Field, Cahokia Mounds Historic Site, Madison County, Illinois. Report of Investigations 51. University of Wisconsin-Milwaukee, Archaeological Research Laboratory.

Bourne, Edward G. (editor)
1922 Narratives of the Career of Hernando de Soto, 2 vols. Allerton, New York.

Brain, Jeffrey P.
1978 Late Prehistoric Settlement Patterning in the Yazoo Basin and Natchez Bluffs Regions of the Lower Mississippi Valley. In *Mississippian Settlement Patterns,* edited by B.D. Smith, pp. 331-368. Academic Press, New York.

Brose, David S.
1989 From the Southeastern Ceremonial Complex to the Southern Cult, "You Can't Tell the Players without a Program." In *The Southeastern Ceremonial Complex: Artifacts and Analysis,* edited by P. Galloway, pp. 27-40. University of Nebraska Press, Lincoln.

Brown, A. J., J. M. Collins, B. L. Gums, G. R. Holley, M. Skele, C. L. Wells, and W. I. Woods
1986 Recent Archaeological Investigations by Southern Illinois University at Edwardsville. *Illinois Archaeological Survey Newsletter* 1 (1/2):2-3, Springfield.

Brumfiel, Elizabeth M., and Timothy K. Earle
1987 Specialization, Exchange and Complex Societies: an Introduction. In *Specialization, Exchange, and Complex Societies,* edited by E. M. Brumfiel and T. K. Earle, pp. 1-9. Cambridge University Press, Cambridge.

Cobb, Charles R.
1989 An Appraisal of the Role of Mill Creek Chert Hoes in Mississippian Exchange Systems. *Southeastern Archaeology* 8:79-92.

Conrad, Lawrence A.
1989 The Southeastern Ceremonial Complex on the Northern Middle Mississippian Frontier: Late Prehistoric Politico-Religious Systems in the Central Illinois Valley. In *The Southeastern Ceremonial Complex: Artifacts and Analysis,* edited by P. Galloway, pp. 93-113. University of Nebraska Press, Lincoln.

Drennan, R. D., and C. A. Uribe (editors)
1987 *Chiefdoms in the Americas.* University Press of America, Lanham, Maryland.

Emerson, Thomas E.
1989 Water, Serpents, and the Underworld: An Exploration into Cahokian Symbolism. In *The Southeastern Ceremonial Complex: Artifacts and Analysis,* edited by P. Galloway, pp. 45-92. University of Nebraska Press, Lincoln.

Flannery, Kent V., and M. C. Winter
1976 Analyzing Household Activities. In *The Early Mesoamerican Village,* edited by K. V. Flannery, pp. 34-47, Academic Press, New York.

Fortier, Andrew C.
1985 *The Robert Schneider Site.* American Bottom Archaeology, FAI-270 Sites Reports 11 (Part 2). University of Illinois Press, Urbana and Chicago.

Fowler, Melvin L.
1974 Cahokia: Ancient Capital of the Midwest. *Addison-Wesley Module in Anthropology* 48, Reading, MA.
1978 Cahokia and the American Bottom: Settlement Archaeology. In *Mississippian Settlement Patterns,* edited by B. D. Smith, pp. 455-478. Academic Press, New York.

1989 *The Cahokia Atlas: A Historical Atlas of Cahokia Archaeology.* Studies in Archaeology 6. Illinois Historic Preservation Agency, Springfield.

Fowler, M. L., and R. L. Hall
1972 *Archaeological Phases at Cahokia.* Research Series, Papers in Anthropology 1. Illinois State Museum, Springfield.

Gibbon, Guy E.
1974 A Model of Mississippian Development and Its Implications for the Red Wing area. In *Aspects of Upper Great Lakes Anthropology, Papers in honor of Lloyd A. Wilford*, edited by E. Johnson, pp. 129-137. Minnesota Prehistoric Archaeology Series 11. Minnesota Historical Society, St. Paul.

Griffin, James B.
1983 The Midlands. In *Ancient North Americans*, edited by J. D. Jennings, pp. 243-302. W. H. Freeman, New York.

Hall, Robert L.
1975 Chronology and Phases at Cahokia. In *Perspectives in Cahokia Archaeology*, pp. 15-31. Bulletin 10. Illinois Archaeological Survey, Urbana.
1986 Upper Mississippi and Middle Mississippi Relationships.*Wisconsin Archaeologist* 67:365-369.

Harn, A. D.
1971 Archaeological Survey of the American Bottom in Madison and St. Clair County, Illinois. Reports of Investigations 21 (Part 2). Illinois State Museum, Springfield.

Hudson, Charles
1976 *The Southeastern Indians.* University of Tennessee Press, Knoxville.

Keeley, Lawrence H.
1982 Hafting and Retooling: Effects on the Archaeological Record. *American Antiquity* 47:798-809.

Koldehoff, Brad
1987 The Cahokia Flake Tool Industry: Socio-economic Implications for Late Prehistory in the Central Mississippi Valley. In *The Organization of Core Technology*, edited by J. K. Johnson and C. A. Morrow, pp. 151-186. Westview Press, Boulder.
1989 Cahokia's Immediate Hinterland: The Mississippian Occupation of Douglas Creek. *Illinois Archaeology* 1:39-68.

Mason, R. J., and G. Perino
1961 Microblades at Cahokia, Illinois. *American Antiquity* 26:553-57.

Milner, George R.
1990 The late prehistoric Cahokia Cultural System of the Mississippi River Valley: Foundations, Florescence, and Fragmentation. *Journal of World Prehistory* 4:1- 44.

Moberg, Carl-Axel
1983 Mississippian Seen from La Tène: On Comparisons of Prehistoric Social Disorganizations. In *Lulu Linear Punctated: Essays in Honor of George Irving Quimby*, edited by R.C. Dunnell and D.K. Grayson. Museum of Anthropology, University of Michigan, Anthropological Papers 72: 167-184, Ann Arbor.

Moorehead, Warren K.
1929 *The Cahokia Mounds.* University of Illinois Bulletin 26(4), Urbana.

Morse, D. F.
1974 The Cahokia Microlith Industry. *Newsletter of Lithic Technology* 3:15-19.

Muller, Jon
1984 Mississippian Specialization and Salt. *American Antiquity* 49:489-507.
1986 Pans and a Grain of Salt: Mississippian Specialization Revisited. *American Antiquity* 51:405-409.
1987 Salt, Chert, and Shell: Mississippian Exchange and Economy. In *Specialization, Exchange, and Complex Societies*, edited by E. M. Brumfiel and T. K. Earle, pp. 10-21. Cambridge University Press, Cambridge.

O'Brien, Patricia J.
1972 Urbanism, Cahokia, and Middle Mississippian. *Archaeology* 25(3):189-97.

Oswalt, Wendell H.
1988 *This Land was Theirs* (4th ed.). Mayfield, Mountain View, California.

Parmalee, Paul W.
 1958 Marine Shells of Illinois Indian Sites. *Nautilus* 71(4):132-139.
Pauketat, Timothy R.
 1987 Mississippian Domestic Economy and Formation Processes: A Response to Prentice. *Mid-Continental Journal of Archaeology* 12:77-88.
Peebles, C. S., and S. M. Kus
 1977 Some Archaeological Correlates of Ranked Societies. *American Antiquity* 42:241-448.
Porter, James W.
 1974 Cahokia Archaeology as Viewed from the Mitchell Site: A Satellite Community at A.D. 1150-1200. Unpublished Ph.D. dissertation, Department of Anthropology, University of Wisconsin-Madison.
Sears, William H.
 1968 The State and Settlement Patterns in the New World. In *Settlement Archaeology*, edited by K. C. Chang, pp. 134-153. National Press, Palo Alto.
Service, Elman R.
 1962 Primitive Social Organization: An Evolutionary Perspective. Random House, New York.
 1963 *Profiles in Ethnology.* Harper and Row, New York.
 1975 Origins of the State and Civilization: The Process of Cultural Evolution. Norton, New York.
Spence, Michael W.
 1985 Specialized Production in Rural Aztec Society: Obsidian Workshops of the Teotihuacan Valley. In *Contributions to the Archaeology and Ethnohistory of Greater Mesoamerica*, edited by W. J. Folan, pp. 76-125. Southern Illinois University Press, Carbondale.
Steponaitis, V. P.
 1986 Prehistoric Archaeology in the Southeastern United States, 1970-1985. *Annual Review of Anthropology* 15:363-404.
Swanton, John R.
 1911 Indian Tribes of the lower Mississippi Valley and adjacent coast of the Gulf of Mexico. Bulletin 43. Bureau of American Ethnology, Washington, D.C.
Titterington, Paul F.
 1938 The Cahokia Mound Group and its Village Site Materials. P. F. Titterington, St. Louis.
Vogel, Joseph O.
 1975 Trends in Cahokia Ceramics: Preliminary Study of the Collections from Tracts 15A and 15B. In *Perspectives in Cahokia Archaeology*, pp. 32-125. Bulletin 10. Illinois Archaeological Survey, Urbana.
Williams, Joyce
 1989 Lithic Assemblage. In *The Holding Site: A Hopewell Community in the American Bottom*, by A. C. Fortier, T. O. Maher, J. A. Williams, M. C. Meinkoth, K. E. Parker, and L. S. Kelly, pp. 319-428. American Bottom Archaeology, FAI-270 Sites Reports 19, University of Illinois Press, Urbana and Chicago.
Winston, J. H.
 1963 Lithic Analysis II. In *Second Annual Report: American Bottoms Archaeology, July 1, 1962-June 30, 1963*, edited by M. L. Fowler, pp. 12-13. Illinois Archaeological Survey, Urbana.
Yerkes, R.W.
 1983 Microwear, Microdrills, and Mississippian Craft Specialization. *American Antiquity* 48:499-518.
 1986 Licks, Pans, and Chiefs, a Comment on "Mississippian Specialization and Salt". *American Antiquity* 51:402-4.
 1987 Prehistoric Life on the Mississippi Floodplain. University of Chicago Press, Chicago.
 1989a Shell Bead Production and Exchange in Prehistoric Mississippian Populations. In *Proceedings of the 1986 Shell Bead Conference*, edited by C. R. Hayes III and L. R. Ceci, Rochester Museum and Science Center, Research Records 20:113-124, Rochester.
 1989b Mississippian Craft Specialization on the American Bottom. *Southeastern Archaeology* 8:93-106.
 1989c Lithic Analysis and Activity Patterns at Labras Lake. In *Alternative Approaches to Lithic Analysis*, edited by D. O. Henry and G. H. Odell, pp. 183-212. Archaeological Papers of the American Anthropological Association 1.

4

The Evidence for Prehistoric Exchange and Its Implications for the Development of Cahokia

John E. Kelly

School of Social Sciences, Contract Archaeology
Southern Illinois University at Edwardsville

Exchange has often been viewed by a number of archaeologists as an important ingredient in the development of complex societies (cf. Renfrew and Shennan 1981). On the other hand there are those researchers who acknowledge the presence of such interaction but clearly consider its role to have been secondary in the evolution of complex societies. Regardless of one's position in this debate, exchange as a process can not be readily ignored and must be considered in any discussion of cultural complexity.

For the eastern woodlands of North America, Mississippian culture epitomizes the highest level of socio-cultural evolution. For those archaeologists engaged in Mississippian research, such societies are often categorized as complex chiefdoms (Steponaitis 1986). Of the numerous Mississippian town-and-mound centers, the large center of Cahokia is the culmination of such complexity. It is truly unique not only in its enormous size but also in its early position in the Mississippian developmental trajectory and its geographic position on the northwestern edge of Mississippian culture.

The emergence of Cahokia and its variant of Mississippian culture can be attributed to a number of transformations occurring over several hundred years. The initial changes are related to specific demographic and subsistence modifications with Late Woodland society between A.D. 600 and 750 (J. Kelly 1990). The actual transition to Mississippian culture in the American Bottom has been referred to as Emergent Mississippian (Kelly et al. 1984, Kelly 1987). A number of rapid changes occurred among the various groups in this region between A.D. 750 to 1000 that ultimately culminated in the Mississippian center of Cahokia. While no attempt will be made to detail the nature of these transformations, exchange played an important role in Cahokia's rise to dominance. The purpose here is to examine the evidence for trade; the context of such exchange; and its role in Cahokia's development.

Evidence

The evidence for exchange with groups outside a particular geographic locality is generally based on finished products or raw materials that differ from those produced or available locally but are similar to ones from another region. In most instances simple megascopic or visual comparisons are made to distinguish those items from external sources. More rigorous physio-chemical techniques have been developed in the past thirty years to provide better quantitative means for differentiating items of prehistoric trade.

For the American Bottom, a number of studies have been conducted on artifacts and raw materials considered to be derived from external sources. The earliest study was published on a ceramic vessel recovered from Cahokia (Bareis and Porter 1965) and involved the use of petrographic analysis. Certain stylistic attributes seemed to indicate a Caddoan vessel, while the nature of the paste in thin section led Porter to suggest a lower Mississippi river valley source.

In addition to this study Porter (1963) had earlier initiated a program of petrographic analysis on many of the different ceramics from the region. He commented on the diversity of clays available and the fact that "we have missed the importance of trade in the area 1000 years ago. A great deal more trade is going on than is presently thought" (Porter 1963:18). Except for Porter's work, there has been no other comparable analysis, although Holley (1988) has started a program involving chemical analysis and Pauketat (personal communication) will employ petrographic analysis in conjunction with neutron activation on samples from Cahokia.

O'Brien's (1969 and 1972) analysis of the Powell Tract ceramic assemblage described a number of ceramic sherds that were attributed to the Caddoan area and the lower Mississippi river valley. This was based on the similarity of pastes, surface treatment, and decoration to comparable types in those areas. A similar approach was employed by Kelly (1980) in the analysis of Emergent Mississippian ceramics recovered from the Merrell Tract at Cahokia. The presence of a number of distinctive vessels from outside the American Bottom was used to suggest that Cahokia emerged as a result of cultural interaction between the central and lower portions of the Mississippi river valley. It is these data from the Merrell Tract that form the core of this paper.

In addition to ceramics a variety of other finished objects and raw materials have been recovered from the American Bottom that are not indigenous. The analysis of these materials has been restricted to Walthall's (1981) study of galena for eastern North America in which a number of samples from Cahokia and the American Bottom were examined. Woolverton's (1974) electron microprobe analysis of copper artifacts from North America included a sample from the Horseshoe Lake site, a single-mound center several kilometers north of Cahokia (Figure 4.1). Except for these studies, source identification has been based almost exclusively on visual examination and comparison with comparable materials or artifacts from other regions. Clearly there is a need to employ more rigorous, quantitative methods for systematic studies. These, however, are often expensive and still must be interpreted.

In order to examine the present evidence for prehistoric exchange at Cahokia this discussion is organized along diachronic lines. Based on almost three decades of intense archaeological investigation, a relatively tight cultural chronology has been developed. While this sequence initially focused on the Late Woodland and Mississippian complexes (Fowler and Hall 1975), the recent work associated with FAI-270 has not only extended this chronology back in time but also refined the earlier complexes (Bareis and Porter 1984). It is the Late Woodland-Emergent Mississippian-Mississippian

portion of this sequence (Figure 4.2) that is of concern here in examining trade and Cahokia.

Late Woodland

The Late Woodland occupation of the American Bottom has been subdivided into three phases. At the end of this sequence in the northern portion of the American Bottom, a fourth phase, Sponemann, is evident. It is the latter portion of this sequence, that is, the Patrick and Sponemann phases, that will be briefly examined. In general the Late Woodland occupation is characterized by population increases that are related to certain subsistence changes (cf. Buikstra et al. 1986). Maize is present in small quantities from the earlier Mund phase and subsequent Patrick phase contexts; however, by the Sponemann phase it has increased in ubiquity (Parker 1986).

Patrick phase sites are ubiquitous. Excavations at over 25 Patrick phase sites indicate the presence of a variety of settlement types ranging from small farmsteads to larger villages with as many as 100 people. Despite the demographic and subsistence changes, there is little evidence for exchange with areas outside the region. One example, however, was the presence of copper in association with a Sponemann phase ceramic vessel in one of the mounds excavated by Moorehead (1929) at the Grassey Lake site in the northern part of the American Bottom. It is also difficult to evaluate the role of intraregional exchange at this time. The strong similarity of ceramic styles over a large portion of southern and west central Illinois and contiguous areas, however, does indicate some type of interaction network.

Emergent Mississippian

The Emergent Mississippian occupation represents the transition from Late Woodland to Mississippian culture in the American Bottom. It is characterized by a suite of changes, one of which was the increased ubiquity of maize. Two major traditions have been identified for the American Bottom. The Late Bluff is distributed in the northern portion of the American Bottom (Figure 4.1). To the south in the central portion of the region (Figure 4.1) was the Pulcher tradition, which persisted into early Mississippian times.

The first century (A.D. 750-900)

The initial Emergent Mississippian activity in the region consisted of small agricultural villages and hamlets. Although a variety of crops were cultivated, maize had become a major item. At Cahokia several areas have such components present. Whether the site

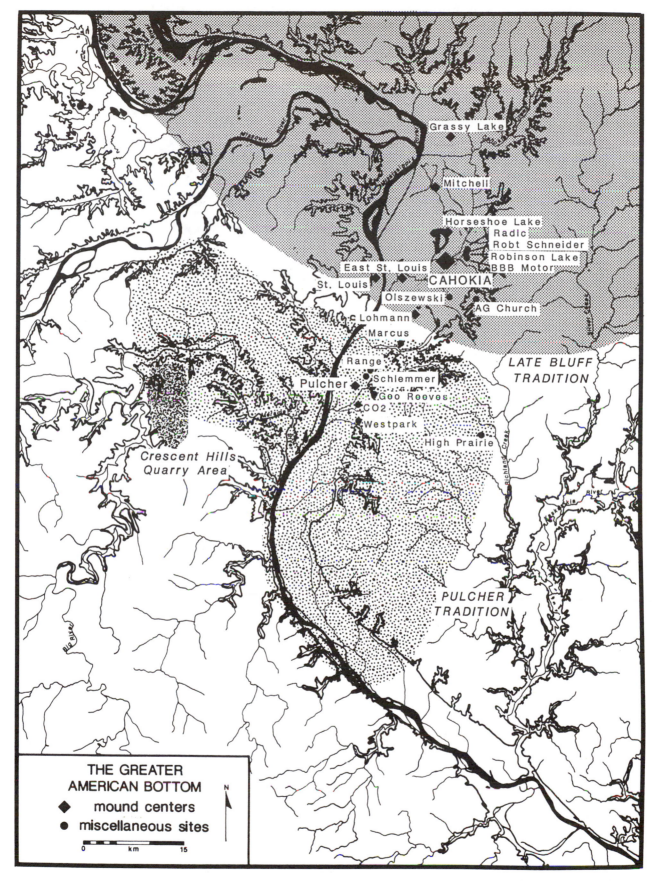

Figure 4.1. Distribution of Selected sites and Mound Centers in the American Bottom Region.

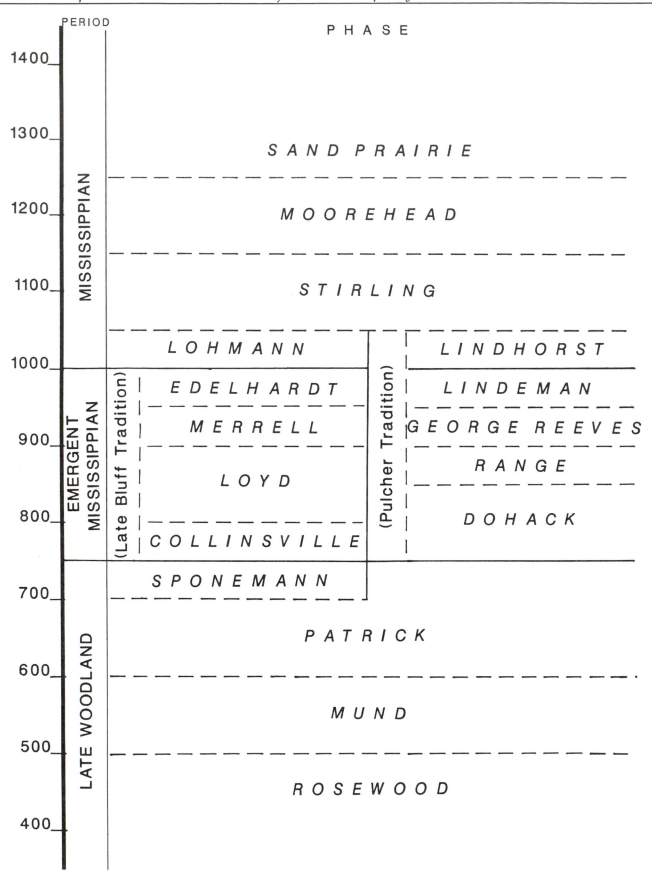

Figure 4.2. Late Prehistoric Chronology for the American Bottom Region.

was a major center or not is inconclusive. Investigations on the Merrell Tract (Figure 4.3) recovered evidence of a Loyd phase community of unknown dimensions with some degree of local importance suggested by the presence of a large residential house and copper (Kelly 1980).

There is considerable evidence throughout the region for intraregional exchange of cherts and ceramic vessels. Since Cahokia and many other sites in the northern American Bottom were located in an area devoid of suitable lithic raw materials, they were dependent upon other locales for these materials (cf. Kelly 1980). For example, most of the chert (82%) from Loyd phase contexts on the Merrell Tract at Cahokia (Figure 4.4) was derived from the Crescent Hills Quarry Area some 45 km to the southwest (Figure 4.1). Other cherts such as Ste. Genevieve (13%) were obtained from sources in the central part of the region some 20 to 30 km to the south.

A variety of other lithic raw materials, such as lime-

stone, sandstone, and hematite, were also recovered from Loyd phase contexts and were available in the aforementioned areas. While it is certainly possible that these other lithic raw materials were traded into the site, it should be noted that limestone, sandstone, and hematite were also present in limited quantities in the upland streams east of Cahokia.

In the central portion of the region these lithic resources were more readily accessible. While Ste. Genevieve cherts dominated the local assemblages, some Burlington cherts (11 to 25% from the Range phase) (Williams 1990b) were imported from the Crescent Hills Quarry Area across the river, 25 to 30 km away. It is important to emphasize that many of the woodworking tools, such as adzes and gouges, were manufactured from the Burlington cherts. Except for a few small Burlington arrow points, these large bifaces were the primary lithic items that were imported.

In addition to the lithic raw materials and artifacts, Late Bluff ceramic vessels were obtained from sources

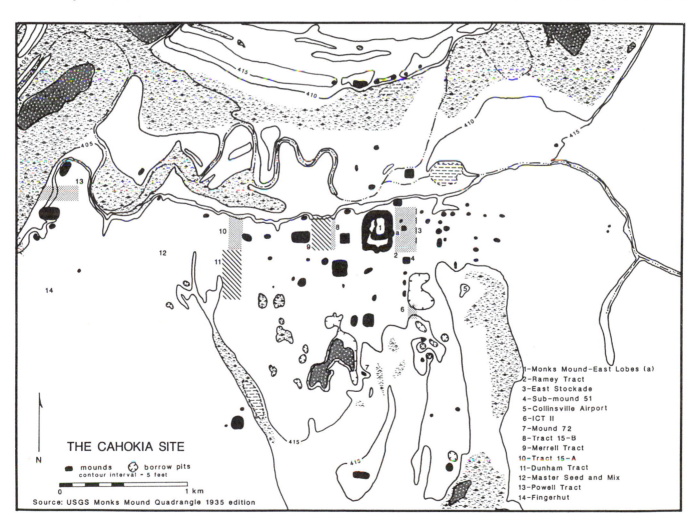

Figure 4.3. The Cahokia Site.

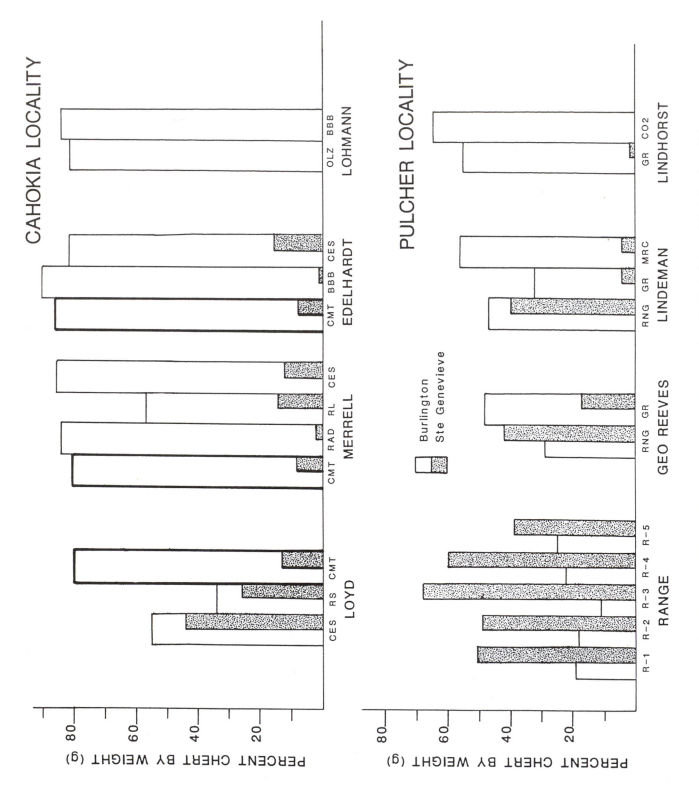

Figure 4.4. Distribution of Local Cherts for Sites by Phase within the Cahokia and Pulcher Localities.

in the uplands north of Cahokia. These were manufactured from a distinctive paste referred to as Madison County Shales (MCS) (Porter 1984). During the Dohack phase at the Range site, they comprise 3% of the assemblage (Ozuk 1990a). By the subsequent Range phase they increase to 13% of the assemblage (Ozuk 1990b). These jars were also imported to Cahokia, and in the Loyd assemblage on the Merrell Tract 39% were manufactured from MCS (Figure 4.5). Limestone-tempered vessels derived from the central portion of the region composed 9% of the Loyd assemblage (Figure 4.5). As emphasized elsewhere (Kelly 1980), Cahokia and the other Emergent Mississippian occupations at this time were involved in a considerable amount of local exchange. As previously postulated (Kelly 1980), this exchange was to a large degree precipitated by an increase in population, which resulted in increased competition for resources that were unevenly distributed throughout the region. This coupled with ties to agricultural lands that were also unevenly distributed undoubtedly resulted in the formation of a local exchange network. While the context of some of the exchange was of an economic nature, other aspects of it may have been embedded in certain social relations and religious ceremonies. This intense pattern of intraregional trade undoubtedly set the stage for exchange with other regions, particularly those to the south.

The actual evidence for extraregional trade during the initial Emergent Mississippian is meager. There is some evidence that Mill Creek hoes made their appearance at this time (Figure 4.6). On the Merrell Tract and the East Stockade (Koldehoff 1990) at Cahokia, Mill Creek flakes represented one half of one percent of or less of the total chert by weight from Loyd contexts (Kelly 1984). Apparently no Mill Creek chert was recovered from the Loyd midden under the east lobes of Monks Mound (Williams 1985). Just east of Cahokia excavation of the Robert Schneider site recovered Mill Creek flakes that comprised 29% of the chert debris (Fortier 1985). The paucity of ceramics recovered from this site make its placement in the Loyd phase tentative. Farther south at the Range site, polished Mill Creek hoe flakes and fragments were recovered from both the Dohack and Range phase components. Although a full inventory of chert types was not completed, these items composed .05% of the total Dohack phase chert by weight and .1% of the Range phase chert (Williams 1990a, b). Although this probably does not represent all of the Mill Creek chert recovered, it suggests that a few Mill Creek hoes were being imported into the region. Unfortunately, it is difficult to determine the actual number of items being imported given the sole presence of flakes derived from maintenance activities and the tendency for subsequent curation of the hoes (cf. Kelly 1984).

In addition to the Mill Creek chert from the Range site, anculosa shell beads were recovered from Dohack and Range phase contexts (L. Kelly 1990a, b). Anculosa is a freshwater gastropod (*Anculosa praerosa*) prevalent in the lower Wabash, Tennessee, and Ohio river drainages (Parmalee 1973). The actual number recovered was small. As with the Mill Creek chert hoes, it is difficult to estimate the quantity obtained since they were probably subject to curation. These items are also present in coeval Late Woodland mortuary contexts of the lower Illinois river valley (Perino 1973).

The only other evidence for exchange at this time is restricted to a few ceramic vessels and rare occurrences of copper. Marine shell beads have been retrieved from coeval mortuary contexts to the north in the lower Illinois river valley (Perino 1973). The only copper evident at this time consists of a copper pendant from Dohack phase contexts at the Range site (Williams 1990a) and a small piece of worked copper from Loyd phase contexts on the Merrell Tract at Cahokia (Kelly 1980). Whether the copper was from the Great Lakes or elsewhere has not yet been determined. Copper may also be present in glacial drift deposits (Brown et al. 1990) and in the Ozarks to the southwest (Morse and Morse 1980). Virtually all of the non-local ceramics recovered are from Loyd phase contexts on the Merrell Tract (Figure 4.7). These vessels comprise about 4.0% of the assemblage. Grog-tempered cordmarked jars (Figure 4.8a) are similar to Mulberry Creek varieties of the Mississippi river valley to the south, either in southern Illinois, western Kentucky, or southeast Missouri. A plain jar with pinched decoration may also be derived from this area (Figure 4.8b). A shell-tempered jar with handle exhibits a red-slipped interior (Figure 4.8c) and is similar to the Varney Red Filmed vessels of southeast Missouri (Williams 1954, Marshall 1965) and northeast Arkansas (Morse and Morse 1980). A shell-tempered red-slipped seed jar (Figure 4.8d) was also recovered and is related to similar vessels from southeast Missouri (Marshall 1965). These red-slipped seed jars also have affinities with the Varney Red Filmed hooded bottles in that both forms represent gourd or squash effigies (Kelly 1980). The neck and shoulder of a grog-tempered, red-slipped vessel may be part of a hooded bottle similar to ones recovered from later Emergent Mississippian contexts at the Range site (Ozuk 1978) and the Marcus site (Emerson and Jackson 1987).

The aforementioned vessels are classified as non-local based on attributes such as paste, mode of surface treatment and details of vessel morphology that differentiate them from local vessels and in turn link them with similar ceramics recovered from an area that is within a 125 km radius of the Ohio river's confluence

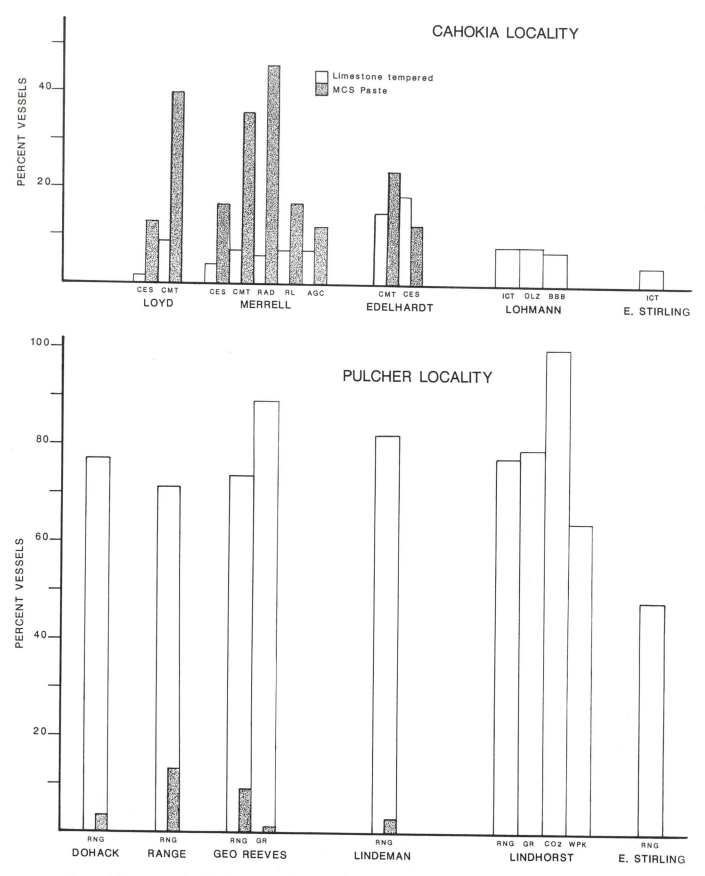

Figure 4.5. Distribution of Limestone Tempered Vessels and Vessels from Madison County Shales (MCS) for Sites by Phase within the Cahokia and Pulcher Localities.

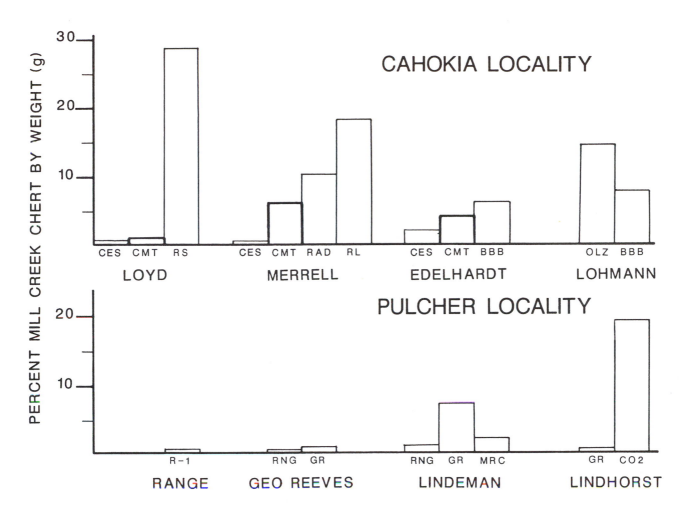

Figure 4.6. Distribution of Mill Creek Chert for Sites by Phase within the Cahokia and Pulcher Localities.

with the Mississippi river. Clearly more rigorous means of assessing these identifications need to be made.

The only other ceramic evidence consists of a Officer Punctate rim recovered from a possible George Reeves phase feature at the Range site (Figure 4.8e). It is possible that this item was redeposited from earlier Dohack or Range phase contexts since this type dates to the ninth century in east central Arkansas and northwest Mississippi (Rolingson 1982). Except for this isolated example, the lack of comparable items from coeval sites in the American Bottom is difficult to evaluate. This may very well reflect the nature of the Loyd phase occupation as part of Cahokia's development as a center at this time. It also may relate to the fact that the phases for the two traditions are not entirely synchronous. The Loyd phase occupation on the Merrell Tract, for example, appears to be relatively late and more in line with the beginning of the George Reeves phase to the south. Regardless of these problems, there is good evidence at this time that exchange was occurring between the American Bottom and an area centered about the confluence of the Ohio and Mississippi rivers.

The second century (A.D. 900-1000)

By A.D. 900 the extra-regional exchange network that had begun to develop was well underway and continued to intensify throughout the rest of the Emergent Mississippian occupation of the American Bottom. In fact this interaction with other regions, in many respects, was one of the primary ingredients in Cahokia's rise to dominance.

In general the Emergent Mississippian settlements during the tenth century continued to be quite varied, with substantial evidence of settlement nucleation involving larger villages (J. Kelly 1990). Given the present evidence, there is some indication that the larger town-and-mound complexes of Cahokia and Pulcher were in place by A.D. 1000. This settlement nucleation

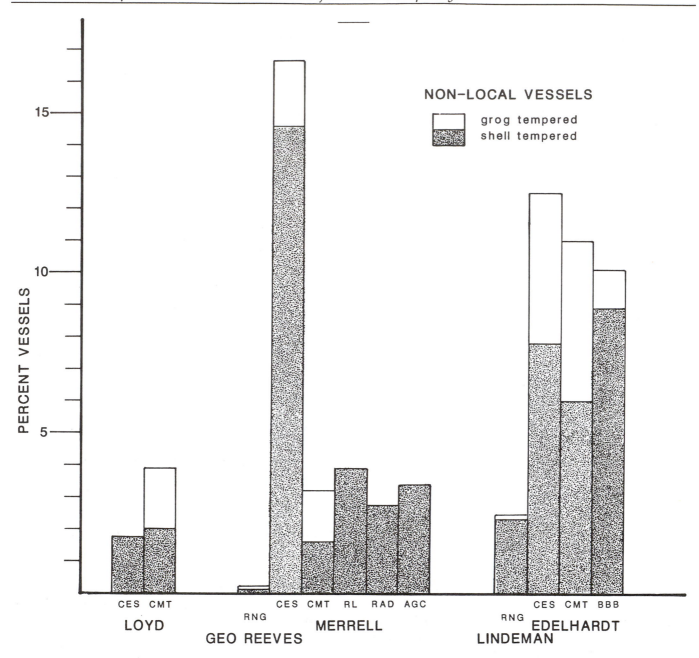

Figure 4.7. Distribution of Non-local Ceramics for Sites by Phase within the Cahokia and Pulcher Localities.

is undoubtedly related to increases in population and the need to manage agricultural lands more effectively (J. Kelly 1990). The larger settlements may have also served an important economic role, in addition to being politico-religious centers.

Although the intraregional exchange network continued to flourish, a number of differences do occur. For example, initially there was a decrease in limestone-tempered vessels between the end of the ninth century and the tenth century at the two localities at Cahokia. However, during the tenth century on the Merrell Tract and the East Stockade at Cahokia there

was a reversal in this trend with increases in the frequency of limestone-tempered vessels being imported while at outlying sites the frequency of limestone-tempered vessels remained relatively stable (Figure 4.5). The amount of Ste. Genevieve chert decreases both at Cahokia and at the outlying sites, but is generally more prevalent at Cahokia (Figure 4.4).

To the south the frequency of jars manufactured from MCS (Figure 4.5) decreases while the amount of Burlington chert being imported increases (Figure 4.4). This increase in Burlington cherts occurs despite the local availability of Ste Genevieve cherts. Again, the

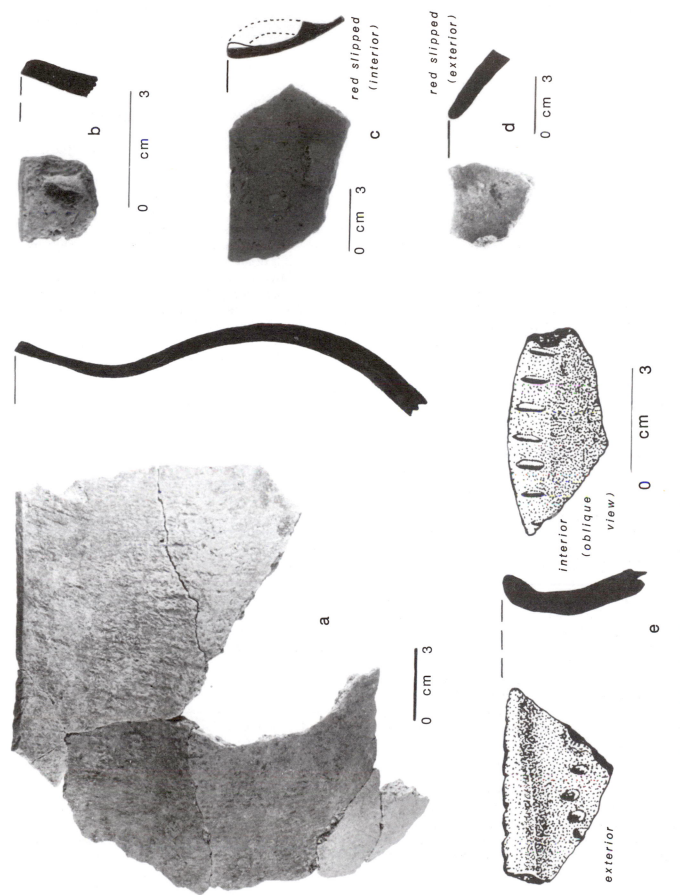

Figure 4.8. Non-local Ceramics from Early Emergent Mississippian Contexts. (a) grog-tempered, cordmarked jar; (b) grog-tempered, pinched jar; (c) shell-tempered seed jar; (d) shell-tempered jar; (e) grog-tempered Officer Punctated jar. (a–d) from Cahokia Merrell Tract (Kelly 1980); (e) from Range Site.

Burlington cherts were imported in several finished forms including woodworking tools, hoes, small arrow points, as well as cores that were subsequently reduced in order to produce expedient tools (Koldehoff 1987). The Ste. Genevieve chert occurs locally in small nodules that were used to produce expedient tools and small arrow points. Presumably the Burlington chert became more accessible through some form of local exchange network.

In contrast with the initial Emergent Mississippian occupations, extra-regional exchange increased in intensity throughout the last half of the Emergent Mississippian and into the early Mississippian occupations. The area of interaction is again centered about the confluence of the Ohio and Mississippi rivers and includes Mill Creek chert hoes, anculosa shell beads, and a variety of ceramic vessels from different parts of this region. By the end of the Emergent Mississippian there is evidence that this interaction sphere had been extended farther south into the lower Mississippi river valley. It may have also included the Gulf of Mexico and the south Atlantic coast sources of marine shell.

Mill Creek chert continued to be imported as large ovate hoes. Except for a single hoe from the Lindeman phase component at the Marcus site and several hoes from George Reeves and Lindeman phase contexts at the Range site, the remaining Mill Creek materials were restricted to flakes and fragments derived from hoe maintenance. The amount present is variable and hence difficult to evaluate. Presumably such debris should reflect the amount of ongoing maintenance activity. Thus a higher frequency of such debris would be expected at the smaller settlements. This appears to be the case for the Cahokia area. However, farther south the smaller settlements, such as George Reeves (McElrath and Finney 1987) and Marcus (Emerson and Jackson 1987) had a much lower frequency of Mill Creek (Figure 4.6). This may reflect the manner in which these tools were being imported into the region, in that they were coming directly to the Cahokia site or nearby sites and subsequently redistributed from there. This pattern presumably continued into the Mississippian. For example, at the East St. Louis site a cache of 70 hoes, some of which had not been used, along with small marine shell beads and "boulders" of chert and greenstone was uncovered over a century ago (Rau 1869).

During the Merrell phase on the Merrell Tract at Cahokia, non-local ceramic vessels comprise 3% of the assemblage. Half of these vessels were shell-tempered and consisted of a red-slipped pan (Figure 4.9a, b) and seed jar (Figure 4.9c). The remainder were grog-tempered, cordmarked jars (Figure 4.9d). There is an unusually high frequency, 15%, of shell-tempered vessels recovered from the East Stockade excavations at

Cahokia (Pauketat 1990). At the outlying Merrell phase sites of Robinson's Lake (Milner assisted by Cox and Meinkoth 1984), A.G. Church (Pauketat n.d.), and Radic (McElrath et al. 1987), these vessels made up 3.9%, 3.4%, and 2.7% of the assemblages, respectively. At all three sites these were shell-tempered, with a number of different vessel forms present, including Varney Red Filmed jars, Varney Red Filmed hooded bottles (Figure 4.9e), red-slipped seed jars (Figure 4.9f), and red-slipped bowls from Robinsons Lake and AG Church. Of the three non-local vessels from Radic only one, a bowl, was identifiable to form.

Of particular interest is the apparent lack of other non-local vessels at these outlying sites, particularly those that are grog-tempered. Farther south at the Range site during the George Reeves phase, grog-tempered vessels occur in conjunction with shell-tempered vessels. However, their frequency is small, less than 1.0%. The shell-tempered vessels are not as diverse and appear to be restricted to Varney Red Filmed and Mississippi Plain jars. The grog-tempered vessels include cordmarked jars and at least one red-slipped hooded bottle (Figure 4.9g). Thus in marked contrast to the Cahokia area, the Pulcher area was not as intensely involved in the exchange network. This may reflect the manner in which these goods were being brought into the American Bottom through centers to the north such as Cahokia. This parallels the manner in which Mill Creek chert hoes were being distributed in the American Bottom.

During the Edelhardt phase at Cahokia the intensity of interaction with the lower Mississippi river valley increased (Figure 4.7). This is evident in the increase in shell and grog-tempered vessels. Shell-tempered containers comprise 6.0% of the Merrell Tract assemblage and include red-slipped, punctated seed jars (Figure 4.10a); Varney Red Filmed and Mississippi Plain jars (Figure 4.10b-d); and an occasional red-slipped bowl.

The grog-tempered vessels comprise 5% of the Merrell Tract assemblage. Four percent are jars which include a plain jar manufactured from a paste similar to ones observed on vessels from the Obion site of

---

Figure 4.9. Non-local Ceramics from Late Emergent Mississippian, George Reeves, and Merrell Phase Contexts. (a, b) shell-tempered, cordmarked pan with punctated lip; (c) shell-tempered seed jar; (d) grog-tempered, cordmarked jar; (e) shell-tempered hooded bottle; (f) shell-tempered seed jar; (g) grog-tempered hooded bottle with frog applique. (a-d) from Cahokia Merrell Tract (Kelly 1980); (e-f) from Robinson's Lake (Milner assisted by Cox and Meinkoth 1984); (g) from Range Site.

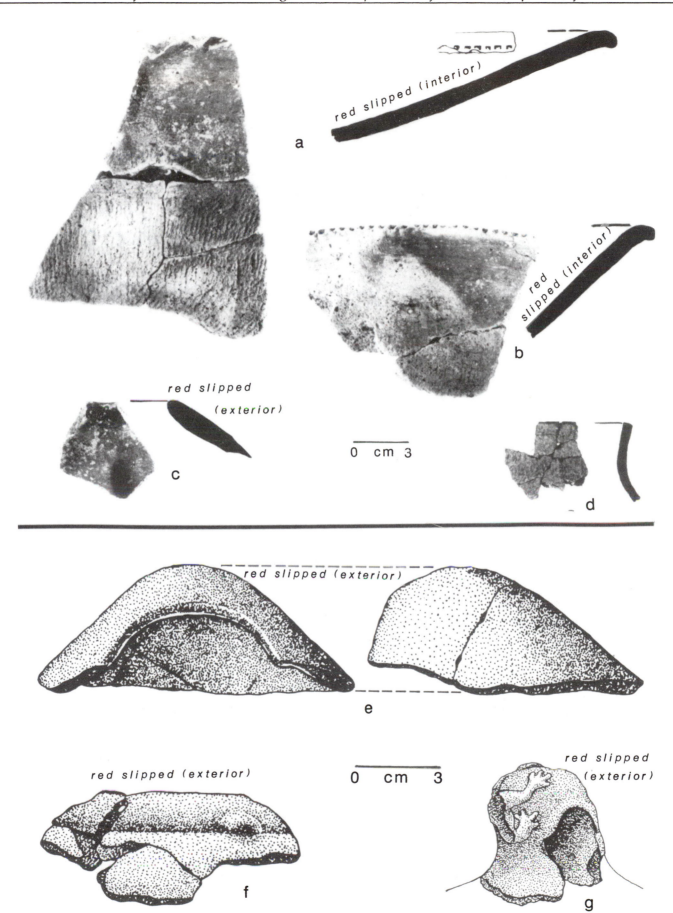

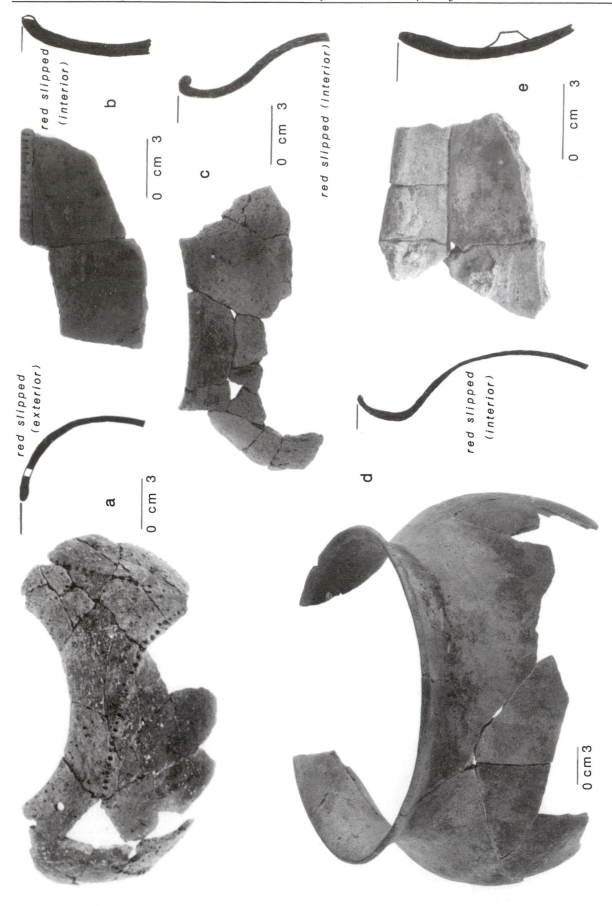

Figure 4.10. Non-local Ceramics from Late Emergent Mississippian, Edelhardt Phase, Contexts, at the Merrell Tract, Cahokia (Kelly 1980). (a) shell-tempered, punctated seed jar; (b–d) shell-tempered, plain jars with red-slipped interiors; (e) grog-tempered, plain jar.

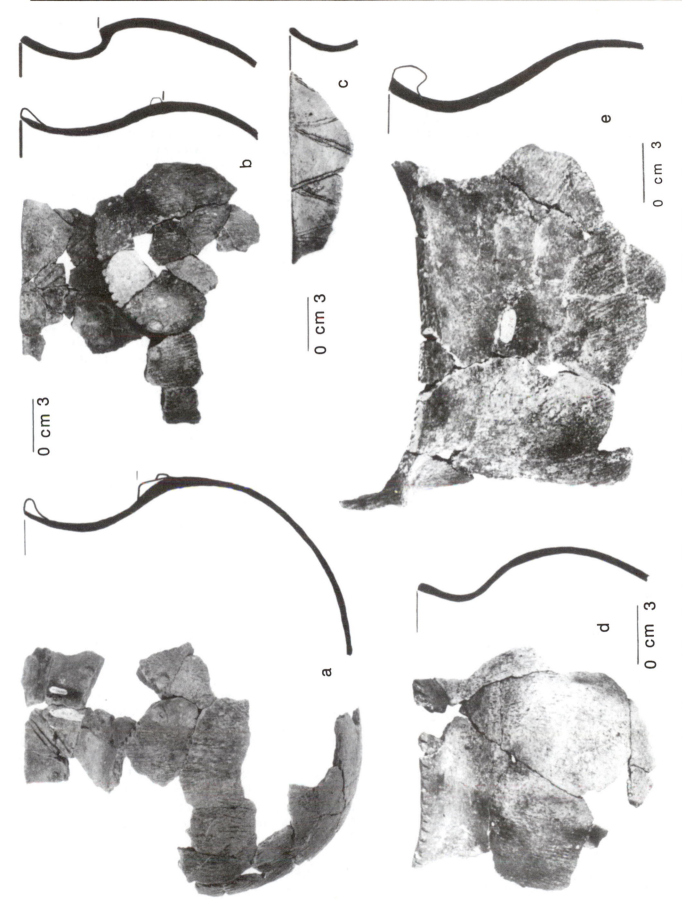

Figure 4.11. Non-local Grog Tempered Ceramics from Late Emergent Mississippian, Edelhardt Phase, Contexts, at the Merrell Tract, Cahokia (Kelly 1980). (a–b) Kersey Incised jar with plain neck and cordmarked body; (c) Kersey Incised jar; (d–e) jars with smoothed over cordmarked neck and cordmarked body. (d) also exhibits notched exterior lip.

northwestern Tennessee (Figure 4.10e); two incised vessels that were classified as Kersey Incised (Figure 4.11a-c), a southeast Missouri type (Marshall 1965); those that are cordmarked to the lip (Figure 4.11d); and several plain necked vessels with cordmarked bodies (Figure 4.11e). Body sherds from Yankeetown Incised jars were also recovered. This type is related to Kersey Incised but is distributed in an area centered about the confluence of the Wabash and Ohio rivers (Redmond 1987).

The remaining one percent of the grog-tempered vessels on the Merrell Tract consists of three bowls (Figure 4.12a, b, c). They are all finely tempered and exhibit well polished surfaces. One is a shallow pan or platter; another is a straight-walled bowl with the distinctive tapered Vicksburg rim; and the remaining bowl with bone tempering exhibits circumferential incising characteristic of Coles Creek Incised *var. Blakely* (Schambach personal communication 1989). These vessels are all undoubtedly derived from Coles Creek contacts farther south in the lower Mississippi river valley. Several body sherds include one that is incised and red-slipped (Figure 4.12d) and another that is burnished and engraved with a white pigment filler (Figure 4.12e). Frank Schambach (personal communication 1989) indicates that the former sherd is part of a red-filmed Crockett Curvilinear Incised bowl probably from the Red river valley. The latter vessel, a bottle or seed jar fragment may resemble Crenshaw Fluted, another type from the Red river valley. A small Homan point of an "olive-gold" jasper was also recovered. This raw material is apparently common to the Red and Sulpher river drainages of northeast Texas (Shafer 1973:189).

From the East Stockade excavations two Coles Creek Incised polished bowls were recovered from Edelhardt phase contexts. One (Figure 4.12f) with an incised line on the superior lip surface is probably comparable to Coles Creek Incised *var. Greenhouse* (Pauketat 1990:58). The other (Figure 4.12g) is probably Coles Creek Incised *var. Blakely* (Pauketat 1990:52).

At the nearby BBB Motor site, the Edelhardt phase occupation includes many of the same non-local vessel types (Emerson and Jackson 1984). Of particular interest is the much higher frequency of shell-tempered vessels, i.e., 16%. Many if not most of these are of local manufacture, based on vessel morphology. A number of the Merrell Tract Bluff jars were tempered with shell indicating the local adoption of shell as a tempering agent by this time. Certainly by A.D. 1000 shell had become the dominate temper, especially for sites located on the floodplain near Cahokia. It was not possible, however, to determine if any of the BBB Motor shell-tempered jars were non-local by simply examining the report. Likewise, there is sufficient time

depth at this site based on structure superposition to suggest that at least three occupational episodes are evident within the Edelhardt occupation. It is evident from inventory data that there was an increase in shell-tempered vessels and vessels with plain and red-slipped surfaces. Thus the shift locally to shell tempering was rapid.

In addition to Varney Red Filmed jars and red-slipped seed jars and bowls, there was at least one incised jar that is a shell-tempered counterpart to Kersey Incised. A large shell-tempered body sherd was from a jar that exhibited a brushed exterior and a red-slipped interior similar to some vessels from southeast Missouri (Marshall 1965).

The non-local grog-tempered vessels included a Kersey Incised jar; Yankeetown Incised body sherds; and a plain jar with an effigy loop handle. The grog in this latter vessel also contained shell. Similar jars have been observed elsewhere at Cahokia (Hall 1975) and are more common in the area of the Ohio and Mississippi confluence. Apparently the only other non-local vessel was a grit-tempered, cordmarked jar with a collared rim. Collaring occurs on many of the jars from eastern and northern Illinois. In general it appears that grog-tempered vessels comprise a small percentage, about 1%, of the assemblage at BBB Motor. The only indication of Coles Creek contacts was one Coles Creek Incised bowl (Figure 4.12h) (Emerson and Jackson 1984).

Farther south, in the Pulcher locality, there was also increase in the frequency of non-local vessels. However, as in the preceding George Reeves phase, these vessels comprised a much smaller percentage than their counterparts to the north. Virtually all of the same ceramic types have been recovered. The major difference, in addition to their lower relative frequency, is the lack of any ceramics related to those of the Coles Creek type. A jasper Alba point was recovered from the Schlemmer site located between the Pulcher and Range sites (Berres 1984). It was probably associated with the Lindeman component and is

---

Figure 4.12 Non-local Grog-Tempered Ceramics from Late Emergent Mississippian, Edelhardt Phase, Contexts. (a) polished pan; (b) polished bowl with Vicksburg rim; (c) Coles Creek Incised variety Blakely (bone tempered) bowl; (d) red-slipped Crockett Curvilinear Incised bowl fragment; (e) engraved bottle or seed jar body sherd with polished exterior and traces of white pigment in engraved lines; (f-h) Coles Creek Incised polished bowls. (a-e) from Cahokia, Merrell Tract (Kelly 1980); (f-g) from Cahokia, East Stockade (Pauketat 1990); (h) from BBB Motor Site (Emerson and Jackson 1984).

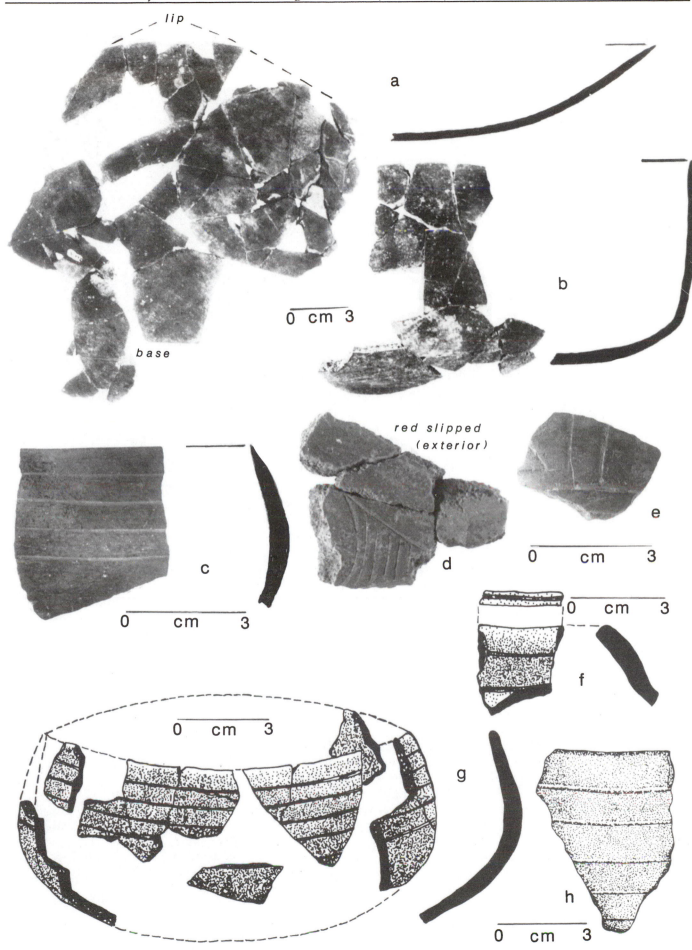

lip

a

base

0 cm 3

b

c

0 cm 3

red slipped (exterior)

d

e

0 cm 3

0 cm 3

f

0 cm 3

g

h

0 cm 3

the only substantive evidence of lower Mississippi river valley connections for this region.

During the final segment of the Emergent Mississippian occupation at Cahokia, there is increased interaction with a much larger geographic area. Except for the incorporation of the Red river valley of the Caddo area and the lower Mississippi valley groups south of the Arkansas river into this extraregional network, most of the same goods and raw materials continued to be exchanged within both intra and extraregional spheres. Although there was continuity, there were also a number of transformations, both in the increased intensity of this interaction and in the manner in which these materials were being distributed. Intraregionally, it appears that most of the materials being exchanged between the southern and northern portions of the American Bottom are more apt to be concentrated in the larger nucleated settlements such as Cahokia, Range, and, presumably, Pulcher. A similar pattern is evident for extraregional items, with a site such as Cahokia serving as a central location for redistribution to outlying settlements. This redistribution was related to the site as a central place for ceremonies and other social gatherings and not necessarily to a particular individual.

Based on several lines of evidence, it is certainly possible that Cahokia had emerged as an early center. The actual evidence for mound construction is not conclusive but certainly possible. The proof for Cahokia's role as a major center consists, in part of the high frequency of raw materials and finished goods from an extensive geographic area, more so than any other site in the region.

A second line of evidence consists of the large size of residential structures. Based on the distribution of the larger houses at sites such as Range and the small size of structures at nearby sites such as BBB Motor, the larger facilities on the Merrell Tract at Cahokia (Kelly 1980), undoubtedly were associated with a large nucleated community. In turn these were probably the abode of high ranking individuals within the settlement.

Finally, the extensive area of the Merrell and Edelhardt phase occupations in the central area of Cahokia, particularly flanking the central feature, Monks Mound, presumably reflects a single large center covering several hundred hectares. It is this distribution that leads one to postulate not only Cahokia's role as a central place, but one in which mound construction was initiated. By the end of the Edelhardt phase on the Merrell Tract, the residential area had probably shifted to the west on Tract 15-A, and the Merrell Tract had become a special use area, such as a plaza in which large posts were erected.

Mississippian

The Inception

The origins of the Mississippian occupation at Cahokia are indigenous and well rooted in the Emergent Mississippian presence in the region. Undoubtedly some rapid transformations occurred toward the end of the Emergent Mississippian occupation. These included the abandonment of the Merrell Tract and the adjacent Tract 15-B as residential areas and their use as some type of specialized precinct along with the commencement of construction on Monks Mound. The initial Mississippian phase (Lohmann) has been recognized in a number of areas of the site (Figure 4.3). These include sub-mound 51 (Chmurny 1973), a reclaimed borrow pit just southeast of Monks Mound; the residential area of the ICT-II (Collins 1987) several hundred meters southeast of Monks Mound; the residential area of Tract 15-A 1000 m west of Monks Mound (Hall 1975); the premound and beginning stages of the Powell Mound (Ahler and DePuydt 1987) and some of the residential area on the Powell Tract (cf. O'Brien 1972); and the Mound 72 mortuary complex (Fowler and Anderson 1975). Unfortunately the analyses of these data are either incomplete or currently in progress, thus it is difficult to compare these data adequately with those of the Emergent Mississippian. There are, however, some general observations that can be made.

First, there is evidence of continued interaction between the Cahokia area and its neighbors in the central portion of the American Bottom, particularly the mound center at the Pulcher site. It is important to emphasize that the Pulcher tradition persisted into early Mississippian times as the Lindhorst phase (Kelly 1990). It is the continued presence of limestone-tempered vessels at Cahokia and other sites in the northern portion of the American Bottom that delineates this interaction. These vessels comprise 8% to 19% of the assemblages at Cahokia (Chmurny 1973; Hall 1975; and Holley 1989). Although a range of limestone-tempered vessel forms was present, a majority were Monks Mound Red bowls (cf. Chmurny 1973). Outlying Lohmann phase farmsteads to the south had assemblages with 20% to 35% limestone tempering (Milner assisted by Williams 1983). Likewise, many of the shell-tempered vessels that appear in early Mississippian assemblages to the south are derived from the Cahokia area (cf. Mehrer 1982). Artifacts and cores of Burlington chert are distributed throughout the region (Koldeoff 1987). Thus the intraregional exchange network continued to thrive.

The evidence for extraregional exchange is also widespread with essentially the same items of

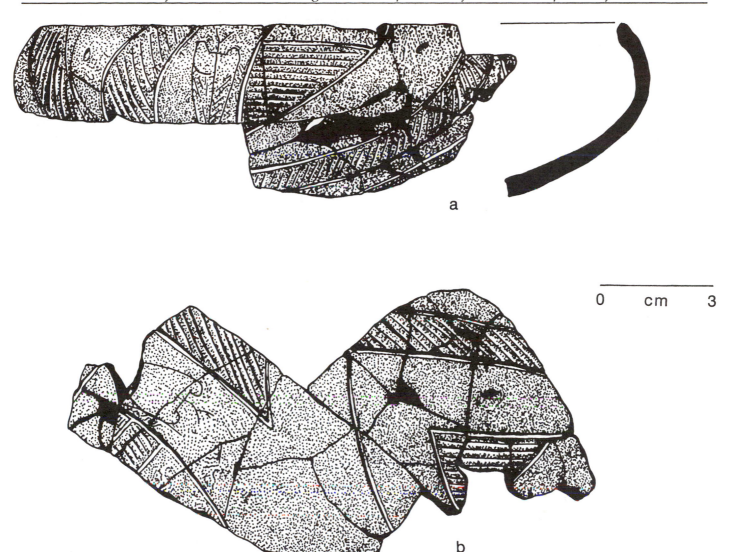

Figure 4.13 French Fork Incised Bowl from Early Mississippian, Lindhorst Phase, Contexts at the High Prairie Site (Koldehoff 1982). (a) side view with profile; (b) view of base.

exchange. This includes Mill Creek hoes, ceramic vessels, and marine shell. Mill Creek hoes prevail as perhaps the primary item of import and were distributed among settlements throughout the region. Ceramic vessels continue to be imported from the area of the Ohio-Mississippi confluence; however, it appears that in contrast to the Emergent Mississippian, they are not as prevalent. Most of these appear to be Varney Red Filmed jars or grog-tempered plain jars. As before, elaborately decorated vessels related to ceramics of the Coles Creek tradition are present (Figure 4.13); however, they comprise less than 2% of any assemblage. Holley (1989) has suggested that some of his "fine-grog" wares from the ICT-II tract show affinities with types of the lower Mississippi valley and Caddoan area.

Perhaps the most important of the imported items was marine shell. At least 3 taxa (Chmurny indicates 4 taxa, but only 3 are evident in his tables) were identified from sub-mound 51 contexts (Chmurny 1973). One of these taxa was a marine scallop (*Pectinidae*) which was worked into spoons. The primary species here and on the Powell Tract (Ahler and DePuydt 1987), however, were marine whelks (*Busycon* spp.) and Atlantic marginella (*Prunum apicinum*), which occurred in the form of beads. The former were presumably imported whole and subsequently manufactured into beads based on the ubiquity of microdrills at Cahokia at this time. This process occurred not only at Cahokia, but also at many of the outlying sites where microdrills have also been recovered (Yerkes 1983). While these materials were accessible to most of the population, the massive blanket of beads recovered from Mound 72 (Fowler and Anderson 1975) perhaps best epitomizes the importance of such items to the elite. Hence the distribution of marine shell may have been under the direct "control" of the ruling elite in terms of their acquisition and subsequent distribution.

In addition to the aforementioned marine shell, freshwater anculosa shells were also recovered from sub-mound 51 (Chmurny 1973). These had been manufactured into beads and represent a continuation of the connections with the drainages of the lower Ohio river valley. Also recovered was a drilled alligator tooth (*Alligator mississippiensis*). This species was known to occur as far north as the mouth of the Arkansas river (Chmurny 1973:230).

Beside the numerous marine shell beads, other items directly associated with the mortuary materials at Mound 72 were bundles of arrows with points derived from different parts of the mid-continent; sheets of mica; a rolled sheet of copper; and a cache of discoidals. The ceramics recovered from Mound 72 (see Fowler this volume), in my opinion, appear to be derived from a residential area that predates the mound and associated mortuary complex. The ceramics present were all fragments of vessels that had been broken and discarded. The lack of whole vessels in direct association with the burials can be viewed as evidence of the lack of importance attributed to such items by the elite at this time.

Other exotics that have been recovered from Lohmann phase residential contexts include galena, hematite, and quartz crystals (Gums 1987). Hixton silicified sandstone cores and projectile points have also been recovered from the Lohmann phase residential area of the ICT-II (DeMott 1987).

As in the Emergent Mississippian occupations, the Lohmann phase web of exchange was widespread. The intensity of exchange may have waned, but the strong similarity of the ceramic assemblage with other early Mississippian assemblages like Obion in western Tennessee; Martin's Farm in eastern Tennessee; and Macon Plateau in central Georgia suggests that widespread cultural interaction persisted. Likewise new contacts were also established with a number of areas to the north that include northwest Iowa (Anderson 1988); southwest Wisconsin (Stevenson et al. 1983); central Illinois (McConaughy 1986); and east central Illinois (Douglas 1976). As discussed elsewhere, this represents the first stage in Cahokia's development as a Gateway center (Kelly 1991).

The Climax

During the subsequent Stirling phase, Cahokia rose to dominance as the largest Mississippian site in Eastern North America. Prior to this, evidence for Cahokia's influence outside the American Bottom was minimal, especially in the lower Mississippi valley where the occurrence of Burlington cherts at a number of sites as far south as northwest Mississippi (Johnson 1987) constitutes the sole evidence of Cahokia-area contact. This, of course, assumes that Cahokia was in some way involved in its distribution, however indirectly.

By the Stirling phase evidence of Cahokia's influence is widespread, especially to the north and northwest where Cahokia may have functioned as a gateway for an elite populace of Mississippians (cf. Kelly 1991). This is based on the distribution of Ramey Incised and Powell Plain jars, whose ultimate source was undoubtedly the American Bottom, if not Cahokia. On the other hand there appears to be a reduction in the amount of certain materials, such as ceramics, derived from outside the region. Excavations at a number of areas at Cahokia have revealed evidence of Stirling phase activities. Residential areas were evident on the Powell Tract (O'Brien 1972) and the ICT-II (Collins 1987) while Tracts 15-A and 15-B were characterized by the presence of specialized facilities such as the Woodhenge (cf. Fowler and Hall 1975). Unfortunately these data have yet to be fully reported upon, which affects this perception of a trade reduction.

In terms of the intraregional network Burlington chert continued to be a primary trade commodity both in the form of completed bifaces, such as woodworking tools and hoes, and as a source of material for arrowpoints, microdrills and other flake tools (Koldehoff 1987). The frequency of limestone-tempered vessels decreased from 4% early in the Stirling phase at Cahokia to 1% by the end of the phase (Holley 1989). This corresponds not only to the disappearance of the Pulcher tradition and its ultimate integration, along with other areas, into a distinctive Mississippian complex that was widespread by the Moorehead phase. The reduction in limestone tempering is also evident at the smaller outlying sites (Milner assisted by Williams 1983). Thus the nature of the intraregional network was being restructured along different lines.

Extraregional materials still being imported include Mill Creek hoes, ceramic vessels, marine shell, and a variety of other exotics. Mill Creek hoes were still a dominant item. Another item manufactured from this material is the classic Ramey Knife. While large maces and spuds were also made from Mill Creek chert, it is difficult to determine when they first appear in the archaeological record. Another chert from southern Illinois, Kaolin, was also used in the manufacture of the aforementioned items.

Ceramic vessels from sources near the confluence of the Ohio and Mississippi rivers appear to be non-existent, while ceramics from areas farther south may be better represented. A small percentage (1.6%) of the ICT-II Stirling assemblages exhibit the "fine-grog" ware vessels that were burnished to varying degrees, slipped and decorated with incising or engraving (Holley 1989). A higher frequency (9.3%) of these vessels have been described by O'Brien (1969 and 1972) for the Powell Tract. It is not clear why the differences in these two assemblages are so pronounced. It may relate to the nature of the activities conducted in these two areas in that there was a greater emphasis on ceremonial or social activities on the Powell Tract.

As to the derivation of these vessels, such items have in the past often been attributed to the Caddoan area or in some instances the lower Mississippi valley (O'Brien 1969). More recently it has been suggested that many of these are actually derived from the lower Mississippi valley or Red river valley (J. Brown personal communication). Holley (1989) feels that many of these "exotic" vessels are in fact of local manufacture. Thus they may represent an attempt by local potters to emulate similar types. This is reminiscent of the impact of Ramey Incised on the production of similar types by various groups to the north of Cahokia. Certainly the ultimate sources of inspiration for the "fine grog" wares were the aforementioned areas, which does represent some form of interaction. Some of the motifs, such as the scroll on Ramey Incised, were certainly inspired by similar designs on some of the earlier Coles Creek ceramics.

As in the Lohmann phase, marine shell was an important item that was available to a large segment of the population. Presumably the elite at Cahokia were involved in its acquisition and distribution both locally and with groups to the north and northwest. Although these materials are conspicuous at many sites to the north, the amount of non-local materials returned to Cahokia appears to have been meager. One would suspect that much of what was being imported was destined for the elite and thus not available for circulation among the rest of Cahokian society. Unfortunately, the only possible elite, Stirling phase mortuary areas to have been "investigated" were the large mortuary facilities of the Big Mound of the St Louis mound group (Williams and Goggins 1956); the large mound at Mitchell (Howland 1877, Winters 1974); the Powell Mound (Titterington 1938); and the large mound at East St. Louis (Kelly 1989), all of which were essentially destroyed between 1870 and

1930. The only data recovered were by interested observers, including tremendous quantities of marine shell, objects of copper or with copper coverings, and, in the case of Mitchell, the remnants of what undoubtedly was a bison skull (Howland 1877, Winters 1974).

Most of the remaining exotics that were present during the Lohmann phase are also evident from Stirling phase contexts, both at Cahokia and its satellites. These materials include galena, hematite, quartz crystals, mica, copper, and Hixton silicified sandstone. To this repertoire of exotics can be added a catlinite tube pipe from the ICT-II tract at Cahokia (Gums 1987) and the distinctive "fireclay" figurines that were retrieved from a number of smaller sites east of Cahokia (Emerson 1982).

The Fall

During the subsequent Moorehead and Sand Prairie phases, Cahokia declined in importance. In the meantime other Mississippian centers to the south began to grow in importance, while to the north Oneota societies were rapidly rising to dominance. The role of Cahokia in extraregional exchange was greatly diminished although many of the same commodities made their way into the American Bottom and to Cahokia, but in what appear to be much lower frequencies. Evidence for interaction with these societies, particularly those to the south, is evident in the strong similarities of certain ceramic vessels such as incised plates and effigy bowls. The strong stylistic congruence in these ceramics emphasizes the continued web of interaction among the various Mississippian groups.

Discussion

In assessing Cahokia's interaction with other areas and in particular the lower Mississippi valley one must rely on certain assumptions regarding what are considered items foreign to the area. In the case of this paper most of the information about items considered to be non-local was derived from the existing literature. The accuracy of this information is ultimately contingent upon the application of more rigorous quantitative techniques. Regardless of these limitations, it is still possible to examine the role of exchange in Cahokia's development. In pursuing this topic there are several areas of discussion that need to be considered. These include the types of materials being exchanged; the context of such materials; the mechanisms by which such exchange was accomplished; and the impact on Cahokia's development.

First, the primary types of non-local materials imported into the American Bottom include Mill

Creek and other cherts from Southern Illinois; anculosa shells from the lower Ohio river drainage; ceramic vessels from a number of different areas; and marine shell. Other items that may be present include various raw materials such as quartz crystals, galena, fireclay, hematite, and copper. Each of these materials will be examined as to their context and possible mechanism of dispersal.

Perhaps the most important items being obtained were the Mill Creek hoes. These appear to make their initial appearance during the ninth century and coincide with the increased importance of maize as a food crop. They increase in ubiquity during the tenth century and continue to be a major item of exchange throughout the Mississippian occupation of the American Bottom. Hoes were an important utilitarian item and readily obtained by most of the population.

The immediate area of Cahokia exhibits the highest density of these tools, second only to the source area. A preliminary study (Brown et al. 1990) attempted to quantify and determine the mode of distribution for these tools over a much larger geographic area. The results were inconclusive as to the mechanisms of distribution.

Ceramics from external sources are in certain respects a difficult item to evaluate, since individuals in most communities were capable of producing ceramic vessels. Thus, the actual utilitarian need for such vessels can not always be explained, especially when such items do not necessarily represent a better product. On the other hand these vessels may simply represent containers for food stuffs or other materials such as shell that were the actual items of import.

Beginning in the ninth century, vessels manufactured from a number of distinctive pastes were produced within the American Bottom and traded through an intraregional network that also involved the distribution of other raw materials, especially lithics. This intraregional sphere of exchange set the stage for extraregional trade. The first non-local vessels appear by the end of the ninth century and were derived from a variety of sources within a 125 km radius of the confluence of the Ohio and Mississippi rivers. Types, such as Kersey Incised, Mulberry Creek Cordmarked, Yankeetown Incised, Varney Red-filmed, and Larto Red-filmed appear, primarily as jars but also as hooded bottles and occasional bowls, with a peak in their occurrence by the end of the Emergent Mississippian occupation. The highest frequency occurs at Cahokia, while populations in the Pulcher locality were less fortunate but certainly not excluded. Based on their distribution in terms of relative frequency, it appears that these vessels, as well as other items such as Mill Creek hoes, were being directly imported to a central location such as Cahokia and then presumably "redistributed" through this intraregional exchange network.

During the latter half of the tenth century the extraregional exchange network was expanded to include the Coles Creek culture of the lower Mississippi river valley and parts of the Red river valley. This expansion may be related to the acquisition of marine shell whelks from the Gulf of Mexico. While ceramics continue to come in from the lower Mississippi river valley and the Caddoan area to the west during the early part of the Mississippian occupation, their frequency appears to have been reduced. During the later, Stirling and Moorehead phase, Mississippian occupation, the "fine grog" wares may have been produced locally and hence represent attempts to emulate those to the south. Since their source is inconclusive, this does not preclude the ongoing interaction between Cahokia and its southern neighbors.

While some of the imported jars may have had utilitarian value, there are others, such as the red-slipped seed jars, hooded bottles, and occasional bowls from Emergent Mississippian contexts that probably had less mundane functions. Basically these vessels represent gourd or squash effigies, whose presence may be related to fertility ceremonies that were pan-Mississippi valley in distribution. They may represent gifts presented to or obtained by local elites during such ceremonies. Vessels comparable to these were ultimately manufactured locally in the form of the limestone-tempered, Monks Mound Red and its grog-tempered kin, Merrell Red Filmed from the area near Cahokia. In many respects these ceremonies may have served as an integrative mechanism not only for social and religious reasons, but also as a means of reaffirming exchange relationships with trade partners outside the region. This may well have involved individual traders. Such evidence is difficult to verify short of finding a canoe full of such individuals buried in the muddy sediments of the Mississippi river.

The elaborately incised and engraved, "fine grog" vessels of the subsequent Mississippian phases presumably reflected a different interpretation of gourd decorations, one more in line with those further south in the lower Mississippi valley. Some of the symbolism (in the scrolls on some of the French Fork Incised) had an impact on the decorative motifs of Ramey Incised. The drop in the frequency of such vessels undoubtedly mirrors changes in the overall nature of the interaction and its direction. Hence, such interactions may have been more directly under the control of the elite at Cahokia and a reflection of the ongoing interaction among the various elite up and down the Mississippi river valley. Their concern was undoubtedly with those items and raw materials that served to enhance and maintain their position within society.

The items recovered from Mound 72, a relatively small mortuary facility early in Cahokia's history, certainly reinforces this notion.

The most prevalent non-local items recovered from Mound 72 were marine shell disk beads. While marine shell was an important item of exchange throughout prehistory, its ubiquity fluctuated. For example, marine shell was common during the Middle Woodland, but its occurrence waned during the subsequent Late Woodland. One of the more common types of shell ornaments recovered from Late Woodland and Emergent Mississippian contexts were the anculosa shell beads derived from the lower Ohio river drainage. These beads appear to have been popular during the ninth and tenth centuries and are distributed as far north as northwest Iowa where they occur in the lower part of Mill Creek middens (cf. Kelly 1991).

The evidence for marine shell is sporadic during the Late Woodland and most of the Emergent Mississippian occupation of the American Bottom. The shell trade appears to have increased in importance by the end of the latter occupation, since marine shell and resultant artifacts are ubiquitous during the early Mississippian. This is clearly the case at Cahokia where at least 19 taxa have been reported from all Mississippian contexts (Chmurny 1972). The most common taxa were the whelk and marginella. Microdrills and other items used in the manufacture of shell ornaments are present not only at Cahokia but also at many of the outlying settlements and farmsteads (Yerkes 1983).

It was marine shell, along with Ramey Incised and Powell Plain jars, that were subsequently distributed to settlements to the north of Cahokia during the Stirling phase, although evidence from the Mill Creek culture of northwest Iowa suggests that this exchange network had probably been initiated by the end of the Emergent Mississippian (Kelly 1991). Presumably the unmodified marine shell, such as whelks were imported directly to Cahokia and other centers where they were subsequently cut and manufactured into various ornaments. One can only assume that such activities were under the control of elite personages. Whether some of the unworked shell and ornaments were "redistributed" to the outlying populace or simply the scrap materials scavenged by these peoples is not entirely clear.

In many respects Cahokia's rise to dominance is related to its role in a number of different webs of exchange that operated both locally and externally. The establishment of the intraregional exchange network occurred early and was a result of at least two primary factors. The first can be attributed to the uneven distribution of raw materials and Cahokia's geographic location on a wide expanse of the Mississippi floodplain devoid of many essential raw materials. The adjoining uplands were similarly lacking in many of these raw materials. The second factor is related to high population densities due to increases in population during the Late Woodland and initial part of the Emergent Mississippian occupations. This ultimately required the establishment of mechanisms by which different types of raw materials, such as chert and salt, could be readily obtained by different segments of the population. While it is possible that local agents or traders were involved, certain agricultural ceremonies may have served as a means by which people within the region could gather and exchange raw materials and finished items at some of the larger and more centrally located settlements.

A chain of these smaller mound centers is distributed the entire length of the American Bottom (Porter 1974) and may have arisen some time after A.D. 900 in response to many of these local needs. Most of those south of Cahokia (Figure 4.1) were located in close proximity to the Mississippi river; along a major tributary exiting the Illinois uplands; and in a downstream position from the source of the larger tributaries along the eastern edge of the Ozarks (Kelly 1980). For the area to the north there is a higher number distributed about Cahokia, which reflects the expansion of the American Bottom in this area.

By the latter half of the Emergent Mississippian occupation this network was expanded to include a large area centered about the confluence of the Ohio and Mississippi rivers. This was subsequently extended farther south into the lower Mississippi river valley and the Gulf of Mexico and ultimately encompassed a larger portion of the Mississippi river drainage north of Cahokia. Through time there was a deemphasis on the exchange of utilitarian products and increased emphasis on decorative and sociotechnic items whose distribution was related to the elite and a prestige-goods economy.

Acknowledgements

This chapter is in part based on a paper presented at the 1988 Mid-south meeting at Paducah, Kentucky. I would like to thank James B. Stoltman for including this paper in his volume and the patience he has shown since extending the invitation. A number of individuals have shared their research and ideas, especially, Tim Pauketat and Brad Koldehoff. Dr. Frank Schambach took the time to examine and comment on the various Merrell Tract sherds and his help is greatly appreciated. Also helpful over the last decade were the many other insightful comments by numerous individuals from the lower Mississippi valley on the handful of exotic sherds at Cahokia. Others who have contributed in various ways include Dr.

George Milner, Thomas Emerson, Douglas Jackson, Dale McElrath, Joyce Williams, Steve Ozuk, Fred Finney, and Dr. George Holley. The photographs used herein were produced by Jeff Abrams; the line drawings were redrafted from the originals by Liz Kassly Kane. I also would like to express appreciation to Dr. John Walthall of the Illinois Department of Transportation and Prof. Charles Bareis of the University of Illinois for the use of the FAI-270 data especially from the Range site; Dr. William Woods of Southern Illinois University Edwardsville for use of his facilities; and Dr. Robert Salzer of Beloit College who led me to the wonderful world of Cahokia. I, however, am responsible for any misuse or misinterpretation of the data.

References Cited

Ahler, Steven R., and Peter J. DePuydt

1987 A Report on the 1931 Powell Mound Excavations, Madison County, Illinois. *Illinois State Museum Reports of Investigations 43.* Springfield.

Anderson, Duane C.

1987 Toward a Processual Understanding of the Initial Variant of the Middle Missouri Tradition: The Case of the Mill Creek Culture of Iowa. *American Antiquity* 52(3):522-537.

Bareis, Charles J. and James W. Porter

1965 Megascopic and Petrographic Analysis of a Foreign Pottery Vessel from the Cahokia Site. *American Antiquity* 31(1):95-101.

1984 *American Bottom Archaeology: A Summary of the FAI-270 Project Contribution to the Culture History of the Mississippi River Valley.* University of Illinois Press. Urbana.

Berres, Thomas Edward

1984 *A Formal Analysis of Ceramic Vessels from the Schlemmer Site (11-S-382): A Late Woodland/ Mississippian Occupation in St. Clair County, Illinois.* M.A. Thesis. Department of Anthropology, Western Michigan University.

Brown, James A., Richard A. Kerber, and Howard D. Winters

1990 Trade and the Evolution of Exchange Relations at the Beginning of the Mississippian Period. In *The Mississippian Emergence*, edited by Bruce Smith, pp 251-280. Smithsonian Press, Washington.

Buikstra, Jane E., Lyle W. Konegsberg, and Jill Bullington

1986 Fertility and the Development of Agriculture in the Prehistoric Midwest. *American Antiquity* 51(3):528-546.

Chmurny, William Wayne

1973 *The Ecology of the Middle Mississippian Occupation of the American Bottom.* Unpublished Ph.D. dissertation, Department of Anthropology, University of Illinois, Urbana.

Collins, James M.

1987 The ICT-II: An Evolutionary Model of Micro- Cahokia Residence. Paper presented at the 25th Annual Workshop of Illinois Archaeology, November 7, 1987, Collinsville, Illinois.

DeMott, Rodney Charles

1987 A Brief Descriptive Summary of the Chipped Lithic Material from the ICT-II. Paper presented at the 25th Annual Workshop of Illinois Archaeology, November 7, 1987, Collinsville, Illinois.

Douglas, John Goodwin

1976 *Collins: A Late Woodland Ceremonial Complex in the Woodfordian Northeast.* Unpublished Ph.D. dissertation, Department of Anthropology, University of Illinois, Urbana.

Emerson, Thomas E.

1982 *Mississippian Stone Images in Illinois.* Illinois Archaeological Survey, Circular No. 6. University of Illinois, Urbana.

Emerson, Thomas E. and Douglas Jackson

1984 The BBB Motor Site (11-Ms-595). *American Bottom Archaeology, FAI-270 Site Reports*, Vol. 6. University of Illinois Press, Urbana.

1987 Emergent Mississippian and Early Mississippian Homesteads at the Marcus Site (11-S-631). *American Bottom Archaeology FAI- 270 Site Reports*, Vol. 17, No. 2. University of Illinois Press, Urbana.

Fortier, Andrew C.

1985 The Robert Schneider Site (11-Ms-1177). In The Carbon Dioxide Site (11-Mo-594), by Fred A. Finney, and The Robert Schneider Site (11-Ms-1177), by Andrew C. Fortier. *American Bottom Archaeology FAI-270 Site Reports*, Vol. 11: 169-313. University of Illinois Press, Urbana.

Fowler, Melvin L., and James P. Anderson
   1975 Report of 1971 Excavations at Mound 72, Cahokia Mounds State Park. In *Cahokia Archaeology: Field Reports*, edited by Melvin L. Fowler, pp 25-27. Illinois State Museum Research Series, Papers in Anthropology 3, Springfield.
Fowler, Melvin L. and Robert L. Hall
   1975 Archaeological Phases at Cahokia. In *Perspectives in Cahokia Archaeology*. Illinois Archaeological Survey Bulletin 10, pp. 1-14. University of Illinois-Urbana.
Gums, Bonnie
   1987 ICT-II Groundstone Tools, Modified Rock, and Exotic Materials. Paper presented at the 25th Annual Workshop on Illinois Archaeology, November 6, 1987, Collinsville, Illinois.
Hall, Robert L.
   1975 Chronology and Phases at Cahokia. In *Perspectives in Cahokia Archaeology*. Illinois Archaeological Survey Bulletin 10: 15-31. University of Illinois, Urbana.
Holley, George R.
   1988 Ceramic Production and Exchange in the American Bottom: Problems and Prospects. A First Approximation. A paper presented at the 1988 Mid-south conference, Paducah, KY.
   1989 *The Archaeology of the Cahokia Mounds ICT-II: Ceramics.* Illinois Cultural Resources Study No. 11. Illinois Historic Preservation Agency, Springfield.
Howland, Henry R.
   1877 Recent Archaeological Discoveries in the American Bottom. *Buffalo Society of Natural Sciences Bulletin* 3(5):204-211. Buffalo.
Johnson, Jay K.
   1987 Cahokia Core Technology in Mississippi: The View from the South. In *The Organization of Core Technology*, edited by Jay K. Johnson and Carol A. Morrow, pp. 187-206. Westview Press, Boulder.
Kelly, John E.
   1980 *Formative Developments at Cahokia and the Adjacent American Bottom: A Merrell Tract Perspective.* Unpublished Ph.D. Dissertation, Department of Anthropology, University of Wisconsin, Madison.
   1984 Late Bluff Chert Utilization on the Merrell Tract, Cahokia. In *Prehistoric Chert Exploitation: Studies from the Midcontinent*, edited by Brian M. Butler and Ernest E. May, pp. 23-44. Center for Archaeological Investigations, Southern Illinois University at Carbondale, Occasional Paper 2.
   1987 Emergent Mississippian and the Transition from Late Woodland to Mississippian: The American Bottom Case for a New Concept. In *The Emergent Mississippian*, edited by Richard A. Marshall. Proceedings of the Sixth Mid- South Archaeological Conference, June 6-9, 1985. Cobb Institute of Archaeology, Mississippi State University, Occasional Papers 87-101.
   1989 Archaeological Investigations of the East St. Louis Mound Center: Past and Present. Paper presented at the 46th Annual Meeting of the Southeastern Archaeological Conference, Tampa, Florida.
   1990 The Emergence of Mississippian Culture in the American Bottom Region. In *The Mississippian Emergence*, edited by Bruce D. Smith, pp. 113- 152. Smithsonian Institution Press, Washington, D.C.
   1991 Cahokia and its Role as a Gateway Center in Interregional Exchange. In *Cahokia and its Neighbors*, edited by Thomas E. Emerson and R. Barry Lewis. University of Illinois Press. Urbana.
Kelly, John E., Steven J. Ozuk, Douglas K. Jackson, Dale L.McElrath, Fred A. Finney, and Duane Esarey
   1984 Emergent Mississippian Period. *In American Bottom Archaeology: A Summary of the FAI-270 Project Contribution to the Culture History of the Mississippi River Valley*, edited by Charles J. Bareis and James W. Porter. University of Illinois Press, Urbana.
Kelly, John E., Steven J. Ozuk, and Joyce A. Williams
   1990 The Range Site 2 (11-S-47): The Emergent Mississippian Dohack and Range Phase Occupations. *American Bottom Archaeology FAI-270 Site Reports*, Vol. 20. University of Illinois Press, Urbana.
Kelly, Lucretia S.
   1990a Dohack Phase Faunal Analysis. In The Range Site 2 (11-S-47): The Emergent Mississippian Dohack and Range Phase Occupations, by John E. Kelly, Steven J. Ozuk, and Joyce A. Williams. *American Bottom Archaeology FAI 270 Site Reports*, Vol. 20. University of Illinois Press, Urbana.
   1990b Range Phase Faunal Analysis. In The Range Site 2 (11-S-47): The Emergent Mississippian Dohack and Range Phase Occupations, by John E. Kelly, Steven J. Ozuk, and Joyce A. Williams. *American Bottom Archaeology FAI 270 Site Reports*, Vol. 20. University of Illinois Press, Urbana.

Koldehoff, Brad

1982 A Coles Creek Vessel from Cahokia's Hinterland. *Illinois Antiquity* 14(2-3):20-23.

1987 The Cahokia Flake Tool Industry: Socio- economic Implications for Late Prehistory in the Central Mississippi Valley. In *The Organization of Core Technology,* edited by J. Johnson and C. Morrow, pp. 151-188. West- view Press, Boulder.

1990 Lithics. In *The Archaeology of the Cahokia Palisade: East Palisade Investigations* by William R. Iseminger, Timothy R. Pauketat, Brad Koldehoff, Lucretia S. Kelly, and Leonard Blake. Illinois Cultural Resources Study No. 14. Illinois Historic Preservation Agency, Springfield.

Marshall, Richard A.

1965 *An Archaeological Investigation of Interstate Route 55 through New Madrid and Pemiscot Counties, Missouri, 1964.* Highway Archaeology Report 1. University of Missouri, Columbia.

McConaughy, Mark A.

1986 The Rench Site Late Late Woodland / Mississippian Farming Hamlet from the Central Illinois River Valley: Food for Thought. Paper presented at the Annual Meeting of the Society for American Archaeology, New Orleans, April 23-26.

McElrath, Dale L., and Fred A. Finney

1987 The George Reeves Site (11-S-650). *American Bottom Archaeology FAI-270 Site Reports,* Vol. 15. University of Illinois Press, Urbana.

McElrath, Dale L., Joyce A. Williams, Thomas O. Maher, and Michael C. Meinkoth

1987 Emergent Mississippian and Mississippian Communities at the Radic Site (11-Ms-584). *American Bottom Archaeology FAI-270 Site Reports,* Vol. 17, No. 1. University of Illinois Press, Urbana.

Mehrer, Mark W.

1982 *A Mississippian Community at the Range Site (11-S-47), St. Clair County, Illinois.* Department of Anthropology, University of Illinois at Urbana-Champaign, FAI-270 Archaeology Mitigation Project Report 52.

Milner, George R. assisted by Joyce A. Williams

1983 The Turner (11-S-50) and DeMange (11-S-447) Sites. *American Bottom Archaeology, FAI-270 Site Reports,* Vol. 4. University of Illinois Press, Urbana.

Milner, George R. assisted by Kelly R. Cox and Michael C. Meinkoth

1984 The Robinson's Lake Site (11-Ms-582). *American Bottom Archaeology FAI-270 Site Reports,* Vol. 10. University of Illinois Press, Urbana.

Moorehead, Warren K.

1929 *The Cahokia Mounds: Part 1, Explorations of 1922, 1923, 1924, and 1927.* University of Illinois Bulletin 26(4):1-106. Urbana.

Morse, Dan F. and Phyllis A. Morse

1980 Zebree Archeological Project Excavation, Data Interpretation and Report on the Zebree Homestead Site, Mississippi County, Arkansas. Report submitted to Memphis District U.S. Army Corps of Engineers, by the Arkansas Archeological Survey, Fayetteville.

O'Brien, Patricia Joan

1969 Some Ceramic Periods and their Implications at Cahokia. In *Explorations into Cahokia Archaeology,* Illinois Archaeological Survey Bulletin 7. University of Illinois, Urbana.

1972 *A Formal Analysis of Cahokia Ceramics from the Powell Tract.* Illinois Archaeological Survey Monograph 3. University of Illinois, Urbana.

Ozuk, Steven J.

1977 Ceramics from Feature 1. In *Report of Investigations and Proposed Mitigation for the Range Site (11-S-47), St. Clair County, Illinois.* FAI-270 Archaeological Mitigation Project, edited by Charles J. Bareis, James W. Porter, and John E. Kelly. University of Illinois, Urbana.

1990a Dohack Phase Ceramics. In The Range Site 2 (11-S-47): The Emergent Mississippian Dohack and Range Phase Occupations by John E. Kelly, Steven J. Ozuk, and Joyce A. Williams. *American Bottom Archaeology FAI 270 Site Reports,* Vol. 20. University of Illinois Press, Urbana.

1990b Range Phase Ceramics. In The Range Site 2 (11-S-47): The Emergent Mississippian Dohack and Range Phase Occupations by John E. Kelly, Steven J. Ozuk, and Joyce A. Williams. *American Bottom Archaeology FAI 270 Site Reports,* Vol. 20. University of Illinois Press, Urbana.

Parker, Kathryn
    1986 Family Gardens and Communal Fields: 600 Years of Farming at the Range Site. Paper presented at the 51st Annual Meeting of the Society for American Archaeology, New Orleans, Louisiana.
Parmalee, Paul W.
    1973 Identification of Faunal Materials from the Koster Site Mounds, Greene County, Illinois. In *Late Woodland Site Archaeology in Illinois I*. Illinois Archaeological Survey Bulletin No. 9. University of Illinois, Urbana.
Pauketat, Timothy R.
    n.d. An Analysis of Pottery from the A.G. Church Site. Manuscript on file. University of Michigan Museum of Anthropology, Ann Arbor.
    1990 Ceramics. In *The Archaeology of the Cahokia Palisade: East Palisade Investigations* by William R. Iseminger, Timothy R. Pauketat, Brad Koldehoff, Lucretia S. Kelly, and Leonard Blake. Illinois Cultural Resources Study No. 14. Illinois Historic Preservation Agency, Springfield.
Perino, Gregory
    1973 The Koster Mounds, Greene County, Illinois. In *Late Woodland Site Archaeology in Illinois I*. Investigations in South-central Illinois. Illinois Archaeological Survey Bulletin 9:141- 210.
Porter, James W.
    1963 *Bluff Pottery Analysis—Thin Section Experiment No. 2: Analysis of Bluff Pottery from the Mitchell Site, Madison County, Illinois*. Southern Illinois University Museum, Lithic Laboratory Research Report 4.
    1974 *Cahokia Archaeology as Viewed from the Mitchell Site: A Satellite Community at A.D. 1150-1200*. Ph.D. dissertation, University of Wisconsin. University Microfilms, Ann Arbor.
    1984 Thin Section Analysis of Ceramics. In The Robinson's Lake Site (11-Ms-582), by George R. Milner, pp. 133-140. *American Bottom Archaeology FAI-270 Site Reports*, Vol. 10. University of Illinois Press, Urbana.
Rau, Charles
    1869 A Deposit of Agricultural Flint Implements in Southern Illinois. *Smithsonian Institution Annual Report for 1868*, pp. 401- 407. Washington, D.C.
Redmond Brian G.
    1987 Yankeetown, Duffy, or Duffytown?: An Examination of Ceramic Variability in the Lower Ohio Valley. Paper presented at the 1987 Midwest Archaeological Conference, October 17, 1987, University of Wisconsin- Milwaukee, Milwaukee.
Renfrew, Colin and Stephen Shannon, editors
    1982 *Ranking, Resources and Exchange: Aspects of the Archaeology of Early European Society*. Cambridge University Press, Cambridge.
Rolingson, Martha (editor)
    1982 *Emerging Patterns of Plum Bayou Culture: Preliminary Investigations of the Toltec Mounds Research Project*. Toltec Papers II. Arkansas Archaeological Survey Research Series 18.
Shafer, Harry J.
    1973 *Lithic Technology at the George C. Davis Site, Cherokee County, Texas*. Ph.D. dissertation, University of Texas, Austin. University Microfilms, Ann Arbor.
Steponaitis, Vincas P.
    1986 Prehistoric Archaeology in the Southeastern United States, 1970-1985. *Annual Review of Anthropology* 15:363-404.
Stevenson, Katherine, William Greene, and Janet Speth
    1983 The Middle Mississippian Presence in the Upper Mississippi Valley: The Evidence from Trempealeau, Wisconsin. Paper presented at the Midwest Archaeological Conference, Iowa, October 21-23, 1983.
Titterington, P.F.
    1938 *The Cahokia Mound Group and its Village Site Materials*. St. Louis, Missouri.
Walthall, John A.
    1981 Galena and Aboriginal Trade in Eastern North America. *Illinois State Museum, Scientific Papers*, Vol. XVII, Springfield.

Williams, Joyce A.

1990a Dohack Phase Lithics. In The Range Site 2 (11-S-47): The Emergent Mississippian Dohack and Range Phase Occupations, by John E. Kelly, Steven J. Ozuk, and Joyce A. Williams. *American Bottom Archaeology FAI 270 Site Reports,* Vol. 20. University of Illinois Press, Urbana.

1990b Range Phase Lithics. In The Range Site 2 (11-S-47): The Emergent Mississippian Dohack and Range Phase Occupations, by John E. Kelly, Steven J. Ozuk, and Joyce A. Williams. *American Bottom Archaeology FAI 270 Site Reports,* Vol. 20. University of Illinois Press, Urbana.

Williams, Kenneth R.

1985 Final Report of Investigations at the East Lobes of Monks Mound. Unpublished report on file at the Department of Anthropology, University of Wisconsin-Milwaukee.

Williams, Stephen

1954 *An Archaeological Study of the Mississippian Culture in Southeast Missouri.* Ph.D. dissertation, Yale University. University Microfilms, Ann Arbor.

Williams, Stephen and John M. Goggin

1956 The Long-Nosed God Mask in Eastern United States. *The Missouri Archaeologist* 18(3):1-72.

Winters, Howard D.

1974 Some Unusual Grave Goods from a Mississippian Burial Mound. *Indian Notes,* Vol. X, No. 2, pp. 34-6. Museum of the American Indian, Heye Foundation, New York.

Woolverton, Donald G.

1974 Electron Microprobe Analyses of Native Copper Artifacts. *Missouri Archaeological Society Memoir* 11: 207-212.

Yerkes, Richard W.

1983 Microwear, Microdrills, and Mississippian Craft Specialization. *American Antiquity* 48(3):499-518.

PART II

Beyond the American Bottom

5

Cahokia From the Southern Periphery

Jeffrey P. Brain
Peabody Museum, Salem, Massachusetts

There is good evidence of Cahokia presence on the southern periphery in the Lower Mississippi Valley. But there are two interesting temporal and spatial observations that must be made at the outset. Temporally, the contact appears to have occurred during the Moorehead phase, not Stirling or earlier, and geographically we have yet to find artifactual evidence south of the Yazoo region in west-central Mississippi. In respect to the lower reaches of the valley, these are very interesting phenomena.

We do have in the Yazoo and contiguous regions of the valley a well-developed culture-historical sequence that is documented in some detail. As background to the events and points of interest to be described here, it must be recognized that there was in this part of the valley a strong native development that was fundamentally different from the Cahokia influence that came in contact with it. The best way to explain this is to describe that culture—Coles Creek—and then the archaeological manifestation of the contact, and then the subsequent developments. Finally, some contextual speculations about that contact will be considered.

Coles Creek was an indigenous development in the Lower Mississippi Valley that had deep roots in the preceding phases of occupation and began to take distinctive form during the eighth century A.D. (Figure 5.1). It is characterized by a number of innovations that became so well integrated and apparently were so highly successful that once established the cultural

pattern was widely replicated throughout the southern part of the valley (Figure 5.2). The resulting configuration is unusually homogeneous in its archaeological manifestations, and it would seem that it maintained a remarkable resistance to major cultural change (i.e., change archaeologically identifiable in basic structural categories) for a period of more than half a millennium.

Coles Creek sites are modest. The centers have mounds that average but three in number, the biggest of which is usually about 4-to-7 m high. They were bona fide ceremonial centers that must have served many social and economic needs, as well as religious, yet they were "vacant" in the sense that they were not primarily residential loci and probably were occupied only by small groups of people who presumably were religious caretakers and/or privileged personae. While the existence of such groups indicates a certain amount of social segmentation in a population that otherwise was dispersed in small hamlet settlements, they have left little evidence beyond the fact of the mound centers themselves. For example, no social ranking is apparent in the mortuary practices that certainly were among the most important functions of the centers. Even if only a portion of the population is represented among the known burials, it is still most illuminating that all ages and sexes were processed in charnel houses and disposed of equally without grave furniture. Sepulture was usually in but one of the mounds, probably the one on which the charnel house

Figure 5.1 Late prehistoric regional phases in the central portion of the Lower Mississippi Valley

		Lower Yazoo	Tensas	Natchez	Lower Red
Plaquemine Mississippian	1500	Wasp Lake	Transylvania	Emerald	
	1400	Lake George	Fitzhugh	Foster	?
	1300	Winterville		Anna	
			Routh		
	1200	Cahokia Horizon			
Coles Creek	1100	Crippen Point		Gordon	Spring Bayou
	1000				
		Kings Crossing	Balmoral		Greenhouse
	900				
Baytown	800	Aden	Ballina		Bordelon
	700	Bayland	Sundown		

was placed. This mortuary pattern is found throughout the distribution of Coles Creek, and the lack of overtly displayed distinction is consistent with other aspects of the culture. If there was significant social ranking, it is not expressed in differential burial practices, nor in the artifactual inventory, mound features, or site plans.

Overall settlement patterning also contributes to the impression of a lack of sociocultural differentiation. It would seem that there were multiple contemporary centers, even in a given region, but there is no indication that there was a hierarchy among these sites since they were approximately equal in size and proximity to each other. Thus, the interpretation is that the mound centers represented the nuclei of relatively equal and autonomous sociocultural units. But that they were in close contact with each other is evident from the remarkable degree of cultural homogeneity described for the Coles Creek culture area. These sites are positioned along all of the major water courses throughout the area and must have maintained close contacts thereby. At the same time, they were serving the local populations that were exploiting the strips of natural levee land found along these courses.

Thus, for a period of 500 years, continuities were overwhelming, while change was minimal. Small changes, of course, are observable over the long period of time and provide the data for phase distinctions, but they are subtle indeed. Whether the lack of change more accurately reflects conscious resistance to any alteration of the status quo, or was due to the fact that the southern part of the Lower Valley was relatively unbothered by external influences during this period, remains the question.

Early Mississippian influences from upriver, probably originating in southeast Missouri or northeast Arkansas, are apparent in the upper Yazoo Basin by the end of the first millennium A.D. For whatever reason, however, these northern elements did not seem to have a major impact upon the Coles Creek culture immediately to the south. A few artifactual modes, such as shell tempering and some vessel forms, are found in small amounts in a few late Coles Creek contexts in the lower Yazoo, but no farther downriver (Williams and Brain 1983; Brain 1969, 1978, 1989; Brain, Brown, and Steponaitis n.d.). Even in the lower Yazoo, the innovations are clearly the result of the introduction of ideas, so far recognized only in ceramic technology, that had no other apparent impact on Coles Creek culture.

Towards the end of the 12th century, however, a striking intrusion appears in the archaeological record of the Yazoo Basin. At a number of sites, artifacts diagnostic of Cahokia have been found (Brain 1969, 1989;

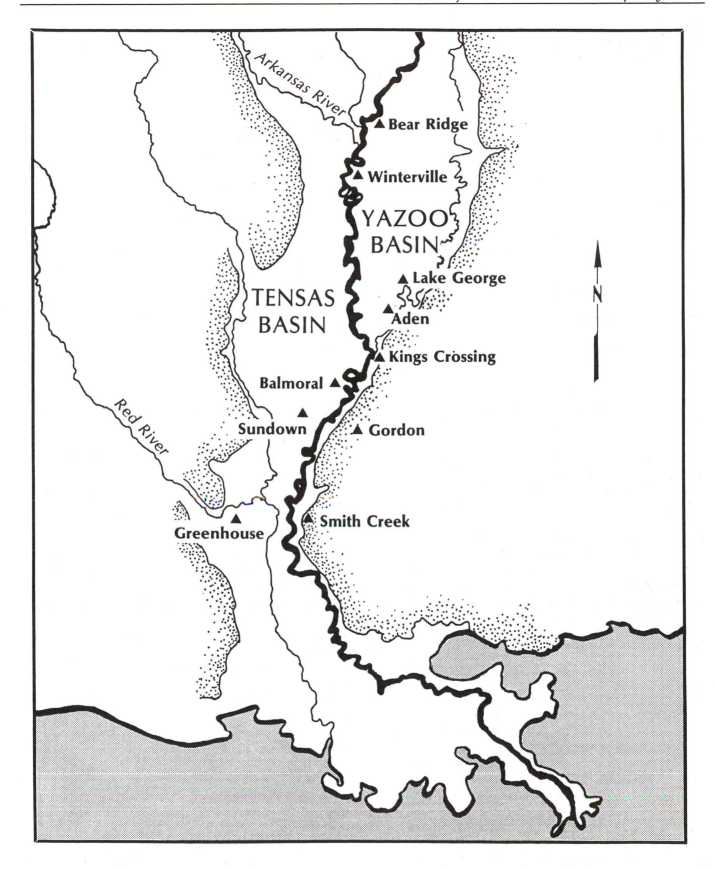

Figure 5.2. Coles Creek Mound sites in the central regions of the Lower Mississippi Valley.

Phillips 1970; Williams and Brain 1983). These sites are more widely dispersed than the late Coles Creek occupation, but most of the contact seems to have occurred at strategic demographic and/or geographic points within that context. The nature and possible motivations for this contact will be discussed below, but first let us review the evidence and the subsequent developments.

The artifactual evidence for this contact is solid, if not plentiful. There are well-dated, late Coles Creek contexts dating to the late Crippen Point phase (A.D. 1100-1200) at both Winterville and Lake George, as well as other sites (Figure 5.4; see also Williams and Brain 1983, Figure 12.15), that manifest distinctive foreign artifacts—not just modal changes, such as had already occurred as a result of secondary diffusion, but whole artifacts that may be derived from a nonlocal source. Pottery types including Powell Plain, Ramey Incised, Tippets Incised (on the distinctive "bean pot" form), Cahokia Cord Marked, and various red-slipped wares are present (Figure 5.3). Also appearing at Lake George is a special variety of the Mississippi Triangular point made from Dongola chert (Williams and Brain 1983: 236). All of these diagnostic artifacts indicate a particular origin: namely, Cahokia, or a closely related satellite.

In addition to the Cahokia diagnostics, other innovations are apparent. One of these is found in the local pottery manufacture as close, although somewhat inept, imitations of the above-named types were fabricated. This development indicates a conscious attempt by the local Coles Creek peoples to copy the new introductions, and represents a radical departure from their own traditions. Behavioral changes in other categories also attest to the fundamental importance of the contact: there were basic departures from Coles Creek mortuary custom, settlement pattern, and site plan, as well as inferred social structure and religious practice.

The most striking manifestation in the Lower Valley of the 13th-14th centuries is a grand florescence. In the area of focus, this was the zenith of prehistoric aboriginal achievement, if the construction of major mound centers is adequate criterion. Pyramidal mounds arranged around a plaza were noted to be characteristic of the Coles Creek culture, but there is marked quantitative and qualitative change that now occurs in the Yazoo and contiguous regions. There are more mound sites than ever before, they are considerably larger, and they have more mounds, sometimes arranged around multiple plazas. Furthermore, the mounds themselves are larger: the principal mounds at Winterville and Lake George are nearly 20 m high and cover more than a hectare, which is four times the size of the average Coles Creek mound. Both sites also boasted more than two dozen mounds each, and,

although there may already have been modest Coles Creek mounds present on the site, they represent but a small portion of the great bulk of earthen construction. Thick mantles were added to those structures and many more new mounds were built from scratch. At Winterville and Lake George, too, new plazas were defined to the east of the large focal mound and all the mounds around the eastern plaza were added at that time. The emphasis upon one mound above all others and its placement on the west side of the principal plaza are distinctly non-Coles Creek traits, but were characteristic of Mississippian sites at this period.

The evidence from excavation at Winterville and Lake George is convincing in detailing the fact that the major construction probably occurred within a relatively brief period of 50-100 years, or even less. Such a massive public works campaign is itself an important change from the comparatively modest organizations to be inferred for the Coles Creek culture. There was clearly a major change in direction and scope of public endeavor.

With this background, a few speculations may be offered. First, while it is possible that what the archaeological record reveals was the result of Coles Creek peoples going upriver, interacting with Cahokia, and then returning home with new ideas and products, it is far more likely that Cahokia initiated the contact—as it seems to have done in many other regions of the eastern part of the continent. The question then is: what were the motivations, at least on this southern periphery? And it must also be asked: given this contact, why was it so seemingly successful?

The latter question may seem gratuitous in light of the traditional model that has cast Mississippian expansion and interaction as basically the result of a superior culture moving in upon one less organized and, thus, overcoming it This model has been substantiated by putative cases of site-unit intrusion reinforced by evidence of fortifications and even possible warfare. However, more recent thinking has questioned this model (e.g., Smith 1984) and, indeed, such overwhelming intrusion apparently was not the situation in this case, at least at this particular time. There are no demonstrable fortifications at the prime sites in the Yazoo, yet there is widespread evidence of Cahokia interaction. Furthermore, the artifactual material from Cahokia is found in small quantities at already-occupied sites. Thus, the contact was occurring within local contexts, and without a major introduction of new peoples. This was not a case of site-unit intrusion involving a large-scale demographic input isolated from, or destroying, a native population. Rather, the widely dispersed, multicomponent horizon in late Coles Creek contexts indicates a coordinated event that seems to have been peacefully

Figure 5.3. Cahokia-derived pottery and imitations from the Winterville and Lake George sites in the lower Yazoo Basin: a, Powell Plain (Winterville); b, Powell imitation (Lake George); c, Ramey Incised (Lake George); d, Ramey imitation (Winterville); e, red-slipped Ramey Incised (Lake George); f, red-slipped Tippets Incised (Winterville); g, Cahokia Cord Marked (Winterville); h, locally made "bean pot" (Winterville).

accepted. The significance of this pattern is important to the consideration of the Cahokia climax, as well as the later prehistory of this part of the Lower Valley.

The Cahokia climax was obviously a complex event, and the motivations for the interaction described here were probably dictated by a number of factors: demographic, economic, perhaps even religious. Each of these has been considered in the literature, and it is not necessary to review the theories here, except insofar as the Lower Valley evidence would seem to support one or the other, or indicate particular motivations. Unfortunately, no definitive evidence presently exists that satisfies our quest for those particular motivations that inspired the contact. The artifacts noted are indeed Cahokia diagnostics, mostly of the Moorehead phase (ca. A.D. 1150-1250), but they are not subsystemic specific. As markers they describe direct contact, but they do not define the nature of the event. However, a close analysis of the distribution of these markers in the lower Yazoo does provide some interesting inferences about the Cahokia horizon in this region, and ultimately perhaps about Cahokia itself.

The known proveniences of Cahokia diagnostics in the Yazoo have a distinctive distribution: they are restricted to the major riverine systems of the Mississippi, itself, and the Yazoo (Figure 5.4). All of the sites were probably in direct association with the active channels of these rivers. Moreover, the sites that have produced the strongest evidence were located at the prime junctures of these systems. Thus, along the Mississippi the sites are situated at what were then major confluences, as with the Arkansas (Winterville and related sites) and the Yazoo (Duck Lake); and also at the major distributary points, as demonstrated at the Winterville and Griffin locales, which provided direct communication with the interior of the region through secondary systems. Along the Yazoo, Cahokia-contact sites such as Haynes Bluff, Shellwood, and Shell Bluff were also located at important confluences within that system almost as far upriver as the modern city of Greenwood. The most notable Yazoo River site was Lake George, which was situated at the most central point geographically within the entire regional riverine system, being at what was then the Sunflower-Yazoo confluence (it was also only a short distance from Deer Creek, the other most important interior stream). Other than these prime junctures, the rest of the region displays an absence of Cahokia diagnostics.

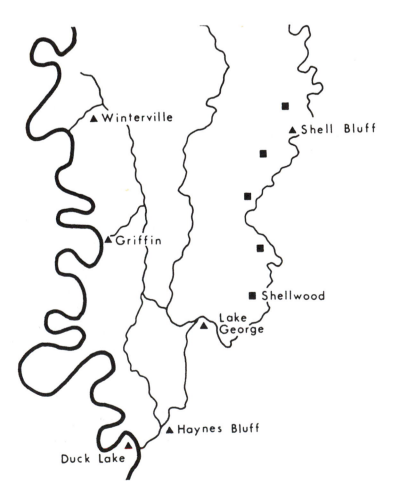

Figure 5.4. Sites in the lower Yazoo Basin at which Cahokia-derived pottery (▲) and local imitations (■) have been found.

The pattern described here is very specific and suggests a highly organized contact that was carefully selective in its establishment. The evidence for the contact is found at the most important junctures of the riverine system, locations that could have effectively controlled the local routes of water-borne communication. One inference, therefore, is that the Cahokia contact was specifically directed toward the control of the region. Furthermore, since there is no indication in any of the archaeologically known contexts of a significant demographic introduction, but rather it seems to have been a case of influence exerted upon resident populations, it might be inferred that this contact was carried out by small groups, presumably directly from Cahokia.

The question of motivation remains. The hypothesized emphasis upon regional control suggests that there were specific reasons for the Cahokia contact. As has been discussed, the reasons do not seem to have been demographic. Nor do they seem to have been political, for there was no apparent attempt to integrate the region into a larger Cahokia polity (a geographic impossibility in any event). Thus, the other major motivations often ascribed to Mississippian expansion at this time must be considered: the economic and religious. Possibly these indeed were the motivating forces, although the evidence at hand is largely inferential.

What economic potential the Yazoo Basin could have offered Cahokia is unknown. It is difficult to think of a single resource unique to the Yazoo that might have been vital to Cahokia. It was a region naturally rich in flora and fauna, but these resources were important only at the local subsistence level. There was no mineral wealth or other exotic resource; there was not even salt. In the absence of archaeological verification, such possible intangibles as feathers or alligator hides would seem to be less than compelling motivation for an event of the magnitude indicated.

If resource extraction was not the motivation, it might be considered whether this was instead a case of economic colonization, that is, trade at a more sophisticated and integrated level. There was, after all, a large population in the Yazoo region that could have been a lucrative market. But again the archaeological evidence does not support this, at least not on any grand organized scale. To date, no specific exotic foreign trade items have been discovered in the appropriate Yazoo contexts. The Cahokia pottery diagnostics listed above would seem to be insufficient cause for establishing great trade networks (unless, of course, they served as containers for some unknown perishable product).

Thus, even if the motivations were at least in part economic, there must have been yet other considerations. One possibility might be that the real objective of Cahokia in this endeavor was to safeguard its overall trade network. The Yazoo, itself, may not have been the primary focus of attention, but perhaps the development and expansion of a particularly viable indigenous culture in the region was sufficient cause to prompt Cahokia to protect its trade connection with the Gulf Coast, a known source of desired materials at that time. The theory becomes suspect, however, when the pattern of Cahokia contact in the Yazoo is scrutinized. The establishment along the Mississippi is perfectly consistent, but why also along the Yazoo River? Two speculations may be offered: that there was an attempt at minor trade interaction by the Cahokians since they were in the neighborhood, or that there was an effort to exert a more positive control of the large population. For the latter effort to have been successful in the apparent absence of a strong economic exchange or significant demographic introduction, it is necessary to find a second major motivation for the contact.

In an earlier consideration of the problem (Brain 1969), based solely on the evidence from Winterville, great importance was ascribed to a putative religious proselytism on the part of Cahokia. There is no good evidence for such activity in the actual archaeological contexts of the relatively short-lived Cahokia horizon in the Yazoo, but the developments that followed immediately thereafter support just such an interpretation. On the basis of this interpolation, it may be suggested that the Cahokia interaction with the Lower Mississippi Valley was economically motivated, but carried out under religious auspices.

Of course, these hypotheses are predicated on the assumption that Cahokia was at its height at this time, and that the observed phenomena are thus the local expression of the inter-areal impact of the mature development cast in economic and religious terms. Whatever the fault of that model, there is the even greater risk that the schedule, as well as the nature, of Cahokia dynamics have been misunderstood. Cahokia may already have been in decline by A.D. 1200, and what is being observed is a case of the "rats deserting the sinking ship." Such a simple dispersal is sufficient motivation for the events described, but is inconsistent with the known facts in the Yazoo. It does not satisfactorily explain the apparently limited demographic nature of the contact, nor the predilection for establishment at specific control points. On the other hand, if the introduction of refugee groups could be archaeologically demonstrated, then the dramatic florescence that followed would be more explicable. There is a certain quantum leap from the late Coles Creek to the following florescent developments that is difficult to explain solely in terms of internal changes in the resident population.

In summary, the direct Cahokia contact occurred within the indigenous late Coles Creek context, and it affected that context profoundly. Whatever the reasons for the contact might have been, the distribution was distinctive: artifactual diagnostics are manifest at widely separated sites that generally were located at critical junctures of the riverine system. It would seem that small numbers of people were involved, but that they were in positions of great social and geographic influence. Although the Cahokia diagnostics soon disappear from the archaeological record, an intensely viable development ensued that represented the reaction of the Coles Creek peoples and their culture to the strong, organized, external influence. Whatever the Cahokians had to offer was accepted, adapted, and transformed into a new expression that became the late prehistoric climax in the region.

Clearly, there were many faces to the influence of Cahokia. In future investigations, it would be well to consider each case as a unique phenomenon until proven otherwise. As for the rest of the Lower Valley south of the Yazoo, the current lack of evidence may be due to our failure to find relevant material, or it may in fact be reality. If the latter is the case, then we must presume either that Cahokia was highly selective in its extraregional establishments, or else that its influence sometimes lacked substance. That ideas rather than artifacts were the real contribution of Cahokia to the Lower Valley is clearly indicated by the developments that followed this contact.

To conclude, then, it must be acknowledged that still we really can do no better than what James B. Griffin said 18 years ago: "There is not very much that can be said with certainty except that the contact with Cahokia was definite and someone carried the Ramey style pottery to the southern Delta [Yazoo] area during the Stirling phase at Cahokia" (Griffin 1973: 378). It can only be added that the contexts of these artifacts in the lower Yazoo region indicate that it was more likely that this contact occurred during the Moorehead phase.

References Cited

Brain, Jeffrey P.
> 1969 Winterville: A Case Study of Prehistoric Culture Contact in the Lower Mississippi Valley. Ph.D. dissertation. Yale University, New Haven.
> 1978 Late Prehistoric Settlement Patterning in the Yazoo Basin and Natchez Bluffs Regions of the Lower Mississippi Valley. In B. D. Smith, ed., *Mississippian Settlement Patterns*. Academic Press, New York.
> 1989 *Winterville. Archaeological Report* 23. Mississippi Department of Archives and History, Jackson.

Brain, Jeffrey P., Ian W. Brown, and Vincas P. Steponaitis
> n.d. Archaeology of the Natchez Bluffs. Manuscript in preparation, Peabody Museum, Harvard University, Cambridge.

Griffin, James B.
> 1973 Review of Phillips' "Archaeological Survey in the Lower Yazoo Basin, Mississippi, 1949-1955." *American Antiquity* 38: 374-380.

Phillips, Philip
> 1970 *Archaeological Survey in the Lower Yazoo Basin, Mississippi, 1949-1955*. Papers of the Peabody Museum, Harvard University, 60, Cambridge.

Smith, Bruce D.
> 1984 Mississippian Expansion: Tracing the Historical Development of an Explanatory Model. *Southeastern Archaeology* 3 (1): 13-32.

Williams, Stephen, and Jeffrey P. Brain
> 1983 *Excavations at the Lake George Site, Yazoo County, Mississippi, 1958-1960*. Papers of the Peabody Museum 74, Harvard University, Cambridge.

6

The Rench Site Late Late Woodland/Mississippian Farming Hamlet from the Central Illinois River Valley: Food for Thought

Mark A. McConaughy
The State Museum of Pennsylvania, Harrisburg

The Rench site (11P4) is situated on a Pleistocene terrace at the base of the western bluffs of the central Illinois River about 20 km north of Peoria, Illinois. Excavations were conducted at Rench by the Illinois State Museum (ISM) between 1980 and 1983 for the Illinois Department of Transportation (IDOT) to mitigate potential impact from construction of a proposed interchange for I-474 near Mossville, Illinois. These excavations discovered Archaic, early Late Woodland (Weaver), and late Late Woodland/Mississippian (LLW/M) components within the IDOT right of way. This paper will focus on the last of these, the LLW/M occupation. Any features from Rench that are discussed in the following paper are LLW/M pits unless otherwise noted.

The late component at Rench has been labeled "late Late Woodland/Mississippian" instead of "Emergent Mississippian" because (1) the term "Emergent Mississippian" implies that the people are on the way to becoming "Mississippian" (i.e., eventually their descendants are full participants in the Mississippian life style), but at this time it remains to be determined just what happened to the descendants of the Rench occupation and (2) the Rench inhabitants appear to represent a local late Late Woodland group that has come in contact with early Mississippian peoples from the American Bottom. It is possible that future work will indicate that they should be considered Emergent Mississippian, but until such data are available, it is felt that LLW/M more accurately describes the Rench occupation.

The Rench Site LLW/M Occupation

The LLW/M component at Rench consists of two burned structures (McConaughy et al. 1985), ten refuse/storage pits, one hearth, and one rock concentration (Figure 6.1). House #1 appears to have been a rectangular wall trench structure (Figure 6.2). However, most of the structure was apparently destroyed by modern agricultural activities, and the remaining wall trench only extended 2 to 4 cm deep beneath the plow zone. The structure may also have been built in a basin since soil overlying it was loosely compacted. House #1 measures 4.2×2.8 m (length/width ratio 1.5:1) inside the wall trenches for a floor area of 11.8 m^2 (126.5 ft.^{2}). Three posts aligned along the central long axis of the structure provided support for a probable hipped or gabled roof (Figure 6.2). There were no LLW/M features located inside of House #1 (note: the pits depicted in Figure 6.2 are all superimposed Weaver features). A charred hickory (Carya sp.) log from House #1 produced a radiocarbon date of 1000 B.P. ± 70 years (A.D. 950, ISGS-1217).

House #2 (Figure 6.3) apparently was built in a much deeper house basin than House #1 and was not heavily disturbed by modern farming activities. The house basin extended 25 cm below the modern, 30 cm

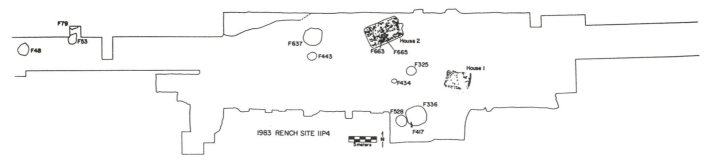

Figure 6.1 The main excavation trench showing the location of late Late
Woodland/Mississippian features and dwellings

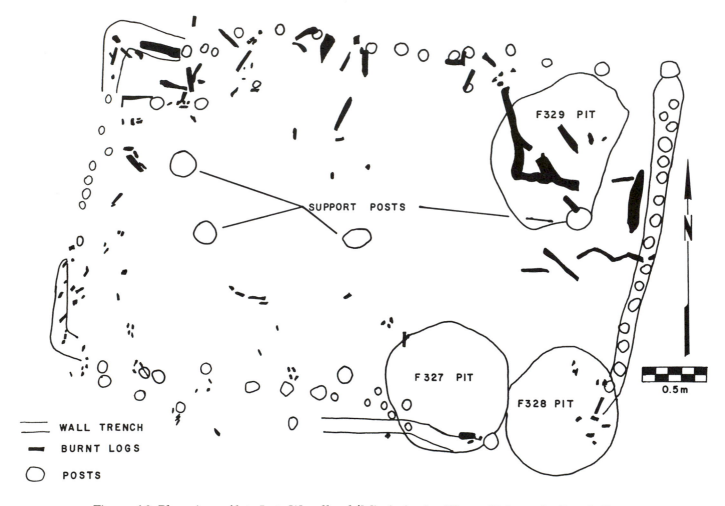

Figure 6.2 Plan view of late Late Woodland/Mississippian House #1 from the Rench Site.

thick, plow zone. Well-preserved charred structural elements (Figures 6.3 to 6.5) permit an accurate reconstruction of House #2 as a rectangular wigwam with vertical end walls (McConaughy 1985). House #2 measures 6.1×3.9 m (length/width ratio of 1.56:1) along the interior of the basin for a floor area of 23.8 m² (255.8 ft.²). A charred hickory (*Carya* sp.) cross beam

from the roof of House #2 produced a radiocarbon date of 930 B.P. ± 70 years (A.D. 1020, ISGS-1216), while charred butternut recovered from the floor provided a date of 940 B.P. ± 70 years (A.D. 1010, ISGS-1215).

A hearth, F-663, was built in the south central portion of House #2 and a small basin-shaped feature, F-

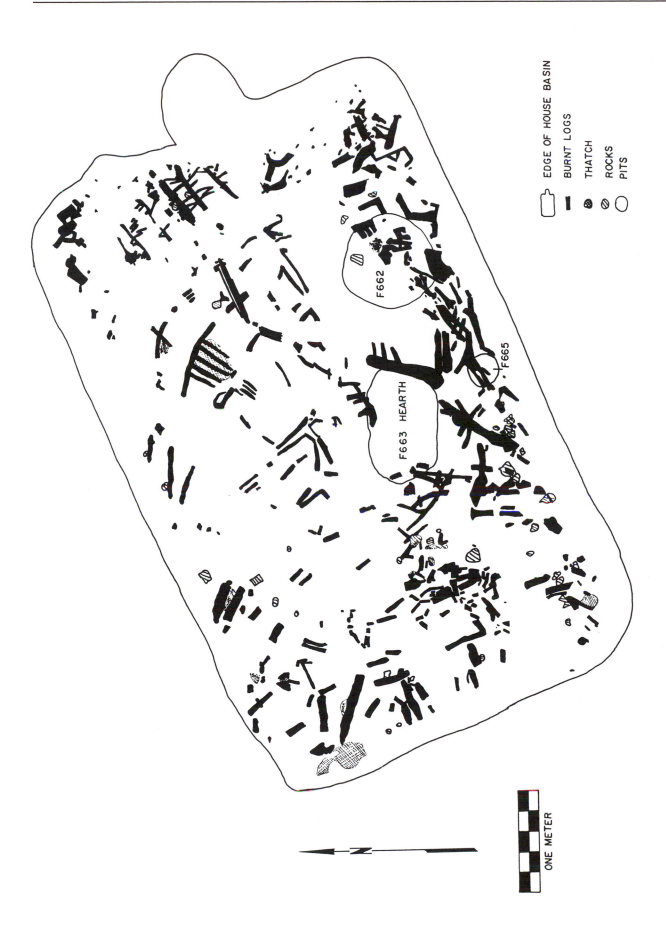

Figure 6.3 Plan view of late Late Woodland/Mississippian House #2 from Rench Site 11P4.

Figure 6.4 Photograph of excavated late Late Woodland/Mississippian House #2 from Rench site 11P4.

Figure 6.5 Reconstruction of late Late Woodland/Mississippian House #2 from Rench site 11P4.

665, was placed beside the hearth along the southern wall (Figure 6.3). The small size of F-665 (Table 6.1) and rounded profile suggest that it may have functioned as a pot stand near the hearth. There were no other LLW/M features located within House #2 (Note: F-662 is a superimposed Weaver pit).

Large pit features were discovered near each house (Figure 6.1). The largest feature, F-336, with a diameter of over 3.5 m is located 5 m southwest of House #1 (Figure 6.1, Table 6.1). F-637, the second largest pit feature at Rench, is located 7.5 m west of House #2 and is over 3 m in diameter (Figure 6.1, Table 6.1). F-336 is over 1 m deep while F-637 is about 0.5 m deep measured from the base of the plow zone. When they were first discovered, it was thought that they might be sweat lodges similar to those found on other Mississippian sites (Caldwell 1967; Hargrave 1983:139-140; Smith 1977:58-61), and they were excavated assuming this premise to be true. However, evidence of foundation wall trenches or postmolds that would indicate structural frameworks, or interior hearths to produce heat for the assumed sweat lodges, were not

discovered. Therefore, it is unlikely that they were sweat lodges or some other form of pit dwelling. They apparently were only very large storage facilities that were later used as refuse pits.

Seven other smaller refuse/storage features were found, located primarily to the west of the dwellings (Figure 6.1, Table 6.1). One rock concentration was superimposed on the edge of F-336 and probably represents the discard of rocks used in a hearth or from use in stone boiling. The lack of associated charcoal and burned earth also implies that these do not represent an in situ hearth.

Charcoal from pit F-53 produced a radiocarbon date of 1140 B.P. ± 70 years (A.D. 810, ISGS-980). This date is thought to be erroneous since the presence of Cahokia Red Filmed sherds in F-53 suggests that it is contemporaneous with the structures. F-53 and all the other LLW/M pits were excavated through various Weaver middens and features. The presence of Weaver pottery in most of them (Table 6.2; Note: Table 6.2 also lists Weaver features contaminated with a few later sherds; consult Table 6.1 for a list of those

Table 6.1
Rench Late Late Woodland/Mississippian Features

Feature Number	Disturb/ Undist.	Profile Form	Length in cm	Width in cm	Depth in cm	Diam Base in cm	Vol Spher in liter	Vol Para in liter	Feature Type
F-48	Undist.	Flat Bot	248	208	100	155	2984.9	2984.9	Ref pit
F-53	Undist.	Basin	196	156	18	Exca-	vated	219	Ref pit
F-79	Undist.	Basin	Only	Part-	ially				Ref pit
F-325	Disturb	Flat Bot	183	156	70	140	1328.6	1328.6	Ref pit
F-336	Disturb	Flat Bot	375	350	110	360	11274.7	11274.7	Ref pit
F-417	Disturb	Unknown	70	20					Rock con
F-434	Undist.	Basin	103	79	24		80.6	78	Ref pit
F-443	Disturb	Basin	180		40				Ref pit
F-528	Disturb	Basin	192	188	23		319.1	326.1	Ref pit
F-637	Disturb	Flat Bot	326	312	52	266	3522.9	3522.9	Ref pit
F-663	Undist.	Basin	116	69	12		37.1	40.3	Hearth
F-665	Undist.	Basin	32	31	10		4.2	3.9	Ref pit
		Totals	2021	1569	459	921	19762.5	19778.4	
		Mean	183.72727	156.9	45.9	230.25	2195.8333	2197.6	
		S.D.	104	112.2	36.4	103.2	3656.6	3655.5	
		Median	183	156	32	210.5	319.1	326.1	
		N	11	10	10	4	9	9	

Note: Volumes for basin pits estimated with spherical and parabolic formulae while flat bottom uses only conical section estimate.

Table 6.2

LATE LATE WOODLAND/MISSISSIPPIAN POTTERY DISTRIBUTION

Fea. #	Havana	Weaver Plain	Weaver Cm	Mossville Cm	Mossville Plain	Mossville Bowl	Powell Plain	Cahok Red Filmed	Miss Bowl	Cahok CM	Maples Mills	Starved Rock	Pinch Pot	Other	Miss Shrdl	Sherdlet
F-48	0	5	6	9	2	0	0	0	0	0	0	0	0	2	0	39
F-53	0	5	6	10	1	0	3	2	0	0	0	0	0	1	1	34
F-79	0	0	0	2	0	0	0	0	0	0	0	0	0	1	0	12
F-146	0	2	3	0	1	0	0	0	0	0	0	0	1	0	0	18
F-298	0	28	17	0	2	0	0	0	0	0	0	0	0	0	0	84
F-304	1	24	19	0	1	0	0	0	0	0	0	0	0	0	0	50
F-325	1	59	35	33	7	0	22	8	1	0	0	0	0	3	5	457
F-325/342	0	1	0	0	0	0	1	0	0	0	0	1	0	0	2	7
F-336	2	81	67	57	14	2	35	9	1	1	4	1	9	1	2	690
F-337	0	30	3	0	0	0	0	1	0	0	0	0	0	2	0	96
F-344	0	25	31	0	1	0	0	0	0	0	0	0	0	0	0	36
F-417	0	0	2	0	0	0	0	0	0	0	0	0	0	0	0	0
F-434	0	4	5	0	2	0	0	0	2	0	0	0	0	0	0	15
F-443	1	63	34	1	6	0	32	15	0	1	0	0	3	3	0	289
F-443 mix	0	39	21	33	0	0	1	0	0	0	0	0	0	0	0	110
F-458	0	3	3	0	0	0	1	0	0	0	0	0	0	0	0	12
F-507	0	5	1	0	1	0	0	0	0	0	0	0	0	0	0	14
F-511	0	15	3	0	0	0	0	0	0	0	0	0	0	0	0	21
F-528	0	16	22	0	1	0	17	0	0	0	0	0	0	1	7	28
F-561	0	15	19	0	0	0	0	0	0	0	0	0	10	0	0	81
F-611	0	13	8	0	1	0	0	0	0	0	0	0	0	0	0	61
F-637	1	87	81	36	5	0	20	3	0	2	1	0	2	0	1	635
F-637/638	0	2	5	1	0	0	0	0	0	0	0	0	0	1	0	13
F-638	0	3	7	0	0	0	0	0	0	0	0	0	0	0	0	24
F-655	0	9	2	0	0	0	0	0	0	0	0	0	3	1	0	2
F-665	0	0	0	0	0	0	0	2	0	0	0	0	0	0	0	0
Subtotals	5	534	400	182	45	2	132	40	4	4	5	2	28	15	18	2827
LW/M STR1	2	28	35	48	1	0	8	0	0	0	0	0	1	1	0	117
LW/M STR2	0	161	113	46	11	0	15	5	0	0	0	0	3	3	0	365
Stratum I	15	109	61	11	2	0	7	7	0	0	0	0	0	0	0	898
Stratum II	4	109	77	0	0	0	0	0	0	0	0	3	0	2	0	466
F-4 Mid	18	815	501	14	1	0	17	3	0	0	2	0	0	5	15	2774
F-40 Mid	3	1352	854	37	2	0	7	0	0	0	0	0	0	9	0	6454
F-145 Mid	1	86	111	0	0	0	0	0	0	0	0	0	1	1	0	633
F-338 Mid	0	109	27	1	0	0	3	0	0	0	0	0	0	0	3	31
Totals	48	3303	2179	339	62	2	189	55	4	4	7	5	33	36	36	14565

identified as LLW/M features) demonstrates that their fill included earlier debris and suggests that the radiocarbon sample from F-53 was contaminated with charcoal from the Weaver occupation. The dates from the structures are more reliable since they were run on materials that had to have been gathered by the LLW/M inhabitants.

Maize was recovered from 90% of the features (including houses) that were analyzed and is missing only from F-417, the rock concentration (King n.d.). Most of the nuts (52.7 g, 77.2%-based only on analyzed flotation data) that were recovered came from House #2. Butternut, black walnut, and hickory nut are relatively abundant, while hazelnut occurs in lesser quantities.

A cluster analysis using floral data indicates that House #1 and pits F-637, F-528, F-325, and F-665 are most similar to each other, in that order (King n.d.). They produced relatively few floral remains as opposed to the other features. F-665 is a small feature in House #2 that has been interpreted as a pot rest, and these data do not conflict with such an interpretation. However, all the materials recovered from the features represent refuse, and these remains may not have anything to do with the original function(s) of the facilities.

F-53 and F-443 cluster apart from the other features since they have relatively large amounts of maize and starchy seeds (knotweed, maygrass, and chenopods). It is possible that the starchy seeds represent contamination since they are a staple of the Weaver diet, and other definite Weaver Phase remains were recovered from the fill of these features (Table 6.2). Also, F-53 was dug through a Weaver midden while F-443 was superimposed on two Weaver pit features.

Houses #1 and #2 sorted out as the most widely divergent features of the cluster analysis (King n.d.). The presence of most of the nutshell in House #2 and relative lack of it in House #1 implies that they were occupied during different seasons of the year, House #1 during the spring and summer while House #2 is more likely used during the fall and winter. However, nuts can be stored and are not totally reliable indicators of seasonality.

White-tailed deer is the most ubiquitous animal species from features at Rench (Martin n.d.). However, fish contributed more individuals than any other class of animals, and House #1 produced far more fish and turtle remains than House #2 (Martin n.d.). This suggests that House #1 was more likely utilized in the spring and summer since the prime fishing period would be during the spring spawning season or during the summer when water levels would be reduced. Similarly, turtles would have been available primarily during the warmer months. However, fish may be obtained year round and are not a totally reliable indi-

cator of seasonality. Thus, the faunal data suggest, but do not conclusively prove, that the two houses were used during different periods of the year.

House #1 lacks any evidence of an interior hearth and this implies a warm weather use for this structure. Cooking fires were more likely built outdoors during the spring and summer months, while an indoor hearth for cooking and heating, as was found in House #2, would have been beneficial in a cold weather dwelling. The larger floor area of House #2 also may have been due to the need to avoid cramped conditions during extended periods of occupancy associated with the colder months.

Radiocarbon dates from the dwellings have overlapping standard deviations and are consistent with an interpretation that the LLW/M occupation of Rench is temporally restricted. Therefore, although none of the individual data bases conclusively indicates seasonality, taken together, they strongly suggest that the two houses from Rench represent seasonal dwellings for one family.

Rench LLW/M Material Culture

Ceramics from Rench provide the most direct evidence of contact with the American Bottom and its influence on the inhabitants of the central Illinois Valley. Grit and sand tempered Canton Ware varieties predominate the Rench LLW/M ceramic assemblage and represent locally manufactured pottery. However, a number of finely made, shell tempered Mississippian pottery types were also recovered, and these are identical to forms from the early Mississippian Phases from the American Bottom. Grit and sand tempered ceramics account for 63% of the LLW/M pottery recovered from plow zone, midden, pit features, and house floor contexts, while shell tempered Mississippian forms amount to 37% overall.

Mississippian pottery was recovered from most of the features and structures. Some sherds were also recovered from a few Weaver features and midden deposits, most probably due to bioturbation and other processes of pedogenesis (Table 6.2). Most of the Mississippian pottery was assigned to the Powell Plain type (Griffin 1949:49-51; Perino 1971:73; Vogel 1975:90-94; Wray 1952:159) since these specimens were shell tempered and had plain or completely smoothed-over surfaces. They tended to have a brown to gray or black exterior surface color, and the exterior surface was burnished or polished on about 21% of the sherds (however, the amount of polishing and burnishing probably is under-represented since the surfaces of some sherds were slightly eroded). Three body sherds were slipped black on the exterior surface, and several rims may also have been slipped black (Figure 6.6).

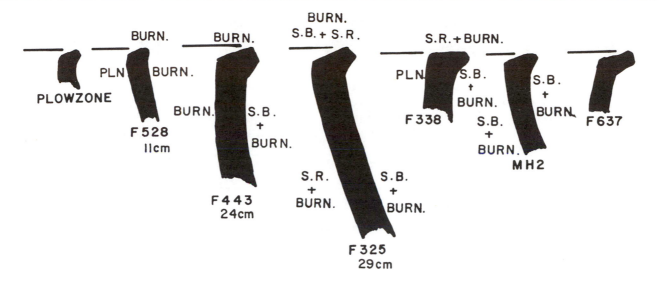

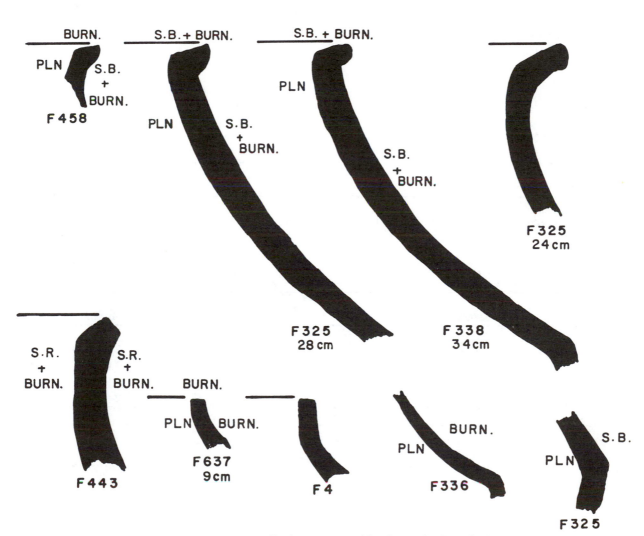

Figure 6.6 Powell Plain rim profiles from the Rench site.

Powell Plain, and most of the other Mississippian types from Rench, have cores that are a uniform gray color. The paste and shell temper are well mixed and usually lack any addition of sand temper. Powell Plain and Cahokia Red Filmed vessels that the author has examined from the American Bottom commonly have this same type of well sorted paste and core color. Conversely, the local late Late Woodland (LLW) pot-tery from Rench usually has sand included in the paste, probably because the potters used local sandy clays to make the vessels. Central Illinois Valley LLW pottery usually is not well made, the paste is not well mixed, and grit temper often is unevenly distributed through it. A petrographic analysis of selected Mississippian and local LLW sherds by Stoltman (Tables 6.3 to 6.5) indicates that the composition of the

Table 6.3 Body and Paste Properties of Mossville Cord Marked and Starved Rock Collared Sherds from the Rench Site.

Body Composition				
Specimen Type	%Matrix	%Sand	%Grit	Temper
Mossville Cord Marked	76	19	5	GABBRO
Mossville Cord Marked	69	19	12	GABBRO
Mossville Cord Marked	63	21	16	GABBRO+?
Mossville Cord Marked	78	17	5	GABBRO+?
Mossville Cord Marked	69	16	15	GABBRO+?
Mean	71 ± 6.0	18 ± 1.9	11 ± 5.3	
Starved Rock Collared	86	3	11	GABBRO

Paste Composition (Excludes Temper)			
Specimen Type	%Matrix*	%Silt	%Sand
Mossville Cord Marked	70	10	20
Mossville Cord Marked	72	7	21
Mossville Cord Marked	70	5	25
Mossville Cord Marked	77	6	17
Mossville Cord Marked	70	11	19
Mean	72 ± 3.0	8 ± 2.6	20 ± 3.0
Starved Rock Collared	85	11	4

*Primarily clay-sized particles.
Analysis conducted and data provided by James B. Stoltman (See Stoltman 1991).

Table 6.4 Body and Paste Properties of Powell Plain Sherds from the Rench Site.

	Body Composition			
	%Matrix	%Sand	%Shell	Shell Size
	67	0	33	2.51
	77	0	23	3.00
	78	1	21	3.02
	69	0	31	2.62
	74	1	25	2.50
MEAN	73 ± 4.8	0.4 ± 0.6	26.6 ± 5.2	2.73 ± 0.26

	Paste Composition (Excludes Temper)		
	%Matrix*	%Silt	%Sand
	97	3	0
	95	5	0
	98	1	1
	96	4	0
	90	9	1
MEAN	95.2 ± 3.1	4.4 ± 3.0	0.4 ± 0.6

*Primarily clay-sized particles.
Analysis conducted and data provided by James B. Stoltman (See Stoltman 1991).

Table 6.5 Body and Paste Properties of Cahokia Red Filmed sherds from the Rench Site

Body Composition			
%Matrix	%Sand	%Shell	Shell Size
79	0	21	2.00
67	0	33	2.57
76	1	23	2.54
MEAN 74 $\pm$ 6.2	0.3 $\pm$ 0.6	26 $\pm$ 6.4	2.37 $\pm$ 0.32

Paste Composition (Excludes Temper)		
%Matrix *	%Silt	%Sand
96	4	0
96	4	0
98	1	1
MEAN 97 $\pm$ 1.2	3 $\pm$ 1.7	0.3 $\pm$ 0.6

*Primarily clay-sized particles.
Analysis conducted and data provided by James B. Stoltman (See Stoltman 1991).

LLW pots differed from the Mississippian forms. These data support an interpretation that the Mississippian ceramic types were not made from local materials by local potters but were trade vessels from an external source, perhaps the American Bottom.

A majority of Powell Plain rims (10, 66.7%) have flattened extruded lips (Figure 6.6). Three specimens have squared-off or flat lips while one rim has a rolled and another a rounded lip. Rim diameters range from 9 to 34 cm and average 22.7 cm, indicating that most of the vessels had relatively large orifices and probably were large jars. Three subangular shoulder sherds were also recovered.

Cahokia Red Filmed pottery (Griffin 1949:57; Perino 1971a:84; Vogel 1975:77-80,100-101) is the only other Mississippian type recovered in any quantity from Rench. However, only two Cahokia Red filmed vessels can be identified based on unique rims (Figure 6.7). One specimen is from a jar that had a rim with a flattened extruded lip, much like most of the Powell Plain jars from Rench (Figure 6.7). The exterior, superior lip and interior surfaces of this specimen are all red slipped. The other specimen is from a bowl that curves to a roughly straight or vertical rim with a flat or squared-off lip (Figure 6.7). Three subangular shoulder sherds were red slipped and assigned to this category (Figure 6.7). The other 50 Cahokia Red Slipped sherds (Table 6.2) are all nondescript body fragments. However, at least nine of these were burnished in addition to being red slipped. It is likely that all of them were burnished, but that subsequent weathering and light erosion of their surfaces prevents accurate determination of this attribute.

Four shell tempered, cord marked body sherds have been tentatively assigned to the Cahokia Cord Marked type (Griffin 1949:55-56; Vogel 1975:96-98). They are gray to brown in color on both interior and exterior surfaces. The twist and ply of the cordage imprinted on the exterior surface cannot be determined. Because of this feature, it is possible that these sherds may be incompletely smoothed-over Powell Plain specimens since the Cahokia Cord Marked type does not appear until the Moorehead Phase in the American Bottom (Milner et al. 1984:175). These four sherds were recovered from three separate LLW/M pits; F-336, F-443, and F-637. However, they are so similar in color and form that it is probable that they are from the same vessel even though they do not join together. This suggests contemporaneity of the three features.

Three shell tempered bowl rims, besides the Cahokia Red Filmed specimen, were recovered. One can be assigned to the St. Clair Plain type (Figure 6.8) (Griffin 1949:54-55; Perino 1971a:65-69; Vogel 1975:77-79). It is an undecorated tan to buff colored rim with a straight or vertical orientation. The incurving bowl rim (Figure 6.8, right specimen of second row) could possibly be assigned to the St. Clair Plain type since it is undecorated. However, it does not seem to match any of the St. Clair Plain forms illustrated by Vogel (1975:77-79), and it is simply classified here as an untyped Mississippian bowl form. The other vertical bowl rim also is classified as an untyped Mississippian bowl. It is slipped black and is burnished on both the interior and exterior surfaces (Figure 6.8, left specimen of second row).

One rim has been classified as a "seed jar" (Emerson and Jackson 1984:69-70, 298) since it has a markedly incurving form (Figure 6.8). This specimen has plain, brown-colored interior and exterior surfaces, and a hole was drilled approximately 25 cm below the lip prior to firing.

The most common locally produced LLW/M ceramics from Rench are Mossville Cord Marked and

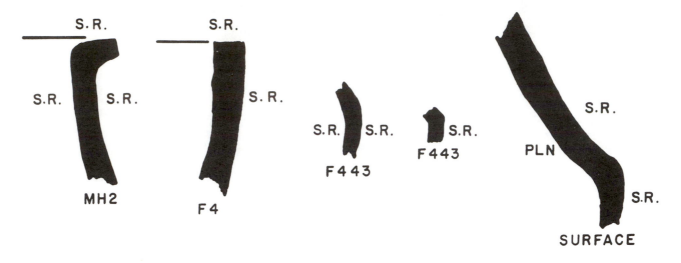

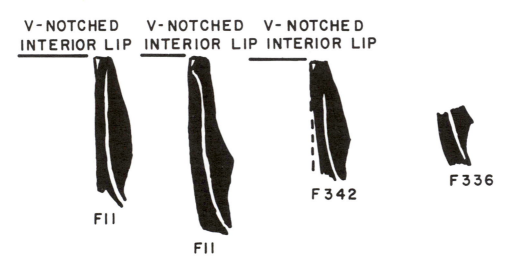

Figure 6.7 Rim and shoulder profiles. Upper row, Cahokia Red Filmed pottery; lower row, Starved Rock Collared pottery from the Rench site.

Mossville Plain. These two types are believed to represent variants of Canton Ware that differ from the Maples Mills Cord Decorated type (Cole and Deuel 1937:48; Fowler 1955:219; Schoenbeck 1946). Mossville Cord Marked and Plain are rarely decorated with cord impressed designs as is characteristic of the Maples Mills type. However, body sherds from all three types would be classified as Canton Ware. Canton Ware is usually tempered with a crushed black-colored grit and sand. Stoltman (Table 6.3) has identified the black grit temper in the Mossville Cord Marked sherds he examined as gabbro. He has also found that sand composes a relatively large percentage of the paste of Mossville Cord Marked pottery. The subsoil at Rench

is a sandy clay and if the pottery was manufactured by the inhabitants of the site from local materials, the sand is unlikely to have been an intentional inclusion.

Mossville Cord Marked and Plain have been briefly mentioned in the literature, but they have never been formally defined. Morse (1963:100,104) mentions that 11 Mossville Cord Marked sherds were collected by the Schoenbecks from the surface of the Steuben site. Morse (1963:104) states that Mossville Cord Marked types are found in "Maples Mills", but that there apparently are two types of Maples Mills assemblages. The first type is heavily influenced by Middle Mississippian ceramic styles (Mossville Cord Marked?) while the other is not directly related to

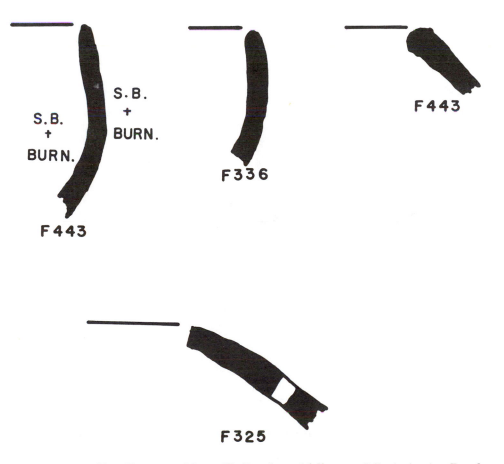

Figure 6.8 Rim profiles. Top row, Mossville Bowls; middle row, Mississippian Bowls; lower row, seed jar rim from the Rench site.

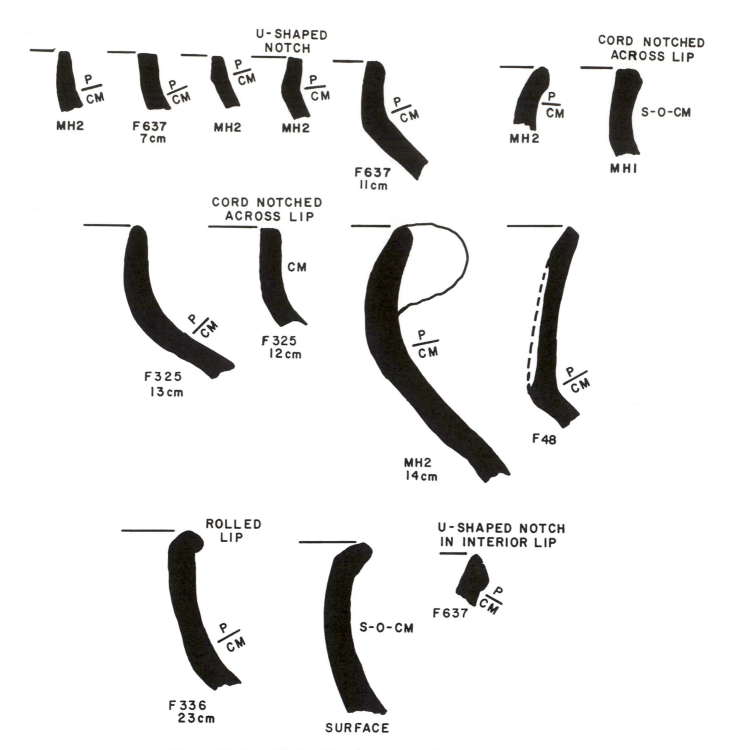

Figure 6.9 Mossville Cord Marked rim profiles from the Rench site.

Mississippian forms (the Maples Mills Cord Decorated type). One Mossville Plain rim sherd has been reported to have come from fill associated with the otherwise Middle Woodland Period Renchville Mound, located approximately 2.7 km southeast of the Rench site (Bluhm and Beeson 1960:169).

The Rench ceramic remains provide a basis for formally defining the Mossville Cord Marked and Plain types. They will be summarized here, and a full description will be provided in the final Rench site

report. Primary exterior surface treatment has been used to separate them into cord marked and plain types.

Mossville Cord Marked rims tend to have short necks, although a few high necked specimens are present (Figures 6.9 and 6.10). Excurving rims only slightly outnumber incurving and vertical forms, and they usually have flattened or rounded lips. Two Mossville Cord Marked rims could be classified as having poorly rolled lips, i.e., versions of the Mossville Cord

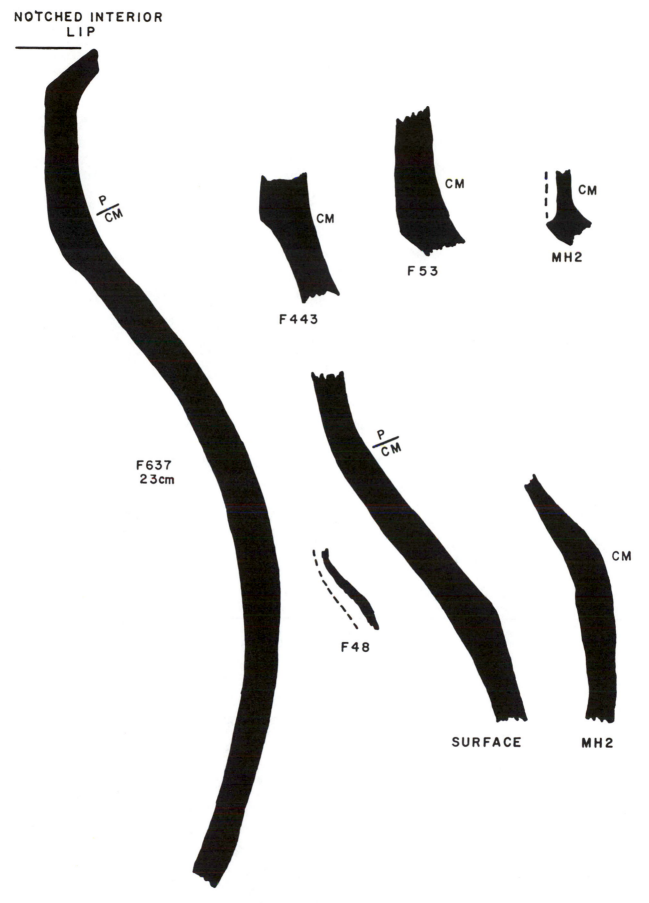

Figure 6.10 Mossville Cord Marked rim and shoulder profiles from the Rench site.

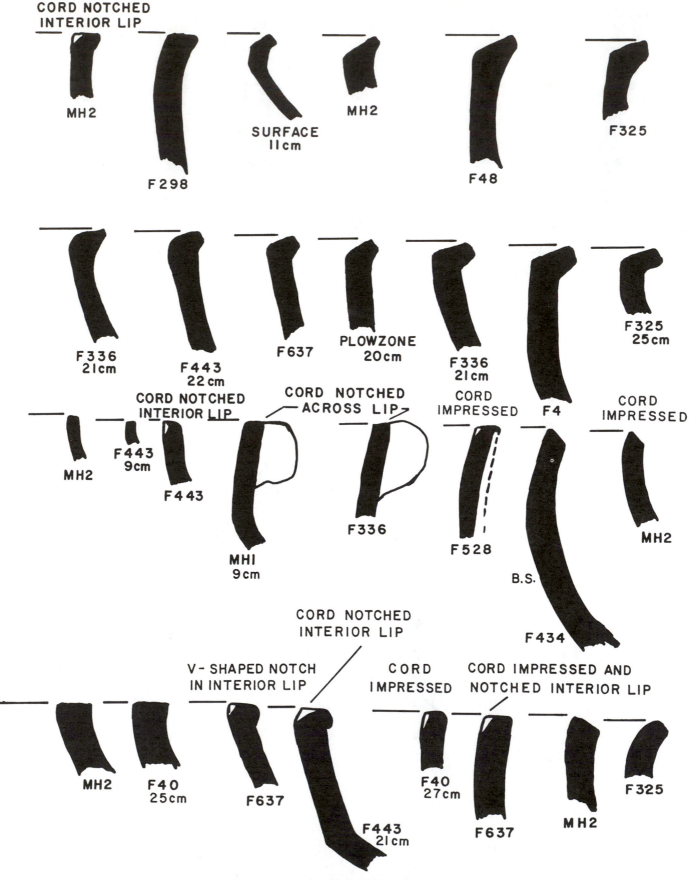

Figure 6.11 Mossville Plain rim profiles from the Rench site.

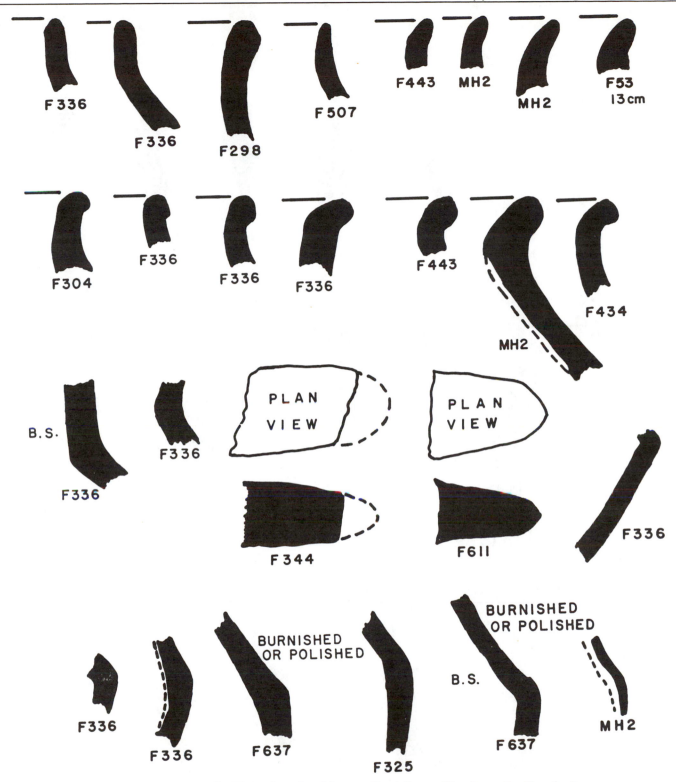

Figure 6.12 Mossville Plain rim, shoulder, and handle profiles from the Rench site.

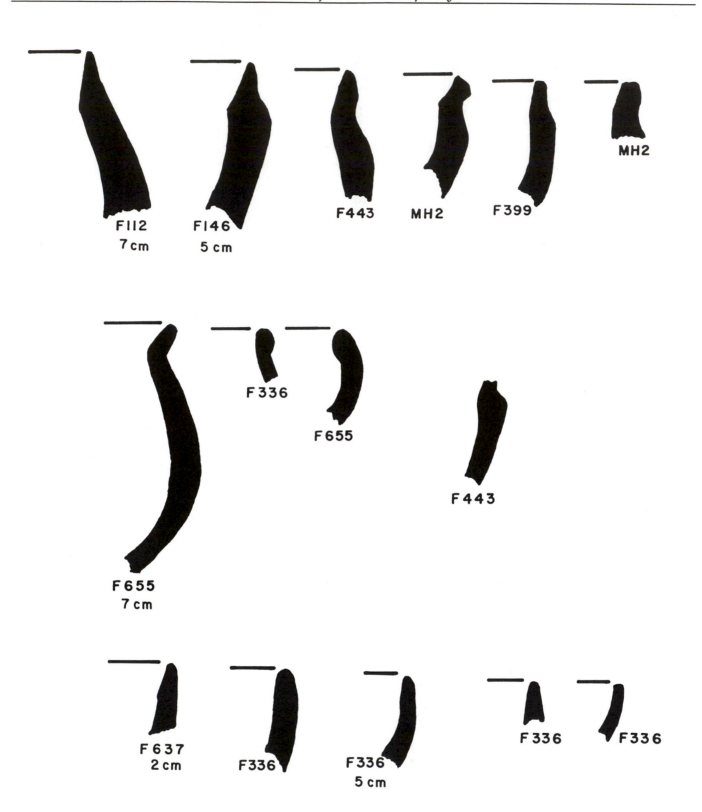

Figure 6.13 Mossville Pinch Pot rim profiles from the Rench site.

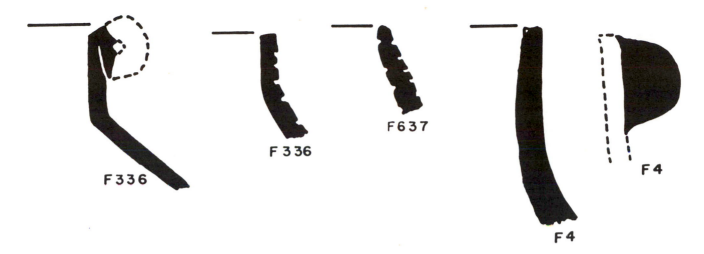

Figure 6.14 Maples Mills Cord Decorated rim profiles from the Rench site.

Marked rounded lip that have been pushed out toward the exterior (Figure 6.9, third row, first two specimens). There also is one example of a flattened extruded lip (Figure 6.10, left specimen). These probably represent attempts by the local potters to imitate the rolled and flattened extruded lip forms of the Mississippian pottery.

Some Mossville Cord Marked rims display a distinct angular break at the base of the neck (Figure 6.10, upper right). This section is often thicker than the rest of the vessel walls and suggests that the rims were formed by applying a strip of clay to the vessel after the body of the jar had been built. Three subangular shoulder Mossville Cord Marked body sherds were recovered, and these are similar to Cahokia Red Filmed and Powell Plain shoulder forms. In all three cases, though, cord marking is present both above and below the shoulder break. However, at the base of the neck of one specimen, the cord marking ends and the neck is smoothed-over or plain. Mossville Cord Marked jars have rounded bases.

The cord marking usually is indistinct, and Mossville Cord Marked characteristically has a dimpled appearance, similar to the surface of a golf ball. The indistinct cord marking may actually represent some type of fabric impression. Conversely, when the cord marking is distinct, it is usually of a two-ply Z-twist cordage. One body sherd of Mossville Cord Marked displays traces of a fugitive red slip. This may be an attempt by the local central Illinois Valley potters to imitate Cahokia Red Filmed. Interior surfaces of most vessels are smoothed-over and intentionally blackened, probably in a fashion similar to that described for historic Cherokee pottery in order to make them water tight (Harrington 1909:226; Holmes 1903:56).

There are fewer Mossville Plain sherds than Cord Marked, 62 sherds versus 339 (Table 6.2). However, 45 Mossville Plain sherds (Figures 6.11 and 6.12) are rims while only 15 rims could be assigned to the cord marked type. Of the 15 Mossville Cord Marked rims (Figure 6.9), representing 15 distinct vessels, only three are cord marked or lightly smoothed-over-cord marked over their entire exterior surfaces up to the lip. Thus, if only the upper portion of the rim had been preserved, most of the Mossville Cord Marked rims would have been classified as Mossville Plain. These data suggest that some of the Mossville Plain rims belong on Mossville Cord Marked bodies.

The 45 Mossville Plain rims recovered represent a minimum of 43 distinct vessels. Mossville Plain rims tend to imitate Powell Plain and Cahokia Red Filmed forms more often than the Cord Marked type. Flattened extruded (Figure 6.11, upper two rows) and rolled lips (Figure 6.12, second row) are relatively common, accounting for 28.9% and 15.6% of the Mossville Plain rims respectively. The rest of the rims are either simply flattened (37.8%) or rounded (17.8%). Excurving and incurving rims occur in equal amounts (19 each) while vertical rims are in the minority (7 examples).

Mossville Plain rims are rarely decorated, but those that are tend to be decorated on the interior lip. Four rims have interior lips impressed with Z-twist cord designs that consist of oblique (to the rim) parallel cords (/ slope) with a bordering horizontal cord at the bottom of the oblique lines. Two rims have cord-wrapped-stick notched interior lips while one is notched with a pointed, V-shaped instrument. The two cord-wrapped-stick notched and one of the cord decorated rims also are decorated with similar designs across the superior lip. One other rim has a narrow V-notched superior lip. Decorations on the exterior lip are rare. One rim has the superior and exterior lip impressed with a cord decoration that is composed of obliquely oriented parallel lines (/ sloped). One other rim may be notched with a V-shaped instrument on the exterior lip. However, it is possible that this last specimen is only an accidental fingernail impression that occurred during manufacture since it is indistinct.

A few Mossville Plain rims had appendages. Two rims, including the specimen that has a cord decoration on the exterior lip, have attached lugs (Figure 6.11). Two plain "ledge" handles were also recovered (Figure 6.12, middle of the third row), but both of these had been broken from the rims. They are rather large to be imitations of small tab-like appendages found on some Bluff jars in the American Bottom (Vogel 1975). They are also small for beaker handles, but they do resemble them. However, no definite beaker style vessel rims have been recovered at Rench.

Eight subangular shoulder sherds have been assigned to the Mossville Plain type (Figure 6.12, bottom row). Two were polished or burnished on their exterior surfaces, and one of these may have been slipped black or intentionally smudged on the interior surface. These indicate that there are Mossville Plain jars that were plain over their entire surfaces.

Two rims were recovered that have been assigned to a tentative Mossville Bowl type (Figure 6.8, top row). Both rims are incurved and have undecorated plain exterior surfaces. One of the rims is slightly folded over toward the interior surface.

Several small, crudely made "pinch pot" forms also were manufactured (Figure 6.13). A majority of these vessels were tempered only with sand, while a few also had grit added to the paste. Pinch pots have rim diameters ranging from 2 cm to 7 cm and may have been been small cups or bowls. They also could represent attempts by apprentice potters to learn the trade since they are crudely made and often retain finger "pinch" marks from manufacture.

Four rims and one lug representing a minimum of three jars have been assigned to the Maples Mills Cord

Decorated type (Figure 6.14) (Cole and Deuel 1937:48; Fowler 1955:219; Schoenbeck 1946). One specimen is from a high necked vessel with a triangular cord impressed design along the exterior surface (Figure 6.14, specimen from F4). Rims from the other two vessels both have horizontal parallel lines cord impressed along their exterior necks, and one also has them along the interior neck. These two rims could also be classified as "Gooden Cord Impressed" (Riggle 1981:6; Schoenbeck 1946:33-34), instead of Maples Mills Cord Decorated. However, the author views them as decorative variants of one type, Maples Mills Cord Decorated. One rim had a lug placed at a slight castelation along the rim, but it had subsequently broken off. One other broken lug was recovered that displayed horizontal cord impressed designs across it.

Four rims, minimally representing three different jars, have been assigned to the Starved Rock Collared type (Hall n.d.; Winters 1967:88). All of the rims have applied collars that bulge out slightly, forming a wedge-shaped profile (Figure 6.7). One rim is castelated and at least two of the vessels have V-shaped notches in the interior lips. Interior lip notching of the third jar cannot be confirmed due to erosion of its interior surface. Stoltman (Table 6.3) indicates one Starved Rock Collared specimen from Rench has a different body and paste composition from the local Mossville Cord Marked pottery. This suggests the Starved Rock Collared pots were produced by different potters from those making Mossville Cord Marked ceramics, and the Starved Rock Collared jars probably represent trade vessels at the Rench site.

Arrow points from Rench are the only chipped stone tools that can be reliably assigned to the LLW/M occupation (Table 6.6). Unfortunately, only one of these is directly associated with any of the features, a Madison point was recovered from the floor of House #1. Most of the rest of the points were surface finds or came from mixed midden deposits.

Most of the arrow points were made from Burlington chert or cobble cherts. The cobbles were probably obtained from nearby glacial till deposits.

Table 6.6 Late Late Woodland/Mississippian Projectile Points from the Rench Site	
Point Type	No. of Specimens
Klunk Side-Notched	16
Koster Corner-Notched	4
Scallorn	3
Schild Spike	1
Madison	9
Mound Stemless	3
Cahokia Double-Notched	4
Cahokia Triple-Notched	1
Total	41

Burlington chert is considered "local" even though the closest source is located over 40 km to the northwest at the Avon Quarries. Burlington chert is also available from the lower Illinois Valley, while Cresent Hills chert, which is similar to the finer grades of Burlington, may be obtained southwest of Cahokia, in Missouri. Thus, although it is assumed that the Burlington chert used is "local" material, it is possible that some was obtained through trade with lower Illinois Valley groups or possibly from the American Bottom.

One Madison point was made from a honey-colored variety of Hixton Silicified Sandstone (Porter 1961), while another is made from quartz crystal. The origins of the quartz crystal is not known, but it is possible that it was found in local glacial till. Conversely, Hixton Silicified Sandstone is available in only one place, Silver Mound, Wisconsin (Porter 1961:78). Silver Mound is located in the northern portion of the Driftless Area of Wisconsin, and the raw material could not have been transported to Illinois by glacial activity. Therefore, this particular Madison point indicates contact with more northerly groups.

Discussion

There are some similarities between the Rench houses and those from the Edelhardt and Lohmann Phases of the American Bottom. Both Edelhardt and Lohmann rectangular single post structures and Lohmann wall trench structures were built in house basins (Emerson and Jackson 1984:117-145; Esarey and Good 1981:22-41; Kelly et al. 1984:153-155; Milner et al. 1984:161-168), as were House #2 and probably House #1 from Rench. The length/width ratios for the Edelhardt Phase houses from the BBB Motor site averaged 1.7 (Emerson and Jackson 1984:115, figured from data presented in Table 35 for interior floor lengths and widths) while averages from four Lohmann Phase sites ranged from about 1.6 to 1.8 (Milner et al. 1984:167). The length/width ratios for the two Rench houses are slightly smaller at around 1.5, but this probably is not significantly different from the American Bottom ratios due to the small sample size.

There are some notable differences between the dwellings from two areas, though. The two Rench houses have larger interior floor areas (H#1 = 11.8 m^2; H#2 = 23.8 m^2) than any of the Edelhardt Phase houses (max. = 10.87 m^2; Emerson and Jackson 1984:115). Lohmann Phase structures are slightly larger, and Rench House #1 would fall in the range listed for them (Milner et al. 1984:167), while Rench House #2 appears to be larger than most Lohmann Phase dwellings. It is not until the Moorehead and Sand Prairie Phases that structures from the American Bottom generally approach the size of Rench House #2 (Milner et al. 1984:167). Conversely, the Moorehead and Sand Prairie structures are more square than the Rench houses and their length/width ratios are smaller (Milner et al. 1984:167).

Rench House #2 is the only rectangular structure that definitely is a wigwam form. The Edelhardt and Lohmann Phase dwellings were not burned and lack any direct evidence of their actual roof form. Thus, they may have had been either wigwam or hipped/gabled-roof structures. However, burned houses from later Mississippian phases in the American Bottom and the Illinois River Valley generally appear to have been hipped- or gabled-roof types (McConaughy 1985), and this implies that the Edelhardt and Lohmann dwellings also had those roof forms. Therefore, Rench House #2 probably represents a late Late Woodland style dwelling from the central Illinois Valley that had not been greatly influenced by contact with Mississippian groups. Conversely, Rench House #1 is much more like Mississippian dwellings in that wall posts were set in a shallow wall trench, and there are centrally located support posts to hold up a hipped, or possibly a gabled, roof. This house may represent a warmer weather house modeled after American Bottom forms.

It has been assumed that the difference between early, well-made, shell tempered Mississippian and grit tempered late Late Woodland wares from the central Illinois Valley indicated production by different societies and was not the result of functional differences (Conrad 1973; Harn 1975:418-420). Later central Illinois Valley peoples became acculturated to a Mississippian life style and began to manufacture local imitations of shell tempered Mississippian forms (Conrad 1973; Harn 1975:418-420 and 1980:19-23). Stoltman's analysis of the Rench ceramics (Tables 6.3 to 6.5) found distinct differences in the pastes and tempers used to produce the Mississippian and late Late Woodland pots. He also suggests these differences were due to production by different societies.

The distribution of the different wares at Rench suggests that the Mississippian pottery represents trade items. Late Late Woodland and Mississippian ceramics occur in frequencies of 86% to 14% in House #1 and 74% to 26% in House #2. Thus, it is not likely that the two dwellings represent two families, one a Mississippian family from the American Bottom and the other from the central Illinois Valley. If this was the case, then one house would presumably have more Mississippian pottery while the other would have more Late Woodland forms. Similarly, it is not likely that the two dwellings represent one family with multiple spouses, one housing a Mississippian and the other a local late Late Woodland potter.

It has been noted that only the late Late Woodland ware from Rench displays charring from use in cooking. The greater quantity of these forms also implies that they were the primary utilitarian ceramics of these people. The presence of painted surfaces or slipping on some of the Mississippian vessels, their overall fine production and their relative rarity all suggest that they were not used for utilitarian purposes at Rench. Thus, it is assumed that some type of ritualistic ideology accompanied the aquisition of Mississippian ceramics.

The Mississippian pottery from Rench most closely resembles types produced during the Lohmann Phase of the American Bottom (Emerson and Jackson 1984:28-90; Esarey and Good 1981:44-90; Kelly et al. 1984:153-154; Milner et al. 1984:161-163). However, Rench does not have any beakers, pans, shallow bowls, water bottles, or funnels, which are all forms found during the Lohmann Phase. The lack of these Mississippian vessel forms in the Rench site assemblage may only indicate the Rench inhabitants did not obtain them. It does not necessarily imply they were not available.

Cahokia Double Notched and Triple Notched points from Rench may also suggest possible contact with American Bottom people. These forms have been assumed to indicate Mississippian (i.e., American Bottom) influences in the central Illinois Valley (Harn 1975:419), probably because so many of them were recovered from burial contexts in Mound 72 from Cahokia (Fowler 1977:21-26). However, Fowler has noted that these points were made into types and from raw materials that "suggest relationships with the Caddo area, some with Tennessee, and some with Wisconsin" (Fowler 1977:23). Thus, the origins of "Cahokia" point types remain speculative. It is possible they were made by many different groups, and the presence of these points at Rench might be due to contact with people from other areas besides the American Bottom.

Based on data from Rench, it is apparent that American Bottom early Mississippian people were already beginning to influence surrounding late Late Woodland groups by A.D. 1000. Unfortunately, it is far more difficult to determine what the Rench inhabitants were sending back to the American Bottom in return for the new ideology and pottery. The only relatively abundant natural resources available at Rench would have been labor, food (i.e., maize, nuts, meat, etc.), and freshwater pearls from the mussel beds of Lake Peoria. Pearls are an item that would have been attractive to higher status people from the American Bottom. However, there is no evidence that the Rench inhabitants were intensively collecting freshwater mussels or pearls.

If people were traveling from the central Illinois Valley to the American Bottom to act as corvee laborers, then it is likely that they would have taken some of their own pottery with them to hold food and water on the journey. After arriving in the American Bottom, some of this pottery would have undoubtedly been broken. If labor was the item used in "trade" for the Mississippian vessels, then central Illinois Valley potsherds should be recovered from some of the American Bottom sites. To date, there apparently has been no Mossville Cord Marked or Plain vessels recovered from Emergent Mississippian or Mississippian sites. Even if they have not been recognized as being Mossville Cord Marked and Plain, an examination of the literature by the author failed to locate anything that resembles them from the American Bottom. Therefore, it seems unlikely that labor was exchanged for the Mississippian ceramics.

The LLW/M component at Rench has been interpreted as a small farming hamlet (McConaughy et al. 1985). Four of the ten features associated with this occupation have estimated capacities of over 1000 liters, and pits F-336 and F-637 are extremely large (Table 6.1). Determining the function of large features is difficult since they were finally used as repositories of general refuse. However, McConaughy (1984) has indicated that there is a correlation between increasing pit size and the number of potential domesticates recovered at sites from the American Bottom and Illinois Valley. This suggests that larger features were storage facilities, and it is probable that the large Rench pits were used for storage.

Demonstrating that all the LLW/M features were used contemporaneously is also difficult. However, as was previously mentioned, four Cahokia Cord Marked sherds that probably came from the same vessel were recovered from the two largest features, F-336 and F-637, and from F-443, indicating that these three pits were at least filled with refuse contemporaneously. Also, only F-325 is clearly stratified, suggesting that most of the pits were filled with refuse over a relatively brief period. In fact, the strata of F-325 most likely represent basket loading and not intermittent reuse since matching sherds were recovered from different layers in this feature. These data imply that the larger features were open and available for use at the same time. Also, although no joins were discovered, the same types of pottery were recovered from the pit features and the two houses, suggesting that they all may have been in use at the same time.

If the large features were used for storage, they could have held an enormous quantity of maize. For example, King (n.d.) has estimated that F-336 could have held nearly 3 million shelled maize kernels. This would have been enough corn to plant over 1000 ha, if it had been stored for this purpose. However, it is likely that most maize would have been stored for use as food.

Wing and Brown (1979:24-25) estimate that an average adult male would require 3200 calories (note: herein calories = kilocalories) of food daily while an average adult female would need about 2300. Requirements for children vary with age and sex from 800 to as much as 3600 calories per day for a 19 year old male (Wing and Brown 1979:24). Therefore, 3000 calories was selected to represent the average caloric intake needed per *person* per day to simplify the following computations. Using this estimate, the average caloric intake per person per year is about 1,095,000 calories.

Comparing the estimated average yearly caloric intake per person per year to the potential calories of stored maize in the larger LLW/M features from Rench indicates that they could have held enough maize to feed 33.4 persons for a year, using the corn stored on the cob estimate, or 44.5 persons if the corn was shelled and if all their caloric intake was from maize (Tables 6.7 and 6.12).

It is certain that maize did not compose the entire diet of these people, and may not have even made up a majority of it. Thus, similar caloric estimates have been made for hickory nut (Table 6.8), black walnut (Table 6.9), butternut (Table 6.10), and *Polygonum* (Table 6.11; smartweed is used as a substitute for knotweed since necessary data for knotweed were not

Table 6.7 Caloric Amounts of Maize that could be Stored in the Four Largest LLW/M Pits from Rench

Feature No.	Feature Vol. in liters	Corn on the Cob Total calories	Shelled Corn Total calories
F-336	11,274.4	21,579,201.6	28,771,141.4
F-637	3,522.9	6,742,830.6	8,990,088.5
F-48	2,984.9	5,713,098.6	7,617,166.3
F-325	1,328.6	2,542,940.4	3,390,454.3
	Totals	36,578,071.2	48,768,850.5

No. pers./yr that total could support   =33.4   = 44.5

Field corn provides 3.48 cal/g (Watt and Merrill 1975:26).

Author's measurements:

0.2 liter Indian corn cob produced 110 g kernals.

5 x 110g = 550 g/l (conversion factor to get 1 liter).

550 g/l x 3.48 cal/g = 1914 cal/l.

110 g = 0.15 l shelled corn.

6 2/3 x 110 = 733.3 g/l shelled corn (conversion factor).

733.3 g/l x 3.48 cal/g = 2551.9 cal/l shelled corn.

Table 6.8 Caloric Amounts of Shagbark Hickory that could be Stored in the Four Largest LLW/M Pits from Rench.

Feature No.	Feature Vol. in liters	Kg. of Nut-meat	Total calories
F-336	11,274.4	1916.6	13,492,864
F-637	3,522.9	598.9	4,216,256
F-48	2,984.9	507.4	3,572,096
F-325	1,328.6	225.9	1,590,336
	Totals	3248.8	22,871,552

No. persons/year that total could support = 20.9

Based on 2 bu. = 32.2 kg nuts (Talalay et al. 1984:341).

2 bu. x 35.328 liters = 70.656 l (coversion factor bu to l).

32.2 kg/70.656 l = 0.46 kg/l of nuts.

Shagbark hickory nutmeat = 0.372 of nut weight (Talalay et al. 1984:344).

Thus 0.372 x 0.46 kg/l = 0.17 kg nutmeat/l.

1 kg of shagbark hickory = 7040 calories (Talalay et al. 1984:344).

Table 6.9 Caloric Amounts of Black Walnut that could be Stored in the Four Largest LLW/M Pits from Rench.

Feature No.	Feature Vol. in liters	Kg. of Nut-meat	Total calories
F-336	11,274.4	1014.7	6,636,112
F-637	3,522.9	317.1	2,073,834
F-48	2,984.9	268.6	1,756,664
F-325	1,328.6	119.6	782,184
	Totals	1720.0	11,248,774

No. persons/year that total could support = 10.3
   Based on 16 bu. = 273 kg nuts (Talalay et al. 1984:342).
   16 bu. x 35.328 liters = 565.248 l (coversion factor bu to l).
   273 kg/565.248 l = 0.48 kg/l of nuts.
   Black walnut nutmeat = 0.194 of nut weight (Talalay et al. 1984:344).
   Thus 0.194 x 0.48 kg/l = 0.09 kg nutmeat/l.
   1 kg of black walnut = 6540 calories (Talalay et al. 1984:344).

Table 6.10 Caloric Amounts of Butternut that could be Stored in the Four Largest LLW/M Pits from Rench.

Feature No.	Feature Vol. in liters	Kg. of Nut-meat	Total calories
F-336	11,274.4	451.0	3,197,590
F-637	3,522.9	140.9	998,981
F-48	2,984.9	119.4	846,546
F-325	1,328.6	53.1	376,479
	Totals	764.4	5,419,596

No. persons/year that total could support = 5.0
   Based on 3 bu. = 32.7 kg nuts (Talalay et al. 1984:342).
   3 bu. x 35.328 liters = 105.984 l (coversion factor bu to l).
   32.7 kg/105.984 l = 0.31 kg/l of nuts.
   Butternut nutmeat = 0.136 of nut weight (Talalay et al. 1984:344).
   Thus 0.136 x 0.31 kg/l = 0.04 kg nutmeat/l.
   1 kg of butternut = 7090 calories (Talalay et al. 1984:344).

Table 6.11 Caloric Amounts of *Polygonum Pennsylvanicum* that could be Stored in the Four Largest LLW/M Pits from Rench.

Feature No.	Feature Vol. in liters	Kg. of smart-weed	Total calories
F-336	11,274.4	5637.2	25,423,772
F-637	3,522.9	1761.5	7,944,140
F-48	2,984.9	1492.5	6,730,950
F-325	1,328.6	664.3	2,995,993
	Totals	9555.5	43,094,855

No. persons/year that total could support = 39.4
Based on 80 cc = 40 g (Murray and Sheehan 1984:290).
1000 cc (i.e. 1 l) = 500 g (coversion factor of 12.5 x cc & g).
100 g smartweed = 451 calories (Murray and Sheehan 1984:294).
Thus, 1 liter or 500 g = 2255 calories.

Table 6.12 Estimated Caloric Amounts of Various Foods that could be Stored in F-336, F-637, F-48, and F-325 from the LLW/M Occupation of the Rench Site (11P4).

Food Species	Est. Total Calories	Est. No. Persons Per Year
Shelled Corn	48,768,850.5	44.5
Smartweed*	43,094,855.0	39.4
Corn on the Cob	36,578,071.2	33.4
Shagbark Hickory	22,871,552.0	20.9
Venison	13,241,261.8	12.1
Black Walnut	11,248,774.0	10.3
Fish	11,229,467.9	10.3
Butternut	5,419,596.0	5.0

*Smartweed used as an estimate for knotweed because data for knotweed were not available.
Nut estimates were based on storage in the shell.

available) because these have also been recovered from Rench features. These data are summarized in Table 6.12.

Dried or smoked meats and fish could also be stored. Deer, fish, and other animals certainly were important sources of protein and other nutrients for the Rench inhabitants. However, only deer and fish would have been available in large quantities from the area surrounding Rench. Unfortunately, volume data for specific weights of these items could not be found. Therefore, the following comparisons with the plant foods are based on gram weights.

Fresh deer meat provides approximately 126 cal/100 g and fish produces about 107 cal/100 g (Keene 1981:136). This can be compared to an estimate of 348 cal/100 g provided by field corn (Watt and Merrill 1975:26). Thus, venison produces roughly 36.2% and fish 30.7% of the calories that a similar weight of maize provides. It is assumed that 100 g of fish or venison probably do not take up more volume than a similar quantity of usable maize stored on the cob. Therefore, if the corn on the cob storage estimates are multiplied by 0.362 for venison and 0.307 for fish, estimates of the possible amounts of stored meat and fish can be made. These estimates suggest that stored venison and fish could feed about 12.1 and 10.3 persons per year respectively if they were the only foods stored in the pits and that was all the people ate (Table 6.12). These are minimum estimates since deer meat and fish would have been dried or smoked for storage, thus removing most of the water content and concentrating the caloric content in a smaller weight and volume.

Assuming that only one nuclear family of five persons was living year round at Rench in warm and cold weather dwellings, surpluses of all of these foods could have been stored in the pits with the exception of butternut. Butternut would have provided just enough food to keep all five individuals alive for a year. Thus, if any combination of foods was stored in

these features, as was most likely the case, the Rench inhabitants had the necessary capacity available to keep a surplus of food.

Based on the preceding data and speculations, it is proposed that the most likely materials exchanged for Mississippian ceramics and accompanying ideology from the American Bottom were various foods. Moreover, it is suggested that maize was the most probable trade good since: 1) corn was actively cultivated by the Rench inhabitants; 2) it was very productive; 3) a greater quantity, in terms of available calories, could be stored in a given space than most other foods; and 4) its availability was more readily under human control.

Conclusions

The LLW/M occupation of the Rench site is interpreted as a small farming hamlet occupied by one nuclear family. These people built separate dwellings to live in during the warmer and colder periods of the year. Maize was grown and probably stored in some of the large pits associated with this occupation. Wild foods utilized included black walnut, hickory nut, butternut, various starchy seeds(?), fish and white-tailed deer.

Mossville Cord Marked and Plain represent locally produced pottery used by the Rench inhabitants. They also obtained Powell Plain and Cahokia Red Filmed ceramics, probably from the American Bottom during the Lohmann Phase. These vessels and associated concepts seemed to have impressed the central Illinois Valley late Late Woodland people to such a degree that they started to produce their own grit tempered imitations of the Mississippian forms. Radiocarbon dates from Rench indicate that this interaction with the American Bottom had begun by at least A.D. 1000.

The large pit features from Rench and the maize recovered suggest that the inhabitants were producing a surplus of food. It is possible that food was traded by the Rench people to the American Bottom for their pottery and ideology. In other words, the exchanges were based on "food for thought".

Acknowledgments

The author would like to thank Harold Hassen, Robert Warren, Jacqueline Ferguson, and Frances B. King for their comments on the paper. However, all interpretations, errors, etc. are solely the responsibility of the author.

Figures 6.2 to 6.5 are used with the permission of the *Midcontinental Journal of Archaeology*, where they first appeared (McConaughy et al. 1985). Marlin Roos of the Illinois State Museum took the photograph of LLW/M House #2 used for Figure 6.4.

The author would also like to acknowledge the analytical work conducted by and data provided by James B. Stoltman on the ceramic wares from the Rench site.

The work at Rench was conducted under contract by the Archaeological Program of the Illinois State Museum Society for the Illinois Department of Transportation. It could not have been accomplished but for the help and aid of M. J. Macchio; Earl Bowman, P.E., Chief of the Bureau of Location and Environment, retired; J. Paul Biggers, current Chief of the Bureau of Location and Environment; John Walthall, Jeff Bruce, and Jerry Jacobson from the Bureau of Location and Environment, Springfield; Steve van Winkle, Roger Rocke, Paula Harris, and James Stone from IDOT District #4, Peoria.

References Cited

Bluhm, Elaine A. and William J. Beeson
  1960 The Excavation of Three Hopewell Mounds at the Caterpillar Tractor Company. In Indian Mounds and Villages in Illinois, pp. 1-24. *Illinois Archaeological Survey Bulletin* No. 2, Urbana.
Caldwell, Joseph R.
  1967 The House that "X" Built. *Living Museum* 28(12):92-93.
Cole, Fay-Cooper, and Thorne Deuel
  1937 *Rediscovering Illinois*. University of Chicago Press, Chicago. Midway Reprint, 1975.
Conrad, Lawrence A.
  1973 The Nature of the Relationships between Cahokia and the Central Illinois River Valley. Paper presented at the fifty-second annual meeting of the Central States Anthropological Society, St. Louis, Missouri, March 29-31, 1973.
Emerson, Thomas E. and Douglas K. Jackson
  1984 *The BBB Motor Site*. American Bottom Archaeology FAI-270 Site Reports, Vol. 6, University of Illinois Press, Urbana.
Esarey, Duane and Timothy W. Good
  1981 Final Report on FAI 270 and Illinois Route 460 Related Excavations at the Lohmann Site, 11-S-49, St. Clair County, Illinois. *Western Illinois University Archaeological Research Laboratories, Reports of Investigations*, No. 3, and *FAI 270 Archaeological Mitigation Project Report*, No. 39. Macomb, Illinois.
Fowler, Melvin L.
  1955 Ware Groupings and Decorations of Woodland Ceramics in Illinois. *American Antiquity* 20(3):213-225.
  1977 The Cahokia Site. In Explorations into Cahokia Archaeology, edited by Melvin Fowler, pp. 1-29. *Illinois Archaeological Survey Bulletin* No. 7, Urbana.
Griffin, James B.
  1949 The Cahokia Ceramic Complexes. *Proceedings of the Fifth Plains Conference for Archaeology Note Book*, No. 1, pp. 44-58. Laboratory of Archaeology, University of Nebraska, Lincoln.
Hall, Robert L.
  n.d. A Newly Designated Pottery Type from Northern Illinois. Ms. on file at the Dickson Mounds Museum, Lewistown, Illinois.
Hargrave, Michael
  1983 Mississippian Wall Trench Structures and Settlement Organization. In The Bridges Site (11-Mr-11), a Late Prehistoric Settlement in the Central Kaskaskia Valley, pp. 121-175. *Center for Archaeological Investigations, Southern Illinois University at Carbondale Research Paper*, No. 38, Carbondale.

Harn, Alan D.
   1975 Cahokia and the Mississippian Emergence in the Spoon River Area of Illinois. *Transactions of the Illinois Academy of Science* 68(4):414-434.
   1980 The Prehistory of Dickson Mounds: the Dickson Excavation. *Illinois State Museum Reports of Investigations*, No. 35, Springfield.
Harrington, M. R.
   1909 The Last of the Iroquois Potters. *New York State Museum Bulletin* No. 133, pp. 222-227.
Holmes, W. H.
   1903 Aboriginal Pottery of the Eastern United States. *Annual Report of the Bureau of American Ethnology* 20:1-201, Washington.
Keene, Arthur S.
   1981 *Prehistoric Foraging in a Temperate Forest: a Linear Programming Model.* Academic Press, New York.
Kelly, John E., Steven J. Ozuk, Douglas K. Jackson, Dale L. McElrath, Fred A. Finney, and Duane Esarey
   1984 Emergent Mississippian Period. In *American Bottom Archaeology*, edited by Charles J. Bareis and James W. Porter. University of Illinois Press, Urbana.
King, Frances B.
   n.d. Late Late Woodland/Mississippian Floral Remains, Ms. that will be included in the final Rench site report, on file at the Illinois State Museum, Springfield.
Martin, Terrance J.
   n.d. Late Late Woodland/Mississippian Faunal Remains, Ms. that will be included in the final Rench site report, on file at the Illinois State Museum, Springfield.
McConaughy, Mark A.
   1984 Feature Volume Estimates as Indicators of Residential Stability and/or Mobility. Paper presented at the 1984 Midwest Archaeological Conference, 19- 21 October, 1984, Evanston, Illinois.
   1985 A Comparison of Burned Mississippian Houses from Illinois. Paper presented at the 1985 Midwest Archaeological Conference, 4-6 October, 1985, East Lansing, Michigan.
McConaughy, Mark A., Claude V. Jackson, and Frances B. King
   1985 Two Early Mississippian Period Structures from the Rench Site (11P4), Peoria County, Illinois. *Midcontinental Journal of Archaeology* 10(2):171-193.
Milner, George R., Thomas E. Emerson, Mark W. Mehrer, Joyce A. Williams, and Duane Esarey
   1984 Mississippian and Oneota Period. In *American Bottom Archaeology*, edited by Charles J. Bareis and James W. Porter. University of Illinois Press, Urbana.
Morse, Dan F.
   1963 The Steuben Village and Mounds: a Multicomponent Late Hopewell Site in Illinois. *Anthropological Papers of the Museum of Anthropology, University of Michigan* No. 21, Ann Arbor.
Murray, Priscilla M. and Mark C. Sheehan
   1984 Prehistoric *Polygonum* use in the Midwestern United States. In Experiments and Observations on Aboriginal Wild Plant Food Utilization in Eastern North America, edited by Patrick J. Munson, pp. 282-298. *Indiana Historical Society Prehistoric Research Series* Vol. 5, No. 2, Indianapolis.
Perino, Gregory
   1971 The Mississippian Component at the Schild Site (No. 4), Green County, Illinois. In Mississippian Site Archaeology in Illinois I, pp. 1-148. *Illinois Archaeological Survey Bulletin* No. 8, Urbana.
Porter, James
   1961 Hixton Silicified Sandstone: a Unique Lithic Material Used by Prehistoric Cultures. *The Wisconsin Archeologist* 42(2):78-85.
Riggle, Stan
   1981 The Late Woodland Transition in the Central Mississippi Valley. *South Dakota Archaeology* 5:5-18.
Schoenbeck, E.
   1946 Cord-Decorated Pottery in the General Peoria Region. *Illinois Academy of Science Transactions* 39:33-42.
Smith, Harriet M.
   1977 The Murdock Mound, Cahokia Site. In Explorations into Cahokia Archaeology, edited by Melvin Fowler, pp. 49-88. *Illinois Archaeological Survey Bulletin* No. 7, Urbana, Illinois.

Stoltman, James B.
1991 Ceramic Petrography as a Technique for Documenting Cultural Interaction: An Example from the Upper Mississippi Valley. *American Antiquity* 56(1)

Talalay, Laurie, Donald R. Keller, and Patrick J. Munson
1984 Hickory Nuts, Walnuts, Butternuts, and Hazelnuts: Observations and Experiments Relevant to Their Aboriginal Exploitation in Eastern North America. In Experiments and Observations on Aboriginal Wild Plant Food Utilization in Eastern North America, edited by Patrick J. Munson, pp. 338-359. *Indiana Historical Society Prehistoric Research Series* Vol. 5, No. 2, Indianapolis.

Vogel, Joseph O.
1975 Trends in Cahokia Ceramics: Preliminary Study of the Collections from Tracts 15A and 15B. In *Perspectives in Cahokia Archaeology*, Illinois Archaeological Survey, Inc. Bulletin No. 10, Urbana.

Watt, Bernice K. and Anabel L. Merrill
1975 *Handbook of the Nutritional Content of Foods*. Prepared for the United States Department of Agriculture, Dover Publications, New York.

Wing, Elizabeth S. and Antoinette B. Brown
1979 *Paleonutrition: Method and Theory in Prehistoric Foodways*. Academic Press, New York.

Winters, Howard D.
1967 An Archaeological Survey of the Wabash Valley in Illinois. *Illinois State Museum Reports of Investigations* No. 10, Springfield.

Wray, Donald E.
1952 Archeology of the Illinois Valley: 1950. In *Archeology of Eastern United States*. edited by James B. Griffin, pp. 152-164. University of Chicago Press, Chicago.

7

The Eveland Site: Inroad to Spoon River Mississippian Society

Alan D. Harn

Dickson Mounds Museum

During the past six decades, considerable information has been accumulated on the development of Cahokia and its socio-economic impact on contemporaneous cultural systems throughout the American Midwest. Such shared core characteristics as temple mounds, plazas, formal town structuring, wall-trench houses, triangular arrowpoints, shell-tempered pottery, and chert-hoe horticulture variously have been used to distinguish bearers of Cahokia Mississippian traditions from their Midwestern neighbors.

That Cahokia was the core area for the development of Mississippian in the upper Midwest is now almost universally agreed upon, even though the mechanisms by which its cultural components were spread continue to be the subject of debate (Caldwell 1967a; Griffin 1960; Hall 1967, 1974; Harn 1975b). Most view the Cahokia Mississippian movement as a neoteric symbiotic-extractive relationship involving varying combinations of acculturation and limited migration of Cahokians into receptive Late Woodland enclaves. However, interregional relationships and contacts involving commodities and exchange that developed in the Cahokia region during the 7th and 8th centuries A.D. probably would later serve as the primary mechanism to facilitate the acceptance and rapid spread of the Mississippian movement.

Certainly by A.D. 600, the presence of the expanding Late Woodland Patrick phase population of the American Bottom region must have been recognized by other contemporaneous populations of the Midwest. Although the most culturally diagnostic item of the Patrick phase, ceramics, is primarily confined to the region later identified as the central Cahokia sphere, by A.D. 600 (ISGS 1392, 1480±70 B.P.; ISGS 1393, 1380±80 B.P.), ceramic jars reminiscent of those of the Patrick phase appeared at the Myer-Dickson site in the Central Illinois River Valley, some 250 river kilometers north of Cahokia. Similar ceramics also were being locally produced over 200 km up the Mississippi River Valley during the 7th and 8th centuries A.D. (McGimsey and Conner 1985).

In neither of these areas is it clear if this distinctive ceramic tradition was a byproduct of acculturation with Patrick phase residents of the American Bottom region or if it developed independently from an indigenous base. What is obvious is that, at least three centuries before the baggage of Mississippian was being assembled at Cahokia, there was some measure of cultural commonality between peoples of the American Bottom and the North-Central Mississippi River Valley and Central Illinois River Valley regions. Yet, strong cultural ties between the American Bottom and its hinterlands do not seem to have developed until Cahokia had blossomed into a Stirling phase Mississippian center. Two interrelated factors, large human populations and intensive corn horticulture, probably were pivotal in the rapid Mississippian expansion that would follow. By A.D. 1100, the Cahokia presence was evident in one form or another throughout a northern frontier that included northern Illinois, southern Wisconsin and southeastern Minnesota, northern Missouri, and much of Iowa.

Instead of a uniform dissemination of Mississippian

culture appearing across the Illinois landscape, pockets of Mississippian developed that may have been partially dependent upon the presence or absence of indigenous host populations. In central Illinois, early Mississippian contact sites such as Shire (Claflin, this volume) and Collins (Douglas 1976) even occur at Woodland isolates positioned well out onto the Grand Prairie, but most of these marginal occupations apparently were short-lived. The most enduring of the early Mississippian occupations were located in two main regions along the heavily forested Illinois River Valley. Many sites were concentrated in the Central Illinois River Valley from the Spoon River northward to the Rench Site area above Peoria Lake, and a smaller number were scattered along the Lower Illinois River Valley south of the Sangamon River. No early Mississippian occupation has been recognized along adjacent stretches of the Mississippi River Valley, even though those areas shared a certain cultural commonality with the Illinois Valley for much of the pre-Mississippian phase of the Late Woodland occupation. This could indicate that indigenous populations had largely abandoned the Mississippi valley for at least 200 km above the mouth of the Illinois River prior to A.D. 1050. A less plausible alternative view might be that this section represented a stronghold of Woodland tradition that successfully resisted acculturation.

Two sites, the small habitation and ceremonial center of Eveland and its associated cemetery, Dickson Mounds, have been most instrumental in assessing cultural development on the northern Mississippian frontier. Close enough to Cahokia to invite frequent contact, these sites were still sufficiently isolated to ensure their own individuality. In addition, they were situated at the margins of several major culture areas linking Cahokia Mississippian with indigenous populations. The cultural personality of the Eveland and Dickson sites resulted from strong Mississippian influences on an indigenous eastern Woodland population that also had established sociopolitical relationships with Woodland contemporaries far into the area that would become the northern Mississippian frontier. Small in size and of short duration, the early components at Eveland and Dickson represent singular episodes of human experience uncluttered by either extensive contemporaneous occupations or population inundation through time. Interregional cultural development may be assessed at these sites with a clarity unattainable at major centers.

The Eveland site represents one of the contact sites from which Cahokia Mississippian was spread into the Central Illinois River Valley. Initially reported by the University of Chicago archaeological survey in the early 1930s, Eveland was first tested in 1958 by Joseph Caldwell of the Illinois State Museum. This test exposed approximately three quarters of Structure 1, a circular building, and several pit features. Larger field crews returned in the summers of 1959 and 1960, exposing the remainder of Structure 1 and excavating a cross-shaped structure, six rectangular buildings, and nearly 40 features associated with the Late Woodland-early Mississippian component. In 1961, excavation emphasis was shifted to the Middle Woodland components at the edges of the site (Cantwell 1980), but one burned, rebuilt Mississippian house was excavated on the gentle talus slope above Eveland.

The Eveland site excavations were undertaken as a part of a larger, informally structured research program emphasizing the Mississippian occupation of the Central Illinois River Valley. However, a secondary purpose of the work was public education. Daily tours of the Eveland excavations were carried out from Dickson Mounds Museum, located on the adjoining property. As the importance of the site became obvious during the first full summer of excavation, the Illinois Department of Conservation purchased the Eveland site property. Excavation emphasis was then shifted toward feature preservation in order to create an in situ habitation display that would complement the burial exhibit at Dickson Mounds. In addition to the circular structure, two burned buildings (Structures 2 and 6) were selected for exhibition. Structure 2 remains one of the structurally best preserved buildings ever excavated and Structure 6 is one of the few cross-shaped houses recorded. All presently are preserved under permanent housing for public viewing.

The desire to preserve the burned structures in place at Eveland created certain research barriers that affect interpretations. Temporary protective covers were positioned over the excavation areas almost from the beginning, and most excavation was done either in complete shade or inside a closed building without adequate lighting. Both the lack of natural lighting and the irregular soil moisture content caused by variable drying and artificial presoaking of excavation units often made tenuous the definition of aboriginal features. In addition, the presence of the labyrinth of charred logs, daub sections, food caches, and other floor artifacts precluded examination of large sections of the floors. Lack of total floor visibility has since resulted in much conjecture concerning the disposition of interior walls in Structure 6 and the presence of double walls on the short sides of Structure 2.

Any analysis of the Eveland site is further compromised by other unavoidable problems. Bone preservation is extremely poor due to high soil acidity. In addition, the excavations were conducted prior to the common employment of such techniques as flotation, and any resulting biological studies will provide limited comparative data for those wishing to quantify the effects of "Mississippianization" on existing subsistence systems. Likewise, field records provide the only written information available for Eveland, since Caldwell had completed only a few manuscript pages of the final report before his death in 1973.

The Dickson Mounds probably served as the cemetery for the Eveland site and possibly for other early Mississippian habitation sites in the area as well. Dickson is located on the bluff edge above Eveland and is best known for its in situ burial exhibit (Harn 1980). This exhibit resulted from a carefully planned excavation program carried out between 1927 and 1929 by Don F. Dickson, a chiropractor whose father owned the mound group, and several relatives. Under the protection of a permanent museum building built to house their excavations, these gentlemen excavated portions of Mounds E and I, exposing the remains of some 248 individuals that were left in situ along with associated burial furniture. The Dickson family museum was operated privately until it was sold to the State of Illinois in 1945.

Major excavations were undertaken at Dickson between 1966 and 1969 by the Illinois State Museum in advance of new museum construction (Conrad 1972; Harn n.d., a). Over 800 burials were recorded by this project, generating considerable new information. Long thought to have been constructed solely by Mississippian people, the excavations soon revealed Woodland components and evidence of the unique intercultural blending of Woodland and Mississippian that Caldwell had first recorded at Eveland a decade before. The Dickson excavations finally provided whole pottery vessels, a great variety of relatively complete artifact inventories, and some tangible evidence of sociopolitical organization to employ in interpretive analyses. An extensive manuscript on the Dickson excavations, completed in the mid-1970s, awaits final revision and publication (Harn n.d., a).

The relationship that existed between peoples of Cahokia and the Illinois River Valley received considerable new attention by researchers following the latest work at Dickson Mounds. Soon extensive excavations at the nearby Mississippian centers of Orendorf and Larson began to yield corroborating evidence of the intensity of the Cahokia connection. Summaries of current research quickly followed (Conrad and Harn 1972; Conrad 1973; Harn 1973, 1975a), with the primary thesis of this present study first being outlined at that time (Harn 1975b).

Much has transpired in the decade since. A series of conferences bringing together researchers focusing on Late Woodland societies throughout western Illinois has substantially increased knowledge of indigenous relationships at the time of Mississippian contact. New radiocarbon dates have been obtained, and considerable excavation and research has been carried out at sites of Late Woodland-early Mississippian amalgamation across western Illinois. Although our understanding of late prehistoric cultural exchange is still far from complete, key elements of social organization have been identified, and new perspectives on Cahokia can be offered from one of its emissaries on the northern frontier.

Eveland Site

The Eveland site is located on the Havana Terrace at the base of the western Illinois River bluff about three kilometers above the confluence of the Illinois and Spoon rivers (Figure 7.1). Surface debris on the site is light and dispersed over an area of less than two hectares. Due to the relatively thin topsoil, house areas at Eveland are sometimes clearly visible through examination of aerial photographs (Figure 7.2). This reconnaissance indicated the presence of few other structures beyond those that were excavated. However, a recent comprehensive surface survey and mapping project revealed concentrations of ceramic and lithic debris that could represent a small number of additional house locations. Short occupancy by a small number of people is indicated for the Eveland site. It is probable that its resident population was less than 50 individuals, based on the presence of perhaps less than ten domestic structures.

All structures at Eveland were oriented to cardinal directions. The central area of the site consisted of several ceremonial wall-trench structures, although contemporaneity among them cannot be demonstrated. Structure 1 is usually referred to as a circular sweat lodge. It has a cylindrical fire pit of prepared clay positioned near its center (Caldwell 1967b). It approaches the extreme size limit (about 5 m diameter) for Mississippian sweat lodges having deep fire pits from the Cahokia area and central Illinois (cf. Harn n.d., b; O'Brien 1972; Porter 1974; Wittry and Vogel 1962), and differs from most others in having internal storage facilities and evidence of domestic activities. Perhaps it was later converted to domestic use.

Thirty meters to the north of this structure were found the burned remains of a large rectangular building (Structure 2). This structure had an extended entryway protecting a south-facing door (Caldwell 1967a). A rectangular fire basin of prepared clay was positioned on the floor slightly to the north of the structure center. A similar, but circular, basin was later superimposed on it, and a fire-reddened, shallow basin was positioned between this central basin and the southeastern building corner. Lending credence to the belief that this was an important public building are the renewed fire basins, series of posts on the northwestern floor that

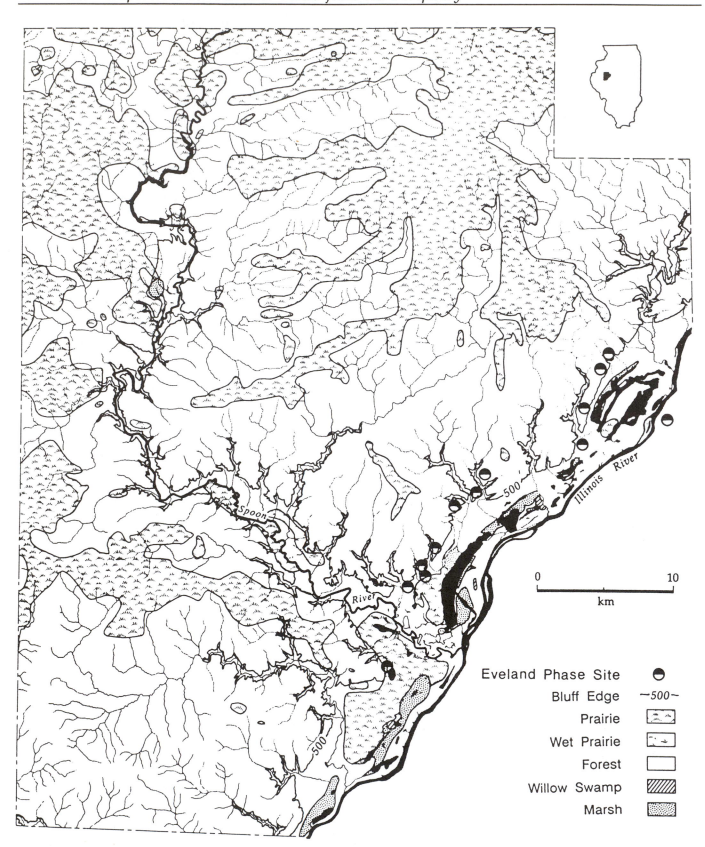

Figure 7.1. The distribution of Eveland phase sites in the Spoon River core area (vegetational communities constructed from notes and plats of the original United States land surveys; hydrology partially based on United States Army Corps of Engineers maps 1902-1904; contour interval in feet from 1949 United States Geological Survey).

Figure 7.2. Aerial photograph of the Eveland site structure clustering (ASCS negative RZ-2T-100, July 6, 1957).

suggest the presence of a raised platform, an unusually clean floor, and the absence of evidence for domestic activity (Conrad 1989:101).

An even larger building (Structure 5) was located 40 meters west of Structure 2 and may have been functionally similar. It had one internal hearth, but lacked an extended entryway. Two restorable Late Woodland Sepo Smoothed-over Cordmarked jars were crushed in the hearth, and numerous Sepo potsherds were scattered across the floor. The latest building in this area, Structure 5 was superimposed over three smaller domestic houses.

Immediately to the north of this large building was Structure 6, an unusual cross-shaped building that had been burned (Conrad 1989: 103). This somewhat asymmetrical structure appeared to be composed of a central room and four adjoining arms of roughly comparable size. However, it is not clear if these areas were open or were separately walled rooms. The in situ preservation of charcoal, a section of plastered clay daub, and preserved vegetal materials on the floor precluded complete examination of many areas and may have obscured evidence of interior walls. At least one interior wall is indicated by a large, flat section of daub along the south central side of the structure interior that had collapsed outward into the south room. Another possible indication of interior wall patterning is the fact that, prior to excavation, there was a marked color variation of the house basin fill that initially led its excavators to anticipate the presence of two superimposed structures. The fill of the east, central, and western segments was characterized by a uniformly light-colored, ashy fill, whereas the fill of the north and south segments was darker, less ashy, and more friable in texture. Possibly only the north and south arms had interior walls, causing differential burning, or perhaps remnants of standing walls across those rooms caused differential siltation in the basin filling process.

Two shallow, hard-baked fire basins were centered on the floor of the structure; one probably was earlier than the other. More materials remained on the floor of this building than in any of the other presumed ritualistic structures. A carbonized ear of corn was to the north of the hearths, and a section of daub collapsed into the south wing partially covered a mass of stored hickory nuts and shelled corn. Scattered to the south of this cache were remains of a Powell Plain jar. Other potsherds and a fragmentary pottery discoidal scattered across the floor may or may not have been associated with the structure at burning. A small pit in the south wing contained a complete miniature jar that may either indicate the presence of subadults in the structure or represent a ritualistic object. Long presumed to be a locus for specialized ceremonial activity, this building was probably functionally similar to the cross-shaped building under the Murdock Mound (Smith 1969:54-56) at Cahokia and may have shared affinities with "L" and "T"-shaped structures from that region (cf. Porter 1974; Bareis 1976).

The three probable domestic houses at the Eveland site were relatively clean of occupational debris and provide little cultural data. They are typical rectangular, wall-trench structures set in basins. Internal hearths occur in the undisturbed structures, but no internal pit features are present. All three were superimposed by Structure 5, a presumed temple or public building.

Dickson Mounds

The Dickson Mounds are located at the point of a bluff spur above the Eveland site. This burial area consists of a premound cemetery, 10 individual "mounds," and a truncated pyramidal mound and its later enlargement, which probably elevated a charnel house above the rest of the cemetery (Harn n.d., a). This complex partially encircled a large borrow pit that resulted from mound construction. The estimated 3,000 burials that comprised this cemetery represented two and one-half centuries of burial, beginning perhaps by A.D. 1000 and continuing to about A.D. 1250. Three distinct Late Woodland burial components are represented (Bauer Branch, Maples Mills, and Sepo), as well as three phases of Mississippian, (Eveland, Orendorf, and Larson). Of the more than 1,050 burials excavated at Dickson Mounds, at least 350 could have been contemporaneous with the Eveland site occupation. Less than 10 percent of these were interred in the premound cemetery, with the remainder divided among five mounds, A-E. The truncated pyramidal mound also dates to this early period. The remaining mounds represent a progressive model of cultural development and associated social and artifactual alignment as the contributing population came increasingly under Mississippian influence.

Indigenous Populations

One problem in examining Cahokia-inspired cultural interaction is the dearth of knowledge about local Late Woodland complexes during and immediately preceding the period of Mississippian expansion.

Although hundreds of Late Woodland pit and hearth features have been excavated in the Eveland site area, no Late Woodland houses have been found. Mortuary data are also scanty, and information is generally meager concerning most aspects of social organization. There exists only a poorly elucidated Late Woodland data base from which to assess the Cahokia-Central Illinois River Valley relationship.

Limestone-tempered, red-filmed ceramics (Cahokia Red-filmed and Monks Mound Red), the first elements to indicate emergent Mississippian cultural interaction between the two regions, appeared in the Central Illinois River Valley during the time of the Lohmann and Edlehardt phase occupations of Cahokia. Although only a few of these sherds have been found on sites in the Spoon River core area, a small assemblage of shell-tempered, red-filmed ceramics occurs 75 km up the Illinois River at the Rench Site (McConaughy, this volume). This may indicate that either Cahokian residency or some other form of direct interregional contact occurred prior to A.D. 1050. If these sites represent early attempts to establish advantageous trading or social relationships, the exercise may have been slow to gain momentum because of the low population density of the Central Illinois River Valley.

Habitation sites of three Late Woodland complexes, Bauer Branch, Maples Mills, and Sepo, are well represented in the Spoon River Mississippian core area. A fourth early late Woodland complex, Myer-Dickson, appears to have flourished and waned before the arrival of Mississippian in the region. This concept is developed shortly. The Bauer Branch complex is primarily centered in the Sugar Creek and LaMoine River drainages 35 km southwest of the Eveland site (Green 1976, 1977). However, small numbers of Bauer Branch pit features, along with some human burials, have been found in the Eveland site area at virtually all sites excavated in recent years. Ceramic analyses indicate that the distinctive Bauer Branch shoulder and rim stamp decorative techniques occur locally on two basic vessel forms that probably represent both Bauer Branch population intrusion and stylistic influence on the local Myer-Dickson phase population. The nature and degree of interaction between the two contemporaneous Woodland groups are currently unknown.

Most local Bauer Branch ceramics fall under Green's (1976) description of densely grit-tempered, slightly rough-textured jars with angular or sharply carinated shoulders. Vessel surfaces are frequently smooth between the rim and shoulder and marked with smoothed-over fabric or a cord-wrapped paddle below the shoulder. Weak rim castellations accompany slightly squared orifices. Other sites such as Weaver (Wray collections), Norris Farms #36, and perhaps Morton (Santure et al. 1990) have produced vessels exhibiting a blending of morphological and stylistic elements of both Bauer Branch and Myer-Dickson. The general vessel form, temper, and surface treatment of these jars is typically Myer-Dickson Smoothed-over Cordmarked, but fingernail punctations are present on shoulders and rims. A squared orifice and castellated rim are present on the only relatively complete vessel from Weaver.

It is assumed that this interaction between Bauer Branch and Myer-Dickson phase peoples took place sometime during the sixth and seventh centuries, according to the dated Myer-Dickson phase contexts. However, only the Bauer Branch complex survived late enough to have adopted such elements as triangular arrowpoints, discoidals, and corn from contemporaneous emergent Mississippian residents of the Cahokia region (Esarey et al. 1982), but the absence of fully developed Mississippian influences such as wall trench houses, formal site structuring, and an advanced level of sociopolitical organization may indicate that Bauer Branch traditions waned prior to the rise of the Stirling Phase in the Cahokia region.

The Maples Mills phase as defined by Cole and Deuel (1937:191-198) seems to have been an intrusive population, perhaps arriving in the Illinois Valley no earlier than the 10th century A.D. Its distinctive cord-decorated pottery, similar in many respects to Madison and Minots wares from the Upper Mississippi River Valley, is probably the most widely distributed Late Woodland pottery in the region. In the Eveland site area, Maples Mills sites are widely distributed in a variety of physiographic settings (Munson and Harn 1966). Aside from limited controlled excavations at the Clear Lake (Cole and Deuel 1937:187-191; Fowler 1952:133-176) and Liverpool sites (McGimsey et al. 1987), no Maples Mills habitation sites have been excavated, and little is known about domestic life patterns. Excavation of mounds F°85 and F°86 of the Gooden mound group, the type site for Maples Mills, produced nearly 100 human burials. The type and paucity of associated burial furniture, consisting primarily of utilitarian equipment and arrowpoints, exhibited neither evidence of Mississippian influence nor of complicated sociopolitical structuring. Despite the discovery of a few shell-tempered Maples Mills sherds at the Garren site and Maples Mills sherds (not vessels) on a Mississippian house floor at Garren (Wray and MacNeish n.d.), the local association between the Maples Mills and Mississippian complexes can best be described as peripheral.

The Late Woodland Sepo tradition was first recognized by Caldwell (1967a:139-142) through his excavations at Eveland in the late 1950s. His cursory description of that tradition, expanded by Harn (n.d., a), requires further revision in light of recent excavations and newly obtained radiocarbon dates that allow more precise temporal control. The Sepo tradition had a much greater time depth than originally thought (Harn 1975b), if the Myer-Dickson dates spanning the 7th century A.D. are an accurate reflection of its beginning.

This ceramic tradition may have undergone only minor transformation from its appearance around the beginning of the 7th century A.D. to its rapid amalgamation with developing Mississippian pottery traditions 500 years later. The greatest body of data concerning its earliest phase (Myer-Dickson) was generated by extensive excavations at the Myer-Dickson village, located on the blufftop behind Dickson Mounds, where well over 200 early Late Woodland pit features were excavated. The latest phase (Sepo) of this tradition is best represented by the Dickson and Eveland excavations. Although not yet analyzed and reported, the nature of the Sepo ceramics is summarized in the following manner.

> The ware is comprised almost entirely of smoothed-over cordmarked jars with semi-conoidal to slightly rounded bases, fairly pronounced shoulders, and medium-high, slightly expanding rims. These vessels are tempered with finely crushed light-colored granite, often supplemented with sand which sometimes contains oversize, smooth quartzitic pebbles. Particles of hematite are occasionally included. . . . Although the rims are frequently plain, notching or stamped decoration of the forward lip border is present in about 41 percent of the sample. This occurs in both vertical and diagonal forms. Plain dowel stamping is probably most common, but cord-wrapped dowel, individual diagonal cord impressions and punctations made with the corner of a cord-wrapped paddle are sometimes employed. Interior stamping on the lip edge is present in a small percentage of the samples from habitation areas but has not occurred in mortuary context. The size of the individual stamped forms is small, rarely exceeding 7 mm. Handles are never present (Harn 1975b:417).

To this description can now be added an additional comment about cordmarking. Although at least two Sepo Smoothed-over Cordmarked jars from the Dickson premound cemetery have "s"- twisted cordmarking, "z"-twisted impressions characterize jar surfaces in later mounds.

It previously had been thought that the Sepo ceramic assemblage developed directly out of Weaver, a terminal Middle Woodland ceramic form. Major excavations since have been undertaken at several key habitation sites in the Illinois Valley (Rench site, McConaughy this volume) and neighboring Mississippi Valley (Deer Track, McGimsey and Conner 1985; Fall Creek and Kuhlman, Hassan 1985; Wet Willie, Morgan 1985), which have provided considerable new data and an extensive series of radiocarbon dates. Although the early ancestry of the Sepo ceramic tradition has not been totally elucidated by this recent attention, some factors have become more clear. The post-A.D. 500 lifeway in the Central Illinois River valley is much more complicated than was once thought and probably involved direct elements of the indigenous Weaver phase as well as elements of extraneous populations. The type of interaction indicated by these elements poses several interesting problems, while providing answers to some other questions of long standing.

Further ceramic seriation within the Sepo phase is now possible in light of these new data. Although vessel pastes, tempering mediums, and surface finishes do not seem to change greatly through time, subtle changes in vessel form and surface treatment are apparent that allow a bipartite division of Caldwell's Sepo phase. It is proposed that the earliest portion of this division be renamed the Myer-Dickson phase. Its ceramics consist of jars similar to those described above (see also Harn n.d., b) with several important differences (Figure 7.3a-d). Myer-Dickson phase jar bases are always semiconoidal; rims are higher but tend to be less expanded in relation to their height; cordmarking is more boldly applied and cordage is predominately "s"-twisted; stamped rim-lip decoration is present on a high percentage of the vessels; and vessels are frequently tempered with dark angular rock (principally gabbro) but are never tempered with shell. Other diagnostic indicators of this proposed phase are small, corner-notched arrowpoints (Figure 7.3e-f) and the absence of corn horticulture, at least early in the occupational sequence. However, little can be said about subsistence or settlement patterns of this phase since only one site has been adequately excavated, and the remains have yet to be analyzed.

The unusually strong similarity between Myer-Dickson cordmarked ceramics from the Illinois River Valley (Figure 7.3a-d) and those of the Deer Track site (White 1985:40-41) in the neighboring Mississippi River Valley suggests that the tradition was not entirely a local expression. The Myer-Dickson phase occupation appears to have been centered in the Eveland site area and probably extended upstream along the Illinois River Valley to at least Rice Lake and downstream to the area of Anderson Lake—a total distance of about 40 kilometers. This complex may have been primarily restricted to the Illinois valley and its western bluff edge. No sites are reported in the Sand Area

Division (Schwegman 1973) on the eastern side of the Illinois River, and no sites are known from tributaries that drain the interior. Unfortunately, only two burials possibly relating to the Myer-Dickson phase have been excavated, and almost nothing can be said about its sociopolitical disposition. Clearly the phase did not extend late enough to become a part of the Mississippian movement. Dates between A.D. 500 and perhaps A.D. 900 would probably bracket the duration of the Myer-Dickson phase, although the apparent absence of corn at the Myer-Dickson site itself might suggest that its occupation was ended before the 8th century A.D.

It is proposed that the term Sepo be retained to identify that portion of the local Late Woodland phase which survived to the point of Mississippianization. As such, the term is more in keeping with Caldwell's (1967a) original proposal that was based on the amalgamated Late Woodland-early Mississippian occupation of the Eveland site.

Isolation of a representative Sepo phase artifact inventory has been impossible for that period immediately preceding the Mississippian presence, and little can be said of either its subsistence patterns or sociopolitical disposition. It is known that corn horticulture was being practiced by Sepo phase peoples, but its relative significance has not been quantified. To date, a trianguloid knife is the only nonceramic item diagnostic of the Sepo phase. Only triangular arrowpoints have been associated with this group, but all contexts are ceremonial and may not be representative of utilitarian equipment. Evidence of Sepo phase habitation has been documented at virtually all excavated sites where an Eveland phase Mississippian component is present, but none of these Sepo occupations is without evidence of Mississippian contact. Nearly 150 Sepo phase burials have been excavated, but evidence for their acculturation to Mississippian is always indicated by the presence of a wide range of Mississippian-derived burial furnishings and related advanced level of sociopolitical organization. The geographic range of Sepo also seems to be confined to the Illinois Valley proper, between the Anderson Lake and Peoria Lake regions.

Pottery representative of two of the four local Late Woodland populations (Maples Mills and Sepo) is present at the Eveland site. However, the few Maples Mills sherds at Eveland probably represent existing surface debris accidentally included in later features. Only in the Eveland phase sections of the Dickson cemetery are there even meager data concerning the temporal relationships of these Late Woodland complexes (Harn n.d., a). Bauer Branch and Myer-Dickson phase ceramics apparently were present in the premound cemetery at Dickson, but the graves and/or

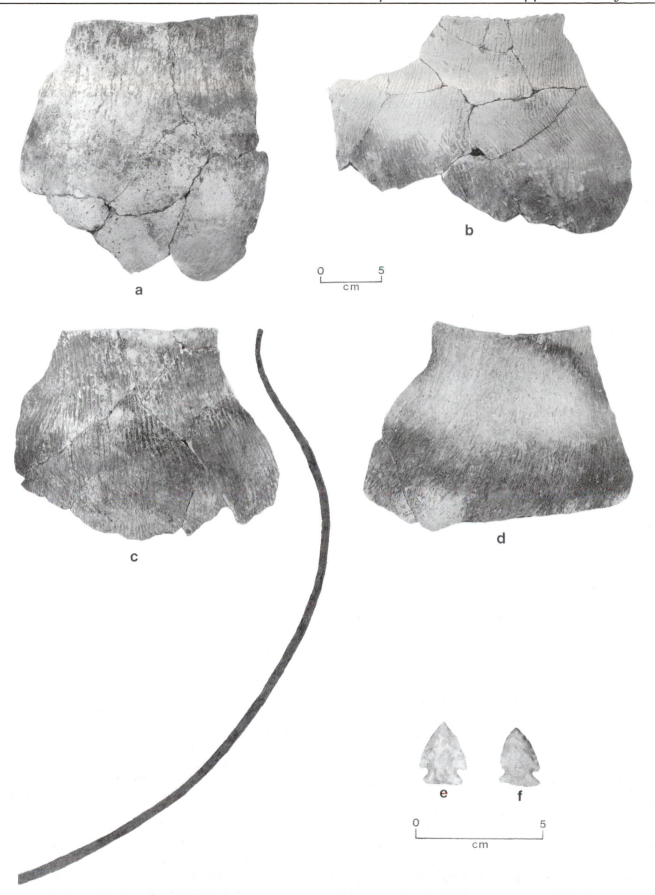

Figure 7.3. Diagnostic Myer-Dickson phase early Late Woodland ceramics and arrowpoints from the Myer-Dickson site.

associated vessels had been disturbed by later Sepo phase and early Mississippian grave-digging activity. Only the probability has been raised that the Bauer Branch and Myer-Dickson phase vessels were with stratigraphically earlier burials.

Similar disturbance compromised the Maples Mills ceramic inventory (Figure 7.4b), but some measure of cultural interaction between this group and the Sepo burial population is evident. Five Late Woodland vessels from Dickson exhibit combined characteristics of both Maples Mills and Sepo phase ceramics (cf. Figure 7.4e-f; Figure 7.5a). Vessel shapes, surface finishes, and paste characteristics are essentially representative of Sepo Smoothed-over Cordmarked, but the rims are either castellated, have four lugs, or have a cord-impressed triangle design, all more characteristic of Maples Mills. A sixth specimen has four lugs placed on a notched rim over a boldly cordmarked, bag-shaped body, creating a vessel that defies traditional categorization. It is not easily attributable to any local Late Woodland complex.

Two other Woodland vessels illustrate further complexity in the composition of Late Woodland society at Mississippian contact (Figure 7.4a; Figure 7.5b). One is a small jar, unclassified as to type, that has diagonally applied cordmarking on the body and a collared rim that is suggestive of Late Woodland ceramics from northern and eastern Illinois (cf. Hall n.d.; Douglas 1976). The second is a typical Sepo jar that has a clay fillet decorated with three horizontally cord-impressed bands applied in a technique that is reminiscent of Woodland cultures from northeastern Iowa westward to the Plains.

Injecting other elements into an already complicated Late Woodland culture history, many vessels are represented at both Eveland and Dickson that were apparently either traded or somehow transported into the Central Illinois River Valley from the Great Oasis area 500 kilometers to the west. Included in this foreign ceramic inventory are rim sherds of Chamberlain Incised, Cambria Type C, McVey Pinched Fillet, McVey Tool Decorated, and one rim similar to Beckman Tool Decorated. One burned domestic structure on the hillslope above the Eveland Site had a restorable McVey Tool Decorated jar on its floor. Foreman Incised ceramics also were represented, and this foreign style was apparently copied by local potters (Harn 1975b: Fig. 2h). The small numbers of recovered ceramics and, with the exception of a bison scapula hoe, the paucity of other artifacts do not seem to indicate a resident population of these western groups, however.

In summary, the Eveland site area had a very complex local Late Woodland history that researchers incompletely understand. Although limited interregional contact seemed to characterize early Late Woodland cultural relationships, external connections gradually developed that linked a mosaic of widely dispersed complexes. The Mississippian intrusion further compounded this complexity but, in a very real sense for the archaeologist, it often instilled order to the cultural complexity by quickly absorbing the evidence.

Eveland Phase Settlement Pattern

Sites producing classic Powell Plain and Ramey Incised ceramics, the earliest indicators of Mississippian presence, are widely scattered throughout the Central Illinois River Valley. They occur in a variety of physiographic situations, but most are limited to either slopewash or terrace locations within the Illinois valley or to bordering blufftops. Few Eveland phase sites are known to be situated in the uplands over one kilometer back of the bluff edge. The spatial distribution of the 13 recorded Eveland phase sites in the central Spoon River area is primarily along the western bluffline of the Illinois River Valley, beginning at a point just below the confluence of the Spoon and Illinois River valleys and continuing for some 30 km up the Illinois (Figure 7.1). Eight sites occur on the Illinois River blufftop, and four are positioned on terraces at the bluff base. Only one Eveland phase habitation site is located on the low, sand bluff bordering the eastern side of the Illinois River, and its position there may have been in response to a unique gardening opportunity (Harn 1976:8). A similar settlement pattern avoiding this sand expanse also is indicated for later Mississippian groups (Harn 1978:244-245).

Well documented information concerning the Eveland phase occupation is limited to only a few sites. Dickson Mounds is the only mortuary site to be carefully excavated, and its archaeological record has sometimes been compromised by previous looting. Five other cemeteries have been partially or totally impacted by local investigators who kept only cursory field records of their digging activities. Although additional information about some of these explorations has been gained by personal interviews with the original participants, much information has been lost. Controlled excavations have been carried out at six Eveland phase habitation sites, but with the exception of Eveland, these usually consisted of limited tests that exposed few features. One eroding pit feature was excavated by the landowner at a seventh habitation site, but only the ceramics were saved. Eveland Phase house structures are recorded only at Eveland and at the Garren site by Wray's poorly documented excavation.

Sites of the Eveland phase are characteristically small, with the majority probably covering less than one hectare. Populations of less than 50 individuals may have characterized a majority of the larger occu-

Figure 7.4. Late Woodland jars from Dickson Mounds: (a) unclassified, collared rim, (b) Maples Mills cord-decorated, (c-d) Sepo Smoothed-over Cordmarked, (e) Sepo Smoothed-over Cordmarked with Maples Mills cord decoration, (f) Sepo Smoothed-over Cordmarked with Maples Mills rim treatment.

Figure 7.5. Amalgamated Late Woodland jars and Eveland phase Mississippian jars from Dickson Mounds: (a) undecorated Maples Mills-like with atypical low rim, (b) Sepo Smoothed-over Cordmarked with Plains-like cord-decorated neck fillet, (c-d) Sepo Plain, (e) Powell Plain, (f) Ramey Incised.

pations, but most sites probably consisted of either a few structures or of single homesteads. Sparse artifact scatters on these sites are indicative of occupational brevity, a proposition generally supported by the limited excavations that have been conducted. Especially in instances of single homesteads, it is probable that some Eveland phase sites have been overlooked by researchers or swamped by later, more intensive Mississippian habitations. However, considering their small size, occupational brevity, and the suggestion that many probably represent succeeding occupations by the same group, the Eveland phase sites of the Central Illinois River Valley did not represent a large population intrusion. Yet, this small population may have been statistically more significant than is now obvious, for present evidence would tend to indicate that the population density of the resident Woodland peoples may also have been low.

The frequency of ritualistic structures at the Eveland site probably is not typical of all sites of this occupation, and it is assumed that Eveland and perhaps a few other sites represent small religious/political centers. However, there is nothing about their size or physiographic location to provide criteria for their apparent emergence as social centers. Perhaps site importance was more closely linked to chance residency by important individuals and/or availability of convertible clients than to the factors of economic or subsistence resource maximization evident with later Mississippian horizons. During the Eveland phase, there is no indication locally of the highly structured community organizational scheme consisting of fortified central towns with plazas and temple mounds that characterized contemporary Stirling Phase Cahokia, or that would characterize succeeding Spoon River Mississippian occupations.

Among Eveland phase sites, there does not appear to have been the intrasite crowding and great functional or seasonal diversity that later characterized Mississippian occupations faced with increased populations and depleted resources (Harn 1978: Figure 13.2, 1986, n.d., c). Sites may have been occupied year round, since internal cooking and heating facilities are present in the few Eveland phase domestic houses to be carefully excavated and recorded (Eveland site field records). Such occurrences often contrast with the seasonally specific occupational schemes of later Mississippian groups.

Although there is a paucity of subsistence data from the Eveland site, such data for the Eveland phase are available from recent excavations at the Norris Farms #26 Site located 1.6 km upriver. Extensive excavations at that site produced a large, shallow midden-filled depression that covered a series of 12 overlapping pit features representing an uninterrupted cul-

tural sequence from Sepo phase Late Woodland through Larson phase Mississippian (Harn 1991). The Sepo-Eveland phase pits, although containing evidence of both corn and wild plant utilization, exhibited greater evidence of animal exploitation with especially high incidences of fish and riverine fauna.

In viewing the dispersed Eveland phase settlement system, one is impressed with the seemingly random site locations, low-level political organization, and varied resource base. Perhaps the environmental richness of the region successfully offset the need for rigid social organization to maintain Mississippian cultural and economic stability—at least to a point when human population pressures began to strain natural resources. Although it is probable that hoe horticulture was practiced at a majority of the Eveland phase sites, it is unrealistic to view such settlements solely as "farmsteads" since such a wide variety of hunting and foraging activities was concomitantly pursued. Lack of integrated sociopolitical aggregations in favor of the maintenance of small, somewhat domestically independent social units is thus indicated for the Eveland phase occupation of the Central Illinois River Valley.

Mississippian Intrusion

Although there is general agreement that some Cahokia Mississippians were residing in the Central Illinois River Valley before A.D. 1100, what social units were represented and what factors underlay their emigration is still the subject of much debate. It seems doubtful that population pressures in the Cahokia region were a major causal factor in light of the small number of sites and individuals represented by the intrusion. However, even relatively minor population pressures could have stimulated movement among certain groups. The fertile and resource rich Illinois Valley would have been an attractive location for anyone seeking greater domestic isolation, and the absence of highly structured sociopolitical organization among Eveland phase sites might argue for this more casual model of emigration.

The Mississippian intrusion also might be viewed in terms of political emigration in the aftermath of social upheaval within the Cahokia sphere, with sites such as Eveland representing residences of subordinate leaders who had been forced out of the Cahokia governing polity. Conversely, these occupations could represent residences of individuals within the governing polity who recognized an opportunity to convert new resources into personal power. The lack of central hierarchy among Eveland phase sites might then suggest that leaders of relatively equal power were initially operating within the Illinois Valley.

Closely tied to this scheme would be a third alternative, colonization. This settlement scheme could have been incidentally stimulated by the political emigration model just proposed, or it could have represented the direct mandate of a Cahokia ruling lineage attempting to dominate regional resources. Since Cahokia was located just below the juncture of the major arteries into its hinterlands (the Missouri, Illinois, and upper Mississippi rivers), it would have been strategically positioned downriver from any colony to facilitate shipment of quantities of goods. However, politically structured colonization would seem to have required the local presence of centralized authority with major regulatory mechanisms to control an area so far removed from the culture center. The absence of important Eveland phase religious/political centers in the Central Illinois River Valley tends to argue against highly structured political domination, although it is obvious that some very important individuals were locally resident.

Many of the Eveland phase contact settlements could represent events no more culturally complex than the return of individuals (who happened to grow up as Mississippian urbanites) to their own homelands or the migration of others to areas occupied by rural (Woodland) relatives. Some of the contact sites could also represent trading outposts of a Cahokia merchant class. Any site with that orientation would have been of pivotal importance in terms of acculturating the indigenous population. Perhaps by these uncomplicated avenues, increasing numbers of Mississippians initially filtered into the Illinois valley before its potential for exploitation became recognized by persons of greater authority.

Present knowledge of the Eveland phase settlement system does not favor one of the above models of Mississippian intrusion over any other. It is suspected that, to some degree, parts of all of the above models might be appropriate for explaining the Mississippian presence into the Spoon River area of Illinois.

The most convincing evidence of the Cahokia influences on the Eveland site area were the shell-tempered ceramic types, Ramey Incised and Powell Plain. These arrived in thin-walled, angular-shouldered, and rolled-rim forms that are virtually indistinguishable from classic Stirling phase wares at Cahokia. Pastes of these vessels have a very smooth texture, lacking the intentional addition of sand that characterizes shell-tempered pastes of chronologically later Spoon River ceramics. The Powell-Ramey jar form and the Ramey decorative mode would be the precursor of several later ceramic styles. A wide variety of other shell-tempered vessel forms arrived with the baggage of Mississippian, including hooded and short-necked bottles, Tippits bean pots, plain and effigy bowls, and plain globular and lobed jars. All of these forms are present in the Dickson cemetery, and most are represented at Eveland as well.

In describing early Mississippian ceramic decorative trends, Harn (1975b:420) states that:

> Common forms of decoration on Ramey Incised jars include single or nested arcs or chevrons, nested straight lines semicurled on one end, "feathered" simple scrolls, diamonds, circles with punctations and, rarely, forked eyes. These elements are arranged around the vessel shoulder and are often connected by single horizontal trails or occasionally separated by single diagonal trails. Elaborate scroll motifs are seldom seen, the decorative elements showing a trend toward rectilinear patterns characteristic of well-developed Ramey.

It cannot be over emphasized how "classic" these early Mississippian vessels are by traditional Cahokia standards. There is little doubt that they were manufactured by potters long experienced in the production of extremely thin-walled, finely executed forms. Because of the relative isolation of the Eveland site, it probably can be assumed that such ceramic purity would only be possible among the original potters retaining traditional Cahokia ceramic standards, or perhaps by "second generation" potters trained by these persons. This period of ceramic purity probably could have been extended by a continued influx of potters from the Cahokia region, but this does not appear to have been the case. Stratigraphically later Powell Plain and Ramey Incised ceramics from the Dickson cemetery are less well executed, and this sequence quickly degenerates into the trailed jar tradition of the following Orendorf phase.

It has been long suspected that many of the classic Powell Plain and Ramey Incised jars in the Spoon River area were originally manufactured in the Cahokia region and transported to the Illinois River Valley. Although researchers have generally stopped short in print of formally identifying these vessels as imports, all other local early Mississippian ceramic forms traditionally have been weighed against these suspected "trade" vessels as a barometer of their relative "Mississippianness."

In order to clarify this problem, eight early Mississippian vessels from the Eveland site and Dickson Mounds were thin sectioned. This sample consisted of four "imported" Ramey Incised and Powell Plain jars and three Ramey jars and one bowl that were suspected, based upon visual observation, to be of local manufacture. In addition to this intracultural comparison, sections of a shell-tempered Sepo Smoothed-over Cordmarked jar from Dickson Mound A and two Myer-Dickson phase jars from the Myer-Dickson site were analyzed as examples from contemporary and chronologically earlier indigenous Woodland populations. Later, several more Myer-Dickson phase vessels were thin-sectioned, along with test tiles of East Creek clay, a local clay source known to have been exploited aboriginally. Two bottomland clay sources in the area also were collected for comparison, but neither was found to approximate the aboriginal samples. The floodplain sample (Norris Farms clay) was far too sandy, and the terrace sample (Eveland clay) from the creek bank behind the Eveland Site was too silty for compatibility (Figures. 7.6 and 7.7.).

Figures 7.6 and 7.7 provide results of the thin section project, which was carried out by James B. Stoltman. Analysis of these data reveals that the eight Powell Plain and Ramey Incised vessels are very uniform with regard to general paste characteristics and tempering percentages. Two of the early Late Woodland Myer-Dickson phase vessels also fall within or near to the Eveland cluster to suggest that they were made from similar clays. The remaining Myer-Dickson phase vessels were all made of sandier clays. The single late Sepo jar closely resembles this Myer-Dickson sample, although it is slightly more sandy.

Stoltman's overall impression of the ceramic sample is that the Late Woodland vessels were being produced from at least two different clay sources, one of which was similar to that source used in the early Mississippian Eveland phase ceramics. All of the Eveland phase sample could have been made from a single clay source, regardless of the individual quality of vessel manufacture, or of social context, and vessel characteristics exhibit such group homogeneity that they seem to be the product of a single people. The use of East Creek clay by indigenous Woodland groups and the plotting of the East Creek clay test tile within the Eveland phase group in Figure 7.6 is very convincing. The common occurrence of Cahokian "trade" vessels in the Central Illinois River Valley must now be viewed with increased skepticism.

Non-ceramic artifacts identified with the Mississippian intrusion at the Eveland-Dickson complex include such domestic equipment as rectangular wall-trench houses set in shallow basins, rectanguloid celts, triangular and notched triangular arrowpoints, potter's trowels, the widespread use of sandstone slot abraders, corn, and perhaps salt. Ritualistic equipment was dominated by marine shell bead ensembles that included a variety of headbands, forelock beads, necklaces, bracelets, anklets, sashes, and beads worn in the hair and sewn on clothing. *Busycon* pendants and a long-nosed god mask of marine shell also occurred.

Other ritualistic equipment included copper-covered earspools of wood and stone, discoidals, Ramey knives, rattles, and tattooing equipment. A circular sweat lodge, extended human burials made in the flesh, and possible human sacrifice provide further confirmation of an early Mississippian presence. Not present at either Eveland or Dickson are block effigy pipes and hoes of Mill Creek chert that are commonly associated with Mississippian culture. One bison scapula hoe at Eveland and widespread distribution of corn in pit features and in Structure 6 indicate that cultivation was a viable part of the Mississippian presence, but whether extensive corn horticulture preceded this acculturation period in the Spoon River area is a possibility that will only be clarified with further excavation.

As mentioned previously, there is nothing locally to suggest that Eveland participated in an interregional settlement or political network involving complex town construction and temple mound ceremonialism. This is not meant to indicate that salient Mississippian religious/political practices were not being followed at Eveland, for indeed they were. The absence of grandiose sociopolitical expressions simply may indicate that Eveland phase populations were small, competition from indigenous populations was fairly light, and natural resources were initially so plentiful that regulation of the people either was not required or could be exercised on a more individualized basis.

The complex, non-egalitarian social organization with a privileged, elite class evidenced in Dickson Mounds burials is undoubtedly attributable to the Mississippian movement. Elements of this organization adversely affected all members of subordinate groups regardless of age or sex, but it had its most severe impact on females, who rarely attained positions of importance within the society (Harn 1980:28-29; n.d., a). There is compelling evidence to suggest that these same Mississippian social patterns severely affected the health of its female population as well. Analyzing vertebral growth patterns of heterochrony, allometry, and canalization that permit inferences into health not possible using traditional paleopepidemiological techniques, George Clark (1985) derived important biocultural data separating the Sepo Late Woodland and Mississippian populations at Dickson Mounds. He concluded that, although Mississippian males enjoyed much better postnatal health than Late Woodland males, Mississippian females declined substantially in both prenatal and postnatal health. Adverse affects of other Mississippian life patterns are discussed in some detail by Blakely (1971), Blakely and Walker (1968), Goodman and Armelagos (1985), Goodman et al. (1980), Goodman and Clark (1979), Lallo (1972, 1973), Lallo et al. (1977, 1978, 1980), Lallo and Rose (1979), Milner (1983, 1984), and Rose et al.(1978).

Figure 7.6. Relationship of three local clay sources to pastes of selected Spoon River area ceramics (temper excluded).

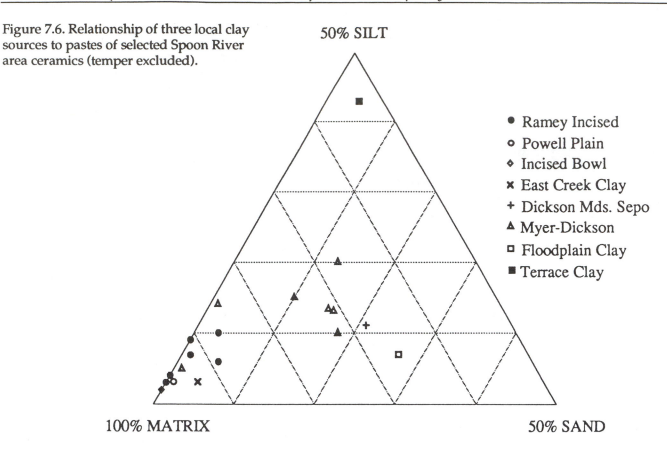

- ● Ramey Incised
- ○ Powell Plain
- ◆ Incised Bowl
- ✕ East Creek Clay
- ＋ Dickson Mds. Sepo
- ▲ Myer-Dickson
- ◻ Floodplain Clay
- ◼ Terrace Clay

Figure 7.7. Relationship of three local clay sources to pastes of selected Spoon River area ceramics (temper included).

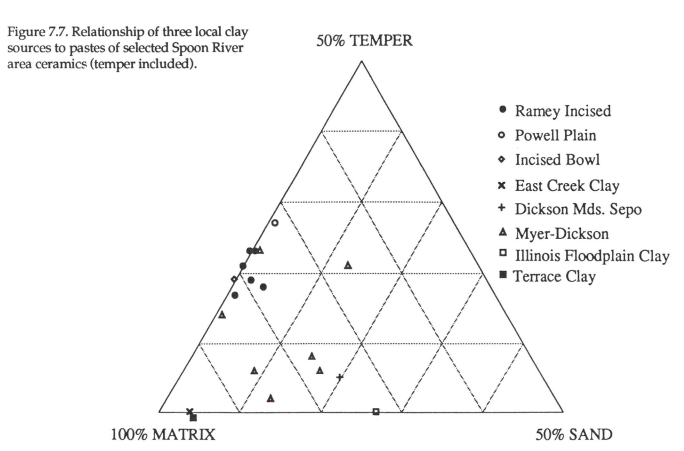

- ● Ramey Incised
- ○ Powell Plain
- ◆ Incised Bowl
- ✕ East Creek Clay
- ＋ Dickson Mds. Sepo
- ▲ Myer-Dickson
- ◻ Illinois Floodplain Clay
- ◼ Terrace Clay

The appearance of large public buildings and smaller structures of specific ritualistic nature at early sites such as Eveland confirm the presence of complex Mississippian social organization. However, the general lack of in situ artifact inventories within the structures leaves a considerable gap in our understanding of what types of activities transpired, how they were undertaken, and who performed them. Many insights into these processes can be gained by examining the mortuary precincts.

Tangible grave goods are associated with approximately one half of the burials at Dickson Mounds and occur in the form of finished and raw materials, tool kits, and facilities. Ownership of most burial furniture is at least partially dependent on age and sex. Burial furnishings frequently include a wide variety of artifacts that relate to the normal day-to-day activities of the individual, contributed goods, gifts not actually owned by the person, pieces sometimes associated with the person's craft skills, and items intimately associated with the deceased. Included in the latter category are certain articles, usually of minor ritualistic nature, that functioned as symbols to distinguish individuals ranking as heads of office or holding other subordinate positions within the local group. Certain of these individuals, such as Burial 1000 in Mound J (who was buried with a large copper gorget with cross, circle, and sunburst repoussé, bead ensemble, and more than 80 other artifacts), were obviously much more important than the others, but it is doubtful that any member of the highest ruling lineage is buried at Dickson Mounds (Harn 1980:27-29; n.d., a).

One additional indicator of distinctive Mississippian ritualistic activity is first evident during the Eveland phase. Probable human sacrifice of ingroup members is recorded in Dickson Mound B and possibly in the premound cemetery at Dickson (Harn 1975b:427-428; n.d., a). The killing and beheading of four males (Conrad 1989:104), followed by the periodic reopening of their burial pit for both addition and removal of other individuals is ritualistically similar to the situation recorded in Cahokia Mound 72 (Fowler, this volume).

Woodland-Early Mississippian Relationships: The Rise of the Spoon River Mississippian Tradition

As evidenced by the discussion of Late Woodland relationships in the Eveland site area, the 11th century was a pivotal period marked by widespread regional contacts that brought together several localized societies and a mosaic of individual technologies. Into this complicated cultural backdrop were injected new elements of Mississippian culture that dramatically altered indigenous lifeways.

The most easily quantified of these influences pertain to the Sepo phase ceramic industry. Although the smoothed-over cordmarked jar remained the most popular Late Woodland ceramic form, its conoidal base had become more rounded and shell tempering was sometimes present by this time (Figure 7.4c-d). Some indigenous potters began production of a second jar form, Sepo Plain (Harn 1975b:418-419), which was unquestionably influenced by the early Mississippian ceramic types Powell Plain and Ramey Incised, although never achieving their design complexities (Figure 7.5c-d). Handles appeared for the first time on some of these jars. Although almost all of these vessels are undecorated, Sepo Plain jars with zig-zag lines and line-filled ovals rudely incised onto their shoulders recently have been excavated at the Norris Farms #26 site. This is presently the best indication that some elements of Ramey symbolism were adapted to the indigenous ceramics as well.

The spatial distribution of Sepo Plain is difficult to assess for one particular reason. Virtually everywhere on the Mississippian frontier that there is evidence of Sterling phase intrusion into a Late Woodland enclave, excavation documents the indigenous production of plain jars that are similar to but rarely the artistic equivalent of Powell Plain. Although lacking the structured stylization of their Mississippian counterparts, these copies are still so ubiquitous in their casual form and surface treatment that they exhibit strong physical similarities among themselves, even though they may be spatially segregated by hundreds of kilometers. Where once many of these regionally aberrant vessels were viewed as Sepo Plain (Harn 1975b:419), we would now discourage the use of that type designation much outside the Sepo phase core area in the Central Illinois River Valley. Although, these "hybridized" vessels do reflect fundamentally similar interactive relationships throughout the Midwest, they obviously were being produced by a host of unrelated Late Woodland populations.

Other Late Woodland-early Mississippian ceramic relationships are not as easily quantified. Although there is ample evidence of cross-cultural relationships among the four indigenous Late Woodland groups just preceding and coeval with the Eveland site occupation, only the Sepo phase group had documented ties with Mississippian that directly affected their technology and mortuary behavior (Harn 1975b:424). On the basis of the few Maples Mills potsherds found at the Eveland site, it cannot be proposed that this group was even interacting with the Eveland occupation, and no Mississippian influences are evident in any of their mortuary contexts in the area. Wray's (Wray and McNeish n.d.) excavation of three Eveland phase houses at the Garren site, 17 km upriver, produced fragments of a Maples Mills jar that was shell-tempered; it remains the most tangible evidence of Mississippian influence on the Maples Mills population in the Spoon River area of Illinois. Likewise, the few Maples Mills sherds on a Mississippian house floor at Garren are viewed as a poor indicator of contemporaneity in light of the possibility of their reposition. Whole vessels would be more convincing. If the two groups were contemporaneous, Maples Mills appears to have been little affected ceramically by the Mississippian presence.

Other aspects of technology and social organization can be employed to quantify the Mississippian presence but, in the absence of recognized effects on other local Late Woodland groups, these aspects are also specific to the Sepo-Eveland phase amalgamation. Although little beyond ceramic seriation can be derived from the Eveland site excavations, widespread evidence of cultural accommodation is present in the Dickson cemetery. There, a wide variety of Mississippian-derived burial furnishings began to appear with the Sepo interments. Initially included were notched triangular arrowpoints, Ramey knives of Mill Creek chert, discoidals, copper-covered stone and wood earspools, ceramic effigy bowls, and beakers that were occasionally smoothed-over cordmarked in a more traditional Sepo technique.

Changes were taking place in other aspects of Sepo ceremonialism, although our understanding of their implications is far from complete. The typical semi-flexed and flexed Woodland burial modes gradually gave way to extended positions during the period of amalgamation represented by the first six burial units at Dickson. As a result, Sepo series Woodland jars placed with extended burials substantially increased in frequency, although, conversely, some semiflexed Woodland burials received classic Ramey Incised and Powell Plain jars. Expressions of wealth and social stature, represented by increased numbers of tools, weapons, and ornaments, became common with flexed interments but varied considerably in quantity among the graves.

Other aspects of exotic ceremonialism are evident within the Dickson cemetery. The Late Woodland society was well represented, at least ceramically, by three of the four pottery vessels placed with the sacrificed headless burials in the highly ritualistic, rectangular burial pit in Mound B (Harn 1975 b:427-428). Flexed burials also characterized the primary figures in a similar grave in the premound cemetery (Harn n.d., a). Woodland participation in important sociopo-

litical activities also may be indicated by the presence of the Sepo jars on the hearth of Structure 5, the largest public building at the Eveland site.

By the middle of the 12th century A.D., the local Late Woodland Sepo community clearly had embarked upon a course of nonegalitarian social organization that contrasted markedly with that of its recent ancestry. For all practical purposes, its people were functioning as integral members of Mississippian society.

Although Late Woodland individuals apparently were not denied lower level leadership positions within this developing society, the following proposal would seem to preclude their initial elevation to pivotal positions within the hierarchy.

> It is doubtful that the impetus behind these particular expressions of so highly an organized and ranked society originated in the Central Illinois Valley. It would be difficult attributing their development to a region so sparsely populated with what was basically a hunting and gathering society. . . . Was the level of Late Woodland sociopolitical organization such that existing ruling lineages might easily have been incorporated into the advanced state-level organization which characterized the Mississippian movement? Nothing in the region would support this position. Nor does it seem probable that the existing Woodland hierarchy was established as the principal prophet of local Mississippianization; for extending the ruling lineage of the vast Mississippian movement so simply surely would have insured the loss of much of its distinctiveness. . . . Furthermore, if the basic motivation behind Mississippian expansion into the hinterlands was exploitive and associated with economic networks focused on Cahokia (as opposed to a more symbiotic extractive-exchange relationship), it is doubtful that retention of indigenous rulers would have been compatible with the aims of the movement (Harn 1975b:429).

Summary

Excavations of an 11th century A.D. occupation at the Eveland site and its cemetery at Dickson Mounds provide unique insights into the processes of cultural change and continuity as the phenomenon called Mississippian spread throughout Late Woodland societies of the upper Midwest. Although neither of the sites was excavated in its entirety nor is yet reported in a form that is readily available to all researchers, sufficient data are generated to document some aspects of the role Cahokia played in the emergence of Mississippian in the Spoon River area of Illinois.

By late in the 11th century A.D., distinctive elements of Mississippian culture, characterized by a highly structured, nonegalitarian society, abruptly appeared in a Late Woodland culture area occupied by groups displaying a much less complex level of social organization. Viewing this phenomenon either in terms of exploitive colonization or as a symbiotic/extractive relationship requires a common prerequisite—commodity exchange. Tangible commodities and innovations coming from the direction of Cahokia were profuse and included a variety of domestic and ceremonial equipment needed to pursue the developing Mississippian lifeway. Domestic technology was dominated by sophisticated engineering, wall-trench houses, deep storage pits, a variety of ceramic forms, triangular and notched triangular arrowpoints, rectanguloid celts, a very few hoes of Mill Creek chert, corn, and perhaps salt. Fortifications soon followed. A wide range of social and ceremonial regalia appeared to validate the various status levels of the new social order. At Dickson, this equipment is dominated by marine shell ornaments which primarily consist of whole ensembles or single examples of beaded items. Marine shell pendants, gorgets, and a long-nosed god mask are also present. Copper items were limited principally to copper-covered wood and stone earspools, although some beads, imitation puma canine ear pendants, and a repoussé gorget appeared in later mounds. Other ritualistic equipment probably traded through Cahokia included Ramey knives of Mill Creek and Kaolin cherts, discoidals, and elbow pipes. Circular sweat lodges, possible human sacrifice, and extended burials were probably other Mississippian-derived traits. Although their initial appearance may have preceded Mississippian by many centuries, the widespread use of rattles and tatooing may be indicative of the Mississippian movement. Not found at either Eveland or Dickson, but present in the area, are stone block effigy pipes.

What then was given in exchange? It is presently impossible to isolate any commodity at Cahokia that could be specifically attributed solely to the Spoon River area of Illinois. Other than coal (which, surprisingly, was never exploited by aboriginal populations), no abundant mineral resources exist in the area, although other natural resources are quite plentiful (cf. Anderson 1951; Harn 1980:4-8). The vast forests would have provided seasonally abundant mast crops, as well as firewood and building materials (although I have much personal difficulty imagining a 250 km Mississippian log flotilla to Cahokia), and such important large animals as the turkey and bear. Deer and elk would have been abundant in the forest margin and prairie edge zones, as would a variety of smaller animals and many fruits and tubers that have good drying and shipping potential. The riverine zone probably held the greatest potential biomass locally, offering a wide variety of fish and other animal and plant resources. The sporadic prairie segments locally provided an abundant source of long grass thatch for house construction, but significant volume requisites per house and transportation distance would have certainly discouraged much extralocal shipping. Rich farmland also abounded in the area, but its exploitation would have required a considerable labor expenditure in deforestation. In addition to the food potential of the region, an endless list of raw materials for manufactured products, ranging from medicine (Harn and Koelling 1974) to canoes, could have been readily garnered from the natural environment. Even the contribution of human labor cannot be omitted from the potential exchange list. Unfortunately, little indication of any of these commodities has survived.

How would any type of exchange system involving potentially perishable products be mirrored in the archaeological record? No extensive midden deposits with bone accumulations are evident at any Eveland phase site, and there is no other evidence locally of surplus production or economic over-exploitation of local resources during the Eveland phase, or probably any succeeding phase for that matter. Of course, most local evidence of over-exploitation would be lost if animals were field processed and shipped out of the region in relatively complete segments without further processing at the local habitation sites.

The relative paucity of corn could be explained in the same manner. Although corn is present at all excavated Eveland phase sites, no large quantities are known. In viewing excavated Mississippian sites of all phases, corn is less well represented at smaller sites, and its increased presence seems to correlate with greater site size and occupational permanence. However, even at the largest local habitation, the Larson site town, corn constituted only a small portion of the diet when weighed against the total volume of other food remains. While still recognizing its potential for adversely affecting Mississippian health in a manner disproportionate to its total ingestion (Goodman and Armelagos 1985), corn becomes even less significant nutritionally when the multitude of non-tangible dietary elements of wild floral produce are also considered (Harn and Baerreis n.d.). However, rather than representing depletion via external exchange, the low incidence of corn may simply reflect modest utilization. Analysis of several Larson phase farmsteads suggests that gardening areas may not have been especially large and individual families were responsible primarily for their own horticultural production (Harn 1991).

Despite the presence of corn and the later influx of beans into the economy (Harn and Baerreis n.d.), basic Mississippian subsistence, emphasizing the exploitation of available natural products, may have continued in much the same form as it had for the previous several centuries of Woodland occupation in the Central Illinois River Valley. Local Mississippian settlement patterns seem more closely to reflect an expediently interrelated extractive system than a complexly interrelated system of sociopolitical organization (Harn 1978, 1983, n.d., c). This is not seen as a departure from traditional Cahokia Mississippian practices so much as it is viewed as a more energy-efficient method of existing in a region rich in natural resources. If populations had been smaller at Cahokia, the heavily horticulturally-based economy of the American Bottom probably would never have developed to the degree that it did. From a subsistence standpoint, the lesser degree that corn horticulture was practiced at sites across the northern Mississippian frontier probably should not be weighted heavily as an indicator of relative "Mississippianness," especially if sufficient natural food resources existed locally. Conversely, if corn is proven to have held important Mississippian religious connotations, as it did among historic groups throughout the American Southeast, it might be more effectively employed as a barometer of Mississippian presence.

Frequencies of certain artifact types, primarily hunting-processing and horticultural equipment, may offer clues to the developing Mississippian economy, but not without raising unanswered questions. We previously outlined interregional proportional differences of these artifact frequencies, contrasting the unusually large numbers of hoes and low numbers of arrowpoints and processing tools in the American Bottom with an opposing emphasis on these tool classes in the Central Illinois River Valley (Harn 1971:37-38; 1980:74). These proportional differences were in part attributed to differing economies influenced by variables of human population pressure and availability of natural resources. Meat packing and hide trading also were identified as additional practices that might have contributed to substantial increases in arrowpoint and butchering and hide-working tool production (Harn n.d., c). However, the continued focus on arrowpoints primarily as hunting equipment could mask the possibility that increased arrowpoint numbers may also be indicators of growing social stresses—an especially important consideration in light of the simultaneous appearance of fortifications in the Central Illinois River Valley.

In discussing nutritional relationships between Cahokia and its hinterlands, physical anthropologists Alan Goodman and George Armelagos (1985:18) proposed that Cahokian exploitation of available food resources was so severe during the post-Eveland phase period at Dickson Mounds that it was detrimental to the health of the local population. Aside from having no artifactual evidence to support this proposed over-exploitation, their argument fails to address some basic causal factors concerning the wide differences in health between the two areas. Recent excavations in the Cahokia area have demonstrated that much of the Mississippian population resided in small farmsteads, usually comprised of one or two structures, which were widely dispersed over the bottomlands (Milner and Williams 1981a-b). Their relative isolation, small numbers of residents, and short term occupations probably resulted in minimal environmental contamination and correspondingly high levels of individual health.

At the other extreme are the Mississippian settlements in the Illinois valley. These occupations often consisted of hundreds of individuals consolidated into a single settlement that was sometimes confined by a fortification wall. Such sites were frequently occupied for several generations (Harn 1978; n.d., b). The spread of disease pathogens by frequent daily contact would have been greatly enhanced by these living conditions, as would transmission of disease through garbage disposal and the accumulation of human waste. One would expect that, without careful sanitary controls, such conditions would have contaminated the soil and associated food products and perhaps nearby water resources as well.

If most researchers in the Central Illinois River Valley are correct in proposing that the Eveland phase population was relatively small, could it really have contributed significantly as a resource base for a Cahokian population often estimated at numbering tens of thousands? If it contributed in this manner without the support of other Midwestern satellites, its major contribution was probably confined to the pockets of members of the governing polity. In discussing this same exchange system, Porter (1969) points out that in addition to its obvious importance as the religious/political center of northern Mississippian life, Cahokia may have served an almost equally important role as market place and redistribution center. Thus, precise determination of the true nature of the Cahokian influence may be a moot point. If residents of the Illinois Valley were not in fact politically dominated by Cahokia, they may have been just as surely ensnared by its munificence.

There is presently no evidence to suggest that the Cahokia presence in the Central Illinois River Valley represented an extension of the Cahokia ruling lineage that was forcibly imposed upon a resisting indigenous population. Neither did the rapid Mississippianization of the Woodland culture appear to have resulted either from population submersion by a superior number of Cahokians or from population decimation. Virtually no indication of warfare or violence is present in the early cemeteries. Implications are that many Woodland occupants of central Illinois were already developing toward a Mississippian lifeway through generations of external contact with terminal Late Woodland and emergent Mississippian populations of the Cahokia region. The phenomenon often viewed as a precipitous and dynamic cultural transformation to Mississippian may have been no more complicated than local Late Woodland adoption of new elements of a lifestyle in which they had long been participating.

Although Cahokia was the progenitor of many key elements of the Mississippian lifeway that developed in the Central Illinois River Valley after A.D. 1050, other regional influences are obvious. Frequent interaction between peoples of the Illinois Valley and coeval cultures as distant as the western Prairie region injected important elements into the local society, but the relationship between these areas was primarily secular in nature. Interaction was generally characterized by an almost exclusive exchange of material items and innovations reflective of daily living that was fostered by common technological adaptations to similar living situations. No structured political confederation of the groups is implied. On the other hand, the mature Mississippian relationship between peoples of the Illinois Valley and Cahokia areas primarily involved a one-sided exchange of religious/political materials and technologies that flowed northward from Cahokia. Material benefits exchanged to Cahokians were undoubtedly many, but little evidence of such transactions is recognized in the archaeological record.

It is presently impossible to quantify accurately the contributions of either Cahokia or the indigenous population to the development of the Spoon River tradition much after the end of the 12th century A.D. By this time, Late Woodland and classic early Mississippian wares had disappeared from the local ceramic assemblages, and a distinctive shell-tempered ceramic tradition emerged that contained diffused elements of both. Although this assemblage remained similar in many respects to that of Cahokia as it developed over the next several generations, strong regional influences remained, affecting not only the complexion of the local ceramic industry, but elements of technology and social organization as well (Harn 1975b:425). The waning of Cahokia's cultural vibrancy is vividly reflected in the Dickson cemetery, if the presence of exotic ceremonialism and profuse regalia are accurate reflections of levels of social organization. In the later burial mounds, burials were increasingly furnished with smaller numbers and less variety of artifacts, with significantly fewer status items being present.

The Eveland site's position at the margins of several major culture areas provides a unique opportunity for assessing the development of Mississippian in the Cahokia hinterlands. Yet considerable clarification must be made of the relationships existing among local Late Woodland populations, and of these to regional Woodland contemporaries, before the causes and effects of Mississippianization can be accurately measured. Just as Cahokia's effect on the indigenous lifeways within its immediate sphere is only beginning to be understood, not enough is known on a regional level to provide an accurate overview of cultural change and continuity as Cahokia Mississippian spread into its northern frontier.

Acknowledgements

Comments on this paper were graciously provided by several individuals whose schedules were already seriously overtaxed. Thanks are expressed to Bonnie Styles, Harold Hassen, and Michael Wiant of the Illinois State Museum and Duane Esarey of Dickson Mounds Museum. James B. Stoltman suggested that thin-section control would be highly beneficial to the Eveland Phase ceramic analysis. The wisdom of his suggestion was borne out by the thin section analysis which he generously supplied. Typing, proofreading, and computer organization of the manuscript were provided by Betty Fawcett, Kim White, and Nicholas Klobuchar of the Dickson Mounds staff, and Diana Day. Photography was done by Marlin Roos of the Illinois State Museum.

References Cited

Anderson, Elsie P.
  1951 The Mammals of Fulton County, Illinois. *Bulletin of the Chicago Academy of Sciences*, Vol. 9:153-188.
Bareis, Charles J.
  1976 The Knoebel Site, St. Clair County, Illinois. *Illinois Archaeological Survey Circular*, No. 1. Urbana.

Blakely, Robert L.
1971 Comparison of the Mortality Profiles of Archaic, Middle Woodland and Middle Mississippian Skeletal Populations. *American Journal of Physical Anthropology*, Vol. 34:43-54.

Blakely, Robert L., and Phillip L. Walker
1968 Mortality Profile of the Middle Mississippian Population of Dickson Mound, Fulton County, Illinois. *Proceedings of the Indiana Academy of Sciences*, No. 78:102-108.

Caldwell, Joseph R.
1967a New Discoveries at Dickson Mound. *Living Museum*, Vol. 29, pp. 139-142.
1967b The House that "X" Built. *Living Museum*, Vol. 28, pp. 92-93.

Cantwell, Anne-Marie
1980 Dickson Camp and Pond: Two Early Havana Tradition Sites in the Central Illinois Valley. *Illinois State Museum Reports of Investigations*, No. 36, *Dickson Mounds Museum Archaeological Studies*.

Clark, George A.
1985 Heterochrony, Allometry, and Canalization in the Human Vertebral Column: Examples from Prehistoric Amerindian Populations. Unpublished Ph. D. dissertation, University of Massachusetts. Amherst.

Cole, Fay-Cooper, and Thorne Deuel
1937 *Rediscovering Illinois*. University of Chicago Press, Chicago.

Conrad, Lawrence A.
1972 1966 Excavations at the Dickson Mound: a Sepo-Spoon River Burial Mound in Fulton County, Illinois. Unpublished Master's thesis, Department of Anthropology, University of Wisconsin, Madison.
1973 The Nature of the Relationships Between Cahokia and the Central Illinois River Valley. Paper presented at the fifty-second annual meeting of the Central States Anthropological Society in St. Louis, Missouri, March 29-31, 1973.
1989 The Southeastern Ceremonial Complex on the Northern Mississippian Frontier: Late Prehistoric Politico-religious Systems in the Central Illinois River Valley. In *The Southeastern Ceremonial Complex: Artifacts and Analysis* (edited by Patricia Galloway), pp. 93-113. University of Nebraska Press, Lincoln and London.
1991 The Mississippian Cultures of the Central Illinois Valley. In *Cahokia and the Hinterlands: Mississippian Cultures of the Midwest* (edited by Thomas E. Emerson and R. Barry Lewis), pp. 119-156. University of Illinois Press, Urbana and Chicago, in cooperation with the Illinois Historic Preservation Agency.

Conrad, Lawrence A. and Alan D. Harn
1972 The Spoon River Culture in the Central Illinois River Valley. Unpublished manuscript on file, Dickson Mounds Museum.

Douglas, John G.
1976 Collins: A Late Woodland Ceremonial Complex in the Woodfordian Northeast. Ph. D. dissertation, University of Illinois, Urbana.

Esarey, Duane, Lawrence A. Conrad, and William Green
1982 Final Report on Phase II Archaeological Investigations on Portions of Amax's Proposed Littleton Mine Field and Littleton Field Haul Road, Schuyler, McDonough, and Fulton Counties, Illinois. *Western Illinois University, Archaeological Research Laboratory, Reports of Investigations*, No. 4. Submitted to Amax Coal Company.

Esarey, Duane, and Lawrence A. Conrad (compilers)
1981 *The Orendorf Site Preliminary Working Papers 1981*. Vols. 1-3. Western Illinois University Archaeological Research Laboratory, Macomb.

Fowler, Melvin L.
1952 The Clear Lake Site: Hopewellian Occupation. *In* Hopewellian Communities in Illinois, edited by Thorne Deuel. *Illinois State Museum, Scientific Papers*, Vol. 5, Springfield.
1972 The Cahokia Site: Summary and Interpretations. Paper presented at the University of Wisconsin-Milwaukee Cahokia Archaeology Project Symposium of the 37 annual meeting of the Society for American Archaeology.

Goodman, Alan H., and George J. Armelagos
1985 Disease and Death at Dr. Dickson's Mounds. *Natural History*, September.

Goodman, Alan H., George J. Armelagos, and Jerome C. Rose
 1980 Enamel Hypoplasias as Indicators of Stress in Three Prehistoric Populations from Illinois. *Human Biology* 52:515-528.
Goodman, Alan H., and George A. Clark
 1981 Harris Lines as Indicators of Stress in Prehistoric Illinois Populations. *In* Biocultural Adaptation: Comprehensive Approaches to Skeletal Analysis, edited by Debra L. Martin and M. Pamela Bumsted, pp. 35-46. *Department of Anthropology, University of Massachusetts, Research Reports* 20. Amherst, Massachusetts.
Green, William
 1976 Preliminary Report on the Bauer Branch Complex, a Late Woodland Manifestation in West-Central Illinois. *Wisconsin Archaeologist*, Vol. 57, pp. 172-188.
 1977 Final Report of Littleton Field Archaeological Survey, Schuyler County, Illinois. *Upper Mississippi Valley Archaeological Research Foundation Reports on Archaeology*, No. 4.
Griffin, J. B.
 1960 A Hypothesis for the Prehistory of the Winnebago. In *Culture in History: Essays in Honor of Paul Radin*. Edited by S. Diamond. Columbia University Press, New York.
Hall, Robert L.
 1967 The Mississippian Heartland and Its Plains Relationship. *Plains Anthropologist*, Vol. 12, No. 36. Lincoln, NB.
 1974 Cahokia Identity and Interaction Models of Cahokia Mississippian. Revised paper originally prepared as a contribution to the proceedings of the advanced seminar "Reviewing Mississippian Development: A Study in the Dynamics of Cultural Growth in the Eastern United States" organized by Stephen Williams and James B. Griffin, sponsored by the School of American Research, Santa Fe, New Mexico.
 n.d. A Newly Designated Pottery Type from Northern Illinois. Unpublished manuscript on file at the Illinois State Museum.
Harn, Alan D.
 1971 An Archaeological Survey of the American Bottoms in Madison and St. Clair Counties, Illinois. *In* Archaeological Surveys of the American Bottoms and Adjacent Bluffs, Illinois. *Illinois State Museum Reports of Investigations*, No. 21, pp. 19-39. Springfield.
 1973 Cahokia and the Mississippian Emergence in the Spoon River Area of Illinois. Paper presented at the 52nd annual meeting of the Central States Anthropological Society in St. Louis, Missouri.
 1975a Another Long-Nosed God Mask from Fulton County Illinois. *Wisconsin Archaeologist*, Vol. 56, pp. 2-8.
 1975b Cahokia and the Mississippian Emergence in the Spoon River Area of Illinois. *Transactions of the Illinois Academy of Sciences*, Vol. 68, pp. 414-434.
 1976 An Archaeological Survey of the Statewide Hatchery Site, Sand Ridge State Forest, Mason County, Illinois. An archaeological assessment and impact statement prepared for Kramer, Chin & Mayo, Inc., Seattle, Washington. Copy on file at the Dickson Mounds Museum.
 1978 Mississippian Settlement Patterns in the Central Illinois River Valley. In *Mississippian Settlement Patterns*, pp. 233-268. Edited by Bruce D. Smith. Academic Press, Inc., New York.
 1980 The Prehistory of Dickson Mounds: the Dickson excavation. *Illinois State Museum, Reports of Investigations* No. 35, Springfield.
 1986 The Marion Phase Occupation of the Larson Site in the Central Illinois River Valley. In *Early Woodland Archeology* (Edited by Kenneth B. Fransworth and Thomas E. Emerson). Center for American Archeology Press. Kampsville.
 1991 Comments on Subsistence, Seasonality, and Site Function at Upland Subsidiaries in the Spoon River Area: Mississippianization at Work on the Northern Frontier. In *Cahokia and the Hinterlands: Middle Mississippian Cultures of the Midwest* (edited by Thomas E. Emerson and R. Barry Lewis), pp. 157-163. University of Illinois Press, Urbana and Chicago, in cooperation with the Illinois Historic Preservation Agency.
 n.d., a The Archaeology of Dickson Mounds. *In* Dickson Mounds: Cultural Change and Demographic Variation in the Life of a Late Woodland-Middle Mississippian Cemetery (edited by Alan D. Harn and George J. Armelagos). Manuscript on file at Dickson Mounds Museum.

n.d., b The Archaeology of the Larson Site (11Fll09). *In* The Larson Site: A Spoon River Variant Town in the Central Illinois River Valley (edited by Alan D. Harn and David A. Baerreis) (in preparation).

n.d., c Variation in Mississippian Settlement Pattern: The Larson Settlement System in the Central Illinois River Valley. Manuscript submitted for publication to Illinois State Museum 1991.

Harn, Alan D., and David A. Baerreis

n.d. The Larson Site (11F1109): A Spoon River Variant Town in the Central Illinois River Valley (in preparation).

Harn, Alan D., and Alfred C. Koelling

1974 The Indigenous Drug Plants of Fulton County, Illinois. *Transactions of the Illinois State Academy of Science*, Vol. 67, No. 3, pp. 259-284.

Hassen, Harold

1985 Late Woodland Diversity in the Fall Creek Locality. *The Wisconsin Archaeologist*, Vol. 66, No. 3, pp. 282-291.

Lallo, John G.

1972 The Paleodemography of Two Prehistoric American Indian Populations from Dickson Mounds. Unpublished M.A. thesis, University of Massachusetts, Amherst.

1973 The Skeletal Biology of Three Prehistoric American Indian Societies from Dickson Mounds. Unpublished Ph. D. dissertation, University of Massachusetts, Amherst.

Lallo, John G., George J. Armelagos and R. P. Mensforth

1977 The Role of Diet, Disease and Physiology in the Origin of Porotic Hyperostosis. *Human Biology*, Vol. 49, pp. 471-485.

Lallo, John G., George J. Armelagos and Jerome C. Rose

1978 Paleoepidemiology of Infectious Disease in the Dickson Mounds Population. *Medical College of Virginia Quarterly*, Vol. 14, No. 11, pp. 17-23.

Lallo, John G., Jerome C. Rose and George J. Armelagos

1980 An Ecological Interpretation of Variation in Mortality Within Three Prehistoric American Indian Populations from Dickson Mounds. In *Early Native Americans: Prehistoric Demography, Economy and Technology* (edited by David Browman). Mouton Publishers: The Hague.

Lallo, John G. and Jerome C. Rose

1979 Patterns of Stress, Disease and Mortality in Two Prehistoric Populations from North America. *Journal of Human Evolution*, Vol. 8, pp. 323-335.

McConaughy, Mark A., Claude V. Jackson and Frances B. King

1985 Two Early Mississippian Period Structures from the Rench Site (11P4), Peoria County, Illinois. *Midcontinental Journal of Archaeology*, Vol. 10, No. 2, pp. 171-194.

McGimsey, Charles R., and Michael D. Conner (editors)

1985 Deer Track, a Late Woodland Village in the Mississippi Valley. *Center for American Archeology Technical Report* l.

McGimsey, Charles R., Duane Esarey, Edwin R. Hajic, Alan D. Harn, Floyd Mansberger, Erich K. Schroeder, and Michael D. Wiant

1987 Archaeological Reconnaissance and Testing at Sites 11-F-2713 and 11-F-25, Liverpool Levee Project, Fulton County, Illinois. Report submitted to the U.S. Army Corps of Engineers, Rock Island District. Contract DACW25-87-C-004. Illinois State Museum Society.

Milner, George R.

1983 The Cultural Determinants of Mississippian Community Health: An Examination of Populations from Two Areas of Western Illinois. Paper presented at the annual meeting of the American Association of Physical Anthropologists, Indianapolis.

1984 Social and Temporal Implications of Variation Among American Bottom Mississippian Cemeteries. *American Antiquity*, Vol. 49, No. 3, pp. 468-488.

Milner, George R., and Joyce A. Williams

1981 The Julien Site (11-S-63): An Early Bluff and Mississippian Multicomponent Site. *FAI-270 Archaeological Mitigation Project Report* 31. University of Illinois, Urbana.

1981 The Turner (11-S-50) and DeMange (11-S-447) Sites: An Early Mississippian Occupation of a Floodplain Locality. *FAI-270 Archaeological Mitigation Project Archaeology*, edited by Charles J. Bareis and James W. Porter. University of Illinois Press, Urbana and Chicago.

Morgan, David T.
   1985 Late Woodland Ceramics from the Fall Creek Locality, Adams County, Illinois. *The Wisconsin Archaeologist*, Vol. 66, No. 3, pp. 265-281.
Munson, Patrick J., and Alan D. Harn
   1966 Surface Collections from Three Sites in the Central Illinois River Valley. *The Wisconsin Archaeologist*, Vol. 47, No. 3. pp. 150-168.
O'Brien, Patricia J.
   1972 A Formal Analysis of Cahokia Ceramics from the Powell Tract. *Illinois Archaeological Survey Memoir* 3.
Porter, James W.
   1969 The Mitchell Site and Prehistoric Exchange Systems at Cahokia: A.D. 1000+300. *In* Explorations into Cahokia Archaeology (edited by Melvin L. Fowler). *Illinois Archaeological Survey Bulletin 7*, pp. 137-164.
   1974 *Cahokia Archaeology as Viewed from the Mitchell Site: A Satellite Community at A.D. 1150-1200.* Ph.D. dissertation, UW-Md. University Microfilms, Ann Arbor.
Rose, Jerome C., George J. Armelagos and John W. Lallo
   1978 Histological Enamel Indicator of Childhood Stress in Prehistoric Skeletal Samples. *American Journal of Physical Anthropology*, Vol. 49, No. 4.
Santure, Sharron K., Alan D. Harn, and Duane Esarey, with contributions by Frances King, Nicholas W. Klobuchar, George R. Milner, Virginia G. Smith, and Bonnie Styles
   1990 Archaeological Investigations at the Morton Village and Norris Farms #36 Cemetery. *Illinois State Museum Reports of Investigations*, No. 45. Springfield.
Schwegman, John E.
   1973 *Comprehensive Plan for the Illinois Nature Preserves System Part Two: The Natural Divisions of Illinois.* Illinois Nature Preserves Commission in cooperation with the Illinois Department of Conservation.
Smith, Harriet M.
   1969 The Murdock Mound, Cahokia Site. *In* Explorations into Cahokia Archaeology (edited by Melvin L. Fowler. *Illinois Archaeological Survey Bulletin 7*, pp. 49-88.
Wittry, Warren L., and Joseph O. Vogel
   1962 Illinois State Museum Projects: October 1961 to June 1962. *First Annual Report: American Bottoms Archaeology* (edited by Melvin L. Fowler). Illinois Archaeological Survey, Urbana.
White, John K.
   1985 Ceramics. *In* Deer Track, a Late Woodland Village in the Mississippi Valley (edited by Charles R. McGimsey and Michael D. Conner). *Center for American Archaeology Technical Report 1*, pp. 27-43.
Wray, Donald E., and Richard S. MacNeish
   n.d. The Weaver Site: Twenty Centuries of Illinois Prehistory. Unpublished manuscript on file at the Illinois State Museum.

8

The Shire Site:
Mississippian Outpost
in the Central Illinois Prairie

John Claflin
Diachronic Research Associates

The Shire site (Illinois State Museum No. Lo^v117), a Mississippian occupation dating to the 12th century A.D., is situated in an agricultural field along Lake Fork Creek in southeastern Logan County, Illinois. In 1972, when test excavations were initiated by the Illinois State Museum, the field in which the site is located was in pasture. Although the landowner allowed a small excavation in a portion of the pasture recommended by a local amateur archaeologist, he was unwilling to plow the pasture or allow shovel testing beyond the excavation boundaries to delineate the areal parameters of the site. Ownership of the property has changed at least twice since the site was tested and subsequent attempts to secure permission to conduct an archaeological survey of the property have been fruitless. Department of Agriculture aerial photographs of the property have also failed to provide any information concerning site size.

Thus, all that is known of this occupation is confined to data recovered from the original five contiguous, three-meter square excavation units. In spite of the small scale of the excavation, the archaeological remains from the Shire site have significant and far-reaching anthropological implications.

Environmental Background

Lake Fork Creek, situated within the central Illinois prairie, is part of the Sangamon River drainage, but it is an anomaly within that riverine system. Prior to 1900, a portion of Lake Fork Creek was a natural lake (Peck 1838). Based on the 1819–1823 United States Government land surveys, this lake was approximately 17 kilometers in length and ranged from .5 to 1.1 kilometers in width. The vegetation surrounding the lake consisted of timber to the north, while the south side was covered with prairie (Johnson 1972, Claflin 1974). At the northwestern edge of the lake water drained from it into a narrow marsh that flowed northward into Salt Creek, near the present town of Lincoln, Illinois. The Shire site was situated on the north side of that natural lake (Figure 8.1).

Although a general geological history has been compiled for the Sangamon River drainage (Miller 1973), specific information about the lake's age and origin is only speculative. Presumably, the lake was created during the Woodfordian as outwash from Kickapoo, Sugar and Salt Creeks, which originate north of Lake Fork on the Shelbyville moraine, dammed Lake Fork Creek, forming the lake.

An archaeological survey conducted in and around the lake in 1972 and 1973 (Claflin 1974) suggested that the lake had existed since the early Holocene. Around 1900 the lake was drained and during the 1930s the present creek channel was excavated. To avoid confusion, the name Lake Fork will apply to the section of the drainage that was a lake. Lake Fork Creek refers to the entire modern tributary.

Because Lake Fork was an upland lake, the physiography around it cannot be directly compared to that in other drainages or even in other parts of the Sangamon drainage. The lake shoreline is succeeded

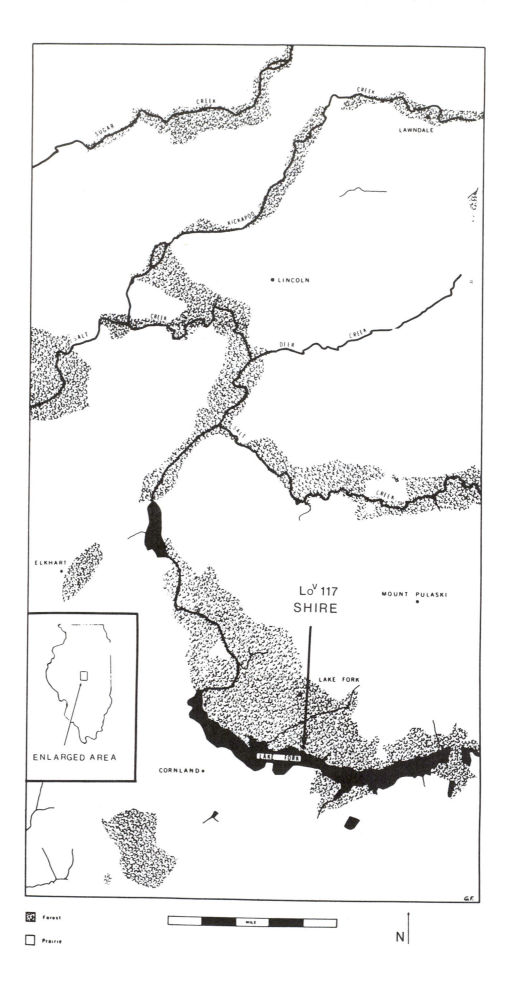

Figure 8.1 Map showing Shire site location.

by upland, but there is a narrow landform between shore and upland that Johnson (1972) has described as "rolling slope." This peculiar environmental setting makes it difficult to compare settlement or even subsistence at Shire with those at sites located in topographic/environmental situations commonly associated with Mississippian or Late Woodland traditions in other drainages.

Cultural Background

In addition to the atypical environmental characteristics around the lake, the location of the Shire site is also anomalous at a cultural level. Although hundreds of archaeological sites had been recorded along the entire length of the Sangamon River drainage (Claflin 1974, Roper 1979, Holland 1965, Lewis 1973 and others) by 1972, the Shire site was one of only two in the entire drainage from which Mississippian ceramics had been recovered. The other was the Lawrenz Gun Club site (ISM No. CS^{v}19), situated near the juncture of the Sangamon and Illinois Rivers, nearly 113 kilometers west of the Shire site. The proximity of the Lawrenz Gun Club site to Mississippian sites in the central Illinois River valley suggests that it may be part of the Mississippian tradition that developed along that segment of the Illinois River (Harn 1980:73).

Research Questions

The motivation for testing the Shire site was a simple one. Since in 1972 Shire appeared to be the only other Mississippian occupation in the entire Sangamon River drainage, and since it was positioned in such an unusual environmental setting, testing was undertaken to determine whether there was any subsurface integrity to the site.

Since 1972, at least three other Mississippian sites have been identified in the Sangamon Drainage, one of which is located near the Lawrenz Gun Club site. Mississippian ceramics were also found with Late Woodland ceramics on a small site in Menard County and on a small site in Sangamon County (Styles et al. 1981). The temporal period(s) or presumed intensity of Mississippian occupation on these, as indicated by the artifacts, has not been reported.

Before proceeding with an examination of the material culture of the Shire site, the following must be stressed: In this discussion, Shire has thus far been described, and will continue to be described, as a Mississippian site, since a Mississippian presence was confirmed by the test excavations. However, intermixed with the Mississippian material is a significant amount of presumably contemporaneous Late Woodland material primarily ceramics and projectile points. Given the presence of Late Woodland and Mississippian material and given the unique environmental conditions of the site's locality, a number of important research questions were posed throughout the analysis:

(1) How do we account for the presence of Late Woodland and Mississippian components at Shire? Are these components separate and distinct?
(2) Is the assemblage at Shire reflective of a Late Woodland population that has lost much of its Late Woodland identity as a result of Mississippian contact?
(3) Is Shire truly a Mississippian occupation, but one which has a special function or a special or unique relationship with indigenous Late Woodland populations?
(4) Why are those areas of the Sangamon River drainage that appear to be environmentally suited for the typical Mississippian settlement pattern unoccupied by Mississippian populations?

Although some of these questions remain unanswered at this writing, an attempt will be made, based on observations of the material culture, to address these and other research problems later in this discussion.

Material Culture

Houses

Luckily, the test units were placed over parts of two and possibly three rectangular, semi-subterranean, wall-trench Mississippian houses (Figure 8.2). House 2, which appears to be burned, may be a double-wall-trench structure or two separate dwellings. No interior features such as hearths or refuse pits occur in the excavated portions of the houses. However, their absence is not unusual for Mississippian wall-trench dwellings in Illinois (Cole et al. 1952, Porter 1969, Harn 1980).

As can be seen in Figure 8.2, sequential house construction is indicated. Rapid filling of the house depressions is also suggested, as provenience data for the ceramics demonstrate a homogeneous mixing of Late Woodland and Mississippian artifacts throughout all levels of the midden inside the houses.

Artifacts

A large quantity of artifactual and faunal material was recovered from the fill of the houses, with ceramics occurring most frequently. It is not the intent of this paper to present a detailed description of this material. However, the analysis performed to identify these ceramic types and to determine the ranges of

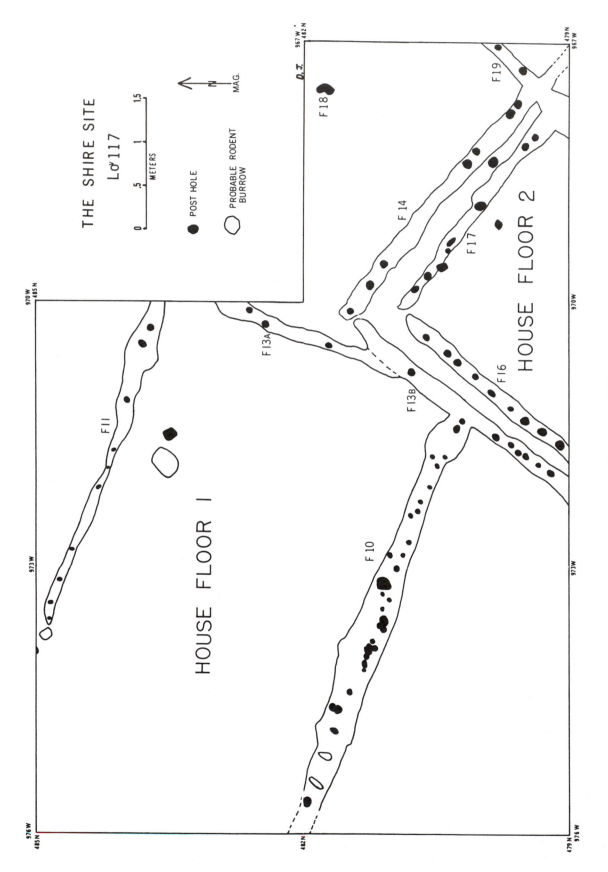

Figure 8.2 Plan map of Shire structures.

variation within those types will be used to organize the data and provide a framework for interpreting site function. It was presumed from this analysis that the number of cultural components at the site could be isolated and their respective temporal positions established. Since the Mississippian component was present at the Shire site, analysis began as a simple procedure to separate the shell-tempered Mississippian ceramics from the grit-tempered Woodland pottery. It was also assumed that since the Shire site excavation was so small, it would be a relatively easy task to identify the "types" present in the temper categories. This proved to be a false assumption.

Eighty vessels have been identified from rim fragments recovered from the houses and at least six additional vessels not represented by rims have been identified among approximately 1500 body sherds from Shire. Thirty of the vessels represented by rims are shell-tempered and 36 vessels are grit-tempered. Tempering agents for the remaining 14 vessels represented by rims include sand (2), crushed hematite (1), chert (1), limestone (1), sand and grit (1), various combinations of grit and shell (6) and grit and (as yet) unidentified materials (2).

Woodland Ceramics

Analysis has revealed a great deal of morphological variability within the non-shell-tempered ceramics. In fact, the variations in rim shape, surface treatment, decorative modes and tempering appearing within such a small sample of vessels suggest that this is more a "collection of pots", than an indicator of any specific Late Woodland ceramic tradition. See Figures 8.3, 8.4, and 8.5.

Further complicating the analysis was the size and physical condition of the rims. Many Late Woodland types are often differentiated by attributes on or below the vessel neck or shoulder, but, in most cases, the Late Woodland rims from Shire were too small to distinguish these areas. This not only precluded comparisons within the collection, but also prevented comparisons with types described in the archaeological literature.

It also became apparent that a number of the non-shell-tempered vessels were attempts at copying Mississippian vessels, while other specimens appear to be experiments combining Late Woodland and Mississippian technologies, forms and/or decorative treatments. For example, one grit-tempered specimen

Figure 8.3 Non-local Late Woodland ceramics from the Shire site. Row 1, Maples Mills; Rows 2 and 3, Bluff; Row 4, Bauer Branch.

was covered with a 1 to 2 millimeter shell-tempered veneer on its interior and exterior surfaces and then fired a second time. Other vessels (Figure 8.4, row 2) display rolled rims and closely resemble the Powell vessel forms from Shire. However, these specimens are all grit-tempered and at least one example displays a cordmarked exterior surface.

Approximately 42 percent of the Late Woodland sample is made of specimens which resemble "Vandalia complex" ceramics (Gardner 1973:219-220) or are similar to Maples Mills (Figure 8.3, row 1) (Fowler 1955:219), Bauer Branch (Figure 8.3, row 4) (Green 1977:32) and Bluff types (Figure 8.3, row 2, 3) (Wittry and Vogel 1962:1-13), along with at least one Sepo-like vessel (Figure 8.4, row 1). The remaining non-shell-tempered vessels, excluding those examples determined to be copies of Mississippian vessels and those presumed to be experiments, have been identified as Late Woodland based on their physical characteristics. However, all are essentially different from each other and are, based on current published data, alien to the Sangamon drainage. Overall, the analysis did little to diminish the initial impression that the Late Woodland rims at Shire represented a collection of different pots rather than a key to the specific identity of Shire's Late Woodland component.

If it is assumed that these Late Woodland vessels are, indeed just a collection of pots, some seemingly unrelated aspects of these ceramics are especially noteworthy, as they are pivotal to understanding the Mississippian component at Shire. First, with one exception (Maples Mills), the Late Woodland ceramic types at Shire are uncommon or non-existent in other parts of the Sangamon drainage. Second, the points of origin or areas of most frequent distribution for the identified types at Shire are outside the Sangamon drainage. Even the unidentifiable Late Woodland specimens have no known antecedants in the Sangamon. Their presence together at Shire implies that the extra-territorial contacts of its inhabitants were multi-directional rather than tied exclusively to a particular region. Third, even though there is some variance in the temporal ranges of these individual Late Woodland types, they are all contemporaneous to each other at circa A.D. 1000-1200. Furthermore, they occur at Shire with Mississippian ceramics which date to the same period.

Since the Late Woodland manifestation at Shire can only be understood within the context of Late Woodland in the Sangamon drainage, the observations presented above will be elaborated upon and evaluated later in this paper.

Mississippian Ceramics

There is far less diversity of types among the Mississippian ceramics from Shire (see Figures 8.6, 8.7,

Figure 8.4 Local copies of Mississippian vessels. Row 1, Sepo-like; Row 2, grit-tempered Powell Plain-like.

8.8, and 8.9). Appearing most frequently in the collection is Powell Plain (Griffin 1949:49-50) with 19 vessels. Ramey Incised (Griffin 1948:51-52), the companion type to Powell Plain, is represented by one vessel. The remaining ten vessels–jars, bowls, plates and beakers and/or bottles–are too small to type more specifically, although their technological characteristics, such as surface treatment, etc., most closely resemble Powell Plain and Ramey Incised vessels. This resemblance would also indicate contemporaneity.

Based upon the Mississippian cultural chronology that has been established for the American Bottom in Illinois, it appears that the Shire site was occupied during the Sterling Phase at Cahokia (A.D. 1050-1150). Not surprisingly, this date coincides with the arrival of these Mississippian ceramic types in other drainages in Illinois (Perino 1971:137, Winters 1967:68-69, Harn 1980, Douglas 1976). The presence of these latter vessel forms, specifically pots and beakers, in the assemblage described above, in addition to two vessels tentatively identified as Cahokia Cordmarked,

suggest that terminal occupation of the Mississippian component may have been as late as A.D. 1200.

One important and distinctive characteristic of the Mississippian ceramics from Shire is a subjective one. Since all the Mississippian ceramics from the Shire site were discovered in house middens, it is assumed that their function was primarily utilitarian. However, there is a great range of variation in the technical and aesthetic quality of the assemblage. A few specimens are outstanding in quality and could be considered archetypical for their respective forms.

A descriptive parallel exists between the Shire specimens and ceramics analysed by Sears (1973) from the Kolomoki site in Georgia. Discussing some particularly well-made specimens from that site, Sears comments that "... these pots are not, then, the products of potters whose training and experience is limited to occasional production of cookpots for their own use, whether these potters be male or female. The mastery of the medium calls for complex training processes which must involve social support" (Sears 1973:39). It

Figure 8.5 Miscellaneous untyped Woodland ceramics.

Figure 8.6 Ramey Incised (upper left) and Powell Plain vessels.

Figure 8.7 Untyped Mississippian vessels.

Figure 8.8 Untyped
Mississippian vessels.

Figure 8.9 Mississippian
rims with appendages.

is felt that Sears' statement is equally applicable to Shire ceramics, since the high quality specimens from the Shire site give every indication of having been manufactured by professional potters.

The logical development of this argument produces questions about the origin of these specimens. The first consideration is whether or not the Mississippian component at Shire was large enough to support an artisan. It is impossible to determine the answer with any degree of certainty, but conversations with local collectors would suggest otherwise.

Lake Fork Creek is extremely rich archaeologically and is, therefore, subject to intensive "relic collecting" by dozens of individuals. When the Shire research was conducted in 1972 and 1973, nearly all of the long-time collectors of Lake Fork archaeological sites were interviewed. Although most of the collectors knew of or had collected the Archaic, Middle Woodland and Late Woodland sites in the drainage, only one knew about Shire's Mississippian component. He had collected it regularly before the area had been converted to pasture.

Given the intensity of relic collecting, it seems unlikely that the Shire site would have escaped detection had the site functioned as a Mississippian ceremonial center or village. Furthermore, specific site information supplied by the individual who collected the site indicated that the Mississippian materials were confined to a very small area.

It is suggested here that the small group of superior quality vessels were not manufactured at the Shire site, but were part of the cultural assemblage physically transported to the site by this immigrant population. Circumstantial evidence, which will be reviewed later, implies that individuals living at Shire emigrated from the American Bottom.

Additional artifacts

Table 8.1 provides an inventory of the remaining artifacts recovered from the five test units. Unfortunately, many of these artifacts contribute little to the resolution of many of the pertinent questions posed regarding this unusual occupation. Neither do the exotic *anculosa*, *busycon* and *marginella* shell beads (Figure 8.10) discovered at Shire contribute greatly to understanding the Mississippian component at Shire, although their presence in the assemblage does hint at ties to the American Bottom.

Some subsistence information can be inferred from the Shire site assemblage. The relatively large numbers of projectile points (Figure 8.11) and the particularly large amount of faunal remains from the five excavation units attest to a reliance on hunting and, to a lesser degree, fishing. In contrast, agriculture, if

practiced at all, seems to have been of minimal importance to the Shire inhabitants. A large corn cob, found directly below the plow zone and possibly modern, and three small, highly polished chert flakes were the only indicators from this test excavation that agriculture was being practiced by this population. Charred seeds and nut hulls recovered from waterscreen samples indicate that gathering was also employed as a subsistence activity to some degree.

Harn (1980:74) has noted that central Illinois valley Mississippian populations appear to rely on hunting rather than agriculture to a degree that contrasts markedly with Mississippian occupations of the Cahokia region. Whether parallels can be drawn from Shire from his observations is unclear at present.

Harn (1980) has argued that, since frontier inhabitants were less likely to deplete faunal and floral resources than were people in a more densely populated area such as Cahokia, agricgulture may not have been employed in remote areas like Lake Fork, where Mississippian populations could more easily subsist without it. While this may explain how and why Mississippian people might adapt their subsistence patterns within a new region, it does nothing to resolve the problem of why a Mississippian population chose to locate in the prairie.

Faunal Remains

The number of species (Table 8.2) represented among the faunal remains from the houses suggests that a healthy natural environment existed around the lake during the occupation of the Shire site. White-tailed deer (*Odocoileus virginianus*) occur with most frequency, accounting for over half of all the bones present. The variety of fish indicates not only that the lake existed during the site's occupancy, but that it was a flourishing aquatic environment. Present were Pike (*Essox* spp.) and Walleye (*Stizostedion* spp.) which had, until recently, been extinct in this part of the Sangamon, along with many fish species that require larger bodies of water to exist and, consequently, no long occur along this section of Lake Fork Creek. To document this, Illinois State Museum archaeologists seined a portion of Lake Fork Creek near Shire in 1972 to identify existing fish species living in the creek. Fish inventoried at that time were primarily minnows and suckers and an occasional sunfish, bullhead catfish or a very small large-mouth bass.

In spite of all the shell-tempered pottery at the site, very few mussels were recovered from the excavations. The excellent state of preservation of the shell in the ceramics and the marine shell beads argues against natural deterioration as a factor in this absence. It would seems that shell was as important

Table 8.1 Shire Artifact Inventory (excluding ceramics).

Category	Comments	Number
PROJECTILE POINTS:		
Unnotched Triangular	Similar to Madison or Mounds Stemless	3
Notched Triangular 1	Similar to Cahokia Side-Notched	7
Notched Triangular 2	Similar to "Bluff" types	5
Notched Triangular 3	Like Notched Triangular 2, but larger	1
Ovate, Side-Notched		1
Ovate, Contracting Stem	Poss. Middle Woodland	1
Proximal Fragment		4
Distal Fragment		6
Medial Fragment		3
Undetermined Fragment		2
Drill		1
	Total	34
OTHER CHERT ARTIFACTS:		
Single Platform Cores		5
Double Platform Cores		3
Retouched and/or Utilized Flakes		169
Unmodified Flakes		646
"Shatter"		220
	Total	1043
BONE:		
Drilled Bone	Drumfish Pendant	1
Cut and Polished	Fragments, probably a type of needle or pin	2
	Total	3
STONE:		
Hammerstone		4
Abraider		3
	Total	7
CLAY:		
Beads		1
SHELL:		
Anculosa Bead		1
Busycon Bead		5
Marginella Bead		3
Freshwater Shell	Cut and drilled	2
	Total	11

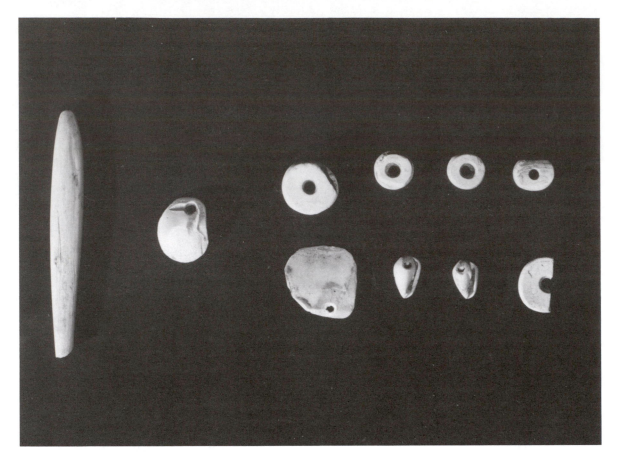

Figure 8.10 Selected bone and shell artifacts.

for tempering material in locally made pottery as it was for a dietary item.

Since it is possible to hunt successfully almost any of the animal species identified at Shire during any time of the year, it is difficult to determine whether the site was occupied year round or only seasonally, but some of the data suggest a warm weather occupation. A relatively large sample of box turtle (*Terrapene* spp.) suggests a summer habitation, since that species is most active and, therefore, most easily taken during that season. It is possible that turtle was collected for cultural rather than dietary use, i.e. for rattles and bowls, in which case the sample size could mean that shells were gathered over a long period, rather than that they were gathered intensively during seasonal occupations.

Deer elements were well represented at Shire, but none of the skulls showed evidence of winter shedding. Particularly interesting was the absence of any migratory bird remains. Assuming that prehistoric waterfowl migration patterns were similar to those of today, it is likely that a lake the size of Lake Fork, lying within the Mississippi fly way, would attract significant numbers of ducks and geese during late autumn and early spring. It seems probable that, if a prehistoric population was in residence at those times, their diet would surely include such a resource. Although these phenomena certainly are not overwhelmingly conclusive indicators of seasonality, it is felt that they support the suggestion that Shire was occupied during the warm-weather months.

Observations and Speculations

The data generated from the excavations failed to resolve many of the questions posed earlier in this report. While presumed Late Woodland copies of, or experiments with, Mississippian forms or technologies suggest a long-term, simultaneous Late Woodland/Mississippian occupation, there is nothing from the site to explain the quantity and variation of the Late Woodland vessels. More Late Woodland vessels were identified from these presumably Mississippian houses than some investigators discover excavating or sampling entire Late Woodland sites, yet there was no single ceramic category or type that contained a sufficient number of vessels to allow a cultural identification of a primary Late Woodland component.

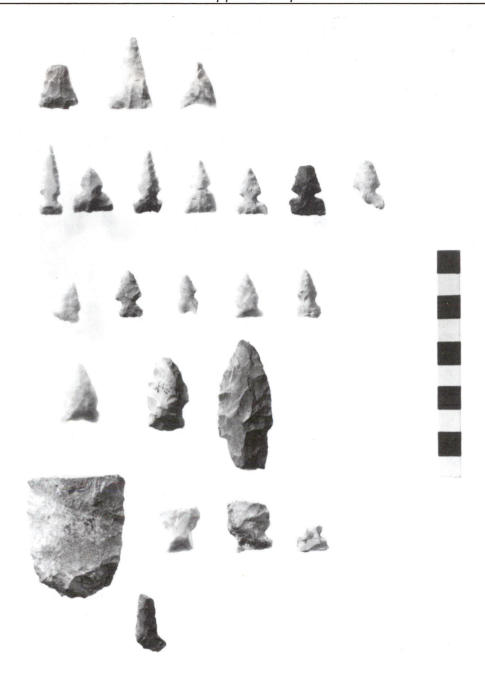

Figure 8.11 Bifacially worked chert artifacts from Shire house middens.

Nor did the excavations determine whether the Mississippian and Late Woodland components were independent entities or were functionally interdependent. To provide some tentative explanations for the phenomena observed at the Shire site, an attempt has been made to synthesize some environmental and cultural information collected in other parts of the Sangamon River drainage. Additionally, since a relationship exists between culture and natural environment, special emphasis has been placed upon the particular environmental characteristics of the lake, the significance of its location within the drainage and the manner in which Late Woodland and Mississippian populations may have adapted to these circumstances.

Since the natural environment of the Sangamon River drainage and its tributaries is so important to this discussion, some background regarding it and its peculiarities is in order. The most complete environmental description and synthesis of the lower and central portions of the region has been provided by Roper

Table 8.2 Identifiable Bone Specimens from the Shire Site

Type	Classification	Number	%	Type	Classification	Number	%
MAMMALS				**FISH**			
White-tailed deer	Odocoileus virginianus	586		Bowfin	Amia calva	11	
Elk	Cervus canadensis	5		Pike/ Muskellunge	Esox spp.	1	
Cottontail	Sylvilagus floridanus	29		Bass	Micropterus spp.	3	
Squirrel	Sciurus sp.	79		Large-mouth Bass	M. salmoides	3	
Raccoon	Procyon lotor	23		Walleye/Sauger	Stizostedion spp.	1	
Plains pocket gopher	Geomys bursarius	1		Sucker	Catostomidae	6	
Eastern chipmunk	Tamias striatus	20		Redhorse	Moxostoma spp.	3	
Beaver	Castor canadensis	1		Smallmouth buffalo	Ictiobus bubalis	1	
Eastern mole	Scalopus aquaticus	8		Minnow	Cyprididae	1	
Gray wolf	Canis lupus	1		Freshwater drum	Aplodinus grunniens	1	
Fox squirrel	Sciurus niger	6		Sunfish	Centrarchidae	1	
Buffalo	Bison bison	1		Bullhead catfish	Ictalurus spp.	10	
Fox	Urocyon sp.	1		Yellow bullhead	I. natalis	2	
Thirteen-lined ground squirrel	Citellus tridencemlineatus	6		Channel catfish	I. punctatus	1	
	TOTAL	767	76.8		TOTAL	45	4.5
BIRDS				**MUSSELS**			
Turkey	Meleagris gallopavo	5		Three Ridge	Amblema costata	1	
Bird	unidentified	5		Blue Point	A. peruviana	3	
	TOTAL	10	1	Purple warty - back	Cyclonaias tuberculata	2	
AMPHIBIANS				Spike/Lady Finger	Elliptio dilatatus	1	
Frog	Rana spp.	2					
	TOTAL	2	.2	Mucket	Actinonais carinata	3	
REPTILES (other than turtle)				Fluted Shell	Lasmigona costata	1	
Snake		10		Pocketbook	Lampsilis ventricosa	1	
	TOTAL	10	1				
TURTLES				Black Sand Shell	Proptera alata	1	
Turtle	Pseudemys, Graptemys	6					
Box turtle	Terrapene spp.	153					
Ornate box turtle	T. ornata	5					
Painted turtle	Chrysemys picta	1					
	TOTAL	165	16.5				
				TOTAL IDENTIFIABLE BONE		999	100

(1979). Although the parameters of her investigations do not encompass the entire drainage, many of her observations are applicable to areas of the Sangamon drainage outside her research universe. Some review is necessary before further discussion can proceed.

As indicated in Figure 8.12, the Sangamon River and its tributaries meander through and drain much of the central Illinois prairie before entering the Illinois River near Beardstown. As Roper (1979:17) points out, "The Sangamon flows away from the 'Grand Prairie'–a frequently glaciated, flat, nearly treeless (prehistorically) area with shallowly entrenched drainage–toward the Illinois Valley–a less frequently glaciated, rather more dissected, thickly forested,

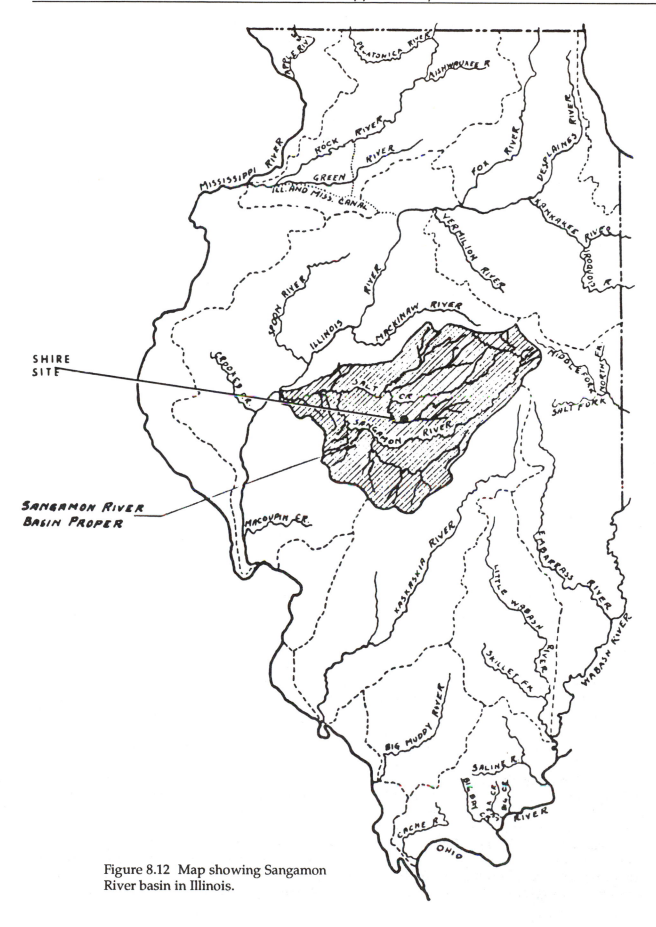

Figure 8.12 Map showing Sangamon
River basin in Illinois.

deeply incised valley. The Sangamon, therefore, has a great range of environmental diversity, at least within Illinois." Lake Fork Creek, situated nearly in the center of the drainage and the prairie, is environmentally more like the upper Sangamon than it is like the lower part of the drainage, which is more like the Illinois River valley.

The proximity of the Sangamon River and its tributaries east of Lake Fork Creek to other central Illinois drainages is also pertinent to this discussion. Many of the tributaries that are part of the upper Sangamon system closely parallel or nearly meet streams that form the Mackinaw, Kaskaskia, Embarras and Vermillion rivers. The Sangamon itself enters the Illinois River approximately 115 kilomenter west of Lake Fork.

Cultural Background in the Sangamon Drainage

Late Woodland (ca. A.D. 1050–1200)

Most of the Late Woodland data from the Sangamon has been derived from site surveys. Few Late Woodland sites have been excavated within the drainage and even fewer date to the time period in question. In spite of this paucity of information from excavated sites, some distributional patterns for particular ceramic types have been documented. At this time no indigenous Late Woodland ceramic types have been identified in the drainage.

During the time period under consideration, Maples Mills, presumably a ceramic type originating in northern Illinois and intrusive into the central Illinois River valley, occurs throughout the drainage and has been documented as far up river as the Hood site in Macon County (Lewis 1975a). Hood (M^{v}56) is situated nearly 50 kilometers east of the Shire site. Maples Mills in the Sangamon is frequently found in association with other ceramic types. For example, ". . . every site in the Sangamon Valley which has Mississippian ceramics also has Maples Mills ceramics, but the reverse is not true" (Roper 1979:38).

Other Late Woodland ceramic types found in the drainage have also been documented with Maples Mills. Albee Cordmarked, a type found frequently in the lower Wabash River valley and east central Indiana (Winters 1967:60-68), and Starved Rock Collared, another northern Illinois type (Hall 1987:65-70), also occur together on Lake Fork Creek sites and on the Hood site (Lewis 1975a) as well. Regarding these occurrences Roper also notes that "every site with Albee and Starved Rock also has Maples Mills, but the reverse is not true (1979:38)." Lake Fork Creek, however, is the only part of the Sangamon in which *all* of Roper's statements regarding Late Woodland

ceramics are true. At present, Lake Fork Creek represents the most western extension of Albee and Starved Rock in the Sangamon drainage. Although no collared ceramics were found at Shire, they do occur on three sites within 2 kilometers of Shire.

In addition to the Maples Mills and the collared ceramics at the Hood site, Lewis (1975a:21) also reports the presence of a sand-tempered Late Woodland variety designated as Paste Category 3. Green (1977:32) has identified these specimens as Bauer Branch. These ceramics, based on the site distributions provided by Green (1977:Figure 5), appear to be concentrated in the central Illinois River valley/west central Illinois area.

At the Miller site, situated along Salt Creek approximately 40 kilometers northeast of Lake Fork, Lewis (1975b:36-37) reports the presence of Late Woodland ceramics, some of which closely resemble "Bluff" jar rim forms, as well as other specimens that he feels resemble some of the Woodland specimens at Shire.

It would seem, then, in spite of the small number of sites that have been examined, that the occurence of multiple Late Woodland ceramic types observed at Shire is not unique, as originally surmised. The multi-drainage interaction noted at Shire may be fairly typical within the drainage. It would also appear that the inhabitants of the upper portion of the Sangamon drainage and Lake Fork Creek in particular, were not culturally isolated during the Late Woodland period, but were, in fact, living at a "cultural crossroads."

Since it could be argued that these conclusions are based on too little survey data and too few excavated sites to be valid, the entire prehistoric sequence represented at Lake Fork has been examined. Not surprisingly, the multi-directional, extra-territorial relationships suggested for the Late Woodland can be documented as far back as the early Archaic and they continue to varying degrees during all subsequent cultural periods (Claflin 1974). Furthermore, ethno-historical sources document widespread intra-regional movements by the Kickapoo–the last aboriginal population to occupy the central Illinois prairies (Temple 1966).

In order to explain why these extra-territorial contacts appear to be so common and include so many sources at Shire, at Lake Fork and in the Sangamon drainage in general, it is necessary to examine closely the natural environment and the way indigenous Late Woodland populations adapted to it. Unfortunately, as noted earlier, little archaeological research beyond the survey level has been conducted in the Sangamon River drainage, but some data from the east central Illinois prairie may be applicable. Regarding Late Woodland settlement/subsistence in that area, Douglas (1976:87) believes Late Woodland peoples were practicing generalized adaptations tailored to their generalized environments and he sees "...frequent and regulated movement as a necessary condition to successfull adaptation to the Woodfordian area." Since the Sangamon drainage, especially its central and upper sections, is environmentally so similar to the east central Illinois prairie, there is currently no reason to suggest that its Late Woodland populations exploited the environment any differently.

Archaeologists tend to conduct research within entire drainages or along segments of drainages and, consequently, there has been an unconscious tendency to think of prehistoric settlement or movement to have been exclusively linear, that is, movement up and down a particular drainage, or movement or settlement across stratified physiographic zones within a segment of a particular drainage. While these patterns of movement are demonstrably true within many research areas, even within the Sangamon, it is argued here that they are not necessarily the exclusive patterns, particularly in the central and upper Sangamon including Lake Fork. Given the homogeneity of the prairie environment and the small size of the streams in the central and upper Sangamon, which inhibit travel by water, overland movement (across the prairie from one forested stream to another) becomes a more efficient means of travel.

Considering the proximity of the upper Sangamon and many of its tributaries to other drainages, an inter-drainage utilization pattern, like a seasonal round encompassing a number of different drainages, could develop. If it can be assumed that populations inhabiting the upper reaches of these other drainages might also locate in the Sangamon, the interaction, contact, etc., indicated by the various ceramic types present at Shire and other Late Woodland sites in the Sangamon is more easily understood. Furthermore, it is not then necessary to posit an elaborate, complicated trade system or involvement in such a trade system to explain the movement of various ceramics from region to region, because this phenomenon would reflect frequent "outside" contacts encountered within a normal subsistence/settlement adaptation.

While the above might explain why multiple pottery types appear together in some single-component Late Woodland sites in the upper Sangamon, it fails to resolve why so many are found together at Shire. It is argued here that the numbers and variations of Late Woodland ceramics are present at Shire because of the lake.

If it is accepted that the central and upper Sangamon acted as a cultural interface or crossroads, as the archaeological record for the region indicates, the Lake Fork Creek drainage in general and the lake in particular, may have been considered an "oasis" in the prairie by some populations, particularly during the local Middle Woodland and Late Woodland periods.

The Lake Fork drainage supported a large Middle Woodland village and mortuary center (Lo^{v}4), as well as a village and mortuary center in the Late Woodland (Lo^{v}24). It is the latter site that is relevant to this discussion. Lo^{v}24 is situated approximately 300 meters west of the Shire excavation units. Originally consisting of six small conical mounds, the site now contains only two. Local informants report that at least three of the mounds, which have been bulldozed away, were situated in the same agricultural field as the Shire site. Examination of Illinois State Museum and local "amateur" collections indicate the ceramic component from the site is no earlier than Late Woodland. Support for this dating is the fact that Maples Mills sherds have been identified. A complete Maples Mills vessel observed in a local collection was supposedly recovered from one of the now-destroyed mounds. Assuming, then, that the Shire excavation units are part of this village and mortuary center, it can be concluded that this locality on the lake was the site of an extremely large Late Woodland complex exceeding 12 hectares in area.

Regardless of whether Shire is considered part of this complex, the physical presence of this mound complex near the lake remains significant. Although other Late Woodland mortuary sites may be present in the central and upper Sangamon, they have yet to be discovered by professional archaeologists. The other archaeological surveys that have been conducted in the central and upper Sangamon (Lewis 1973, Holland 1965, Styles et al. 1979) reflect a paucity of this Late Woodland site type. If, indeed, the lack of large sites is a cultural reality rather than a sampling or survey bias, it would seem reasonable to suspect that Lo^{v}24 functioned as a major religious, social and "political" center for Late Woodland groups living in the central Illinois prairie.

Since the lake appears to be the primary difference between the geographies of Lake Fork drainage and other streams draining this part of the prairie, it was likely the factor that determined placement of this particular site type. The lake and its attendant resources insure the environmental stability necessary to support a large, more permanent settlement.

Given the proximity of the Shire excavation to Lo^{v}24, it is reasonable to suspect that the Mississippian component at Shire might be part of this Late Woodland village and ceremonial complex. Without an archaeological survey, however, this suspicion cannot be heavily relied upon, especially given the density of archaeological sites in this small drainage. Depending on the locality, site densities range from a low of one site every 12 hectares to a high of one site every 2 hectares.

Overall, however, the proximity of Lo⌄24 to Shire, the large amount of Late Woodland material recovered from the Shire excavations and the presumed Late Woodland copies of Mississippian vessels and the contemporaneity of the two localities suggested by the presence of Maples Mills pottery at both sites, constitute a set of circumstantial evidence that is difficult to explain away. Researchers familiar with central Illinois might consider the Collins site in Vermillion County (Douglas 1976) an analog for Shire and parallels can be drawn, but Collins appears to be physically more complex and functionally different from Shire.

Mississippian in the Sangamon

The paucity of Mississippian sites in the Sangamon drainage has already been discussed, as has the apparent uniqueness of a Mississippian presence at Shire. To explain the reasons for these phenomena, it is necessary to examine the factors involved in site selection and assess their relative importance.

These factors can be better isolated if the kind of site type Shire represents can be determined and if its function can be ascertained. For example, the factors important for selecting a site for a farmstead would likely be different from the criteria for selecting a base camp or village location. Unfortunately, no direct data were recovered from the excavations that could be used to determine site type or function. Again, circumstantial evidence and conjecture must be relied upon to supply an explanation.

The large numbers of Late Woodland and Mississippian ceramics found diminish the likelihood that Shire was just an isolated farmstead. Its isolation, along with its distance from other known Mississippian sites in the drainage, also argues against this categorization. Furthermore, there is no evidence that Shire functioned as a Mississippian ceremonial center, even a small one. The mortuary ceremonialism indicated by the nearby mound group seems to be Late Woodland derived.

A small village or hamlet site type seems to be a reasonable function designation, given the information derived both from local informants and from the excavated materials. It could then be argued that the lake locality was chosen because it closely duplicated a floodplain, back-water lake situation–a seemingly preferred Mississippian settlement location in riverine environments. Unfortunately, in this instance, this explanation fails to address why this group by-passed so much of the lower drainage to live by the lake. The idea of Mississippian men and women paddling wooden canoes up the Mississippi, then up the Illinois River and finally up the Sangamon River, Salt Creek and Lake Fork Creek in order to live by a lake,

although possible, seems a bit far-fetched. Yet, professional archaeological survey of the area indicated that the lower Sangamon drainage was essentially unoccupied by Mississippian people.

Site Evaluation

Function

If Shire was functionally different from typical Mississippian sites, that is, if the reasons for its existence were different, it might then follow that its physical placement would be different - in this case, the Illinois prairie. It is suggested here that the Shire site functioned primarily as a commercial embassy for Mississippian people among the indigenous Late Woodland inhabitants of the central Illinois prairies.

Because of the presence of Late Woodland copies of Mississippian ceramics, it is believed that the Shire site represents a simultaneous Late Woodland/Mississippian occupation.

It is assumed, therefore, that Shire functioned as a separate, culturally-distinct trading settlement within the already established Late Woodland community. This situation is seen as analogous to the successful 18th and 19th century European traders in the Midwest and the eastern plains. As described by Lehmer (1977:93), these European tenant-traders "...came individually, or in small groups, and wherever possible, they took up residence in the Indian villages, rather than in forts or trading posts." It is hypothesized that the Mississippian population at Shire acted as tenant-traders in a similar manner, living as members of a large, Late Woodland village, but maintaining their own cultural identity.

Parenthetically, it is interesting to note that this tenant-trader system was extremely successful among historic Indian tribes, no matter where it was employed. In the Illinois and Missouri territories, it was so successful that Auguste Chouteau (1816:104), American agent of Indian Affairs for Upper Louisiana, encouraged the adoption of this system for American traders, noting that the British always out-competed their American counterparts who did not employ the technique.

This functional designation is obviously conjecture, but, given the biophysical and cultural circumstances previously outlined that distinguish Lake Fork from all other parts of the drainage, it is the hypothesis that addresses the greatest number of questions posed in this investigation. To review, Lake Fork is:

1) the only natural lake in the entire region,
2) centrally located in the region, and
3) strategically important as the focus of a cultural interface with other regions throughout the prehistory of the area.

Additionally, it has been hypothesized that, at the time of Mississippian contact, inter-regional and multi-directional interaction and presumed trade were normal to the Late Woodland inhabitants of this region as a result of localized adaptation to its particular envrionmental conditions. One consequence of this constant inter-regional contact would have been that minimal effort was needed by an immigrant Mississippian population to become involved in a multi-regional network of trade. Contact with outside groups was then the norm, rather than the exception for these Late Woodland people. The fact that the lake would closely resemble a familiar Mississippian environment (a riverine, backwater lake) is a fortuitous coincidence.

Origins

It is also suggested that these Mississippian traders at Shire migrated from the American Bottom, rather than from closer Mississippian centers like those in the central Illinois River valley or the upper Kaskaskia River drainage. This argument is based on several separate lines of reasoning. First, during the period under consideration, Mississippian is emergent in both the latter regions and it seems unlikely that people in either drainage would be experiencing a need to establish a trading outpost at that stage in their development. Second, an examination of the Mississippian ceramic sequence in the upper Kaskaskia essentially eliminates it from consideration as the origin of the Shire traders; Mississippian ceramics in the upper Kaskaskia that date to the period under investigation are cord-marked with shell and sand tempering, apparently deriving from Mississippian developments in the Wabash River drainage (Moffat 1987, McGowan 1985, Lipenot et al. 1986).

The arguments based on ceramic comparisons do not as effectively refute the central Illinois valley connection, since the Powell Plain and the Ramey Incised specimens found at the Shire site closely resemble those same types found in the central Illinois valley. However, Harn's (1975:426) overview of the central Illinois Valley provides the strongest argument against a central Illinois valley Mississippian emigration to Shire:

> Early Mississippian habitation sites with associated Powell Plain and Ramey Incised ceramics are widely dispersed in the central Illinois valley. Fewer than twenty such sites are known, most of which are quite small and subsidiary in nature. Even given this small number, it is improbable that a majority were ever occupied simultaneously. If a

population intrusion from the direction of Cahokia is acutally indicated, the paucity and small size of the sites suggest the presence of only a small number of people.

In contrast, Cahokia had a large population with a multiplicity of needs and demands and a documented complex of wide ranging trade mechanisms to satisfy them (Porter 1969), so ties between Shire and Cahokia seem more justifiable. In addition, many Mississippian manifestations observed outside the American Bottom during the period under consideration appear to be derived Cahokia (Harn 1980, Douglas 1976, Perino 1971). Also, Mississippian ceramics associated with the Late Woodland "Albee Complex" of the Wabash River valley suggest close affinities to Cahokia (Winters 1967). There is no direct archaeological evidence indicating the kinds of articles being traded between the Shire and the American Bottom. However, it is felt that the model presented by Porter (1969:151) is a feasible analog.

Transport

It is also speculated that the migration of tenant-traders into the central Illinois prairie and the subsequent trade between the Shire site and Cahokia took place via overland routes rather than by water. In support of this contention, it is noted that several historical accounts refer to the existence of "Indian trails" used by early Euro-American settlers. These accounts cannot be construed as proof of overland travel between Shire and the American Bottom, but they do lend credence to the plausibility of the suggestion.

Zimri Emos, a government surveyor and one of the first residents of Springfield in Sangamon County, Illinois, documented the existence and location of an "Indian trail", which ran north-south just east of the original settlement of Springfield. This trail ran from the American Bottom near St. Louis, Missouri, to Peoria, Illinois. Known to early settlers as the Edwards Trace, it was the route taken by Ninian Edwards and his militia in 1812 to attack Indian villages located near Peoria. The trail "passed through little timber, followed nearly the watersheds or divides of the streams through the prairie (Enos 1911:219). An 1815 map of Illinois by Rene Paul traces the route of the Edwards expedition (Tucker 1942:Plate XL). According to Enos, Indians were utilizing the trail as late as 1821 and it was still well defined when he traveled part of the route in 1833.

The known propinquity of this trail to Lake Fork is based on an account by John Reynolds, a member of Edwards' "Rangers" who made the 1812 trip with Edwards from Fort Russell (Edwardsville, Illinois) to

Peoria. Reynolds (1855:87) reports that the militia ". . . crossed the Sangamon River east of the present city of Springfield and passed not far on the east of Elkhart Grove (Figure 1)." Elkhart Grove is a large, tree-covered moraine rising 60 meters above the flat prairie surrounding it. It is situated 6.4 kilometers northwest of the lake and, like the lake, was a major landmark for the region.

The reason for the absence of Mississippian sites between the mouth of the Sangamon and Lake Fork might be considered more explainable if links between Lake Fork and the American Bottom were by means of overland trails rather than by water. Expanding on this idea, it might also be hypothesized that since this historic Indian trail extended to the central Illinois River valley, it may have also served as a route between that area and the American Bottom during the Mississippian period. Certainly this overland route between the two areas would be shorter and more direct than river travel. Furthermore, unlike river travel, an overland trail could be utilized throughout the year, and, finally, it seems unreasonable to assume that the overland route described above, or even overland travel in general, was strictly a phenomenon of the Historic period.

If the hypothesis concerning overland travel is valid in this instance, then it is reasonable to assume that Mississippian people from the American Bottom could have used overland travel to reach other hinterland regions. Therefore, sites like Shire, while not necessarily commonly occurring, may not have been so unusual as originally surmised.

Conclusions

The excavation at Shire has demonstrated that from as early as A.D. 1050 to possibly as late as A.D. 1200, an apparently intrusive population displaying characteristics of the Mississippian cultural tradition settled along a natural lake in the middle of the central Illinois prairie. These people built rectangular, semi-subterranean, wall-trench houses, and there is evidence of sequential construction that implies a continuing, rather than ephemeral, occupation. The population possessed well-made, shell-tempered pottery and subsisted primarily by hunting, gathering and fishing, although agriculture cannot be totally ruled out as a source of food. A summer occupation is evidenced, but the site could have been inhabited throughout the year.

Other ceramic types and projectile point types indicate Late Woodland components at Shire. The variety of Late Woodland ceramic types represented in the assemblage point to the likelihood of extensive extraterritorial trade and/or contact. Not only was there at least one Late Woodland component that was contemporaneous with the Mississippian component at Shire, but the homogeneous mixing of the ceramics and projectile points of the two cultural traditions, along with the presence of Late Woodland copies of Mississippian ceramics, strongly hint that the two occupations were actually simultaneous.

Since the ethnic identity of the group responsible for the faunal material cannot be determined, hypotheses regarding subsistence and seasonality for the Mississippian component may or may not be equally appropriate for the Late Woodland component. The recovery of relatively large numbers of Late Woodland projectile points, as well as a large quantity of faunal remains attests to the fact that hunting was the primary method of food procurement for the Late Woodland population.

The excavations at Shire did succeed in confirming the presence of a "pure" Mississippian occupation along Lake Fork. Unfortunately, however, they revealed few data that were not surmised before the excavations began. Moreover, the excavations did little to resolve most of the research questions outlined at the beginning of this report, and no direct data were generated that would help explain the entry of a Mississippian population into the central Illinois prairie in general, or into lake Fork in particular. Furthermore, no direct data exist from the site or from survey that would explain why Mississippian failed to flourish in the Sangamon or why its demise occurred when it did. If the hypotheses presented here regarding how and why Shire existed are correct, it would seem that the demise of Shire could relate directly to events occuring in the American Bottom.

References Cited

Chouteau, Auguste
> 1816 Comments, Letters from the Secretary of War Transmitting the Documents Exhibiting Annuities and Presents and the General and Particular View of the Indian Trade.... William A. Davis, Washington.

Claflin, John
> 1974 *An archaeological Survey of a Holocene Lake in Central Illinois.* Manuscript on file, Anthropology Deparment, Illinois State Museum. Springfield, Illinois.

Cole, Fay-Cooper, et al.
    1951 *Kincaid: A Prehistoric Illinois Metropolis.* University of Chicago Press.
Douglas, John G.
    1976 *Collins: A Late Woodland Ceremonial Complex in the Woodfordian Northeast.* Ph.D. dissertation, University of Illinois, Urbana. University Microfilms, Ann Arbor, Michigan.
Enos, Zimri A.
    1911 The Old Indian Trail, Sangamon County, *Journal of the Illinois State Historical Society* 41:218-222, Springfield.
Fowler, Melvin L.
    1955 Ware Groupings and Decorations of Woodland Ceramics in Illinois, *American Antiquity* 20:213-225.
Gardner, William M.
    1973 The Vandalia Complex: A Late Woodland Complex in the Central Kaskaskia River Drainage, *Late Woodland and Site Archaeology in Illinois 1.* Illinois Archaeological Survey Bulletin 9:214-227. Urbana.
Green, William
    1977 Final Report of Littleton Field Archaeological Survey, Schuyler County, Illinois. Upper Mississippi Valley Archaeological Research Foundation Reports on Archaeology, No. 1. Report submitted to Amax Coal Company, Indianapolis, Indiana.
Griffin, James B.
    1949 The Cahokia Ceramic Complexes, *Proceedings of the Fifth Plains Conference for Archaeology.* Laboratory of Anthropology, University of Nebraska, Notebook 1:44-57.
Hall, Robert L.
    1987 Type Description of Starved Rock Collared, *The Wisconsin Archaeologist.* 68(1):65-70.
Harn, Alan D.
    1975 Cahokia and the Mississippian Emergence in the Spoon River Area of Illinois, *Transactions of the Illinois State Academy of Science.* 68(4):414-434.
    1980 The Prehistory of Dickson Mounds: A Preliminary Report, *Dickson Mounds Museum Anthropological Studies No.1.* Illinois State Museum, Springfield.
Holland, C.G.
    1965 *An Archaeological Survey of the Oakley Reservoir,* Illinois State Museum Preliminary Reports 5, Springfield.
Johnson, Judith B.
    1972 Proto-Euro-American Phytogeography of the Lower Sangamon River Drainage in Central Illinois. Manuscript on file, Anthropology Department, Illinois State Museum. Springfield.
Lehmer, Donald J.
    1977 The Other Side of the Fur Trade. *Reprints in Anthropology* 8:91-104. J. and L. Reprint Company, Lincoln, Nebraska.
Lewis, R. Barry
    1975a The Hood Site. *Reports of Investigations No. 31.* Illinois State Museum, Springfield.
    1975b Archaeological Salvage Investigations in the Proposed Clinton Reservoir, DeWitt County, Illinois. Illinois State Museum report submitted to Illinois Power Company, Decatur, Illinois.
Lewis, Sheila D.
    1973 *An Archaeological Survey of the Proposed Clinton Reservoir, Dewitt County, Illinois.* Illinois State Museum report submitted to the Illinois Power Company, Decatur.
Lapinot, Neal H., et al.
    1986 Cultural Resource Testing and Assessments: The 1985 Season at Lake Shelbyville, Shelby and Moultrie Counties, Illinois. *St. Louis District Cultural Resource Management Report No. 30.* U.S. Army Corps of Engineers, St. Louis.
Miller, James Andrew
    1973 Quaternary History of the Sangamon River Drainage System, Central Illinois. *Reports of Investigations No. 27.* Illinois State Museum, Springfield.
McGowan, Kevin P.
    1985 Cultural Resource Testing and Data Sampling at Thirteen Archaeological Sites in the Lake Shelbyville Project Area, Illinois. *St. Louis Cultural Resource Management Report 27.* U.S. Army Corps of Engineers, St. Louis District.

Moffat, Charles R.
  1987 Mississippian Settlement Patterns in the Upper Kaskaskia River Valley, Illinois. *Wisconsin Archaeologist* 68(3):238-265.
Peck, John M.
  1838 *Peck's New Gazeteer of Illinois*. Grigg and Eliot, Philadelphia.
Perino, Gregory H.
  1971 The Mississippian Component at the Schild Site (No. 4), Greene County. *Mississippian Site Archaeology: I*. Illinois Archaeological Survey Bulletin No. 8:1-148. Urbana.
Porter, James Warren
  1969 The Mitchell Site and Prehistoric Exchange Systems at Cahokia: A.D. 1000 ± 300. *Explorations into Cahokia Archaeology*. Illinois Archaeological Survey Bulletin 7:137-175. Urbana.
Reynolds, John
  1855 *My Own Times*. Perrymand and H.L. Davison, Belleville.
Roper, Donna C.
  1979 Archaeological Survey and Settlement Pattern Models in Central Illinois. *Illinois State Museum Scientific Papers, Vol. XVI, Midcontinental Journal of Archaeology, Special Paper Number 2*. Springfield.
Sears, William H.
  1973 Sacred and Secular in Prehistoric Ceramics, *Variation in Anthropology: Essays in Honor of John MacGregor*. Illinois Archaeological Survey, Urbana.
Styles, Bonnie Whatley, et al.
  1979 Archaeological Site Distribution in the Sangamon Drainage and Grand Prairie: Testing and Refinement of Predictive Models for Site Location. Illinois State Museum report submitted to the Illinois Department of Conservation.
Temple, Wayne C.
  1966 Indian Villages of the Illinois Country. *Illinois State Museum Scientific Papers, Vol. 2, Part 2*. Springfield.
Tucker, Sara Jones, ed.
  1942 Indian Villages of the Illinois Country. Part 1, Atlas. *Illinois State Museum Scientific Papers, Vol. 2*. Springfield.
Winters, Howard D.
  1967 An Archaeological Survey of the Wabash Valley in Illinois. *Illinois State Museum, Reports of Investigations No. 10*. Springfield.
Wittry, Warren L. and Joseph O. Vogel
  1962 Late Woodland Ceramics at the Cahokia Site. Council for Illinois Archaeology 3:1-13.

9

Above the American Bottom: The Late Woodland-Mississippian Transition in North-East Illinois

Charles W. Markman
Archaeological Survey
University of Missouri-St. Louis

The Cooke site (11Ck52) is located on a gentle ridge, just east of the Fox River, and sixty kilometers west of the Chicago lake shore (Figure 9.1). Recent investigations at Cooke provide insight into the beginnings of the Langford Tradition, a grit-tempered, Upper Mississippian ceramic tradition that occurred in northern Illinois. The Cooke site ceramic assemblage along with radiocarbon dates provide only a general indication of the position of the site in the cultural chronology of north-east Illinois. These data also raise questions regarding the chronology of interaction with the American Bottom and other Middle Mississippi centers to the south. While it is evident that the cultural transformations which occur between the Woodland and Mississippian period were far more radical at these centers than in northern Illinois, it is not altogether clear what role the cultural dynamism of the south had in transforming cultures upstream and to the north. In this regard, the apparent co-appearance of maize horticulture and Ramey Incised-like decorative motifs in northern Illinois at sites like Cooke by A.D. 1100 (i.e., the time of the Stirling phase at Cahokia) suggests that cultural developments in northern Illinois were somehow related to those occurring in the American Bottom region. However, the presence of 8-row maize at Cooke at a time when 10- and 12-row maize still predominated in the American Bottom complicates the issue.

This paper presents results from fieldwork at the Cooke site conducted during the 1984, 1985, and 1986 seasons by Northern Illinois University summer field schools, under the direction of the author and considers the implications of this research in terms of adaptation in north-east Illinois during the transition from a Late Woodland to an Upper Mississippian pattern.

Investigations at the Cooke Site

Prior to the most recent research at the Cooke Site, limited excavations were conducted by Elaine Bluhm in the late 1950s and by David Wenner and Jane MacCrae in the early 1960s (MacCrae 1968). These earlier projects, and the most recent project as well, were initiated with the encouragement of the landowner, Mrs. Henry Cooke, who has maintained an interest in the site and in seeing that it receive the attention of professional archaeologists. Mrs. Cooke has surface-collected the site since childhood. Her collection includes over one hundred diagnostic projectile points, covering the chronological spectrum from the Paleo-Indian through the Upper Mississippian period, and an Historic kaolinite pipe as well (ibid.).

At first, the prospect of investigating a site with such a broad, mixed assemblage was discouraging. However, in discussing the provenience of materials with Mrs. Cooke, it seemed that temporally discrete deposits might be spatially segregated over the two-and-a-half-hectare collection area. A systematic surface survey was conducted to augment the distribution information provided by the landowner. It was apparent that an intensive early Upper Mississippian

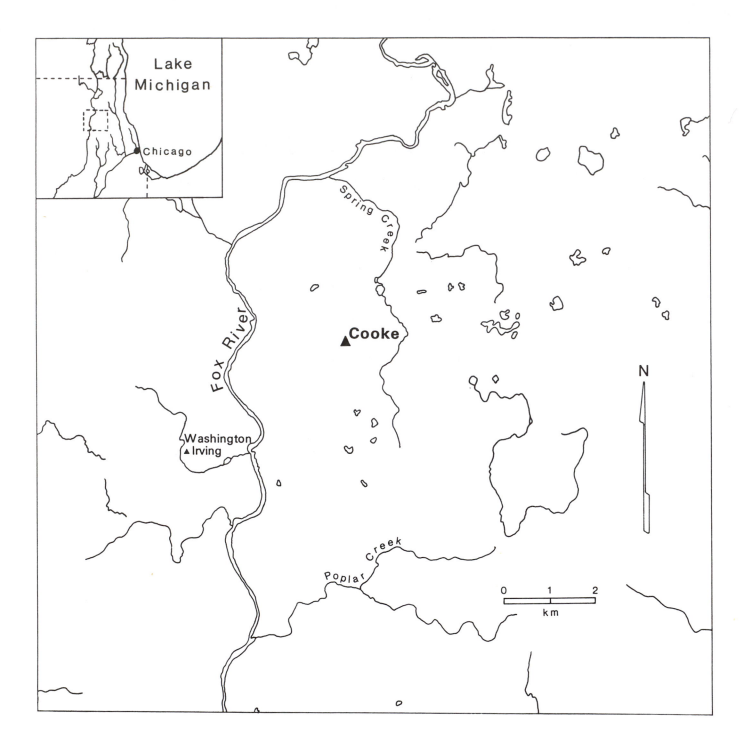

Figure 9.1. The Cooke and Washington Irving site locations in the central Fox River Drainage, north-east Illinois.

period occupation occurred on a low rise along the east edge of the property, next to a pond and marsh (Figure 9.2). The earlier investigations indicated that undisturbed feature deposits existed below the plow-zone in this area but flotation recovery techniques had not been utilized. Thus, the prospect of recovering ethnobotanical and faunal data from datable contexts provided a major impetus for beginning the latest phase of investigation at the Cooke site.

The Northern Illinois University excavations began with a four week session in the summer of 1984 in which an excavation block measuring approximately 4 m × 10 m was opened (Figure 9.3). Excavations were conducted by pealing the plowzone, a dark silty clay loam about 15 cm thick, and exposing the lighter colored subsoil along with the darkened stains of pit features. The site is situated on a morainal ridge, and Holocene deposits are confined to the plowzone, except for features that intrude into the glacial subsoil. Eleven such features were found in the main excavation block in the 1984 season, five of which were possible postmolds and seemed to form a semi-circular configuration, possibly the apsidal end of an elongated structure or a portion of an oval or circular structure. The postmolds are widely spaced, yet considering the effects of plowing and erosion, it is likely that more shallow postmolds as well as remnants of a living floor, had been obliterated. During 1985, the main excavation block was enlarged to the east in hope of exposing a continuation of the postmold configuration. However, the picture that emerged was not a simple one. A cluster of large refuse-filled pits occurred within the additional forty square meters of horizontal extension. In 1986 the main-block excavation was extended to the southeast into an area of thicket that had not been plowed, at least not within recent times. The configuration of closely spaced pit features continued in this area, suggesting that the locale had been occupied repeatedly with new hearths and refuse pits being dug during successive occupations.

During the 1984 season, two one-meter test squares, Test Units 2 and 3, were dug, south of the main block (Figure 9.2). Test Unit 2 was placed in a low-lying area, and the water table was reached at a depth of 60 cm. The very dark loam, which continued to the bottom of the test unit, made it nearly impossible to distinguish soil strata. The pit yielded a high concentration of ceramics, faunal remains, and maize fragments, suggesting that the area may have been used for refuse disposal. Two features, Features 12 and 13, were found in opposite corners of Test Unit 3. During the 1986 season, Test Unit 3 was re-opened and the excavation was enlarged into a 2 m × 2 m test unit, Square 205, so that the remaining portions of these features, could be excavated. Also in the final season,

three 2 m × 2 m test units, Squares 201, 202, and 203 were placed in the field west of the main block in areas where sparse surface debris had been encountered. Two of these units were sterile. A solitary postmold stain, Feature 42, was encountered in the third unit, Square 201.

A total of forty-two features was recorded during three seasons from 1984-1986 (Table 9.1).

Patterns of Resource Utilization

The Cooke site is situated on one of a number of parallel low ridges, together known as the Valparaiso Morainic System (Willman 1971). This geological formation was produced as the ice sheets retreated eastward in a series of pulses as the Wisconsinan glaciation waned. As the ice continued to retreat, high-volume run-off of meltwater scoured out a steep, narrow valley between moraine ridges three kilometers west of the site. Today, the placid Fox River runs along the bottom of this trough.

The Greater Chicago area is characterized by flat terrain dotted with bogs and marshlands, the remnants of Late Pleistocene glacial lakes (Willman 1971). It has been shown that during the Holocene the extent of these wetland environments would have fluctuated with climatic changes that in turn would greatly affect settlement location choices (Brown 1990b; Jeske 1988; Larsen 1985; Markman 1991). The Lake Michigan shoreline was subject to the most radical fluctuations, caused not only by climatic factors, but also by geologic factors. At various times the water level changed dramatically in response to events causing blockage or erosion of existing spillways, or on occasion, the abandonment of an existing spillway for an alternate outlet (cf. Hough 1958; Larsen 1985).

The Cooke site, at an elevation of 285 m above sea level and 108 m above Lake Michigan, is the highest point in Cook County. Because the low ridge would provide relatively dry camping throughout even the wettest episodes of the Holocene, and because the locality has not been affected by colluvial, alluvial, or lacustrine deposition, it is not surprising that archaeological materials from almost all periods of prehistory are represented in the surface collection.

The principal site component, which represents the early Upper Mississippian period, is located on a relatively low-lying portion of the field just above a shallow spring-fed pond. Though reconstruction of the setting at the time of occupation is problematic, it seems likely that the pond was formed in the last century by erosion causing a siltation blockage (Farrell 1987). The pond has since diminished in size through additional siltation. A significant amount of topsoil loss through erosion from the field above the pond has been

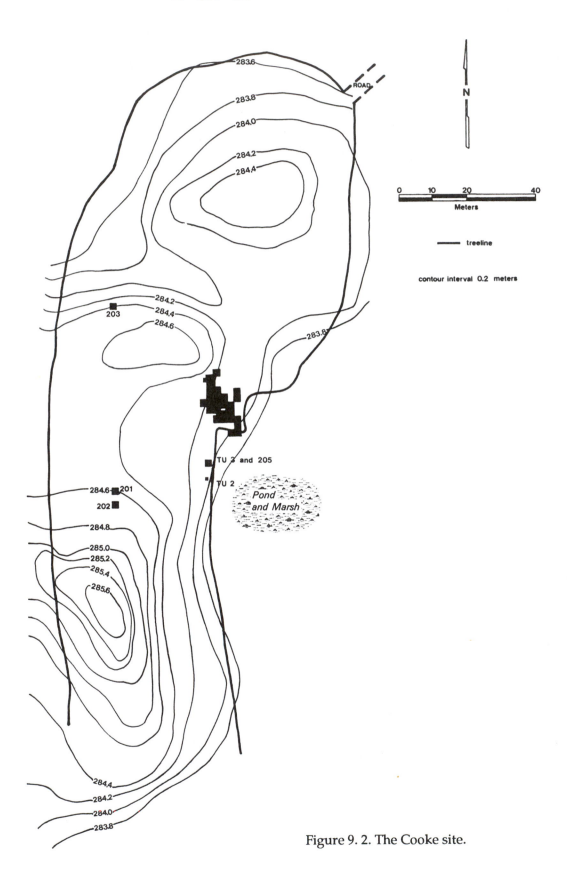

Figure 9. 2. The Cooke site.

THE COOKE SITE   11 CK 52

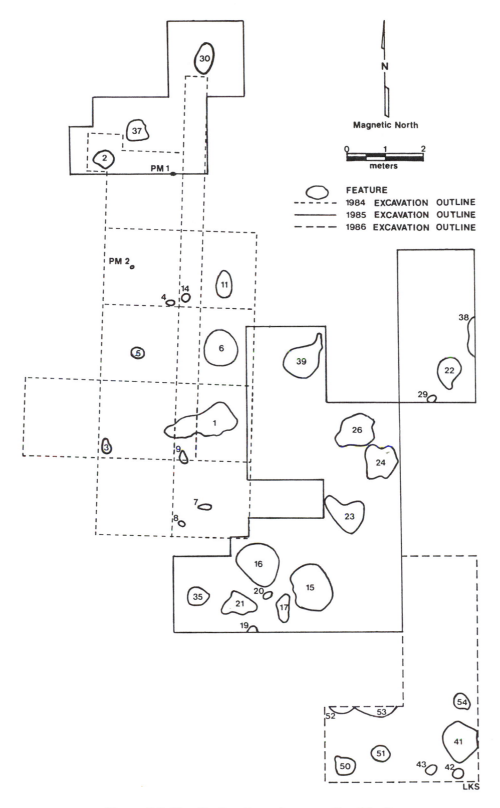

Figure 9.3. The Cooke site main excavation block.

Table 9.1 The Cooke Site (11Ck52) Feature Tabulation

Feature Number	Feature Category	Length x Width x Depth	Fill Description	Contents	Comments
1	Composite Pit	214 x 90 x 46	Dark Loam	Ceramics, Lithics, Charcoal, Bone, Shell, Fired Clay	Burnt pit lining. C_{14} dates, AD 780 $\pm$130 AD 1000$\pm$70
2	Small Basin	51 x 51 x 11	Dark Loam	Ceramics, Lithics, Charcoal, Bone	C_{14} date, AD 910 $\pm$130
3	Small Basin	57 x 40 x 13	Dark Loam	Ceramics, Lithics, Charcoal, Bone	
4	Post Mold	19 x 18 x 18	Dark Loam	Ceramics, Charcoal	
5	Post Mold	21 x 20 x 17	Dark Loam	Ceramics, Charcoal	
6	Small Basin	60 x 55 x 25	Dark Loam with Glacial Cobbles	Ceramics, Lithics, Charcoal, Bone	
7	Indeterminate		Shallow stain		
8	Indeterminate			Bone	Bone concentration
9	Post Mold	20 x 20 x 20	Dark Loam and 1 Large Cobble	Charcoal	
10	Post Mold	25 x 20 x 5	Dark Loam	Charcoal	
11	Small Basin	55 x 40 x 15	Dark Loam	Ceramics, Charcoal, Bone	
12	Rectangular Pit	56 x 47 x 36	Dark Loam with Glacial Cobbles	Ceramics, Lithics, Charcoal, Bone	C_{14} date, AD 1020 $\pm$70
13	Small Basin	72 x 60 x 17	Dark Loam	Lithics, Charcoal, Bone	
14	Post Mold	26 x 24 x 32	Dark Loam Charcoal	Ceramics, Lithics,	C_{14} date, AD 850 $\pm$120
15	Conical Pit	65 x 65 x 45	Dark Loam	Ceramics, Lithics, Charcoal, Bone, Shell	
16	Cylindrical Pit	110 x 90 x 55	Dark Loam	Ceramics, Charcoal, Bone, Shell	
17	Small Basin	60 x 55 x 37	Dark Loam with Glacial Cobbles	Ceramics, Lithics, Charcoal, Bone	
21	Small Basin	60 x 55 x 15	Dark Loam	Ceramics, Charcoal, Bone	
22	Large Basin	2 x 45 x 23	Dark Loam	Ceramics, Charcoal, Bone, Shell	
23	Composite Pit	112 x 35 x 26	Dark Loam with Glacial Cobbles	Ceramics, Charcoal, Bone	
24	Large Basin	85 x 65 x 30	Dark Loam with Glacial Cobbles	Ceramics, Charcoal	

Table 9.1 Continued

Feature Number	Feature Category	Length x Width x Depth	Fill Description	Contents	Comments
26	Large Basin	82 x 58 x 39	Dark Loam with Glacial Cobbles	Ceramics, Lithics, Charcoal, Bone	
29	Post Mold	20 x 18 x 10	Dark Loam	Charcoal	
30	Large Basin	90 x 85 x 50	Dark Loam	Ceramics, Charcoal	
35	Small Basin	51 x 44 x 2	Dark Loam	Ceramics, Charcoal, Bone	
37	Cob/bark-filled	47 x 43 x 55	Very Dark Loam	Charcoal, Bone	Cylindrical shape Pit
38	Small Basin	38 x x 14		Ceramics, Lithics, Charcoal, Bone	
39	Large Basin	125 x 60 x 38	Dark Loam	Ceramics, Charcoal, Bone, Shell	
40	Post Mold	25 x 15 x 12	Dark Loam	Charcoal	
41	Large Basin	110 x 100 x 23	Dark Loam	Ceramics, Lithics, Charcoal, Bone	
42	Small Basin	25 x 25 x 8	Dark Loam	Lithics, Charcoal, Bone	
43	Small Basin	45 x 35 x 12	Dark Loam	Charcoal	
44	Small Basin	65 x x 20	Dark Loam	Ceramics, Lithics, Charcoal, Bone	
45				Same as Feature 13.	
46				Same as Feature 12.	
47	Large Basin	90 x 86 x 40		Ceramics, Charcoal	
50	Small Basin	50 x 35 x 3	Dark Loam	Ceramics, Lithics, Charcoal, Bone	
51	Small Basin	50 x 50 x 18	Dark Loam	Ceramics, Lithics, Charcoal, Bone	
52	Large Basin	80 x x 15	Dark Loam	Ceramics, Lithics, Charcoal	
53	Indeterminate		Dark Loam with Glacial Cobbles	Ceramics, Lithics, Charcoal, Bone	
54	Small Basin	40 x 30 x 8	Dark Loam	Ceramics, Lithics, Charcoal, Bone	
55	Cob/bark-filled	30 x 20 x 35	Very Dark Loam	Ceramics, Charcoal, Shell	Cylindrical shape Pit
PH1	Post Mold	9 x 5 x 10	Dark Loam	Charcoal	
PH2	Post Mold	8 x 7 x 2	Dark Loam	Charcoal	

observed by the landowner during her lifetime. It has also been noted by older residents of the area that the pond was much more extensive early in this century. The early Upper Mississippian occupants may well have been living next to a spring-fed brook, rather than a spring-fed pond. This reconstruction is supported by the absence of aquatic and semi-aquatic species such as American lotus (*Nelumbo lutea*) and a species of bull rush (*Scirpus* sp.), both of which occur at the slightly later Washington Irving site (Egan 1985; Jeske 1990), a Langford Tradition Upper Mississippian site five kilometers from Cooke. Furthermore, the relative paucity of fish also supports the reconstruction. And those species that were found probably came from a larger body of water, most likely the Fox River (Kreisa 1986).

Government Land Office map and survey records of circa 1840 show that the area was characterized by a preponderance of oak forest, occasionally interrupted by patches of prairie (cf. Kilburn 1959). Essentially the same pattern holds today except that the former prairies are now cultivated. Of course, suburban development has also affected the area, but not as severely as areas farther east, toward Chicago. Infrared satellite imagery shows a deep red band around the western edge of the Chicago Region and east of the Fox River, indicating substantial tree cover on the moraine ridges (Lumen et al. 1986). The deep red band becomes wider towards the Wisconsin border. Rectangular farm plots are seen west of the tree-lined Fox River. Before Euro-american colonization, most of the cultivated till plains to the west would have been characterized by prairie.

Presumably the proportions of oak forest and prairie in the immediate vicinity of the site fluctuated in response to changes in moisture and temperature regime. The principal occupation of the site would have occurred during the Neo-Atlantic climatic episode, which ended around A.D. 1150. In the northern Midwest, this was a warm episode of favorable agricultural conditions, not unlike the past fifty years (Bernabo 1981; Larsen 1985:Table 1; Webb and Bryson 1972; Swain 1978). Thus the present landscape provides a reasonable indication of the environment of the site vicinity during its principal occupation. The immediate vicinity would be characterized by extensive edge zones at the interface of prairie and forest, making it prime deer habitat. A five kilometer site catchment radius would encompass the bluffs and narrow bottomlands of the Fox River as well as the marshes that line Spring Creek, a Fox River tributary.

The results of faunal and botanical data analysis show that the inhabitants of the site did not fully exploit the spectrum of available resources within the five kilometer catchment zone (Kreisa 1986; Parker

1985). It appears that the Cooke site represents a specialized extraction camp, mainly an encampment where a primary focus of activity was the procurement of deer that might congregate during the fall to take advantage of the acorn mast (Parker 1985). Though a variety of small mammal and fish bone is present in the faunal sample, deer bone makes up an overwhelming portion of the assemblage (Table 9.2). Likewise, corn dominates in the floral assemblage with gathered seeds represented in small quantities (Table 9.3).

Feature 1 was the largest feature encountered and had one of the highest densities of deposit at the site (Figure 9.4). The feature fill included large quantities of faunal, floral, and artifact debris. Evidently Feature 1 was utilized repeatedly over an extended period of time for different purposes. One portion of the feature contained an extremely heavy concentration of charred bark and corn-cob fragments, which may indicate that one of its functions was as a smudge pit or hide-smoking pit (cf. Binford 1967). Similar concentrations of corn cupules and bark were found at the bottom of Features 37 and 55. The interpretation of these features as hide-smoking pits corroborates other data and adds further support to the notion that a primary function of the site was as a fall deer procurement and processing camp. However, an alternate interpretation of this type of feature has been offered by Patrick Munson (1969) who suggests they may have been used for producing a smudge finish on pottery.

The water source and other habitat features must have made the Cooke site an ideal location for attracting deer and, consequently, an ideal location for ambush hunting. The faunal configuration is similar to that of upland Late Woodland sites that have been studied from southwest Wisconsin (Theler 1987) and north-east Iowa (Benn 1980). The southwest Wisconsin pattern has been interpreted in terms of groups moving into the upland areas in the late fall to exploit white-tailed deer. The analysis of dental cementum annuli from deer remains in Hadfields Cave, an upland site in north-east Iowa, show that the animals were taken in the fall and winter (Benn 1980:155).

Corn is ubiquitous in features at the Cooke site averaging 28.1 fragments per liter. The sample includes kernel fragments as well as cob fragments and cupules. It is evident that corn was either being cultivated at the site or brought to the site as whole cobs. If corn was grown in the upland area within the near vicinity, it is likely that corn hilling techniques were used. This method was used extensively in the Historic period in forested upland settings (cf. Sasso and Brown 1987).

An analysis of cupule dimensions, following the method outlined by Cutler and Blake (1976), suggests

Table 9.2 Taxa Present at the Cooke Site (11CK52) *

SPECIES	AGGREGATED MNI	MNI BY FEATURE	NUMBER OF ELEMENTS	1964 ASSEMBLAGE **
Fish				
Esocidae (Pike)	–	–	1	
Ictaluridae (Catfish)	–	–	1	
Centrarchidae (Sunfish)	–	–	17	
Pisces (Unidentifiable)	–	–	10	
Reptiles				
Terrapene sp. (Box Turtle)	1	3	5	
Testudines (Unidentifiable	–	–	20	
Birds				
Anas sp. (Duck)	1	1	3	
Bucephela albeola (Bufflehead)	1	1	1	
Bubo virginianus (Great-Horned Owl)	1	1	1	
Aves (Unidentifiable)	–	–	7	
Mammals				
Gaucomys volans (Southern Flying Squirrel)	1	1	1	
Microtus sp. (Meadow Vole)	1	2	8	
Sciurus sp. (Squirrel)	1	1	1	
Castor canadensis (Beaver)	1	1	1	
Ondatra zibethica (Muskrat)	1	4	10	
Procuyon lotor (Racoon)	1	4	11	+
Urocyon/Vulpes (Fox)	1	1	4	+
Carnivora (Unidentifiable)	–	–	5	
Cervus canadensis (Elk)	1	1	2	+
Odocoileus virginianus (White-tailed deer)	6	23	234	+
Mammalia (Unidentifiable)	–	–	2111	+
Unidentifiable	–	–	913	
TOTALS	18	44	3367	

* From Kreisa (1985) based on an analysis of 1984 and 1985 materials including Features 1 through 39.
** Identifications by Paul Parmalee, reported by Jane MacCrae (1968:211).

that 8 and 10 row corn was being utilized at the Cooke site by A.D. 1100 during the early Upper Mississippian occupation (Parker 1985) (Table 9.4). The low row numbers suggest that the variety being cultivated was the cold-adapted, Eastern Eight-Row (Cutler and Blake 1976), a type commonly referred to as Northern Flint (Brown and Anderson 1947) and sometimes Eastern Complex (Yarnell 1964:107). Among Northern Flint varieties, it is usual that over 80% of the ears are eight-row, up to 15% are ten-row, and a few twelve-row ears may occur. Unfortunately, the Cooke site corn was not sufficiently intact to discern the cross-section shape of

the cob or the morphology of the kernels, key characteristics by which the Northern Flint identification could be confirmed. Northern Flint cobs tend to have a cross section that is square, pentagonal, or hexagonal rather than one which is round or elliptical and kernels have a distinctive crescent shape. However, Northern Flint has been identified at the Fisher site in Will County, another early Upper Mississippian site (ibid.: 115). It is also prevalent at later sites in north-east Illinois (see Table 9.3).

Interestingly, the more northerly adapted 8 and 10 row races do not become dominant at Cahokia and the

Table 9.3	Summary of Floral Data for the Cooke Site
Total features analyzed	22
Total liters fill analyzed	591
Mean wt. charcoal/10 ltrs. (g)	1.8
Mean wood fragments/10 ltrs. (g)	115.7
Mean nut fragments/10 ltrs. (g)	3.4
Nut:Wood ratio	0.03
Mean seeds/10 ltrs. (g)	1.4
Features with cucurbits, %	0
Features with maize, %	59.1

[*] Data from Parker (1985). Compare with Johannessen (1984: Tables 12-14).

Table 9.4 Summary Corn Data for Northeast Illinois

Site	Reference	Period/ Phase	No. Cobs	Mean Row No.	Median Cupule Width in mm	Row Numbers % Total Sample 8 10 12 14 16
Cooke (11Ck52)	1	Langford		8.7	7.0	56 30 1 -- -- Estimated from cupule dimensions (N=100).
Fisher	2	Langford/ Fisher			7.2	"... Eastern (Northern Flint) in shape but smaller than the typical kernels of that race."
Palos (11Ck26)	3	Huber	21	8.9	8.2	71 19 10 - -
Zimmerman	3	Historic	22	8.6	8.0	19 10 - - -
Plum Island	3	Proto-Historic	38	9.7	7.4	38 41 20 1 -
Hoxie Farm	3	Huber	10	9.8		40 30 30 - -
Knoll Spring	3	Huber			distorted	Northern Flint
Oak Forest	4	Huber			"about 7 mm"	Crescent-shaped kernels. Most 8-row and 10-row estimated from cupule dimensions.

References: 1 - Parker 1985; 2 - Yarnell 1964; 3 - Cutler and Blake 1976;
4 - Asch and Asch n.d.

Feature 1   plan view

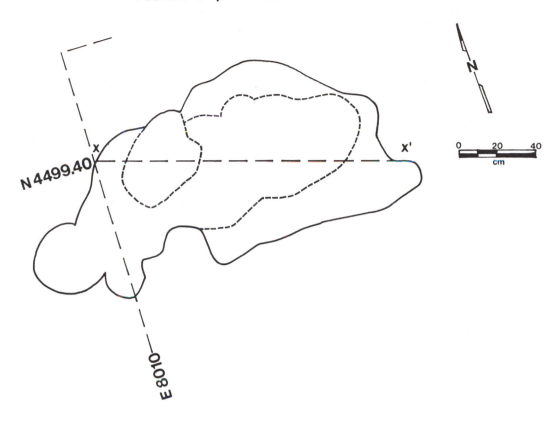

North wall profile

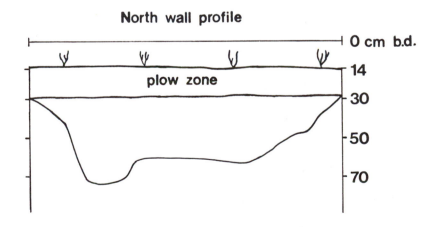

Figure 9.4. Feature 1.

American Bottom until much later (Watson 1988; Wagner 1983). Instead there is a substantial occurrence of maize with higher row numbers (Cutler and Blake 1976). The early predominance of 8-row corn at Cooke is not altogether surprising. By the end of the Woodland period, approximately 800-1000 A.D., vari-

eties showing affinity to later Northern Flint or Eastern Eight-Row had either developed or were introduced to the Central Plains (Adair 1988). For instance, at the Two Deer site in Kansas charred corn from the Bemis Creek phase represents a mixture of 8-12+ rows that may have been evolving toward 8-row dominance (ibid.:74-76). Radiocarbon dates at the site range between A.D. 860 and 1060 (Adair and Brown 1981). Later, true Northern Flint becomes evident or abundant at Steed Kisker sites in the Kansas City area. The Steed Kisker phase occurs between AD. 1000 and 1200 (O'Brien 1978:69-70 and this volume).

Although the question of origins remains largely unresolved, it is generally presumed that the emergence of Northern Flint in its distinctive form took place to the east, perhaps through a process of selection, genetic drift, and isolation (e.g., Doebley et al. 1986; Ford 1985; Galinat 1988; Wagner 1988). In Ohio, for instance, Eastern Eight-Row corn is ubiquitous and sometimes abundant at long-term habitation sites by the initiation of the Fort Ancient period, ca. A.D. 1000 (Wagner 1987). Northern Flint is particularly well suited to the cool, wet climates of the Northeast and, evidently, groups in southern Ontario, western New York and Pennsylvania, and eastern Ohio rapidly embraced corn agriculture once this locally adapted strain had fully evolved (Wagner 1988).

The Cooke botanical assemblage is significantly different from American Bottom assemblages in that Cooke has a very low seed count, averaging 1.4 seeds per 10 liters. The low frequency occurrence of seeds is a common pattern of contemporary northerly sites in southern Michigan (Katherine Parker 1986, personal communication). Also, in the Fort Ancient area and surrounding areas, where Northern Flint establishes an early predominance, similar low-frequencies of native North American starchy seeds have been observed, suggesting that starch requirements were being met almost entirely with corn (Wagner 1988). At the same time, a group of starchy seeds that made up a pre-maize complex—including maygrass, goosefoot, and knotweed—persisted in the American Bottom and elsewhere in the Middle Mississippi drainage, even after large scale maize agriculture appeared. Wagner has noted a correlation between the distribution of Northern Flint and high readings for heavy isotopes of carbon in skeletal samples, confirming the predominance of corn and the relatively low diversity of diet in these areas (ibid.).

The Cooke data seem to suggest a pattern similar to that of the Ft. Ancient area. However, at this point the regional database is insufficient to discern what, exactly, the site represents in terms of local adaptive patterns. Studies elsewhere in the Midwest have indicated that patterns of plant utilization can vary from drainage to drainage and site to site, even during the same period and phase (cf. Keegan 1987). There is no reason to believe that less diversity existed in northeast Illinois. Currently there are fewer than a dozen sites in north-east Illinois where sizable flotation samples have been recovered and analyzed, making it

easy to overstate conclusions regarding regional subsistence patterns and trends.

A very general conclusion which might be drawn from the Cooke site is that the semi-mobile, hunting-farming lifeways witnessed by the earliest explorers of the southern Lake Michigan vicinity, already existed in a recognizable form at the onset of the Mississippian period. Ethnohistoric descriptions of the subsistence-settlement strategies of Contact period Algonquin speaking groups in this same vicinity involved maize agriculture along with seasonal hunting and gathering activities. Hunting involved extended forays by small groups dispersing from semi-permanent agricultural villages, that were usually in riverine settings (Callender 1978a). Thus, settlement patterns changed on an annual cycle with agricultural villages being occupied in summer and outlying hunting camps in the fall, winter, and spring.

The Early Historic pattern described by Callender is a model that has been widely used for interpreting archaeological site locations and subsistence data at the southern end of Lake Michigan and in the Upper Illinois drainage area (e.g., J. Brown 1961, M.Brown 1975, Cremin 1980, 1983, Faulkner 1972, Michalik 1982, Peske 1971). More recently, it has been noted that there are ethnohistoric data to support a seasonal model in which the annual cycle is reversed:

> They [the Illinois] set them [summer hunting cabins] up on the edge of a prairie so as to be in a cool place, and for in the month of June and in order to be in the open all the southern nations establish themselves in the most open spots so as to see what is going on, and so as not to be taken by surprise, ... (Brown 1990b:161, citing Quaife 1947:94).

And,

> . . . [the] same family occupies perhaps a dozen different stops in a year. . . . In winter they generally select some romantically sheltered spot near a lake or stream . . . . In summer they reverse the order, camping on the highest knobs and most airy points on groves; sometimes, though rarely, planting a 'small patch' of corn (Brown 1990b:161-2, citing Kellar 1936:63).

Further research is necessary for explaining the discrepancy in the historic accounts. However, it is likely that the Early Historic pattern is more complicated than previously conceived.

Fission-fusion patterns are described for the Illinois (Callender 1978d:673-74; Deliette 1934) and Miami

(Callender 1978e:682; Trowbridge 1938), the Sauk (Callender 1978c:649; Marston 1912:148-152), Fox (Callender 1978b:637; Forsyth 1912:233-234; Marston 1912:148-153), Kickapoo (Callender et al. 1978:658), and Potowatami (Clifton 1978:727,729) as well as the Mascouten (Goddard 1978:729). Political structures existed, facilitating the summer coalescence of bands into villages, and the fall dispersal into smaller, independent units (eg. Callender 1978c:650; Forsyth 1822).

Recent interpretations of Langford settlement-subsistence patterns suggest that the ethnohistoric data provide an interpretive model that is useful, but only at a general level (Jeske 1990; Markman 1991). Significant changes had occurred in the long interim between the Cooke occupation and European Contact. Thus the Protohistoric and Early Historic models are not entirely appropriate for interpreting earlier settlement-subsistence patterns. The economies had remained diffuse and groups continued to move on an annual round, dispersing and coalescing according to resource availability. However, the Late Mississippian period in north-east Illinois seems to have been a time when population and community nucleation occurred similar to the process that is described in eastern Wisconsin at this same time (Overstreet 1978). It is evident, for instance, that by the late Mississippian period, the narrow stream valleys and uplands north of the Upper Illinois, including the Middle Fox Valley, had been largely abandoned (cf. Markman 1991). Furthermore, the ethnohistoric records indicate that at some point communal hunting of large game, mainly bison, had become an important component of the annual subsistence cycle throughout the Prairie Peninsula (Brown 1965). James Brown has placed this transformation at around A.D. 1400 or slightly afterward, contending that the spread of the communal bison hunt coincides with the spread of an Oneota horizon style. Although there is little evidence of bison at the Huber phase Oneota sites of north-east Illinois (cf. Markman 1991), Early Historic accounts of Central Algonquin groups describe communal buffalo hunts that involved distant forays to upland prairies, sometimes 100 to 150 kms away from the agricultural home-base villages. These took place either during the summer between corn planting and harvesting (e.g., Deliette 1934) or during the winter (e.g., Gibson 1963:32, 91).

On the basis of location and subsistence data, the Washington Irving site—though two hundred to three hundred years later than Cooke—seems to represent a similar Langford tradition, semi-permanent, summer agricultural village (Egan 1985; Yerkes 1985; Kreisa 1986; Jeske 1990). Irving is located by a small stream that runs within an old meander of the Fox River. Soils at Irving and its immediate vicinity are sandy and friable, therefore amenable to pre-plow methods of cultivation, contrasting markedly with the heavy clay loams of the upland Cooke site. Agricultural tools, such as the scapula hoes found at the Huber sites, or the massive chert hoes found at Mississippian sites in the American Bottom, are not evident at Irving, perhaps indicating more perishable implements, such as the digging stick, were used. Evidence for exploitation of lotus (*Nelumbo lutea*) tubers (Egan 1985) may indicate a late spring occupation. The presence of corn in almost all features suggests the site was occupied through the mid- or late-summer harvest.

The Irving faunal and botanical assemblages suggest a broader spectrum exploitation strategy than Cooke. Wetland, prairie, woodland, and floodplain resources are more evenly represented (Kreisa 1986; Yerkes 1985; Egan 1985). Like Irving, most Langford sites that have been investigated to date—Gentleman Farm (J. Brown et al. 1967), Zimmerman (J. Brown 1961; M. Brown 1975), Hotel Plaza (Schnell 1974)—are in riverine settings, and all demonstrate a broader spectrum of resource utilization than does the Cooke assemblage (Kreisa 1986). Even so, the inhabitants of Cooke maintained a relatively diverse diet during their stay. For instance, catfish and pike remains occur at the site indicating that, although strategically located for exploiting upland resources, riverine resources were also being sought. These fish, as well as some species of sunfish, require a fairly large body of water and the nearest available source would probably be the Fox River.

The lithic assemblage also supports an interpretation of the Cooke site as a specialized extraction camp. Using Washington Irving as a point of reference, the Cooke site shows relatively little evidence of primary reduction. Multifaces or cores make up only 6% of the chert tool assemblage compared with 28% at Irving. Pieces with cortical remnants make up only 17% of the Cooke assemblage, compared with 40% at Irving. It seems that lithic manufacturing activity at Cooke was limited to repairing tools that were brought to the site, while primary production of lithic tools took place elsewhere, perhaps at a more permanent, agricultural base camp.

The Ceramic Assemblage

Although the stylistic modes and iconographic motifs that are recognized as Mississippian are clearly a southern phenomenon, a refinement of local chronologies and cross-correlation between them is most important for discerning the time lag between the appearance of ideas in one region and their diffusion elsewhere. A refinement of chronologies is also essential for better understanding the degree to which ideas were filtered and reinterpreted as they moved northward. Unfortunately, radiocarbon methods do not provide sufficient resolution to sort out the phases that mark the rapid development of the Cahokia center (cf. Stoltman 1987), much less to correlate the contemporary chronology of north-east Illinois. Likewise, the standard errors on the Cooke and other north-east Illinois dates allow for a very broad range of dating possibilities, particularly when atmospheric correction factors are taken into account (see Figures 9.5 and 9.6).

The pottery assemblage from the Cooke site suggests that the principal occupation of the site occurred at the beginning of the Upper Mississippian period, just prior or during the beginning of the American Bottom Stirling phase. However, earlier ceramics are evident as well.

Of the 1,634 sherds recovered in the excavations between 1984 and 1986 only 588 exceeded a maximum length of 10 mm, a measurement used to select sherds for coding and analysis. Even within the selected group, the mean length was only 25.3 mm. And only 37 of the 588-sherd sample group were either rims or decorated pieces, that is, sherds that displayed attributes that would place them, without ambiguity, in established descriptive categories. These categories include Langford (J. W. Griffin 1946, 1948; J. Brown 1961; J. Brown et al. 1967), Aztalan Collared (Baerreis and Freeman 1958), Starved Rock Collared (Hall 1987), and Point Sauble Collared (Baerreis and Freeman 1958) (Figures 9.7 to 9.11). Also, Swanson Cordmarked (Brown 1961:39-41) and Madison Cord Impressed (Baerreis 1953) sherds may derive from an earlier occupation corresponding to the earliest of the five

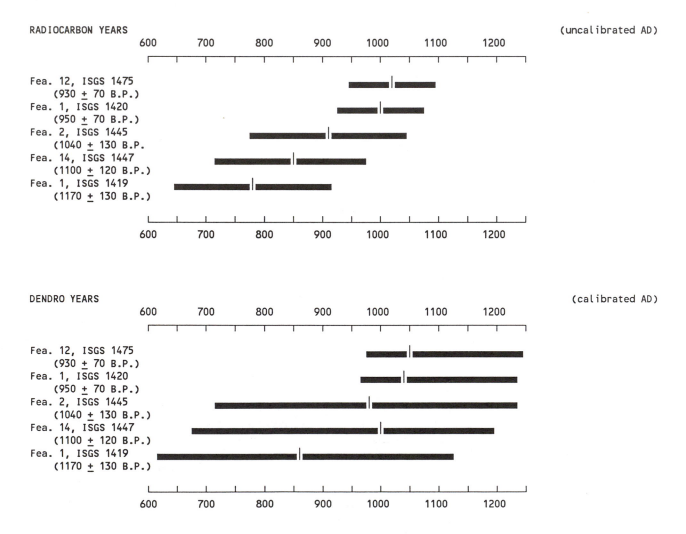

Figure 9.5. The Cooke Site (11Ck52) radiocarbon assays, provided by the Illinois State Geological Survey. All dates are from wood charcoal. TOP: The solid lines represent dates that have been corrected for isotopic fractionation, but not for the error in half-life of C-14, or for variations in the atmospheric concentration of C-14. BOTTOM: The solid horizontal lines represent the 2-sigma date ranges corrected for variations in atmospheric concentrations of C-14 using Method B of Stuiver and Becker (1986).

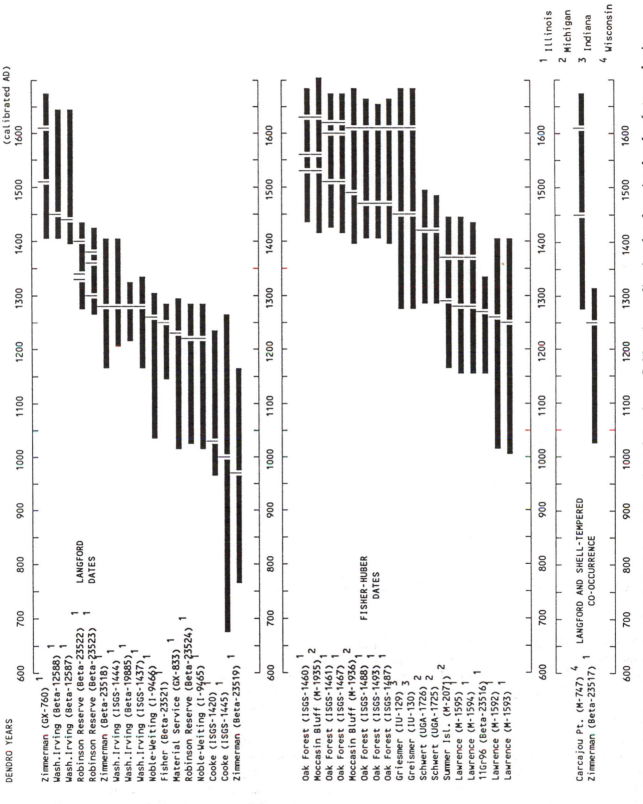

Figure 9.6. The Langford and Fisher-Huber radiocarbon chronology. Calibrations adjusting for changing levels of atmospheric C-14 were provided by Roelf Beukens, Isotrace Laboratory, University of Toronto. Horizontal bars represent the 95% confidence interval and vertical lines the intersection(s) of the radiocarbon dates and dendro calibration curve.

Figure 9.7. Vessel fragment from a Langford Trailed and Cordmarked vessel from the Cooke site, Feature 1.

dates obtained, A.D. 780 ± 130 (Figure 9.5). Middle Woodland ceramics were not encountered but are reported from earlier investigations. Jane MacCrae illustrates Steuben Punctate (1968:Fig. 68a) and two Naples Dentate Stamped sherds (1968:Figure 68 b, c) from the site. Otherwise, the assemblage from the early excavations and surface collecting is similar to that encountered during the Northern Illinois University field work. The Cooke assemblage includes no vessels from which a lip-to-base reconstruction can be made. Only two vessels are even partially reconstructible, one a Langford jar recovered from Feature 1, and the second a Swanson-like vessel recovered

from Feature 47 in test square 205 located 10 m south of the main excavation block (Figure 9.2).

The majority of the undecorated body sherds correspond to whole vessels that would be either Langford or Starved Rock Collared. Rims of both types were recovered. Yet the undecorated body sherds of these two categories are indistinguishable (Hall 1987) and could not be placed in one category or the other. In both types angular particles of dark, crystalline grit is used as tempering and both occur as globular jars. The two are differentiated by rim and neck form and by decorative subtleties only. In fact, Langford, Starved Rock Collared, and Aztalan Collared as well, overlap

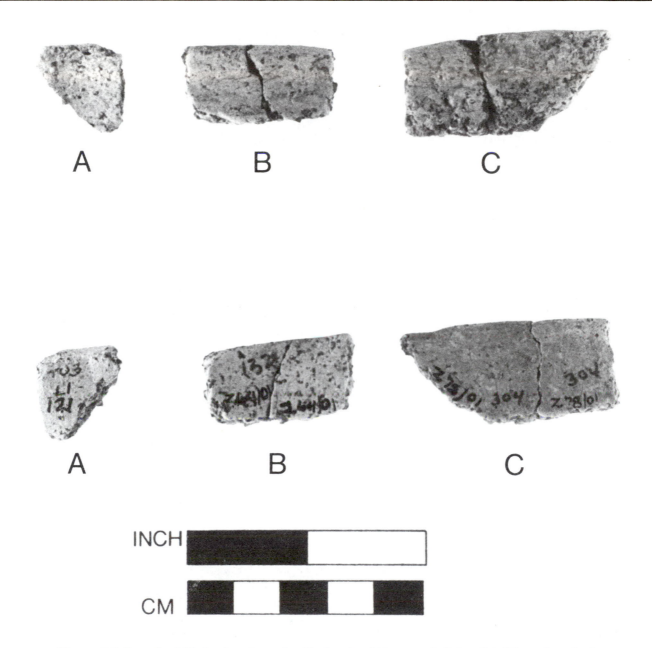

Figure 9.8. Langford Plain rims from the Cooke site. (A) test unit 2, level 4; (B) surface find; (C) surface find.

according to all of the key attributes that might distinguish undecorated body sherds—temper material, temper coarseness, temper density, surface treatment, hardness, thickness, and color.

The Cooke data demonstrate that the Langford ceramic tradition—a tradition that persists, perhaps, into the fifteenth century or beyond—was established by A.D. 1100, a century earlier than previously estimated (cf. Brown et al. 1967:39). Thus the early end of the Langford Series coincided with the occurrence of Starved Rock Collared. The latter appeared in the terminal Late Woodland and probably persisted no later

than the beginning of the thirteenth century (Hall 1987). Feature 2 at Cooke, a pure Langford deposit with smooth, thin, trailed sherds—closely resembling the later Washington Irving materials (Figure 9.9B)-carries a date of A.D. 910 ± 130. Furthermore, the latest of the five dates is only A.D. 1020 ± 70. The early dates are reaffirmed by a recent assay of A.D. 870 ± 80 from a feature at the Zimmerman site that contained the fragmented remains of one or more Langford vessels and a Madison Triangular point (Table 9.5) (Jeske and Hart 1988:87).

Starved Rock Collared and Langford sherds are

Table 9.5   Langford Radiocarbon Chronology

Site	Radiocarbon Date (AD)	Comments
Zimmerman (11Ls13)	870 ± 90	Feature 6 - Langford ware and Madison points (Jeske and Hart 1988).
Cooke (11Ck52)	910 ± 130	Feature 2. Langford Trailed ware
Cooke (11Ck52)	1000 ± 70	Feature 1. Compound feature with Langford and L.Woodland
Noble-Wieting (11ML28)	1120 ± 75	Langford Ware (Brown n.d.)
Robinson Res (11Ck2)	1120 ± 60	Mound 2, Burial 1 - Langford miniature pot (Brown n.d.; Jeske and Hart 1988).
Material Srvc(11Ls50)	1135 ± 85	(Collagen). Langford wares (Brown et al. 1967).
Fisher (11Wi5)	1150 ± 60	Burned post from structure. Langford Ware (Jeske and Hart 1988).
Noble-Wieting (11ML28)	1165 ± 75	Langford Ware (Brown n.d.).
Wash.Irving (11K52)	1230 ± 70	Feature 5 area F. Langford Plain ware (Jeske 1990).
Wash.Irving (11K52)	1240 ± 60	Feature 17 area A. Langford Plain ware (Jeske 1990).
Wash.Irving (11K52)	1240 ± 70	Feature 5 area D. Langford Plain ware (Jeske 1990).
Zimmerman (11Ls13)	1240 ± 80	Feature 2. Langford ware (Jeske and Hart 1988).
Robinson Res(11Ck2)	1330 ± 60	Feature 50. Langford Plain ware (Jeske and Hart 1988).
Robinson Res(11Ck2)	1370 ± 50	Feature 4. Langford Cordmarked ware (Jeske and Hart 1988).
Wash.Irving (11K52)	1510 ± 70	Feature 5 area A (intrusive pit). Langford Plain ware (Jeske 1990).
Wash.Irving (11K52)	1530 ± 70	Feature 6 area A. Langford Cordmarked ware (Brown n.d.; Jeske and Hart 1988).
Zimmerman (11Ls13)	1600 ± 85	Burial 21 (Collagen). Langford Plain ware (Brown et al. 1967:43).

both found at numerous sites besides Cooke (cf. Brown et al. 1967; Hall 1987; Jeske and Hart 1988; Markman and Adams 1986). While contextual data are not sufficiently refined at any site to determine whether or not the two potteries occur in temporally discrete components, the overlap of other attributes, beside tempering, suggests that they have a common derivation. It seems that Langford probably grew out of what has been called the Des Plaines Complex (Gillette 1949), which includes Starved Rock Collared and a number of other collared types (Hall 1987). In fact, the type definition of Langford Cordmarked encompasses both rim collars and plain rims (Brown 1961:35). The definition was written before Starved Rock Collared was defined as a discrete type (Hall 1962), and effectively includes Starved Rock Collared as a variant within the Langford Series. The closeness of the two types is also seen on the Upper Illinois River where even Langford Plain sherds sometimes have visible collars or folds (cf. Fenner 1963:63, Fig. 27c-f). However, in most Langford examples the lip fold is only evident as a slight thickening. The lip or collaring can only be detected by carefully examining the rim in cross-section.

The early Langford vessel reconstructed in Figure 9.7—a constricted orifice jar with an angular shoulder—appears to be a transitional type showing a mixture of both Woodland and Mississippian characteristics. Like most Late Woodland vessels, it is grit tempered with cordmarking. Yet it also has smoothed areas decorated with an incised design.

The vessel profile and surface finish—a combination of smoothed and cordmarked areas—are also seen on numerous Bluff jars in the American Bottom. The zone of smoothing on this vessel, however, is below the shoulder, just the opposite of Bluff examples of the Emergent Mississippian period (cf. Kelly et al. 1986:Plate 26d; Vogel 1975:Fig. 46). The vessel profile compares closely with the vertical and incurved necked jars that make up Type 4 at the Range site (Ozuk 1987; 1990a; 1990b) and is similar to Vogel's generalized outline of a "transitional type" at Cahokia (1975:Fig. 32).

The vertical-neck jar with an angular shoulder is a widespread form that may have persisted slightly longer in northeast Illinois than in the American Bottom. In the American Bottom lips became more everted through time as vessels became more shallow, culminating with the very shallow Powell Plain and Ramey Incised vessels of the Stirling Phase.

The broadly incised or trailed lines on the reconstructed Langford vessel and other Langford sherds at the Cooke site are suggestive of the decorative patterns on Ramey Incised vessels (cf. Griffith 1981) and is a feature that cross dates this material with the Stirling phase. The curvilinear, parallel lines on the bottom examples shown in Figure 9.9 most clearly demonstrate this affinity in contrast to later Oneota

Figure 9.9. (A-B) Langford Trailed, (D) Langford Trailed and Cordmarked. (A) Feature 5; (B) Feature 2; (C, D) Feature 17.

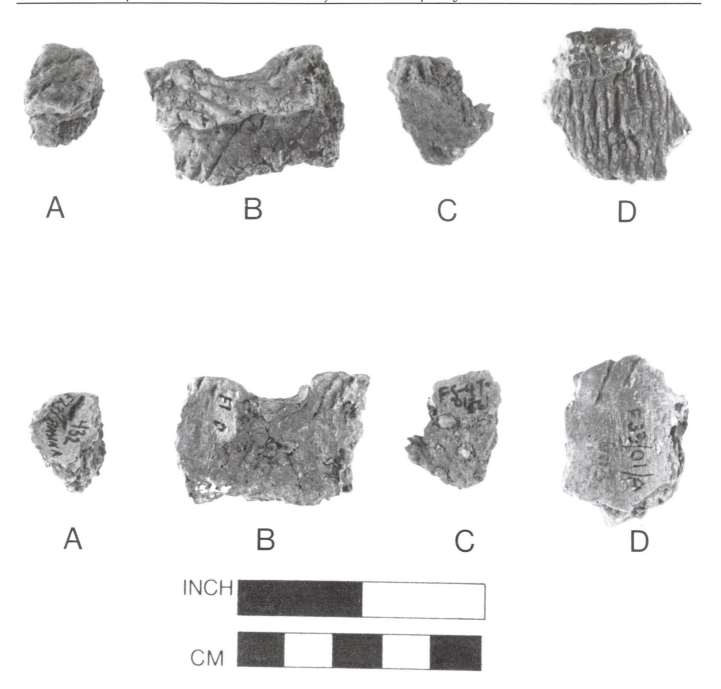

Figure 9.10. Collared rims from the Cooke site. (A, B, D) Point Sauble Collared; (C) unidentified.

designs, which generally show more use of vertical, rectilinear lines (cf., Stoltman 1986:Fig. 3).

The Cooke ceramic assemblage, along with the radiocarbon evidence (Figures 9.5 and 9.6), suggests that attenuated influences from Cahokia were reaching northeast Illinois by the Stirling phase (A.D. 1050-1150). At this time full-fledged Ramey Incised pottery was appearing in the Upper Mississippi drainage both west and north of this area (Stoltman 1986). The evidence suggests connections between Cahokia and northeast Illinois, but connections that were weaker and perhaps less direct than those between the Cahokia center and the upstream areas closer to the Mississippi River.

The vessel fragments illustrated in Figure 9.7 come from Feature 1, a complex pit dug in several stages. Two carbon 14 dates were derived for the feature— A.D. 780 ± 70, most likely not corresponding to the vessel, and A.D. 1000 ± 70 (Figure 9.5). The latter yields a calibrated age of A.D. 1034 with a 1-sigma

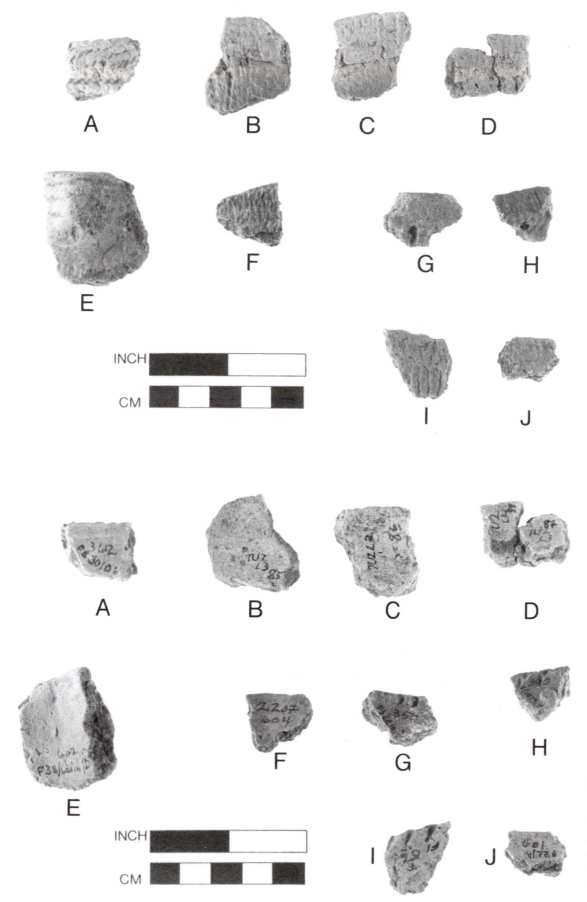

Figure 9.11. Collared rims from the Cooke site. (A-E) Aztalan Collared; (F-J) Starved Rock Collared.

range of A.D. 1012 to 1166 (Figure 9.6) (Markman 1991: Appendix 2). Similar trailed and cordmarked vessel fragments were recovered from Feature 17 along with a Cahokia Notched point (Figure 9.9c-d).

The pottery from Cooke along with that from later Langford sites suggests that in northeast Illinois some of the improvements in ceramics that were occurring during the course of the Woodland period continued in the grit-tempered potteries of the Mississippian period. For example, recorded trends in Woodland ceramics of Illinois include not only a decrease in the girth of vessel walls but also a change from elongated to globular jar forms (Braun 1983). All previously reported Langford jars, and the shell-tempered Mississippian period jars of north-east Illinois as well, never have angular breaks, like that shown in Figure 9.7, but consistently show an uninterrupted spherical profile. Braun (1983) has noted that a change toward smaller, more globular vessels can be viewed as a way of compensating for the loss of flexural strength by potters who sought to produce cooking jars with improved thermal conductivity. Furthermore, the thinning of vessel walls during the Woodland period and later increased thermal conductivity by sacrificing flexural strength.

Braun proposed that ceramic changes during the Woodland period were linked to subsistence trends involving increased consumption of starchy seeds—including corn toward the end of the Late Woodland period. The most effective way of extracting nutrients from starchy seeds is by extended boiling to produce a gruel. The cooking process requires vessels that can resist extended and repeated heat stress.

Braun did not focus his analysis on another apparent trend in pottery that seems to have been geared toward the same technological results, namely the increased attention given to selecting clays and specific rocks for grit temper. While quantified data are lack-

ing, it seems evident that dark mineral constituents became more frequent in Illinois ceramics following the Middle Woodland period, while Middle Woodland pottery, mainly Havana Ware, is characterized by temper that includes considerable quartz, a mineral with a very rapid rate of expansion. As potters began selecting darker rocks for grit, they were effectively selecting rocks that are likely to include mafic minerals that have relatively low expansion rates. The importance of a low rate of expansion is that the clay of traditional pottery is also generally low. And the closer the rates of expansion of clay and temper, the less likely a vessel will crack when heated (cf. Rye 1976).

A group of six sherds from the Cooke site was sent to James Stoltman, at the University of Wisconsin, for thin-sectioning and petrographic analysis. The results are presented in Tables 9.6 and 9.7 and illustrated in Figures 9.12 and 9.13. The sherds represent some of the range of variability seen in the site assemblage, but the sample group is not proportionally representative. Two of the sherds, 9 and 402, are clearly Langford Trailed pieces. Number 402 is a rim sherd, similar in appearance to those shown in Figure 9.8. Number 9 is a light buff sherd similar to the sherds shown in Figures 9A and 9B.

Numbers 143 and 193 are thick body sherds, both having wall thicknesses of 9 mm. Exterior surfaces are smoothed-over-cordmarked. When viewed in cross-section the clay body appears laminated. Corresponding rims could not be identified. Upon macroscopic examination it seemed that the two sherds might be included in an as-yet-unidentified type. However, the thin-section results suggest that number 143 is probably a variant of Langford. Although thicker than most Langford body sherds, which generally measure between 5.0 and 6.5 mm, the paste and temper analysis shows that, like the Langford trailed sherds, it was made from a sandier

Table 9.6 Cooke Site Pottery Thin Section Samples---Paste Analysis*

Sherd No.	Thin Section Number	Type	% Matrix	% Silt	% Sand	Sand Size Index [3]
9	11-114	Langford	89	3	8	1.62
402	11-115	Langford	66	10	24	1.58
143	11-111	Langford-like	74	8	18	1.61
193	11-112	smoothed over cm	93	5	2	1.25
185	11-116	Swanson-like	89	10	1	1.00
173	11-113	Pt. Sauble Collared	90	7	3	1.83

* Temper is excluded. Matrix includes clay only.

Table 9.7 Cooke Site Pottery Thin Section Samples---Body Analysis*

Sherd No.	Thin Section Number	Type	Temper	% Matrix	% Sand	% Grit	Grit Size Index**
9	11-114	Langford	gabbro	61	5	34	3.65
402	11-115	Langford	gabbro	57	18	25	3.09
143	11-111	Lang.-like	gabbro	73	16	11	3.83
193	11-112	socm***	gabbro	78	2	20	3.98
185	11-116	Swanson-like	granite	82	1	17	3.23
173	11-113	Pt. Sauble Collared	syenite	79	2	19	3.79

*   Temper is included. Matrix includes clay plus silt.
** Grit and Sand Size Indices = A Nominal Scale
***Unidentified smoothed-over cord marked

1 Fine = .0625-- .249 mm   4 Very Coarse = 1.00--1.999 mm
2 Medium = .25--.499 mm   5 Gravel = > 2.0 mm
3 Coarse = .50--.999 mm

clay than the other three examples (Figures 9.12 and 9.13). Furthermore, gabbro was used for temper.

Gabbro was identified as the temper in four of the six samples, including the two Langford Trailed sherds (number 9 and 402) and the two sherds that had been provisionally placed in an unidentified category. Gabbro is a dark-colored rock composed principally of pyroxene and plagioclase, with quartz absent. It does not occur in local outcroppings but can be found within the glacial drift as erratics (Porter 1958). Gabbro has been identified as the raw material in manufacturing two celts at Aztalan in southern Wisconsin from roughly the same time as the principal occupation at Cooke (ibid.).

One of the two non-gabbro-tempered sherds is a Swanson-like body sherd (number 185). The temper was identified as crushed granite. The exterior surface is smoothed-over-cordmarked. The wall thickness is 8 mm.

The other non-gabbro-tempered sherd (number 173) is a body sherd that seems to correspond closely with the rim sherd shown in Figure 9.10B, a piece identified as Point Sauble Collared. The rim sherd demonstrates an unusual and deep thumb impression on the lip. The grit-temper is identified as syenite, an intermediate, rather than mafic or felsic rock (Mottana et al. 1978:281).

A surprising result of the thin-section analysis is the coarseness of the grit temper, which has a size index above 3.00 in all six cases (Table 9.7). The figure exceeds most Late Woodland grit and rivals some Havana ware (Stoltman, personal communication). The data are difficult to reconcile with Braun's observation of a general decrease in the size of grit particles during the Woodland period, a change that he also links to concerns with resistance to thermal stress (1983). However, other data indicate that while a decrease in particle size produces improved resistance to thermal stress on the first heating, vessels with a larger temper fair better on subsequent heatings, and thus are better suited for repeated use (Steponaitis 1983:43-45). Analysis of additional samples from the Cooke site and similar analysis of pottery from other Langford sites are needed to provide a comparative sample and more reliable interpretations.

Throughout much of the Midwest there were abrupt cultural changes at around A.D. 1000, the onset of the Mississippian period, that in many areas was also marked by a radical change in the ceramic assemblage. New vessel forms appear and in many areas potters began using crushed shell as a tempering material.

By around A.D. 1400 shell-tempered pottery had become dominant within the Chicago Lake Plain and the drainages of the Lower Des Plaines and the Upper Illinois Rivers. It is not altogether clear why the inhabitants of the Fox Valley, the Upper Des Plaines, and the Middle Rock adhered to the tradition of producing grit-tempered pottery. The rejection of shell tempering probably reflects a stylistic expression of cultural identity as much as a technological decision. Measurements of thermal shock resistance show shell (calcite) and gabbro are roughly equivalent (Rye 1976:116-117). Shell has the disadvantage that at temperatures above 750°C calcite decomposes to carbon dioxide and calcium oxide, which has poor thermal expansion resistance. However, this difficulty can be overcome by adding salts (Rye 1976).

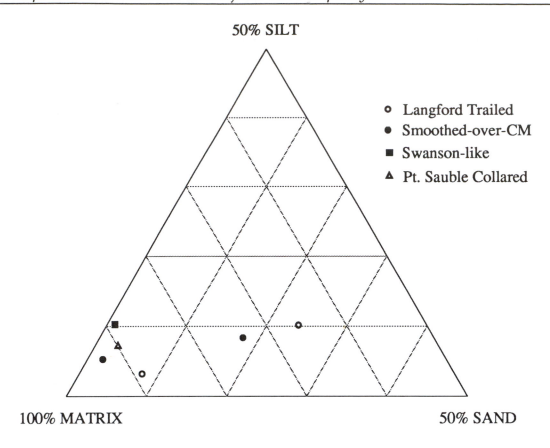

Figure 9.12. Paste composition of Cooke site pottery samples (see Table 9.6).

Mississippian Traditions in North-East Illinois

On the basis of stylistic motifs the ceramics of north-east Illinois have been divided into two Mississippian traditions, one Oneota and the other non-Oneota, which are partially contemporaneous and spatially interspersed (Brown 1965). In the Chicago Area the two decorative styles coincide with distinct temper types, that is, the Oneota pattern is evident on shell-tempered pottery and the non-Oneota on grit-tempered wares. The Oneota ceramic style is known in its "classic" form from sites mostly in the north-west Prairie Peninsula including Iowa, Wisconsin, and Minnesota. The Huber phase pottery of the Chicago Lake Plain also represents a quintessential Oneota ceramic assemblage. A statistical analysis of ceramic decorative patterns was used by James Brown to define the Oneota style (1965). Brown found that the Oneota style could be distinguished from the non-Oneota by a characteristic repetition of vertical elements, a simple repetition of rectilinear units, and a frequent occurrence of what is referred to as the "ABACA" pattern of repeated motifs

(ibid.:123). The non-Oneota style, including Langford, is characterized by a high frequency of arches, festoons, "V"s, and curvilinear elements. In terms of decorative motifs Langford is closely related to Ramey Incised (Griffith 1981) and to early and middle Oneota types (Stoltman 1986). Although the latter are characterized by shell temper, a nearly continuous style zone can be seen to extend from southern Illinois into central Wisconsin during the interval A.D. 1050 to A.D. 1200 (Brown 1983). This style generally corresponds to what John Griffin referred to as a generalized Upper Mississippian (1948) and is eventually superseded by the Oneota style after ca. A.D. 1200/1250.

The Huber site, located on the Sag Channel, was first excavated in the late 1920s (Bennett and Engberg 1929; 1990). From early on the affinities were recognized between the Huber pottery and that of Oneota sites to the west (cf. Griffin 1943). Berrien pottery of the eastern shore of Lake Michigan (Betterel and Smith 1973) is virtually identical to Huber (Brown and Asch 1990). The Oneota affinities and the temporal placement of an earlier shell-tempered pottery, a type later to be known as Fisher, were not immediately apparent. The Fisher site is located above Joliet where

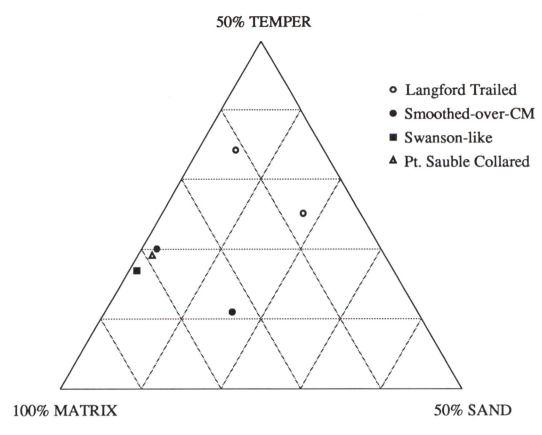

Figure 9.13 Clay body composition of Cooke site pottery samples (see Table 9.7).

the Des Plaines and Kankakee Rivers join to form the Upper Illinois. The site was first excavated by George Langford between 1926 and 1928 (1927, 1928, 1930). Later the stratigraphy was further analyzed by John Griffin who noted that the ceramics of the early level, Fisher A, consisted of shell-tempered Fisher pottery and the upper components, Fisher B and C, of Langford grit-tempered pottery (1944, 1946, 1948). The decoration on Fisher sherds is generally incised on a cordmarked or occasionally a smoothed surface. Non-Oneota arches and festoons occur on the pottery, but rectilinear design elements, including strap handles with rectilinear incisions, demonstrate an Oneota pattern (Brown 1965; 1983). Additional evidence has shown that Fisher and Huber are early and late manifestations of a single Fisher-Huber sequence. Charles Faulkner demonstrated that pottery from Greismer and Fifield in northern Indiana represents an intermediary stage in the sequence of stylistic development (1972). The current data seem to indicate that Fisher coexisted with Langford. Then Langford waned while the distinctive Huber, Oneota pattern emerged. It is now apparent that the Fisher site locality represents a shifting boundary between Fisher and Langford.

While it is evident that there is temporal overlap between the shell-tempered and grit-tempered traditions, just how long this co-occurrence lasted has not been firmly established. The latest Fisher-Huber site to yield Langford sherds is the Hoxie Farm site (ibid.:48), which suggests that after around A.D. 1400 Langford waned in the Fisher-Huber dominated area; that is, the southern edge of Lake Michigan and the Upper Illinois Valley. It is evident, though, that Langford persisted in the Fox Valley. A recent pair of dates from the Washington Irving site (11K52) suggest that Langford persisted into the fifteenth century (Jeske 1990). Questionable claims of Langford pottery occurring with Early European trade goods have been used to suggest that Langford persisted up to the Protohistoric period. The confusion on this issue was initiated by Kenneth Orr's insistence that the Langford material at the Zimmerman site should be included as part of the Historic component (1949). The interpretive error was based on the fortuitous intrusion of historic goods in Langford pits (Brown 1983) and was later compounded by a problematic bone collagen date from Zimmerman (Table 9.5).

Conclusions: The Cooke Site in Regional Perspective

Langford and Fisher-Huber represent roughly contemporary, but spatially discrete ceramic traditions, with Huber evolving from Fisher and persisting several centuries beyond Langford. Langford is more clearly connected to local Late Woodland traditions and may begin slightly earlier than Fisher (Figure 9.6).

The grit-tempered and shell-tempered ceramics occur in complementary niches with little overlap. Langford ceramics do occur in the Chicago Outlet area as well as in northern Indiana, but usually in low frequency along with other wares, implying ongoing interaction between Langford and Fisher groups (Faulkner 1972; J. Brown 1985) and perhaps the early displacement of Langford groups from these areas. On the other hand, shell-tempered ceramics are virtually confined to environmental settings adjacent to extensive marshlands and bottomland, mainly the Upper Illinois River and the low-lying Chicago Outlet area next to Lake Michigan. Shell tempered ceramics are rare to non-existent, not only on the Fox river, but also in sites along the Des Plains River and the Middle Rock River—all streams with undeveloped bottomland environments. Generally, the Langford tradition seems to be associated with groups who not only focussed on areas of extensive bottomlands and marshes, but also on the narrow, wooded stream valleys that protrude into the prairies of northeast Illinois (Jeske 1990).

The archaeological data also suggest that after the crystallization of a Middle Mississippian pattern, the Illinois River developed as a main artery of communication between the Middle Mississippi and the Great Lakes. Shell tempered ceramics are prevalent along the waterway and extend into the marshy sloughs of the Chicago Outlet.

The Langford and Fisher-Huber ceramic traditions represent interacting groups who maintained ethnic boundaries and distinct identities and perhaps contrasted in terms economic patterns as well. However, both are characterized by diverse and flexible modes of subsistence that would be adjusted to fit the configuration of resources of any of the various niches of the Prairie Peninsula. Langford groups, although not totally isolated, were bypassed by the major cultural transformations that occurred in the riverine and lacustrine marshlands as the Mississippian period progressed.

It appears likely that the Langford tradition emerged from a local Late Woodland ancestor between A.D. 1000 and 1100, and the Cooke site seems to represent this early Woodland-Mississippian transition. Maple Mills, Tampico, or Canton Wares, characterized by jar-shaped vessels and gabbro temper, occur earlier than Langford in areas to the west and south, and may represent a forerunner to both Starved Rock Collared and Langford.

It is evident from the early Langford pottery at the Cooke site that ideas and influences emanating from the dynamic areas to the south, ultimately Cahokia during its Stirling phase, were reaching north-east Illinois. On the other hand the early Northern Flint maize recovered from Cooke is more difficult to connect to the Cahokia world since its presence here occurred at a time when this variety was rare or absent in the American Bottom (Cutler and Blake 1969).

Acknowledgements

Mr. and Mrs. Henry Cooke are acknowledged for supporting the Cooke site investigations in so many ways. The project also received supportive donations from members of the Barrington Historical Society. Radiocarbon dates were run by the Illinois State Geological Survey on a no-fee basis. The author is grateful to the Northern Illinois University students who participated in the field and laboratory work, many of whom contributed hours of their time far in excess of course requirements. Those deserving special mention include M.Catherine Bird, Joseph Craig, Frank Farrell, Carole Pescke, Bonnie Redmer, and Elsie Way.

References Cited

Adair, Mary J.
   1988 *Prehistoric Agriculture in the Central Plains.* University of Kansas Publications in Anthropology 16.
Adair, Mary J., and Marie E. Brown
   1981 The Two Deer Site (14BU55): A Plains Woodland-Plains Village Transition. In *Prehistory and History of the El Dorado Lake Area, Kansas (Phase II)*, edited by Mary J. Adair, pp. 237-351. University of Kansas, Museum of Anthropology, Project Report Series No. 47.
Asch, David L., and Nancy B. Asch Sidell
   1990 Archaeobotany. In *The Oak Forest Site: Investigations into Oneota Subsistence-Settlement in the Cal-Sag Area of Cook County, Illinois*, edited by James A. Brown. At the Edge of Prehistory: Huber Phase Archaeology in the Chicago Area, Part II. James A. Brown and Patricia J. O'Brien, general editors, pp. 241-265. Center for American Archaeology, Kampsville.

Asch, David L., and James A. Brown
1990 Stratigraphy and Site Chronology. In *The Oak Forest Site: Investigations into Oneota Subsistence-Settlement in the Cal-Sag Area of Cook County, Illinois,* edited by James A. Brown. At the Edge of Prehistory: Huber Phase Archaeology in the Chicago Area, Part II. James A. Brown and Patricia J. O'Brien, general editors, pp. 174-185. Center for American Archaeology, Kampsville.

Baerreis, David A.
1953 The Blackhawk Village Site (Da5), Dane County, Wisconsin. *Newsletter of the Iowa Archeological Society* 4(4):5-20.

Baerreis, David A., and Joan E. Freeman
1958 Late Woodland Pottery in Wisconsin as seen from Aztalan. *The Wisconsin Archeologist* 39(1): 35-61.

Benn, David W.
1980 *Hadfields Cave: A Perspective on Late Woodland Culture in Northeast Iowa.* University of Iowa, Office of the State Archaeologist, Report 13.

Bennett, Wendell C., and Paul R. Engberg
1929 Huber Site Near Blue Island: Report of Excavation and Survey of Collection. Ms. on file, Illinois State Museum, Springfield.
1990 Huber Site Near Blue Island: Report of Excavation and Survey of Collection. In *Hoxie Farm and Huber: Two Upper Mississippian Archaeological Sites in Cook County Illinois,* edited by Elaine B. Herold, Patricia J. O'Brien, and David J. Wenner. At the Edge of Prehistory: Huber Phase Archaeology in the Chicago Area, Part I. James A. Brown and Patricia J. O'Brien, general editors, pp. 100-103. Center for American Archaeology, Kampsville.

Bernabo, J.C.
1981 Quantitative Estimates of Temperature Changes over the Last 2700 years in Michigan Based on Pollen Data. *Quaternary Research* 15:143-159.

Bettarel, Robert L., and Hale G. Smith
1973 *The Moccasin Bluff Site and the Woodland Cultures of Southwestern Michigan.* University of Michigan, Museum of Anthropology, Anthropological Papers 49.

Binford, Lewis R.
1967 Smudge Pits and Hide Smoking: Use of Analogy in Archaeology. *American Antiquity* 32(1):1-12.

Braun, David P.
1983 Pots as Tools. In *Archaeological Hammers and Theories,* edited by James A. Moore and Arthur S. Keene, pp. 107-134. Academic Press, New York.

Brown, James A.
1965 The Prairie Peninsula: An Interaction Area in the Eastern United States. Unpublished Ph.D. dissertation, Department of Anthropology, University of Chicago.
1983 The Archaeology of the Mississippian Period in the Chicago Area. Paper presented at the Midwest Archaeological Conference, October 1983, Iowa City, Iowa.
1990a Environmental History. In *The Oak Forest Site: Investigations into Oneota Subsistence-Settlement in the Cal-Sag Area of Cook County, Illinois,* edited by James A. Brown. At the Edge of Prehistory: Huber Phase Archaeology in the Chicago Area, Part II. James A. Brown and Patricia J. O'Brien, general editors, pp. 142-144. Center for American Archaeology, Kampsville.
1990b Oneota Subsistence-Settlement Research. In *The Oak Forest Site: Investigations into Oneota Subsistence-Settlement in the Cal-Sag Area of Cook County, Illinois,* edited by James A. Brown. At the Edge of Prehistory: Huber Phase Archaeology in the Chicago Area, Part II. James A. Brown and Patricia J. O'Brien, general editors, pp. 161-173. Center for American Archaeology, Kampsville.

Brown, James A., editor
1961 *The Zimmerman Site: A Report on Excavations at the Grand Village of Kaskaskia, LaSalle, County, Illinois.* Illinois State Museum, Report of Investigations No. 9.
1985 *Preliminary Report of Archaeological Investigations at the Oak Forest Site (11Ck53) Cook County Illinois.* Northwestern University Archaeological Center Contributions No. 3.

Brown, James A., and David L. Asch
1990 Cultural Setting: The Oneota Tradition. In *The Oak Forest Site: Investigations into Oneota Subsistence-Settlement in the Cal-Sag Area of Cook County, Illinois,* edited by James A. Brown. At the Edge of Prehistory: Huber Phase Archaeology in the Chicago Area, Part II. James A. Brown and Patricia J. O'Brien, general editors, pp. 145-160. Center for American Archaeology, Kampsville.

Brown, James A., Roger W. Willis, Mary A. Barth, and George K. Neumann
  1967 *The Gentleman Farm Site, LaSalle County, Illinois*. Illinois State Museum, Reports of Investigations, No. 12.
Brown, Margaret K.
  1975 *The Zimmerman Site: Further Excavations at the Grand Village of Kaskaskia*. Illinois State Museum, Reports of Investigations No. 32.
Brown, William L., and Edgar Anderson
  1947 The Northern Flint Corns. *Annals of the Missouri Botanical Garden* 34(1):1-29.
Callender, Charles
  1978a Great Lakes-Riverine Sociopolitical Organization. In *Handbook of North American Indians. Volume 15, Northeast*. Bruce G. Trigger, volume editor. pp. 610-621. Smithsonian Institution, Washington, D.C.
  1978b Fox. In *Handbook of North American Indians. Volume 15, Northeast*. Bruce G. Trigger, volume editor. pp. 636-647. Smithsonian Institution, Washington, D.C.
  1978c Sauk. In *Handbook of North American Indians. Volume 15, Northeast*. Bruce G. Trigger, volume editor. pp. 648-655. Smithsonian Institution, Washington. D.C.
  1978d Illinois. In *Handbook of North American Indians. Volume 15, Northeast*. Bruce G. Trigger, volume editor. pp. 673-680. Smithsonian Institution, Washington, D.C.
  1978e Miami. In *Handbook of North American Indians. Volume 15, Northeast*. Bruce G. Trigger, volume editor. pp. 681-689. Smithsonian Institution, Washington, D.C.
Callender, Charles, Richard K. Pope, and Susan M. Pope
  1978 Kikapoo. In *Handbook of North American Indians. Volume 15, Northeast*. Bruce G. Trigger, volume editor. pp. 656-667. Smithsonian Institution, Washington., D.C.
Clifton, James A.
  1978 Potawatomi. In *Handbook of North American Indians. Volume 15, Northeast*. Bruce G. Trigger, volume editor. pp. 725-743. Smithsonian Institution, Washington, D.C.
Cremin, William M.
  1980 The Schwert Site: A Fifteenth Century Fishing Station on the Lower Kalamazoo River, Southwest Michigan. *The Wisconsin Archeologist* 61:280-292.
  1983 Late Prehistoric Adaptive Strategies on the Northern Periphery of the Carolinian Biotic Province: A Case Study from Southwest Michigan. *Midcontinental Journal of Archaeology* 8:91-107.
Cutler, Hugh C., and Leonard W. Blake
  1976 *Plants from Archaeological Sites East of the Rockies*. University of Missouri-Columbia, American Archaeology Reports No. 1.
Deliette, Pierre
  1934 Memoir of De Gannes Concerning the Illinois Country [1721]. In *The French Foundations*. Compiled by Theodore C. Pease and Raymond C. Werner, pp. 302-395. Collections of the Illinois State Historical Library 23.
Doebley, John F., Major Goodman, and Charles W. Stuber
  1986 Exceptional Genetic Divergence of Northern Flint Corn. *American Journal of Botany* 73:64-69.
Egan, Katherine
  1985 Analysis of Plant Remains from the Washington Irving Site. (XIRV). Unpublished manuscript on file, Department of Anthropology, Northwestern University, Evanston.
Farrell, Frank, III
  1987 The Cooke Site: Site Catchment Analysis. Unpublished M.A. star paper, Department of Anthropology, Northern Illinois University, DeKalb.
Faulkner, Charles H.
  1972 *The Late Prehistoric Occupation of Northwestern Indiana: A Study of the Upper Mississippi Cultures of the Kankakee Valley*. Indiana Historical Society, Prehistory Research Series 5(1).
Fenner, Gloria J.
  1963 The Plum Island Site, LaSalle County, Illinois. In *Reports on Illinois Prehistory: I*, edited by Elaine A. Bluhm, pp. 1-107. Illinois Archaeological Survey Bulletin 4.

Ford, Richard I.
1985 Patterns of Prehistoric Food Production in North America. In *Prehistoric Food Production in North American*, edited by Richard I. Ford, pp. 341-364. University of Michigan Museum of Anthropology, Anthropological Papers No. 75.

Forsyth, Thomas
1822 Letter, May 12, 1822, Thomas Forsyth to Lewis Cass. (Forsyth Papers, Vol. 4, Draper Collection) State Historical Society of Wisconsin, Madison.
1912 An Account of the Manners and Customs of the Sauk and Fox Nations of the Indian Traditions [1827]. In *The Indian Tribes of the Upper Mississippi Valley Region of the Great Lakes*, vol. 2, edited by Emma H. Blair, pp. 183-245. Arthur H. Clark, Cleveland.

Galinat, Walton C.
1988 The Origins of Maiz de Ocho. *American Anthropologist* 90(3): 682-683.

Gibson, Arrell M.
1963 *The Kikapoos: Lords of the Middle Borders*. University of Oklahoma Press, Norman.

Gillette, Charles E.
1949 The Non-Mississippian Manifestations at the Fisher Site, Will County, Illinois. Unpublished M.A. thesis, Department of Anthropology, University of Chicago.

Goddard, Ives
1978 Mascouten. In *Northeast*, edited by Bruce G. Trigger, pp. 668-672. Handbook of North American Indians, vol. 15. William G. Sturtevant, general editor. Smithsonian Institution, Washington, D.C.

Griffin, James B.
1943 *The Fort Ancient Aspect, Its Cultural and Chronological Position in Mississippi Valley Archaeology*. The University of Michigan Press, Ann Arbor.

Griffin, John W.
1944 New Evidence from the Fisher Site. *Transactions of the Illinois State Academy of Sciences* 37:37-40.
1946 The Upper Mississippian Occupation at the Fisher Site. Unpublished M.A. thesis, Department of Anthropology, University of Chicago.
1948 Upper Mississippi at the Fisher Site. *American Antiquity* 14(2):124-126.

Griffith, Roberta J.
1981 *Ramey Incised Pottery*. Illinois Archaeological Survey, Circular No. 5.

Hall, Robert L.
1962 *The Archaeology of Carcajou Point: With an Interpretation of the Development of Oneota Culture in Wisconsin*. 2 vols. The University of Wisconsin Press, Madison.
1987 Type Description of Starved Rock Collared. *The Wisconsin Archeologist* 68(1):65-70.

Hough, J.L.
1958 *Geology of the Great Lakes*. University of Illinois Press.

Jeske, Robert J.
1988 *The Archaeology of the Chain O'Lakes Region in Northeastern Illinois*. Illinois Historic Preservation Agency, Illinois Cultural Resources Study No. 5.
1990 Langford Tradition Subsistence, Settlement, and Technology. *Midcontinental Journal of Archaeology* 15(2):221-249.

Jeske, Robert J., and John P. Hart
1988 *Report on Test Excavations at Four Sites in the Illinois and Michigan Canal National Heritage Corridor, LaSalle and Grundy Counties, Illinois*. Northwestern Archaeological Center, Contributions No. 6.

Johannessen, Sissel
1984 Paleoethnobotany. In *American Bottom Archaeology*, edited by Charles J. Bareis and James W. Porter, pp. 197-214. The University of Illinois Press, Urbana.

Keegan, William F., editor
1987 *Emergent Horticultural Economies of the Eastern Woodlands*. Southern Illinois University, Center for Archaeological Investigations, Occasional Paper No. 7.

Kellar, Herbert A.
  1936 *Solon Robinson, Pioneer and Agriculturalist, Vol. 1, 1825-1845*. Indiana Historical Bureau, Indiana Historical Collections 21.
Kelly, John E., Steven J. Ozuk, Douglas K. Jackson, Dale L.McElrath, Fred A. Finney, and Duane Esarey
  1984 Emergent Mississippian Period. In *American Bottom Archaeology*, edited by Charles J. Bareis and James W. Porter, pp. 128-157. University of Illinois Press, Urbana.
Kilburn, Paul D.
  1959 The Prairie-Forest Ecotone in Northeastern Illinois. *American Midland Naturalist* 62(1):206-217.
Kreisa, Paul P.
  1986 An Analysis of Faunal Remains from the Cooke Site (11-Ck-52). Unpublished manuscript on file, Department of Anthropology, Northern Illinois University, DeKalb.
Langford, George, Jr.
  1927 The Fisher Mound Group, Successive Aboriginal Occupations Near the Mouth of the Illinois River. *American Anthropologist* 29(3):153-206).
  1928 Stratified Indian Mounds in Will County. *Transactions of the Illinois Academy of Science* 20:247-253.
  1930 The Fisher Mound and Village Site. *Transactions of the Illinois State Academy of Science* 22:79-92.
Larsen, Curtis E.
  1985 Geological Interpretation of Great Lakes Coastal Environments. In *Archaeological Sediments in Contexts*, edited by J.L. Stein and W.R. Ferrand, pp. 91-110. Center for the Study of Early Man, Orono.
Lumen, D.E., R.E. Dahlberg, A. Warren, and R. Vaupel
  1986 *Landscapes of Northern Illinois: Northern Illinois Satellite Image Map*. Northern Illinois Foundation, DeKalb.
MacCrae, Jane Canby
  1968 The Cooke Site, Cook County Illinois. In *Hopewell and Woodland Site Archaeology in Illinois*, edited by James A. Brown, pp. 201-212. Illinois Archaeological Survey Bulletin No. 6.
Markman, Charles W.
  1991 Chicago Before History: The Prehistoric Archaeology of a Modern Metropolitan Area. Studies in Archaeology, No. 8. Illinois Historic Preservation Agency, Springfield.
Markman, Charles W., and Keith W. Adams
  1986 The Swanson Site (11-Ls-18): An Early Mississippian Period Occupation on the Upper Illinois River. *The Journal of Anthropology* 5(2):64-107.
Marston, Morrell
  1912 Letter to Reverend Dr. Jedidiah Morse from Major Marston, U.S.A., Commanding at Ft. Armstrong, Ill., November 1820. In *The Indian Tribes of the Upper Mississippi Valley and the Region of the Great Lakes*, vol. 2., edited by Emma H. Blair. Arthur H. Clark, Cleveland.
Michalik, Laura K.
  1982 An Ecological Perspective on the Huber Phase Subsistence-Settlement System. In *Oneota Studies*, edited by Guy E. Gibbon, pp. 29-53. University of Minnesota Publications in Anthropology No. 1.
Mottana, Annibale, Rodolfo Crespi, and Giusseppi Liborio
  1978 *Simon and Schuster's Guide to Rocks and Minerals*, edited by Martin Prinz, George Harlow, and Joseph Peters. Catherine Athill, Hugh Young, and Simon Pleasance, translators. Simon and Schuster, Inc., New York
Munson, Patrick J.
  1969 Comments on Binford's "Smudge Pits and Hide Smoking: The Use of Analogy in Archaeological Reasoning." *American Antiquity* 34(1):83-84.
O'Brien, Patricia J.
  1978 Steed Kisker and Mississippian Influences on the Central Plains. In *The Central Plains Tradition Internal Development and External Relationships*, edited by Donald J. Blakeslee. University of Iowa, Office of the State Archaeologist, Report 11.
Orr, Kenneth G.
  1949 The Historical Upper Mississippi Phase in Northern Illinois: LaSalle County Excavation, 1947. In *Proceedings of the Fifth Plains Conference for Archaeology*. University of Nebraska Laboratory for Anthropology Notebook 1:100-105.

Ozuk, Steven J.

1987 Patrick Phase Ceramics. In *The Range Site (11-S-47): Archaic through Late Woodland Occupations*, edited by John E. Kelly, Andrew C. Fortier, Steven J. Ozuk, and Joyce Williams, pp. 230-304. American Bottom Archaeology FAI-270 Reports, Vol. 20. The University of Illinois Press, Urbana.

1990a Dohack Phase Ceramics. In *The Range Site 2: The Emergent Mississippian Dohack and Range Phase Occupations*, edited by John E. Kelly, Steven J. Ozuk, and Joyce Williams, pp. 117-182. American Bottom Archaeology FAI-270 Reports, Vol. 20. The University of Illinois Press, Urbana.

1990b Range Phase Ceramics. In *The Range Site 2: The Emergent Mississippian Dohack and Range Phase Occupations*, edited by John E. Kelly, Steven J. Ozuk, and Joyce Williams, pp. 387-448. American Bottom Archaeology FAI-270 Reports, Vol. 20. The University of Illinois Press, Urbana.

Overstreet, David F.

1978 Oneota Settlement Patterns in Eastern Wisconsin: Some Considerations of Time and Space. In *Mississippian Settlement Patterns*, edited by Bruce D. Smith, pp. 21-52. Academic Press, New York.

Parker, Katherine

1985 Plant Remains from the Cooke Site. Unpublished manuscript on file, Department of Anthropology, Northern Illinois University, DeKalb.

Peske, G. Richard

1971 Winnebago Cultural Adaptation to the Fox River Waterway. *The Wisconsin Archeologist* 52:62-70.

Porter, James W.

1958 Petrographic Analysis of Eight Aztalan Celts. *The Wisconsin Archeologist* 39(1):26-35.

Quaife, Milo M., editor

1947 *The French in the Great Lakes Region*. Lakeside Press, Chicago.

Rye, Owen S.

1976 Keeping Your Temper Under Control: Materials and the Manufacture of Papuan Pottery. *Archaeology and Physical Anthropology in Oceans* 11(2):205-211.

Sasso, Robert F., and James A. Brown

1987 Land, Field, and Maize: A Perspective on Oneota Agriculture. Paper presented in the symposium "Prehistoric Adaptations in the Greater Chicago Area: A Century of Archaeological Research", at the American Anthropological Association meetings, Chicago, November 16, 1987.

Schnell, Gail Schroeder

1974 *Hotel Plaza, An Early Historic Site with a Long Prehistory*. Illinois State Museum, Reports of Investigations 29.

Steponaitis, Vincas P.

1983 *Ceramics, Chronology, and Community Patterns, An Archaeological Study of Moundville*. Academic Press, New York.

Stoltman, James B.

1986 The Appearance of the Mississippian Cultural Tradition in the Upper Mississippi Valley. In *Prehistoric Mound Builders of the Mississippi Valley*, edited by James B. Stoltman, pp. 26-34. Putnam Museum, Davenport.

1987 The FAI-270 Project: Rewriting the Prehistory of the American Bottom. *The Quarterly Review of Archaeology* 8(4):4-7.

Stuiver, Minze, and Bernd Becker

1986 High-Precision Decadal Calibration of the Radiocarbon Time Scale, A.D. 1950-2500 B.C. *Radiocarbon* 28:863-910.

Swain, A.M.

1978 Environmental Changes During the Past 2000 Years in North Central Wisconsin: Analysis of Pollen, Charcoal, and Seeds from Varved Lake Sediments. *Quaternary Research* 10:55-68.

Theler, James L.

1987 *Woodland Tradition Economic Strategies: Animal Resource Utilization in Southwestern Wisconsin and Northeastern Iowa*. Office of the State Archaeologist, Report 17.

Trowbridge, Charles C.

1938 *Meearmeear Traditions*, edited by Vernon Kinietz. Occasional Contributions from the Museum of Anthropology of the University of Michigan, No. 7. (The original manuscript is dated 1825.)

Vogel, Joseph O.
　　1975 Trends in Cahokia Ceramics: Preliminary Study of the Collections from Tracts 15A and 15B. In *Perspectives in Cahokia Archaeology*, edited by James A. Brown, pp. 32-125. Illinois Archaeological Survey, Bulletin 10.

Wagner, Gail E.
　　1983 Fort Ancient Subsistence: The Botanical Record. *West Virginia Archaeologist* 35:27-39.
　　1987 Uses of Plants by the Fort Ancient Indians. Unpublished Ph.D. dissertation, Department of Anthropology, Washington University, St. Louis.
　　1988 The Implications of the Adoption of Northern Flint Corn. Paper presented in the session, "Agricultural Adaptations to Marginal Areas of the Upper Midwest", Society for American Archaeology 53rd Annual Meeting, April 28, 1988, Phoenix.

Watson, Patty Jo
　　1988 Prehistoric Gardening and Agriculture in the Midwest and Midsouth. In *Interpretations of Culture Change in the Eastern Woodlands During the Late Woodland Period*, edited by Richard W. Yerkes, pp. 39-67. The Ohio State University, Department of Anthropology, Occasional Papers in Anthropology 3.

Webb, T. III, and Reid A. Bryson
　　1972 Late- and Postglacial Climatic Change in the Northern Midwest U.S.A.: Quantitative Estimates Derived from Fossil Pollen Spectra by Multivariate Statistical Analysis. *Quaternary Research* 2:70-115.

Willman, H. B.
　　1971 *Summary of the Geology of the Chicago Area.*. Illinois State Geological Survey, Circular 460. Urbana.

Yarnell, Richard A.
　　1964 *Aboriginal Relationships Between Culture and Plant Life in the Upper Great Lakes Region*. University of Michigan, Museum of Anthropology, Anthropological Papers, No. 23.

Yerkes, Richard W.
　　1985 Faunal Remains from the Washington Irving Site (11-K-52), A Langford Tradition (Upper Mississippian) Settlement in Kane County, Illinois. Unpublished paper on file, Department of Anthropology, Northwestern University, Evanston.

10

The Implications of Aztalan's Location

Lynne Goldstein
Department of Anthropology
University of Wisconsin-Milwaukee

Archaeologists have debated the nature and definition of Middle Mississippian society for many years, with varying degrees of consensus. Nonetheless, some sites have consistently been labeled Middle Mississippian by all scholars. One such site is Aztalan, located in Jefferson County, Wisconsin. The structure of the site (Figure 10.1), with its palisade, plaza area, pyramidal mounds, and houses, is comparable to other Middle Mississippian centers. Additionally, the artifacts, in particular the presence of shell-tempered Powell Plain and Ramey Incised pottery types, clearly indicate some Middle Mississippian presence. Finally, the radiocarbon dates for the site make a Middle Mississippian connection feasible.

Aztalan is an unusual Middle Mississippian site because it is farther north than most other commonly agreed upon centers, and it is in a region that is generally considered home to Upper Mississippian or Oneota societies. Aztalan has thus appeared to be unique or enigmatic to many scholars, and a number of individuals have devoted a considerable number of pages in attempts to determine Aztalan's origins, nature, and meaning (e.g., Barrett 1933, Baerreis and Bryson 1965, Hall 1986, Hurley 1977, McKern 1946, Peters 1976).

One of the more interesting puzzles about Aztalan has been its location; the Crawfish River has never been a mighty river with a major floodplain, and the setting doesn't fit our general notion of preferred Mississippian settlement locations. Aztalan is apparently not located where scholars expect it to be. To illustrate the significant difference between Aztalan's actual location and where people think Aztalan should be, I have prepared Figure 10.2. Figure 10.2 is a map of Wisconsin indicating Aztalan's actual location, and where various scholars have placed it in maps in the literature (note that the map only includes Wisconsin locations; some scholars have placed the site in Illinois). Aztalan's location, and the possible reasons for selecting this location, will be examined below.

Bruce D. Smith has, in several publications, discussed Mississippian settlement patterns and the physiographic location of Middle Mississippian centers (e.g., Smith 1978, 1985). Smith notes that Mississippian groups lived in river-valley floodplains, in particular in meander belts of major river valleys with their characteristic natural levees and backwater swamps. The soils in these settings were ideal for agriculture, and fish were plentiful in the oxbow lakes and backwater swamps. Waterfowl were also attracted to these settings in abundance, as were other animal and plant species. Smith goes on to describe what he terms the "Mississippian pattern of subsistence," focusing on five groups of wild species of plants and animals (Smith 1985:67): backwater species of fish; migratory waterfowl; white-tailed deer, raccoon, and turkey; nuts, fruits and berries; and seed-bearing pioneer plant species.

Perhaps it is this notion of the Mississippian pattern of settlement and subsistence that confuses scholars when they try to locate Aztalan on a map: the Crawfish River is not a major river system, and flood-

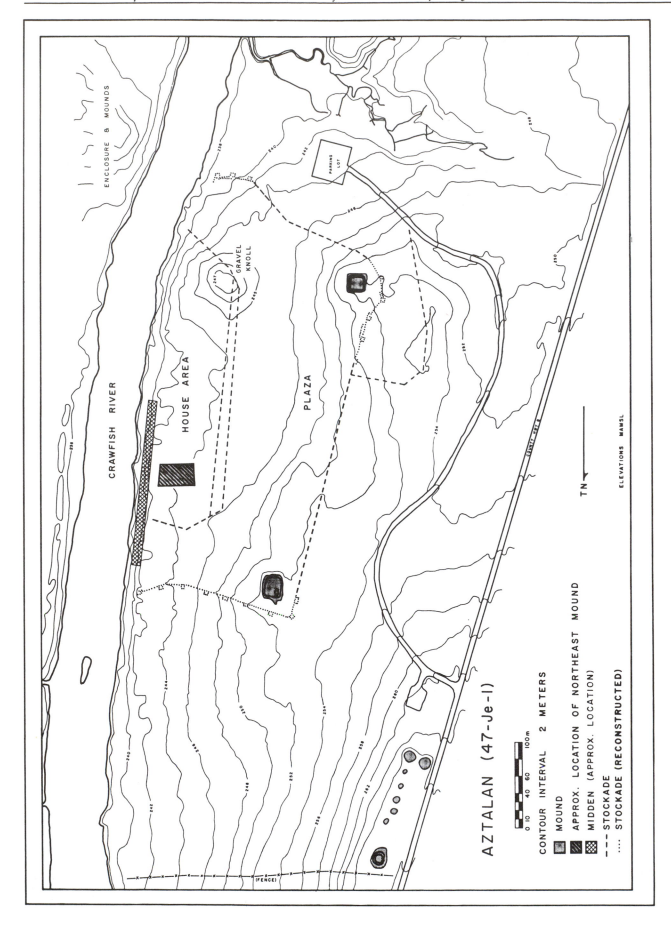

Figure 10.1. Topographic map of the Aztalan site, with major site areas and features indicated.

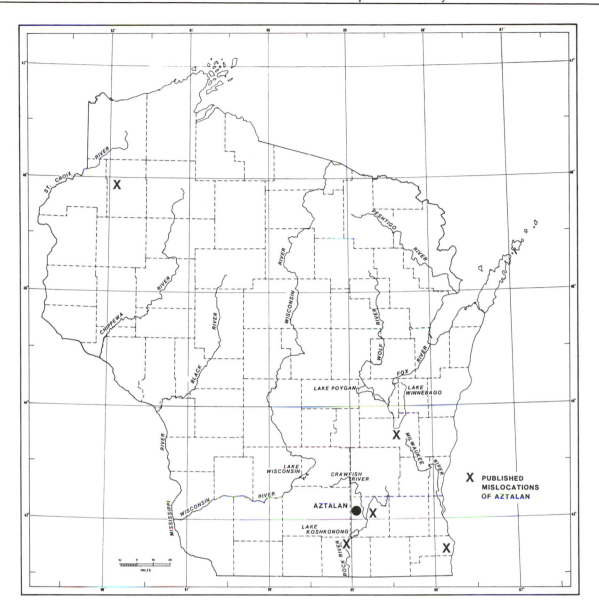

Figure 10.2. Aztalan's actual location in Wisconsin, and several of the places it has been erroneously placed on maps in the literature.

plains, as well as natural levees, etc., are virtually non-existent as compared to those associated with other Mississippian sites. Nonetheless, it is the case that the people living at Aztalan shared the basic Mississippian pattern of subsistence (F. King, personal communication; Parmalee 1960; Richards 1985; Yerkes 1980). Why did they choose the Crawfish River, and how did they manage to maintain their usual subsistence base? These questions are the focus of this paper.

The Physical Setting

Aztalan is located in the western portion of Jefferson County, Wisconsin. The region is in the "Eastern Ridges and Lowland" district of the state (Martin 1965). The area was covered by the Green Bay lobe of the Wisconsin glaciation, with the glaciation's effect having been a general leveling of topography (Martin 1965: 22-224). The landscape is made up of gently rolling hills and valleys — surficial features due to glacial deposition. Among the distinctive surficial features of the region are boulder trains; drumlins; and ground, terminal, and recessional moraines. The pattern of streams, lakes, and wetlands is typical of a young, imperfectly drained, glaciated landscape.

The "greater Aztalan area" lies to the south of Curtis' (1959) "tension zone." The tension zone is the boundary between the northern hardwood province and the southern prairie-forest floristic province. Roughly, the boundary corresponds to a climatic boundary between a northern zone of relatively cool, moist conditions, and a southern zone that is warmer and drier. The southern zone also tends to average at least 160 frost-free days, important for prehistoric agriculture.

The physiographic variability of Southeastern Wisconsin tends to be on a micro, rather than a macro, scale. Relief is relatively small, and protected areas (i.e., small valleys) can be found throughout the region. Martin (1965: 209) notes that early European settlers focused on the area primarily because of "(a) level topography, (b) fertile soil, and (c) favorable climate." It is likely that prehistoric people were drawn to the region for some of the same reasons.

A pre-European settlement vegetation reconstruction for the Aztalan vicinity (Milfred and Hole 1970; Kind 1979) (Figure 10.3) shows a distinctive pattern: the area west of the Crawfish River has large areas of oak openings, the area between the Crawfish and Rock Rivers tends to be mixed oak-maple-basswood forest, and the area east of the Rock River is predominantly climax maple-basswood forest. Wetlands, in particular marshes, are prevalent throughout the region.

There has been considerable debate about the reason(s) for the area's distinctive vegetation pattern, centering on why the oak openings exist, and how they were formed (Curtis 1959; Zicker 1955; Dorney 1980, 1981). Most scholars agree that the oak openings could only have been formed and maintained by burning, with the traditional position being that the burning must have been human-induced (Curtis 1959, Zicker 1955). Zicker (1955), in particular, suggests that the inhabitants of Aztalan were responsible for part of the pattern of regular burning to maintain open land for agriculture. More recently, in an extensive study of the vegetation of Southeastern Wisconsin, Dorney (1980) found no observable relationship of disturbed vegetation with historic Indian sites (n.b.: the same is true if one examines the distribution of prehistoric sites), although there is circumstantial evidence for extensive use of fire by the Winnebago. However, Dorney (1980) has also calculated the rate of lightning-induced fires in the region, and concludes that this natural phenomenon is an equally likely cause. He argues that fire —the most important disturbance factor in the pre-European settlement vegetation pattern—was probably caused by *both* humans and lightning. Significantly, the fires were stopped by the large combination marsh-river systems, and not by rivers alone. Indeed, the distinctive pattern neatly outlines the location of wetland-river complexes.

For archaeologists, the question of when this pattern emerged is perhaps more important and interesting. The evidence (Dorney, personal communication) suggests that there were some lapses between burn-ings since oaks are present in some density. The oaks, once established, would be more resistant to fires (cf. Curtis 1959). The beginnings of this vegetation pattern most likely correspond to the expansion of the prairie during the mid-Holocene (Dorney, personal communication), and the pre-European pattern was likely established by at least 5000 BP. Thus, while some prehistoric groups likely practiced burning or perhaps maintained already burned areas with additional regular burnings, it is unlikely that, for example, the people who inhabited Aztalan were responsible for the initial vegetation pattern.

The Survey and Its Results

In 1976, the University of Wisconsin-Milwaukee (UWM) began a systematic program of survey and test excavation in the area around Aztalan. This work built on initial research conducted under the direction of James W. Porter, then of Loyola University, in 1975 and 1976 (Steube 1976), but took a broader, long-term, and more systematic perspective. The UWM project, termed the Crawfish-Rock Archaeological Project, continued from 1976 through 1984. Figure 10.4 illustrates the area encompassed by the Crawfish-Rock Archaeological Project; the project area includes the lower half of the Crawfish River, extending from a sharp bend in the river near Mud and Chub lakes in southern Dodge County, to just south of the confluence of the Crawfish and Rock rivers in the city of Jefferson. This region includes every vegetation zone present in Southeastern Wisconsin, and also encompasses several rivers, streams, and lakes.

The survey was multi-stage in design, and centered on an overall 15% stratified random sample of approximately 70 square miles; in addition to the sample units (1/4 of 1/4-section, or 40 acres), a number of additional areas were surveyed because of collector tips, threats of development, or other reasons. Figure 10.4 indicates the units (both within and outside of the sample) that were surveyed. Using close-interval pedestrian survey and shovel probing techniques, we surveyed over 7000 acres and recorded over 400 archaeological sites; a total of 14 sites were test excavated and/or mapped. The site patterning is very clear and consistent (especially for sites that date from the Late Archaic period or more recently), and seems related to the patterning of physiographic variables.

Site patterning indicates an orientation toward wetland resources, especially permanent wetlands such as marshes and swamps. These wetlands yield rich food resources even when resources in other vegetation zones may be temporarily unavailable due to severe climatic conditions (e.g., drought or cold). Large and/or dense sites in the region are consistently located near

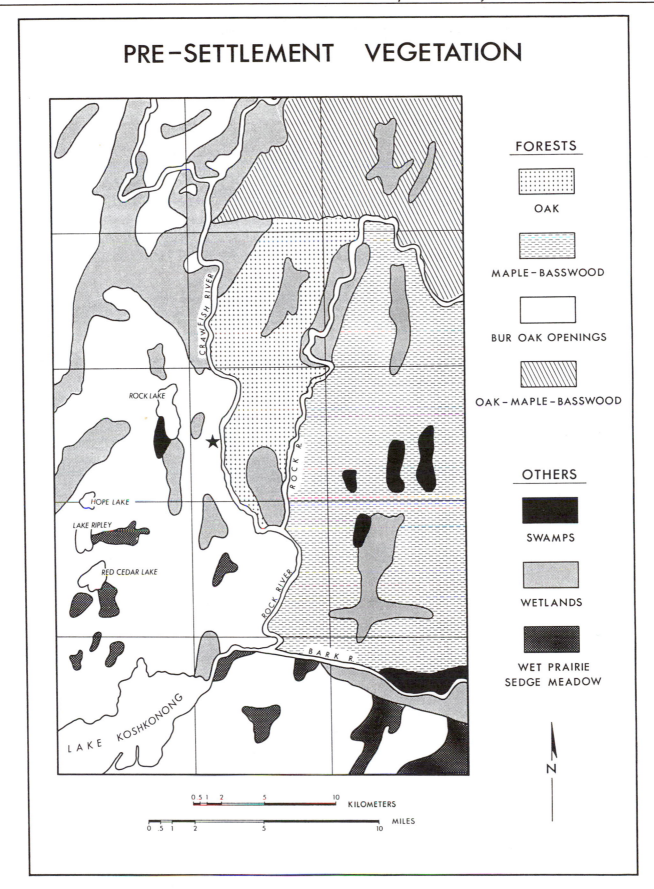

Figure 10.3. The pre-European settlement vegetation reconstruction for the Crawfish-Rock project area (adapted from Milfred and Hole 1970 and Kind 1979). The star indicates the location of Aztalan.

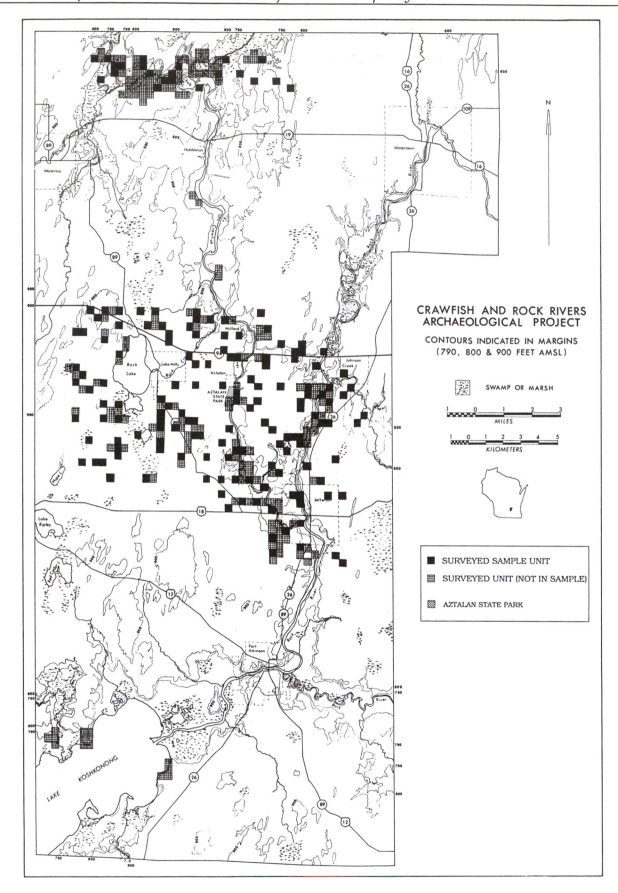

Figure 10.4. Units surveyed by UWM as a part of the Crawfish-Rock Archaeological Project.

productive wetlands *and* near areas of stream confluences; generally, sites are near stream confluences (on the interior bend of rivers) at the intersection of marsh, oak forest, and oak openings. Additionally, the densest, multicomponent sites tend to be on the Crawfish River, but on the east bank. Given this patterning, I have elsewhere (Goldstein 1987) proposed a model of wetland resource utilization, with the suggestion of repeated exploitation of resources through time, rather than extended occupation at one time. Aztalan is one of the few sites that does not fit the general pattern.

Examining the survey and excavation data, it is notable that *very* few sites date to the Mississippian period. The number of sites with shell-tempered pottery [including those sites documented by Porter's survey (Steube 1976)], totals six. If one adds the number of sites with triangular projectile points, the total increases to about 30, but these sites could as easily be Late Woodland, or even Oneota, in affiliation. However, an Oneota affiliation is unlikely since there are presently no known Oneota (Upper Mississippian) sites in the survey area. The distribution of Oneota sites in all of Southeastern Wisconsin indicate that these people used only the edges of the region: in the southwest, there are several sites along the northwest/west shore of Lake Koshkonong; in the northwest, there is a site near Horicon Marsh, and in the east, there is a site in northern Milwaukee County and in southern Ozaukee County. Examining this situation in detail, Rodell (1983) suggested that Oneota sites are associated with large, shallow-basin flow-through (eutrophic) lakes situated along major rivers.

One of the major goals of the Crawfish-Rock survey was to examine the region for insights into the nature of Aztalan and its relationships to other contemporaneous cultural systems. That examination yielded almost no sites that were contemporaneous, unless one hypothesizes that all Late Woodland sites are contemporaneous with Aztalan. Such a hypothesis would seem to be too broad, if not somewhat dubious.

It is of course possible that we simply missed those Mississippian sites or that preservation conditions were such that items such as shell-tempered pottery were not preserved on the surface. While this is possible, it seems most unlikely. All plowed fields were walked systematically at intervals averaging one meter, and any areas shovel probed were sampled at a ten-meter interval. Further, a few sites did yield shell-tempered pottery, and shell-tempered pottery was certainly preserved on the surface of sites in the Lake Koshkonong area, immediately to the south of the Crawfish-Rock area (Goldstein 1987). With no compelling reason to the contrary, we must assume that, based on the over 15% stratified sample, Middle Mississippian occupation in the Aztalan area is limited to the Aztalan site itself and a few small sites (perhaps special activity camps) in the immediate vicinity.

The few Mississippian sites around the town of Milford are possibly associated with the fish dam here, comparable to the fish dam about two miles downriver at Aztalan itself. Other sites might be hunting camps or the result of some other extractive activity. One or more of the sites might also be associated with what may be a "signal mound" on a hill north of Aztalan. About 1-3/4 miles north of Aztalan (immediately north of present-day Interstate 94) is at least one mound on top of a large drumlin. That mound may be a platform mound. It is visible from the linear row of conical mounds along the west edge of the Aztalan site, and Aztalan is easily visible from this mound. It is possible that this mound served as a signal or lookout station. The possible platform mound has not been adequately investigated, but its presence (if it dated to the Middle Mississippian period) would suggest some activity outside the immediate site area. However, no matter what the function and nature of this mound, it seems certain that the kinds of settlement patterns documented for many other Middle Mississippian centers (cf. Smith 1978), do not exist for Aztalan.

What are the implications of this conclusion? We now have strong, unbiased data that Aztalan is unique and is in essence a Middle Mississippian "island" in the region. The arguments for site-unit intrusion become almost overwhelming; how else can one explain a well-developed, highly structured Middle Mississippian center in a region without other Middle Mississippian sites? There are few alternative explanations. Possibilities will be examined in the next section of this paper.

Even though Aztalan was apparently not part of a local well-developed Mississippian settlement pattern, surrounded by contemporaneous settlements of differing sizes and function, we must still account for its location. Although it does not initially appear that a location on the Crawfish makes sense for a Mississippian group following the basic Mississippian pattern of subsistence, the Crawfish is indeed an excellent location for the following reasons:

1. If Aztalan represents a trade center in any sense at all, the Crawfish River can be used as a means of transportation to locations farther north and west, as well as farther south and west. For the kinds and routes of trade proposed for Mississippian cultures, Aztalan's location on the Crawfish River would be suitable for any participation in that trade or interaction. One could, for example, easily come up the Rock River, then the Crawfish, then portage over to the Wisconsin River, and continue north again. Other options in different directions are also available.

2. The specific location of Aztalan allows easy access to all vegetation and resource zones present in the region (cf. Figure 10.3). The wetland resources available from Aztalan's position on the Crawfish are significantly richer than those available from a comparable position on the Rock River.

3. Soils along the west bank of the Crawfish are better drained than those east of the river and are more suitable for maize agriculture (Milfred and Hole 1970). The oak openings on the west bank of the river are also more easily cleared for farming; oak openings do not occur at all along the Rock River.

4. According to long-time local residents, the Crawfish River is apparently not as susceptible to long freezes in the winter because of concentrations of springs; both the river and its resources would be accessible for greater portions of the year. The springs would also be desirable at other times of year.

5. The area on the west bank of the Crawfish River provides a somewhat more level landscape. Drumlins are present north and east of the site, and the terminal moraine begins to the south (cf. Martin 1965).

There are no rivers with wide floodplains and backwater lakes in the region; if Middle Mississippian people wanted to be here, they had to adapt to a different setting. Nonetheless, the characteristics of Aztalan's setting constitute a reasonable facsimile for Middle Mississippian settlement, resulting in the relatively easy exploitation of the same wild plant and animal species, as well as a good position for agricultural fields.

Pottery Types and Excavations at Aztalan

In the previous section, I outlined a number of reasons that, for physiographic/ subsistence motives alone, a location on the Crawfish River would be a reasonable choice for a Middle Mississippian village. However, anyone familiar with Southeastern Wisconsin might ask why not settle at Lake Koshkonong or some other place along the Rock River, south of the Crawfish?

The answer to this question first requires a separate discussion about the nature and extent of late prehistoric societies in the region. During the late prehistoric period, archaeologists have identified several Late Woodland, Middle Mississippian, and Upper Mississippian (Oneota) groups in the Midwestern U.S. Grit-tempered pottery is characteristic of the Late Woodland group, shell-tempered pottery in a variety of forms represents the Middle Mississippian group, and Oneota is represented by shell-tempered pottery in a more limited of number forms.

If one examines the pottery from the Aztalan site, it is clear that the majority of the pottery is not shell-tempered Middle Mississippian ware, but is instead grit-tempered. In fact, examination of the pottery from *all* Aztalan excavations (cf. Bleed 1970; Richards 1985) demonstrates that the 25% shell-tempered pottery/75% grit-tempered pottery ratios noted by Bleed (1970) hold true for all collections from the site (Richards 1985); if anything, the shell-tempered proportion is generous in some site areas. What can one infer from these proportions?

Peters (1976:3) has suggested that the presence of the two ceramic types can be explained in one or more of the following ways: 1) Middle Mississippian people inhabited Aztalan for only a short period of time; 2) Middle Mississippian people were a distinct minority during the occupation of Aztalan; and 3) Middle Mississippian males moved into the area and took Woodland wives/women. Hurley (1977) adds a fourth possibility when he reiterates his position that Aztalan was in part an Effigy Mound Tradition site, and that the grit-tempered ceramics represent this initial occupation — that is, Hurley is arguing for a long-term Effigy Mound and Middle Mississippian occupation. Along this same line, Hurley also disagrees with several other researchers (e.g., Peters 1976; Boszhardt 1977; Stoltman 1976; and Steube 1976) and argues that Aztalan was not occupied for a short period of time, but was used over a period of several hundred years.

In 1984, the UWM Crawfish-Rock Archaeological Project focused its energies on the Aztalan site. In particular, since the systematic survey of the region was complete, we could turn our attention to Aztalan itself to answer some specific questions about the site and its structure. In addition to documentation of extant collections and production of a topographic map of the site (cf. Figure 10.1), we undertook excavations to recover information about site formation processes and to assess the integrity of the archaeological deposits. One set of excavations centered on the river bank midden deposits where Barrett (1933:164) had reported their exposure, and another set of excavations were undertaken in the plaza area of the site in order to gather information on soil genesis, sediment composition, and colluvial process. Part of the following discussion of our 1984 excavations is summarized from an initial field report by John D. Richards, presented in Goldstein (1985).

In terms of site preservation, one concern is that the midden area along the river bank is being destroyed by erosion. However, there has also been some question raised as to whether the midden deposits actually reflect a midden, or whether the deposits are the result of sheet erosion from the upslope portion of the site. Joan Freeman (personal communication) indicates that when excavating in the central portions of the site, many of the features appeared to be bisected, as if the upper portions had been removed. Her impression was confirmed when excavations under the northeast pyramidal mound yielded features of much greater depth and structure. Freeman postulated that much of the site had been washed downslope, and that the midden area may not be exclusively midden, but may also include slope wash of parts of the site that were previously upslope.

The 1984 fieldwork at Aztalan demonstrates several important factors concerning the nature of the site (Richards 1985). The midden area excavations yielded some 70 cm of cultural deposits, and suggest some stratigraphic separation between some of the Late Woodland and Mississippian ceramic types. While no stratigraphic unit contained only Mississippian ceramics, shell-tempered sherds were recovered in association with grit-tempered varieties in the upper strata of the sequence. The lower strata produced only grit-tempered pottery. Although a significant proportion of this grit-tempered pottery appears to mimic Mississippian vessel forms, ceramics from the earliest stratigraphic unit in the sequence show no evidence of Mississippian influence. Most of the rims from the lowest stratum represent Aztalan Collared pottery, with a few Madison Plain rims, and one Madison Folded Lip rim.

Large portions of the upper parts of the river bank deposits are colluvial in origin, but purposeful aboriginal activity is responsible for a significant percentage of the overall accumulation. Features suggest aboriginal dumping of kitchen garbage, hearth cleanings and broken pottery. The archaeological deposits in the river bank area show a high degree of stratigraphic integrity. It is possible that this area of the site constitutes one of the few remaining undisturbed deposits within the site proper.

We expected the plaza area excavations to produce very little in terms of cultural materials; our major purpose in excavating there was as a geomorphic test for information on colluvial deposits near the river. Barrett (1933) and Freeman (personal communication) indicated that this portion of the site appeared comparatively devoid of cultural deposits. Our plaza area excavations demonstrate that remnants of subsurface features exist in this part of the site; we exposed four shallow pit features in association with up to 50 post molds and an isolated section of wall trench (Richards 1985). As noted by Freeman, all features were truncated by erosion and runoff. All of the pottery recovered was grit-tempered, with one Madison Plain rim and five Aztalan Collared rims. Five other rims resemble Mississippian vessel forms rendered in grit-tempered paste. Although the integrity of the plaza deposits has been seriously compromised by modern agricultural practices, a substantial amount of information may still be recoverable.

The stratigraphic data, along with a series of radiocarbon dates, present some new perspectives on the question of what the combination of grit-tempered and shell-tempered pottery represents. Table 10.1 is a summary of the radiocarbon dates from UWM's excavations.

Some of these dates are earlier than expected, in particular the A.D. 820 date from the lower portion of the midden excavations. Only one Aztalan date is earlier than this, sample M-1037 at A.D. 750 ± 150 (Boszhardt 1977:131-133). A great deal of discussion has been generated by the early date, with Griffin (1961) and Hurley (1977) arguing for its acceptance, and many others (Ritzenthaler 1961, Baerreis and Bryson 1965, Peters 1976, Stoltman 1976, Steube 1976, and Boszhardt 1977) suggesting that it is far too early. We note that our A.D. 820 date comes from the same section of the site (Barrett's Section VI) as sample M-1037.

While we cannot conclude that there was a distinctly separate Late Woodland and Middle Mississippian occupation of the site, it does seem that the site may have been occupied for a longer time than was previously thought, with the initial occupation dating somewhat earlier than expected. Our excavations would suggest that the initial occupation of Aztalan might have no associated Middle Mississippian pottery, being instead represented solely by grit-tempered wares.

Let us return to the possible explanations for mixed pottery types that were outlined at the beginning of this section. While it is possible that Middle Mississippian people inhabited Aztalan for only a short period of time, this explanation does nothing for our understanding of the Late Woodland materials, particularly since we have previously indicated that Late Woodland sites in this region are generally in different physiographic locations. Peters' (1976) second possible explanation (that Middle Mississippian people may have been a distinct minority during the occupation of Aztalan) is true *only* on the basis of pottery types—the organization of the site clearly suggests a Middle Mississippian structure. Peters' final argument about Middle Mississippian males moving into the area and taking Woodland wives is intriguing, but is hardly the most parsimonious explanation for pottery type distributions. Likewise, while Hurley (1977) is probably correct about a somewhat longer occupation for Aztalan, his reasoning is not precise. Hurley suggests that the combination of pottery types represents Effigy Mound people mixing with Middle Mississippian folks; while this is possible, it is not a sufficient explanation—why aren't there similar mate-

Table 10.1. UW-Milwaukee's Radiocarbon Dates from Aztalan

Number	Date (BP)	Date (A.D.)	Original expectations	Context
DIC-3044	870 ± 50	1080 ± 50	A.D. 900-1200	Plaza area. From fill of pit; associated with Late Woodland ceramics.
DIC-3133	950 ± 65	1000 ± 65	A.D. 1200-1300	From midden excavations; Feature 20, Stratum 5. Should date the later Mississippian/ Late Woodland occupation.
DIC-3134	850 ± 45	1100 ± 45	A.D. 1000-1100	From midden excavations; surface in Stratum 11. Should help date Late Woodland occupation.
DIC-3135	1130 ± 55	820 ± 55	A.D. 1000-1100	From midden excavations; Feature 6, Stratum 11; assoc. with Aztalan Collared rim — should be Late Woodland
DIC-3136	850 ± 50	1100 ± 50	A.D. 1000-1100	From midden excavations; Feature 10, Stratum 11; should be Late Woodland occupation

rials elsewhere in the region? Does every instance of co-occurrence of different pottery types have to mean culture contact?

In the author's opinion, what is most intriguing about the distribution of pottery types at Aztalan is the presence of the Aztalan Collared vessels. Collared pottery is very distinctive (Figure 10.5), and the large majority of Late Woodland pottery at Aztalan is collared—about 75% of the pottery is grit-tempered, and about 75% of the grit-tempered pottery is Aztalan Collared (Baerreis and Freeman 1958, Bleed 1970, Hurley 1977). Stoltman (1976) has noted that Aztalan Collared and Madison Cord Impressed pottery types co-exist at several other sites in the state, and he has discussed the implications of this co-occurrence. Aztalan Collared has been closely associated with the Aztalan site, and its occurrence in separate (possibly earlier) contexts with other Late Woodland pottery, but no Mississippian pottery, has been the cause of some interest (cf. Stoltman 1976). Was Aztalan Collared made and used elsewhere, prior to the Mississippian presence at Aztalan? Stoltman (1976) concludes that such sites both predated and co-existed with Aztalan.

The relative abundance of Madison Cord Impressed pottery across the region (cf. Hurley 1986, Stoltman 1976) suggests that the type may extend for a long period in prehistory. But, it is interesting to note that, with the exception of the few Madison pottery types, the kinds of grit-tempered vessels found at Aztalan are not found anywhere else in the immediate vicinity. The majority of grit-tempered sherds at

Aztalan are either Aztalan Collared or are Mississippian forms created with a grit-tempered paste (cf. Richards 1985). The number of collared rimsherds (Aztalan Collared or any other collared variety) found during our survey of the Crawfish-Rock area is minimal; likewise, few such rims have been generally recorded for Southeastern Wisconsin, with the exception of some Upper Mississippian sites and a few Late Woodland sites.

Salkin (1987) has noticed a similar pattern, based on his excavation of a series of sites in southern Wisconsin. His work focused in Dodge County, on the eastern margins of the Horicon Marsh, and north of Aztalan. Salkin (1987:78) has proposed two separate archaeological phases, partially based on the differential distribution of collared ceramics. The Horicon Phase is represented by small upland camps near wetlands/lake or river interfaces. Effigy mounds are often associated, and the pottery is Madison series ceramics; projectile points include triangular styles as well as various stemmed forms. By contrast, the proposed Kekoskee Phase places a greater emphasis on riverine locations, with semi-permanent or permanent villages, some of which are fortified. Maize horticulture is present, but there is no firm evidence for mounds. Pottery includes collared types and Madison ceramics, and the projectile points are small and triangular. Salkin places the Horicon Phase at A.D. 650-1200, and the Kekoskee Phase at A.D. 800-1300.

The questions raised previously about Aztalan now change a bit since we have to account not only for the Middle Mississippian presence, but also for the people

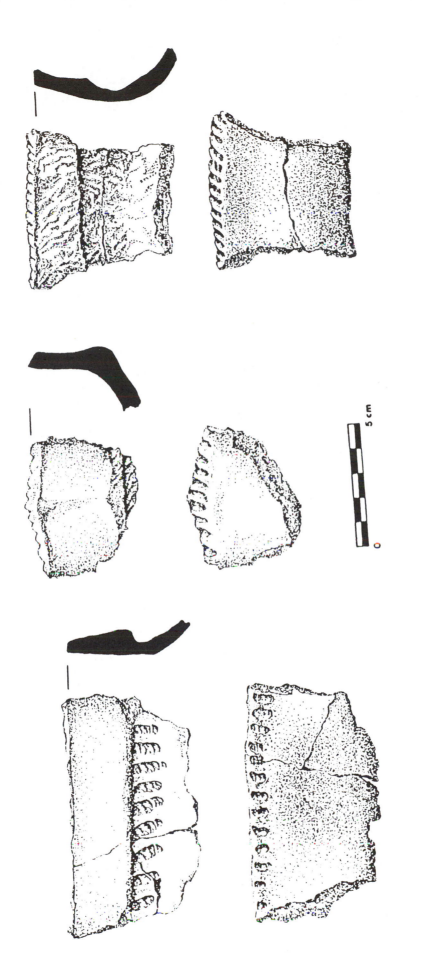

Figure 10.5. Some examples of Aztalan Collared pottery from the University of Wisconsin-Milwaukee's 1984 excavations at Aztalan.

who made the collared pottery. The grit-tempered collared vessels could also be Middle Mississippian, or they may represent some other, possibly earlier, intrusive presence into southern Wisconsin. Many Middle Mississippian sites have so-called Late Woodland pottery on them (cf. Harn 1971, Hall 1986), but not all such sites have exotic Late Woodland pottery. That is, I suggest that the collared, grit-tempered pottery at Aztalan (as well as at what Salkin [1987] calls Kekoskee Phase sites) may be as foreign as the shell-tempered vessels.

In a popular discussion of Middle and Upper Mississippian societies in Wisconsin, Hall (1986) notes that there are problems in deriving Aztalan directly from Cahokia. Not only is shell-tempered pottery in the minority at Aztalan, the grit-tempered pottery at Aztalan is not at all like the grit-tempered pottery at Cahokia. Hall suggests that perhaps people came to Aztalan from the Sangamon Valley in central Illinois or the Wabash Valley in east-central Illinois and adjacent Indiana (see Figure 10.7), where grit-tempered and shell-tempered pottery occur on sites in about the same proportion as they do at Aztalan. Hall sees Aztalan as an outpost of Illinois or Indiana Woodland peoples in the process of becoming Mississippian, rather than as Mississippians who moved north from Cahokia itself. Further examination of the archaeological data from northern Illinois suggests that collared grit-tempered pottery is present, but is also quite limited in its northern Illinois distribution to the area north of Peoria, and focused around Starved Rock, as well as the Rock River valley and the Fox and northern Illinois valleys (Elizabeth Benchley, personal communication; M. Catherine Bird, personal communication; Birmingham 1975; Douglas 1976; Hall 1962; Alan Harn, personal communication).

Archaeologists have devoted a considerable amount of discussion to the nature and development of Mississippian chiefdoms, as well as the nature of frontier settlements in complex societies (e.g., Green and Perlman 1985, Griffin 1985, Paynter 1985, Peebles and Kus 1977, Service 1971, Smith 1986). Given this background, an Illinois source, north of Cahokia, for the people who settled Aztalan makes quite a bit of sense. Rather than a group of people moving north from Cahokia to Wisconsin, it is perhaps more logical to assume that people living a more generalized Woodland/Mississippian lifeway in northern or central Illinois separated into smaller groups and moved into new territories. This process of social fissioning of society would be particularly likely on the boundaries or margins of eventual Mississippian influence, such as central and northern Illinois. Groups in these frontier regions would be more self-sufficient, more spatially separate, and less directly influenced by any central chiefdom authority. That some of these groups

might move into new territories, yet still maintain ties with central Mississippian society, is not unlikely or surprising. While in one sense such a process might suggest the disintegration of Mississippian society, it also would result in the spread of that society, particularly as viewed from an archaeological perspective.

Aztalan Collared pottery appears to be associated with the first movement of such groups from the south into Wisconsin. The type both predates and co-exists with Middle Mississippian forms. Whether the pottery style more clearly represents Late Woodland or Mississippian cultures can be debated, but this association is perhaps less important than the style's apparent foreign origin. Aztalan Collared pottery has certainly been documented from other sites in Wisconsin (cf. Baerreis and Freeman 1958, Hurley 1977, Stoltman 1976), but, except for Salkin's (1987) Kekoskee sites, in no case other than Aztalan does collared pottery appear to be the majority type. The people represented by this style may or may not have achieved the level of organization we commonly associate with Mississippian societies, but they likely were agriculturalists. In any event, either initially or at a somewhat later time, these people became integrated into a Middle Mississippian lifeway, at least at Aztalan.

But Why the Crawfish River?

If the movement of people into southern Wisconsin represents social fissioning or frontier movements of Woodland/Mississippian groups in northern and central Illinois, why would these people have selected this particular spot for their settlement, and why did they not develop the kind of widespread community settlement patterns one sees in other Middle Mississippian areas? Let's examine each of these questions in turn.

If one were coming into Wisconsin, especially on the Rock River, why not stop and settle at Lake Koshkonong, a shallow lake/marsh complex that is resource rich? The simplest explanation is that the Koshkonong area was bypassed because someone else was already there—namely, Oneota groups. Radiocarbon dates from the Carcajou Point and Crabapple Point sites lend some support to this notion. Figure 10.6 indicates the mean radiocarbon dates (presented as calendric dates) for all Aztalan samples and Lake Koshkonong Oneota samples (Carcajou Point, Crabapple Point, Crescent Bay Hunt Club); standard deviations are omitted for clarity (data from Boszhardt 1977, Richards 1985). The amount of overlap between the dates, especially at the early end of the range, indicates contemporaneity.

However, given the distribution of Oneota sites and the possible relationship between the first people at Aztalan and areas of northern and central Illinois, other possible motives should also be considered in

Aztalan & Koshkonong Radiocarbon Dates

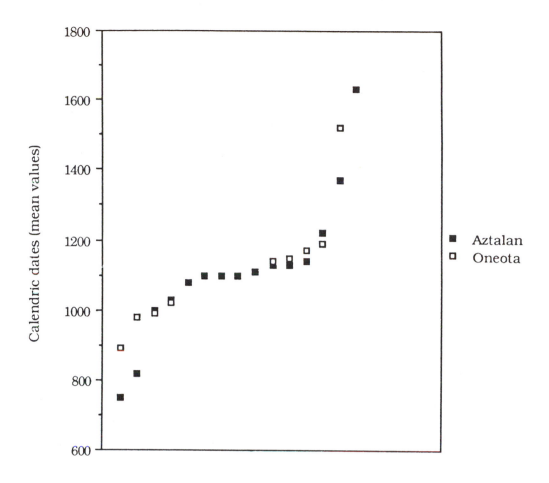

Figure 10.6. A comparison of mean radiocarbon dates from Aztalan and from Oneota sites in the Lake Koshkonong area (data from Boszhardt 1977 and Richards 1985).

settlement decisions. Where were these people living in Illinois?

Birmingham (1975) examined the distribution of Langford Tradition sites in the Rock River Valley. He divides the Rock River in Illinois into three parts (Figure 10.7): 1) the lower valley, from the confluence with the Mississippi River at Rock Island to Sterling; 2) the middle valley, which includes the area between Sterling and Rockford; and 3) the upper valley, which covers the area from Rockford to the Wisconsin state line. Birmingham notes that the lower and upper portions of the valley are characterized by broad flood-plains, surrounded by predominantly prairie uplands, with some forest. The middle valley "is characterized by an extremely narrow river valley, the uplands often bordering the river channel. Floodplains, when they

occur, rarely exceed one mile" (Birmingham 1975:3). Birmingham finds that Langford sites are almost exclusively within the middle portion of the valley, and concludes that "if the Langford peoples were choosing locations that featured riverine proximity, together with immediate accessibility to bottomland, timber, and prairie as analysis indicates, the middle region would seem ideal" (Birmingham 1975:27). He notes that other Langford sites are in similar regions. While not suggesting that the Langford Tradition represents the source for the inhabitants of Aztalan, I note that many of these middle Rock River Valley sites also have collared pottery.

It is beyond the scope of this paper to examine the origins of Oneota in Wisconsin, or the origins of the Langford Tradition in Illinois. However, it is interesting

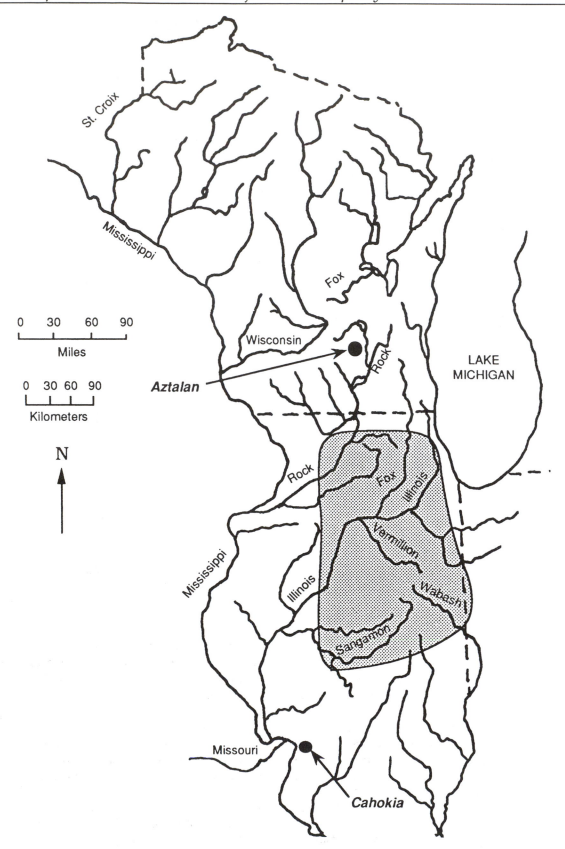

Figure 10.7. Aztalan's location relative to potential areas of origin. In Illinois, the Rock, Wabash, Vermillion, and Sangamon river valleys have specifically been suggested as areas of origin for Aztalan.

to note that the distribution of collared vessels in Illinois seems to mirror the kinds of locations Birmingham notes for Langford sites. Specifically, the distribution of collared pottery types seems to be associated with what Douglas (1976) has termed the Woodfordian Northeast; this term refers to the portions of the Midwest affected by the Woodfordian stage of the Wisconsin glaciation. Douglas discusses the distinctive character of the region in some detail, noting that although some of the larger rivers have a slightly different and more complex character, the region in general can be described as follows:

> Broad expanses of level ground bounded by low lunate ridges, very minimally developed drainage systems . . . with relatively shallow, narrow, simple stream valleys, weakly developed soils (with some outstanding exceptions), and in some areas unstable land surfaces—all provide clues to even the slightly-trained eye that this land is of a different nature from that surrounding it (Douglas 1976:8).

The general character of the landscape in northern Illinois and southeastern Wisconsin is similar, with a few notable exceptions. Although wetlands are characteristic of a young, glaciated landscape, there is more prairie in northern Illinois than there is in Wisconsin; Wisconsin wetlands (which include more swamps and marshes than wet prairie) tend to have a higher food and resource value, which may account for the more specific wetland orientation noted in southeastern Wisconsin (Goldstein 1987).

Following this pattern, if people moved up the Rock River to settle in Wisconsin, they would find that the Rock Valley in Rock County, Wisconsin, is very similar to the upper Rock Valley in Illinois (Figure 10.7). If the upper valley in northern Illinois was not particularly desirable for late prehistoric inhabitants, it probably was not desirable in Wisconsin either. The author knows of no recorded Mississippian sites or sites with collared pottery along the Rock River in Rock County. While this may well reflect survey bias and/or lack of survey work, it may also reflect deliberate prehistoric choice.

The Rock River changes its character at Lake Koshkonong (Figure 10.7), widening into a broad, shallow lake with extensive wetlands. Earlier, I suggested that the Koshkonong area may have been avoided because Oneota people were already there. It is also possible that Koshkonong was avoided because it did not resemble the landscapes that these people knew. Farther north, in particular along the Crawfish River, one could find the kind of settings similar to those in Illinois. The Crawfish location provides the narrow stream valley setting within a mile of all physiographic zones. I outlined before some of the reasons for that *particular* location on the Crawfish (as opposed to the Rock), but this more cognitive argument places the setting in an even broader context.

To put it simply, people may have settled at Aztalan because, as they moved north along the Rock River, it was one of the first locations that fit their notions and their knowledge of a good place to live. Koshkonong may have been avoided because of earlier settlers, but it may also have been avoided because it was not a setting that was familiar. Cognitively (and physiographically), the Crawfish River location looked most like home, and therefore, was a setting that these people knew how to use. Salkin's (1987) Kekoskee Phase sites are in similar settings.

The second portion of the question posed at the beginning of this section asked why a Mississippian settlement pattern did not develop around Aztalan. Even if our greater than 15% stratified random sample missed some sites, it should provide a good understanding of the general character of the region, and it seems unlikely that it missed an entire settlement pattern.

To propose a slightly speculative scenario, if Aztalan represents a settlement of people who moved north from Illinois, and if Oneota people were settled at Koshkonong at the same time, it is possible that the development of Aztalan occurred in some isolation. Given a longer time span for the site, it is possible that a relatively small group of people settled here first, then gradually grew into the village that we see archaeologically. If the site were inhabited for 200-300 years, even a small initial population of 20-30 could effectively grow to a population of several hundred over that period. If this were the case, it is possible that there was no need for outlying settlements since the population never reached the point where that kind of expansion was necessary or desirable. It may also have been desirable to protect against possible Oneota raids or other perceived dangers.

Initial intentions may have been to develop and expand the site into another Middle Mississippian center, with surrounding populations. The distance may have proved to be too great, or it is possible that the fissioning or dispersion of Middle Mississippian groups to other areas was great enough that the organization could not support another full-blown center of population.

If Aztalan represents two separate movements of people (a Woodland collared occupation and a later Mississippian occupation), this scenario is still not totally unlikely. There is clearly a relationship, in parts of Wisconsin and in parts of Illinois, between the people represented by the collared pottery and the Middle

Mississippian folk. Whether the former developed into the latter, or the former were influenced by the later is unclear. Nonetheless, the Middle Mississippian presence at Aztalan (and almost exclusively at Aztalan) might still reflect the first Mississippianization of the collared group in Wisconsin, and for the reasons discussed above, the only real Middle Mississippian development in the region.

Summary and Conclusions

The Aztalan site in Jefferson County, Wisconsin represents a puzzle to archaeologists from several different perspectives:

1. The visual structure of the site and many of the artifact classes and types clearly suggest a Middle Mississippian level of organization.

2. The collared grit-tempered pottery and the location of Aztalan do not follow the pattern noted for other Middle Mississippian centers (cf. Smith 1985). There is no hierarchical settlement pattern nor outlying settlements, and the majority of the pottery on the site is grit-tempered and generally collared.

3. Although Aztalan does not fit the Mississippian settlement pattern, it also does not fit the clear settlement pattern and location preferences of other prehistoric groups who have lived in the area — other groups focused on the margins of resource-rich wetlands and interior river bends.

4. Even given a different setting and a different pattern of living, evidence from the site indicates that Aztalan is classic Middle Mississippian in both its formal structural elements and its subsistence patterns. All of the foodstuffs outlined by Smith (1985) as characteristic parts of the Middle Mississippian pattern are present, even though the physiographic location is totally different.

In an attempt to address this puzzle systematically, this paper has proposed a model, albeit an incomplete model, to account for Aztalan's placement and origin.

When was Aztalan first occupied, and where did these people originate? I have proposed, based on the radiocarbon dates and stratigraphic evidence, that people moved to the site around A.D. 800-900. The argument for an early settlement is compelling, in particular when one considers that not only the Middle Mississippian shell-tempered pottery, but also the grit-tempered collared pottery, is foreign in the region. Collared pottery is limited in its distribution, with one locus being the northern and central portions of Illinois. The people who first settled at Aztalan made

collared, grit-tempered pottery, and probably came up the Rock River from northern and/or central Illinois. It is likely that not a lot of people were part of that early group of settlers. These Woodland people were already engaged in some maize horticulture, and settled not only at Aztalan, but also at other sites in south-central Wisconsin that have recently been termed Kekoskee Phase (Salkin 1987). We still need to determine the precise route of the people who moved into the area, including their origin(s) in a more specific sense. We also need additional information on the extent and diversity of collared ware throughout the Illinois and Wisconsin area — to understand the development of Aztalan, we need to know these distributions in better detail. This scenario suggests that the Middle Mississippian presence at Aztalan would represent the *second* movement north of people (or at least ideas) from the south. Given the sedentary, semi-agricultural lifeways of these Woodland folks, it would not be surprising that Middle Mississippian might be readily accepted or added on to what they already did. This seems especially likely given the spread of Mississippian influence into the regions of Illinois where this collared pottery seems to have originated.

Another part of the origins question is why people decided to move north, either initially or at a later time. I have suggested that movement into the area was part of a natural social fissioning process. Sedentary, agricultural groups would eventually need to search for more land to support an expanding population. Additionally, groups in the Woodfordian Northeast would have been at the margins or frontiers of Middle Mississippian society, and would have been more independent and under less direct control of central authorities. Spread and expansion of these groups might be part of the natural maintenance and development process.

Why did they select the Aztalan location? If we do not argue for a direct Cahokia home for the settlers, Aztalan's location makes a great deal of sense. If these people were adapted to what Douglas (1976) calls the Woodfordian Northeast, they were adapted to narrow, shallow, and young river systems with a series of resources in close proximity. If they were moving north along the Rock River, the Aztalan location was one of the first places that offered subsistence resources in a setting that was familiar. Aztalan would look like home. Additionally, a Crawfish River location offered several distinct physiographic and resource advantages over a location on a similar portion of the Rock River.

Lake Koshkonong, a rich and desirable place to anyone who had lived in southeastern Wisconsin for very long, was unfamiliar ground to these people (although it might appear much more familiar to someone from

Cahokia), and was probably also already occupied by Oneota groups. Whoever these settlers were, they came to stay, but they also engaged in trade and regular contact along the Crawfish-Rock-Mississippi river systems. Exactly when the site took on its Middle Mississippian character is not clear, but clearly it happened.

What happened to these people? Here is where the model is most incomplete. Did Aztalan fail as a settlement? Why didn't they develop the characteristic Middle Mississippian settlement pattern? I have suggested that if the initial population at Aztalan was small, the rate of population growth over a 200-300 year period was probably sufficient to account for a population of several hundred people at Aztalan's maximum. It seems possible that with this kind of population it may not have been necessary to spread out into associated farmsteads and villages. Also, there may have been real or perceived dangers in an expanded settlement system. Perhaps they thought that others would move up to Aztalan later, or perhaps the distance was just too great for additional settlers. It is also possible that the Oneota groups at Koshkonong discouraged additional settlers. Whatever the reason(s), it appears that Aztalan developed in relative isolation and maintained its nucleated single settlement as a means of maintaining its society.

If the initial settlement of Aztalan was a part of an expansion process of Woodland/Mississippian societies, especially along the margins of what became Middle Mississippian influence, perhaps this expansion speeded the disintegration and decentralization of Middle Mississippian society. Is it a coincidence that the Middle Mississippian materials at Aztalan date to the Stirling Phase, and that it is during the subsequent Moorehead Phase that Cahokia itself seems to undergo population decline and retrenchment? Perhaps the question of what happened to the people at Aztalan is better answered from the perspective of Cahokia.

This has been an attempt to model a complex series of developments based on a number of lines of independent evidence. While I may have raised more questions about Aztalan than I have answered, the questions are becoming more specific, and thus more easily attempted.

References Cited

Baerreis, David A. and R.A. Bryson
    1965 Climatic Episodes and the Dating of the Mississippian Cultures. *The Wisconsin Archeologist* 46:203-220.

Baerreis, David A. and Joan E. Freeman
    1958 Late Woodland Pottery as Seen from Aztalan. *The Wisconsin Archeologist* 39(1):35-61.

Barrett, Samuel A.
    1933 Ancient Aztalan. Bulletin of the Public Museum of the City of Milwaukee, Vol.XIII.

Birmingham, Robert A.
    1975 The Langford Tradition and its Environmental Context in the Rock River Valley, Illinois. Unpublished Masters paper, Department of Anthropology, University of Wisconsin-Milwaukee.

Bleed, Peter
    1970 Notes on Aztalan Shell-Tempered Pottery. *The Wisconsin Archeologist* 51(1):1-20.

Boszhardt, Robert
    1977 Wisconsin Radiocarbon Chronology — 1976, a Second Compilation. *The Wisconsin Archeologist* 58:87-143.

Curtis, John T.
    1959 *The Vegetation of Wisconsin.* University of Wisconsin Press, Madison.

Dorney, John R.
    1980 Presettlement Vegetation of Southeastern Wisconsin: Edaphic Relationships and Disturbance. Masters thesis, Department of Botany, University of Wisconsin-Milwaukee.
    1981 The Impact of Native Americans on Presettlement Vegetation in Southeastern Wisconsin. Paper presented at the annual meeting of the Wisconsin Academy of Sciences.

Douglas, John G.
    1976 Collins: A Late Woodland Ceremonial Complex in the Woodfordian Northeast. Unpublished Ph.D. dissertation, University of Illinois, Urbana.

Goldstein, Lynne
    1987 *The Southeastern Wisconsin Archaeology Project: 1986-87 & Project Summary.* Report to the Historic Preservation Division, State Historical Society of Wisconsin. UWM Archaeological Research Laboratory, *Reports of Investigations*, No. 88.

Green, Stanton and Richard Perlman (editors)
   1985 The Archaeology of Frontiers and Boundaries. Academic Press, Inc., New York.
Griffin, James B.
   1961 Some correlations of climatic and cultural change in eastern North American prehistory. *Annals of the New York Academy of Sciences*, Vol. 95, Art. 1; pp. 710-717.
   1985 Changing Concepts of the Prehistoric Mississippian Cultures of the Eastern United States. In *Alabama and the Borderlands: From Prehistory to Statehood* (R. Reid Badger and Lawrence A. Clayton, eds.); pp. 40-63. The University of Alabama Press, University, Alabama.
Hall, Robert L.
   1962 A Newly Designated Pottery Type from Northern Illinois. Paper presented at the Midwest Archaeological Conference. Springfield, Illinois.
   1986 Upper Mississippi and Middle Mississippi Relationships. *The Wisconsin Archeologist* 67(3-4):365-369.
Harn, Alan D.
   1971 Comments on the Spatial Distribution of Late Woodland and Mississippian Ceramics in the General Cahokia Sphere. Paper presented at the Cahokia Ceramics Conference, Collinsville, Illinois, July 19-23, 1971.
Hurley, William M.
   1977 Aztalan Revisited. *The Wisconsin Archeologist* 58:256-294.
   1986 The Late Woodland Stage: Effigy Mound Culture. *The Wisconsin Archeologist* 67(3-4):283-301.
Kind, Robert J.
   1979 An Environmental Reconstruction of the Crawfish and Rock Rivers Archaeological Project's Study Area and its Implications for Prehistoric Settlement-Subsistence Behavior. Masters paper, Department of Anthropology, University of Wisconsin-Milwaukee.
Martin, L.
   1965 *The Physical Geography of Wisconsin* (third edition). The University of Wisconsin Press, Madison.
McKern, William C.
   1946 Aztalan. The Wisconsin Archeologist 27:41-52.
Milfred, C. J. and F. D. Hole
   1970 Soils of Jefferson County, Wisconsin. *Bulletin 86, Soil Series 61.* University of Wisconsin, Geological and Natural History Survey, Soil Survey Division.
Parmalee, Paul W.
   1960 Animal Remains from the Aztalan Site, Jefferson County, Wisconsin. *The Wisconsin Archeologist* 41:1-10.
Paynter, Robert
   1985 Surplus Flow between Frontiers and Homelands. *The Archaeology of Frontiers and Boundaries* (Stanton Green and Richard Perlman, eds.); pp. 163-211. Academic Press, Inc., New York.
Peebles, Christopher S. and Susan M. Kus
   1977 Some Archaeological Correlates of Ranked Societies. *American Antiquity* 42(3):421-448.
Peters, Gordon R.
   1976 A Reevaluation of Aztalan: Some Temporal and Causal Factors. *The Wisconsin Archeologist* 57:2-11.
Richards, John D.
   1985 Aztalan Compilation, Mapping and Excavations. In *The Southeastern Wisconsin Archaeology Project: 1984-85* (Lynne Goldstein, editor); pp. 63-109. Report to the Historic Preservation Division, State Historical Society of Wisconsin. UWM Archaeological Research Laboratory,*Report of Investigations*, No. 81.
Ritzenthaler, Robert E.
   1961 Radiocarbon dates for Aztalan. *The Wisconsin Archeologist* 44:180.
Rodell, Roland
   1983 The Late Prehistory of Eastern Wisconsin: A Survey of the Archaeological Research and Interpretations Pertaining to Oneota Settlement and Subsistence. Masters paper, Department of Anthropology, University of Wisconsin-Milwaukee.
Salkin, Philip H.
   1987 A Reevaluation of the Late Woodland Stage in Southeastern Wisconsin. *Wisconsin Academy Review* 33(2):75-79.

Service, Elman R.
  1971 *Primitive Social Organization* (second edition). Random House, New York.
Smith, Bruce D.
  1978 Variation in Mississippian Settlement Patterns. In Mississippian *Settlement Patterns* (Bruce D. Smith, editor); pp. 479-503. Academic Press, Inc., New York.
  1985 Mississippian Patterns of Subsistence and Settlement. In *Alabama and the Borderlands: From Prehistory to Statehood* (R. Reid Badger and Lawrence A. Clayton, eds.); pp. 64-79. The University of Alabama Press, University, Alabama.
  1986 The Archaeology of the Southeastern United States: From Dalton to De Soto, 10,500-500 B.P. *Advances in World Archaeology* (Fred Wendorf and Angela E. Close, eds.); Volume 5, pp. 1-92. Academic Press, Orlando, Florida.
Stoltman, James B.
  1976 Two New Late Woodland Radiocarbon Dates from the Rosenbaum Rockshelter (47 DA 411) and Their Implications for Interpretations of Wisconsin Prehistory. *The Wisconsin Archeologist* 57(1):12-28.
Steube, Fred K.
  1976 Site Survey and Test Excavations in the Aztalan Area. *The Wisconsin Archeologist* 57:198-259.
Yerkes, Richard W.
  1980 Flotation, Fish Scales, and Seasonal Patterns in the Abundance of Charcoal, Maize, and Nuts at the Site of Aztalan, Jefferson County, Wisconsin. Unpublished manuscript.
Zicker, Wilma A.
  1955 An Analysis of Jefferson County Vegetation Using Surveyors' Records and Present Data. Masters thesis, Department of Botany, University of Wisconsin-Madison.

11

The Fred Edwards Site: A Case of Stirling Phase Culture Contact in Southwestern Wisconsin

Fred A. Finney and James B. Stoltman
Department of Anthropology
University of Wisconsin-Madison

Much popular and scientific attention has been focused on the large, extensive mounded sites of the Central Mississippi River valley, especially the site of Cahokia. Early archaeological research at Cahokia concentrated on documenting its mounds and defining a chronological sequence, while more recent research has emphasized the emergence and subsequent areal expansion of the complex socio-political system associated with the florescent period of the site's occupancy. During its heyday, ca. A.D. 1000-1250, Cahokia exhibited the highest degree of socio-political complexity so far known among the native peoples of Eastern North America. Along with the sheer enormity of the site, important evidence for this complexity includes elite-class burials and an extensive trade in non-local materials and ritual artifacts (See Fowler, this volume). A number of sites in the Upper Midwest (e.g., Aztalan, Mills, Silvernale, and Cambria) have been suggested as sources for many of the exotic materials found at Cahokia. These sites exhibit Middle Mississippian ceramics, particularly Powell Plain and Ramey Incised, the hallmarks of the Stirling phase at Cahokia, as evidence of cultural interaction with Cahokia. Scholars have variously interpreted this evidence of cultural interaction between Cahokia and the Upper Midwest to represent systematic trade, migration, or random contact, as well as different combinations of the above.

The main subject of this paper is a recently discovered Late Woodland site in southwestern Wisconsin at which there is unequivocal evidence of cultural interaction with the Cahokia cultural sphere. Fred Edwards (47-Gt-377), as the new site is called, is located in the Grant River valley about 13 kilometers upstream from its confluence with the Mississippi River (Figure 11.1). Archaeological field work at the Fred Edwards site has involved four controlled surface collections (1982, 1984, 1985, and 1987) and three seasons of excavation (1984, 1985, and 1987) by personnel from the Department of Anthropology, University of Wisconsin-Madison, under the direction of James B. Stoltman (Finney and Stoltman 1986; Finney 1990, 1991; Stoltman 1991).

The principal archaeological component at the site may be characterized as Late Woodland with extensive evidence of Middle Mississippian culture contact in the form of a wide range of exotic or non-local items. Included among these non-local items are Ramey Incised and Powell Plain jars, Mill Creek chert, Dongola chert, Kaolin chert, Burlington chert, marine shell (both beads and larger fragments), and polished stone earspools, all of which presumably originated from a source or sources well to the south of Wisconsin. In addition a number of additional non-local items, such as Hartley Fort ceramic types, Aztalan Collared jars, copper, Hixton silicified sandstone, red pipestone (possibly catlinite), and Knife River flint, indicate cultural interaction with other Late Woodland peoples. The wide diversity of non-local items recovered is unparalleled at any other known site in the Upper Mississippi Valley region, except possibly Aztalan, and suggests that the site's

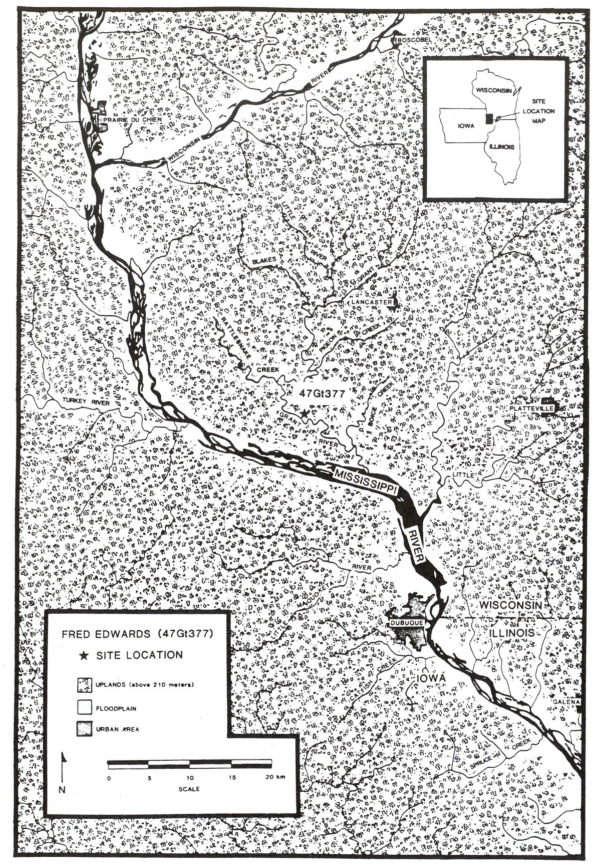

Figure 11.1. Fred Edwards site location in Southwest Wisconsin.

residents were actively engaged in a far-flung exchange system that almost certainly had Cahokia as the ultimate moving force.

Research Objectives

While our research objectives at the Fred Edwards site were multiple, consonant with the theme of this volume, our primary objective in this paper is to shed new light on the nature of cultural interaction that linked Cahokia to its northern hinterlands through a detailed analysis of a single, well-controlled example, the Fred Edwards site. An important supposition underlying our analysis is that attempts to understand a subsystem (i.e., the Fred Edwards site) are relevant to the endeavor of trying to understand the larger system (i.e., a Cahokia-centered interaction network) of which it was a part.

At least three factors are especially germane to any archaeological investigation of the problem of inter-site cultural interaction: (1) relative age of the sites involved, (2) evidence of reciprocity, and (3) context of exchanged goods in both producing and consuming societies. Cultural interaction could only occur between contemporary sites, a factor that should be confirmed based upon independent evidence, not merely assumed. Secondly, it is important to ascertain the kinds and amounts of materials and goods that were being produced for exchange both in the centers and in the peripheries. After all, cultural interaction is a two way process that can only be fully understood when evidence is available from all partners to the exchange. Third, knowledge of the context of both imported items and production activities in both the center and the peripheries is requisite to the construction of any comprehensive models of cultural interaction. For example, are imported items found uniformly distributed among all social classes within a society? Or, are all social segments or households engaged in the production of items for exchange? Did archaeological site formation processes (e.g., Schiffer 1987) severely alter artifact distributions? It is through efforts to answer questions like these that we can hope to understand the dynamics underlying inter-site cultural interaction.

The methods used to investigate this research problem at the Fred Edwards site included controlled surface collection and block excavation to recover the spatial arrangement of subsurface pits, structures, and posts, along with their associated artifacts and faunal and floral remains. The excavations revealed what appears to be a single community composed of a series of household clusters (i.e., structures and associated pits) arranged around the northern and southern edges of a central, open area, presumably a plaza.

Our view that the prehistoric occupation of the site can be attributed to a single archaeological component warrants further discussion. As can be seen from Figures 11.5 and 11.6, there are relatively few instances of feature superimposition at the site. There are, however, at least three instances of pits superimposed upon house basins (Features 2, 6, and 50) and two instances of overlapping house basins (Features 50/73 and 115/158), indicating that not all features were precisely contemporary. Nevertheless, the cultural content of all features is so clearly uniform that the cases of overlapping features are best interpreted as rebuilding activities on the part of peoples whose material culture was basically uniform throughout the period of site occupation. Thus, while not maintaining that the all features so far excavated were precisely contemporary, the overall evidence strongly suggests that all were built within a relatively brief interval of time and that only a single archaeological component is represented at the site.

The Fred Edwards Site

The Fred Edwards site is a unique late prehistoric village in the Upper Mississippi Valley region. It is situated five to six m above the modern floodplain of the Grant River on a late Woodfordian terrace (Figures 11.1 and 11.2). The terrace extends southward from a prominent upland ridge that rises about 60 m above it. The area has been under intensive cultivation since the 1870's. The known limit of surface cultural material scatter is approximately 3.5 ha. Two gullies divide the terrace into three lobes, with the primary surface concentration corresponding closely to the central lobe (Figure 11.2). The central lobe concentration covers an area of about 1.2 ha and is the location of the main village area, which was at least partially enclosed by a palisade.

Radiocarbon Dates

Eighteen radiocarbon dates from 14 different features are available for the Fred Edwards site (Figure 11.3). Twelve of these features contain ceramics diagnostic of the Fred Edwards phase. The two exceptions are the palisade (Feature 148) and a pit (Feature 8) located inside a structure. All dates were run at the Center for Climatic Research, University of Wisconsin-Madison (Steventon and Kutzbach 1986, 1987, 1989). The radiocarbon dates are one of two main methods for dating the Fred Edwards occupation. The second method is cross-dating by well known ceramic types, e.g., Ramey Incised.

The median values of the eighteen dates range between A.D. 800 and A.D. 1300. Taking the one sigma values into consideration, 13 of the dates can be seen to cluster between A.D. 1050 and A.D. 1150,

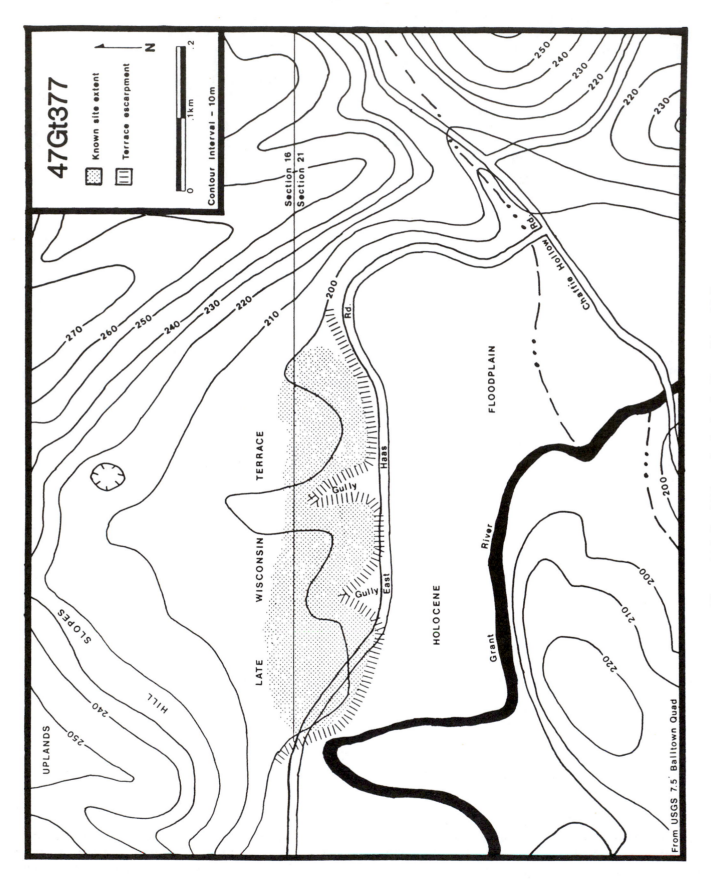

Figure 11.2. Fred Edwards site in the Grant River Valley.

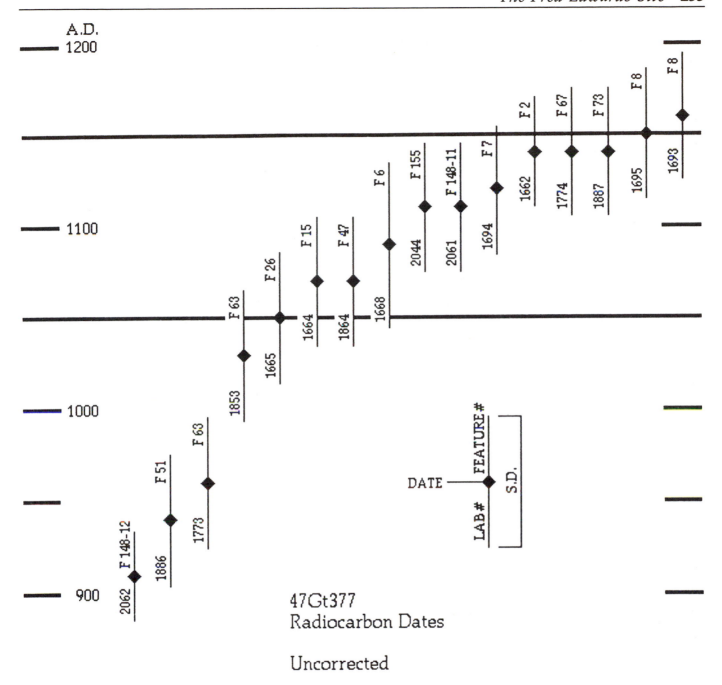

47Gt377
Radiocarbon Dates

Uncorrected

Figure 11.3. Uncorrected radiocarbon dates from Fred Edwards. Two dates - A.D. 800 ± 70 (WIS-1663) and A.D. 1300 ± 70 (WIS-1854) - are not shown on this figure.

the age of the Stirling phase at Cahokia (cf. Fowler and Hall 1975). Of the five remaining dates, two comfortably overlap the A.D. 1050-1150 range if their two sigma values are taken into consideration, leaving only three of the 18 radiocarbon dates as incongruous with this age estimate. Since the evidence from ceramic cross dating of such types as Aztalan Collared (Stoltman 1976; Baerreis and Freeman 1958),

Hartley Crosshatched (Tiffany 1982), and Powell Plain and Ramey Incised (Fowler and Hall 1975; Bareis and Porter 1984) is also entirely consistent with this evidence, we accept A.D. 1050 to A.D. 1150 as the best estimate for the age of the occupation of the Fred Edwards site. Further information about specific radiocarbon dates, is provided in the following section.

Community Organization

Excavations at the Fred Edwards site involved the removal (by shovel scraping) of 731 m² of plowzone and exposed 165 features (Figure 11.4). Features were normally clearly discernible at the base of the plowzone, being brown to dark brown in color in contrast to the yellow loess subsoil. The intensity of occupation was not uniform over the site. Both the density of artifacts recovered in the surface collections and feature densities were observed to be greatest along the southern and northern margins of the central lobe. This observation may be biased to some extent due to plowinduced erosion along the sloping eastern and western peripheries of the central lobe, where it is possible that some subsurface features have been destroyed.

The excavations revealed a community composed of a series of household clusters, that is, structures and associated pits (Winter 1976), arranged around two sides of a central courtyard or plaza. That the central area served as a plaza is suggested by the low density of artifacts recovered there in the controlled surface collections along with the paucity of features encountered during excavations—an area of 46 m² excavated near the center of the lobe uncovered no features (Figure 11.4). Evidence for a palisade (Feature 148) was encountered on the south end of the lobe, where a post line borders the Feature 50 and Feature 73 household clusters (Figure 11.6). Unfortunately, the palisade could be followed for only a short distance at this location since each end had apparently been destroyed by erosion. A sheet midden (Feature 164) is located outside the palisade line. This midden extends for an undetermined distance along the edge of the central lobe.

Features identified at the Fred Edwards site are nine semi-subterranean basin structures, two other structures that are probable sweatlodges, 118 pits, 34 posts (located outside of structures), one midden, and one palisade line. The semi-subterranean structures (Features 2, 6, 50, 73, 115, 118, 155, 158, and 162) have shallow, rectangular basins that exhibit wall posts set in individual postholes. Six structures had interior, subfloor pits, while exterior pits were near all structures. Artifacts, including especially ceramics and lithics, were abundant in both plowzone and subsurface feature contexts, while fauna and charred floral remains were abundant only in feature contexts.

Seven structures had apparently been used as single-family dwellings. Their floor areas ranged from 8 to 12 square meters. In addition there are two larger structures whose function is less certain. Features 118 and 162 had floor areas of ca. 18 and 23 square meters. Considering the relatively small size of the majority of the structures, their larger size is more probably attributable to use as communal structures rather than as extended family dwellings (e.g., Conrad 1989).

Six household clusters were thoroughly investigated. The spatial distribution of the known, excavated household clusters is on the north and south ends of the central lobe. Aerial photographs suggest the presence of additional structures on the north, west, and south sides of the "plaza". We estimate that at least 20 structures were constructed on the central lobe. There appears to be one rebuilding episode during the site occupation, reflected in the superimposition of Features 50 and 73 on the south and Features 115 and 158 on the north (Figures 11.4 to 11.6).

Feature 2 Household Cluster

Feature 2 and its associated pits were positioned at the northwest edge of the community (Figures 11.5-11.6). Long axis orientation of the Feature 2 basin was east–west. The semi-subterranean basin was 3.50 m long, 2.63 m wide, 14 cm deep, and had a floor area of 8.04 m². No interior pits were associated. A cluster of 12 pits was located several meters east of the structure, and three were found to the north. One pit, Feature 3, superimposed the west edge of the structure basin.

Posts for the walls had been positioned along the inner edge of the structure basin. A total of 55 postmolds was recorded in the floor of the basin after removal of the fill. The charred remains of three wall members were recovered from the basin fill just inside the east post row (Figure 11.5). A radiocarbon sample derived from these charred logs produced a dated of A.D. 1140 ± 60 (WIS-1662; Figure 11.3). A wigwam type construction is suggested for Feature 2. When the number of posts from the east (N=13) and west (N=10) walls and the north (N=16) and south (N=16) walls were compared, the numbers suggest the pairing of wall posts from east to west and north to south. In some cases there are apparent groupings or concentrations of posts.

Feature 6 Household Cluster

Feature 6 and it's associated pits were centrally located at the north end of the central lobe (Figures 11.4 and 11.5). Long axis orientation of the basin is east-west, similar to Feature 2. The semi-subterranean basin was 4.26 m long, 3.41 m wide, and 12 cm deep and had a floor area of 12.20 m². Feature 6 is notable for its abundant internal features and distinctive entryway. The internal features include two storage pits, two hearths, and three posts. A west-facing entryway is marked by posts extending outside the basin on the south side. One of the hearths (Feature 8) is located within the entryway, while the second hearth (Feature 18) and the two storage pits (Features 15 and 17) are located within the structure basin. One storage pit located outside of Feature 6 (Feature 9) was probably associated with it, but a second external pit (Feature 7) postdates the structure since it is superimposed upon

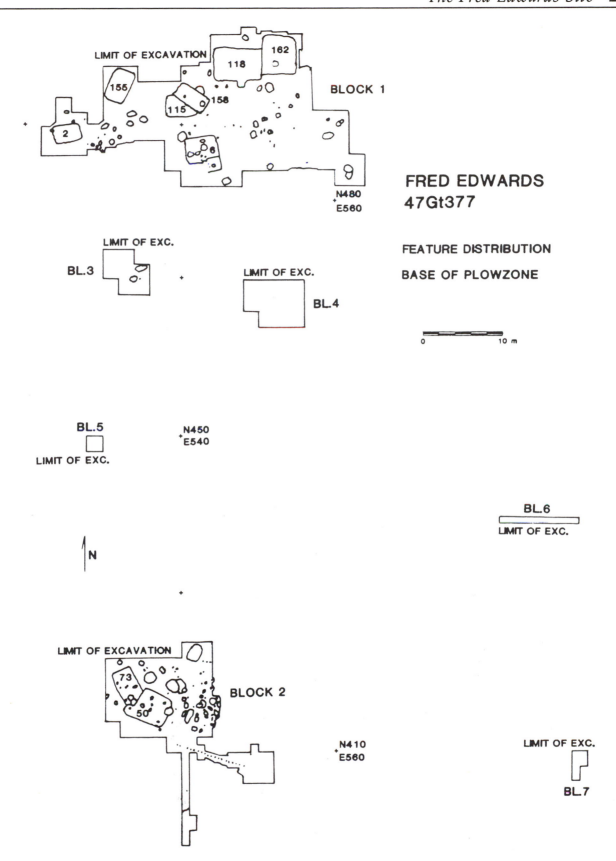

Figure 11.4. Site Plan at Fred Edwards.

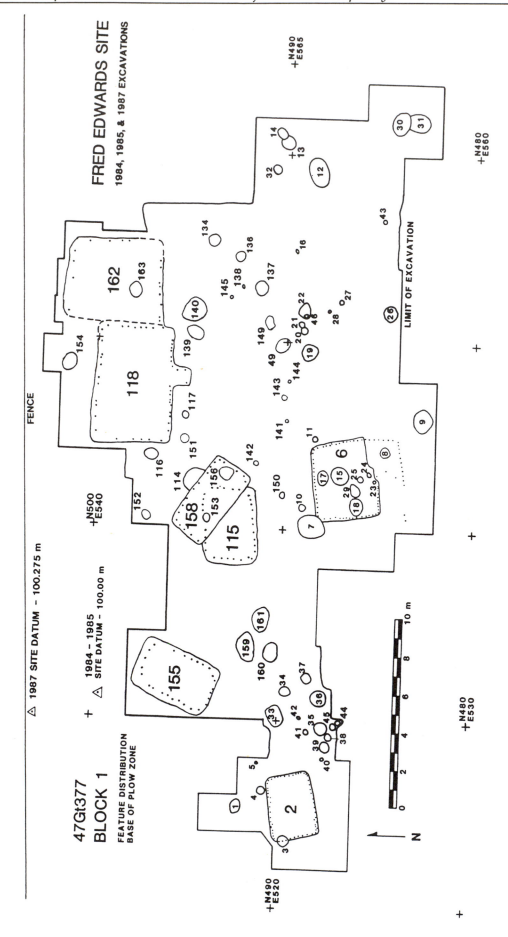

Figure 11.5. Block 1 at Fred Edwards.

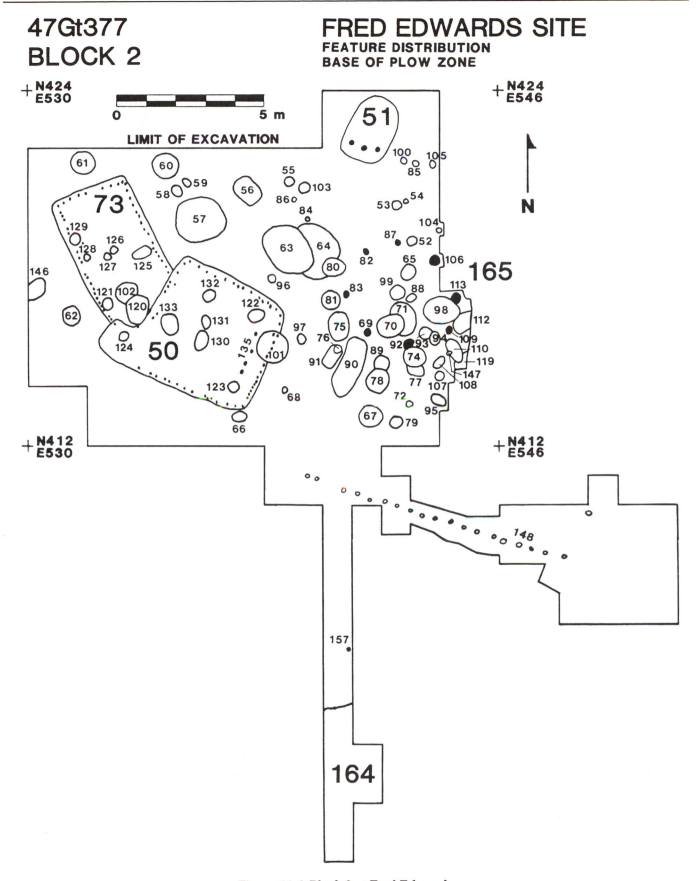

Figure 11.6. Block 2 at Fred Edwards.

the northwest corner of the basin. Seventy-seven post-molds were found along the interior margin of the basin and in the entryway. A gabled roof construction is implied by the presence of three internal posts (Features 23-24-25).

Four radiocarbon dates provide a consistent and seemingly reliable age estimate for the Feature 6 household cluster (Figure 11.3): A.D. 1070 ± 70 (WIS-1664), A.D. 1090 ± 90 (WIS-1668), A.D. 1150 ± 70 (WIS-1695), and A.D. 1160 ± 70 (WIS-1693). A charcoal sample from Feature 7, which should postdate Feature 6, produced a radiocarbon date of A.D. 1120 ± 70 (WIS-1694), suggesting that its construction must have followed quickly on the heels of the abandonment of Feature 6. In addition one anomalously early date was obtained from Feature 8, a hearth within the entryway–A.D. 800 ± 70 (WIS-1663). This date was run on a large piece of wood charcoal. When the results were obtained, additional radiocarbon samples, this time of bark (WIS-1693) and nut shell (WIS-1695) were extracted from the Feature 8 soil samples and submitted for dating. The results of these newer dates suggest that the early age of WIS-1663 can probably be attributed to the dating of wood charcoal derived from the inner rings of a large log and that this date should be rejected as inappropriate for dating the period of occupation at Fred Edwards.

Feature 155 Household Cluster

Feature 155 was positioned at the northwest edge of the community (Figures 11.4 and 11.5). The semi-subterranean basin in which the structure was set measures 4.50 m long, 2.96 m wide, 30 cm deep, and has a floor area of 9.36 m². The long axis of the basin is oriented northeast-southwest. No internal pits were associated. Nearly all of the Kaolin chert found at the site was recovered from Feature 155. A cluster of 12 pits is located several meters south of the structure.

Numerous (N=127) charred wall or roof members were found on the basin floor, concentrated in the north half. A charcoal sample from one of these logs produced a radiocarbon date of A.D. 1140 ± 70 (WIS-2044). Twenty-six postmolds were positioned along the interior margin of the basin. When the number of posts from the east (N=7) and west (N=9) walls and the north (N=5) and south (N=5) walls were compared, the numbers suggest the pairing of wall posts across the structure. A wigwam type construction is suggested for Feature 155.

Feature 115 Household Cluster

Feature 115 was positioned on the north side of the community (Figures 11.4 and 11.5). Other structures were found to the west, east, and south. Feature 115 had been superimposed by Feature 158, another structure

basin. The semi-subterranean basin in which the structure had been set measures 4.19 m long, 2.98 m wide, 28 cm deep, and had a floor area of 10.00 m². One internal pit, Feature 153, was associated with Feature 115. In addition an unusually large number of artifacts was found scattered throughout the basin fill, including 13 ceramic vessels, 19 projectile points, and 6 endscrapers.

Thirty-two postmolds were positioned along the interior margin of the basin. When the number of posts from the east (N=6) were matched with those from the west (N=7), and those from the north (N=8) were matched with those from the south (N=11), the pairing of wall posts was suggested. (Postmolds could not be defined along a portion of the north wall near Feature 153). A wigwam type of construction is suggested for Feature 115.

Feature 158 Household Cluster

Feature 158 and its associated pits were positioned on the north side of the community (Figures 11.4 and 11.5). Other structures were to the west, east, and south. The semi-subterranean basin was 4.52 m long, 2.24 m wide, 22 cm deep, and had a floor area of 8.28 m². The orientation of its long axis is northwest-southeast. One internal pit, Feature 156, was associated with the structure. Feature 158 had been superimposed onto Feature 115, a basin structure with a different long axis orientation, and onto Feature 114, a pit. Only 19 postmolds could be identified along the interior margin of the basin. None was found on the south side, although their existence was probable. Like the other structures at the site, it seems likely that Feature 158 was of wigwam type construction.

Feature 118 Household Cluster

Feature 118 is located at the north edge of the community (Figures 11.4 and 11.5). Its semisubterranean basin measures 6.38 m long by 4.12 m wide, is 8 cm deep, and has a floor area of 22.98 m². The long axis of the basin is oriented east-west. An entryway, measuring 99 cm × 99 cm, extends from the south wall. No internal pits were associated, but scattered pits were located south of the structure. Forty-five postmolds were identified along the interior margin of the basin. Few postmolds were defined along the north wall, which is adjacent to the modern field boundary, because of a large number of root and rodent disturbances. Feature 118 overlaps and apparently superimposes Feature 162, a second basin structure located immediately to the east, but a clear boundary between them could not be defined. Considering the large floor area of the Feature 118 basin, it is possible that the structure served some kind of communal function. Unfortunately, the artifact inventory from the feature was too sparse to confirm such an interpretation.

Feature 162 Household Cluster

Feature 162 and its associated pits are located on the north edge of the site immediately adjacent to Feature 118 (Figures 11.4 and 11.5). The size of the semi-subterranean basin can only be estimated because the exact position of the west wall was obscured by Feature 118. Our estimate of its size is as follows: 5.18 m long, 4.39 m wide, and 10 cm deep, with a floor area of 18.03 m². Perhaps this structure shared a common wall with Feature 118. In any event, the large size of Feature 162 also implies it had been a communal building. The long axis of the basin is oriented north-south. Only 17 postmolds were identified along the interior margin of the basin. As with Feature 118, postmolds along the north wall were difficult to discern. One pit, Feature 163, was located within the structure basin, while two external pits located several meters to the south were also apparently associated with Feature 162.

Feature 73 Household Cluster

Feature 73 and its associated pits are located at the south end of the central lobe (Figures 11.4 and 11.6). The structure basin is oriented northwest-southeast and measures 4.84 m long, 3.77 m wide, and 22 cm deep. The floor area of the basin is 11.78 m². Feature 73 is notable for the presence of a number of shallow internal pits in the south half and a hearth and a post in the center. Fifty-nine postmolds were recorded along the interior margin of the basin, their arrangement suggesting a wigwam type construction. Three external storage pits located to the north and east were probably also associated with this structure. A second structure, Feature 50, superimposed Feature 73.

Feature 50 Household Cluster

Feature 50 and its associated pits are located at the south end of the central lobe (Figures 11.4 and 11.6). The Feature 50 basin is 31 cm deep and measures 4.21 m long X 4.16 m wide, with a floor area of 15.83 m². The long axis orientation is roughly northwest-southeast. Sixty-four postmolds were positioned along the interior margin of the basin, with a gap in the southwest corner marking the location of an entryway. Feature 50 is notable for the presence of a number of interior features, including six shallow pits, a central post, and a bench or platform along the southeast wall (Figure 11.6). At least one large storage pit (Feature 63) to the northeast of Feature 50 appears to be associated with it, as do at least some of the dense cluster of pits to the east of the structure. Four charcoal samples from the Feature 50 household cluster were dated. Of these four dates, two are acceptable, a third (WIS-1773) is acceptable at two sigma, while the fourth (WIS-1854) is inexplicably too young:

WIS-1773	A.D. 960 ± 70	F. 63
WIS-1853	A.D. 1030 ± 70	F. 63
WIS-1774	A.D. 1140 ± 70	F. 67
WIS-1854	A.D. 1300 ± 70	F. 50

Feature 51, Possible Sweatlodge

Feature 51 is a unique subrectangular basin located northeast of the Feature 50 household cluster at the south end of the central lobe (Figure 11.6). It measures 2.23 m NE/SW × 1.66 m NW/SE, with a floor area of 3.70 m² and a depth of 32 cm. Three internal postmolds along the southern wall mark the position of an apparent bench or platform. The most distinctive property of Feature 51 was the concentration of fire-cracked rock, all limestone/dolomite of local derivation, that comprised a substantial portion of the basin fill. In all, 227 kg (501 lbs) of fire-cracked rock fragments were recovered from Feature 51. Beneath this rock concentration on the floor of the basin was a charcoal-rich layer. Virtually no other cultural materials were recovered from the basin, leaving its function undetermined. It is possible that this small structure served as an oven for roasting various foodstuffs, but the absence of associated faunal or flora remains inclines us to view it as a sweatlodge, presumably with a pole framework positioned outside of the basin. In this regard, however, it must be admitted that it differs from other reported sweatlodges in the Midwest, which tend to be circular in shape and to have continuous walls (cf. Hargrave et al. 1983; Mehrer 1982; Milner 1984; Porter 1974). Charcoal from this basin provided a C-14 date of A.D. 940 ± 70 (WIS-1886), which appears to be bit too old for the main period of site occupancy. We regard it, like WIS-1773, as unacceptable within the range of its one sigma value, but acceptable within the two sigma range.

Feature 165, Possible Sweatlodge

Feature 165 is a circular post structure located at the east side of Block 2 (Figure 11.6). This feature is approximately 3.40 m in diameter and has eight wall posts (Features 69, 82, 83, 87, 92, 106, 109, and 113). The posts have an average spacing of 139 cm. While the wall posts occur in pairs across the structural feature, the pairings are not apparent in the post profiles. It is assumed that this reflects post removal during site occupation. Such activities could easily distort post profiles. The arrangement of the exterior pits adjacent to Feature 165 is notable. On the west and southwest sides a number of pits are carefully arranged outside the wall post arc of Feature 165. This is good evidence for the contemporaneity of these pits with Feature 165. Seven possible interior features occur inside the circular wall. It is not known how many of these pits are contemporary with the Feature 165 structure. Candidates for association with Feature 165 are Features 88 and 99, small basin pits located virtually at the exact center of the structure. Feature 99 is an excellent candidate for a hearth pit associated with the sweatlodge.

Subsistence Data

Soil samples were collected from all features excavated at the Fred Edwards site, with the primary objective being the recovery of paleobotanical remains. The laborious recovery of these materials through flotation and their analysis is being conducted by Constance Arzigian as a portion of her doctoral dissertation research. Recently published preliminary results of this research establish that the Fred Edwards site ". . . contains clear evidence for the cultivation of corn, squash, maygrass, sunflower, and tobacco, with extensive use, if not cultivation, of goosefoot and knotweed, along with a variety of wild plant foods such as hickory, walnut, acorn, and a variety of fruits and berries" (Arzigian 1987:232). The tobacco is the oldest so far reported in Wisconsin. In addition a species of *Hordeum* identified as little barley was also recovered. This, together with the maygrass, constitute the first reported occurrences of these probable cultigens in an archaeological context north of central Illinois. The presence of these southern plants well beyond their known natural range further accentuates the non-local character of the Fred Edwards assemblage.

Faunal remains recovered from feature contexts include mammal, fish, bird, turtle, and snake. These materials are still undergoing analysis, but mammals are clearly predominant, with deer, elk, and beaver being the most important. The combined evidence from the faunal and floral assemblages suggests year-round occupancy of the Fred Edwards site. Warm season (i.e., spring, summer, and fall) indicators include the cultivated plants, nuts, fish, and migratory waterfowl, while two deer skulls with shed antlers from the Feature 6 Household Cluster confirm a winter occupancy for at least a portion of the site. A concentration of fur-bearing mammals was also recovered from the same household cluster, further suggesting winter activity (Finney et al. 1986).

Ceramic Assemblage

The ceramic assemblage recovered from the Fred Edwards site is comprised of a unique blend of Late Woodland and Middle Mississippian technological and stylistic attributes. With the benefit of petrographic thin section analysis in combination with conventional typological analysis, we have subdivided this assemblage into three major classes: (1) Late Woodland, (2) Middle Mississippian, and (3) Late Woodland/Mississippian Hybrid. In addition, the Late Woodland and Middle Mississippian classes can be further partitioned on the basis of paste characteristics into local and non-local manufactures. All Hybrid vessels appear to be of local manufacture. Recurrent associations of all three classes in sealed feature contexts argues that the 331 individual vessels currently recorded for the site derive from a single archaeological component.

Late Woodland Ceramics

Of the 331 vessels 149 (45%) have been classed as Late Woodland. The preponderance of these vessels—129—have been assigned to a new ceramic series, Grant, that has not previously been recognized in Wisconsin (Figures 11.7 and 11.8). Corded surfaces and moderately thick vessel walls (5-8mm) tempered with crushed hematite characterize this ceramic series. Sandstone occasionally accompanies hematite as part of the temper, a reflection of the derivation of the hematite in the local sandstone bedrock. Granite also occurs, but relatively rarely, as temper. Vessel forms are generally globular jars with moderately constricted necks and uncollared rims (Figure 11.11), although nine vessels have added rim strips (i.e., fillets) below the lip. An additional four vessels appear to have true collars (i.e., thickened lips due to folding of the rim) and are believed to be of local manufacture based upon limited petrographic evidence (one was thin sectioned).

Over half of the vessels are decorated on the exterior upper rim with cord-impressed designs, while the filleted vessels normally are characterized by interior upper rim cord impressions only. Castellations and/or lugs occur on some vessels, but have been observed so far only on the types Grant Cord-Impressed and Grant Filleted. Based upon the presence or absence of the diagnostic attributes of either cordmarked or plain surfaces, filleting, and exterior cord-impressed decoration, the Late Woodland Grant ceramic series has been subdivided into types as follows:

	N
Grant Cordmarked	35
Grant Plain	24
Grant Filleted	9
Grant Cord-Impressed	32
Other Cord-Impressed	19
Other Collared	4
Miniature Vessels	6
Totals	129

The "Other Cord-Impressed" category above is comprised of miscellaneous fragments that for various reasons are difficult to classify reliably. Most are almost certainly attributable to the Grant series, but a few could be from the Madison series (e.g., Hurley 1975; Benn 1980).

A petrographic analysis of a sample of 16 Grant series vessels produced the following mean value for

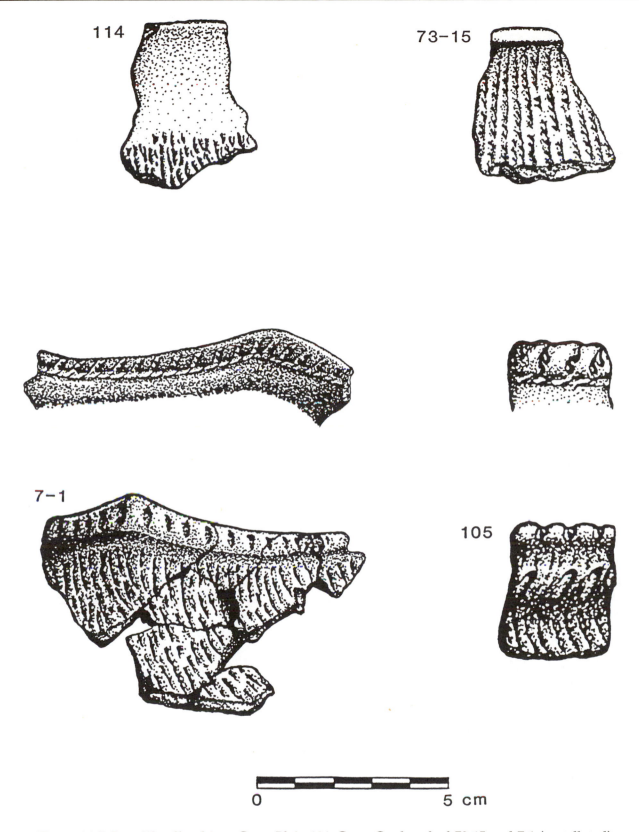

Figure 11.7. Late Woodland jars: Grant Plain 114; Grant Cordmarked 73-15 and 7-1 (castellated); and Grant Collared (filleted) 105.

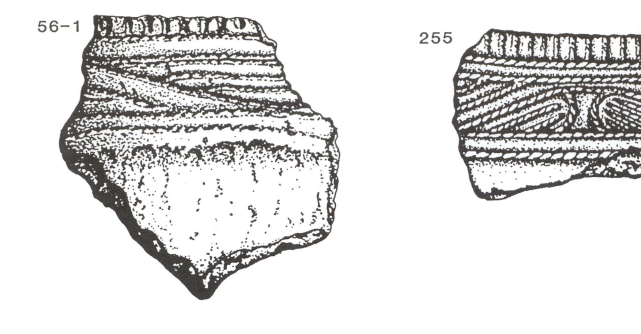

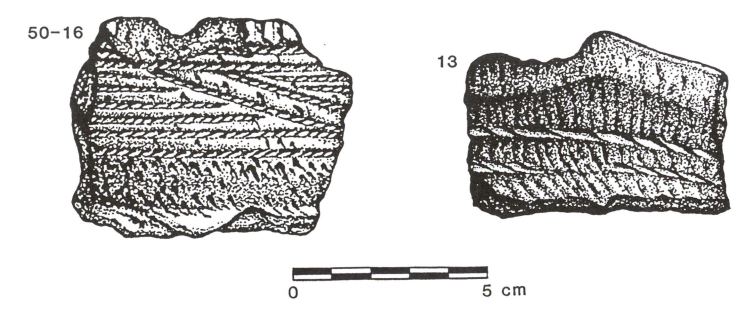

Figure 11.8. Late Woodland jars: Grant Cord Impressed 56-1 to 50-16; and Aztalan Collared 13 (castellated).

the basic paste constituents, excluding temper: 80% matrix, 18% silt, and 2% sand (Stoltman 1991). Since these values are precisely identical to those for a sample of clay collected from the subsoil of the loess that underlies the Fred Edwards site, it is concluded that these vessels were of local manufacture. Hematite, the normal temper, occurs as a common concretion in the local St. Peter sandstone. A substantial number of hematite fragments were recovered in our excavations.

The Grant ceramic series is unique in the current archaeological record of Wisconsin. Its closest analogues, we believe, are not to be found in the Madison ceramic series associated with Effigy Mound Culture in southern Wisconsin (e.g., Baerreis 1953; Rowe 1956; Geier 1978; Storck 1972; Hurley 1975), but with Canton Ware associated with the poorly understood Maples Mills complex of northwestern Illinois and adjacent portions of Iowa (e.g., Fowler 1955; McConaughy et al. 1985; Riggle 1981). We interpret the dominance of this ceramic series at the Fred Edwards site (in conjunction with other aspects of the assemblage) to reflect an actual influx of new peoples into the Grant River Valley from the south in the form of a site-unit intrusion (Willey et al. 1956).

An additional 20 Late Woodland vessels in the Fred Edwards assemblage are considered to be of non-local manufacture and most probably trade vessels. These non-local vessels consist of 11 Aztalan Collared (Figure 11.8) and ten Hartley series vessels (Hartley Cross-Hatched, Hartley Tool Impressed, Hartley Plain, Mitchell Modified Lip, French Creek Cord-Impressed, and an untyped incised-over-cordmarked vessel [Tiffany 1982; Figure 11.9]). A comparative petrographic analysis of five of the 10 Hartley series vessels from Fred Edwards with a sample of nine vessels from the Hartley Fort site (Tiffany 1982), suggests that the Hartley series vessels at Fred Edwards are actual imports from northeastern Iowa (Stoltman 1991). In a similar vein two of the eleven Aztalan Collared vessels were thin sectioned and compared both with local clays and with the suspected external source, in this case the Aztalan site. The results show conclusively that these collared vessels were not locally manufactured, but their source must currently remain unknown since their pastes and tempers do not resemble those so far observed from the Aztalan site. We feel that these non-local vessels are especially important for they connote evidence of extensive cultural interaction with other Late Woodland peoples at the same time as the occupants of the Fred Edwards site were clearly in close interaction with the Cahokia cultural sphere (see below).

Middle Mississippian Ceramics

A substantial minority of the Fred Edwards ceramic assemblage is readily attributable to the broad episode of Middle Mississippian culture contact in the Upper Mississippi Valley region associated primarily with the Stirling phase at Cahokia (Figures 11.10 and 11.11; Fowler and Hall 1975; Bareis and Porter 1984). Eighty (24%) of the 331 vessels in the Fred Edwards assemblage are of the following Middle Mississippian types:

Powell Plain	60
Ramey Incised	12
Cahokia Red Filmed	8
	80

Petrographic thin section analysis of 7 Powell Plain vessels suggests that this category is comprised of both locally manufactured and imported vessels. Five of the thin-sectioned vessels have paste characteristics closely similar to the Grant series, indicative of manufacture from local clays: the mean paste values for these five are 82.8% Matrix, 15.6% Silt, and 1.6% Sand. By contrast two Powell Plain vessels were made from very different pastes: their mean indices are 97% Matrix, 3% Silt, and 0% Sand, clearly profoundly different from the local clays. Also, when temper is included in the calculations, the amount of shell added is seen to be clearly different for the nonlocal vessels (a mean of 26.5% shell) in contrast to the local vessels (a mean of only 10.2% shell).

The Ramey Incised and Cahokia Red Filmed vessels are all presently regarded as imports. Three of the Ramey Incised vessels were thin-sectioned. Their combined paste indices are so closely similar to the two non-local Powell Plain vessels (mean values for paste indices are 96.7% matrix, 3.3% Silt, and 0% Sand plus 29.3% shell temper) that a common non-local origin seems probable.

A comparative petrographic analysis of Ramey/Powell ceramics from other sites within the Cahokia contact sphere is currently underway in an effort to ascertain the derivation of these imports. Virtually identical paste and temper features have so far been identified from Aztalan and Rench, suggesting that a common derivation of imports over a wide area exists. That the source for these presumed trade vessels is the American Bottom remains to be confirmed, but it does seem probable. No thin sections have so far been made of any of the Cahokia Red Filmed vessels, so their non-local origin remains an untested hypothesis. Another bit of evidence suggestive of the non-local origin of the five Powell Plain/Ramey Incised vessels that have been thin sectioned is the unambiguous presence of slipping on the exterior surfaces of all, whereas none of the local Powell Plain vessels, including the five that have been thin sectioned, show such evidence.

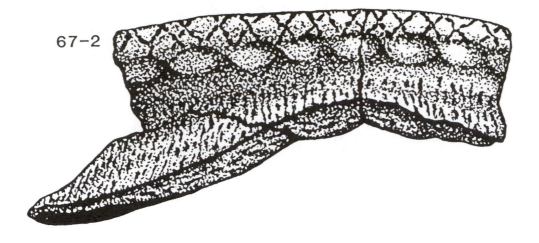

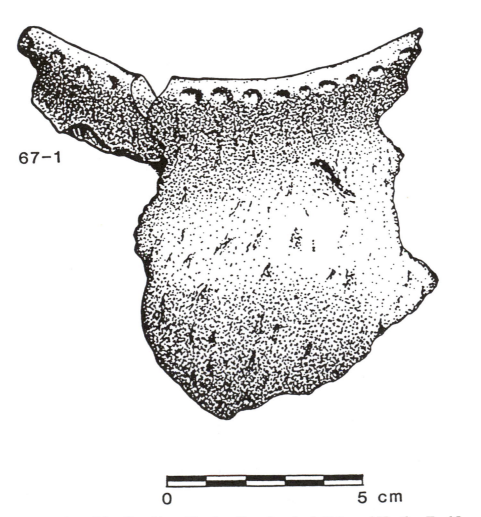

Figure 11.9. Late Woodland jars: Hartley Crosshatched 67-2; and Hartley Tool Impressed 67-1.

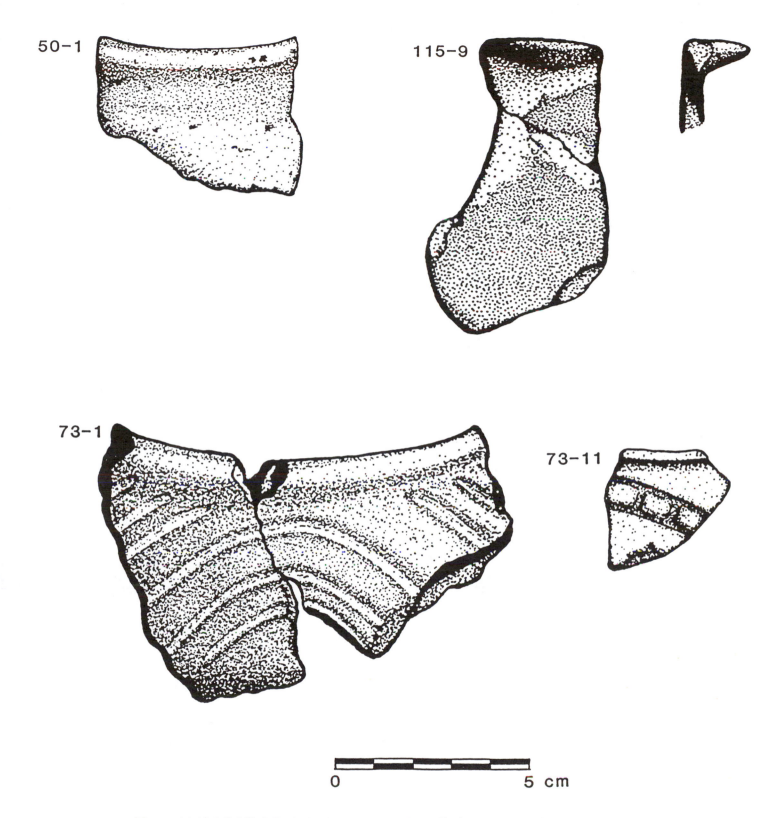

Figure 11.10. Middle Mississippian ceramics: Powell Plain jar 50-1; Cahokia Red Filmed bowl 115-9; and Ramey Incised jars 73-1 and 73-11.

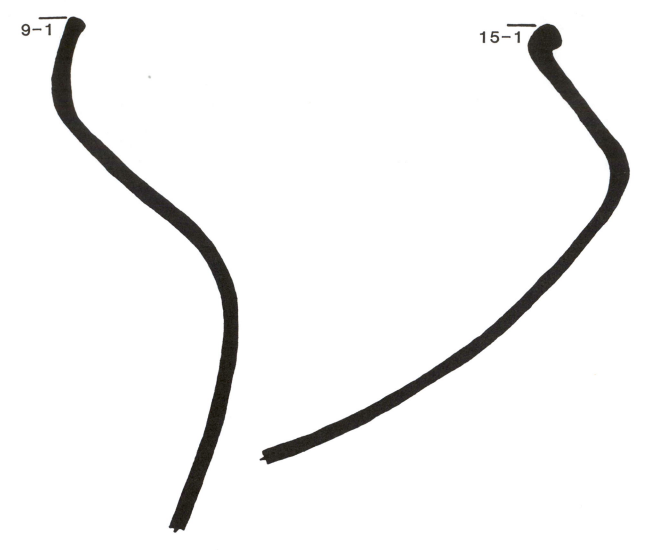

Figure 11.11. Late Woodland (9-1) and Middle Mississippian (15-1) jar shapes.

Late Woodland/Mississippian Hybrid Ceramics

A total of 102 vessels (31%) display a mixture of attributes that reflect the interaction of the two distinct ceramic traditions (informally we often refer to this class as "Woodissippian"). For example, 22 vessels with smooth (i.e., uncorded) surfaces are characterized by the diagnostic Powell/Ramey jar form—low rim with extruded lip combined with a prominent shoulder—but are grit tempered. The paste characteristics of these vessels are identical to those of the local Grant ceramic series, but the vessel form reflects what can only be interpreted as a Middle Mississippian style. To this type we have given the name Potosi Plain (Figure 11.12). One additional vessel, left untyped, has the same paste and vessel form as Potosi Plain but also has incised decoration—a sort of Ramey Incised on a local Woodland paste.

Another 62 vessels are mainly simple, globular jars (i.e., have non-Ramey/Powell forms) similar to the Grant Plain and Grant Cordmarked types, but differ significantly in possessing shell temper. The preponderance of these vessels (48) have plain surfaces, while a notable minority have cordmarked surfaces (9, including 4 bowls) or cord-impressed decoration (5). These vessels have been assigned to a new ceramic series comprised of three types as follows: Edwards Plain, Edwards Cordmarked, and Edwards Cord-Impressed (Figure 11.12). We have assigned this ceramic series to the hybrid class because of the obvious intermixture of Late Woodland and Mississippian ceramic-making practices that are its hallmarks.

Six vessels–three plain jars, two cordmarked jars, and one cordmarked bowl–are distinctive in possessing a mixture of both grit and shell temper. These have been excluded from the Edwards ceramic series, but are considered part of the general Hybrid class at the site.

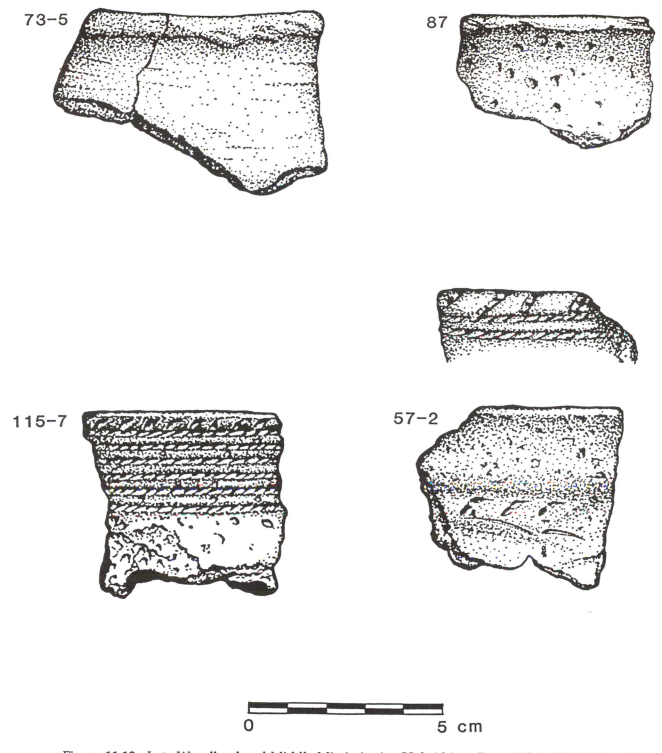

Figure 11.12. Late Woodland and Middle Mississippian Hybrid jars: Potosi Plain 73-5; Edwards Plain 87; and Edwards Cord Impressed 115-7 and 57-2.

Because of the many individual vessels in the Hybrid class that possess what we interpret to be both Late Woodland and Middle Mississippian attributes (e.g., grit tempering and the Powell/Ramey jar form, or cordmarking and shell tempering, or cord-impressed decoration and shell tempering), we inter-pret this class as evidence of close cultural interaction among potters (women?) from both cultural traditions at the Fred Edwards site. Rounding out the Hybrid inventory are eight miniature vessels with Powell-Ramey-like shapes made of untempered pastes.

Lithics and Other Artifacts

Several aspects of the cultural assemblage other than ceramics are also particularly noteworthy. One of the most distinctive features of the site is a lithic industry extraordinarily rich in projectile points and endscrapers. Over an area of approximately 1.2 ha on the central lobe 438 projectile points and 246 endscrapers have so far been recovered. The vast majority of the projectile points are simple, unnotched triangles, but a number of side-notched and one tri-notched triangle are present, as well as a few corner-notched points. All are in the size range of arrow heads.

Although less abundant than the projectile points, the endscrapers are far more distinctive (Figure 11.13). Many are unifacially retouched, but the vast majority, have been bifacially retouched. Indeed, the bifacial finishing is so complete on many that initially we mistook them for leaf-shaped knives or projectile points. More careful macroscopic examination of these artifacts revealed a consistent pattern of asymmetry along the "basal" edges (i.e., the edges opposite the pointed ends) coupled with recurrent abrasion of these edges, indicating that it was these edges rather than the "tips" that were the business ends of the tools. Subsequently, microscopic examination revealed the consistent presence of use-wear polishes along these edges, which Helle Jensen, a Danish expert in lithic edge wear analysis, has identified as unambiguous dry hide polish.

The inference that we draw from these data is that the killing of deer and elk, minimally, and the processing of their hides was conducted at the Fred Edwards site on a scale that far surpassed the immediate needs of the local residents. In short, we postulate that a major economic activity of the Fred Edwards villagers was the surplus production of elk and deer products, especially hides, for exchange with other participants in a larger economic sphere that centered, ultimately, upon the Cahokia site during its Stirling phase.

Another important item in the Fred Edwards site cultural inventory is the lead-rich mineral galena. Fifty six pieces of galena have been recorded for the site. Most of these are small, natural cubes, some of which show evidence of ground surfaces, but a single, exquisite tubular bead was also recovered. To the best of our knowledge this is the largest number of galena fragments so far reported for any prehistoric site in the Upper Mississippi Valley lead district. As with elk and deer, it seems to us that galena procurement by the Fred Edwards villagers can be reasonably postulated to have occurred on a scale far greater than their own immediate needs. Considering the site location in the heart of the Upper Mississippi Valley lead district, it seems reasonable to postulate that galena procurement for exchange into a Cahokia-centered exchange network was a major *raison d'etre* for the character

and placement of the Fred Edwards site.

The likely mode of aboriginal galena procurement was placer mining along the Grant River. This technique was used by historic miners to discover productive bedrock sources to be mined. It is doubtful that prehistoric peoples employed mine shafts to get galena, but rather walked clear-running, rocky stretches of rivers like the Grant where the heavy, silvery mineral would either be readily visible or readily separable from natural gravels (Hodge 1842; Owen 1840). This technique is no longer employable along the streams in this region because agriculturally-induced slope wash has choked the streambeds with extensive deposits of silt.

One additional local lithic material, hematite, occurs in large quantities implying its importance at the Fred Edwards site. A total of 549 pieces of hematite was recovered from our investigations. Again, this figure appears to be the highest known for any site in the Upper Mississippi Valley. Several activities at the Fred Edwards site would have required hematite, including use as ceramic vessel temper and/or making red ocher for hide processing (Keeley 1980). While there are at least two probable local uses for hematite, the large scale of hematite procurement suggests that the mineral itself could also have been collected for exchange.

While not attempting to go into detail, it is important to note one additional important feature of the Fred Edwards non-ceramic cultural inventory: the great diversity of non-local materials that somehow found their way to the site. Included in the inventory of exotic items recovered from the site are the following: 1) from the south, Burlington, Kaolin, Dongola, and Mill Creek chert; marine shell beads and fragments; and polished stone earspools; 2) from the west, Knife River flint and red pipestone (or catlinite ?), and 3) from the north, copper and Hixton silicified sandstone. Although none of these materials is individually abundant, their diversity, coupled with the wide range of non-local ceramic vessels that are also present (including Powell Plain, Ramey Incised, Hartley ware, and Aztalan Collared), strongly suggests that the Fred Edwards villagers were engaged in an extraordinary amount of cultural interaction with their neighbors in all directions. This is all the more noteworthy when it is realized that the site, by all indications, was never much larger than 100 people (probably a maximum of 20 single-family dwellings at any one time) and was situated in a relatively isolated portion of the Grant River Valley deep in the "hill country" of southwestern Wisconsin's Driftless Area.

Conclusions

The Fred Edwards site has proved to be especially important for shedding new light on the nature of cultural interaction between the Cahokia cultural

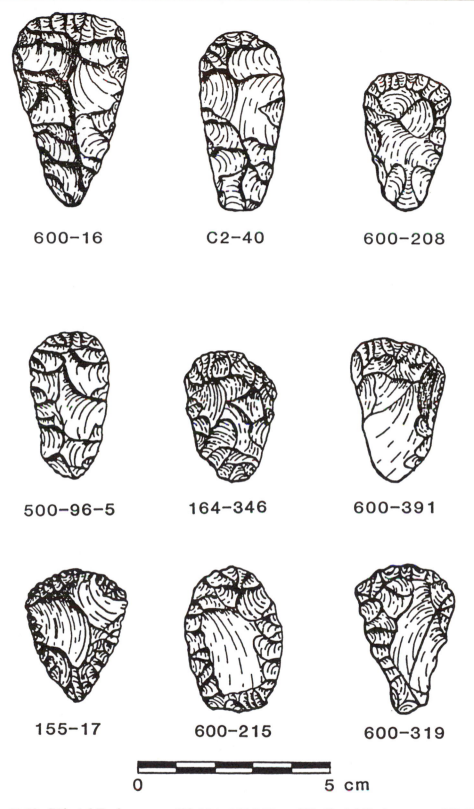

600-16   C2-40   600-208

500-96-5   164-346   600-391

155-17   600-215   600-319

0   5 cm

Figure 11.13. Bifacial Endscrapers 600-16 to 164-346; and Unifacial Endscrapers 600-391 to 600-319.

province and its northern hinterlands. In line with the three factors stated in "Research Objectives" as being germane to the investigation of inter-cultural interaction, we summarize what we believe to be the significance of the Fred Edwards site.

First, on the basis of a large and consistent battery

of radiocarbon dates, the age of the Fred Edwards site can be confidently placed within the century A.D. 1050 to A.D. 1150, precisely the same age as the Stirling phase at Cahokia. While there is evidence of sequential occupational activity at the site in the form of some feature overlap, the homogeneity of the cultural inventory in all undisturbed contexts confirms that, within the limits of normal archaeological resolution, the site represents a single component of relatively short duration, probably less than a century. The main occupation of the site clearly parallels the heyday at Cahokia and was neither preceded nor followed by any other substantial occupation.

Second, not only is there ample independent radiocarbon evidence to document the contemporaneity of Fred Edwards with Cahokia's Stirling phase, but there is direct evidence at the site of cultural contact with the Cahokia cultural province. This evidence appears most convincingly in the form of Powell Plain and Ramey Incised ceramic vessels whose paste characteristics can be demonstrated to be more closely similar to comparable vessels from such Cahokia outlier sites as Rench and Aztalan than they are to vessels at the very same site. Clearly, these are trade vessels at all three sites and presumably derive from a common source, although that source cannot yet be identified. In addition to these diagnostic Cahokia-style ceramics it is reasonable to hypothesize that such non-local materials in the Fred Edwards cultural inventory as Burlington, Mill Creek, Kaolin, and Dongola cherts, marine shell, and polished stone ear spools also derive from cultural interaction with the Cahokia cultural sphere. Assuming that some form of reciprocity is involved in any pattern of cultural interaction, attempts to understand the character of Cahokia-hinterland interaction will always be incomplete so long as hinterland sites are conceived of primarily as recipients of Cahokia influences. In the case of the Fred Edwards site there is strong suggestive evidence that the occupants of the community were actively engaged in the procurement of galena and deer and elk products, especially hides, for consumption by peoples elsewhere within the Cahokia cultural sphere.

Third, efforts to understand more fully the nature of the exchange relationships that stimulated and facilitated the circulation of goods and services within a prehistoric interaction sphere must consider the contextual evidence of visible exchange items within the archaeological record. In the case of the Fred Edwards site it was hoped that the differential distribution among the various households of imported items and local commodities presumably being prepared for export would provide valuable evidence as to the units of production and consumption within the village. In particular it was hypothesized that uniform versus clustered distributions of such items within the community would serve to discriminate individual household from communal control over production and consumption (e.g., Brown et al. 1990; Brumfiel and Earle 1987; Smith 1990; Tosi 1984; Wright 1984). Without going into detail here, suffice it to say that the distribution of both imported items and artifacts indicative of local surplus production of export items reveals a generally uniform distribution within the community. No central or specialized storage or production facilities were encountered within the portions of the site excavated. The available archaeological evidence is consistent with the view that the Fred Edwards community was comprised of a loose aggregate of independent household units, each of which was probably self-sufficient in maintaining themselves and producing items for exchange within the Cahokia interaction sphere. If there was any centralized or coercive control over these household units, we failed to uncover any evidence of it in our excavations.

In sum we interpret the Fred Edwards site to have been a site-unit intrusion of Late Woodland peoples into southwestern Wisconsin from northwestern Illinois or Northeastern Iowa. These people were probably motivated by economic demands emanating ultimately from Cahokia during the time of its Stirling phase, though possibly they were responding to contacts from more proximate Cahokia-related communities like Eveland, Rench, Mills, or Lundy. In any case it is hypothesized that these outsiders settled in a relatively sparsely populated portion of the Grant Valley where they planted a variety of crops to sustain themselves while at the same time engaged in the relatively intensive procurement and production of galena and deer and elk hides, commodities that were in high demand among Cahokia-affiliated communities farther to the south. Despite its relatively small size and comparative isolation, the archaeological evidence clearly indicates that the occupants of the Fred Edwards site were actively engaged in cultural interaction not only with Middle Mississippian peoples to the south, but with local peoples to the west and north as well. As with the other major northern hinterland sites like Aztalan, Mills, Silvernale, Diamond Bluff, and Hartley Fort, all of which revealed clear evidence of Stirling phase cultural contacts with the Cahokia world, the Fred Edwards site was abandoned roughly coincident with the termination of the Stirling phase ca. A.D. 1150. It seems reasonable to hypothesize that the cultural changes occurring at Cahokia during the mid-12th century A.D. were directly correlated with profound changes occurring widely in the northern hinterlands at the same time.

References Cited

Arzigian, C.M.
  1987 The emergence of horticultural economies in southwestern Wisconsin. In Emergent horticul-
    tural economies of the Eastern Woodlands. *Occasional Paper* 7: 217-242, edited by W. Keegan,
    Center for Archaeological Investigations, Southern Illinois University at Carbondale.
Baerreis, D.A.
  1953 Blackhawk Village site (Da-5), Dane County, Wisconsin. *Journal of the Iowa Archeological Society*
    2: 5-20.
Baerreis, D.A. and J.E. Freeman
  1958 Late Woodland pottery in Wisconsin as seen from Aztalan. *The Wisconsin Archeologist* n.s. 39:
    35-61.
Bareis, C.J. and J.W. Porter (editors)
  1984 *American Bottom Archaeology*. University of Illinois Press, Urbana.
Benn, D.W.
  1980 Hadfields Cave: a perspective on Late Woodland culture in northeastern Iowa. *Report* 13, Office
    of the State Archaeologist, University of Iowa, Iowa City.
Brown, J.A., R.A. Kerber, and H.D. Winters
  1990 Trade and the evolution of exchange relations at the beginning of the Mississippian Period. In
    The Mississippian Emergence: 251-280, edited by B. Smith. Smithsonian Institution Press,
    Washington, D.C.
Brumfiel, E.M. and T.K. Earle
  1987 Specialization, exchange, and complex societies: an introduction. In *Specialization, exchange, and
    complex societies*: 1-9, edited by E. Brumfiel and T. Earle. Cambridge University Press, Cambridge.
Conrad, L.A.
  1989 The Southeastern Ceremonial Complex on the northern Middle Mississippian frontier: late pre-
    historic politico-religious systems in the Central Illinois River Valley. In *The Southeastern
    Ceremonial Complex: artifacts and analysis:* 93-113, edited by P. Galloway, University of Nebraska
    Press, Lincoln.
Finney, F.A.
  1990 Late Woodland and Middle Mississippian culture contact at the Fred Edwards site in the Upper
    Mississippi River Valley. Paper presented at the 55th Annual Meeting of the Society for American
    Archaeology, Las Vegas.
  1991 Cahokia's Northern Hinterland as viewed from the Fred Edwards site in Southwest Wisconsin:
    examining the evidence for central control and prestige goods economy. Unpublished Ph.D. dis-
    sertation, University of Wisconsin-Madison.
Finney, F.A., J.S. Boaz, and J.R. Graves
  1986 Faunal exploitation at the Fred Edwards (47Gt377) site, Grant County, Wisconsin. Manuscript
    on file, Department of Anthropology, University of Wisconsin-Madison.
Finney, F.A. and J.B. Stoltman
  1986 The Fred Edwards site: a case of Stirling phase culture contact in southwest Wisconsin. Paper
    presented at the 51st Annual Meeting of the Society for American Archaeology, New Orleans.
Fowler, M.L.
  1955 Ware groupings and decorations of Woodland ceramics in Illinois. *American Antiquity* 20: 213-225.
Fowler, M.L. and R.L. Hall
  1975 Archaeological phases at Cahokia. In Perspectives in Cahokia Archaeology. *Bulletin* 10: 1-14,
    Illinois Archaeological Survey, Urbana.
Geier, C.R.
  1978 An analysis of the pottery assemblage from the Hog Hollow site: a transitional Middle-Late
    Woodland habitation site in the Mississippi River Valley. *The Wisconsin Archeologist* n.s. 59: 151-245.
Hargrave, M.L., G.A. Oetelaar, N.H. Lopinot, B.M. Butler, and D.A. Billings
  1983 The Bridges sites (11-Mr-11): a late prehistoric settlement in the Central Kaskaskia Valley. *Research
    Papers* 38, Center for Archaeological Investigations, Southern Illinois University at Carbondale.
Hodge, J.T.
  1842 On the Wisconsin and Missouri Lead Regions. *The American Journal of Science and Arts* o.s. 43: 35-72.

Hurley, W.M.
  1975 An analysis of Effigy Mound complexes in Wisconsin. *Anthropological Papers* 59, Museum of Anthropology, University of Michigan, Ann Arbor.
Keeley, L.H.
  1980 Experimental determination of stone tools uses: a microwear analysis. University of Chicago Press, Chicago.
McConaughy, M.A., C.V. Jackson, and F.B. King
  1985 Two Early Mississippian period structures from the Rench site (11P4), Peoria County, Illinois. *Midcontinental Journal of Archaeology* 10: 171-193.
Mehrer, M.W.
  1982 A Mississippian community at the Range site (11-S-47), St. Clair County, Illinois. Unpublished M.A. thesis, University of Illinois at Urbana-Champaign.
Milner, G.R.
  1984 The Julien site. *FAI-270 Site Reports* 7, University of Illinois Press, Urbana.
Owen, D.D.
  1840 Report of a geological exploration of a part of Iowa, Wisconsin, and Illinois. U.S. House of Representatives Document 239: 11-115, 26th Congress, 1st Session, Washington, D.C.
Porter, J.W.
  1974 Cahokia Archaeology as viewed from the Mitchell site: a satellite community at A.D. 1150-1200. Unpublished Ph.D. dissertation, University of Wisconsin-Madison.
Riggle, S.
  1981 The Late Woodland transition in the Central Mississippi Valley: A.D. 700-1000. *South Dakota Archaeology* 5: 5-18.
Rowe, C.W.
  1956 The Effigy Mound culture of Wisconsin. *Publications in Anthropology* 3, Milwaukee Public Museum.
Schiffer, M. B.
  1987 *Formation processes of the archaeological record*. University of New Mexico Press, Albuquerque.
Smith, B.D. (editor)
  1990 *The Mississippian Emergence*. Smithsonian Institution Press, Washington, D.C.
Steventon, R. and J. Kutzbach
  1986 University of Wisconsin Radiocarbon Dates XXIII. *Radiocarbon* 28: 1206-1223.
  1987 University of Wisconsin Radiocarbon Dates XXIV. *Radiocarbon* 29: 397-415.
  1988 University of Wisconsin Radiocarbon Dates XXV. *Radiocarbon* 30:367-383.
  1990 University of Wisconsin Radiocarbon Dates XXVI. *Radiocarbon* 32:209-228.
Stoltman, J.B.
  1976 Two new Late Woodland radiocarbon dates from the Rosenbaum Rockshelter (47Da411) and their implications for interpretations of Wisconsin prehistory. *The Wisconsin Archeologist* n.s. 57: 12-28.
  1991 Ceramic petrography as a technique for documenting cultural interaction: an example from the Upper Mississippi Valley. *American Antiquity* 56.
Storck, P.L.
  1972 The Archaeology of Mayland Cave. Unpublished Ph.D. diss. University of Wisconsin-Madison.
Tiffany, J.A.
  1982 Hartley Fort ceramics. *Proceedings of the Iowa Academy of Science* 89: 133-150.
Tosi, M.
  1984 The notion of craft specialization and its representation in the archaeological record of early states in the Turanian Basin. In *Marxist perspectives in archaeology*: 22-52, edited by M. Spriggs. Cambridge University Press, Cambridge.
Willey, G.R. et al.
  1956 An archaeological classification of culture contact situations. In Seminars in Archaeology 1955, edited by R. Wauchope, *Society for American Archaeology Memoirs* 11: 1-30.
Winter, M.G.
  1976 The archaeological household cluster in the Valley of Oaxaca. In *The Early Mesoamerican Village*: 25-31, edited by K. Flannery. Academic Press, New York.
Wright, H.T.
  1984 Prestate political formations. In *On the evolution of complex societies: essays in honor of Harry Hoijer 1982*, edited by Timothy Earle, pp. 41-77. Undena Publications, Malibu, California.

12

The Diamond Bluff Site Complex and Cahokia Influence in the Red Wing Locality

Roland L. Rodell
Mississippi Valley Archaeology Center

Cahokia influence in the northern reaches of the upper Mississippi Valley is recognized among a handful of sites in the Red Wing Locality that have Middle Mississippian-inspired traits. Within this group of sites is the Diamond Bluff mound and village site complex. Although known to local antiquarians during the 19th century (cf. Svec 1985), Diamond Bluff was not identified with Mississippian culture until the late 1940s, when Middle Mississippian related artifacts were recovered from the site area (Lawshe 1947; Maxwell 1950a, 1950b). Since then Diamond Bluff has periodically been referenced in writings pertaining to Middle Mississippian in the upper Mississippi Valley (Gibbon 1974, 1991; Griffin 1960; Hall 1962; Kelly 1991; Stoltman 1986; Williams and Goggin 1956).

The Diamond Bluff site complex is comprised of at least two large village areas and a large mound group that includes a variety of mound types characteristic of Late Woodland mound building traditions in the Upper Midwest. What has made Diamond Bluff interesting (as well as confusing) is that not only have Late Woodland and Oneota artifacts been recovered from both mound and village contexts, but mixed with them are Middle Mississippian-inspired artifacts. Most notable are the Ramey Incised motif on locally made ceramic jars and artifacts identified with the Southeastern Ceremonial Complex. These Middle Mississippian-inspired artifacts are the signature traits of the Silvernale Phase and are found at a number of sites in the Red Wing Locality, most notably the Bryan, Silvernale, and Energy Park sites. Since these sites are discussed elsewhere in this volume, this presentation will focus primarily on the archaeology of the Diamond Bluff site complex.

The objective of this paper is to address two areas that are specific to understanding the archaeology of the Diamond Bluff site complex and the theme of this volume. First, a review of archaeological investigations of Diamond Bluff is presented. The site complex has been of interest to antiquarians and archaeologists for over a century, from the early mound surveys to more recent excavations and surface collection investigations. A major portion of this segment of the paper will focus on the 1948 Wisconsin Archaeological Survey (WAS) excavations (Maxwell 1950a, 1950b). Recently, through the generosity of Dr. Moreau Maxwell of Michigan State University and students who participated in the WAS project, the University of Wisconsin-Milwaukee Archaeology Laboratory obtained field notes, maps, profiles, and photographs of the WAS excavations. These materials have provided insightful information about the mound excavations and testing of the village area. Regrettably, the artifacts from the WAS excavation are not available for study. The illustrations of pottery motifs that are presented below are taken from pencil and paper rubbings that accompany the WAS notes, while rim profiles are derived from Hall (1962).

The second part of the paper will address the more elusive problem of the Middle Mississippian presence at Diamond Bluff and in general the Red Wing Locality. The thesis favored here is that the Middle Mississippian presence in the Red Wing Locality was

253

limited to contact between Cahokian traders and the indigenous population sometime in the early to mid 11th century A.D. The impetus that led to this contact was the expansion of the Cahokian "symbiotic-extractive exchange system" (Gibbon 1974:133) into an area that was an established locality in a regional Woodland trade network. For the indigenous Red Wing population, Cahokian contact initiated the Silvernale Phase that is recognized archaeologically by a limited variety of Middle Mississippian-inspired traits found among Late Woodland and Oneota remains. What has remained an unresolved issued is the cultural identity of the Red Wing population at the time of Cahokian contact (e.g., Gibbon 1991; Stoltman 1986). While evidence from Diamond Bluff, as well as the general Red Wing Locality, is thin, it would appear that Late Woodland peoples were utilizing the area at the time of initial Cahokian contact.

Before proceeding, some comment regarding the different site names for Diamond Bluff is in order. Depending on the source, the reader may find one or more names used to refer to the site setting. They include the "Diamond Bluff mound group," (cf. Svec 1985, 1987), the "Mero group" (Brower 1903) and "Mero site" (Lawshe 1947; Wendt and Dobbs 1989), and the "Trimbelle River Group" (Squier 1914) and "Trimbelle site" (Wendt and Dobbs 1989). The "Trimbelle site" is identified in the State Historical Society of Wisconsin site code files as 47-Pi-93, while the other names are associated primarily with site area 47-Pi-2. The name Mero refers to one of three families that owned land on the Diamond Bluff terrace near the end of the 19th century. Trimbelle comes from the name of the stream that enters the Mississippi Valley at the terrace. Without exception these names identify either specific site phenomena, such as mounds, or only a portion of the overall site setting. The name Diamond Bluff is derived from the small community about a mile north of the site area. It is also the name of the terrace on which the site complex is located (Martin 1916:151), and it is the name assigned by one of the first investigators, T. H. Lewis, to the large mound group that dominated the terrace (cf. Svec 1985). Due to the intricate makeup of the site area, the name preferred by this writer and used here is the Diamond Bluff site complex.

The Site Setting

The Diamond Bluff site complex (47-Pi-2, 93) is located in the upper Mississippi Valley at 44° 38' north latitude and 92° 36' west longitude. The Diamond Bluff terrace is on the Wisconsin side of the valley and is approximately 5 miles directly north of Red Wing, Minnesota. The site complex is found over much of the 220 acre (89 hectares) terrace, which is 1.3 miles (2.1 km) long, up to 0.4 miles (0.6 km) wide, and elevated 60 feet (18.3 meters) above the surrounding floodplain. The gently undulating terrain on the terrace is comprised of twelve soil types with textures ranging from silt loams to sand (Haszel 1968).

In the Red Wing Locality the Mississippi Valley is about 3 miles wide. The valley is defined by steep bluffs—made of Ordovician sandstone and dolomite (Paull and Paull 1977)—that rise over 350 feet above the floodplain. Reconstructions of early 19th century vegetation patterns reveal the close proximity of a variety of plant communities (Finley 1976, Marchner 1974). In the Mississippi floodplain hardwood forests of soft maple, ash, basswood, elm, willow, and cottonwood were prevalent. Many of the elevated river terraces, like the Diamond Bluff terrace, were covered by oak and prairie communities, as were extensive areas of uplands on the Minnesota side of the valley (Marchner 1974). On the Wisconsin side, the uplands had sugar maple-basswood-oak forests and tracts of oak openings (Finley 1976).

Several streams converge in the Red Wing Locality, including the Trimbelle River that enters the Mississippi Valley at the Diamond Bluff terrace, and the Cannon River on the Minnesota side of the valley opposite the Diamond Bluff terrace. Also from Minnesota, the Vermillion River enters the Mississippi River at Red Wing, and 15 miles upstream is the confluence of the Mississippi and St. Croix Rivers. Wisconsin's Chippewa River enters the Mississippi 25 miles downstream from Red Wing.

Pre-1948 Investigations

In an 1869 presentation on prehistoric earthworks in the Red Wing Locality, Dr. W. M. Sweney mentions a large mound group on the Wisconsin side of the Mississippi Valley: "...there are vast numbers of mounds dotted over the sandy plain between the river and bluffs. Some of these deviate from the regular circular form, being composed of a main body oblong shape..., resembling the prostrate position of a bird with wings outstretched" (from Brower 1903:63). Given the more detailed survey data of subsequent investigators, Diamond Bluff is the one mound group on the Wisconsin side of the valley that would have fit this description. Although Sweney does not indicate how many mounds were on the Diamond Bluff terrace, it is estimated that there must have been around 500.

The investigation conducted by T. H. Lewis provides us with the most detailed record of the Diamond Bluff mound group. Lewis surveyed the Diamond Bluff terrace in the spring of 1887 and recorded 396 mounds (Figure 12.1). At the time of the survey, Lewis estimated that nearly 150 mounds had already been destroyed by cultivation (Svec 1985). Therefore, his total may represent only 75% of the mounds observed by Sweney. Among the extant mounds were 308 conicals that ranged in height from 1 to 9 feet and diameters up to 100 feet. There were 77 linear mounds extending to lengths of 184 feet and heights of 7.5 feet. The 8 oval mounds attained heights of 7 feet and lengths of up to 80 feet. Finally, the effigy mounds included a bird effigy at the southern end of the terrace that had a wing span of 92 feet, and "wolf" and "panther" forms at the north end of the terrace. The effigies averaged 141 feet in length and 2.5 feet in height (Svec 1985).

The value of Lewis's investigation can not be overestimated. Unfortunately, however, his notes on Diamond Bluff provide no information on artifacts or village sites (Svec 1985). There can be little doubt that Lewis observed artifact debris while mapping the mounds, especially since much of the site area was cultivated. Apparently Lewis believed in a moundbuilder race unrelated to Native American Indians and, therefore, reasoned that the Indian artifacts found scattered among the mounds did not belong to the mound builders and should not be considered part of the survey data. According to Charles Keyes, "...there is nothing...to show that Lewis had any interest in

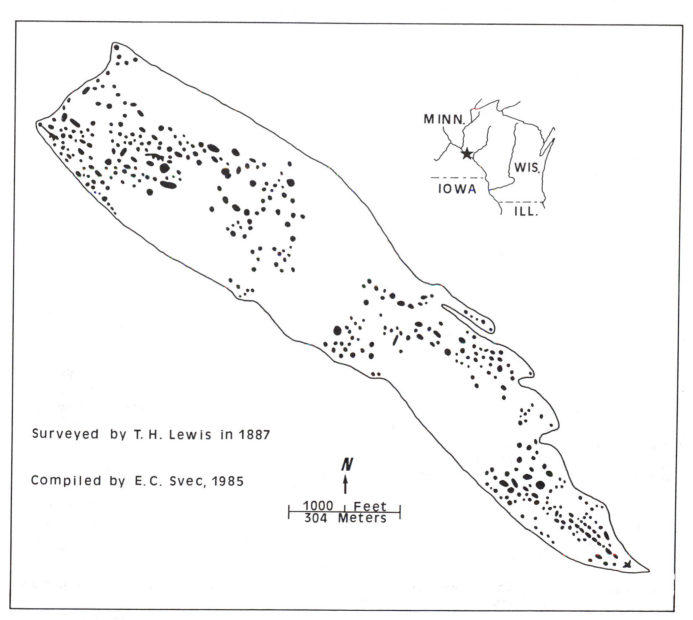

Surveyed by T. H. Lewis in 1887

Compiled by E.C. Svec, 1985

Figure 12.1. The Diamond Bluff mound group mapped by T. H. Lewis in 1887 (derived from Svec 1985).

fragmentary relics of any kind, ...his interest even in perfect relics...was rather moderate" (1928:103).

In 1903 J. V. Brower published a report of mound explorations in the upper Mississippi Valley that focused on the Red Wing Locality where, "at Diamond Bluff, an extraordinary mound region was encountered" (1903:47). Brower estimated that approximately 300 mounds—including the "panther" and "wolf" forms—were still visible on the terrace. Although an accompanying sketch map of the Red Wing Locality provides little detail, it does show two village sites associated with the Diamond Bluff terrace (Brower 1903). One is near the north end of the terrace, while the other is located at the south end off the edge of the terrace (Figure 12.2). Unfortunately, there is very little discussion in the text about the Diamond Bluff mounds, and there is no mention of the habitation sites.

Within a decade of Brower's survey, George Squier of Trempealeau, Wisconsin, visited the Diamond Bluff terrace (1914). Squier describes the Diamond Bluff mound group not only as having some of the largest mounds he had encountered, but the largest mound group recorded during his investigations (1914:138-139). Squier's sketch map of the Diamond Bluff group depicts only 100 mounds on the north half of the terrace, of which approximately 60 were under cultivation (Figure 12.3). It is of specific interest that the map does not clearly show the "panther" effigy on the north end of the terrace. This is curious since the mound is in an area that was most likely in pasture. Squier did note that one of the mounds suggested an effigy, but its form "was doubtful for the outlines are by no means distinct" (1914:139). The fact that later investigators readily identified the "panther" effigy, suggests that Squier's visit to Diamond Bluff was brief and his map hastily prepared (Svec 1985).

Sometime around 1940, portions of the Diamond Bluff terrace were surface collected by members of the Minnesota Archaeological Society. An account of the survey notes the presence of a fairly large mound group at the north end of the terrace that includes an effigy (Lawshe 1947). Presumably, the effigy is the "panther" mound mapped by Lewis. Furthermore, Lawshe refers to two village sites on the north half of the terrace where over 2000 artifacts were collected. "Two spots seem to have been occupied on the site (terrace?), one at the *northern end* and the other *near the mounds*, the mound site being larger and apparently longer occupied" (Lawshe 1947: 77; parentheses and emphasis added). These artifact scatters may or may not represent two distinct occupation areas. The area identified as *near the mounds* would be the north village site depicted on Brower's map (Figure 12.2), and subsequently the focus of excavations by the Wisconsin Archaeological Survey and the University of Wisconsin-Milwaukee. It is possible that this village extends into the area identified as the *northern end*, although many of the artifacts could have just as easily come from mounds destroyed by cultivation.

The artifacts recovered by the collectors included simple notched and unnotched triangular points, scrapers, a variety of ground stone items, modified mussel shells, a copper ornament shaped like a mace, and a small engraved "short-nosed" god mask made of marine shell. Most of the pottery is tempered with crushed shell and displays a variety of curvilinear and rectilinear motifs (Lawshe 1947). A brief description identifies many of the pottery types as belonging to the "Oneota Aspect," although one of the illustrations is of a rolled rim that is labeled "resembles Cambria" (Lawshe 1947:74). Although no specific reference is provided, most likely Lawshe was comparing the sherd to "Cambria pottery type C" from the Cambria site in the lower Minnesota River valley, which Wilford suggested was Aztalan-Middle Mississippi influenced (1945:39).

The 1948 Excavations

By 1948, only 47 mounds remained intact on the north end of the Diamond Bluff terrace in an area used for pasture. Maxwell notes that remnants of mounds were still visible in the adjacent cultivated field (1950a). Among the extant mounds were 30 conicals, 16 ovals, and the "panther" effigy, with only four of the mounds having evidence of major disturbance (Maxwell 1950a, 1950b). Figure 12.4 illustrates 43 of the mounds and is derived from a base map of the WAS project area (see Maxwell 1950b:429). Six mounds were selected for excavation, and test pits were opened in the village area southeast of the existing mounds.

The WAS excavation took place during the summer of 1948 and included a field school under the supervision of Dr. Moreau Maxwell of Beloit College and Mr. Chandler Rowe from Lawrence College. Before discussing the excavations, some comment is necessary regarding the available information. The quality of the field notes varies considerably, not only collectively but also in regard to specific excavations. For example, the notes for Mound 4, and to a lesser extent Mound 26 (the "panther" effigy), are more detailed and informative than the notes for the other mound excavations and village area. Although some individuals recorded the presence of debitage, faunal remains, etc., their remarks are inconsistent, often brief, and lack detail. During the project, excavation fill was not screened nor were matrix samples collected. Therefore, information regarding the composition of mound fill, density of artifacts, kinds of artifacts, and faunal or floral remains is incomplete. By noting these shortcomings it is not my intent to be critical of the WAS project, its participants, or field procedures, but simply to indicate the limitations and problems with the data that are available. Overall, the field notes and photographs have been a valuable source of information that have

provided insights on the WAS project.

Mound 4

With a base diameter of 50 feet and height of 7 feet, Mound 4 is the largest conical among the extant

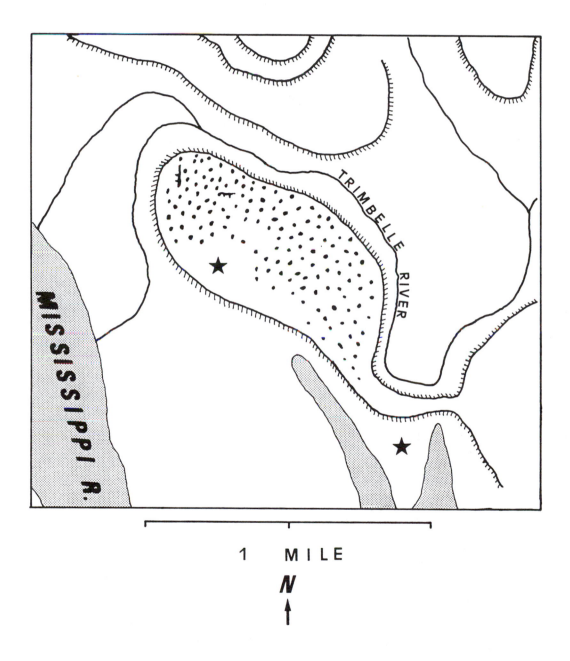

Figure 12.2. Brower's map of the Diamond Bluff terrace. The stars identify village areas (derived from Brower 1903).

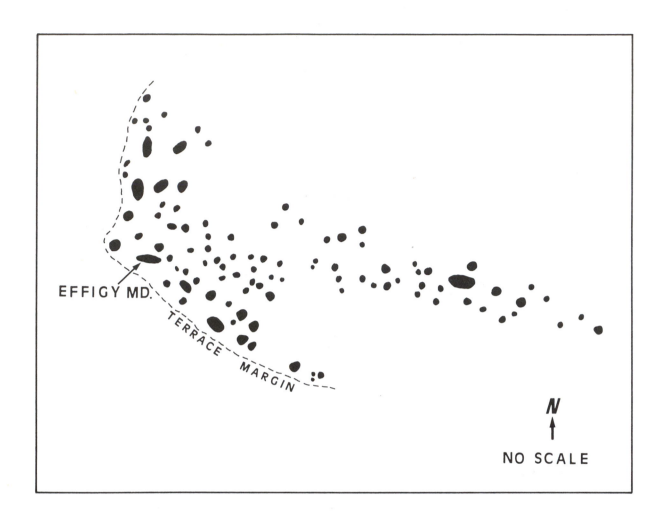

Figure 12.3. Squier's map of the mounds on the north end of the Diamond Bluff terrace (derived from Squier 1914).

mounds (Maxwell 1950b:438). When Lewis measured the mound in 1887, the diameter was 44 feet and the height was 8.5 feet. Its size was second only to one other conical that had a wider diameter (Svec 1985). The discrepancy between Lewis's measurements and those recorded by the WAS may be due to the methods of measurement. Over the span of 61 years, however, soil erosion and slumping—accelerated by grazing animals—would tend to decrease mound height while increasing its width at the base.

Two intersecting 5-foot-wide trenches were cut through the center of Mound 4. Profiles of the mound show basket loads and soil boundaries described as seepage lines, and at the base an area of midden bordered by a mottled loam. Some of the loads contained concentrations of organic remains and artifacts described as village refuse. Field notes indicate that

basket loading was more evident than what is depicted on the composite profiles of the east and west walls (Figure 12.5). There were also numerous seepage lines that are most likely the boundaries of basket loads modified by soil processes. There is no evidence of multiple building episodes. Instead, it appears that the mound was constructed during a single event, or over a short period of time.

Below the humus layer that covers the mound, most of the mound fill texture is described as sandy loam. The textural variation within the sandy loam class, along with the introduction of midden during construction, would create significant textural differences within the matrix of the mound. The development of seepage lines is probably related to these textural differences and the movement of water through the mound. The differences in soil texture will either

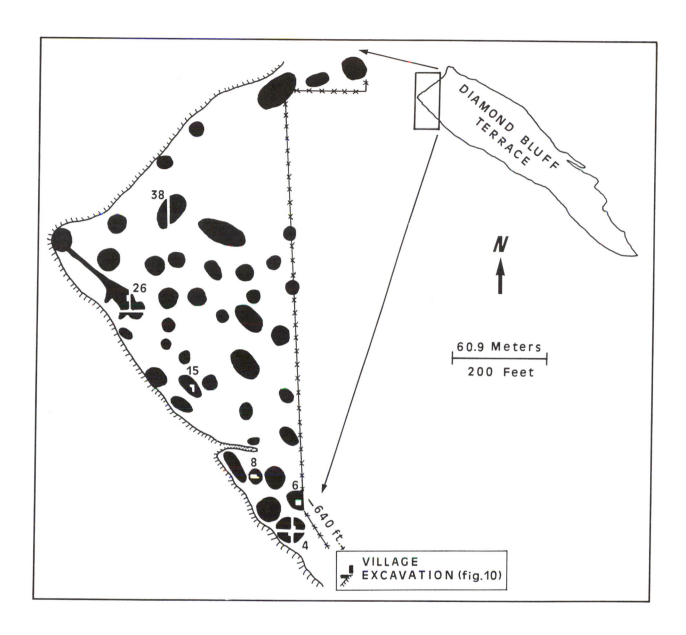

Figure 12.4. The mounds excavated by the Wisconsin Archaeological Survey in 1948 (base map from Maxwell 1950a).

facilitate or impede the movement of water. As water moves downward, contact with a finer textured soil would tend to redirect its movement laterally. Depending on soil textural differences, the effects of these processes through time may enhance or breakdown the boundaries between basket loads.

At the base of the mound are two areas described as mottled loam and midden that appear to be a remnant A soil horizon bordering a concentration of midden. A plan view of the Mound 4 excavation reveals that nearly 150 square feet of midden were exposed at the base of the mound (Figure 12.6). When the borders of the midden are connected, the estimated area increases to roughly 225 square feet. The nature of the midden is not clear; however, with a village site adjacent to the mounds and basket loads containing village refuse, it is not unreasonable to assume that some of the mounds were constructed over a preexisting habitation area. By extrapolating and connecting the limits of the midden, the shape and orientation of the projected area corresponds closely with the 200 square foot house feature excavated by UWM in the nearby

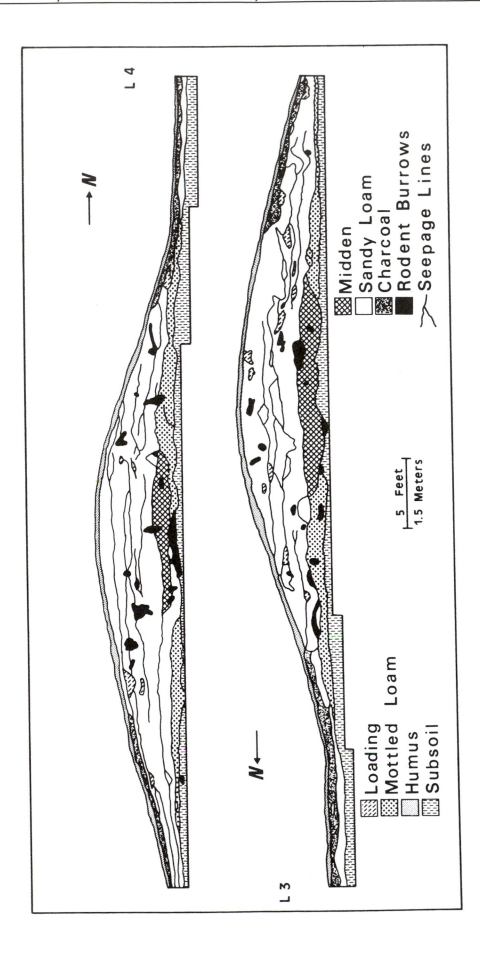

Figure 12.5. The east and west wall profiles of Mound No. 4 at Diamond Bluff.

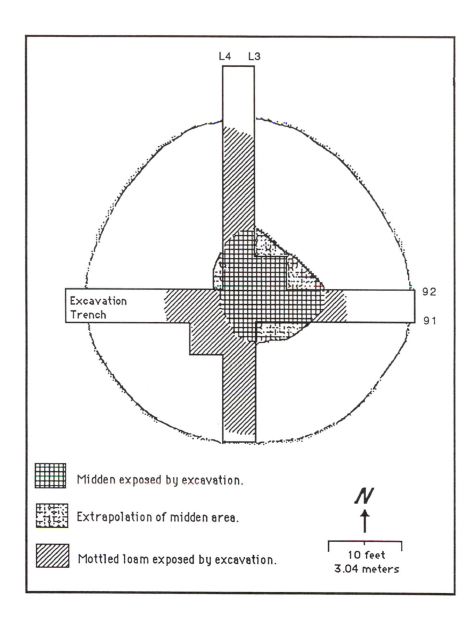

Figure 12.6. A plan view of Mound No. 4 showing the location of midden and mottled loam.

habitation area (Alex 1974; Van Dyke 1983; and below). This, however, remains speculative since there is no evidence of submound features suggesting storage pits, hearths, or postholes, nor are there any specific details regarding the recovery of artifacts from either the midden or the mottled loam.

The human remains uncovered in Mound 4 (Figure 12.7) are believed to represent five adults and one juvenile (Maxwell 1950a, 1950b). Poor preservation made it difficult or impossible to determine sex or disposition of the burials. The only identifiable elements

were fragments of larger bones, portions of the skull, and teeth. Since there are no indications in the profiles of an intrusive pit, it can only be concluded that the interments took place during construction of the mound. What appeared to be one adult in an extended position was encountered in units 89 and 90 L3 approximately 3 feet below the surface. The remains consisted of two femurs, a portion of the cranium and molars. Three interments representing two adults and one juvenile were in the north trench. In unit 93 L3, right and left humeri, a clavicle fragment, along with

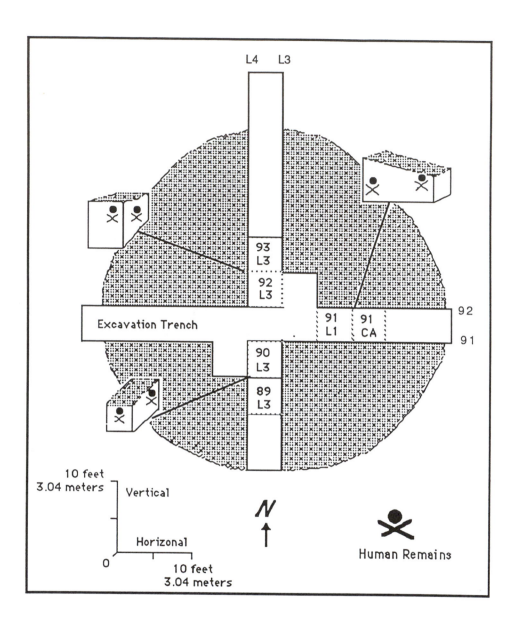

Figure 12.7. The location of burials in Mound No. 4.

maxilla and mandible fragments were uncovered approximately 4.5 feet below the mound surface. In close proximity were a humerus and teeth identified as belonging to a juvenile. In unit 92 L3, a femur was uncovered in the fill close to the mound surface. The human remains found in the east trench were interpreted as two individuals. Approximately 2 feet below the mound surface in unit 91 L1, a celt, burnt bone, and teeth were uncovered, while in unit 91 CA two unidentifiable bone fragments believed to be human were found in the fill approximately one foot below the mound surface.

Artifacts were found throughout the mound fill, although little information is available on proveniences. With the exception of the celt noted above, all the other artifacts were simply part of the general mound fill. In addition to the celt, the other lithics include a stemmed projectile point and a small triangular point. Among the 245 fragments of pottery were 188 grit-tempered and 57 shell-tempered sherds. This included 16 rim sherds representing four vessels. Two of the shell-tempered vessels and one grit-tempered vessel appear to be local variants of Ramey Incised. Both the shell-tempered jars have bolstered lips, relatively straight necks, and angular shoulders (Figure 12.8: E). The grit-tempered jar has a rolled or bolstered lip, a straight neck, and angular shoulder with a scrolled motif (Figure 12.8: F). The fourth vessel is an aberrant grit tempered jar that has vertical tool incisions on the interior of the rim and a combination of punctates, diagonal and horizontal incised trails on the rim exterior (Maxwell 1950b; also see Hall 1962: plate 41, R & S).

Mound 6

When Lewis mapped this mound in 1887, it was 60 feet long, 38 feet wide, and had a height of 5.5 feet (Svec 1985). By 1948 over half of the mound had been destroyed and the remaining portion was pitted. The remnant measured 28 feet in length, 33 feet in width, and did not exceed 2.5 feet in height. The texture of the mound fill ranged from sand to sandy loam. There was also evidence of charcoal in some of the basket loads used to construct the mound. Among the artifacts recovered in the fill were two small, shell-tempered sherds with smoothed surfaces, two small, cord-marked, grit-tempered sherds, and a small cube of galena (Maxwell 1950b:3). No human remains were found in the mound nor was there evidence of prehistoric disturbance after construction of the mound.

Mound 8

Mound 8 is described as a low conical with a diameter of 30 feet and height of 2 feet. These dimensions correspond closely with the 28 foot diameter and 2 foot height recorded by Lewis (Svec 1985). Although no evidence of human remains or diagnostic artifacts were found in the mound (Maxwell 1950a:440, 1950b:3), field notes indicate some of the basket loads contained concentrations of organic material. In particular one reference notes an abundance of charred material that appeared to be corn stalks and wood. There is also a reference to lithic debris in the mound fill.

Mound 15

In 1887, Mound 15 had a length of 62 feet, a width of 25 feet, and height of 4.5 feet (Svec 1985). The WAS recorded a length of 66 feet , a maximum width of 40 feet, and a height was slightly over 4 feet. On top of the mound and near the center was a pit roughly 8 feet in diameter and approximately 2 feet deep. Two small, grit-tempered sherds and bone fragments believed to be human were found in the mound fill. Information about the mound fill is limited to brief notations about pockets of clay that were periodically encountered above a relatively uniform clay layer. The latter bordered a small primary mound that was

encountered at approximately 2.5 feet below the surface. The primary mound was only partially exposed and excavated during which a human premolar was found. The dimensions of the primary mound were estimated to be approximately 4 feet in diameter and 2 feet in height. Beneath the primary mound was a rectangular-shaped feature measuring 2 × 3 feet with a depth of 0.75 feet. No cultural remains were recovered from this feature.

Mound 26

When Lewis mapped the "panther" effigy in 1887, it had a length of 180 feet and body width of 29 feet from the hump on the back to the underside (Svec 1985:75, table 2). These dimensions correspond closely with a length of 175 feet and body width of 34 feet recorded by the WAS. The mound was excavated by two intersecting trenches cut through the upper body and head of the effigy (Figure 12.9). Notes provide few details on the mound fill. It is assumed that the general composition of the fill was similar to that found in the other excavated mounds. In one of the profiles a dark loam is identified just above the subsoil horizon, suggesting the presence of a buried A soil horizon similar to that in Mound 4. Also, midden is noted as being present in the mound fill. Among the artifacts reported mixed in the fill were a triangular projectile point, some grit-tempered sherds, and two sherds with angular shoulders from which the temper (shell?) had been leached out. Near the base of the mound at approximately the original ground surface, shell-tempered pottery sherds from an angular shouldered jar were found (Maxwell 1950a 441).

Approximately 2 feet below the mound surface, unidentified burnt material, a shell tempered jar, and human remains were encountered (Figure 12.9). The fragmentary cranium, maxilla, and mandible were identified as belonging to a juvenile. It appears that the burial and jar were interred during mound construction. The excavators found no evidence of disturbance or an intrusive pit that could account for the burial after the mound was completed. The shell-tempered vessel is described as having a scalloped lip and a slightly everted rim. On the angular shoulder are a series of lobes, and above each lobe are six incised concentric loops. Below the shoulder the cordmarked surface is smoothed over (Maxwell 1950b).

Also in the north trench—the exact proveniences are not provided—two more discoveries were made. A second vessel was recovered in darkly stained soil at a depth of approximately 1.5 feet below the mound surface. It is described as a small, globular-shaped, shell-tempered jar with a plain surface and loop handles (Maxwell 1950a:441, 1950b). Toward the center of

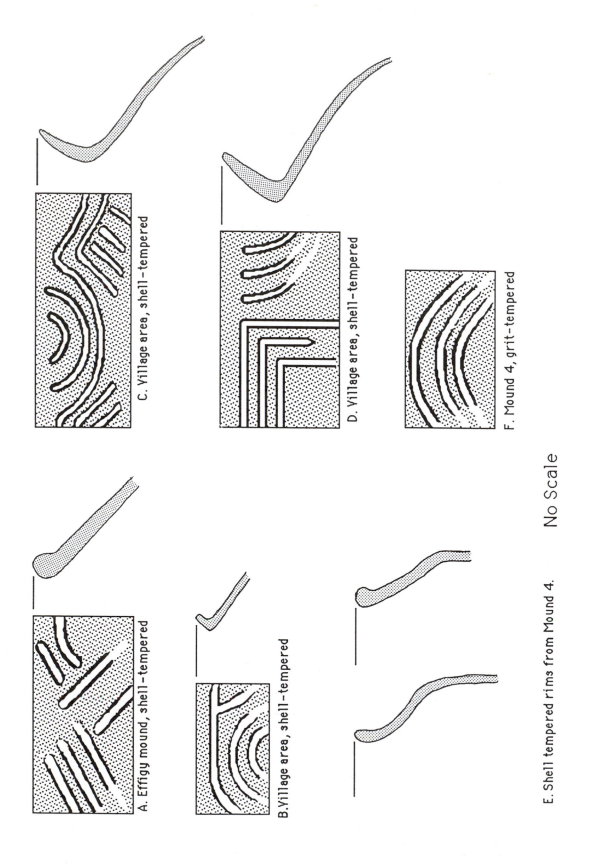

Figure 12.8. Pottery motifs and rim profiles recovered by the Wisconsin Archaeological Survey at Diamond Bluff (derived from field notes and Hall 1962, Vol. II).

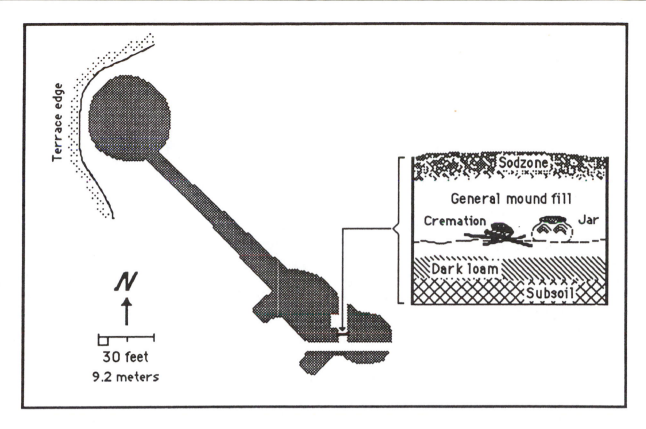

Figure 12.9. The excavation plan of the effigy mound (No. 26) and locations of cremation burial and decorated jar.

the trench and at the pre-mound ground surface, a submound pit with an oval shaped orifice was uncovered. Near the top of the feature was a shell-tempered sherd with a bolstered or rolled-like lip, a straight neck, and a Ramey-like motif on the shoulder (Figure 12.8: A). Within the pit were the skeletal remains of an adult female and a child (Maxwell 1950a:442, 1950b). In the mound fill above the feature there was no evidence of an intrusive pit through the mound leading to the feature. Therefore, prehistoric excavation of the pit and introduction of the shell-tempered sherd apparently took place sometime prior to construction of the mound. Although submound burial pits have been found beneath effigy mounds (e.g., McKern 1928), it is also possible that the pit was a pre-mound feature associated with the village area.

Mound 38

Number 38 is described as a large oval mound measuring 75 feet long, 50 feet wide, and 7.5 feet high. These dimensions compare favorably with the measurements of 80 × 48 × 7 feet, recorded by Lewis in 1887 (Svec 1985). Excavation uncovered human skeletal

remains in the upper levels of the mound in three locations. Bone preservation was poor, and it could not be determine if three or four individuals had been found. The fragmentary remains were identified as adults and consisted of some teeth, along with mandible, skull, femur, tibia, and scapula fragments. One of the interments appeared to have been in a semiflexed position (Maxwell 1950a:3). There were no pottery vessels or tools associated with the human remains, although field notes indicate that a small piece of mica was found with one of the burials. The notes also indicate evidence of basket loading, the presence of deer bone and charcoal flecks in the fill, and that the sandy loam mound fill was darker than that found in the other excavated mounds. Artifacts recovered in the mound fill include two grit-tempered and two shell-tempered sherds and a small triangular point.

Village Testing

In addition to the mound excavations, the WAS conducted some excavation in an adjacent village area. This is the same village site noted on Brower's 1903 map (Figure 12.2) and encountered by Lawshe (1947).

Maxwell reports that two Oneota village sites were located near the extant mounds (1950a:428, 430); however, the notation of two sites served more to distinguish surface finds in the plowed area from the artifacts recovered in the test pit excavations near the edge of the terrace. The field notes have no information on the surface collections in the plowed field other than a listing of some of the artifacts. The walkovers in the cultivated area were conducted when rain prevented work on the excavations (Maxwell, personal communication). Among the artifacts listed are a number of triangular-shaped projectile points and shell-tempered pottery sherds.

Excavation in the village area was initiated when midden material was discovered eroding from a ravine at the edge of the terrace approximately 640 feet southeast of Mound 6 (Figure 12.4). Six 5 × 5 foot test units were opened near the ravine in an area that had not been disturbed by plowing. Initially, the units were excavated in arbitrary 6-inch levels. This was soon changed to 3-inch intervals when it became apparent that strata could not be clearly defined below the humus layer. Three features were recorded (Figure 12.10). All are described as having straight sides and rounded bottoms and containing village refuse.

The diameter of feature 1 was approximately 3 feet, with a depth of 2 feet. The excavation recovered several shell-tempered sherds and a triangular projectile point. Feature 2, along the edge of the bank, was represented by two overlapping pits that measured 7.5 feet in length with a maximum width of 5 feet. No information is available on depth. The feature(s) contained a large milling stone, shell tempered pottery, charcoal fragments, along with mollusca, fish, and faunal remains. Three large bones are not described in detail, but notes indicate that they appeared to be bison remains. Feature 3 was approximately 3 feet in diameter with a depth of over 1.5 feet. It contained faunal remains and shell-tempered and grit-tempered pottery.

Other artifacts recovered in the village area included "thumbnail" scrapers, abrading stones, and shell-tempered pottery (Figure 12.8: B, C, D). Maxwell reports that about one year after the WAS project a gravel removal operation near the village excavation area exposed more features. Mixed with Oneota pottery were, "...shell tempered, angular shouldered rim sherds with horizontal rims, rolled lips, and scrolls and curvilinear elements..." indicating the village also had a Middle Mississippian-related component (Maxwell 1950b:4).

In summarizing the WAS excavations, Maxwell (1950a, 1950b) recognizes three components at Diamond Bluff: Late Woodland Effigy Mound, Middle Mississippian, and Oneota. Regarding the specific nature of these relationships Maxwell concludes,

"...that all of the mounds sampled were constructed after the arrival of elements of Mississippian culture" (1950b:4). Specifically, the effigy mound was built by Oneota or peoples in direct contact with Middle Mississippian after the introduction of Middle Mississippian traits (1950b). Although both Oneota and Middle Mississippian traits were found in the village area, it was unclear if the two were contemporary or if Oneota developed out of Middle Mississippian (Maxwell 1950a: 443).

Post-1948 Investigations

In 1974 the University of Wisconsin at Milwaukee conducted an excavation on the Diamond Bluff terrace under the direction of the late Dr. Robert Alex (Alex 1974; Van Dyke 1983). The UWM excavation was located near the edge of the terrace approximately 130 feet west of the WAS village excavations. Attempts to relocate the WAS test pits were unsuccessful. It is possible that the WAS excavation area no longer exists because the quarrying operation noted above may have destroyed that portion of the site.

The UWM crew opened 138.75 square meters (1497.4 sq. ft.) of the site area by excavating n 10 centimeter levels (Figure 12.11). Over 40 features were uncovered—some that extended to depths of over 1.5 meters—along with a semi-subterranean house and a problematic house (Alex 1974). The floor of the semi-subterranean house was encountered approximately 50 centimeters (20 inches) below the surface. Its semi-rectangular shape measured approximately 5 meters by 3.75 meters, encompassing an area of approximately 18.75 square meters (202 sq. ft.). Although bordered by several post holes, there was no evidence of wall-trench construction. The entrance was not excavated, but is believed to have been at the north end. Associated with the structure were three pit features and a hearth. The problematic structure was in an area identified by numerous post holes and midden. The exposed midden covered approximately 4 square meters (43 sq. ft.) and was bordered on the west side by post holes that extend a distance of nearly 6 meters (19.7 ft.). The time constraints of a field school prevented completion of the excavation in this area (Alex 1974).

The lithic artifacts include a variety of cherts, silicified sandstones, and some Knife River Flint. The most common tools types are unnotched and side-notched arrowheads, "thumbnail" or humpback scrapers, sandstone abraders, hammerstone cobbles, and a variety of bone tools. The pottery assemblage is dominated by shell tempered wares that include Oneota types and Middle Mississippian-inspired Silvernale wares (Figure 12.12). Grit-tempered pottery comprises only a small fraction of the assemblage.

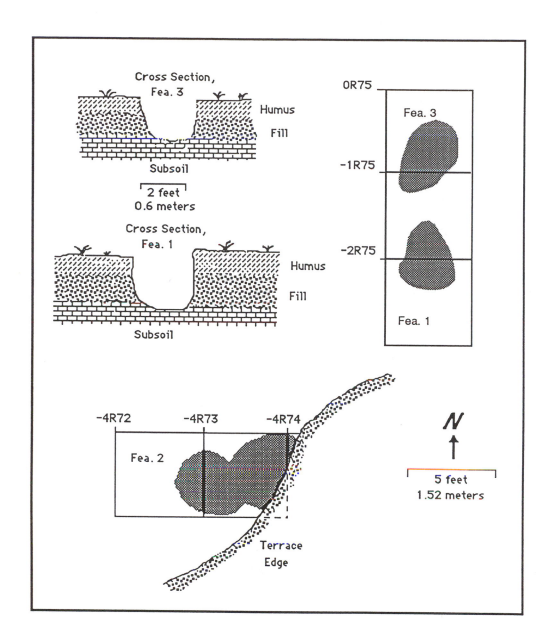

Figure 12.10. The Wisconsin Archaeological Survey test excavation in the village area.

Although an extensive analysis of faunal remains has yet to be conducted, elements from a variety of terrestrial mammals have been identified. They include bison, beaver, elk, squirrel, muskrat, white-tail deer, raccoon, rabbit, black bear, gray and red fox, badger, skunk, wolf, and dog (Van Dyke 1983). Examination of a small sample of fish remains revealed several species known to inhabit both the main channel and backwaters of the Mississippi flowage (McInnis 1977). An analysis of maize from three excavation units identified North American Popcorn, Midwest 12-row, and Eastern 8-row. The samples also contained wild plum seeds (Cutler and Blake 1976).

Human remains represented by several cranium fragments, complete and fragmented mandibles, and loose teeth were recovered from midden filled pit features. There are three mandibles with cut marks on the posterior aspect of the ramus and two mandibles that display cut marks on the anterior of the horizontal

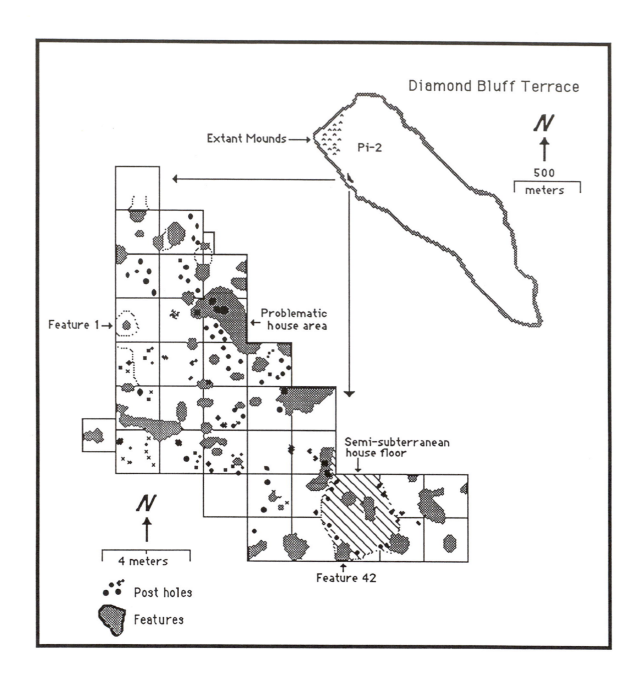

Figure 12.11. Plan view of village excavation by the University of Wisconsin-Milwaukee.

ramus. A number of parallel cut marks are also visible on cranium fragments of occipital and parietal bones. Among the several individual teeth are three canines, one incisor, and one premolar that are notched near the tip of the root suggesting they were worn as pendants on a necklace (Rodell n.d.).

Five radiocarbon dates are available from the UWM excavation area (Table 12.1). Three of the radiocarbon dates were obtained from wood charcoal recovered in

feature 42, a pit in the floor of the semi-subterranian house. The two radiocarbon dates from feature 1 were also derived from wood charcoal (Figure 12.11). Both features were filled with midden debris. The uncorrected dates (Bender, et al. 1978) have been recalibrated by the method proposed by Stuiver (1982; also Stuiver and Reimer 1986). Recalibration of conventional dates adjusts for past fluctuations in atmospheric C-14 and is based on dendrochronological determina-

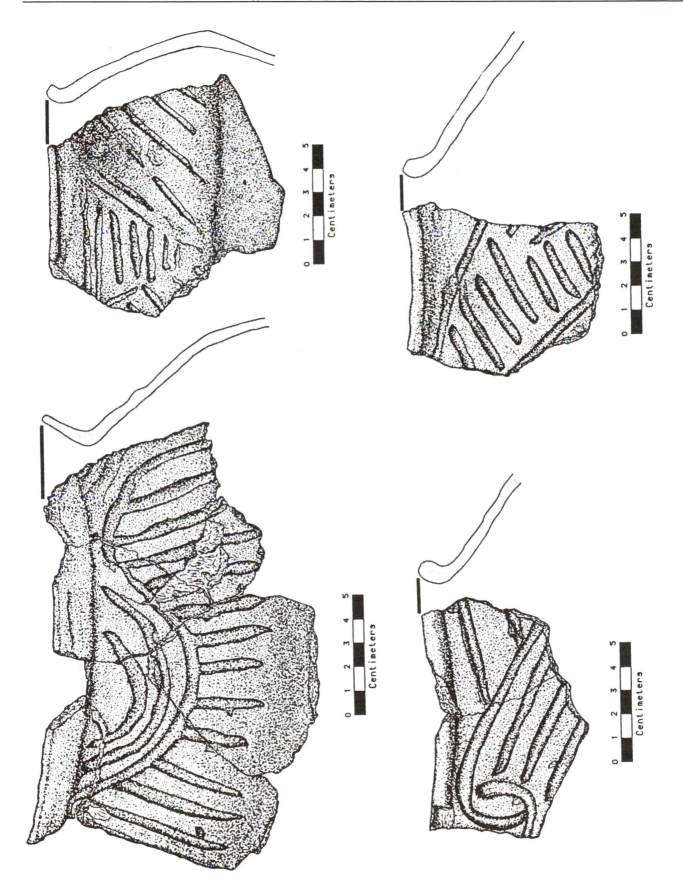

Figure 12.12. Silvernale ware recovered in the village area excavated by the University of Wisconsin-Milwaukee.

tions. The dendro-age dates indicate that in the millennium before A.D. 1250 conventional radiocarbon ages err toward being too old (Stuiver 1982:5). The conversion of an uncorrected date may intercept the dendroage calibration curve more than once resulting in more than one age per corrected date as is evident with three of the dates in Table 12.1. In these cases all of the corrected ages must be considered (Stuiver and Reimer 1986).

Within a decade of the UWM excavation, the Diamond Bluff terrace was subject to more archaeological investigation. In 1980 and 1981 the State Historical Society of Wisconsin (SHSW) surveyed the north half of the terrace in the site area listed as 47-Pi-2 (Penman 1981:12-13, 1984:35-36). The SHSW collections include lithic debris and tools, along with shell-tempered and grit-tempered pottery. Shell-tempered pottery was recovered in the general area where mounds had existed (Penman 1984:36). This suggests that the village excavated by the WAS and UWM extended several hundred feet eastward from its confirmed location along the west side of the terrace edge, or that the mounds had contained shell-tempered pottery either in the general fill, as intentionally buried vessels, or both.

Following the SHSW investigations, the Institute for Minnesota Archaeology (IMA) conducted a series of surface collections over the entire terrace (Wendt and Dobbs 1989). The IMA survey relocated 192 of the 396 mounds mapped by Lewis and identified four concentrations of artifact scatters that are viewed as being habitation settings. Two of the sites are listed as Woodland occupations. They are site 47-Pi-93, located at the southern tip of the terrace within an area that had a dense concentration of mounds, and Mero No. 3 situated in the center of the terrace between two clusters of mounds. The sites designated Mero No. 1 and Mero No. 2 are bordered by mounds and are identified as Silvernale villages.

The IMA surveys (Wendt and Dobbs 1989) have provided some insights on the spatial relationships of habitation areas and mounds on the Diamond Bluff terrace (Figure 12.13). The two Woodland site areas—47-Pi-93

and Mero No. 3—are represented by thin scatters of lithic debris and cord marked, grit-tempered pottery. Mero No. 3 covers roughly 1.7 acres (0.7 hectares) and is in the approximate center of the terrace in an area where apparently no mounds had been built. This site may represent a small habitation site or an activity area associated with the other site areas. Site 47-Pi-93 is at the south end of the terrace, covers roughly 3.5 acres (1.4 hectares), and is where several mounds existed. While 47-Pi-93 may represent an activity area or habitation setting, it is equally likely that this artifact scatter may represent the remains of mound fill and burial offerings strewn about by plowing.

The artifact scatters identified as site areas Mero No. 1 (47-Pi-2) and Mero No. 2 are located on the west side of the terrace. In comparison to the Woodland sites, Mero No. 1 and No. 2 have greater densities of artifacts over larger areas, and the assemblages are represented by mixtures of Woodland, Silvernale, and Oneota artifact types. Both sites are estimated to cover about 17 acres (6.9 hectares). Wendt and Dobbs (1989) note the limits of Mero No. 1 and No. 2 are marked by distinct declines in artifact densities, and that these boundaries appear to correspond with the mounds that once bordered the respective site areas on three sides. There is, however, good reason to suspect that some mounds were constructed over a previously existing Oneota habitation area, given the findings of the WAS mound excavations near the site area 47-Pi-2 (Mero No. 1). As presented above, at the base of Mound 4 (Figure 12.6), a concentration of debris described as village midden was uncovered, and at the base of Mound 26 (effigy) the submound pit containing the human remains can arguably be interpreted as a village pit burial. Pit burials in habitation settings are reported at the Bryan site (Gibbon 1979: 9-10) and are known at other Oneota sites (Hall 1962; Kreisa 1987; Mc Kern 1945). Whether or not the pattern of the Mero No. 1 and Mero No. 2 habitation areas bordered by mounds began during the Woodland period, or is indicative of the Silvernale period occupation, or is the result of later Oneota settlement will only be resolved by continued investigation.

Table 12.1: Radiocarbon dates from the UWM excavation at Diamond Bluff.

Feature	Depth	Lab No.	Uncalibrated date B.P.[1]	Calibrated date [2]
No. 1:	50-60 cm.	WIS-841	910±55 (A.D. 985-1095)	A.D. 1025 (1070, 1085, 1127, 1137, 1154) 1207
	70-80 cm.	WIS-842	890±55 (A.D. 1005-1115)	A.D. 1033 (1158) 1215
No. 42:	80-90 cm.	WIS-846	955±55 (A.D. 940-1050)	A.D. 1001 (1031, 1144, 1146) 1157
	100-110 cm.	WIS-849	790±55 (A.D. 1105-1215)	A.D. 1208 (1257) 1278
	110-120 cm.	WIS-845	755±55 (A.D. 1140-1250)	A.D. 1222 (1263, 1273, 1275) 1281

[1]Bender, et al. 1978.
[2]Stuiver and Reimer 1986.

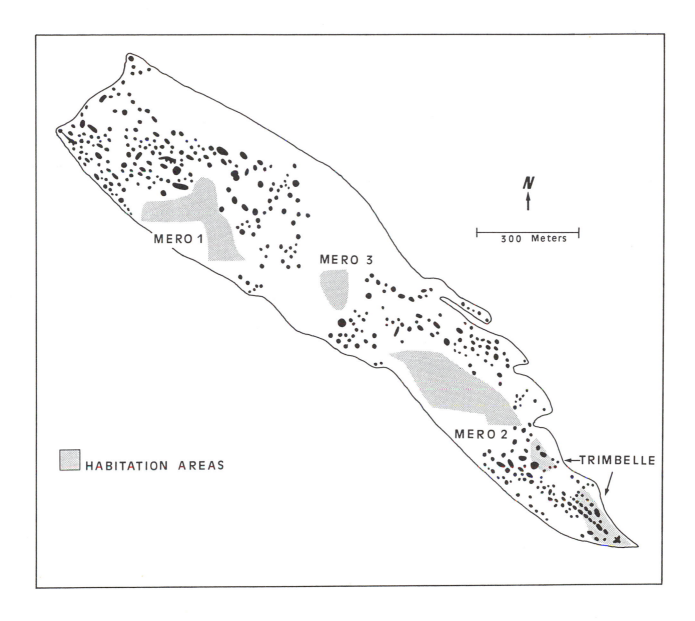

Figure 12.13. Site areas on the Diamond Bluff terrace identified by the Institute for Minnesota Archaeology survey (derived from Wendt and Dobbs 1989).

Discussion

With the kinds of data presently available from the Diamond Bluff site complex, and other sites in the Red Wing Locality (Dobbs 1984; Gibbon 1979), what can be said regarding both the nature of Middle Mississippian contact and the identity of the indigenous Red Wing population at the time of contact? In Oneota studies there has been a long standing debate revolving around the origins of Oneota culture and its relationship to Middle Mississippian culture (e.g., Griffin 1960; Gibbon 1972, 1974; Stoltman 1983, 1986).

One position favors the emergence of the Oneota culture *in situ* and prior to expansion of Cahokian influence into the northern Mississippi Drainage around circa A.D. 1050 (Gibbon 1982). Supporters of this position point out that, ". . . radiocarbon dating revealed that Oneota arose as a coherent cultural complex too early to be a 'simple' offshoot of more complex, Mississippian type cultures to the south, mainly . . . Cahokia" (Brown 1982:107). While there is agreement here that Oneota culture cannot be viewed simply as a by-product of Middle Mississippian culture, the statement that "Oneota arose as a coherent cultural complex" prior to the spread of Middle Mississippian influence in the 11th century is misleading. In the upper Mississippi Valley, many of the traits that would become the hallmarks of the Oneota cultural complex—large village sites, shell tempered globular jars with chevron motifs, triangular points, humpback scrapers, catlinite pipes and tablets, sandstone abraders, a riverine adaptation, bison hunting, maize horticulture, etc.—do not appear collectively as cultural units before the time of the Cahokian trade network. Furthermore, it has been argued that Oneota symbolism, displayed on pottery, in copper ornamentation, etc., was greatly influenced by Middle Mississippian (Benn 1989; Hall 1991).

The alternative position recognizes the emergence of Oneota culture during the 11th century A.D. as a result of Middle Mississippian interaction with Late Woodland peoples (Stoltman 1986). This would appear to be a more tenable position, especially in light of the empirical data and speculations on Oneota symbolism noted above. Gibbon (1972, 1982), however, has stressed the point that the emergence of Oneota lifeways involved a variety of processes that took place over a period of time. These processes culminated with Middle Mississippian contact during the eleventh century. There is, unfortunately, a poor understanding of these processes. And while there can be little doubt that the roots of the Oneota cultural tradition extend back to Late Woodland, the kinds of data relevant to this problem have remained elusive, resulting in interpretations based primarily on inferential evidence and speculation (Gibbon 1982:86). The Red Wing Locality is no exception to this problem. With the data presently available from Diamond Bluff and related sites in the area, the evidence for a pre-Silvernale Oneota occupation is based primarily on conjecture.

The argument for a pre-Silvernale Phase Oneota population in the Red Wing Locality relies upon radiocarbon dates that predate A.D. 1050 (Gibbon 1974:130, 1991). What has not been made explicit however, is if the early dates came from contexts clearly associated with early Oneota/pre-Silvernale remains, or if the dates were from mixed contexts containing Silvernale/ Oneota remains. This is clearly a problem with the radiocarbon dates from Diamond Bluff (Table 12.1). The Diamond Bluff radiocarbon dates were derived from samples of wood charcoal that had been recovered from arbitrary 10 centimeter levels. Although it is not my intention to be critical of the UWM field methods, the excavation of features by arbitrary levels was not adequate enough to document the complex strata of the midden deposits, which presumedly were the result of both cultural and natural episodes of filling and mixing. The three dates from Feature 42 came from a 40 cm vertical segment. The

two extreme dates—A.D. 1001 (1031,1144,1446) 1157 and A.D. 1222 (1263,1273, 1275) 1281—are so far apart that their one sigma ranges do not overlap (at the two sigma range there is a 48 year overlap). Furthermore, their location in the stratigraphic sequence is in reverse order to their chronometric relationship. The same situation also exists for the two dates recovered from Feature 1, however, the one sigma ranges are in close harmony. In addition, a nearly complete Silvernale vessel came from the level with the date of A.D. 1033 (1158) 1215. Although the five radiocarbon dates from the Diamond Bluff village area (47-Pi-2) correspond to the time of Middle Mississippian influence and Oneota presence in the Red Wing Locality, it remains equivocal if the radiocarbon ages can clearly be assigned to specific components.

At Diamond Bluff there is evidence that Woodland groups periodically utilized the terrace from late Middle Woodland times through the Late Woodland period. Woodland culture at Diamond Bluff is most evident by the conical, linear, and effigy mounds that are characteristic of Late Woodland mound types in the upper Mississippi Valley. A Woodland presence is also recognized by other artifacts, most notably pottery. Although investigations indicate that the amount of Woodland pottery is small in proportion to the number of shell temper wares, cordmarked, grit-tempered pottery has been recovered in both mound and village contexts. According to Lawshe only a few of the pottery sherds collected by his party were tempered with sand or crushed stone, and had designs made by, "grass, beads and possibly ears of corn... (and) cord-wrapped paddle" (1947:83). Most of the pottery recovered by the WAS is described as being grit tempered with nearly equal numbers of sherds having cordmarked or smoothed surfaces (Maxwell 1950b). From a total of 107 rims, 77 (72%) are grit-tempered and 30 (28%) are shell-tempered. None of the grit-tempered, cordmarked rims are attributed to specific types. The IMA survey identified concentrations of Woodland pottery on the Diamond Bluff terrace, although the number of sherds is small in comparison to the amount of shell-tempered pottery. Some of the grit-tempered pottery is identified as Late Woodland Madison Cord Impressed (Wendt and Dobbs 1989). The Woodland pottery recovered by the UWM excavation represents only a small fraction of the ceramic assemblage. Although many of the sherds are simply grit tempered and cordmarked fragments, there are a few identifiable types. They include Angelo Punctate, a late Middle Woodland/ early Late Woodland type (Hurley 1974a) and two Late Woodland wares: Madison Cord Impressed, and Clam River ware (McKern 1963).

Madison Cord Impressed is a relatively common

pottery type associated with Late Woodland mound sites (e.g., Hurley 1974b). The presence of Clam River ware, which has a more restricted distribution, is neither spatially nor temporally out of place at Diamond Bluff. Although this pottery type is best known among Late Woodland sites in the region bordering the St. Croix River (Caine 1974; Gibbon and Caine 1980:63; McKern 1963; Van Dyke and Oerichbauer 1988), approximately 100 miles north of the Red Wing Locality, Clam River pottery has been reported at the Plum Creek site (47-Pe-38) 25 miles east of Diamond Bluff (Ford 1982). Radiocarbon dates place the Clam River tradition during the Late Woodland period, ca. A.D. 400 to 1100 (Gibbon and Caine 1980; Van Dyke and Oerichbauer 1988).

Among the lithic artifacts recovered from the Diamond Bluff terrace (Lawshe 1947; Van Dyke 1983; Wendt and Dobbs 1989), there are only a few tools that have been specifically identified as Woodland. Lawshe illustrates a variety of chipped stone and ground stone tools that may be Woodland artifacts (1947:76, 80, 82), and Maxwell reports that a projectile point recovered from Mound 26 was Woodland (1950a:442). In the UWM lithic assemblage there are some point types, as well as a significant amount of chert debitage, that could be of Late Woodland origin. The findings of the IMA survey indicate that Woodland groups may have relied more heavily on cherts than the later Oneota component (Wendt and Dobbs 1989).

In the Red Wing Locality investigators have reported that there were from 2000 to as many as 4000 mounds (Brower 1903; Schmidt 1941). Like Diamond Bluff, neighboring mound groups contained a variety of mound forms (cf. Winchell 1911). The Red Wing Locality was on the northwestern periphery of the effigy mound region, while to the north there was the Clam River mound tradition, and to the west were other contemporary mound building groups (Anfinson 1984; Gibbon and Caine 1980; Mallam 1976; McKern 1963). Given the generally accepted view that Woodland mound sites were the focus of annual gatherings where people conducted ceremonial, social and economic activities (Green 1986; Mallam 1976), it is suggested that the Red Wing Locality served this function for a variety of regional cultural traditions. The reason for the focus on Red Wing is not entirely clear. An important consideration, however, is its geographic location in relation to a number of major rivers and streams that converge in the area. In addition to the Mississippi River, the Cannon River provides a route to the Minnesota River Valley and access to west-central Minnesota (Wilford 1955:139). There is easy passage to Lake Superior, via the St. Croix and Brule Rivers, and there are major streams leading into the

interiors of northern Minnesota and northern Wisconsin. It would appear then that the Red Wing Locality was a natural hub through which regional trade and information was channeled (Rodell 1989).

Middle Mississippian interest in the upper Mississippian Valley may have been initiated during the period A. D. 950-1050 (Kelly 1991). While no concrete proof for this exists in the Red Wing Locality, 70 miles downstream at Trempealeau, Wisconsin, there is some evidence, albeit tenuous at this time, of early Middle Mississippian influence. At Trempealeau there is a terraced, pyramidal, flat-topped mound and, from the unpublished notes of George Squier (Stevenson, et al. 1983), descriptions of red slipped pottery that are akin to pottery types associated with late Emergent Mississippian and early Mississippian phases at Cahokia. The finds at the Stull site (47-Tr-159), and the recent test excavations at the Squier Garden site (47-Tr-156) conducted by the Mississippi Valley Archaeology Center, have recovered small samples of red slipped rim sherds. Notwithstanding the speculative nature of the available data, it appears that the Trempealeau locality represents a Middle Mississippian presence in the upper Mississippian Valley that predates the Silvernale Phase in Red Wing (Green 1988; Squier 1905; Stevenson, et al. 1983). If, as suggested above, Red Wing was already the focus of regional trade and social interaction, the pull northward to the Red Wing Locality would have required little incentive on the part of the Cahokian trade network.

Mound building on the Diamond Bluff terrace was not limited to pure Woodland groups but continued after the introduction of Mississippian-inspired traits. As revealed by the WAS excavations some of the mounds were constructed after the introduction of Middle Mississippian symbolism, most notably the Ramey motif displayed on sherds recovered in mound fill and on a buried jar. In the American Bottom, the Ramey Incised motif is most closely identified with the Stirling Phase, circa A. D. 1050-1150 (Bareis and Porter 1984; Fowler and Hall 1974; Holley 1988). Emerson has presented a persuasive argument regarding the function of the Ramey Incised vessel as "utilitarian symbolic ware" (1989:67). Ramey Incised vessels were used in a variety of social functions, including rituals to "... reaffirm intragroup relations... (and)... integrate outsiders, traders, allies, and such into the social system" (Emerson 1989:67). If indeed Ramey Incised vessels were used in such observances, not only within the American Bottom but at other Midwest localities interacting with Cahokians, Emerson's thesis has implications for interpreting Mississippian in the Red Wing Locality.

In the Red Wing Locality a significant proportion of ceramic assemblages are dominated by Silvernale wares. In following the logic of Emerson's thesis (1989), Ramey Incised vessels were functionally part of everyday use—not just among a select group people but throughout the greater Red Wing community—while symbolically the Ramey motif linked the Red Wing communities to the Cahokian "symbiotic-extractive exchange system" (Gibbon 1974:133; 1982:89). The Ramey Incised motif on locally manufactured ceramic vessels is by far the most common of the Middle Mississippian-inspired traits in the Red Wing Locality and is a hallmark of Silvernale ware (Anfinson 1979:183- 190; Wilford 1955). Among the Silvernale wares, the Ramey motif occurs on the classic Ramey-Powell jar form as well as on the basic globular Oneota vessel form. Of particular interest are the 77 grit-tempered rim sherds recovered by the WAS, 40 of which are described as having "Old Village" designs. Although this sample is small, it raises the possibility that the Ramey motif was adopted before other Mississippian ceramic traits such as shell tempering.

The context in which Ramey Incised sherds have been found in the Red Wing Locality is almost exclusively midden debris. A notable exception is the effigy mound (No. 26) at Diamond Bluff. As described above, two relatively complete shell-tempered vessels were recovered from this mound. The first vessel was a small undecorated jar with a smoothed surface and loop handles. Although plain wares are rare at Diamond Bluff, as well as in the general Red Wing Locality (cf. Gibbon 1979), it is not unusual to find them in early Oneota ceramic assemblages in other regions (cf. Hall 1962). The second jar had a scalloped lip, and incised concentric loops above a series of lobes on an angular shoulder. The motif of incised concentric loops is in the style of Ramey Incised, and is found on other vessels from Diamond Bluff and nearby sites (cf. Gibbon 1979). The lobed body effect is also found on a minority of vessels from the nearby Bryan site (Stortroen 1957: 41-42, Plate II; Gibbon 1979: Plate S18), as well as at Cahokia (Holley 1988:270, Figure 48-D). Although few in number, the lobed bodied vessels fit nicely within the local pottery sequence of Silvernale wares.

Also, from the Red Wing Locality there are a small number of artifacts relating to the Southeastern Ceremonial Complex. The Diamond Bluff site complex has revealed a limited variety of Southeastern Ceremonial Complex traits including a marine shell "god mask," the baton or mace-shaped motif depicted in copper ornamentation and incised on pottery (Figure 12.14), and chunky stones. A shell-tempered sherd with the mace motif was excavated by UWM from the floor of the semi-subterranean house. The shell mask, chunky stones, and copper artifact were

recovered from the surface (Lawshe 1947), so it is not known if these items were from plowed down mounds, a village area, or some other context. At the Bryan site, small copper mace pendants (Gibbon 1979) and falcon symbolism, depicted by a bird motif on both a ceramic jar (Link 1982:34) and a bone pendant (Stortroen 1957: plate VII, figure B-4), have been found. Stylized falcons can also be derived from the feathered-Ramey scroll motifs on Silvernale wares (cf. Benn 1989; Hall 1991). Other artifacts found in the Red Wing Locality that are possibly related to the Southeastern Ceremonial Complex include small stones with engraved faces and a small pottery head, and an ear spool (Gibbon 1979, 1991).

Like the Ramey motif, the artifacts identified with Southeastern Ceremonial Complex have ties to the theme of interregional relationships, prestige, and sanctioned authority (Brown 1976; Emerson 1989). A number of writers have interpreted the "god masks" as being symbolic of traders or trade alliances (e.g., Gibbon 1991; Griffin 1967; Hall 1990; Kelly 1991). Hall has even suggested that the "god masks" signified ". . . a ceremonial relationship between the participants through a fiction of kinship, and that the ceremony was specifically used to establish friendly relations between otherwise unrelated groups" (1991:88).

In addition to the Ramey motif and the ceremonial artifacts, there are other artifact types in the Red Wing Locality that may be Middle Mississippian-inspired. Among them are a pyramidal flat-topped mound, notched triangular arrowheads, and semi-subterranean house forms (Gibbon 1991). A pyramidal flat-topped mound between the Bryan and Silvernale sites was mapped by T. H. Lewis in the late 1800s (cf. Schmidt 1941; Winchell 1911:153). For whatever reason(s), Wilford did not include this mound type in his definition of the Silvernale Focus (1955:139-140). Other researchers, however, believe the association to be more than a coincidence (Griffin 1960; Hall 1962; Gibbon 1974, 1979). In fact, recent excavations conducted by the IMA at the Energy Park site have identified a Silvernale Phase component at the locality of this mound (Dobbs and Breakey 1987).

It is not uncommon to find small, side-notched, triangular arrowheads among the Silvernale Phase sites. At Diamond Bluff these points are made of cherts, silicified sandstone, and Knife River Flint (Lawshe 1947; Van Dyke 1983). Whether or not this point type is derived from Middle Mississippian influence or is the result of Plains influence is not clear since it was common in both spheres of influence (Kelly 1991; Kehoe 1966). From the Silvernale and Bartron sites there are isolated examples of tri-notched points that are more closely aligned to some Cahokian point styles (Gibbon 1991). In addition to the semi-subterranean house

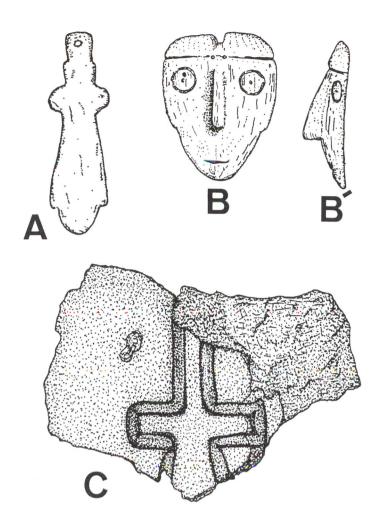

Figure 12.14. Artifacts attributed to the Southeastern Ceremonial Complex found at Diamond Bluff. (A) Copper mace pendant, (B-B´) marine shell God Mask (derived from Beadle 1942; Lawshe 1947), (C) mace pendant motif on pottery in University of Wisconsin-Milwaukee collection.

floor uncovered at Diamond Bluff (Alex 1974; Van Dyke 1983), the remains of similar structures were excavated at the Bryan site (Gibbon 1979). Like the notched points, it is also not clear if semi-subterranean house forms in the Red Wing Locality are of Middle Mississippian or Plains influence.

While point types and house forms are suggestive of Plains influence, other artifact types leave little doubt that the Red Wing communities were in contact with Plains groups. In the Diamond Bluff lithic assemblage there is a small percentage of Knife River Flint, and pottery sherds identified as Mitchell Modified Lip (Alex 1974; Van Dyke 1983), a pottery type of the Middle Missouri Tradition. The pottery was recovered from the semi-subterranean house feature and

appears to represent one vessel, although not enough sherds exist for a reconstruction. The sherds are tempered with a fine grit, have smooth surfaces, and thin trailed line decoration. The lone rim sherd is relatively short and everted outward and has a singular zigzag trailed line on the lip. Similar Plains and related Cambria pottery types have also come from the Bryan and Silvernale sites (Gibbon 1979,1991).

Found among the Red Wing sites are a variety of conventional Oneota artifacts (Gibbon 1979; Lawshe 1947; Van Dyke 1983). At Diamond Bluff, as well as other Red Wing sites, the style of the Oneota pottery is very similar to Blue Earth wares. The shell-tempered jars have medium to high everted rims, rounded shoulders, and chevron motifs (cf. Anfinson 1979:39-

44; Gibbon 1979). In the UWM assemblage handles are rare although both the loop and strap types are present. Motifs illustrated by Lawshe (1947: 74, 87) include the target design and chevrons bordered by punctates. Similar motifs are also present in the UWM assemblage, although they are not as common as the Ramey motif that precedes adoption of the chevron (Hall 1962). Lip-rim decoration is rare. However, when present, it is most often found on the interior surface of the rim. The lithic assemblages include sandstone abraders along with numerous humpback scrapers and small unnotched triangular arrowheads made of cherts, silicified sandstone, and Knife River Flint. The lithic artifacts are not only characteristic of conventional Oneota assemblages, but more specifically they are indicative of the Silvernale Phase in the Red Wing Locality.

Summary

During the latter half of the 19th century the pioneering investigations on the Diamond Bluff terrace recorded a large and complex mound group comprised of a variety of mound types that are characteristic of Late Woodland culture (cf. Svec 1985, 1987). In the 1940s, two independent investigations found evidence of Oneota and Middle Mississippian-inspired artifacts on the terrace (Lawshe 1947; Maxwell 1950a, 1950b). In particular, the WAS project investigated both mound and village areas. Most revealing were the excavations in six mounds that clearly indicated some of the mounds were constructed after the indigenous population adopted the Ramey motif and shell tempering of ceramic jars. Subsequent studies include excavations in one of the village settings by UWM in 1974 (Alex 1974; Van Dyke 1983), Svec's reconstruction of the Diamond Bluff mound group (1985, 1987), and the surface collections by the SHSW (Penman 1981, 1984) and the IMA (Wendt and Dobbs 1989). The UWM excavation uncovered several midden-filled features and a semi-subterranean house floor. The five radiocarbon dates from these excavations fall within the period of the early 11th century to late 13th century A.D. The other projects have provided important information on the size of the mound group(s), artifact densities, and spatial relations of mounds and habitation areas on the terrace.

What remains poorly understood is the archaeological identity of the indigenous Red Wing population at the onset of the 11th century A.D. Late Woodland on the Diamond Bluff terrace is identified with the Effigy Mound and Clam River traditions. In addition to the mound types, Late Woodland is represented by a widely scattered but low density of artifacts on the terrace. Late Woodland utilization of the terrace was not continuous, but recurring over several centuries by relatively small groups that occupied the site on a seasonal basis for both social and economic reasons. In contrast, the major occupation of the Diamond Bluff site complex is represented by the Oneota cultural tradition.

While it is not known what attracted Middle Mississippian interests to the Red Wing Locality, it is suggested here that this area had been the focus of trade and interaction among regional Late Woodland groups. Initial attempts by Cahokia to establish a foothold in the upper Mississippi Valley may have taken place as early as A.D. 950-1000 at Trempealeau, Wisconsin. This, in turn, was followed by the establishment of trade relations with the Red Wing Locality in the 11th century A. D. (cf. Kelly 1991).

The evidence for a Middle Mississippian site-unit intrusion in the Red Wing Locality is, at best, equivocal. Archaeological investigations at Diamond Bluff and related sites have not revealed Middle Mississippian artifact assemblages comparable to Mississippian site assemblages to the south. Instead a Middle Mississippian "presence" is represented by a small fraction of artifact types, such as the marine shell "god mask," and Ramey symbolism. Presumedly, these were introduced to the local population by Middle Mississippian traders. A weak link in drawing any conclusions about Middle Mississippian in the Red Wing Locality is the absence of human skeletal data and burial assemblages that could be used for comparative study with other Mississippian, Late Woodland or Oneota populations. Although the WAS documented mound burial at Diamond Bluff, the kinds of information required for comparative study does not exist. Human skeletal remains recovered from the village area by UWM are limited to cranial fragments, mandibles, and teeth. The context of these bones and the presence of cutmarks on several of the fragments suggests the remains of trophies and not a resident burial population (Rodell n. d.). The study by Glenn (1974) of Late Prehistoric crania from the Red Wing Locality was limited to three individuals from the Bryan site. Although the sample was too small to have any statistical significance, Glenn suggested that the physical attributes of the crania resemble the Middle Mississippian type (1974:138).

The Silvernale Phase was a local response to the Cahokian trade network with the indigenous population emulating certain aspects of Middle Mississippian culture. Whether this population was Oneota (Gibbon 1974, 1979,1991) or Late Woodland (Stoltman 1986) is not entirely clear. The evidence from Diamond Bluff favors Late Woodland. For the duration of the Silvernale Phase, circa A.D. 1025 to 1200, the indigenous Red Wing population preserved much of its local autonomy. Initially only those traits of Mississippian culture needed to articulate with the Cahokian trade network were adopted. These artifacts were limited to items of the Southeastern Ceremonial Complex and Ramey symbolism, and they functioned to maintain the "magico-religious sanctions and guarantees" required to insure success of the Cahokian trade system (Gibbon 1974:136). As involvement with the Cahokian trade system declined or became modified, the Mississippian symbolism was modified to emphasize the regional character of cultural groups. Most notable being the falcon symbolism that Benn (1989) has argued became the unifying social identity of the Oneota cultural tradition (also see Hall 1991).

Acknowledgements

I would like to thank Dr. James Stoltman for inviting me to contribute to this volume. This chapter is a revised version of a paper presented in the symposium, "Pattern, Phase and Focus: a Symposium Honoring Will C. McKern," at the annual Midwest Archaeological Conference, October 16-18, 1987, Milwaukee, Wisconsin. I am grateful to Dr. Moreau Maxwell, and Elmer Denlinger, John Forde, Thomas Kehoe, Charles Jacobs, and Owen Miles. Through discussion and correspondence they provided information on the 1948 WAS excavation and graciously contributed field notes, maps, and photographs. Dr. Robert Salzer of Beloit College also provide information on the 1948 excavation. The University of Wisconsin-Milwaukee has provided access to artifacts, notes, and materials from the 1974 excavation.

Robert Boszhardt, James Stoltman and Allen Van Dyke provided comments on earlier drafts of this paper. Michael Kolb of the UWM Soils Laboratory patiently explained soil relationships and formation processes; and Ronda Ulrath drew the illustrations for Figures 12 and 14. I appreciate their efforts and contributions. Any errors or misinterpretations reflect my own shortcomings.

References Cited

Alex, Robert
   1974 UWM 1974 Summer Field School. Newsletter of the Wisconsin Anthropological Society, 3(1):4-5.
Anfinson, Scott F. (editor)
   1979 *A Handbook of Minnesota Prehistoric Ceramics*. Minnesota Archaeological Society, Fort Snelling.
Anfinson, Scott F.
   1984 Cultural and Natural Aspects of Mound Distribution in Minnesota. *The Minnesota Archaeologist*, 43(1):3-30.
Bareis, Charles and James W. Porter (editors)
   1984 *American Bottom Archaeology*. Illinois Department of Transportation. University of Illinois Press, Urbana.
Beadle, B. V.
   1942 A Recent Find of Carved Shell Effigies. *The Minnesota Archaeologist*, 8(4):169.
Bender, Margaret M., Reid Bryson, and David A. Baerreis
   1978 University of Wisconsin Radiocarbon Dates XV. *Radiocarbon*, 20(1):157-167.
Benn, David W.
   1989 Hawks, Serpents, and Bird-Men: Emergence of the Oneota Mode of Production. *Plains Anthropologist*, 34(125):233-260.
Brower, J. V.
   1903 Minnesota Discovery of its Area 1540-1665. *Memoirs of Explorations in the Basin of the Mississippi*, Vol. 6. H. L. Collins Co., St. Paul.
Brown, James A.
   1976 The Southern Cult Reconsidered. *Midcontinental Journal of Archaeology*, 1(2):115-135.
   1982 What Kind of Economy did the Oneota Have? In *Oneota Studies*, edited by Guy E. Gibbon, pp. 107-112. Publications in Anthropology No. 1, University of Minnesota, Minneapolis.
Caine, Christy A. H.
   1974 The Archaeology of the Snake River Region. In *Aspects of Upper Great Lakes Anthropology: Papers in Honor of Lloyd A. Wilford*, edited by Elden Johnson, pp. 55-63. Minnesota Prehistoric Archaeology series No. 11, Minnesota Historical Society, St. Paul.
Cutler, Hugh C. and Leonard W. Blake
   1976 Corn form the Diamond Bluff Site (47-Pi-2), Wisconsin. Unpublished manuscript on file, Mississippi Valley Archaeological Center, UW-La Crosse.

Dobbs, Clark A.
  1984 Excavations at the Bryan Site: 1983-1984. *The Minnesota Archaeologist*, 43(2):49-58.
Dobbs, Clark A. and Kim Breakey
  1987 A Preliminary Report on Investigations at the Energy Park Site (21GD158): A Silvernale Phase Village at the Lake Pepin Locality. Paper presented at the Midwest Archaeological Conference, Milwaukee, Wisconsin, October 16-18.
Emerson, Thomas E.
  1989 Water, Serpents, and the Underworld: An Exploration into Cahokian Symbolism. In *The Southeastern Ceremonial Complex: Artifacts and Analysis*, edited by Patricia Galloway, pp. 45-92. University of Nebraska Press, Lincoln.
Finley, R. W.
  1976 Original vegetation cover of Wisconsin (map; scale 1:500,000). United States Department of Agriculture, Forest Service, North Central Forest Experiment Station, St. Paul.
Ford, Benjamin W. Jr.
  1982 Plum Creek Bridge Site (47-Pe-38): A Late Woodland Campsite in Pepin County, Wisconsin. *The Wisconsin Archeologist*, 63 (1):18-46.
Fowler, Melvin L. and Robert L. Hall
  1972 Archaeological Phases at Cahokia. Research Series, *Papers in Anthropology*, No. 1, Illinois State Museum, Springfield.
Gibbon, Guy E.
  1972 Cultural Dynamics and the Development of Oneota Life-way in Wisconsin. *American Antiquity*, 37(2):166-185.
  1974 A Model of Mississippian Development and Its Implications for the Red Wing Area. In *Aspects of Upper Great Lakes Anthropology: Papers in Honor of Lloyd A. Wilford*, edited by Elden Johnson, pp. 129-137. Minnesota Prehistoric Archaeology series No. 11, Minnesota Historical Society, St. Paul.
  1979 *The Mississippian Occupation of the Red Wing Area*. Minnesota Prehistoric Archaeology series No. 13, Minnesota Historical Society, St. Paul.
  1982 Oneota Origins Revisited. In *Oneota Studies*, edited by Guy E. Gibbon, pp. 85-90. Publications in Anthropology No. 1, University of Minnesota, Minneapolis.
  1991 The Middle Mississippian Presence in Minnesota. In *Cahokia in the Hinterlands: Middle Mississippian Cultures of the Midwest*, edited by Thomas E. Emerson and R. Barry Lewis, pp. 207-220. University of Illinois Press, Urbana.
Gibbon, Guy E. and Christy A. H. Caine
  1980 The Middle to Late Woodland Transition in Eastern Minnesota. *Midcontinental Journal of Archaeology*, 5 (1):57-72.
Glenn, Elizabeth J.
  1974 *Physical Affiliations of the Oneota Peoples*. Office of the State Archaeologist, Report 7, The University of Iowa, Iowa City.
Green, William
  1986 Prehistoric Woodland Peoples in the Upper Mississippi Valley. In *Prehistoric Mound Builders of the Mississippi Valley*, edited by James B. Stoltman, pp. 17-25. The Putnam Museum, Davenport.
  1988 An Early Mississippian Mound Center in the Upper Mississippi Valley. Paper presented at the annual meeting of Central States Anthropological Society, St. Louis, March 24-27.
Griffin, James B.
  1960 A Hypothesis for the Prehistory of the Winnebago. In *Culture in History: Essays in Honor of Paul Radin*, edited by Stanley Diamond, pp. 809-865. Columbia University Press, New York.
  1967 Eastern North American Archaeology: A Summary. *Science*, 156(3772):175-191.
Hall, Robert L.
  1962 The *Archeology of Carcajou Point* (2 volumes). The University of Wisconsin Press, Madison.
  1991 Cahokia Identity and Interaction Models of Cahokia Mississippian. In *Cahokia in the Hinterlands: Middle Mississippian Cultures of the Midwest*, edited by Thomas E. Emerson and R. Barry Lewis, pp. 3-34. University of Illinois Press, Urbana.
Haszel, Orville L.
  1968 *Soil Survey Pierce County, Wisconsin*. USDA, Soil Conservation Service, University of Wisconsin-Madison.

Holley, George R.
   1988 *Analysis of Ceramics from Excavated Features—ICT-II*. Contract Archaeology Program, Southern Illinois University-Edwardsville.
Hurley, William M.
   1974a *Silver Creek Woodland Sites, Southwestern Wisconsin*. Office of the State Archaeologist, Report 6, The University of Iowa, Iowa City.
   1974b Culture Contact: Effigy Mound. In *Aspects of Upper Great Lakes Anthropology: Papers in Honor of Lloyd A. Wilford*, edited by Elden Johnson, pp. 115-128. Minnesota Prehistoric Archaeology series No. 11, Minnesota Historical Society, St. Paul.
Kehoe, Thomas F.
   1966 The Small Side-Notched Point System of the Northern Plains. *American Antiquity*, 31(6): 827-841.
Kelly, John E.
   1991 Cahokia and Its Role as a Gateway Center in Interregional Exchange. In *Cahokia in the Hinterlands: Middle Mississippian Cultures of the Midwest*, edited by Thomas E. Emerson and R. Barry Lewis, pp. 61-80. University of Illinois Press, Urbana.
Keyes, Charles R.
   1928 The Hill-Lewis Archeological Survey. *Minnesota History*, 9(2):96-108.
Kreisa, Paul P.
   1987 Oneota Burial Patterns in Eastern Wisconsin. Paper presented in symposium: Pattern, Phase and Focus: a Symposium Honoring Will C. McKern. Midwest Archaeological Conference, Milwaukee, October 16-18.
Lawshe, Fred E.
   1947 The Mero Site-Diamond Bluff, Pierce County, Wisconsin. *The Minnesota Archaeologist*, 13(4):74-95.
Link, Adolph W.
   1982 Handles, Lobes and Appendages on Ceramics from the Bryan Site. *The Minnesota Archaeologist*, 41(1):30-44.
Mallam, Clark R.
   1976 *The Iowa Effigy Mound Manifestation: An Interpretive Model*. Office of the State Archaeologist, Report 9, The University of Iowa, Iowa City.
Marchner, Francis J.
   1974 The original vegetation of Minnesota (map; scale 1:500,000). United States Department of Agriculture, Forest Service, North Central Forest Experiment Station, St. Paul.
Martin, Lawrence
   1916 *The Physical Geography of Wisconsin*. Wisconsin Geological and Natural History Survey, Bulletin No. XXXVI. Madison.
Maxwell, Moreau S.
   1950a A Change in the Interpretation of Wisconsin's Prehistory. *Wisconsin Magazine of History*, 33(4):427-443.
   1950b A Preliminary Report on the Diamond Bluff Site. Paper Presented at the Society for American Archaeology Meeting, May 19-20, 1950, University of Oklahoma, Norman.
McKern, Will C.
   1928 The Neale and McClaughry Mound Groups. *Bulletin of the Public Museum of the City of Milwaukee*, Vol. 3, No. 3, pp. 213-416.
   1945 Preliminary Report on the Upper Mississippi Phase in Wisconsin. *Bulletin of the Public Museum of the City of Milwaukee*, Vol. 16, No. 3, pp. 109-285.
   1963 The Clam River Focus. Milwaukee Public Museum, *Publications in Anthropology*, No. 9, Milwaukee.
McInnis, Peggy
   1977 Fishscale Analysis from Diamond Bluff. Unpublished manuscript on file, Mississippi Valley Archaeological Center, UW-La Crosse.
Paull, Rachel Krebs, and Richard A. Paull
   1977 *Geology of Wisconsin and Upper Michigan*. Kendall/Hunt Publishing Co., Dubuque.
Penman, John T.
   1981 Archaeology of the Great River Road. Wisconsin Department of Transportation, *Archaeological Report* No. 5. Madison.

1984 Archaeology of the Great River Road: Summary Report. Wisconsin Department of Transportation, *Archaeological Report* No. 10. Madison.

Rodell, Roland L.
1989 Oneota, Space and Time in the upper Mississippi Valley. Paper presented in symposium: Oneota and Related Late Prehistoric Cultures: Current Research. Midwest Archaeological Conference, Iowa City, October 13-15.
n. d. Post-mortem alterations on human skeletal remains at Diamond Bluff. Unpublished manuscript, Mississippi Valley Archaeological Center, UW-La Crosse.

Schmidt, E. W.
1941 A Brief Archaeological Survey of the Red Wing Area. *The Minnesota Archaeologist*, 7(2):71-80.

Squier, George H.
1905 Certain Archaeological Features of Western Wisconsin. *The Wisconsin Archeologist*, o.s., 4(1):25-38.
1914 Archaeological Resources of Western Wisconsin. *The Wisconsin Archeologist*, o.s., 13(3):121-150.

Stevenson, Katherine, William Green and Janet Speth
1983 The Middle Mississippian Presence in the Upper Mississippi Valley: The Evidence from Trempealeau, Wisconsin. Paper presented at symposium entitled "Cultural Development and Adaptation along the Upper Mississippi River: Recent Investigations." Midwest Archaeological Conference, Iowa City, October 21-23.

Stoltman, James B.
1983 Ancient Peoples of the Upper Mississippi River Valley. In *Historic Lifestyles in the Upper Mississippi River Valley*, edited by John Wozniak, pp. 197-255. University Press of America, Lanham.
1986 The Appearance of the Mississippian Cultural Tradition in the Upper Mississippi Valley. In *Prehistoric Mound Builders of the Mississippi Valley*, edited by James B. Stoltman, pp. 26-34. The Putnam Museum, Davenport.

Stortroen, Charles E.
1957 The Bryan Site: A Prehistoric Village in Southern Minnesota. Unpublished M. A. thesis, the Department of Anthropology, University of Minnesota.

Stuiver, M.
1982 A High-Precision Calibration of the AD Radiocarbon Time Scale. *Radiocarbon*, 24(1): 1-26.

Stuiver, M. and P. J. Reimer
1986 A Computer Program for Radiocarbon Age Calibration. *Radiocarbon*, 28(2B):1022-1030.

Svec, E. Christopher
1985 The Diamond Bluff Site: Location of former Mounds using Historical Documents and Aerial Photography. Unpublished Senior's Thesis, Department of Anthropology, The University of Wisconsin-Madison.
1987 The Diamond Bluff Site: Locating Plowed Mounds Using Historical Documents and Aerial Photography. *The Wisconsin Archeologist*, 68(3):175-211.

Van Dyke, Allen P.
1983 An Initial Briefing on the 1974 Excavation at Diamond Bluff, Wisconsin. Paper presented at conference on Western Oneota Ceramics, April 16-17, Red Wing, Minnesota.

Van Dyke, Allen P. and Edgar S. Oerichbauer
1988 The Clam River Focus Revisited: Excavations at 47-Bt-36, Burnett County, Wisconsin. *The Wisconsin Archeologist*, 69 (3):139-162.

Wendt, Dan and Clark A. Dobbs
1989 A Reevaluation of the Mero (Diamond Bluff) Site Complex. The Institute for Minnesota Archaeology, *Reports of Investigation* No. 59. Minneapolis.

Wilford, Lloyd
1945 Three Village Sites of the Mississippi Pattern in Minnesota. *American Antiquity*, 11(1):32-40.
1955 A Revised Classification of the Prehistoric Cultures of Minnesota. *American Antiquity*, 21(2):130-142.

Williams, Stephen and John M. Goggin
1956 The Long Nosed God Mask in Eastern United States. *The Missouri Archaeologist*, 18(3):4-72.

Winchell, N. H.
1911 *The Aborigines of Minnesota*. The Pioneer Company, St. Paul.

13

The Mississippian Presence
in the Red Wing Area, Minnesota

Guy E. Gibbon
Department of Anthropology, University of Minnesota
Clark A. Dobbs
Institute for Minnesota Archaeology

Middle Mississippian traits are concentrated in two areas of Minnesota, at the confluence of the Cannon and Mississippi rivers near Red Wing and along the main trench of the Minnesota River from Mankato to the Red River of the North. Few other Middle Mississippian traits have been found in the state outside of these two areas (Gibbon 1991). Even though there are significant differences in the physical environment of these areas, both can be characterized as northern deciduous gallery forest habitats with adjacent areas of tall-grass prairie. Elden Johnson's paper in this volume summarizes our present understanding of the Middle Mississippian presence along the trench of the Minnesota River. This paper reviews the nature and distribution of Middle Mississippian traits near Red Wing, the area of the state where these traits occur in greatest abundance and in purest form.

In order to contribute most directly to the concerns of this volume—the nature of Cahokia-periphery interaction—we have structured our discussion around the four culture contact situations suggested for consideration by Stoltman in his symposium prospectus (for a more complete discussion of these situations see Stoltman 1986). These contact situations are: (1) a 'pure' Middle Mississippian intrusion into a non-Mississippian region; (2) an intrusion of a Middle Mississippian population segment, perhaps an elite, into the Cahokia hinterland; (3) a site-unit intrusion of Late Woodland emissaries; (4) culture contact without

permanent population displacement, probably involving trade.

We first review the history and results of archaeological research in the Red Wing area, and then summarize our own understanding at the time of the symposium of the Middle Mississippian and Oneota presence there. We conclude by assessing the applicability of Stoltman's four contact situations to our region of study.

Archaeological Research in the Red Wing Area: A Review

The Red Wing area has long been known as one of the richest archaeological regions in Minnesota. As early as 1823, the exceptional density of prehistoric earthworks scattered across the landscape at the juncture of the Mississippi and Cannon rivers was noted by Major Stephen Long and Ensign James Colhoun (Kane, Holmquist, and Gilman 1978:151, 279). The Rev. J. F. Aiton investigated stone 'cairns' on the bluffs above the Cannon River in 1848 and produced the only substantive account of these unusual structures that survives today (in Winchell 1911:165).

During the mid-1880s, T. H. Lewis, the field surveyor and partner of A. J. Hill in the Northwestern Archaeological Survey, recorded and mapped more than 2,000 mounds on the Wisconsin and Minnesota sides of the Mississippi River near Red Wing (see Winchell 1911; Dobbs 1986a). The records of this survey are particularly valuable to modern scholars, since almost all of these mounds are now destroyed. At the turn of the century, J. V. Brower and Dr. W. M. Sweeney also recorded a number of mounds in the region, particularly on Prairie Island, and documented the presence of several major village sites (Brower 1903: frontispiece, 49-68).

Modern archaeological investigations began in the late 1940s with Moreau Maxwell's excavations for Beloit College at the Mero site (Maxwell 1950; Rodell, this volume) and Lloyd A. Wilford's University of Minnesota excavations at the Bartron, Silvernale, and Bryan sites (Figure 13.1; Wilford 1952, 1955, 1956, 1958, 1985, n.d.; Stortroen 1957, 1985; Gibbon 1979). Wilford recognized that the clearest expression of Middle Mississippian traits in Minnesota occurred within this complex of sites, which he referred to as the Silvernale focus, a focus whose ceramics were "clearly related to Aztalan, to Apple River, and to the Monks Mound aspect" (Wilford 1955:140). Nonetheless, he included the Silvernale focus within the Upper Mississippi phase, which he regarded "as due to a fusion of Middle Mississippi elements with older Woodland elements..." (ibid.:141).

Excavations were also carried out on both sides of the Mississippi River during the 1960s and early 1970s, with Elden Johnson (University of Minnesota) excavating portions of the Bartron site and the Birch Lake Mound group on Prairie Island in the late 1960s (Johnson et al. 1969; Gibbon 1979), and Robert Alex (University of Wisconsin-Milwaukee) excavating additional portions of the Mero (Diamond Bluff Complex) site in the early 1970s (Rodell, this volume). Other small-scale excavations and tests were conducted at the Bryan and Silvernale sites (Dobbs 1985b; Gibbon 1979).

The first systematic survey of Goodhue County was carried out by Christina Harrison for the State Wide Archaeological Survey in the late 1970s (Harrison 1981), and in 1983 the Institute for Minnesota Archaeology (IMA) initiated a long-term research program in the area. To date, the IMA has conducted both extensive surveys (Dobbs 1985a) and excavations at a number of sites, including Bryan (Dobbs 1985b, 1987), Energy Park (Dobbs 1986b; Dobbs and Breakey 1987), and Adams (see below).

Site Content and Distribution

Although these surveys and excavations clearly document a Middle Mississippian presence in the Red Wing area, they also document the presence of other archaeological complexes in the same area, including Woodland, Oneota, Cambria, and Silvernale. Selected information about this entire array of complexes is summarized here, for familiarity with both types of

evidence — Mississippian and non-Mississippian — is essential, we believe, in assessing the applicability of Stoltman's four contact situations to our region of study.

Types of Sites and Their Distribution

An underlying assumption of the IMA's recent surveys in the Red Wing area is that Silvernale phase sites, if derived from a Middle Mississippian base via site-unit intrusion, should have a characteristic Middle Mississippian settlement pattern, both internally and regionally. More precisely, if site-unit intrusion from the south occurred, then one or more sites should be present that (1) were year-round settlements, (2) contained typical Mississippian house forms and material culture configurations, and (3) were organized around a central plaza and, possibly, platform mounds. This pattern should differ markedly from that of sites affiliated with local complexes, such as Oneota and Late Woodland, which we assume (1) were seasonally occupied, (2) contained local house forms and material culture configurations, and (3) lacked associations with either central plazas or platform mounds.

A brief discussion of internal site patterning and content is included in the following sections. Here we will consider two general types of sites (mound and habitation) that have been provisionally defined for the area and the association of Oneota and Silvernale sites with local landforms (Dobbs 1985a:51-61).

Five different types of mound groups are present in the region. These are: (1) mound groups containing many (>50) mounds that are principally or exclusively conical and/or linear in form; (2) smaller mound groups (<50) containing linear, conical, and effigy mounds; (3) small (<10) groups containing only conical mounds; (4) specialized groups containing mounds and/or other features like rock cairns; (5) sites containing earthen embankments and/or fortifications. Some of these groups undoubtedly contain earthworks constructed during different time periods and by members of different archaeological cultures. Nonetheless, we suggest that Oneota and/or Mississippian people were involved in the construction of most of these mounds, for shell-tempered sherds with Oneota and/or Mississippian decorative styles were in the fill or with burials in the few that have been excavated (Maxwell 1950; Johnson et al. 1969; Gibbon 1979, 1991). Two platform mounds are also present, a flat-topped conical mound on Prairie Island and a rectangular platform mound in a group of mounds (21GD52) between the Bryan and Silvernale sites (Figure 13.1; Winchell 1911:153). The flat-topped pyramidal mound was 4 feet high and 40 by 60 feet on a side when surveyed by T. H. Lewis in the mid-1880s.

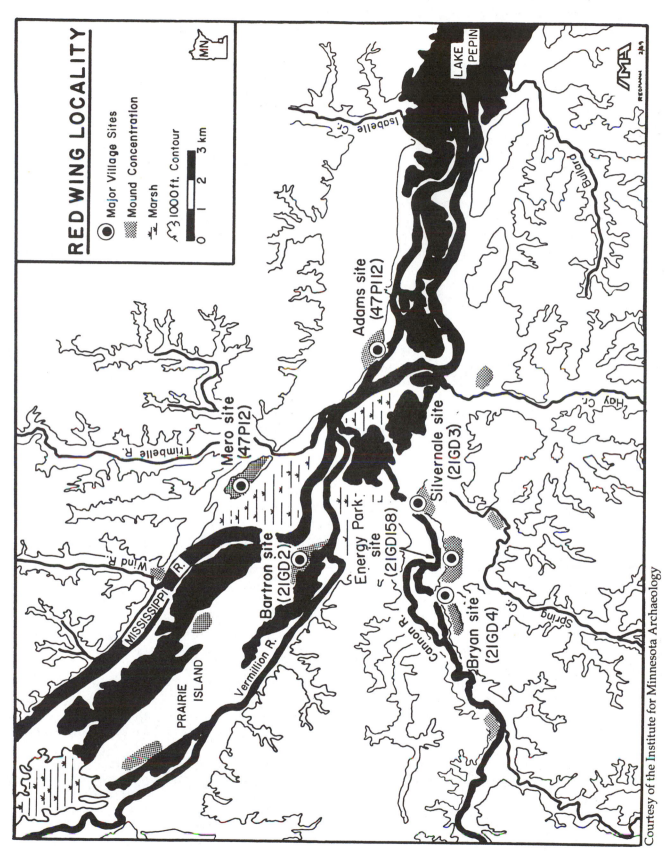

Figure 13.1. The Red Wing Locality.

Courtesy of the Institute for Minnesota Archaeology

It now has been largely destroyed by cultivation.

Five types of habitation site have also been defined (Figure 13.1): (1) large villages including Bryan (21GD4), Silvernale (21GD3), Adams (47PI12), and Mero (47PI02); (2) smaller villages including the Energy Park site (21GD158), the Double site (47PI81), Bartron (21GD2), and possibly the Belle Creek site (21GD72); (3) small outlying sites that may represent farmsteads or minor communities (e.g., 21GD96 and 21GD109); (4) small special-function sites that contain few formal tools but relatively large numbers of cores and flakes (e.g., 21GD91 and 21GD170 in Spring Creek Valley between the Bryan and Silvernale sites); (5) small special-function sites characterized by the absence of pottery and formal tools, the presence of a moderate to very low artifact density, and a high proportion of retouched or utilized flakes. Of the village sites, Adams and Bartron are Oneota, while the remainder are either exclusively Silvernale or at least dominated by Silvernale components. At present, site types 3 through 5 are lumped together as 'Oneota-Silvernale,' for diagnostic traits other than, for example, small 'undiagnostic' shell-tempered sherds have not been found. Future test excavations should define more clearly the cultural associations of many if not most of them.

The distribution of Oneota and Silvernale phase village sites across the landscape does not display a consistently different pattern. Bryan and Energy Park are situated on a well-drained glacial outwash terrace underlain by sands and gravels. Both overlook the Cannon River and are at least 100 feet above the floodplain. Both are also immediately adjacent to terrace margins with steep slopes. Mero is located in a similar setting overlooking the confluence of the Trimbelle and Mississippi rivers. Adams is also located on a well-drained glacial terrace, but it overlooks the back channel of the Mississippi, rather than one of its tributary streams. Moreover, the principal habitation area at Adams is located several hundred feet back from the margin of the terrace.

Silvernale and Bartron are in physiographic settings markedly different from Bryan, Adams, and Mero. Silvernale is on a bench between 20 and 25 feet above the Cannon River floodplain. The bench is composed of silt-loam and fine sandy loam sediments. Bartron is near the southern end of Prairie Island also at an elevation of about 20 feet above Sturgeon Lake and the backwater floodplain of the Mississippi.

Several conclusions can be drawn from these settings and provisional site types: (1) Oneota and/or Mississippian people were involved (somehow) in the construction of earthen burial mounds; (2) the presence of two platform mounds has been documented, but one is a conical mound and the other is not direct-ly associated with a large habitation site (although it may be associated with the smaller Energy Park site); (3) Oneota and Silvernale village sites occur in both high terrace and lowland settings; (4) Silvernale and/or Oneota villages were associated with smaller special activity localities; (5) Oneota villages, although fewer in number than Silvernale villages, fall within the same general size categories established for Silvernale villages.

Site Content and Patterning

In this review of the content and internal patterning of the Bryan, Silvernale, Bartron, Adams, and Energy Park village sites, only information bearing directly on the nature of the Middle Mississippian presence in the Red Wing area will be presented. More complete discussions of each of these sites can be found in Dobbs (1985b, 1986b, 1987) and Gibbon (1979).

The Bryan Site (21GD4)

As indicated in our review of archaeological investigations in the area, the most extensive excavations at Bryan were conducted by Wilford in the 1950s (in 1951, 1954, 1955, 1957) and by Dobbs in the mid-1980s (in 1983 and 1984). These two samples are discussed separately below for several reasons. First, while Wilford's sample has been analyzed in detail, he did not apply fine-scale recovery techniques, and a portion of his sample is missing. Second, the processing and analysis of Dobb's sample, which contains a large amount of floated material, in not yet complete. Although the following review may seem overly detailed, it is only at this level of detail, we believe, that an assessment of Stoltman's four contact situations can be made in the Red Wing area.

Only two aspects of Wilford's Bryan assemblage will be discussed here: (1) the nature of the relationship of Oneota and Mississippian-like ceramics in the assemblage, and (2) other features of the site discovered at the time of Wilford's excavations that might have a bearing on the Cahokia area–Red Wing contact situation.

Several problems exist in using Wilford's ceramic sample for comparative purposes. First, many of the sherds and rims are missing (presumably traded for similar comparative collections); for example, 40% of all rim sherds were unavailable for Gibbon's 1979 study. Second, Wilford's classification system shifted during the 1950s, so (without the missing sherds) it remains impossible today to determine precisely what, for instance, 'rolled rim' meant in 1954 as compared to 1957. Still, the general characteristics of the sample are known and a large enough collection remains for some pit-to-pit comparisons.

Of the 13,818 sherds recovered from Bryan by Wilford, approximately 92% were shell-tempered and 8% grit-tempered. Wilford regarded nearly all of the grit-tempered sherds he recovered as Cambria rather than Woodland, an interpretation supported by the 1979 study. Wilford assigned the profiles of rims in his 1955 and 1957 samples to four basic types. For convenience, they will be called rolled, short-thick, short-thin, and high (Figure 13.2). He regarded the rolled rims as Middle Mississippian, the high as Oneota, and the short as transitional between the other two, for he assumed that an intrusive Middle Mississippian people had gradually evolved into the Oneota. Table 13.1 records the numbers of rims in each category according to various samples. If the 1955-1957 sample is taken as the least distorted, then rolled rims account for about 39% of the sample, short rims 41% and high rims 10%. In the earlier and larger 1951-1954 sample, however, 28% of the rims were high. One can conclude (1) that the proportions of high and rolled rims

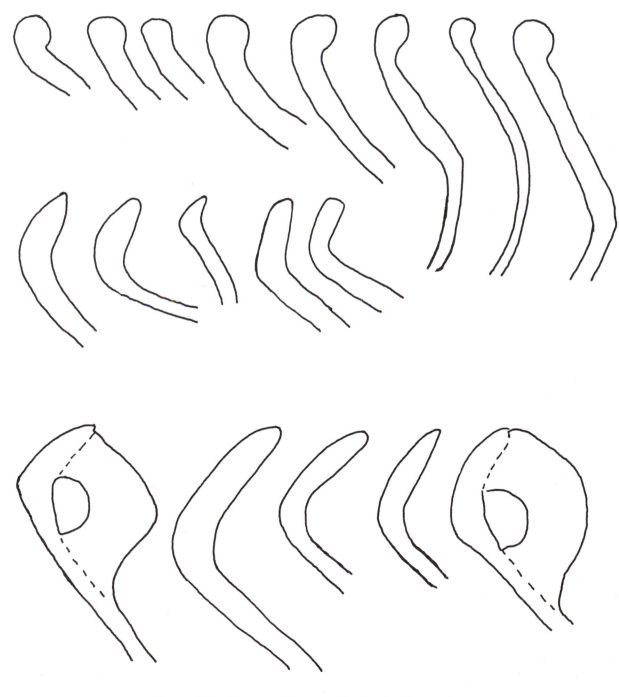

Figure 13.2. Rim profile categories for the Bryan site.

Table 13.1. Numbers of rims in profile categories from Bryan in Wilford's sample.

	1951-54*		1955-57		1979 Study	
Rolled	212	48%	65	39%	94	30%
Short-Thick	0	0%	12	7%	66	21%
Short-Thin	59	28%	56	34%	13	4%
High	123	28%	17	10%	126	40%
Misc.	46	11%	16	10%	17	5%
	440	100%	166	100%	316	100%

(* Since Wilford's profile categories were not defined until his analysis of the 1955-57 sample, it remains unclear what 'rolled' rim means in this column; it seems that 'rolled' and 'short-thick' rims were combined.)

vary across the site, and (2) that rim profiles usually not associated with an Oneota assemblage (all but high rims) dominate (72–90%) the Bryan ceramic assemblage.

Although these are informative statistics, they may well be statistics for a fabricated universe, that is, a universe formed by the analyst by combining several temporally and culturally distinct ceramic assemblages. Attempts to isolate distinct components at Bryan using Wilford's ceramic assemblage have not, however, been successful. Analyses by Wilford and by Stortroen (1957), who worked with the 1954 sample, can be summarized as follows: (1) grit-tempered sherds (Cambria ware), while always a small minority, are more common proportionately in lower levels than in upper levels; (2) in the site area excavated in 1955 and 1957, rolled rims are more common in lower levels and high rims more frequent in level 1, while short rims are fairly equally distributed among levels (Stortroen [1957:94], however, could find "no significant stratigraphic differences ... among either the major pottery types or among the various types of artifacts" in his analysis of the 1954 material); (3) Oneota traits are most commonly found in the western part of the site; (4) in general the results of the analyses of artifact and feature distributions within the site have been inconclusive in isolating separate components or in identifying significant trends in distribution other than those mentioned above.

Gibbon's 1979 study found some support for each of these four conclusions, although the small numbers of sherds associated with the first two indicate that these trends may lack significance. For example, in the 1955-1957 sample 41 grit-tempered sherds (11.2% of all sherds in the level) were in level 2 and 7 sherds (6.7%) in level 1; in unit B of the 1954 excavation, a unit containing a fairly high proportion of grit-tem-

pered sherds, 55 grit-tempered sherds (55.1%) were in level 2 and 20 (51.2%) in level 1. And, in one sample studied by Wilford, 13 rolled rims, 9 short rims, and 2 high rims were in level 2 and 1 rolled rim, 5 short rims, and 11 high rims in level 1. Since Wilford's excavations usually began after the midden had been stripped by gravel removal operations and pits exposed, the sample of sherds outside pits was small and is, therefore, difficult to interpret.

Stronger support is available for conclusions (3) and (4). Excavation units in the western part of the Bryan site do seem to have a greater proportion of 'Oneota' traits than units in other parts of the site. For instance, unnotched triangular projectile points, high rims, and punctate decoration on bodysherds all demonstrate a higher incidence of occurrence in the western, and especially the southwestern corner, of the area of the site excavated by Wilford (Gibbon 1979:59). Nonetheless, other artifact distribution and association studies have failed to support the existence of more than one clearly defined component (but see the discussion of Dobb's excavation at Bryan below). A Q-type factor analysis of material within 98 pits and excavation units revealed a wide horizontal dispersion of in general only loosely related units, for example, rather than clusters of units tightly grouped together by similar artifact and debris content. An R-type factor analysis of the same material also failed to isolate distinctive tool kits or associations of materials.

Ceramic studies also support this conclusion. Table 13.2 records the numbers of storage/refuse pits in Wilford's assemblages associated with particular rim profile categories. High and rolled rims occur together in approximately 32% of the pits. It is also apparent that the greater the number of rims in a pit, the more likely rims of all three categories (high, rolled, short) will be associated together. Even more significant is

Table 13.2. Rim profile associations in pits in Wilford's Bryan sample.

Rolled Only	5	9%
Short Only	1	22%
High Only	7	12%
Rolled and Short	15	26%
Rolled and High	4	7%
Short and High	11	19%
Rolled, Short, and High	14	25%
	57	100%

(The sample used here includes only those pits containing two or more rims available for examination in the 1970s. 'Short' here refers to both short-thin and short-thick rims.)

the association of rim profiles and shoulder design elements on all available vessels in Wilford's sample. Oneota chevrons, Mississippian scrolls, and plain shoulders are associated with all four of Wilford's rim profile categories (Table 13.3; Figure 13.3). When rims with only small fragments of shoulder attached are considered (Table 13.4), the percentages of rims in all four categories with shoulder fragments decorated with straight lines (Oneota?), curved lines (Mississippian?), or both straight and curved lines seem about the same. Although these are very rough measures of trait associations, they support the general conclusion that Oneota-like and Mississippian-like traits occur together in many instances rather than being consistently separated in Wilford's Bryan ceramic assemblage.

Other artifacts and structures that might be Middle Mississippian-related discovered by Wilford and others at Bryan before the IMA excavations can be quickly summarized. Two small copper 'Southern Cult' mace-like batons, a silver-colored 'pulley' ear spool, a Thunder Bird shoulder design motif on a high rim ceramic vessel, and the central axis of a shell columella are in private collections and lack other than a general site provenience. It is perhaps worth noting that a few undecorated fragments of catlinite from the site are also in private collections. A crude face with what Wilford thought were feline features was carved on a small piece of sandstone found in pit 72 during the 1954 excavations. This piece of sculpture was associated with both rolled rim and short rim vessels. Of the 83 triangular projectile points found by Wilford, 61 are unnotched and 22 have a single set of side notches. These latter points could as easily be related to the Plains side-notched point complexes as to a Mississippian presence.

Although the semisubterranean (probably posthole) houses excavated by Wilford are too general in structure to attribute to one cultural source (Mississippian, for example), their ceramic associations are very informative. A rectangular house (pit 70) 7.5 by 6.7 feet in outline with a floor about 1.6 feet below the surface of the C horizon was associated with rolled rim and short rim vessels and Cambria ware. A circular house (units F and G) was 8.5 feet in diameter with a floor about 2.2 feet below the surface of the sod. This house was associated with 6 high rims, 1 short rim, and a scroll design on a bodysherd. All three high rim vessels (the other three rims were fragments) have atypical Oneota shoulder decoration, such as external nodes. A human skull on (or in) the floor of this house was considered a 'trophy skull' by Wilford; it is probably this skull that Glenn (1974) identified as Muskogid

Table 13.3. Cross-Tabulations of rim profile and shoulder design in Wilford's Bryan sample.

	High	Rolled	Short-Thin	Short-Thick
Oneota Chevron	8	4	3	1
Oneota Misc.	4	3	2	0
Miss. Scrolls	4	4	2	2
Miss. Misc.	2	1	0	1
Plain	1	1	2	2

Available for Study in the 1970s

Table 13.4. Cross-tabulations of rim profile and shoulder fragment design in Wilford's Bryan sample.

	High	Rolled	Short-Thin	Short-Thick
Straight Line	15	19	14	14
Curved Line	6	13	6	4
Straight and Curved Line	8	9	8	4

Available for Study in the 1970s

Figure 13.3. Shoulder decoration motifs on ceramics from the Bryan site.

(i.e., as similar to skeletal populations associated with core Mississippian sites to the south). Both houses had apparently burned with walls and ceiling falling and smothering the blaze.

Still other features of Bryan known from Wilford's excavations that might have a bearing on the nature of the Cahokia area-Red Wing contact situation can also be quickly summarized. (1) Although faunal and floral food debris was not saved, a number of crude measures based on percentages of artifact classes and numbers of pits suggest that the inhabitants of Bryan relied upon plant foods (presumably maize) to a greater extent than the inhabitants of a number of Oneota sites (Bartron, Sheffield, Bornick, Walker-Hooper) (Gibbon 1979). (2) Radiocarbon dates indicate the site could have been occupied for several hundred years (Table 13.5). (3) The chipped stone material seems local to the Upper Mississippi River Valley (a fine gray chert, oolitic flint, jasper, quartzite, agate). (4) Many characteristic Middle Mississippian traits were not found during Wilford's excavations. These include wall-trench structures, tri-notched triangular projectile points, Mississippian hoes, spades, and knives, discoidals, pottery trowels and pans, water bottles, beakers, and plates. (5) The artifact assemblage is characterized by chipped stone end scrapers and by an extensive worked bone-antler-tooth complex that seems more typical of sites to the west than of Cahokia-area sites. This latter complex includes deer third phalange projectile points, fishhooks, bison scapula hoes and picks, elk antler picks, bone and antler punches, beaver tooth incisors, bone and antler awls of a variety of types, needles, battens, shuttles, deer jar sickles, antler tool handles, spatulas, antler gaming counters, tubes, bird bone pins, armlets or pendants, perforated deer phalanges (for the pin-and-cup game?), whistles, and fish teeth beads.

The IMA 1983-1984 excavations at Bryan opened seventy 2 × 2 meter units, examined 557 features, discovered the remains of several structures and two sides of a log palisade, and recovered tens of thousands of pieces of cultural debris using water-screening and flotation methods (Figure 13.4). Although an initial report has been prepared on the project (Dobbs 1987, 3 vols.), initial processing and sorting of the material is only now being completed. The following observations must, therefore, be regarded as preliminary.

In general the ceramic assemblage is broadly consistent with earlier descriptions of ceramics from the site, that is, there is considerable variation in vessel and rim form, decorative motif, and vessel size. Both classic, rolled rim ceramics of the Silvernale phase and ceramics associated with the Oneota were recovered (Figures 13.5 and 13.6). It is of interest to note that the frequency of ceramics and other artifacts clearly referable to 'classic' Middle Mississippian forms is quite low. Only one vessel that might fall within the range of variation of Ramey Incised was found. However, numerous variations on the rolled rim theme were observed and several of these vessels appeared to have been either burnished or fired in a special fashion. There is considerable variability in the size, form, and decoration of Oneota ceramics in the sample. Straight-rimmed vessels with typical chevron motifs are present. However, other vessels are decorated with a continuous design of wavy trailed lines or modifications of the 'guilloche' motif commonly associated with the Silvernale phase. Most vessels in the sample appear, however, to be low rim Silvernale varieties.

Five radiocarbon determinations were obtained from the 1983-1984 assemblage (Table 13.5; Dobbs 1985b:58; also see Dobbs 1982). These age determinations bracket the period from A.D. 1050–1350 and are consistent with other interpretations of the chronology of the Red Wing area (Gibbon 1979; Shane 1981).

Samples dated from features 109 and 202 were in association with Silvernale phase ceramics and with pottery that appears to have its origins to the west (Cambria and/or Mill Creek?) (Figures 13.7 and 13.8).

During the course of Wilford's excavations, he observed a 0.5 foot high ridge that appeared to run the entire length of the site. He placed two excavation squares over this ridge to evaluate the possibility that it represented a stockade line. Although posts were found in one of the excavation squares, they did not appear to continue into the other. As a result, he concluded that the ridge and postmolds were the product of modern activities. Elden Johnson, who was visiting the site at the time, thought, however, that the posts did indeed represent a palisade (E. Johnson, personal communication; Gibbon 1979:11). The presence of a palisade at the site remained, then, unresolved.

The remains of the western palisade wall and it's southwestern corner were discovered in May, 1983. It was possible to trace this segment of the palisade for almost forty meters up to the edge of the site destroyed in the 1930s (Figures 13.9 and 13.10). In May 1984, the northwestern edge of the palisade was discovered as well (Figure 13.11). At present, it is estimated that the palisade surrounded an area of approximately 10 acres. This enclosure is quite large when compared to similar structures in the Upper Mississippi Valley (e.g., the Valley View site near La Crosse - see Stevenson 1985). The Bryan palisade was composed of upright posts with an estimated height of between 7 and 9 feet. The postmolds comprising the wall were consistently between 18 and 22 cm. in diameter and spaced at 60 cm. intervals. Small cobbles, in particular chunks of dolomite from the nearby bluffs, were commonly used as chinking for the posts. However, no evidence of a daub covering or interwoven material within the wall was found during the excavation.

Four structures, including two houses, were discovered. Two of these are incomplete and their form is still not fully understood. Structure 4 appears to have been associated with the northern wall of the palisade and consists of a double line of posts bordering the palisade wall to the north (Figure 13.11). Structure 1 is a house that consists of a square pattern of postmolds surrounding an essentially sterile area devoid of features (Figure 13.11). The house area, however, is surrounded by a circle of refuse pits. Structure 3 appears to be a complex circular dwelling or other structural type that was rebuilt on several different occasions (Figure 13.11).

The importance of maize and horticulture at Bryan was reinforced by the 1983-1984 excavations. Numerous bell-shaped pits, bison scapula hoes, deer mandible 'sickles,' and other maize-processing tools

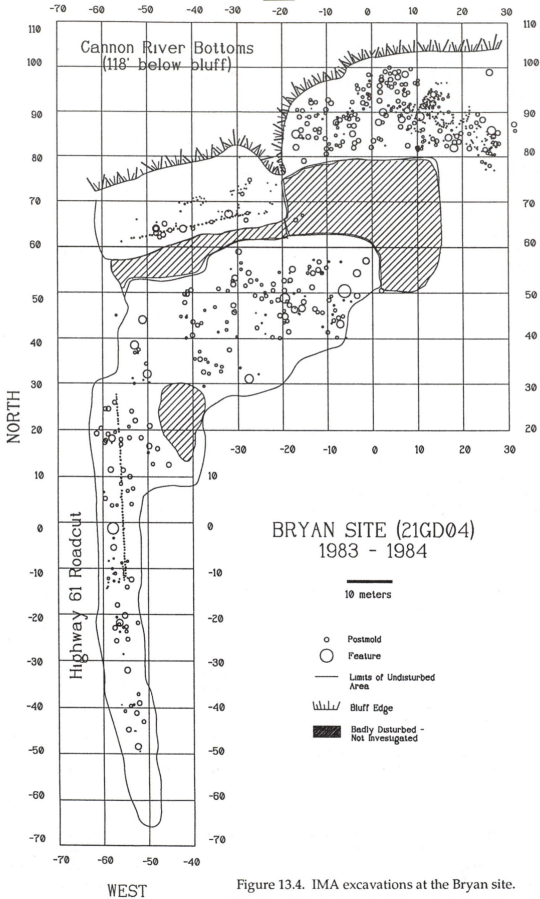

Figure 13.4. IMA excavations at the Bryan site.
Courtesy of the Institute for Minnesota Archaeology.

Table 13.5. Radiocarbon dates from Red Wing area archaeological sites.

Site	Uncalibrated Dates			Calibrated Dates	
	BP	s	AD	Dates AD	Sample No.
Bryan	825	150	1125	905-1355	I-781
	760	90	1190	1055-1350	I-782
	500	120	1450	1310-1515	I-783
	740	50	1210	1215-1330	Beta 8840
	870	50	1080	1035-1255	Beta 8841
	920	50	1030	930-965 1015-1235	Beta 8842
	780	100	1170	1045-1340	Beta 8843
	840	70	1110	1050-1265	Beta 8844
Silvernale	740	130	1210	1230+/-140	GX-7036
	830	125	1120	1180-1150+/-135	GX-7037
	650	120	1300	1300+/-130	GX-7038
Bartron	815	125	1135	1180+/-135	GX-7034
	405	130	1545	1440+/-140	GX-7035
	890	55	1060	1070+/-65	WIS-434
	850	55	1100	1120-1090+/-65	WIS-423
Mero	910	55	1040	1050+/-65	WIS-841
	890	55	1060	1070+/-65	WIS-842
	955	55	995	1020+/-65	WIS-846
	790	55	1160	1190+/-65	WIS-849
	755	55	1195	1220-1200+/-65	WIS-845

(Dates corrected using the calibration table published in Klein et al., 1982.)

were recovered. A unique type of feature termed 'corn concentrations' (Dobbs 1987:49) was also identified during these excavations. These features contain charcoal and large numbers of corn kernels and cobs; ash deposits and artifacts are rarely found in them. In general, they are circular in horizontal plan with a diameter of less than 0.4 meters and rounded in vertical cross-section with a depth of less than 0.4 meters. Although their function remains unknown, one hypothesis is that they are the bases of smudge pits used for hide smoking (Binford 1967).

More than 5 liters of carbonized maize cobs and kernels were recovered. A preliminary analysis of some of this maize by Robert McK. Bird indicates that there are at least four distinct categories of maize in the sample. The best defined of these types has between 8 and 12 rows with cupule widths ranging from 6.4 to 8.2 mm. McK. Bird regarded some of this maize as "possibly Northern Flints" (see Attachment E, Dobbs 1987:458).

The higher concentration of Oneota traits in the western portion of the site noticed by Wilford is also evident in the artifacts and features discovered in 1983-1984. Dobbs feels that there is evidence for an Oneota component in the northwestern portion of the site that is spatially and temporally distinct from the Silvernale phase component. The primary area covered by the Oneota component appears to be on the edge of the terrace overlooking the Cannon River immediately adjacent to and outside the palisade, while the Silvernale occupation appears to be set back from the terrace edge by approximately 20 meters. This hypothesis is based on the following field observations: (1) Silvernale phase ceramics seem to occur only within or immediately adjacent to the area delineated by the palisade; (2) Oneota ceramics occur within the palisade area, but are most common outside the palisaded portion of the site; (3) ground stone tools, particularly mullers, are common outside the palisaded portion of the site but rarely found within this area; (4) the types of features outside the palisade area are distinctly different from those within the palisade.

The Silvernale Site (21GD3)

Wilford conducted small-scale excavations at Silvernale in 1947 and 1950. Since the recovered sample of artifacts was small, only a few of its characteristics are summarized here. Only about 53% of Wilford's original ceramic sample is presently available for study. Of 53 rim sherds without attached shoulders, 11 have rolled rims, 20 short rims, and 22 high rims. Of 212 small decorated shoulder sherds,

Staff photo, Institute for Minnesota Archaeology

Figure 13.5. Two Oneota jars nested inside one another in Feature 401 at Bryan.

Staff photo, Institute for Minnesota Archaeology

Figure 13.6. Interior vessel of two Oneota jars nested inside one another in Feature 401 at Bryan.

Figure 13.7. Unusual grit-tempered sherds from Bryan. The lower sherd was found in Feature 202 in association with a rolled rim vessel; the sherds in the upper part of the plate are in the Adolf Link collection.

Staff photo, Institute for Minnesota Archaeology

Figure 13.8. Portion of a vessel found in Feature 388 at Bryan. Note the presence of cord-marking below the shoulder.

Staff photo, Institute for Minnesota Archaeology

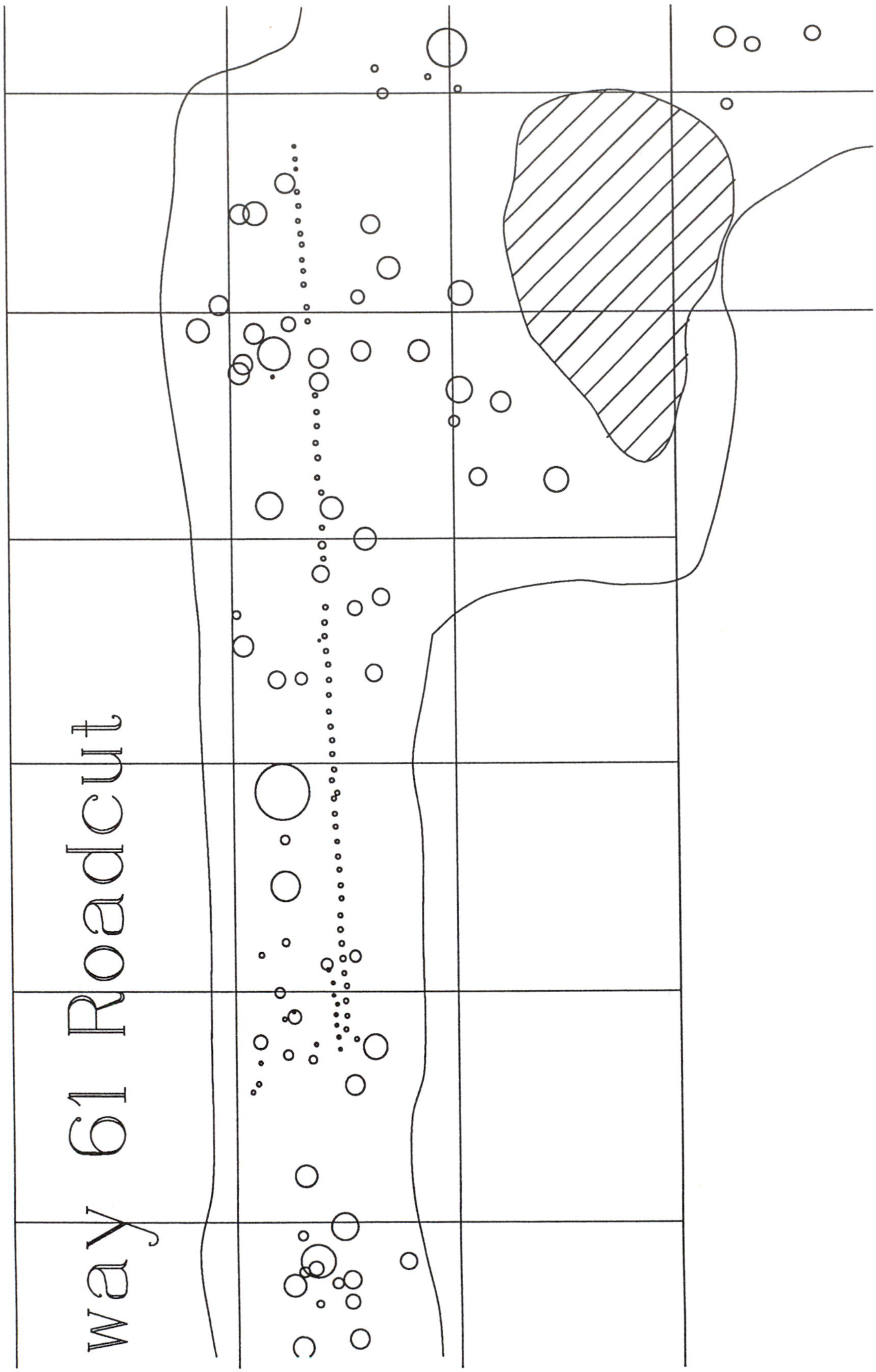

Figure 13.9. The southwestern palisade wall at Bryan.

Courtesy of the Institute for Minnesota Archaeology.

Figure 13.10. West wall of the palisade at Bryan (looking north from the southwest corner of the palisade; note the second set of postmolds immediately to the left of the palisade line). Photo by Clark A. Dobbs, Inst. Minn. Archaeo.

ficult to draw many sound conclusions from this sample and the information provided above. However, we can tentatively conclude that the Silvernale ceramic sample is in general similar to that of Wilford's Bryan sample.

Other relevant information from Silvernale can be as briefly summarized. (1) Of 35 triangular projectile points recovered by Wilford, only 6 have side notches. One of the latter points also has a shallow basal notch. (2) A small shell-tempered human head modeled in clay is in a private collection and lacks specific provenience. The head is about 1 3/4 inches in diameter and has a round hole at the base (presumably for attachment). The eyes are formed from relatively large pieces of mussel shell, while other features are indicated by incisions. (3) Although less varied (presumably due to sample size), the bone-antler-tooth complex observed at Bryan is also present at Silvernale. (4) The chipped stone material seems similar to that at Bryan. (5) The characteristic Mississippian traits absent at Bryan are also absent at Silvernale, with the exception of the single tri-notched projectile point. (6) In general, the assemblage at Silvernale seems sufficiently similar to that described for Bryan to consider both occupations as approximately contemporaneous. This conclusion seems supported by radiocarbon determinations for the site (Table 13.5; Dobbs 1982:103).

Wilford excavated 270 square feet of the site in 1947 and 200 square feet west of the 1947 excavations in 1950. He also excavated two conical mounds (nos. 36 and 45) in 1947. With this additional background, the following conclusions concerning spatial and stratigraphic trends at Silvernale can be drawn from the meager amount of available information: (1) there is no firm evidence to demonstrate which people (possibly represented by Cambria, Woodland, Silvernale, and Oneota traits) were the first inhabitants of the village area; (2) Cambria and Woodland traits are most frequent in the 1947 excavation area; (3) Cambria sherds seem to decrease in proportion from lower to upper levels in the 1947 site area; (4) the use of curved lines and punctate decoration decreases in popularity from lower to upper levels in 1950 units, although curved line decoration becomes more common in upper levels of 1947 units; (5) a vertical trend from rolled rims to high flared rims is apparent in the 1947 units; (6) a greater proportion of Oneota ceramic traits are present in 1950 units, as seen, for example, in the percentage of high flared rims in the sample (80%) as compared to the 1947 sample (40.4%); (7) greater leaching of shell tempering from ceramics in the 1947 sample could indicate that the 1950 area is more recent; (8) some conical mounds of the Silvernale group were probably built by Cambria, Silvernale (Mississippian), or Oneota peoples.

160 have straight-line decoration (including 3 definite chevrons), 27 curved lines (with 2 definite scrolls), 17 straight lines and punctates, 3 curved lines and punctates, 3 curved and straight lines, and 2 with punctates only. Seven additional large shoulder sections are decorated with chevron designs. Of the 12 vessels in the sample, 6 have rolled rims, 2 short rims, and 4 high rims. Two of the high rim vessels have typical Oneota shoulder design elements; one is plain, and the other has straight lines on a fragment of shoulder. One of the short rims has a scroll design on the shoulder, and the other has curved lines on a shoulder fragment. Three of the rolled rims have straight lines on shoulder fragments and the other three have curved line decoration on the shoulder (with one shoulder large enough to display a typical Middle Mississippian design motif). The only vessel shape present is the jar. Of the 2,793 sherds recovered from Silvernale by Wilford, 51 are grit-tempered. Wilford classified 36 of these sherds as Cambria and 15 as Woodland. It is dif-

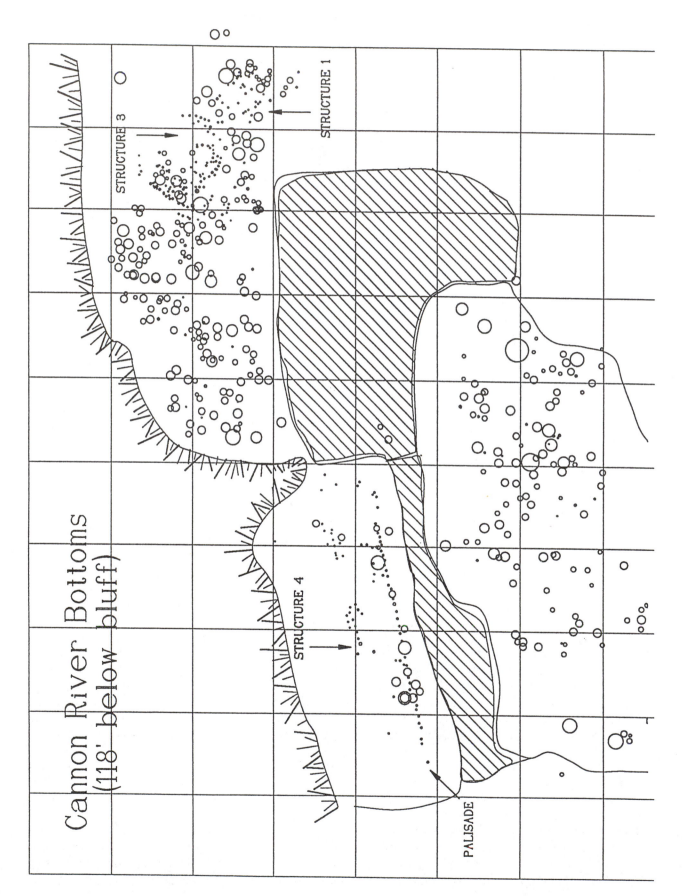

Figure 13.11. The northwestern palisade wall at Bryan.
Courtesy of the Institute for Minnesota Archaeology.

The Bartron Site (21GD2)

Portions of the Bartron site were excavated by Wilford in 1948 and by Elden Johnson in 1968 and 1969 (Gibbon 1979). Unlike Bryan and Silvernale, Bartron is a Blue-Earth related Oneota village site containing few traits that could be Middle Mississippian-related. The traits include: (1) a few scroll motifs (2 vessels and 4 bodysherds in a sample of 679 vessels and decorated bodysherds); (2) one side-notched and one tri-notched triangular projectile point in a sample of 85 points (70 unnotched triangular, 2 stemmed, 4 corner-notched, and 9 side-notched); (3) the corner of a possible wall-trench structure (unusual in that the wall is almost a meter thick and the corner a real squared corner rather than the juncture of two walls that do not quite meet; whether this structure is Mississippian-related or even prehistoric remains unclear); (4) a few angular shoulders on ceramic vessels. Except for the side-notched triangular point, one jar with an angular shoulder, and the possible wall-trench structure, these Mississippian traits (the tri-notched point, scroll motifs, several angular jar shoulders) were concentrated in the area of a nearly square (9 × 9.5 meters) posthole house with a black 'depressed' floor and an Oneota artifact assemblage. One or possibly two additional houses with depressed floors were also found at the site; the most extensively excavated was rectangular (4 × 5.5 meters) and had a black 'greasy' floor beginning 45 cm. below the soil surface. It is also pertinent to note that both ceramic vessels with scroll motifs had high 'Oneota' rims.

Other bits of information about Bartron that could be relevant to the central problem of this volume are: (1) two uncalibrated radiocarbon determinations for the site are A.D. 1060±55 (WIS-434) and A.D. 1100±55 (WIS-423) (Table 13.5); (2) of 221 vessels and rim fragments examined in Gibbon's 1979 study, only 3 are grit-tempered (all are non-Woodland and could be either Oneota or Cambria); (3) of 648 decorated bodysherds examined in the 1979 study, 11 are grit-tempered and non-Woodland (3 have curved line decoration, 2 punctate decoration, 1 straight line decoration, and 5 large pieces have straight line 'Oneota' designs); (4) of 221 rim profiles drawn for the 1979 study, 3 represent one variety of short-thin rim and the remainder are high 'Oneota' profiles (rolled and pseudo-rolled or short-thick rims are absent); (5) of 4,455 sherds in Wilford's original 1948 ceramic sample, only 8 (0.2%) were grit-tempered, and only one of these was non-Woodland (Oneota or Cambria); (6) although maize horticulture was practiced, subsistence seems to have been based on hunting to a greater extent than at Bryan or at Oneota sites such as Walker-Hooper and Bornick (Gibbon 1979); (7) a bone-antler-tooth complex similar to that at Bryan and Silvernale is present at Bartron; (8) the cult items (thunderbird motifs, copper batons, figurines) at Bryan have not been found at Bartron; (9) Bartron was probably palisaded (Gibbon 1979); (10) a single circular, flat-topped mound was described by T. H. Lewis in a group of 23 mounds just south of Bartron on the same island (two additional flat-topped circular mounds were also located by Lewis in western Hennepin County); (11) Bartron is no more than 7 to 10 acres in extent (Bryan was probably 15 to 20 acres in extent); (12) excavations by Elden Johnson (Johnson et al. 1969) at the Birch Lake Mound group near Bartron recovered Mississippian-Oneota artifacts in the fill of a Woodland mound (leading Johnson to conclude "...that the Birch Lake mound group was constructed by a Woodland group in contact with an intruding Mississippian population and perhaps trading with them").

The Adams Site (47PI12)

Adams is a large Oneota village site located on the east side of the Mississippi River in Pierce County, Wisconsin. As mentioned earlier, it is situated on the edge of an extensive post-glacial terrace overlooking a back channel of the Mississippi River. Surface investigations by Dobbs (1986a) in 1984 indicated that there were discrete concentrations of cultural debris at the site, and that these concentrations had distinctly different debris profiles. Limited excavations were conducted by the IMA in 1985. Although analysis of the recovered material is also still in progress, several observations can be made.

First, Adams appears to be a single component Oneota site. The only Middle Mississippian traits found are a number of chunky stones (more than 10). Several copper items were also recovered. Second, Adams appears to belong to the same archaeological culture as the Armstrong site in Trempealeau County, Wisconsin. This conclusion is based on an attribute analysis of the two ceramic assemblages which indicated no statistical difference between them. It is assumed that the two components date to the same approximate time period, that is, to ca. A.D. 1100-1150 (Hurley 1978). Third, there appears to be structural differences between Adams and the Bryan and Silvernale sites. Rather than the deep storage pits characteristic of those sites, the only features found at Adams are the bases of what appear to be trash heaps or middens.

Finally, the horizontal distribution of 'concentrations' at Adams is well-defined and discrete, with the space in between low in artifact density. Based on this information, the homogeneity of the artifactual assemblage, and the similarity of the ceramic assemblage with that of Armstrong, it is possible that the site represents a large, single-component village occupied for a brief period of time in the twelfth century.

The Energy Park Site (21GD158)

The Energy Park site was discovered during the course of an IMA archaeological survey of the City of Red Wing in 1984. Like all other Silvernale phase villages in this region, the habitation portion is surrounded by a mound group (21GD52), although this particular mound group contains the flat-topped pyramidal mound mentioned previously (Figure 13.1). The presence of a village site in probable association with this Middle Mississippian architectural feature is particularly intriguing. Moreover, unlike all other known Silvernale phase sites in the region, the village portion of the site has not been destroyed by gravel mining or other severely disruptive activities. Energy Park has the potential, then, to provide answers about the nature of the Middle Mississippian presence in the Red Wing area that are otherwise unavailable.

Limited fieldwork was conducted at the site during October 1986, and during the summers of 1987 and 1988. The principal goal of the investigations was to examine a Silvernale phase site as a functioning community and to move beyond purely artifact-based studies. Two controlled surface collections of artifactual debris from the entire site have been completed (1986 and 1988), and roughly 60% of the site has been examined using soil resistivity. Since laboratory analysis of materials recovered during the surveys is still in progress, the discussion here summarizes Dobb's preliminary interpretations of these data.

The controlled surface collections indicate that there is a well-defined internal plan at the site. A contour map of the distribution of total numbers of artifacts obtained in 1986 (Figure 13.12) shows a major concentration on the western edge of the site and a somewhat less dense concentration on the eastern edge. These artifact scatters were composed mostly of debitage and stone tools, with only a few small pieces of pottery. Smaller debris scatters surround the center of the site. These concentrations contain far more pottery than do those along the eastern and western edges, and are tentatively interpreted as domestic activity areas.

The drought of 1988 produced a series of 'crop marks' that were visible both from the air and on the ground. Aerial photographs taken in July clearly show 'patches' of darker vegetation similar in location to the debris concentrations identified during the 1986 controlled surface collection. Small patches about 5 meters in diameter were grouped in a circle roughly 40 meters in diameter around the central portion of the site. It is possible that these discolorations in vegetation represent structures or refuse pits near struc-

tures, in which case there may have been an open area in the center of the village.

The debris profile of the various concentrations defined during the controlled surface collections are quite different. Excavations conducted within the limits of three of them confirmed these differences both in the types of artifacts recovered and in the nature of subsurface deposits.

A series of deep trash pits was discovered in a 1987 excavation block located along the northeastern edge of the site. These pits contained characteristic village refuse, and freshwater mussel shells, which probably indicates that they were filled during the late spring or early summer. In 1988 an excavation block was placed in the area of high artifact density in the western portion of the site. Although the material recovered replicated the debris profile obtained from the controlled surface collection, the subsurface density of features was markedly lower than in the northeastern block. Only one deep pit feature, containing a few pieces of debitage and pottery, was found. The remaining features were mostly shallow, basin-shaped pits containing few artifacts and two discolored areas apparently subjected to high heat. The two latter features may represent hearths.

In general the artifactual assemblage at the Energy Park site is typical of other Silvernale phase sites in the region. The ceramic assemblage is composed of Silvernale phase-like, Oneota, and grit-tempered (only two pieces) sherds (Figures 13.13 and 13.14). Groundstone implements are relatively rare, while items like bison scapula hoes, ferruginous sandstone abraders, triangular projectile points, snub-nosed scrapers, and the like are common. The only Middle Mississippian artifact found to date is a complete notched triangular point made of a non-local raw material of unknown origin. It has five notches, one large and one small notch on each side and a basal notch (Figure 13.15).

Cubes of galena are relatively common, with at least five recovered from processed samples thus far. Galena is not a particularly common material at sites in the Red Wing area, and its relative frequency at Energy Park is intriguing.

The limited information available so far for the site makes interpretation difficult at this time. However, two hypotheses are offered here by Dobbs for consideration. First, it is hypothesized that Energy Park represents a 'central place' for Silvernale phase occupants of the Red Wing area. Its location almost halfway between Bryan and Silvernale, the presence beside it of the flat-topped pyramidal mound, and the Cahokia point and galena lend support to this hypothesis. A corollary of this hypothesis is that the village was occupied principally by elite individuals. Second, it is hypothesized that the village was relatively short-

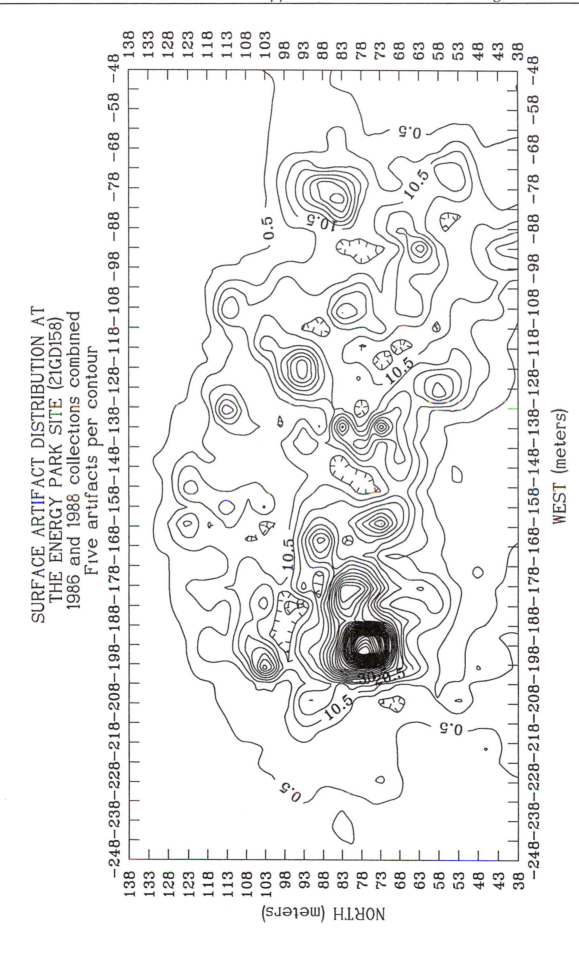

Figure 13.12. Surface contours of artifact density at Energy Park.
Courtesy of the Institute for Minnesota Archaeology.

Figure 13.13. Blue Earth-like vessel found in Feature 2 in Excavation Block 1 at Energy Park.

Figure 13.14. Vessel found in Feature 1 in Excavation Block 1 at Energy Park.

Figure 13.15. Cahokia tri-notched projectile point found in Unit 273 in Excavation Block 4 at Energy Park. Staff photo, Institute for Minnesota Archaeology.

lived. This hypothesis is supported by the site's low artifact density when compared to other Silvernale phase sites in the area, the relatively clear patterning visible from the controlled surface collection, and the near absence of subsurface feature-overlap.

An Interpretation of the Mississippian Presence in the Red Wing Area

Although the authors of this paper disagree on details of the Mississippian presence in the Red Wing area, they do agree on the broad outlines of this presence. This broad outline will be sketched first. A few of its main contentions will then be defended or briefly elaborated.

Our understanding of the Mississippian presence in the Red Wing area can be summarized in four claims. First, the Red Wing area was inhabited by Oneota peoples before the appearance of the Mississippian-related Silvernale cultural complex. This pre-Silvernale Oneota occupation began ca. A.D. 1000 and is represented by Bartron, possibly the Adams and Double sites, and possibly the Oneota component in the northwest corner of Bryan. Second, the Silvernale cultural complex emerged in the late eleventh or in the twelfth century as an amalgam of Oneota and Mississippian traits. Dobbs would bracket the presence of this com-

plex in the Red Wing area between ca. A.D. 1175 and A.D. 1300, while Gibbon prefers a short occupation period beginning ca. A.D. 1100. Within this time span, changes occurred in the Silvernale settlement-subsistence system and in its artifactual assemblage, but the cultural complex always differed in certain important respects from both 'pure' Cahokia-centered and Oneota complexes. Third, the Silvernale cultural complex functioned as a prairie-oriented northern node in a Mississippian-centered extraction and magico-religious network (e.g., Gibbon 1974). Fourth, the complex ceased to exist sometime in the thirteenth century, if not earlier, probably in response to the demise of Cahokia as a major center and the collapse of its far flung economic-religious network. The Red Wing area was abandoned, apparently experiencing little more than transient occupation until the arrival of the Santee Dakota in the seventeenth century. Although Oneota peoples had occupied the Blue Earth Valley before these events, the focus of Oneota activity in the state shifted to this south-central Minnesota river valley in the thirteenth or early fourteenth century.

Stoltman (1986:29-32) has argued that Silvernale, Bryan, and Diamond Bluff represent a pre-Oneota complex in the Red Wing locality, one reflecting cultural interaction between the Cahokia cultural province and local Late Woodland peoples. In his view, "the first fully Oneota assemblages post-date A.D. 1075 or 1100," with the real prominence of Oneota culture occurring only after the waning of Cahokia influence in the region after ca. A.D. 1200. We and others are taken to task for adopting the view "that Oneota origins were not in any way correlated with the spread of Cahokia influences into the Upper Mississippi Valley during the Lohman/Stirling phases," that is, for not adopting the view that Oneota origins have their roots in the movements of peoples and/or ideas out of "the great Middle Mississippi center of Cahokia in the American Bottom" (ibid.).

A careful reading of the literature should convince the reader that the origins of Oneota culture remain an unresolved problem (e.g., Gibbon 1972, 1982; Dobbs 1982; Stoltman 1983:230-242; Benn 1984). There is general agreement, however, that Oneota emergence was largely an in situ process involving Late Woodland peoples. Debate focuses on the dynamics of this process and (especially) on the role played by the Cahokia cultural system in this transformation.

Our position can be quickly summarized. We believe that regarding the Cahokia cultural system as the sole source of the transformation throughout the northern periphery fails to distinguish between two widespread and equally important transformations. These transformations occurred in the northern tier of the eastern United States and in adjacent portions of the Plains and Canada during the A.D. 800-1200 interval. The first involved the emergence of what might loosely be called 'horticultural lifeways,' and the second a process of 'mississippianization.' We regard the emergence of Oneota culture as a phenomenon of the first transformation, just as we regard Mill Creek, Great Oasis, Fort Ancient, the Iroquoian cultures, and the Cahokia cultural system itself, for example, as products of this transformation. The second transformation, of which the Cahokia cultural system was a florescence, was centered within the Upper Mississippi Valley. By failing to pay sufficient attention to the broader context out of which the Cahokia cultural system itself emerged, one conflates, in our opinion, the process of 'mississippianization' and the geographically more extensive and in general earlier transformation to a horticultural lifeway. Each requires, again in our opinion, a separate if somewhat intertwined explanation. As a consequence of this conflation, one is unable to ask, 'What was the nature of the interaction between Cahokia-related populations and the Oneota (and the Mill Creek and Fort Ancient people, and so on) '? Our position—that early Oneota developed coevally with and interacted with Mississippian cultures in the Upper Mississippi Valley—remains a working-hypothesis, but a hypothesis, nonetheless, that does justice to our data base by not requiring us to reject all Oneota radiocarbon dates before A.D. 1075 or 1100 (Stoltman 1986:33). We do agree, however, that Oneota culture surged southward after A.D. 1200 into southwestern Wisconsin (e.g., the La Crosse area), Iowa, and Illinois. We assume that it is the late entry of Oneota people in these southern areas, where Stoltman and others who maintain that Oneota emerged as a result of Mississippian (Cahokia) contact work, that accounts in part for their position.

We should add that the evidence for a vigorous Late Woodland presence in the Red Wing area remains meager at the present time, perhaps because of the more mobile lifeway of Late Woodland peoples in the region. As we demonstrated earlier, Late Woodland ceramics are either absent or rare at Bryan, Silvernale, Bartron, Adams, and Energy Park. Harrison's (1981) survey for the Minnesota Historical Society in 1978 discovered only a light scatter of Late Woodland sites, a phenomenon also documented by Dobb's (1985a) more recent surveys. The only examples of a Late Woodland presence that possibly supports Stoltman's model of cultural interaction between the Cahokia cultural province and local Late Woodland peoples are the content of several burial mounds (Maxwell 1950; Johnson et al. 1969), but the non-Woodland portions of these mound inclusions do not seem to represent 'pure' Cahokia-derived assemblages. The publication in detail of the University of Wisconsin-Milwaukee's early 1970s excavations at the Mero site and the IMA's planned 1991 excavations at the site might help resolve this problem. Since the focus of this paper is the nature of the Mississippian presence in the Red Wing area, we will forego comment on the relationship between Oneota and Late Woodland cultures in the area.

We believe that the brief review of the Silvernale phase artifact assemblage provided in the last section is sufficient to demonstrate that it differs from Cahokia and Oneota assemblages, that it is in fact an amalgam of the two. This is especially apparent in the ceramic assemblage, which is an unusual blend of Oneota and Cahokia sphere inspired stylistic traits. Although the evidence remains tenuous, we believe it is sufficient to argue that this amalgam resulted from the transformation of a resident Oneota population through Mississippian contact.

We see the presence of a small amount of Middle Mississippian material and the flat-topped conical mound at Bartron, as well as the chunky stones at Adams, as possible indicators of contact with the Cahokia sphere. Contact was initiated and the transformation to the Silvernale cultural system completed sometime within the A.D. 1050-1200 interval. Although some Middle Mississippian peoples most likely participated in this transformation (some of the possibilities are reviewed below), we find no evidence, as yet, for a site-unit intrusion by a 'pure' Middle Mississippian group. Classic Powell Plain and Ramey Incised vessels, for example, are rare and scattered at both Bryan and Silvernale, and wall-trench structures, tri-notched points, Cahokia hoes, and a host of other items are either absent (which is usually the case) or even rarer than the vessels.

In addition we fail to see, as yet, any specific functional context for materials and traits derived from the Cahokia sphere; they appear jumbled in the midden and in pits with a range of other traits and materials. Still, the life-histories of Silvernale phase sites remain poorly known and, as a result, subject to varying interpretations. As mentioned, we disagree on the time span within which the Silvernale cultural complex dominated the Red Wing area. What we do see, however, is: (1) a few 'classic' Ramey Incised and Powell Plain vessels; (2) a predominant amount of locally made pottery emulating Middle Mississippian forms and decorations; (3) the presence of only a few Middle Mississippian stone artifacts (mainly chunky stones and tri-notched points); (4) some elements of a Mississippian settlement pattern and village organization; (5) an iconography (Southeast Ceremonial Complex) and platform mounds reflecting some aspects of Mississippian religious beliefs (though the associations of the iconography could be more diverse in the upper Midwest); (6) an array of Oneota traits, including ceramic traits, the bone-antler-tooth complex, and a high proportion of chipped stone scrapers.

Since a working-model of Cahokia-Red Wing interaction has been presented in some detail elsewhere (Gibbon 1974, 1979), only an overview of this model will be presented here. In brief the Silvernale phase has been interpreted as a prairie-oriented node in a Cahokia sphere economic-religious network. The purpose of this network was extraction of resources from peripheral areas. The Silvernale node articulated with Cambria peoples along the trench of the Minnesota River. These western peoples may have provided dried buffalo meat and other items for the network. They may also have acted as middlemen, connecting the Silvernale node with other Initial Middle Missouri Tradition peoples still farther to the west. We find the presence of Cambria ware, Plains side-notched points, and semi-subterranean house forms in major Silvernale phase sites, as well as the presence of both Middle Mississippian-inspired and Initial Middle Missouri Tradition ceramics at the Cambria site itself, as possible support for this model. The presence at some Cambria sites of unusual amounts of bison bone, and of extensive bone and scraper complexes at both Silvernale phase sites and Cambria, suggests that dried buffalo meat, as mentioned above, worked skins, and other items may have been entering the network from the north. This model has not, however, been adequately tested as yet by new field excavations. Elden Johnson's paper in this volume provides additional thoughts on the possible role that Cambria may have played within a Cahokia sphere extraction system.

Cahokia-Inspired Contact Situations: An Evalution

What conclusions can be drawn from these data and interpretations as regards Stoltman's four Cahokia-inspired contact situations? First, the only one of the four options that can be clearly rejected is a site-unit intrusion of Late Woodland emissaries. Second, a 'pure' Middle Mississippian intrusion into a non-Mississippian area also seems unlikely, if by this is meant a site-unit intrusion into a Late Woodland geographic area. Extensive surveys have failed to isolate anything at all that resembles an assemblage of this nature with the possible exception of some mound inclusions. Nonetheless, the possibility remains that a small and as yet undetected 'pure' Middle Mississippian component could be present at one or more sites. Dobb's surveys should resolve this issue within the next few years.

Having voiced this caution, it seems clear to us that the existing evidence best supports some version of one of the remaining contact situations, that is, "culture contact without permanent population displacement, probably involving trade" or "an intrusion of a Middle Mississippi population segment, perhaps an elite, into the Cahokia hinterland." Since, as stated, these options are not logically exclusive (there could, for instance, have been an amalgamation of an intrusive population segment and a hinterland group for purposes of trade that did not involve permanent population displacement), we will interpret the two options as implying that a Mississippian population segment was either present or not.

Evidence can be marshalled to support either of the latter options. The first option is supported by the presence of Cahokia sphere traits (small amounts of Ramey Incised and Powell Plain pottery, some tri-notched points, the flat-topped pyramidal mound, the Mississippian flavor of the settlement-subsistence system) and the possible presence of a southern physical type at Bryan (Glenn 1974). The contact-for-trade-without-population-intrusion scenario is supported, on the other hand, by the absence of numerous other Cahokia sphere traits (wall-trench structures, Cahokia hoes, plates and a variety of other ceramic items, the Cahokia sphere lithic assemblage, and so on), the curious blend of ceramic stylistic traits, the continuity of regional Oneota bone-antler-tooth and lithic assemblages, and the presence of flat-topped conical mounds.

The contact situation we favor is a version of the first of these two options. According to this version, a local Oneota population was heavily influenced by the Cahokia cultural system; this influence included the movement into the Red Wing area of a Middle Mississippian population segment and an amalgamation of this segment with at least some portion of its resident Oneota population. There is no evidence, as yet, to support the contention that this segment was an elite or largely an elite. For instance, neither elite class Middle Mississippian mortuary structures nor other indicators of the presence of a socially stratified Middle Mississippian society have been found (but note Dobb's hypothesis that Energy Park may have been occupied by a Silvernale phase elite). One possibility worth exploring is that this segment was composed largely of women; this would help explain the strong Mississippian flavor of the ceramic assemblage. We find it difficult to believe that this assemblage could result from distant trading contacts alone. Whatever the answer, while the Silvernale system disappeared at about the same time as the demise of Cahokia, Oneota peoples continued to flourish in the Upper Mississippi River Valley.

Our interpretations constitute a rough-edged working model whose function is to direct research. It should be clear that we still lack a highly confirmed picture of what happened in the Red Wing area during the A.D. 900-1300 interval. The captious reader will have little difficulty in unraveling our model, for loose-ends abound. For instance, the nature of the Late Woodland occupation of the area remains largely unknown; the dynamics leading to the presence of Oneota peoples at Bartron, Adams, and other sites remain a matter of speculation; the internal histories of all sites remain largely opaque; it remains unclear whether some Oneota and Silvernale phase settlements were contemporaneous or not; although a model of Silvernale interaction within the region has been presented, it remains untested. The strong research program currently underway in the Red Wing Locality should continue to provide new data to resolve the differences between these competing models of the Middle Mississippian presence in the region.

Acknowledgements

Funding for the 1983-1984 Bryan Data Recovery Project was provided by the Minnesota Department of Transportation. Additional funds were provided by the Minnesota Historical Society. Funding for the investigations at the Energy Park Site were provided by The Red Wing Area Fund, The City of Red Wing, and private patrons., Investigations at the Adams Site were funded by a survey planning grant from the National Park Service through the State Historical Society of Wisconsin. Funding for the City of Red Wing Survey was provided by the Legislative Commission on Minnesota Resources and the City of Red Wing. Additional funding and support for all of these projects was provided by the Institute for Minnesota Archaeology.

References Cited

Benn, D. W.

1984 *Excavations at the Christenson Site (13PK407), Central Des Moines River Valley, Iowa.* U. S. Army Corps of Engineers Contract Report DACW25-82-0049. Rock Island District.

Binford, L. R.

1967 Smudge Pits and Hide Smoking: The Use of Analogy in Archaeological Reasoning. *American Antiquity* 32:1-12.

Brower, Jacob V.

1903 *Memoirs of Explorations in the Basin of the Mississippi*, vol. VI, Minnesota. H. L. Collins Co., St. Paul.

Dobbs, Clark A.

1982 Oneota Origins and Development: The Radiocarbon Evidence. In *Oneota Studies*, edited by Guy E. Gibbon, pp. 91-105. University of Minnesota Publications in Anthropology, No. 1. University of Minnesota, Minneapolis.

1984 *Oneota Settlement Patterns in the Blue Earth River Valley, Minnesota.* Ph.D. thesis. University of Minnesota.

1985a *An Archaeological Survey of the City of Red Wing, Minnesota.* Reports of Investigations No. 2. Institute for Minnesota Archaeology, Minneapolis.

1985b Excavations at the Bryan Site: 1983-1984. *Minnesota Archaeologist*, 43:49-58.

1986a *Wisconsin Mounds Recorded by the Northwestern Archaeological Survey and an Evaluation of the Adams Site (47PI12).* Reports of Investigations No. 7. Institute for Minnesota Archaeology, Minneapolis.

1986b *A Preliminary Report on Investigations at the Energy Park Site (21GD158).* Reports of Investigations No. 16. Institute for Minnesota Archaeology, Minneapolis.

1987 *Archaeological Investigations at the Bryan Site (21GD4). Goodhue County, Minnesota: 1983-1984.* Reports of Investigations No. 8. Institute for Minnesota Archaeology, Minneapolis.

Dobbs, Clark A. and Kim Breakey

1987 A Preliminary Report on Investigations at the Energy Park Site (21GD158): A Silvernale Phase Village at the Lake Pepin Locality. Paper presented at the 1987 Midwest Archaeological Conference, October 1987, Milwaukee.

Gibbon, Guy E.

1972 Cultural Dynamics and the development of the Oneota Life-Way in Wisconsin. *American Antiquity*, 37 (2): 166-185.

1974 A Model of Mississippian Development and Its Implications for the Red Wing Area. In *Aspects of Great Lakes Anthropology*, edited by E. Johnson, pp. 129-137. Minnesota Prehistoric Archaeology Series, No. 11. Minnesota Historical Society, St. Paul.

1979 *The Mississippian Occupation of the Red Wing Area*. Minnesota Prehistoric Archaeology Series, No. 13. Minnesota Historical Society, St. Paul.

1982 Oneota Origins Revisited. In *Oneota Studies*, edited by Guy E. Gibbon, pp. 85-89. University of Minnesota Publications in Anthropology, No. 1. University of Minnesota, Minneapolis.

1991 The Middle Mississippian Presence in Minnesota. In *Cahokia and the Hinterlands*, edited by Barry Lewis and Thomas B. Emerson, pp. 206-220. University of Illinois Press, Urbana.

Glenn, Elizabeth

1974 *Physical Afflictions of the Oneota Peoples*. Report No. 7, Office of the State Archaeologist. University of Iowa, Iowa City.

Harrison, Christina

1981 An Archaeological Survey of Dakota and Goodhue Counties, Minnesota. Manuscript notes. Minnesota Statewide Archaeological Survey. Minnesota Historical Society, St. Paul.

Hurley, William M.

1978 The Armstrong Site: A Silvernale Phase Oneota Village in Wisconsin. *Wisconsin Archaeologist*, 51 (1): 1-145.

Johnson, E., M. Q. Peterson, and J. Streiff

1969 Birch Lake Burial Mound Group. *Journal of the Minnesota Academy of Science*, 36 (1): 3-8.

Kane, L. M., J. D. Holmquist, and C. Gilman

1978 *The Northern Expeditions of Stephen H. Long*. Minnesota Historical Society, St. Paul.

Klein, J., J. C. Lerman, P. E. Damon, and E. K. Ralph

1982 Calibration of Radio Carbon Dates. *Radiocarbon* 24 (2): 103-150.

Maxwell, Moreau S.

1950 A Change in the Interpretation of Wisconsin's Prehistory. *Wisconsin Magazine of History* 33: 427-443.

Shane III, Orrin C.

1981 *Radiocarbon Chronology for the Late-Prehistoric Period in Southern Minnesota*. American Philosophical Society Yearbook.

Stevenson, K. P.

1985 *Oneota Subsistence-Related Behavior in the Driftless Area: A Study of the Valley View Site Near La Crosse, Wisconsin*. Ph.D. thesis. University of Wisconsin-Madison.

Stoltman, James B.

1983 Ancient Peoples of the Upper Mississippi River Valley. In *Historic Lifestyles in the Upper Mississippi River Valley*, edited by John Wozniak, pp. 197-255. University Press of America, New York.

1986 The Appearance of the Mississippian Cultural Tradition in the Upper Mississippi Valley. In *Prehistoric Mound Builders of the Mississippi Valley*, edited by J. B. Stoltman, pp. 26-34. The Putnam Museum, Davenport, Iowa.

Stortroen, C. E.

1957 *The Bryan Site: A Prehistoric Village in Southern Minnesota*. Master's thesis, University of Minnesota.

1985 The Bryan Site: A Prehistoric Village in Southern Minnesota. *Minnesota Archaeologist*, 43: 37-48.

Wilford, Lloyd A.

1952 The Silvernale Mound and Village Site. Ms. on file, Department of Anthropology, University of Minnesota, Minneapolis.

1955 A Revised Classification of the Prehistoric Cultures of Minnesota. *American Antiquity* 21:130-142.

1956 The Ralph Bryan Site (1951-1952). Ms. on file, Department of Anthropology, University of Minnesota, Minneapolis.

1958 The Ralph Bryan Site (1955 and 1957). Ms. on file, Department of Anthropology, University of Minnesota, Minneapolis.

1985 The Ralph Bryan Site, 1951-1952. *Minnesota Archaeologist*, 43: 21-36.

n.d. The Bartron Site. Ms. on file, Department of Anthropology, University of Minnesota, Minneapolis.

Winchell, N. H.

1911 *The Aborigines of Minnesota*. Minnesota Historical Society, St. Paul.

14

Cambria and Cahokia's Northwestern Periphery

Elden Johnson
Institute for Minnesota Archaeology

The Cambria phase of western Minnesota is best known from published data on a single site located on a Minnesota River terrace some 80km west of Silvernale phase sites in the Red Wing area of eastern Minnesota and 150km northeast of the Mill Creek sites of northwestern Iowa. Previous analyses of the Cambria site all suggest a relationship with Cahokia as seen in the ceramic assemblage but leave that relationship undefined (Wilford 1945; Knudson 1967).

This paper reviews the published data on the Cambria site, summarizes relevant data on other sites grouped in the Cambria phase, and places the Cambria phase in its temporal and geographic setting. The purpose is to define its relationship to Cahokia through a review of the settlement and subsistence patterns, ceramics, lithics, human burial practices, the interrelationships among sites grouped in the Cambria phase, and their role in a Cahokia-based trade network.

Sites of the Cambria phase can be grouped into four categories: 1) large village sites on Minnesota River terraces, 2) smaller Minnesota River or tributary-situated sites located near the large village sites, 3) upland prairie-lake and riverine sites, and 4) burial sites. The two large village sites are the Cambria site (21BE2) and the Gillingham site (21YM3); the smaller adjacent village sites are the Owen Jones site (21BE2), the Price site (21BE36), and the Gautefeld site (21YM1) (Figure 14.1). None of the reports on the latter sites has been published. Sites in the third and fourth categories are numerous and are not listed individually, except as referred to later.

Placement of the Cambria phase in time is secure with the publication of radiocarbon dates on charred wood from the Cambria and Price sites. Those dates are A.D. 1135± 125 (GX6778) and A.D. 1175±130 for the Cambria site; A.D. 950±80 (I-8883), A.D. 1105±80 (I-8881), and A.D. 1065±80 (I-8882) for the Price site (Shane 1980). Mean dates thus range from A.D. 950 to A.D. 1175, all but the earliest date within the range of the Stirling and Moorhead phases at Cahokia (Fowler and Hall 1972). The cultural classificatory placement of the Cambria phase in the Initial Middle Missouri Tradition is clearly demonstrated in Tiffany's recent (1983) work. The Mill Creek sites and the Over focus sites are contemporary, as are those of the Silvernale phase in the Red Wing area, which Shane (1980), on the basis of radiocarbon age determinations, places between A.D. 1000 and 1300.

The antecedent Woodland cultures of the region show considerable stability in settlement pattern and subsistence through the Fox Lake and Lake Benton phases. Shane (1982) and Anfinson (1982) discuss some aspects of this stable pattern that includes larger villages located on prairie lake islands and peninsulas and on smaller Minnesota River tributaries, though rarely in the Minnesota River Valley itself. The subsistence pattern is dominated by bison hunting but with a supplementary range of utilization of smaller mammals, fish, and waterfowl (Shane 1982:47; Anfinson 1982:67). There is little evidence of plant

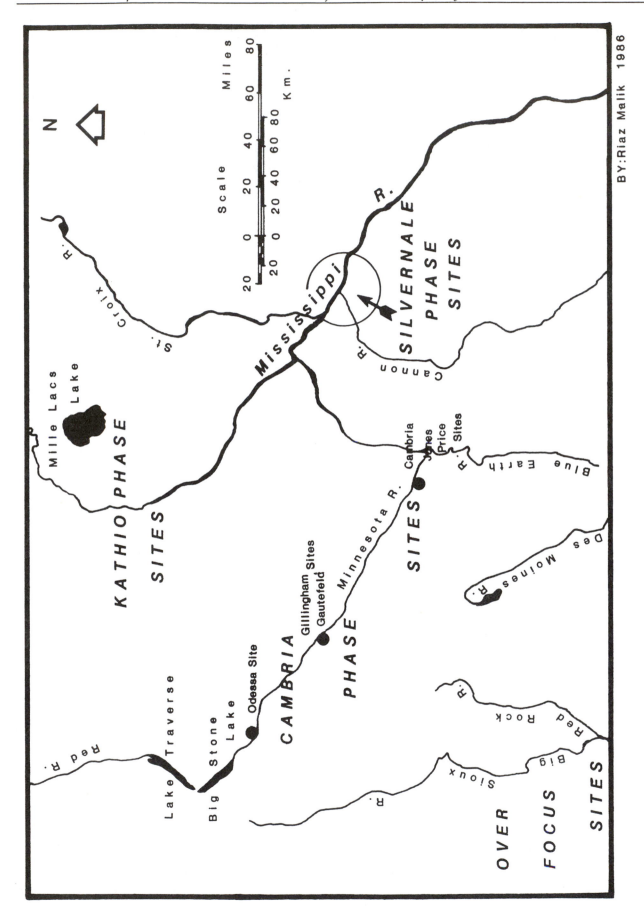

Figure 14.1. Map of Cambria Phase sites.

utilization, probably a function of the lack of small scale recovery techniques in the earlier excavations, and there is no evidence that horticulture was present. Burial in earthen mounds was practiced, with the burial mode dominated by secondary bundle burial.

The ceramics of the late prehistoric Lake Benton phase of the prairie region south and southwest of the Minnesota River are grit-tempered, globular vessels with cordmarked exterior surfaces, straight to slightly flared rims, and cordwrapped dowel decoration on the exterior rim. Anfinson labels these as Lake Benton Cord Wrapped Stick Impressed and Lake Benton Vertical Cord Marked (1982:110). A radiocarbon date from the Pederson site (21LN2) of A.D. 1245± 80 (Hudak 1974; 1976:3) indicates the contemporaneity of the upland populations with the Cambria developments in the Minnesota River Valley.

The Woodland cultures of the Kathio phase in the prairie region north of the Minnesota River Valley are less well known, though similar subsistence and burial patterns are present. The ceramics in the late prehistoric period of that region are Kathio (Wilford 1955) and Onamia (Bleed 1969). Vessel form is like that of the Lake Benton Series, temper is grit, exterior surface treatment is cord marking, and exterior rim decoration is cordwrapped dowel. Rim form, decorative motifs, and lip treatment differentiate Kathio and Onamia ceramics from Lake Benton.

Cambria phase sites are located in the prairie region of western Minnesota, a region of low relief glacial moraine, and outwash, once dotted with small lakes and sloughs, now mostly drained for agriculture. The tall grass and wet prairie vegetation was interrupted by arboreal vegetation on fire-shielded shores of lakes and by riverine gallery forests. Tree species included oak, cottonwood, box elder, and willow as the most numerous forms.

Through this prairie region flows the Minnesota River, moving southeast from its source at the outlet of Big Stone Lake on the South Dakota-Minnesota border to a point midway in the state where it turns northeast to join the Mississippi River at Ft. Snelling. The present river is a small stream that meanders through wide bottom lands in a valley that is in some places 5km wide and over 60m deep. After the river has turned northeast, and only a few kilometers east of the Cambria site, the vegetation pattern changes to a mosaic of forest and prairie openings in a region in historic times dominated by the maple-basswood "Big Woods". Grim (1985) has shown that the extensive Big Woods is historic in origin and suggested that it developed as a result of the discontinuance of burning practices that had their origins in the late prehistoric period.

On the Minnesota River slopes leading to the uplands, occasional remnants of a four-terrace system are found, and it is on these terraces that the two large and the four smaller Cambria habitation sites are located.

Relationships to Cahokia and the questions of the origins of the Cambria phase can best be seen in the archaeological record from the Cambria site. The majority of the data on the site come from the excavations of William B. Nickerson, who worked at the site in 1913 and again in 1916 under the auspices of the Minnesota Historical Society and under the direction of Warren Upham and N. H. Winchell, the latter the state geologist at the University of Minnesota. Nickerson's written excavation report, together with his site assemblage, remain in the Historical Society collections. Lloyd Wilford excavated at the site in 1938 and again in 1947. His data are in the University of Minnesota collections. Wilford published a summary of his Cambria data (1945a) in a paper comparing Cambria with what was then known of Great Oasis and Blue Earth Oneota of south central Minnesota. Wilford, in that paper, provided the first broad typology of Cambria ceramics. Ruthann Knudson (1967), who provided a detailed analysis of the ceramics, and Watrall (1968), who analyzed the bone, shell, and lithic artifacts, used the combined Nickerson and Wilford collections.

The Cambria site is built upon a projecting terrace nose some 20m above the valley floor (Figure 14.2). The limits of the site toward the interior of the terrace have not been determined, but Nickerson noted (1917:3) that though he began his excavations "... at what looked like a wall, nothing indicative of timbers or posts was found, and Mr. Jones (the property owner) thought the appearance of a wall was due to the making of a 'dead furrow' in cultivating the land". Such a protective device was mapped at the other large Cambria site, Gillingham, by T. H. Lewis in 1883 (Figure 14.3). Should the present owners of the Cambria site allow further excavation at some time in the future, it is probable that subsurface evidence of a palisade line would be found.

Knudson's type-variety ceramic analysis defines 4 types and 12 varieties. The preponderant varieties are Linden Everted Rim, accounting for 60+% of the 1,128 rim sherds analyzed. Linden Everted and its varieties are Initial Middle Missouri similar to Chamberlain ceramics (Knudson 1967:263-267; Figure 14.4, a-c). Her Judson Composite type, constituting only 12% of the total, shows an interesting combination of Missouri River and Over focus S-shaped rims on vessels with angular shoulders and chevron or curvilinear design (Figure 14.4, e-f). Most important for this paper are the rolled rim vessels that are varieties of Ramey Incised and Powell Plain—here labeled Ramey Broad Trailed: New Ulm variety

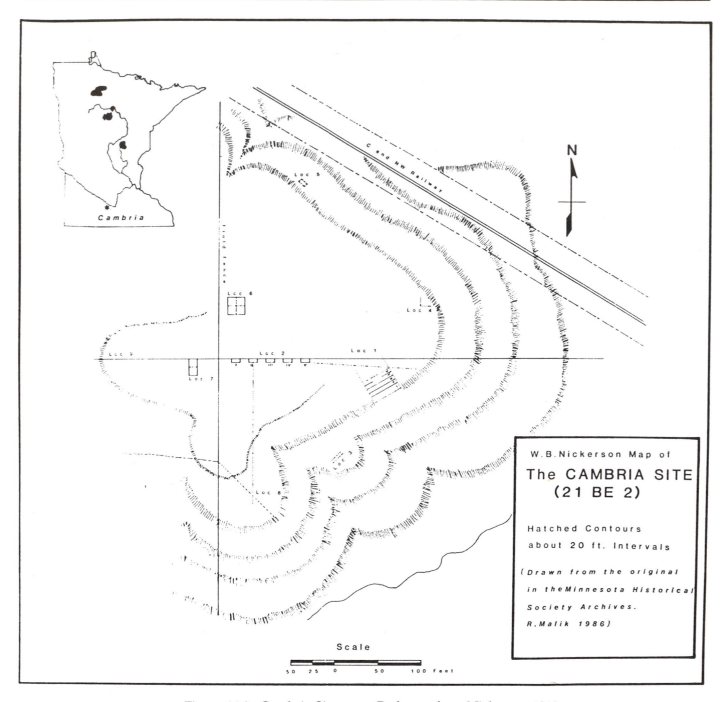

Figure 14.2. Cambria Site map. Redrawn from Nickerson 1913.

(Figure 14.5), and Powell Plain. These types constitute 14.5% by sherd count and 14.6% by vessel count
of the total ceramic assemblage. That these vessels
are locally made is clear. They have a crushed granite, grit temper, and while the exterior surfaces are
smooth, and occasionally burnished in the area from
the shoulder to the neck, the surface below the shoulder is, in most cases, characterized by smoothed over
cord marking. Wilford noted the local character of

the rolled rim ceramics when he stated that
"Cambria is not a Middle Mississippian site, and type
C pottery is not a Middle Mississippian pottery, for it
is grit- rather than shell-tempered" (1945a:39).
Knudson reaffirms this when she states that
"...Cambria ceramics from southern Minnesota are
overwhelmingly Middle Missouri-like and appear to
provide an eastern boundary for that tradition"
(Knudson 1967:280).

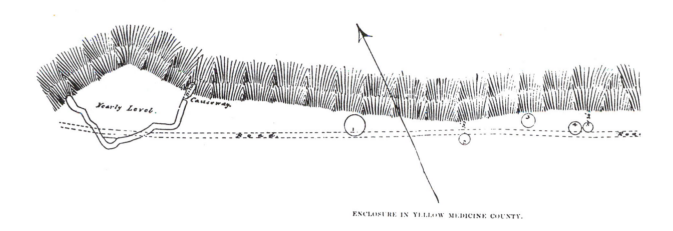

Figure 14.3. T. H. Lewis map of the Gillingham Site. From Winchell 1911:110-117.

The Cambria site is unique among the others classed in the Cambria phase, for it is only at this easternmost site that sherds representing Knudson's Ramey Broad Trailed or Wilford's Type C are found.

The lithic assemblage shows even less interaction with Middle Mississippian. Of the 153 projectile points that were complete, only 4, or 2.5% of the total, are tri-notched. Some 37+% are small, straight-based, side-notched points of the kind described by Kehoe (1966:123), while the majority are small un-notched triangles (Watrall 1968:9-11). The materials from which these points are made are local cherts, true also of most of the other lithic artifacts. Of the 280 end scrapers and side scrapers, for example, only six are of Knife River flint, two of local Sioux quartzites, and none is made of the quartzites seen in some frequency in the knives and scrapers of the Red Wing area. The other Minnesota River Valley Cambria sites lack the tri-notched points and, like Cambria, utilize local cherts and red quartzites as raw material.

Watrall (1974) describes the subsistence pattern at the Cambria site to be one of maize horticulture, growing a flint variety, with a dependence upon large game resources dominated by bison, deer, and elk. A large number of faunal species from river bottom habitats is also represented, though remains of other plant domesticates and flora from the native vegetation do not appear in the assemblage. He correctly attributed this to the lack of small-scale recovery methods in the early excavation (1974:141). Another horticultural marker at Cambria is the bison scapula hoes (N=21), an artifact type that is also western in origin.

Human burials are not found in the Cambria site nor are they found in the other sites of the phase. Near each Minnesota Valley Cambria site is a series of small circular burial mounds, some of which are of Cambria phase origin. Mound 1 of the Lewis group (21BE6) near the Cambria site produced five extended primary burials on the subsoil or in a shallow pit in the subsoil. While Mound 2 of the group produced only 2 human vertebrae and no complete burial, 14 grit-tempered, smooth-surfaced body sherds were found, as were two miniature mortuary vessels, one with a rolled rim and a second with an extruded beveled lip decorated by incised cross hatching (Wilford 1956).

In an earlier paper (Johnson 1961), I described the Miller Mound (21BS4), Schoen Mound No. 1 (21BS2), and Schoen Mound No. 2 (21BS1) located near the headwaters of the Minnesota River, which were exca-

Figure 14.4. Linden Everted Rim and Judson Composite Types. (a) Linden Variety (Cambria Site); (b) Searles Variety, interior rim view (Cambria Site); (c) Nicollet Variety (Cambria Site); (d, f) Judson Composite vessel, 2 views (Cambria Site); (e) Cottonwood Variety (Silvernale Site).

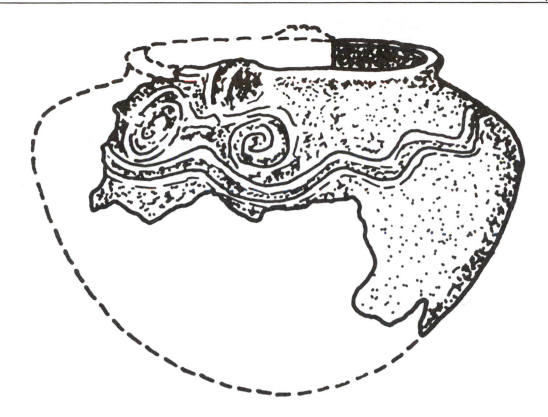

Figure 14.5. Ramey Broad Trailed: New Ulm Variety.

vated earlier by Wilford and attributed by him to Cambria: "At Big Stone Lake some of the Mounds contain primary burials. A few Cambria sherds were found in one of these, and another contained a small mortuary pot of Cambria type with loop handles" (1955:139). I suggested at that time that the Schoen mounds, which had been mapped by T.H. Lewis, who described them as circular with flat tops, represented a more widely distributed Cambria form. Over 80 mounds of that form were mapped by Lewis in his surveys, and the distribution of mounds of that form coincides with the distribution of Cambria phase sites (Johnson 1961:72).

Most suggestive of a Middle Mississippian affinity is the truncated, four-sided, pyramidal structure mapped by Lewis at the Odessa site (Figure 14.6). This site is on the northeast side of the Minnesota River Valley on the 20m terrace. At the time it was mapped, the pyramidal structure measured 54' by 42' at the base and had a flat top measuring 20' by 28'. No elevation is given. An associated long embankment measured 722' long, 20' wide, and 1 1/2 to 2' in height. Unfortunately, the mounds have been destroyed, and the area is now the playground for the Odessa town school.

Further testing of the proposition that these flat topped mounds are associated with Cambria and rep-

resent a distant version of a Cahokia pattern is impossible now given the prohibition on mound excavation in Minnesota.

The data from the Cambria site itself, and, as will be seen later, data from other Cambria sites, suggest that settlement growth on river valley terraces was probably associated with the development of maize horticulture and the need for alluvial soils that could be cleared for gardens. Accompanying this new settlement-subsistence trend was the modification of Late Woodland ceramic styles into Initial Middle Missouri types, a shift in burial mode to extended primary burials, sometimes with associated mortuary vessels, continuation of the bison hunting systems that dominated the subsistence practices of the Woodland cultures of the region, and a persistence of smaller upland settlements. All of the evidence points to the development of those Cambria villages from regional Woodland antecedents. The source of these changes, given the Initial Middle Missouri affinities of Cambria, would appear to have been Middle Mississippi culture, perhaps via Mill Creek (Ives 1962; Tiffany 1983) and the localized Great Oasis developments of extreme southwestern Minnesota and adjacent southeastern South Dakota (Wilford 1945).

Cambria phase sites, both in the Minnesota River Valley and in the uplands, are grouped in the phase

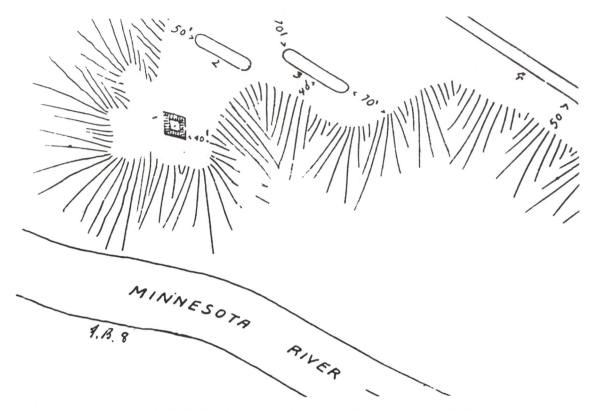

Figure 14.6. T. H. Lewis map of the Odessa Site. From Winchell 1911:121.

on the basis of Initial Middle Missouri ceramics, predominantly varieties of the Linden type that occur with high frequency at the Cambria site. The Gillingham site, located on a high south bank terrace immediately below Granite Falls and the confluence of the Yellow Medicine and Minnesota Rivers, was tested in the 1940s by Lloyd Wilford (1948). Mapped by T. H. Lewis in the 19th century, he indicated a transverse ridge and depression inland from the terrace point that appears to be a palisade. Wilford's excavations were frustrating to him in that the site had been severely disturbed by house construction associated with the nearby Riggs-Williamson Upper Sioux Agency Mission of the 19th century. The minimal excavations provided no evidence of structures or storage pits. Linden, Chamberlain, and Mitchell ceramics were found associated with some "Woodland" forms of Lake Benton varieties. There are no Ramey varieties as seen at the Cambria site, and no scapula hoes were found. The site no longer exits because of recent gravel pit operations, thus the function of the site and its role in the proposed trade network must remain speculative.

The nearby Gautefeld site is located at the juncture of Spring Creek and the Yellow Medicine River, slightly upstream from the juncture of the latter stream with the Minnesota River. Wilford's (1953)

unpublished report on Gautefeld describes the presence of two components separated horizontally, with Blue Earth phase materials on a low area below a small, low terrace or ridge that produced Woodland and Initial Middle Missouri ceramics. Wilford lists general Cambria (Linden) ceramics as comprising 70.5% of the total from the surface collection in the possession of the farmer, but only 50% of the 131 sherd total from his excavations. He found no Ramey-like sherds, but noted a few in the surface collection—warning the reader that Gautefeld, the owner, had collected at the Cambria site and that his material from that site and his own cultivated fields were mixed and not identified as to source.

The two secondary sites located within a few kilometers of the Cambria site are the Price site and the Owen D. Jones site. The former is located on a high Minnesota River terrace extending slightly upstream in the Morgan Creek Valley at the juncture of that stream with the Minnesota River. The Price site has not been published but is described as Cambria (Shane 1980). The small Owen D. Jones site, located on a high terrace near the Cambria site, was excavated by Wilford in 1941. His site report (1950b) describes all of the 347 sherds as Cambria type A using his nomenclature, or Linden varieties, using Knudson's more detailed typology. Only seven projectile points were found, three are Eastern triangular, one is side-notched, and three are broken and cannot be classed. As at Gautefeld, no storage pits, scapula hoes, or other evidence of horticulture were found.

These Minnesota River Valley or adjacent tributary sites are all located on the southwest side of the river trench. All are located at or near the juncture of larger tributary streams that flow northeast to the large valley and drain the prairie uplands. The two large sites appear to be defensively located, each with one or more nearby small sites. Of these, the Cambria site itself is best known archaeologically and is distinctive in that it is the only site that has Ramey-like ceramics, numerous storage pits, and tri-notched triangular points. It is the most easterly of sites in the Cambria phase.

The relationship of the smaller valley Cambria sites to Cambria and Gillingham is conjectural. They may represent early developments in the movement of upland populations into the valley or they may represent what Watrall (1974) suggests as a budding off of segments of the Cambria and Gillingham populations with population growth associated with an intensification of horticulture. The lack of chronological controls prevents a solution to this question at the present time.

The upland sites with Initial Middle Missouri components are numerous, and most occur on Fox Lake and Lake Benton phase sites that continue to be occupied during the Cambria phase. The extension of Cambria sites of this sort into the headwaters area of the Minnesota River to the northwest and thence to both east and west sides of Lakes Big Stone and Traverse (Streiff 1972) is seen at sites such as Stielow (21BS14), Artichoke Island (21BS23), Strader (21TR9), Browns Valley (21TR5), and at Hartford Beach (Haug 1982) on the west side of Big Stone Lake. Anfinson (1982:67) suggests that most of these sites were "warm season" sites on the basis of the faunal assemblages, with movement of these groups to sheltered river valleys and more heavily timbered regions during the winter season. Evidence for this pattern and for upland bison kill and processing sites here is lacking, a function of the lack of research toward those ends. Upland bison kill and processing sites may be difficult to identify and associate with phases identified by ceramics, but the effort should be made.

I also suggest that if Cambria and Gillingham were protected by palisades, that protection was probably there to defend against attacks from Woodland populations north of the Minnesota River living in the prairie-forest mosaic region, a climatic zone north of where effective maize cultivation is possible. Those groups, probably antecedents of the historic Dakota, who produced Kathio and Onamia ceramics, depended upon wild rice, bison, deer, numerous smaller mammals, and fish for subsistence, would have been attracted to the stores of maize and perhaps other cultigens at sites like Cambria. The nature of that northern system has been described (Johnson 1985).

The Cambria phase is thus a prairie-lake and river valley complex with a series of differing site types, subsistence patterns, and settlement locations. I suggest that populations in this larger region were interacting in a system of exchange dominated by populations at the Cambria site and that their system was tied to a larger Cahokia-based trade network. Within the Cambria phase this system involved upland groups hunting and processing bison in a tall grass and wet prairie environment that Shay (1978:199) calculates has a bison density ranging from 4-14 bison per km^2. This practice could take place during the entire year, with communal hunting in the summer and smaller group winter hunting as the bison scattered to more easterly protected winter ranges. The practice of processing bison at the kill sites is demonstrated by the osteological remains at the larger upland sites where Anfinson notes that ". . . the high frequency of bison limb elements and scarcity of trunk elements at the Big Slough. . . Pederson. . . and Mountain Lake sites indicates that the bison were butchered away from the habitation sites" (1982:63).

The larger Minnesota Valley sites were both horticultural and hunting, utilizing locally produced maize, and perhaps other cultigens—bison, deer, elk, and numerous small mammals from river bottom habitats—and fish and shellfish. Dried bison meat from the upland interacting groups was funneled down the major river tributaries to Gillingham and Cambria, probably in exchange for dried maize, and possibly tobacco and other cultigens.

The Cambria site seems to be dominant in this system and appears to be a major trade network node in the larger Cahokia-centered system. That larger system as seen in the Upper Mississippi Valley has been presented in the form of a model by Gibbon (1984) where he describes the system in this northern zone as "extractive" (1984:9). The analysis of Cambria presented here suggests that the Cambria phase was one sub-set of that extractive network, Mill Creek another, and Silvernale the third along the northwest margin of a Cahokia-centered system.

How the Cambria phase was tied to that network and what its role may have been is seen in the relationships of Cambria with sites and populations in the Red Wing area. That Cambria contacts were present in Silvernale phase sites is demonstrated by the presence of Cambria ceramics at the Silvernale site (Wilford 1950a; Figure 14.4d). In this model, Cambria, as a major node in that exchange network, collected dried meat and hides from its westerly contemporaries and funneled those items to populations at the

Silvernale phase sites who participated more directly in the Cahokia-inspired trade network. Goods received in exchange from the Silvernale groups were preponderantly maize and perhaps other dried cultigens, for it is unlikely that the limited production of domesticated food resources at Cambria, possibly Gillingham, and the smaller river valley "satellite" sites or outliers would have been sufficient to supply both the resident populations and the upland groups. Cambria's supplying of bison scapulae hoes to the Red Wing area is also likely.

The artifact assemblage at the Cambria site suggests that there may have been an additional trade item stemming from a specialized craft at the Cambria site. In that assemblage Watrall (1968:40-58) describes 54 bone awls, 8 deer cannon bone beamers, 10 bison scapula fleshers, and 19 bone quill flatteners. All are tools associated with hide working and clothing manufacture and are objects not represented or represented in low frequencies at the other Cambria phase sites. This suggests that not only were bison hides and scapulae moved east to the Red Wing area, but that finished, quill-decorated robes moved in that direction as well. A craft specialization in what may have been a product for an elite—Silvernale or Cahokia—is probable.

In summary, it is clear that Cambria developed in place from a Woodland population. I suggest that Cambria phase riverine and upland sites of the upper Minnesota River watershed form an exchange subset in a larger-based Cahokia network. Lacking any evidence of direct Cambria-Cahokia interaction, that Cambria exchange subset operated through the Silvernale sites in the Red Wing area. Cambria thus consisted of a varied series of interrelated sites whose populations were engaged in differing activities in bison procurement, processing, and distribution in a prairie region remote for Cahokia.

References Cited

Anfinson, Scott F.

1979 A Handbook of Minnesota Ceramics. *Occasional Publications in Minnesota Anthropology* No. 5. Minnesota Archaeological Society, St. Paul.

1982 Faunal Remains from the Big Slough Site (21MU1) and Woodland Cultural Stability in Southwestern Minnesota. *Minnesota Archaeologist* 41:1:53-71.

1987 A Regional Perspective of Southwestern Minnesota Prehistory. Mss Minnesota Historical Society, St. Paul.

Bleed, Peter

1969 The Archaeology of Petaga Point. *Minnesota Prehistoric Archaeology Series* No. 2, Minnesota Historical Society, St. Paul.

Dobbs, Clark

1983 Oneota Origins and Development: The Radiocarbon Evidence. in G. Gibbon, ed., Oneota Studies, *University of Minnesota Publications in Anthropology* No. 1. Minneapolis.

Fowler, Melvin L. and Robert L. Hall

1972 Archaeological Phases at Cahokia. Illinois State Museum Research Series, *Papers in Anthropology* No. 1. Springfield.

Fugle, Eugene

1962 Mill Creek Culture and Technology. *Journal of the Iowa Archaeological Society* 11:4:1-126.

Gibbon, Guy E.

1984 The Middle Mississippian Presence in Minnesota. Mss. Department of Anthropology, University of Minnesota.

Grimm, Eric C.

1985 Vegetation History along the Prairie-Forest Border in Minnesota. In, J. Spector and E. Johnson, eds., Archaeology, Ecology and Ethnohistory of the Prairie-Forest Border Zone of Minnesota and Manitoba. *Reprints in Anthropology* 31:9-30, Lincoln.

Haug, James K.

1982 Excavations at the Winter Site and Hartford Beach Village 1980-81. South Dakota Archaeological Research Center, Ft. Meade.

Hudak, G. Joseph

1974 The Pederson Site. M.A. Thesis, University of Nebraska.

1976 Woodland Ceramics from the Pederson Site. *Scientific Publications*, Science Museum of Minnesota, St. Paul.

Ives, John C.

1962 Mill Creek Ceramics. *Journal of the Iowa Archaeological Society* 11:3:1-59.

Johnson, Elden
    1961 Cambria Burial Mounds in Big Stone County. *Minnesota Archaeologist* 23:3:53-81.
    1985 The 17th Century Mdewakanton Dakota Subsistence Mode. In J. Spector and E. Johnson, eds., Archaeology, Ecology and Ethnohistory of the Prairie-Forest Border Zone of Minnesota and Manitoba, *Reprints in Anthropology* 31:154-166. Lincoln.
Kehoe, Thomas F.
    1966 The Small Side-Notched Point System of the Northern Plains. *American Antiquity* 31:827-841.
Knudson, Ruthann
    1967 Cambria Village Ceramics. *Plains Anthropologist* 12:37:247-299.
    1985 Late Prehistoric Selection of Wild Ungulates in the Prairie-Forest Transition. In J. Spector and E. Johnson, eds., Archaeology, Ecology and Ethnohistory of the Prairie-Forest Border Zone of Minnesota and Manitoba, *Reprints in Anthropology* 30:31-64. Lincoln.
Nickerson, William B.
    1917 Archaeological Evidences in Minnesota: Explorations of the Minnesota Historical Society in 1913 and 1916 in the Valley of the Minnesota River. Mss. Minnesota Historical Society Archives. St. Paul.
Scullin, Michael
    1979 Price Site (21BE36): Preliminary Notes on a Previously Unidentified Site of the Cambria Focus. Mss. Department of Anthropology, Mankato State University, Mankato, MN.
Shane III, Orrin C.
    1978 The Vertebrate Fauna of the Mountain Lake Site, Cottonwood County, Minnesota. *Scientific Publications*, Science Museum of Minnesota (New Series) 4:2. St. Paul.
    1980 *Grantees' Reports 1980.* American Philosophical Society, Philadelphia.
    1982 Fox Lake Subsistence and Settlement: New Evidence from Southwestern Minnesota. *Minnesota Archaeologist* 41:1:45-52.
Shay, C. Thomas
    1978 Late Prehistoric Bison and Deer Use in the Eastern Prairie-Forest Border. In, L. Davis and M. Wilson, eds., Bison Procurement and Utilization: A Symposium. *Plains Anthropologist Memoir* 14:194-212.
Streiff, Jan E.
    1972 Roster of Excavated Prehistoric Sites in Minnesota to 1972. *Minnesota Prehistoric Archaeology Series* No. 7, Minnesota Historical Society, St. Paul.
Tiffany, Joseph A.
    1983 An Overview of the Middle Missouri Tradition. In, G. Gibbon, ed., Prairie Archaeology, *University of Minnesota Publications in Anthropology* No. 3. Minneapolis.
Watrall, Charles R.
    1968 An Analysis of Bone, Stone and Shell Materials from the Cambria Focus. M.A. Thesis, University of Minnesota, Minneapolis.
    1974 Subsistence Pattern Change at the Cambria Site: A Review and Hypothesis. In, E. Johnson, ed., Aspects of Upper Great Lakes Anthropology, *Minnesota Prehistoric Archaeology Series* No. 11, Minnesota Historical Society, St. Paul.
Wilford, Lloyd A.
    1945a Three Villages of the Mississippian Pattern in Minnesota. *American Antiquity* 11:1:32-40.
    1945b The Cambria Village Site. Mss. Department of Anthropology, University of Minnesota, Minneapolis.
    1948 The Gillingham Site. Mss. Department of Anthropology, University of Minnesota, Minneapolis.
    1950a The Silvernale Site. Mss. Department of Anthropology, University of Minnesota, Minneapolis.
    1950b The Owen D. Jones Site. Mss. Department of Anthropology, University of Minnesota, Minneapolis.
    1953 The Gautefeld Site. Mss. Department of Anthropology, University of Minnesota, Minneapolis.
    1955 A Revised Classification of the Prehistoric Cultures of Minnesota. *American Antiquity* 21:120-142.
    1956 The Lewis Mound. Mss. Department of Anthropology, University of Minnesota, Minneapolis.
Winchell, N. H.
    1911 *The Aborigines of Minnesota.* Minnesota Historical Society, St. Paul.

15

Modeling Mill Creek-Mississippian Interaction

Joseph A. Tiffany

California State Polytechnic University

The Mill Creek culture of northwest Iowa was first defined by Charles R. Keyes in 1927 and has been the subject of on-going archaeological research for over 50 years (Anderson 1985:53, 1987; Tiffany 1987). Known from 23 sites dating between A.D. 900 and 1300, the Mill Creek culture is generally considered to be part of the Initial variant of the Middle Missouri tradition (Anderson 1987; Henning 1971; Tiffany 1983).

Mill Creek sites are typically small, compact villages 1 ha or less in extent characterized by middens up to 3 m or more in depth. Most are located on alluvial terraces in the valleys of the Big Sioux and Little Sioux rivers and their tributaries where two major regional variants, the Big Sioux and Little Sioux phases, have been recognized (Anderson 1969; Henning 1971). Some Mill Creek sites, apparently those in the latter portion of the sequence, like Wittrock, were fortified (Anderson 1986). Others may also have been fortified, but years of cultivation have obscured the evidence.

Mill Creek houses are semi-subterranean, rectangular structures with either internal or external entryways. Village plans from the Chan-ya-ta (13BVl), Wittrock (130B4), and Kimball (13PM4) sites suggest the houses were laid out in rows (Tiffany 1982a:4). Mill Creek house size and form, however, are generally more variable than at other sites of the Initial variant of the Middle Missouri tradition (Tiffany 1982a:30). The superstructures of Mill Creek and Lower James phase (Over focus) houses also vary

from the reported norm for Initial variant houses (Wood 1967). Wattle and daub houses with earthen banked exterior walls were found at the Mitchell site of the Lower James phase and the Chan-ya-ta site of the Little Sioux phase (Alex 1973; Baerreis and Alex 1974; Tiffany 1982a:27).

Other aspects of the Mill Creek settlement system are not well known. For example, several burial patterns have been suggested including primary burials within villages, bluff top ossuaries, mounds, and scaffold burials (Orr 1963; Anderson et al. 1979; Alex 1971:39, 1981). A burial of a child was found in the midden overlying a structure at the Chan-ya-ta site; several human bone fragments and jaws were found in the storage pits and house fills as well (Tiffany 1982a:5).

The current Mill Creek settlement model (Tiffany 1982a:90; Anderson 1987:529-531) proposes that a limited number of base villages were occupied at any one time; satellite or budded villages were also present from time to time, formed as a result of population dynamics, societal disputes or specific resource exploitation. The base villages were probably in local environmental settings most conducive to agriculture and hunting, with the budded villages, like Chan-ya-ta, in more marginal areas. Villages would have been moved from time to time as local resources were depleted, with some villages later reoccupied. This settlement model accounts for the number, distribution, and nature of known Mill Creek sites, and allows for a reasonable population size and growth within the accepted time range for the Mill Creek occupation of northwest Iowa (Tiffany 1982a:91). Recent research by Anderson (1987:532) provides operational tests of this settlement model and variations on it.

Only a few Mill Creek sites have been excavated. These are the Phipps (13CK21), Wittrock (130B4), Chan-ya-ta (13BVl), and Brewster (13CK15) village sites of the Little Sioux phase, and the Broken Kettle (13PMl) and Kimball (13PM4) village sites of the Big Sioux phase. Others have been surface collected, had limited test excavations, or had salvage excavations (Henning 1968; Tiffany 1982a:5; Anderson 1981). Subsistence data recovered from these excavations show the Mill Creek economy follows the general Plains Village pattern of corn agriculture and big game hunting (bison, elk, and deer) supplemented by fishing and wild plant food gathering (Dallman 1983).

Stone, bone, and shell artifacts of the Mill Creek culture fall within the range of similar assemblages found on Initial variant sites (Lehmer 1971:73-95; Fugle 1957, 1962) (Figure 15.1). Important Mill Creek artifact types include elbow pipes and ornaments of red pipestone, side and basal notched projectile points resembling Cahokia points and discoidals (Figure 15.2). Stone hoes and pulley shaped earspools have been reported (Fugle 1957:132), but marine and fresh-water (*Anculosa*) shell beads are more common (Figure 15.2). Large sections of cut marine shell as well as whole marine shells have been found on Mill Creek sites (Baerreis 1968:188-191; Fugle 1957). Two Long-Nosed God masks have been recovered from Mill Creek sites; one is from an ossuary, the other from a village site (Anderson 1975; Anderson et al. 1979; Figure 15.3). Copper artifacts are virtually nonexistent. A single copper fragment from the Wittrock site is the only specimen reported for the Mill Creek culture (Tiffany 1983).

Mill Creek pottery is most similar in frequency of pottery types with the Lower James phase (Over focus; Alex 1981) of the Initial variant (Figure 15.4). Trailed rather than cord-impressed decoration is more common on Mill Creek pottery than in the Initial variant villages of the Missouri trench. A hallmark of the Mill Creek ceramic assemblage is the presence of locally made Mississippian vessel forms such as bowls, seed jars, high-neck water bottles, and small rolled-lip jars with carinated shoulders. Effigy lugs and handles and decorative iconography also occur. Even though the locally made Mississippian-like pottery can constitute up to 20 percent of a given Mill Creek ceramic assemblage, usually less than 1 percent of the pottery is trade vessels (Alex 1971:34; Tiffany 1983:17-18). It is important to note that the frequency of various locally made Mississippian-like vessels apparently changes coevally with the popularity of

similar vessel forms in the Mississippian ceramic sequence at Cahokia (Milner et al. 1984:158-186; Henning 1982:283; Anderson 1981).

There is no evidence for interaction between Mill Creek and the Oneota tradition (Henning 1968:191-192). The relationship between Mill Creek and Great Oasis, however, continues to be a matter of speculation. Mill Creek ceramic assemblages occasionally contain Great Oasis pottery as well as pottery from Late Woodland period groups in western and eastern Iowa (Anderson 1981; Tiffany 1982b; Figure 15.4). With the exception of sites like Larson (13PM61), which contain mixed deposits, Great Oasis sites do not have Mill Creek pottery on them. Final reports are not yet available on important sites like West Broken Kettle (13PM25) which could clarify the situation. Although Great Oasis and Plains Village pottery have been reported from the Spoon River culture (Henning 1967:189), the trade items, copied decorative styles, and pottery forms characteristic of Mill Creek and indicative of Mill Creek-Mississippian contact after A.D. 1000 are virtually absent from Great Oasis sites. As Alex (1981:42) notes "before we spill too much ink describing the symbiotic relationships of the adjacent Great Oasis and Mill Creek villages, we should prove beyond question that these villages are in fact contemporary." Great Oasis is seen as a separate cultural manifestation largely antecedent and developmentally related to the Mill Creek culture where the distribution of the two complexes occur.

In addition to Mill Creek-Great Oasis interaction, evidence in eastern Iowa for interaction between Mill Creek and Late Woodland groups adds a significant dimension to the understanding of Mill Creek-Mississippian relationships. Mill Creek pottery has been found at the Hartley Fort (13AM103) in the Upper Iowa valley in northeast Iowa, and Hartley Fort pottery has been found at the Chan-ya-ta Mill Creek culture site (Tiffany 1982a, b) and the Fred Edwards Late Woodland site in southwest Wisconsin. The Late Woodland pottery at the Hartley Fort is heavily influenced by Mill Creek. The Hartley Fort ceramic assemblage also contains Mississippian trade pottery (Tiffany 1982b). The radiocarbon dates from the Hartley Fort and the Mississippian pottery show that the Hartley Fort was occupied during the Stirling phase at Cahokia (McKusick 1973; Tiffany 1982b).

Mill Creek and Ramey Incised pottery have been recovered from northeast Iowa rockshelters and open sites (Logan 1976; Tiffany 1983:94; Orr 1963). Additionally, the Waterville Rockshelter (13AM124) produced a Mississippian red-slipped seed jar. One of the open sites consists of surface finds of Mill Creek pottery from the confluence of Pleasant Creek with the Mississippi, directly across the Mississippi from the

a

b

Figure 15.1. Stone and bone artifacts from Mill Creek sites in the Charles R. Keyes Collection. (a) stone tools; (b) bone tools.

2a

2b

2c

Figure 15. 2. Mill Creek artifacts from Big Sioux and Little Sioux phase sites (Tiffany 1986b). (a) discoidals; (b) projectile points; (c) marine shell and marine shell beads.

Apple River culture. Excavation notes on all these sites are unclear, but the Mill Creek and Ramey Incised pottery were apparently in association with local, Late Woodland assemblages (Logan 1976:173).

Two southeast Iowa sites, however, Gast Farm (13LA12) and 13WS61, have Late Woodland components in association with Mississippian pottery forms (William Green, personal communication 1987; Tiffany 1986a, 1991). This constellation of eastern Iowa sites provides support for linkage among Mill Creek, Mississippian and Late Woodland groups in this reach of the Mississippi valley.

The Problem

Two models have been proposed over the years to explain both the nature of Mississippian interaction with the Mill Creek culture and the role that Mississippian culture, as manifested at the Cahokia site, had in the formation and development of the Mill Creek culture. In the migration model proposed by Griffin (1946, 1960), Mill Creek culture was seen as the result of the migration of Mississippian peoples from

Cahokia through sites like Aztalan in Wisconsin and Cambria in southwestern Minnesota into northwest Iowa. Griffin also suggested the possibility of a broader Mississippian expansion from Cahokia where Mississippian peoples around A.D. 1000 "moved up the Illinois to the Peoria area [Spoon River culture], up the Mississippi into Wisconsin [Aztalan] and eastern Minnesota [Red Wing area, Bryan-Silvernale] and up the Missouri to Kansas City [Steed-Kisker], Sioux City [Mill Creek culture], and into South Dakota [Over focus]" (Griffin 1967:189).

The other model proposes in situ development of the Mill Creek culture and on-going interaction with Mississippian groups. Mill Creek researchers since the 1960s have argued that the Mill Creek culture is part of the Middle Missouri tradition and that the Mill Creek culture developed out of resident Late Woodland groups such as Great Oasis as a result of contact and acculturation (Henning 1968, 1971; Anderson 1969; Tiffany 1982a).

These two models hinge a great deal upon how "Mississippian" is defined and used, what evidence there is for Mississippian interaction and when and

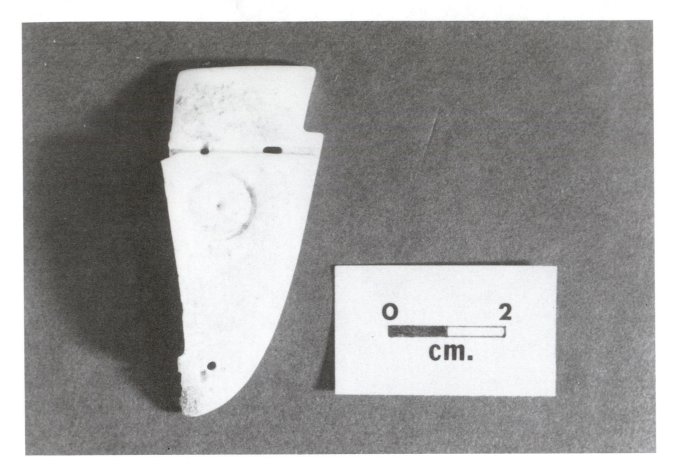

Figure 15.3. Long-nosed god mask, Siouxland Sand and Gravel site (13WD402).

4a

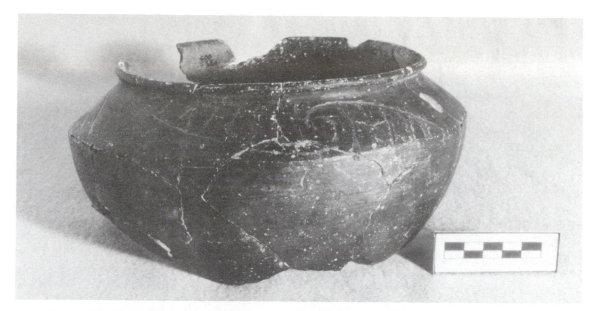

4b

4c

Figure15.4. Pottery from Mill Creek and Great Oasis sites (Tiffany 1986b). (a) restored Mill Creek pottery from the Charles R. Keyes Collection; (b) Ramey Incised vessel from the Chan-ya-ta site (13BV1); (c) Great Oasis Wedge Lip and Great Oasis Incised pottery.

how Mississippian-Mill Creek contact took place. As used in Iowa and the eastern Plains border, Mississippian refers to the variant of Middle Mississippi culture manifested in what was formerly referred to as the Old Village focus at the Cahokia site (Henning 1967; Griffin 1949, 1952). Recent research in the Cahokia site region has resulted in the definition of several phases during the main period of Mississippian utilization of the area. These are the Lohmann (A.D. 1000-1050), Stirling (A.D. 1050-1150), Moorehead (A.D. 1150-1250), and Sand Prairie (A.D. 1250-1400) phases (Bareis and Porter 1984:12; Milner et

al. 1984). The Stirling phase corresponds most closely to the Old Village focus (Fowler and Hall 1975:6; Milner et al. 1984:168-173).

Mississippian culture is characterized by distinctive forms of shell tempered pottery, intensive agriculture, and a nucleated settlement pattern consisting of communities of varying sizes. Mississippian sites are often fortified and commonly contain flat-topped pyramidal mounds and rectangular wall-trench houses of wattle and daub construction (Griffin 1967; Gibbon 1974; Stoltman 1978:725; Smith 1978:479-498). The Mississippian temple-plaza community pattern is thought to represent socially stratified societies where territoriality and land ownership were predominant (Griffin 1967:189; Stoltman 1978:725). Extensive trade networks in marine shell, salt, chert, and copper occurred among Mississippian and non-Mississippian groups (Griffin 1967:190; Cobb 1989); Southeast Ceremonial Complex artifacts and iconography found in Mill Creek and Plains Village sites are also attributed to Mississippian contact through Cahokia (Henning 1967:185).

Henning (1967:185) states that Mississippian contact in the western Prairie Peninsula is identified by trade pottery and locally made ceramics emulating Mississippian forms and decoration, occurrence of elements of Mississippian settlement patterns and village organization, and artifacts and iconography reflecting Mississippian religious beliefs. Except for ceramics, not all the elements that define Mississippian culture or Mississippian contact appear consistently in Mill Creek sites.

Recent thinking downplays the migration models and favors an in situ model because of the increasing number of radiocarbon dates which show that the Mill Creek culture developed coevally with Mississippian culture in the Upper Mississippi valley (Tiffany 1981). Furthermore, as Henning correctly observed:

> No evidence for the construction of flat-topped pyramidal mounds by Mill Creek peoples or any other local groups has been forthcoming. The ceramic complex does yield evidence for Mississippian influence, but it is definitely not "pure" Mississippian at the base of the earliest sites. The earliest ceramics indicate the use of indigenously derived ceramic traits. . . . (Henning 1967:188)

In his comprehensive study of Mill Creek technology, Fugle further elaborated on this viewpoint.

> There is little doubt that the Mill Creek archaeological culture is related to the Old Village focus at Cahokia because of the close similarity in ceramics and projectile points. However, the small Mill Creek villages lacking temple mounds stand in contrast to the large Cahokia culture center with many large temple mounds. The remainder of the Middle Mississippi traits characteristic of Mill Creek sites are more generalized and are not particularly diagnostic of the Cahokia center. The close similarity of Mill Creek with the Middle Mississippi phase is borne out by such

items as stone pulley type earspools, chunkey stones, profuse amounts of marine shells for ornamentation, stone hoes (rare), triangular shaped retouched drills, double conoidal elbow pipes, large numbers of polished celts, shell columella pendants, the scalloped shell disc gorget and the use of wattle and daub in house construction. However, there are more differences between Mill Creek archaeological culture and the Middle Mississippi phase than there are similarities. . . . (Fugle 1957:346-347)

Mill Creek radiocarbon dates, the lack of a discrete Mississippian component in any Mill Creek site, and the predominant use of pottery types indigenous to the Middle Missouri tradition throughout the Mill Creek culture sequence all suggest a trait-unit rather than a site-unit intrusion (Willey et al. 1956:7-8) to account for the presence of Mississippian material culture in Mill Creek villages. According to Willey et al:

> . . . a trait-unit is an object modified or transported by human agency, a stylistic or technological feature or complex or a characteristic archaeological association. In ethnological terms . . . diffused traits or traded objects would appear archaeologically as intrusive trait-units (Willey et al. 1956:7-8).

The central issue under consideration in the earlier migration model and in the current in situ model is how Mill Creek-Mississippian interaction occurred, the reasons for it, and verification with archaeological data. In the migration model, which is no longer tenable, the explanation was simple: Mill Creek assemblages had Mississippian elements in them because Mill Creek people were Mississippians and they kept in contact with their own groups. With the in situ model, the identification of processes is more complex. The in situ model presumes a cultural development in the western Prairie Peninsula that parallels Mississippian, such as formation of nucleated, fortified, agricultural village cultures and utilization of the bow and arrow by societies with languages and social systems different from Mississippian. Mississippian cultural development probably played an important role in the formation of societies like Mill Creek, but characterization of the nature, extent, and reasons for Mississippian involvement are less clear in the in situ model.

For example, evidence for contact between the Mill Creek culture and Mississippian centers like Cahokia is abundant on Mill Creek sites, but virtually non-existent on Mississippian sites. Except for instances mentioned earlier, Late Woodland sites in eastern and southeastern Iowa show little or no evidence for either Mississippian or Mill Creek contact. Trade is considered to be the interactive mechanism between Mill Creek and Mississippian groups (Henning 1967:190; Alex 1971). The archaeological record supports a largely one-way Mill Creek-Mississippian exchange, and archaeologists have suggested that these trading contacts were probably initiated and dominated by the Mississippians (Griffin 1967:189-190; Porter 1973).

Henning (1967:190, 1982:288-289) and Alex (1971) argue for the presence of a large-scale trade network between Mill Creek and Cahokia; the archaeological evidence presented and the in situ model indicate that this trade would have been extensive, continuous and direct. Henning and Alex saw marine shell as a key exchange item. Alex (1971:43-45) further argued that Mill Creek groups served as intermediaries or gateway communities in a reciprocal, down-the-line exchange network where buffalo hides and dried meat were obtained from Northern Plains groups by Mill Creek traders and by hunters of the Mill Creek culture. These items were exchanged at Cahokia for marine shell which in turn was made into beads and other goods at Mill Creek villages for trade with Northern Plains cultures. The presence of whole marine shells, large pieces of cut marine shells, and finished marine shell artifacts in Mill Creek sites all indicate trade in marine shell was present and possibly substantial (Figure 15.2). There is abundant evidence from Mill Creek sites that bison, deer, and elk were hunted and processed. Bison hides and especially meat attainable by Mill Creek groups may have been in demand in large, agricultural centers like Cahokia where the diet was high in carbohydrates but deficient in certain proteins.

The archaeological record clearly shows on-going contact between the Mill Creek culture and Mississippian centers like Cahokia. If trade is the operative mechanism of the currently accepted in situ model of Mill Creek culture, then all aspects of Mill Creek-Mississippian trade need to be clearly spelled out and verified archaeologically. The extensive trade network hypothesis proposed by Henning and Alex is provocative, for it has a basis in ethnographic and historic fact and can be confirmed by empirical data in the archaeological record. The remainder of this paper is directed towards this end.

Mill Creek-Mississippian Exchange

An extensive trade network between the Mill Creek culture and Mississippian centers, notably Cahokia, has been proposed to account for the presence of Mississippian and Mississippian-influenced artifacts in Mill Creek culture. The rationale and mechanisms for this exchange system can be derived from ethnohistoric and historic information. Jablow (1950), Ray (1974), and others (Bowers 1950; Spicer 1961; Bruner 1961; Wood 1980) provide well-documented analogies among historical period hunting and gathering groups and Plains Village farming cultures like the Mandan for the kind of trade proposed for Mill Creek and Cahokia. Although other tribes could be cited as examples (Wright 1967), the use of the Mandan is appropriate since the Middle Missouri tradition, which includes Mill Creek, is believed to culminate in the Mandan and Hidatsa cultures.

Summarizing from Bruner (1961:219-226), the Mandan tribe consisted of several independent villages that were economically, politically and, with the exception of portions of the Okipa ceremony, ceremonially autonomous. All social and economic activities were performed by the thirteen exogamous, matrilineal clans. The clans served as the corporate bodies in each village. For example, a lodge may have been built and used by females of a given lineage, but the lodge was owned by the clan to which that lineage belonged.

The women of each village performed agricultural and household-related tasks; the men hunted and were involved in ceremonial activities. The women grew the corn and other produce, tanned the hides, and dried the meat. As a consequence, the women owned what they produced, which included not only the agricultural goods, but also the game killed by the men.

Most technological skills, special knowledge, and ceremonial information were purchased in Mandan society. The ceremonial life of the Mandan revolved around medicine bundles, both personal and tribal. Some bundles were inherited, others purchased. The result was a social structure based on bundle ownership where some lineages or clans were more influential than others. Village leaders, for example, were lineage or clan heads who owned tribal bundles.

The Mandan had a number of loosely age-graded, secular societies for both men and women. The criterion for membership in a secular society was not age but collective purchase by a group of individuals of the songs, rites, paraphernalia, and so forth. These societies served as the means for establishing an individual's position in the social structure as well as defining the composite behavior and responsibilities expected by Mandan society for individuals of a general age.

The transfer ritual in a Mandan secular society or the exchange of bundles or valued information provides an important key to understanding Mandan intertribal relations. A superordinate-subordinate, fictive kin relationship (father-son) was established between buyer and seller. Gifts were exchanged as well as the ritual, bundle, or commodity being purchased. In addition, the buyer's wife was surrendered to the ceremonial father. Mandans spent their lives in the accumulation of prestige through wealth, bundles, inheritance, prowess in warfare, and the giving and taking of sexual favors.

Not surprisingly the earliest historical accounts show the Mandan conducted intertribal trade in much the same way as their intratribal social relationships (Jablow 1950:22, 45-46; Ray 1974:38-40, 55-57, 75; Wood 1980:100). In trading situations the Mandan men first established a fictive kin relationship between buyer and seller involving a public ceremony and exchange of expensive gifts of generally equal value between buyer and seller. Once completed and solidarity established, the entire village and trading party would barter items individually with respect to what each group was most concerned about, notably commodities such as bison hides, meat, and agricultural produce (Jablow 1950:46). These goods, as mentioned, were owned by the Mandan women, consequently, the trade in these items was the purview of the women. The resulting atmosphere of exchange following the public ceremony has been described as resembling a county fair (Jablow 1950:48).

In the Fur Trade period the Mandan served as brokers, being both producers and suppliers of aboriginal goods and European manufactured items (Bruner 1961:199). The main Mandan commodity was corn and other agricultural produce which they traded to the nomadic tribes for hides, furs, and leather goods. They exchanged these with European traders for guns, ammunition, and other items of European manufacture. In the Fur Trade period, the European goods, guns, and ammunition were used in the ceremonial exchange and traded by the Mandan men with Plains nomadic groups for horses. The basic commodity exchange, however, continued apparently as it had prior to European contact. The European items used in the ceremonial exchange probably replaced or supplemented other valued aboriginal goods such as feathers and shell ornaments (Jablow 1950:13-14, 46; Ewers 1955:435).

The Mandan provide a well-documented analogy for Mill Creek-Mississippian interaction. Furthermore, ethnohistoric accounts show that important elements of the Mandan exchange system were prevalent among Indian tribes throughout the Western Great Lakes and eastern prairies regions (Wright 1968). With respect to the trade network proposed, Mill Creek traders (men and women) would have traveled to Cahokia. Fictive kin relationships would have been established among the Mill Creek men and the ruling elite of Cahokia. A ceremonial exchange would have

taken place including the gift of women by the Mill Creek men in exchange for a wide spectrum of Mississippian rituals, paraphernalia, iconography, and ceremonial artifacts. Following this, a commodity exchange would have taken place involving the trade of bison hides and dried meat for marine shell, pottery, and utilitarian items.

An excerpt from a Mandan origin myth pertaining to the Okipa ceremony as presented by Bowers (1950:360-361) is instructive regarding Mandan (and presumably Mill Creek) trading relationships and the importance to the Mandan of shell:

> . . . Once our people lived beside a large lake. They had a large boat in those times that was able to carry twelve people. On the other side of the lake was a large tribe of people whose chief was named Maniga. This boat would go by its own power; all the people needed to do was to point it and say "Go." In the middle of this lake there was a rough place, and sometimes it seemed that the boat would surely tip over. When the people neared the shore, the red willows would turn into warriors and wrestle with them. Beyond the willows was the village of which Maniga was chief. The Mandan crossed this lake for shells which were very numerous on that shore, but they could not get them without being seen by these people. Maniga always called his People together whenever the Mandan came across. He would supply so much food, water, tobacco, and women that many of the Mandan died of excessive indulgence. If they did as they were ordered, Maniga gave them great quantities of shells. They crossed every summer, and the hardships encountered always killed several of the party. Lone Man said he would go over. He took along a man named Bull Spirit who had the medicine of the water plants and could drink forever. Another man had the medicine of the buffalo that eats all the time. The third man had the medicine of the tobacco bee that lives on the tobacco plant but never gets sick. Lone Man went to protect his people and free themselves from the Maniga. He quieted the rough water and weakened the young men who were the red willows of the bank. They went directly to Maniga's village and ordered the women to bring out the food, water, and tobacco which was already prepared for them. The man with the spirit of the water plants com-

plained of not having enough to drink; the man with the spirit of the buffalo complained of not having enough to eat; the man with the spirit of the tobacco bee complained of the weak tobacco; Lone Man complained that not enough women had been supplied him. Maniga observed that none of the Mandan died and that this party was not like the others. He realized that Lone Man had outwitted him. Maniga said, "You people have gone too far." Lone Man replied, "It is you who have gone too far, doing all these things before giving my people the shells they need so much. . . . (Bowers 1950:360-361)

The folklore and fact on the shell trade underscore important points. First, the Mississippian pottery and artifacts found on Mill Creek sites reflect a social mechanism which, when used by Mississippians in an exchange context, helped develop and sustain a more general interactive economic system with non-Mississippian groups that was beneficial to both parties. In this vein, the use of Mississippian goods parallels the mutualistic exchange system described by Spielmann (1982, 1983) for the Late Prehistoric period Pueblo-Southern Plains trade. Second, while the number and kind of Mississippian artifacts may appear to have less value than the meat and hides being exchanged for them, these gifts to the Mill Creek traders were more than symbolic or a trinket trade. The exchange system proposed reflects the interrelationship of political and economic systems found in ranked societies like Cahokia where exchange of valuables is used as a means to negotiate and maintain alliance networks (Cobb 1989:90). Using the historical analogy and the folklore example, the Mill Creek traders would have exchanged quality items they thought were of equal value in the ceremonial exchange. Further, given the hardships, time, labor, and expense of a trading venture, the Mississippian items may have had considerably more value in Mill Creek society than in Mississippian, where following the Mandan analogy, such items would be an important means of obtaining prestige through the purchase of medicine bundles, songs, rituals, and so forth, matters that lay at the heart of Mandan and presumably Mill Creek social structure.

The other side of the trading equation in this model of Mill Creek-Mississippian interaction is the assumed need for a reliable protein source and hides by Mississippian centers like Cahokia. Results of recent research at the Cahokia site locality show that portions of the population suffered from dietary stress and diseases related to a high carbohydrate diet (Milner et al.

1984:236-240). The faunal remains from Mississippian sites contain very few deer or other large game; the preponderance of the faunal assemblages by bone count are fish remains (Kelly and Cross 1984:231).

These data are complementary in that corn agriculture can support a relatively large, stable population. A large population living in one area like Cahokia and the American Bottom over an extensive period of time would have quickly decimated local resources such as wood and large game. Fish are an excellent source of protein and are readily available in the American Bottom area. Since the faunal information available is based on bone counts, it is difficult to assess the relative importance of fish, or beans for that matter, in the overall diet of Mississippians in the American Bottom at this time. Following the trading model proposed, the Mississippian elite would be controlling the Mill Creek trade locally, meaning these individuals would have a more balanced diet than others. Biological anthropologists can test this assumption against the Cahokia archaeological record, and zooarchaeologists can also further evaluate the Mississippian diet at Cahokia with a comprehensive analysis of the faunal remains. Regardless of the Mississippian data base, however, information is available from Mill Creek sites to evaluate this model.

The model of Mill Creek-Mississippian interaction proposed is based upon ethnographic and historical accounts of the Mandan. This extensive, on-going prehistoric exchange involved direct contact between two cultures for trade of commodities needed by the Mississippians for items considered to be of high value by the Mill Creek traders. This trade network was centered at Cahokia and reflects one aspect of the spread of Mississippian culture into the Upper Mississippi valley. This proposed exchange network fits what Linton (1940:501) described as a directed situation. As discussed by Spicer:

. . . directed contact involves interaction in specific roles between members of two different societies and effective control of some type and degree by members of one society over another. Members of the superordinate society have an interest in changing the behavior of members of the subordinate society in particular ways. In directed contact the societies are interlocked in such a way that the participants in one social system are subject not only to sanctions of their own but also those operative in the other system. (Spicer 1961:520)

The iconography, mimicry of Mississippian pottery forms, and the presence of Long-Nosed God masks in the Mill Creek culture all suggest directed trade. An excellent example is use of biconcave discoidals by the Mill Creek culture, coupled with the fact that historically the Mandan were playing the Chunkey game in a manner similar to southeastern tribes (Will and Spinden 1906:125). The Arikara also played Chunkey and considered it "to some extent as a religious ceremony" (Will and Spinden 1906:125). The archaeological linkage of the Mill Creek culture to the Mandan and the fact that the Arikara spoke a Caddoan dialect are important. For the Mandan, clearly this game and the use of discoidals are borrowed traits with no real context in a Plains Village society. While the game may have been learned from the Arikara, it is equally possible the game has a long history in Mandan culture extending back to Mississippian or Caddoan influence on Initial Middle Missouri tradition cultures like Mill Creek.

The directed trade situation proposed for Mill Creek-Mississippian interaction fits with current in situ models of Mill Creek cultural development presented earlier. Directed trade also provides an effective means of accounting for the extensive Mississippian influence present in Mill Creek sites without resorting to movement of peoples as proposed in earlier migration models.

Evaluation of the Model

Earle and Erickson (1977:3) note that a variety of differing methods of exchange can produce similar distributional patterns in the archaeological record. The model of Mill Creek-Mississippian interaction proposed is based on ethnographic data and provides both the reasons for and the mechanisms by which Mill Creek-Mississippian trade could have occurred. The archaeological record shows that there was contact, but this record superficially appears to be a one-way activity with Mill Creek sites providing ample evidence for Mississippian contact, but not vice versa. It has been suggested that this information is in all likelihood present in Mississippian centers like Cahokia if the existing data on human populations and faunal remains were examined thoroughly.

The model purports that Mill Creek subsistence goods, specifically bison meat and hides, were being exchanged for high value Mississippian controlled items such as shell ornaments. For the proposed model to be of interpretative value, it has to be both possible and probable. The Mill Creek archaeological data must show evidence for a surplus of processed animals and the presence of Mississippian trade goods in frequencies relative to the potential number of adults who could afford them. Additionally, the means for feasible transport of the goods involved must be identified.

The model must be based in archaeological data and evaluated in terms of archaeological data. To accomplish this, meaningful comparative units have to be established. The archaeological data must consist of comparably sized samples from comparably sampled units derived from either single component sites of short duration, sites of longer duration where the rate of midden accumulation can be determined, or a combination of both kinds of site data. Without controlling for these limiting factors or data constraints, the potential sources of error in the data resulting from length of occupation, site age or time, and population size represented are so great that any comparisons made would not be of much value.

To examine the model, multiple methods will be employed to estimate population size, length of occupation, and subsistence needs for five Mill Creek culture sites chosen for this analysis. Presumably, if each set of methods used in this study produces similar results, then it can be argued that the formal, temporal, and spatial variability in the data has been controlled and evaluation of the model can proceed. Since manipulation of the original site report information is necessary to meet the analytical constraints identified for this analysis, each step of the following data evaluation is detailed as thoroughly as possible. The data are presented in the metric system, and the figures have been rounded. Variations on the methods and results presented in this study with respect to analysis of dietary needs and population dynamics have been attempted on Plains Village and food gatherer groups (Gilbert 1969; Ascher 1959; Cook and Treganza 1950).

The five Mill Creek sites include three base villages, Phipps, Kimball, and Wittrock, and two budded villages, Brewster and Chan-ya-ta. Four are part of the Little Sioux phase; Kimball is a Big Sioux phase site. Phipps and Kimball are deep tell-like middens; Wittrock is shallower and presumably of shorter duration. Chan-ya-ta is a small, single component site; Brewster is deeper and may contain more than one component. These sites were chosen because they are the best documented sites in the literature (Table 15.1).

Table 15.1. References for Values Cited in Table 2.

Site Name	References
Brewster	Anderson 1981:11, 68-69, 51, 53, 130-33, 1985; Dallman 1983:6, 29
Chan-ya-ta	Tiffany 1982:13, 86, Appendices
Wittrock	Henning 1968:42, 222, 225, 228, 234
Phipps	Henning 1968:70, 197-198, 200, 205, 221; Ruppé 1955; Ives 1962:11
Kimball	Keyes and Orr 1939; Ives 1962; Henning 1968:80-81, 100-101 241-245, 248-249, 261-262

Table 15.2. Basic Data from Five Mill Creek Sites.

Site Name	Site Number	Site m³	Size m²	Excavation m³	Percent Excavated	Total Rims	Shell Tempered Pottery
Brewster	13CK15	2,124	1,642	61	2.88	3,196	12
Chan-ya-ta	13BV1	3,431	5,574	210	6.12	2,474[4]	17
Wittrock	13OB4	7,000	4,700	14	0.20	197	0
Phipps-1 [1]	13CK21	11,111	4,611	10	0.09	635	3
Phipps-2 [2]	-	-	-	52	0.46	2,511	24
Phipps-3 [3]	-	-	-	62	0.55	3,146	27
Kimball	13PM4	13,846	5,827	18	0.13	740	2

[1] Henning 1963 excavation
[2] Ruppé 1955 excavation
[3] Phipps site combined totals
[4] Chan-ya-ta house floors: Total Rims- 503; Percent Excavated- 1.05

Table 15.3. Comparison of Estimated Length of Occupation between Ceramic Breakage and Subsistence Years.

Site Name/ Population	Ceramic Years					Subsistence Years				
	50	70	100	150	200	50	70	100	150	200
Brewster	44	32	22	15	11	55	39	27	18	14
Chan-ya-ta	16	12	8	5	4	18	13	9	6	5
Phipps-2	229	163	114	76	57	309	21	55	103	77

Total Subsistence Days: Brewster 995,972; Chan-ya-ta 329,609; Phipps-2 5,647,174.

The data for the Brewster site are derived from the 1970 excavation (Dallman 1983; Anderson 1981), and the information on Chan-ya-ta is from a 1974 excavation (Tiffany 1982a) (Tables 15.1 and 15.2). Kimball was extensively excavated in 1939 as part of a WPA project and tested again in 1963 (Keyes and Orr 1939; Henning 1968). The data for Wittrock are from a 1963 test excavation (Henning 1968:42). The information on Phipps is from a 1955 excavation and a 1963 test excavation (Ruppé 1955; Henning 1968). The WPA excavation materials from Kimball represent a highly selective sample and were not used.

Three different sets of values are shown for the Phipps site in Table 15.2, one each for the two excavations (Phipps 1, 1963 excavation; Phipps 2, 1955 excavation) and a third representing a combined figure. These were used in the initial ceramic evaluation to follow to provide comparative information on one site. With the exception of the fill units over the Chan-ya-ta houses (Tiffany 1982a:12-15), all the excavations were conducted in a comparable manner on the five sites.

Different excavation reports for Phipps and Kimball cite different estimates of the size of these sites. Ruppé's (1955:335-336) estimate of 87 × 53 m (285 × 175 ft; see also Fugle 1962:17) was checked against the base map of the Phipps site on file at the Office of the State Archaeologist of Iowa; it was found to be correct and was used instead of Ives's figure (1962:6; Henning 1968:70). Keyes and Orr's (1939:13) dimensions for the Kimball site (60 × 97 m; 196 × 320 ft) were used instead of those provided by Henning (1968:80-81). Additional values are presented in Table 15.2 for the Chan-ya-ta floors only.

The depth for each site is derived from published reports (Dallman 1983:29; Tiffany 1982a:13, 86; Henning 1968:197, 222, 241). Dallman (1983:6) noted that part of the Brewster site had been destroyed. Dallman's (1983:29) estimate of 2,124 m³ (75,005 cu ft) was used (Table 15.2) even though the dimensions Dallman cited earlier (1983:6) would have given a much larger volume. The disparity in values can be resolved by the fact that Brewster is a midden mound like Phipps, thus the average depth of the Brewster site is probably less than the 2 m (6 ft) figure Dallman cited. Also, the 2.88% excavated for Brewster (Table 15.2) is based on Dallman's (1983:29) figures and not the approximate value of 1/35 (2.86%) he used in his analysis.

There is also some disparity between the figures for total subsistence days for Brewster and Chan-ya-ta used in this analysis (Table 15.3) and those cited in the respective excavation reports. The estimate in the Chan-ya-ta site report is based on 1,800 calories per day (Tiffany 1982a:86). The value used in Table 15.3 for Chan-ya-ta has been recalculated for 2,400 calories per day, however, to correspond with Dallman's (1983:29, 53) procedure for Brewster and Phipps. The Chan-ya-ta faunal sample reported earlier was derived from 2.3% of the total excavated site area. The figure for subsistence days for Brewster faunal remains in Table 15.3 was calculated using 2.88%, not the approximate 1/35 value Dallman (1983:29) used. Finally, the subsistence information for Phipps was based on faunal remains recovered from Ruppé's (1955) excavation and not Henning's (1968) later work in which the faunal remains underwent only preliminary analysis (Dallman 1983:53). Dallman was apparently unaware of Ruppé's (1955:336) report which placed the total excavated area at 52 m³ or .46% of the total site area. Faunal material from a slit trench excavated by Ruppé was used in Dallman's study (1983:45-47), but it is not shown on the map of the Phipps site excavations in Dallman's (1983:46) report. Using Dallman's (1983:53) estimate of 25,977 subsistence days and the corrected percent excavated of .46, a total of 5,647,174 is obtained (Table 15.3), not the value of 1,588,620 given by Dallman (1983:53).

Population estimates and length of occupation of the five Mill Creek sites were computed in the following manner with the Brewster site data as an example. Using the 2.88% "percent excavated" and the 3,196 "total rims" values for Brewster (Table 15.2), the total number of rims at the site can be estimated at 1,109,722. Applying Drennan's (1984: 32) formula of 2.5 pots per year consumed with 20 rims per pot (Table 15.4), 2219 pot/years are represented in the Brewster site. Using different population values (50, 70, 100 and so forth), the estimated length of the occupation at Brewster and the other sites examined based on ceramic use and breakage can be determined (Table 15.4). Based on Table 15.4, the population esti-

mates of 70 people at Brewster and Chan-ya-ta, 100 people at Wittrock and 200 each at Phipps and Kimball are considered reasonable.

The values from the floor units of the Chan-ya-ta site parallel the figures derived for the whole site. This is important because, as noted earlier, the house fills at Chan-ya-ta were excavated differently from the floors with respect to the other sites under study. The three sets of data from Phipps also produced roughly parallel results. The data based on the test excavation (Phipps-1, Henning 1968) are probably less reliable because of sample size. The values of 200 people and 57 years, representing the totals of both excavations (Phipps-3, Table 15.4), are close to the Kimball figures. The Phipps-1 values are used for the analyses of trade shell and endscrapers because these data are derived solely from this excavation.

Next, total subsistence years for the three sites with subsistence data were computed by taking the subsistence days value for each site (Table 15.3), dividing it by 365 and then dividing it by varying population sizes (50, 70, 100, and the like). These results were then compared with the ceramic breakage results in terms of population size and length of occupation (Table 15.3). The subsistence years exceed the length of occupation based on ceramic breakage by as much as 20 years for Phipps (200 people) and as little as 1 year at Chan-ya-ta (70 people). These figures are significant as will be shown shortly. Essentially, the faunal remains from three Mill Creek sites indicate the population at each site could have subsisted totally on meat with plenty to spare. From the commonly held viewpoint that Plains Village farmers' diets consisted of an equal mix of game and agricultural produce, and they did not occupy the villages year-round, the amount of available meat from these three Mill Creek sites is considerable. Even a short-lived budded village like Chan-ya-ta was producing surplus food.

The final phase of this part of the analysis provides one more check on the ceramic breakage and subsistence years figures by examining an independent data

Table 15.4. Estimated Length of Occupation in Years of Five Mill Creek Sites.
Based on Ceramic Breakage for Various Populations.

Site Name	Number of People						Number of People Chan-ya-ta Floors		
	50	70	100	150	200	250	70	100	150
Brewster	44	32	22	15	11	9	-	-	-
Chan-ya-ta	16	12	8	5	4	3	14	10	6
Wittrock	39	28	20	13	10	8	-	-	-
Phipps-1	282	202	141	94	71	56	-	-	-
Phipps-2	218	156	109	73	55	44	-	-	-
Phipps-3	229	163	114	76	57	46	-	-	-
Kimball	228	163	114	76	57	46	-	-	-

Table 15.5. Household Size Based on Wedel's Formula.   [1]

Site Name	Number	Unit	m^2	Individuals/ House (5 m^2/person)	Mean
Kimball	13PM4	House A	46	9	
		House B	58	12	11
		House C	53	11	
Wittrock	130B4	1-1	30	6	
		1-2	49	10	9
		2-1	54	11	
Chan-ya-ta	13BV1	East Floor	31	6	
		West Floor	11	2	5
		6 Floor	37	7	
		9-1	13	3	6[2]
		9-2	25	5	

[1]From Tiffany 1982:32 and Wedel 1979:94.
[2]Mean computed using East Floor, 6 Floor and 9-2.

set from Mill Creek sites, namely population estimates derived from house sizes. Wedel's (1979:84) estimate of 5 m^2 per individual is conservative and may slightly underestimate the actual population (Blakeslee 1989:4, 14). It was used, however, to compute household size from three of the Mill Creek sites under study (Table 15.5). In terms of size the Mill Creek houses fall well within the range of Wedel's (1979) sample. Even though Wedel's formula is for Central Plains tradition structures, it is applicable to Mill Creek because of the generally smaller size of Mill Creek culture houses when compared to other Initial Middle Missouri sites (Tiffany 1982a:28, 30, 32). Interestingly, the Mill Creek houses, especially those at Chan-ya-ta, are of comparable size to Mississippian houses of the same age in the Cahokia area (Milner et al. 1984:170-172).

The 11 Mill Creek houses range in floor size from 12 to 58 m^2 resulting in household size estimates of 2 to 12 individuals with an average of 8 people per house (Table 15.5). The houses are from both base villages (Kimball and Wittrock) and a budded village (Chan-ya-ta). Dallman (1983:30) had suggested a figure of 21 people per house based on a figure of 2.97 m^2 (32 ft^2) per person. While 2.97 m^2 is obviously more conservative, Dallman's (1983:30) calculations resulted in an estimate that was too high because he assumed all the Wittrock houses to be much larger than the excavation data show (Tiffany 1982a:29).

In the case of Wittrock, which probably had 15 houses in use at any one time, Dallman's figures give a population of 315 people. Using the data in Table 15.5 and Wedel's (1979) formula, Wittrock's population would have been 135 people. If the population figure of 135 is used with the ceramic breakage formula in

Table 15.4, an occupation of 15 years is obtained for Wittrock. Even though Henning (1968; Vis and Henning 1969:256) felt the Wittrock site contained two components, the figure for the length of the Wittrock occupation supports Anderson's (1986) analysis, which suggests Wittrock was a briefly occupied, single component, base village. Population estimates based on Chan-ya-ta household size (at least 10 houses occupied at any one time) also result in values similar to those derived from ceramic breakage. When the household size is taken into consideration with ceramic breakage figures and subsistence years, it should be clear that each data set is producing comparable, and hence, presumably reliable information on Mill Creek population size, length of village occupation, and available total animal resources represented at each site.

The population parameters of the Mill Creek culture can be further evaluated by looking at information provided by Weiss (1973, citing Acsádi and Nemeskeri 1957). These authors place the mean life expectancy of proto-agriculturalists at 19.8 years and the life expectancy of Neolithic groups at 19.1 years (Weiss 1973:49; Acsádi and Nemeskeri 1957:133-147). Weiss (1973:49) also notes a juvenile mortality rate between 30 and 50 percent among "anthropological populations." Using this information, two life tables characterizing the Mill Creek population are provided in Table 15.6 (Weiss 1973:128, 132). Weiss's information assumes a stationary (zero growth) population. With a population of 1,000 people, the number of adults (percent of population between 15 and 50 percent, Table 15.6) would range from 466 to 484. With sexual parity assumed, the number of adult male or female Mill Creek people ranges from 233 to 242.

Table 15.6. Mill Creek Population Characteristics.

Statistic	Mortality Rates	
	30%	50%
Birth Rate	.0391	.0527
Gross Reproductive Rate	2.50	3.51
Completed Family Size (with sexual parity)	5.00	7.02
Mean Age at Reproduction	26.69	26.69
Adult Survival (percent)	19.00	19.00
Population under 15 (percent)	45.30	47.40
Population 15-50 (percent)	48.40	46.60
Population over 50 (percent)	6.30	6.00
Average Age	20.50	19.90
Average Age of Adults	31.60	31.60

Table 15.7. Mill Creek Population Dynamics.

Initial Populations	50	100	150	200	250	300	350	400
1,000	1,051	1,105	1,162	1,221	1,284	1,350	1,419	1,492
233	245	258	271	285	299	315	331	348
242	254	268	281	296	311	327	343	361

Formula: $N = N_o e^{(rt)}$
N = final population
r = growth rate
t = time
N_o = initial population

As mentioned earlier, radiocarbon dates suggest a 400-year time span for the Mill Creek culture (Anderson 1981; Tiffany 1982a:1). Most Mississippian trade items in northwest Iowa appear to bracket the Stirling and Moorehead phases, A.D. 1050-1250, however (Bareis and Porter 1984:12). With this information in mind, using a Neolithic annual population growth rate of .1% (Hassan 1973:540) and an initial population of 1,000, Mill Creek population growth can be computed using the formula shown in Table 15.7. The potential population increase in adult men or women is also shown in Table 15.7.

The assumption of an initial population of 1,000 and a very slow growth rate for the Mill Creek culture considers Mill Creek in terms of both the total Initial Middle Missouri population and the population of the Mandan historically (Kroeber 1963:139). For Mill Creek a population of 1,000 would permit an initial settlement pattern of five base villages, two on the Big Sioux and three along the Little Sioux River. With approximately 200 people in each base village and 70 per budded village, in 200 years in the middle of the Stirling phase, the Mill Creek population would have expanded the equivalent of one base village (221 people, Table 15.7). By the end of the Moorehead phase (A.D. 1250) or 350 years from the "start" of the Mill

Creek culture, the population would have increased by 42 percent or 419 people. These population data "fit" with respect to the total number of Mill Creek sites, seriation of the sites in the Little Sioux valley, the range of Mississippian ceramics present in Mill Creek sites, and the settlement model presented earlier. They will be used in the remaining analyses.

Data on shell tempered trade pottery were computed in the manner described earlier for population estimates based on ceramic breakage using the information contained in Tables 15.2 and 15.3 (Table 15.8). Although Mississippian trade pottery with other tempering agents are in the collections from Mill Creek sites, shell tempering was singled out because it is easily tabulated from the research reports used without resorting to detailed reexamination of all the collections. The pots per person per year figures in Table 15.8 indicate that the mean figure of seven pots per year for a population estimate of 540 people in the five sites represented is probably reliable for all villages regardless of size, location, or chronological order in the Mill Creek culture irrespective of the number of people who may have actually participated in the trading. With these limiting assumptions in mind, the total number of shell tempered vessels in Mill Creek sites was computed (Table 15.9). The

Table 15.8. Data on Shell Tempered Trade Pottery in Four Mill Creek Sites.

Site Name	Total Shell Tempered Pots	Pots/Year	Pots/Person/ Year	Length of Occupation	Population Estimates
Brewster	21	1	.014 ±.004 [1]	32	70
Chan-ya-ta	14	1	.014 ±.003	12	70
Phipps-3	245	4	.020 ±.004	57	200
Kimball	77	1	.005 ±.003	57	200
Totals	357	7	Mean .013	-	540

[1] Formula for estimated error $n(1/\sqrt{N})$ where n = pots per person per year and N= actual values (Table 15.2).

Table 15.9. Shell Tempered Vessels in Mill Creek Sites.

Time A.D.	Cahokia Phases	Mill Creek Population	Year Intervals	Vessels per Person	Total Vessels-Mill Creek Occupation Years			
					100	200	300	350
950		1,000	Initial	13	1,300	2,600	3,900	4,500
	Lohmann							
1,050		1,105	100	14	1,400	2,800	4,200	4,900
	Stirling							
1,150		1,221	200	16	1,600	3,200	4,800	5,600
	Moorehead							
1,250		1,350	300	18	1,800	3,600	5,400	6,300
	Sand Prairie							
1,300		1,419	350	18	1,800	3,600	5,400	6,300

Mean pots/year = 16
Mean total pots @ 350 years = 5,520

Table 15.10. Traded Shell in Three Mill Creek Sites.

Site	Sample			Total			Shell/Year		Shell/Person/Year	
	Marine	Anculosa	Total	Shell	Marine	Anculosa	Total	Marine	Total	Marine
Wittrock	1	0	1	500	500	0	25	25	25	.25 ±.25
Phipps-1	4	30	34	37,778	4,444	33,333	532	63	2.66	32 ±.16
Kimball	8	5	13	10,000	6,154	3,846	175	108	.88	.54 ±.19
Totals	13	35	48	48,778	11,098	37,179	732	196	1.26 (mean)	.37 (mean)

results show an average of 16 pots per year with a total between 4,800 and 5,600 vessels. These totals are the absolute minimums because it is not known how many shell tempered vessels were traded into the Dakotas after reaching the Mill Creek culture. With the population figures supplied earlier (Tables 15.6 and 15.7), only 3 to 4% of the adult Mill Creek population at any time need to have been involved in trading to account for all the shell tempered pottery in Mill Creek sites.

Similar data were prepared on traded shell objects (*Anculosa* sp. and marine shell) in three Mill Creek sites (Tables 15.10 and 15.11). These data are far less reliable because of lack of comparative ethnoarchaeological information. For this analysis it is assumed that the sole source of Mill Creek marine shell is Cahokia. This seems plausible given the evidence for Late Woodland-Mississippian-Mill Creek contacts along the Mississippi valley in eastern Iowa presented earlier and the presence of craft specialization at Cahokia (Yerkes 1989). The recent reporting of a Caddoan trade vessel from a Mill Creek ossuary, however, opens the possibility for a Central Plains route (Anderson and Tiffany 1987). Evidence for Mill Creek-

Table 15.11. Estimates of Total Traded Marine Shell.

Time A.D.	Cahokia Phases	Mill Creek Population	Year Intervals	Shell per Person Marine Shell Number	Weight (g)	Total Shell
950		1,000	Initial	392	498	1,464
	Lohmann					
1,050		1,105	100	436	553	1,627
	Stirling					
1,150		1,221	200	478	607	1,785
	Moorehead					
1,250		1,350	300	530	673	1,978
	Sand Prairie					
1,300		1,419	350	560	711	2,091

Table 15.12. Available Hides from Three Mill Creek sites.

Site Name	Minimum Number Bison	Deer	Elk	Total Estimate Bison	Deer	Elk	Hides/Year Bison	Deer	Elk
Brewster	89	40	8	3,090	1,389	278	98	44	8
Chan-ya-ta	48	13	4	2,087	565	174	181	49	15
Phipps-2	94	52	12	20,435	11,304	2,609	374	207	48
Totals	231	105	24	25,612	13,258	3,061	653	300	71

Table 15.12 Continued

Site Name	Hides/Person/Year Bison	Deer	Elk
Brewster	1.4 ± .15	.6 ± .09	.3 ± .11
Chan-ya-ta	2.6 ± .38	.7 ± .19	.2 ± .10
Phipps-2	1.9 ± .20	1.0 ± .14	.2 ± .06
Totals	1.9	.8	.2

Central Plains tradition interaction comparable to that recorded for eastern Iowa is lacking.

Regardless, the results show 1.26 shell objects per person per year entering the Mill Creek culture and .37 marine shell objects per person per year (Table 15.10). The latter is close to Drennan's Mesoamerican value of .44 shell objects per year (Drennan 1984:33-34). As a result, Drennan's low value of 1.27 g per shell object was also computed to determine the total mass of shell irrespective of the artifact (shell bead, columella pendant, etc.). The results in Table 15.11 for marine shell only show a mean total per year of 480 shell objects, a minimum of marine shell in Mill Creek sites at 168,000 objects over 350 years at a total weight of 213 kg. In total shell objects the average is 1,789 objects per year for a total of 626,000 shell objects at 795 kg over the same time period. Although this may sound like a lot of shell, the total shell figures represent only around 2.3 kg (5 lbs) per year coming into the Mill Creek culture. So again, as with the trade pottery, only a small number of adults would have to have been involved in the shell trade to account for all the shell potentially present on all Mill Creek sites. Like the trade pottery, however, these figures are conservative because it is not known how much shell was traded out of the Mill Creek culture for goods supplied to them or placed with burials and thus taken out of the archaeological recovery system.

The last set of figures deals with what would appear to be the "hidden" data, i.e., the dried meat and hides Mill Creek traders were presumably bringing to Mississippian centers like Cahokia in exchange for visible artifacts such as shell and pottery, as well as other objects, rituals, and the like which are not preserved archaeologically. Data derived from Mill Creek sites are used because, as noted earlier, bioanthropological and subsistence data are lacking from Cahokia or have undergone only preliminary analysis.

Table 15.13. Available Bison Meat from Three Mill Creek sites.

Site Name	Total Bison	Total kg (250 kg/Bison)	Total kg/year	Total kg/ Person/Year	Population Estimate	Length of Occupation
Brewster	3,090	772,500	24,140	345 ± 2	70	32
Chan-ya-ta	2,087	521,750	43,479	621 ± 6	70	12
Phipps-2	20,435	5,108,750	92,886	464 ± 3	200	55
Totals	25,612	6,403,000	160,505	477 (mean)	340	-

Table 15.14. Available Endscrapers from Five Mill Creek sites.

Site Name	Excavated Totals	Site Totals	Scrapers/Year	Scrapers/ Woman/Year	Number of Women
Brewster	125	4,340	137	9	16
Chan-ya-ta	316	5,163	449	28	16
Wittrock	29	14,500	884	32	28
Phipps-1	16	17,778	252	5	47
Kimball	33	25,385	446	10	47

Table 15.15. Minimum protein requirements.

RDA g/kg	Ave. Daily Allowance (g)	Ave. Yearly Allowance (kg)	Bison Meat Needed Yearly (kg)
.45	31	11	55
.59	40	15	75
.66	45	16	80

Table 15.16. Bison hides and meat available for trade.

Value	Total Hides Yearly	Local Use 1.5/year	Hides for Trade	Kg of Bison Meat Yearly	Local Use 80 kg Person/Year	Kg of Bison Meat for Trade
Range	1,702-2140	-	-	468,672-475,476	-	-
Estimate	1,921	1,500	421	472,074	80,000	392,074

The amounts of available hides and meat were computed from three Mill Creek sites with subsistence data (Tiffany 1982a:appendices; Dallman 1983: 114-116). These figures are based on the minimum number of animals present at each site, the percent of the site excavated, and a conservative average (male, female, and juveniles) for the bison of 250 kg of usable meat per animal (Watt and Merrill 1963:11; Dallman 1983:21; Tables 15.12 and 15.14; Wheat 1972:107-108).

Looking at bison only, large numbers result based on three Mill Creek sites. These sites are producing nearly two bison hides per year per person with 477 kg of available meat per person per year (Tables 15.12 and 15.13). The 477 kg value is consistent with Ewer's (1955:168) "conservative estimate" of 1.36 kg daily or 496 kg annually (Wheat 1972:109).

The number of endscrapers on the five Mill Creek sites supports the view that apparently numerous hides were being processed (Table 15.14). The figures in Table 15.14 are for a total population of 1,000 23.3 percent of which were adult women (Table 15.6).

Considering the range of minimum protein requirements for adults (average weight 68 kg) (Reidhead 1981:207; Minor 1983:164; National Research Council 1980:42; Table 15.15), using the highest possible estimate (80 kg per person per year), the Mill Creek culture is producing a surplus of over 392,000 kg bison meat alone each year (Table 15.16). This surplus is based on the assumption mentioned earlier, that the Mill Creek population consisted of 1,000 adults who were subsisting entirely on meat, which was not the case. These figures also take into consideration that there are only 20 kg of protein per 100 kg of bison meat (Wheat 1972:112-113; Reidhead 1980:54; Watt and Merrill 1963:11-15, beef values).

In the case of hides, assuming local use of 1.5 bison hides per year per person, the number of bison hides available for trade is 421 per year (Table 15.16). For comparison, in 1808-09 Native American tribes, principally the Sauk, Mesquakie, and Ioway, in a single season brought in over 14,000 deer hides for trade at the factory in Fort Madison, Iowa (Kurtz 1979:24). The hides were in packs weighing about 45kg (100 lbs) each (Kurtz 1979:21). It is not clear whether the packs were carried using dogs, horses, people, or a combination of all three transportation modes.

Even though there are numerous problems when comparing historical patterns with prehistoric ones in this particular regard, these numbers do indicate that the estimates used for this analysis are conservative. The Mill Creek figures and the amount of available meat are based on a Mill Creek population of 1,000. Again, both values for hides per person per year (Table 15.12) and kg per person per year (Table 15.13) indicate the data from the three Mill Creek sites are probably representative and can be used to characterize the entire culture at any one time.

Turning to the Cahokia area, assuming a population ranging between 20,000 and 50,000 people (Gregg 1975) with 6 to 10% of that population representing the elite, the total population of the upper class could range from 1,200 to 5,000 people. The 20,000 figure is within the population range based on Milner's (1986:223) most recent estimates which do not include the "downtown" Cahokia area. Using the values in Table 15.15, the yearly protein requirements of the Cahokia elite were computed (Table 15.17). These data show a range of 13,200 to 80,000 kg of protein would be needed yearly, the average being 39,200 kg. When compared against the potential kilograms of bison meat available in the Mill Creek culture, a range of 1,316 to 7,128 people could have received their minimum yearly protein needs from bison meat potentially available in the Mill Creek culture (Table 15.18). Table 15.18 also shows an absolute "bottom line" of potential kilograms based on the estimated number of traded hides (421 at 250 kg each, 105,250 kg total). As a gateway community, the Mill Creek culture could have minimally supplied all the protein for the elite; at maximum, the Mill Creek culture apparently had enough surplus bison meat to supply the protein needs for a substantial portion of the Cahokia population.

The last issue to address refocuses on the central concern of demonstrating an ethnographically derived model with archaeological evidence. The data presented all indicate that the kind of trade envisioned in the model was possible. The remaining question is one of probability in terms of how practical and feasible it would have been to move such enormous quantities of foodstuffs from northwest Iowa and the Northern Plains to Cahokia. First, the maximum of 400,000 kg of bison meat per year needed at Cahokia (80,000 kg × 5; Table 15.17) for the elite can be reduced in weight by 80% with no protein loss if dried meat was shipped (Spielmann 1982). Obviously, dried meat would be easier to move, and the technology for drying beef was in all likelihood present among prehistoric Plains Village groups. The 400,000 kg of bison meat reduces

Table 15.17. Kilograms of protein yearly for Cahokia elite.

Cahokia Elite Population	31 g Daily (11 kg Yearly)	40 g Daily (15 kg Yearly)	45 g Daily (16 kg Yearly)
1,200	13,200	18,000	19,200
2,000	22,000	30,000	32,000
3,000	33,000	45,000	48,000
5,000	55,000	75,000	80,000

Table 15.18. The number of people potentially fed by the Mill Creek culture.

Bison kg/Yr/Person	Cahokia Population Receiving Yearly Protein Requirement from Mill Creek Bison	
	105,250 kg	392,074 kg
55	1,914	7,128
75	1,403	5,228
80	1,316	4,901

to 80,000 kg (176,370 lbs or 88 tons). The mean value of 196,000 kg needed yearly at Cahokia (Table 15.17) reduces to 39,200 kg (86,421 lbs or 43 tons).

The average distance from the Mill Creek culture to Cahokia is 845 km (520 mi, a range of 490 to 550 mi), a little over three times the distance Drennan (1984:28) felt it was feasible to move food staples profitably overland in Mesoamerica. In her analysis of Southern Plains-Pueblo trade, Spielmann (1983:259) documents archaeological and ethnohistorical movement of dried meat from the Texas panhandle area into the Rio Grande pueblos, presumably by dog travois, a distance of 225 km (140 mi).

Mill Creek trade with non-Cahokian Mississippian groups, which seems probable given the information on the Hartley phase presented earlier, could have been overland or via river travel. The average distance from the Mill Creek culture to the nearest non-

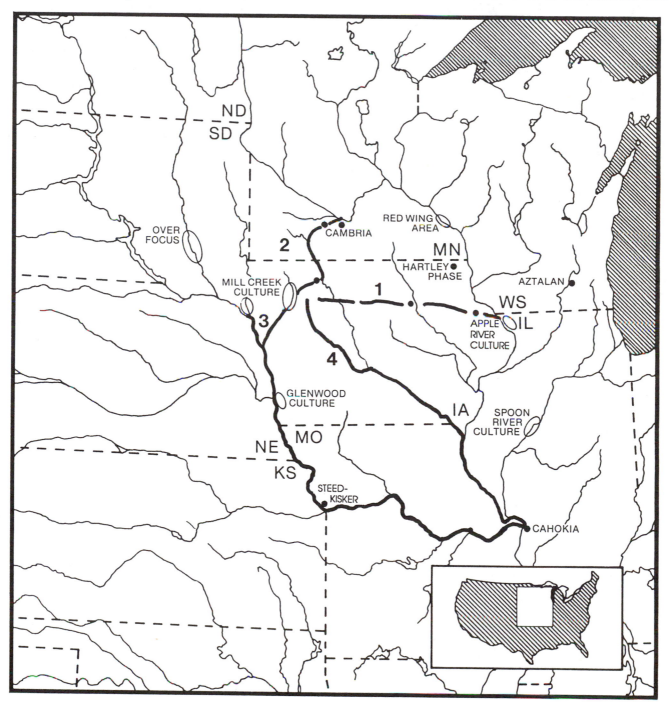

Figure 15.5. Map showing the location of archaeological manifestations and probable trade routes discussed.

Cahokian center is the 483 km (300 mi) to the Apple River culture in northwest Illinois. Mill Creek trading parties could have either traversed the prairie lakes region of north-central Iowa—tough sledding at best (Route 1, Figure 15.5)—or they could have gone north by canoe and portage to the Cambria site (Route 2) (Johnson 1986). It is certain that contact between Cambria and the Mill Creek culture occurred since Mill Creek pottery is reported from the Cambria site and vise versa (Knudson 1967:271; Ives 1962).

Although historical accounts indicate Indians and their dogs commonly carried loads ranging from 36 to 45 kg, the amount of dried meat, hides or both that could have been transported by either humans or dogs for subsistence and on-going trading would have been small (Wilson 1924:227-228; Lowie 1954:39-40; Wheat 1972:117-119). Thus, for Mill Creek traders to have supplied a critical subsistence resource in a regular exchange system, as the model proposes, the only feasible method would have been river travel. One route could have been down the Big Sioux River to the Missouri River and to Cahokia (Route 3). A check of the location of the Big Sioux phase Mill Creek sites will show they are strategically located on the Big Sioux just north of its confluence with the Missouri River. Traders on the Little Sioux had a couple of possible routes: down the Little Sioux River to the Missouri and then to Cahokia or down the Raccoon or the West Branch of the Des Moines River to the Mississippi, then to Cahokia (Route 4). Cahokia seems also to be strategically located to intercept trade either down the Mississippi or Missouri rivers.

Ray (1974) and Wood and Thiessen (1985) provide historical documentation on long-distance trade with the Mandan applicable to Mill Creek. With respect to the Assiniboine, who traded with the Mandan, Ray (1974:38-39), citing La Verendrye's 1737 account, notes that the Assiniboine usually set out for trading expeditions to the Mandan villages in the summer and stayed until fall. Unlike their trade with Europeans in which only men participated, whole Assiniboine bands including women, children, the old, and the disabled went south to the Mandan villages to trade. The Assiniboine made the trip from Portage la Prairie, Manitoba, to the Bismarck-Stanton, North Dakota area (ca. 480 km, 300 mi) in 45 days (Ray 1974:39), an average of 11 km (7 mi) a day overland. Hidatsa informants also reported that 11 km per day was an easy pace on hunting forays where dogs were utilized as pack animals (Wilson 1924:227). Ray (1974:39) notes, however, that La Verendrye claimed the Assiniboine route could be covered in 20 days. Wood and Theissen (1985:48) also provide much faster travel times for late 18th century European fur traders. Regardless, these accounts indicate that the Mill Creek people presumably could have traveled at a speed comparable with early contact Native American tribes with a broad spectrum of their population.

Little (1987) used ethnohistoric data on canoe travel times on the inland waterways of the northeastern United States to establish probable travel times for prehistoric trade centered on Cahokia. Her results show that Mill Creek traders could have made a round trip journey to Cahokia in 30 days which is well under the 118 day limit suggested by Drennan (1984) for feasible and profitable economic interaction (Little 1987:66). Other ethnohistoric accounts of long-distance trade by river travel have been reported by Wright (1967) for the Western Great Lakes region and Waselkov (1989) for the southeast. Intertribal trade among groups 804 km (500 mi) or more apart was common-place (Wright 1967:182). Furthermore, the methods of exchange and the kinds of items traded, such as foodstuff and ceramics, among these tribes parallel the Mandan system and that proposed for the Mill Creek culture (Wright 1967:185, 187). Thus, it can be argued that given the Mississippian trade objects in Initial Middle Missouri sites, long-distance trade in commodities and material goods via river travel was occurring in prehistory.

In a recent paper Brose (1986) noted that prehistoric dugout canoes in the Ohio area may have had a maximum practical load of 680 kg. He also pointed out that these boats could be unstable, especially if loaded with subsistence goods of varying specific gravities. With Mill Creek, meat and hides would more likely have been rafted as described in ethnographic and historical accounts using the equivalent of Mandan bull boats (Wilson 1924:285-286; De Voto 1947:116-117; Lowie 1954:45-46; Figure 15.6a). Bull boats were hard to navigate, but they could be built quickly and transported overland with relative ease, and they could carry large loads (Wilson 1924:285-286; Bowers 1965:40; Boller 1972:79-81). In the Fur Trade period large numbers of bull boats were amassed to move goods, and Euro-American traders used a variety of the native bull boat to transport hides and goods (De Voto 1947:116-117; Boller 1972:172; Figure 15.7). Ethnographic accounts indicate that bull boats were commonly used to move hides and dried meat; to do so, the boats were often lashed together to form large flotillas to increase their stability with heavy loads (Wilson 1924:254-255; Bowers 1965:57; Figure 15.6b). Wilson's (1924:255, 285-286; Bowers 1965:145) figures indicate Hidatsa bull boats could carry between 230 and 900 kg.

Assuming the Mill Creek traders could muster 30 bull boats, with one adult weighing 68 kg (150 lbs) in each bull boat, and each bull boat capable of carrying four adults and gear or 272 kg (600 lbs), one Mill Creek

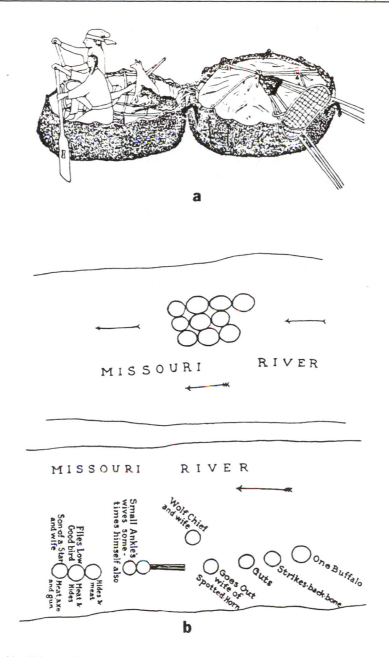

Figure 15.6. Use of bull boats by the Hidatsa, Goodbird artist. From Wilson 1924: 254, 296. (a) Goodbird's parents paddling one bull boat and towing another laden with meat and hides (note dog travois); (b) diagrams showing methods of lashing bull boats together to increase stability.

trading venture by bull boat to Cahokia could have carried as much as 6,120 kg (13,500 lbs) of dried meat. This is 16% of the mean total of 39,200 kg of dried meat and 7% of the maximum of 80,000 kg of dried meat estimated as needed annually by the Cahokia elite population. Obviously, much more meat and hides as well could have been transported if more people, larger boats, or both were used. Of equal importance is the fact that Mill Creek may have been only one source of meat for Cahokia (Goodman et al. 1984).

Summary

The model of Mill Creek-Mississippian interaction based on ethnographic accounts involves a regular, direct, and controlled trade in meat and hides for marine shell and other Mississippian objects. The model is both demonstrable based on archaeological evidence and feasible given the probable technology and means available to the Mill Creek traders. This analysis has dealt with artifacts and avoided terms

Figure 15.7. Bull boating on the Platte river, Alfred Jacob Miller artist. From De Voto 1947:Plate 22.

like "luxury" or "utilitarian" because the underlying assumption is the Mill Creek traders, like the Mandan, traded for items that met or exceeded in quantity and quality what they were bartering. These objects, by Mandan analogy, had importance within Mill Creek culture perhaps much different from Mississippian culture because of the power (medicine bundles and so forth) they could buy. In other words, the numbers of shell objects or trade vessels in Mill Creek sites may have the appearance of a historical period trinket trade. Such a viewpoint, however, represents the values modern researchers might place on these objects as well as the survivability of these items in the archaeological record, both of which are considered to be biased in this study.

Another point stressed was that Mississippians in trade centers like Cahokia may well have tried to direct the interaction between themselves and groups like the Mill Creek culture through alliance networks in order to insure a smooth flow of goods they needed. In this sense, as Porter (1973:152, 158) notes, the extent of Cahokia as a cultural center and its sphere of influence may be seen as a result of a controlled exchange system throughout the Upper Mississippi Valley. A Mississippian center the size of Cahokia needed raw materials and resources; Cahokia could not have developed without controlled exchange of the type proposed with the Mill Creek culture nor could groups like Mill Creek have developed as they did without extensive exchange with centers like Cahokia.

Further study of the proposed model can extend in several directions. The ceramics from deep midden sites like Phipps can be reanalyzed and compared with ceramics from Cahokia and the Illinois valley to measure more accurately Mississippian influences on Mill Creek sites through time. As a large base village, Phipps is ideal in this regard because the subsistence data have been analyzed and the nearby Brewster site, a probable budded village, has undergone extensive analysis, all published. Perhaps the best means of exploring the model further, however, would be to analyze a single tightly clustered community of related base and budded villages through time. The sites along Waterman Creek in the Little Sioux phase provide such an opportunity. New excavation of Mill Creek sites utilizing flotation techniques not used at Phipps could substantially add to and refine the subsistence information on the Mill Creek culture through time, a matter which is at the heart of this study.

The other side of the trading relationship could also be examined. As mentioned earlier, there is considerable new subsistence evidence which has undergone preliminary analysis only from the Cahokia site area as a result of the FAI-270 project. Analysis of fish remains and determination of the importance of beans in the Cahokia diet are important in this regard. Bioanthropological data on protein consumption by the Cahokia elite with respect to other Mississippian populations could add an independent source of verification of the model. Finally, species identification and trace element study of marine shell from Cahokia and Mill Creek sites may be useful in confirming Cahokia as a major or sole source of marine shell in Initial Middle Missouri sites. In the mean time hopefully it has been shown that hinterland areas on the periphery of Cahokia, like Mill Creek, can provide more substantive information than before believed possible about Mississippian culture history.

Acknowledgements

I would like to thank Stephen C. Lensink, William T. Billeck, James B. Griffin, Robert Burchfield, Dale R. Henning, W. Raymond Wood, John Ludwickson, an anonymous reviewer, and Duane Anderson for their timely insights and suggestions. I would also like to thank Lynda Ostedgaard for the dietary data and Eunice Prosser for typing a draft of the manuscript. Modeling Mill Creek-Mississippian Interaction is Iowa Quaternary Studies Contribution 12.

References Cited

Acsádi, G., and J. Nemeskeri
   1957 Palaodemographische Probleme am Beispiel des fruhmittelalterlichen Graberfeldes des Hamlinba-Cseres, Kom. Veszprem/Ungarn. *Homo* 8:133-147.

Alex, R. A.
   1971 Upper and Plains Mississippian. Unpublished manuscript on file in the Office of the State Archaeologist of Iowa, Iowa City.
   1973 Architectural features of houses at the Mitchell site (39DV2), eastern South Dakota. *Plains Anthropologist* 18:149-158.
   1981 The village cultures of the Lower James River valley, South Dakota. Unpublished Ph.D. dissertation, Department of Anthropology, The University of Wisconsin, Madison.

Anderson, D. C.
   1969 Mill Creek culture: a review. *Plains Anthropologist* 14:134-143.
   1973 Brewster site (13CK15); lithic analysis. *Journal of the Iowa Archeological Society* 20.
   1975 A long-nosed god mask from northwest Iowa. *American Antiquity* 40:326-329.
   1981 Mill Creek ceramics: the complex from the Brewster site. *Report* 14. Office of the State Archaeologist of Iowa, Iowa City.
   1985 Models of Mill Creek midden formation: implications for future research. *The Proceedings of the Iowa Academy of Science* 92:53-57.
   1986 The Wittrock excavations: implications for the study of culture process within the Initial variant of the Middle Missouri tradition. *North American Archaeologist* 7:3:215-241.
   1987 Toward a processual understanding of the Initial variant of the Middle Missouri tradition: the case of the Mill Creek culture of Iowa. *American Antiquity* 52:522-537.

Anderson, D. C. and J. A. Tiffany
   1987 A Caddoan trade vessel from northwestern Iowa. *Plains Anthropologist* 32:93-96.

Anderson, D. C., J. A. Tiffany, M. Fokken, and P. M. Williams
   1979 The Siouxland Sand and Gravel site (13WD402): state law protecting ancient cemeteries. *Journal of the Iowa Archeological Society* 26:119-146.

Ascher, R.
   1959 A prehistoric population estimate using midden analysis and two population models. *Southwest Journal of Anthropology* 15:168-178.

Baerreis, D. A.
   1968 Artifact descriptions: bone, stone and shell. In Climatic change and the Mill Creek culture of Iowa, edited by D. R. Henning, pp. 107-191. *Journal of the Iowa Archeological Society* 15.

Baerreis, D. A., and R. A. Alex
   1974 An interpretation of midden formation—the Mill Creek example. In Aspects of Upper Great Lakes Anthropology, edited by E. Johnson, pp. 143-148. *Minnesota Prehistoric Archaeology Series* 11. Minnesota Historical Society, St. Paul.

Bareis, C. J., and J. W. Porter
   1984 Research design. In *American Bottom Archaeology: A Summary of the FAI-270 Project Contribution to the Culture History of the Mississippi River Valley*, edited by C. J. Bareis and J. W. Porter, pp. 1-14. The University of Illinois Press, Urbana.

Blakeslee, D.
    1989 On estimating household populations in archaeological sites, with an example from the Nebraska phase. In Plains Indian Historical Demography and Health, edited by G. R. Campbell, pp.3-16. *Plains Anthropologist, Memoir* 23.
Boller, H. A.
    1972 *Among the Indians--- four years in the Upper Missouri, 1858-1862*. Edited by M. M. Quaife. Bison Book edition. University of Nebraska Press, Lincoln.
Bowers, A. W.
    1950 *Mandan Social and Ceremonial Organization.* The University of Chicago Press, Chicago.
    1965 Hidatsa social and ceremonial organization. *Bulletin* 194. Bureau of American Ethnology, Smithsonian Institution, Washington, D.C.
Brose, D.
    1986 Logs and logistics. Paper presented at the 51st annual meeting of the Society for American Archaeology, New Orleans.
Bruner, E. M.
    1961 Mandan. In *Perspectives in American Indian Culture Change*, edited by E. H. Spicer, pp. 187-277. The University of Chicago Press, Chicago.
Cobb, C. R.
    1989 An appraisal of the role of Mill Creek chert hoes in Mississippian exchange systems. *Southeastern Archaeology* 8:79-82.
Cook, S. F. and A. E. Treganza
    1950 The quantitative investigation of Indian mounds. *University of California Publications in American Archaeology and Ethnology* 40:223-262.
Dallman, J. E.
    1983 A choice of diet: response to climatic change. *Report* 16. Office of the State Archaeologist of Iowa, Iowa City.
De Voto, B.
    1947 *Across the Wide Missouri.* Reprint. Bonanza Books, New York.
Drennan, R. D.
    1984 Long-distance movement of goods in the Mesoamerican Formative and Classic. *American Antiquity* 49:27-43.
Earle, T. K., and J. E. Ericson (editors)
    1977 *Exchange Systems in Prehistory.* Academic Press, New York.
Ewers, J.
    1955 The horse in Blackfoot Indian culture. *Bulletin* 159. Bureau of American Ethnology, Smithsonian Institution, Washington, D.C.
Fowler, M. L., and R. L. Hall
    1975 Archaeological phases at Cahokia. *Bulletin* 10:1-14. Illinois Archaeological Survey, Urbana.
Fugle, E.
    1957 Introduction to the artifact assemblages of the Big Sioux and Little Sioux foci. Unpublished M.A. thesis, Department of Sociology and Anthropology, The University of Iowa, Iowa City.
    1962 Mill Creek culture and technology. *Journal of the Iowa Archeological Society* 11:4.
Gibbon, G.
    1974 A model of Mississippian development and its implications for the Red Wing area. In Aspects of Upper Great Lakes anthropology, edited by E. Johnson, pp. 129-137. *Minnesota Prehistoric Archaeology Series* 11. Minnesota Historical Society, St. Paul.
Gilbert, B. M.
    1969 Some aspects of diet and butchering techniques among prehistoric Indians in South Dakota. *Plains Anthropologist* 14:277-294.
Goodman, A. H., J. Lallo, G. J. Armelagos and J. C. Rose
    1984 Health changes at Dickson Mounds, Illinois (A. D. 950-1300). In *Paleopathology at the Origins of Agriculture*, edited by M. N. Cohen and G. J. Armelagos, pp.271-305. Academic Press, New York.
Gregg, M.
    1975 A population estimate for Cahokia. In *Perspectives in Cahokia Archaeology*, pp.126-136. Bulletin 10. Illinois Archaeological Survey, Urbana.

Griffin, J. B.

1946 Cultural change and continuity in the eastern United States. *Papers of the Robert S. Peabody Foundation for Archaeology* 3: 37-95.

1949 The Cahokia ceramic complexes. In Proceedings of the 5th Plains Conference for Archeology, pp. 44-57. *Notebook* 1. Laboratory of Anthropology, University of Nebraska, Lincoln.

1952 Culture periods in eastern United States archeology. In *Archeology of Eastern United States*, edited by James B. Griffin, pp. 352-364. University of Chicago Press, Chicago.

1960 A hypothesis for the prehistory of the Winnebago. In *Culture in History: Essays in Honor of Paul Radin*, edited by S. Diamond, pp. 809-865. Columbia University Press, New York.

1967 Eastern North American archaeology: a summary. *Science* 156:175-191.

Hassan, F. A.

1973 On mechanisms of population growth during the Neolithic. *Current Anthropology* 14:535-540.

Henning, D. R.

1967 Mississippian influences on the eastern Plains border: an evaluation. *Plains Anthropologist* 12:184-194.

1971 Origins of Mill Creek. *Journal of the Iowa Archeological Society* 18:6-13.

Henning, D. R. (editor)

1968 Climatic change and the Mill Creek culture of Iowa. *Journal of the Iowa Archeological Society* 15:parts l and 2.

Henning, D. R. (compiler)

1982 Subsurface testing program: proposed Perry Creek dam and reservoir area, Plymouth County, Iowa. *Technical Report* 82-05. Division of Archaeological Research, Department of Anthropology, University of Nebraska, Lincoln.

Ives, J. C.

1962 Mill Creek pottery. *Journal of the Iowa Archeological Society* 11.

Jablow, J.

1950 The Cheyenne in Plains Indian trade relations 1795-1840. *Monographs of the American Ethnological Society* 19.

Johnson, E.

1986 Cambria and Cahokia's northwestern periphery. Paper presented at the 51st annual meeting of the Society for American Archaeology, New Orleans.

Kelly, L. S., and P. G. Cross

1984 Zooarchaeology. In *American Bottom Archaeology: A Summary of the FAI-270 Project Contribution to the Culture History of the Mississippi River Valley*, edited by C. J. Bareis and J. W. Porter, pp. 215-232. University of Illinois Press, Urbana.

Keyes, C. R., and E. Orr

1939 Report of an archaeological survey of the Broken Kettle and Kimball prehistoric Indian refuse-mound village sites. Project 3600, Works Progress Administration. Report on file, Charles R. Keyes Collection, State Historical Society, Iowa City.

Knudson, R. A.

1967 Cambria village ceramics. *Plains Anthropologist* 12:247-299.

Kroeber, A. L.

1963 *Cultural Areas and Natural Areas of Native North America*. University of California Press, Berkeley.

Kurtz, R.

1979 Deer, fur and Indians in the midwest. Unpublished manuscript on file, Office of the State Archaeologist, Iowa City.

Lehmer, D. J.

1971 An introduction to Middle Missouri archaeology. *Anthropological Papers* 1. National Park Service, Washington, D.C.

Little, E. A.

1987 Inland waterways in the northeast. *Midcontinental Journal of Archaeology* 12:55-76.

Linton, R. (editor)

1940 *Acculturation in Seven American Indian Tribes*. Appleton-Century-Crofts, New York.

Logan, W.D.
1976 *Woodland Complexes in Northeastern Iowa*. Publications in Archaeology 15. National Park Service, Washington, D.C.

Lowie, R. H.
1954 Indians of the Plains. *Anthropological Handbook* 1. The American Museum of Natural History, New York.

McKusick, M. B.
1973 The Grant Oneota village. *Report* 4. Office of the State Archaeologist of Iowa, Iowa City.

Milner, G.R.
1986 Mississippian period population density in a segment of the central Mississippi river valley. *American Antiquity* 51:227-238.

Milner, G. R., T. E. Emerson, M. W. Mehrer, J. A. Williams, and D. Esarey
1984 Mississippian and Oneota period. In *American Bottom Archaeology: A Summary of the FAI-270 Project Contribution to the Culture History of the Mississippi River Valley*, edited by C. J. Bareis and J. W. Porter, pp. 158-186. The University of Illinois Press, Urbana.

Minor, L. J.
1983 *Nutritional Standards*. AVI Publishing Company, Westport, Connecticut.

National Research Council
1980 *Recommended Daily Allowances*. 9th Edition. National Academy of Sciences, Washington, D.C.

Orr, E.
1963 Iowa archaeology reports, 1934-1939. Ten volumes. *Archives of Archaeology*. Society for American Archaeology.

Porter, J. W.
1973 The Mitchell site and prehistoric exchange systems at Cahokia: A.D. 1000 300. *Bulletin* 7:137-164. Illinois Archaeological Survey, Urbana.

Ray, A. J.
1974 *Indians in the Fur Trade: Their Role as Trappers, Hunters, and Middlemen in the Lands Southwest of Hudson Bay*. University of Toronto Press, Toronto.

Reidhead, V. A.
1981 A linear programing model of prehistoric subsistence optimization: a southeastern Indiana example. *Prehistory Research Series* 6:1. Indiana Historical Society, Indianapolis.

Ruppé, R.
1955 Archaeological investigations of the Mill Creek culture of northwest Iowa. *Yearbook of the American Philosophical Society*, pp. 335-339.

Smith, B. D.
1978 Variation in Mississippian settlement patterns. In *Mississippian Settlement Patterns*, edited by B. Smith, pp. 479-503. Academic Press, New York.

Spicer, E. H.
1961 Types of contact and processes of change. In *Perspectives in American Indian Culture Change*, edited by E. H. Spicer, pp. 517-544. The University of Chicago Press, Chicago.

Spielmann, K. A.
1982 Inter-societal food acquisition among egalitarian societies: ecological analysis of Plains/Pueblo interaction in the American southwest. Unpublished Ph.D. dissertation, Department of Anthropology, University of Michigan.
1983 Late prehistoric exchange between the southwest and southern Plains. *Plains Anthropologist* 28:257-272.

Stoltman, J. B.
1978 Temporal models in prehistory: an example from eastern North America. *Current Anthropology* 19:703-746.

Tiffany, J. A.
1981 A compendium of radiocarbon dates for Iowa archaeological sites. *Plains Anthropologist* 26:55-73.
1982a Chan-ya-ta: a Mill Creek village. *Report* 15. Office of the State Archaeologist of Iowa, Iowa City.
1982b Hartley Fort ceramics. *Proceedings of the Iowa Academy of Science* 89:133-150.

1983 An overview of the Middle Missouri tradition. In Prairie archaeology: papers in honor of David A. Baerreis, edited by G. Gibbon. *Occasional Publications in Anthropology* 3:87-108. University of Minnesota, Minneapolis.

1986a Ceramics from the F-518 project. In Archaeological Investigations along the F-518 corridor: Phase III mitigation at 13WS61, 13WS65 and 13WS122, edited by S. C. Lensink. *Iowa Quaternary Studies Contribution* 9:227-245. Office of the State Archaeologist of Iowa, Iowa City.

1986b The Mississippian tradition and Iowa's prehistoric peoples. In *Prehistoric Mound Builders of the Mississippi Valley*, edited J. B. Stoltman, pp. 35-39. Putnam Museum, Davenport, Iowa.

1991 Models of Mississippian Culture History in the Western Prairie Peninsula: A Perspective from Iowa. In *Cahokia and the Hinterlands, Middle Mississippian Cultures of the Midwest* edited by T. E. Emerson and R. B. Lewis, pp. 183-192. University of Illinois Press, Urbana.

Vis, R. B. and D. R. Henning
1969 A local sequence for Mill Creek sites in the Little Sioux valley. *Plains Anthropologist* 14:253-271.

Waselkov, G. A.
1989 Seventeenth century trade in the colonial southeast. *Southeastern Archaeology* 8:117-133.

Watt, B. K., and A. L. Merrill
1963 Composition of foods. *Agriculture Handbook* 8. United States Department of Agriculture, Washington, D.C.

Wedel, W. R.
1979 House floors and native settlement populations in the Central Plains. *Plains Anthropologist* 24:85-98.

Weiss, K. M.
1973 Demographic models for anthropology. *Memoirs* 27. Society for American Archaeology, Washington, D.C.

Wheat, J. B.
1972 The Olsen-Chubbuck site. a Paleoindian bison kill. *Memoirs* 26. *American Antiquity* 37: Part 2. Society for American Archaeology.

Will, G. F. and H. J. Spinden
1906 The Mandans. *Papers of the Peabody Museum of American Archaeology and Ethnology* 3:80-219.

Willey, G. R., C. C. DiPeso, W. A. Ritchie, I. Rouse, J. H. Rowe, and D. W. Lathrop
1956 An archaeological classification of culture contact situations. In Seminars: in archaeology, 1955, edited by R. Wauchope, pp. 1-30. *American Antiquity, Memoirs* 11:part 2.

Wilson, G. L.
1924 The horse and dog in Hidatsa culture. *Anthropological Papers* 15:part 2:125-312. American Museum of Natural History, New York.

Wood, W. R.
1967 An interpretation of Mandan culture history. *Bulletin* 198. Bureau of American Ethnology, Smithsonian Institution, Washington, D.C.

1980 Plains trade in prehistoric and protohistoric intertribal relations. In *Anthropology on the Great Plains* edited by W. R. Wood and M. Liberty, pp.98-109. University and Nebraska Press, Lincoln.

Wood, W. R. and T. D. Thiessen
1985 *Early fur trade in the northern Plains.* University of Oklahoma Press, Norman.

Wright, G. A.
1967 Some aspects of early and mid-seventeenth century exchange methods in the Western Great Lakes. *Michigan Archaeologist* 13:181-197.

1968 A further note on trade friendship and gift giving in the western Great Lakes. *Michigan Archaeologist* 14:165-166.

Yerkes, R. W.
1989 Mississippian craft specialization in the American Bottom. *Southeastern Archaeology* 8:93-106.

PART III

Synthesis and Conclusions

Cahokia as Seen from the Peripheries

James B. Stoltman

University of Wisconsin-Madison

Cahokia, as any natural phenomenon, may be perceived from many different perspectives. It may be viewed up close, on a micro-scale, from afar, on a macro-scale, or from any intermediate position between these extremes. Each perspective has its own inherent strengths and limitations. The issue in considering the differences among the various perspectives is not one of truth and falsity, but, rather, one of reconciliation, of appreciating that each perspective can add a new dimension to our understanding of the phenomenon under investigation. Because there is a huge literature concerning the Cahokia site, i.e. viewing the site on a micro-scale (see Fowler 1989), this volume was intended as a complement to that literature by emphasizing the macro-scale. A major goal of this volume, then, is to provide a context for viewing Cahokia more effectively from afar as a participant in a larger culture-historical matrix of interacting cultures.

For analytical purposes, this larger culture-historical matrix shall be conceived as a system, that is, parts and their interrelationships (Hall and Fagen 1956), and shall be viewed at a scale that is both supra-regional and multi-cultural. The parts of this system are defined minimally as those sites that have produced Powell Plain and/or Ramey Incised ceramic types, including recognizable local imitations thereof, while the interrelationships linking the system parts are defined as the various cultural processes, for example, migration, trade, diffusion, wife exchange, etc., that produced the observed distribution of the parts.

There are a number of reasons for employing the Powell/Ramey ceramic types to define the boundaries of our analytical system. First, these distinctive types are easily and reliably identified, have a wide geographic distribution, and have been widely reported in the literature. Second, they appear to be reliable indicators of at least indirect, if not direct, contact with American Bottom culture (At the present time this is the only known region that has a local, developmental sequence from Late Woodland to Mississippian in which these types have recognizable precursors.). And, third, they are reliable horizon markers for the time interval from ca. A.D. 1000 to A.D. 1200. In thus recognizing such a system it should be explicitly understood that it is intended to serve as a convenient and simplified analytical construct, a conceptual tool with a job to do, not a replica of some past actuality. It is important to realize that, insofar as sites that interacted with the American Bottom in ways that did not involve the transmission of Ramey/Powell-like ceramics are excluded from consideration, this system is an inadequate model of American Bottom/periphery interaction. Nonetheless, there is such a diversity of sites included in the analysis that it is reasonable to assume that a consideration of them *in toto* will provide a valuable macro-scale analytical unit within which to view the Cahokia site.

In considering this system let us first turn to the archaeological evidence pertinent to the subject of inter-site *relationships* as seen from the peripheries of the American Bottom. The eleven chapters in Part II of this volume document a wide range of types of culture contact situations involving American Bottom culture and its hinterlands during the A.D. 1000-1200 period. In order to provide an overview of these data I shall follow Stoltman 1986 (with some modification) in recognizing five types of culture contact situations. As will be seen, these culture contact situations are characterized by distinctive combinations of American Bottom-like and local cultural practices and thus presumably reflect different processes of cultural interaction. These culture contact situations will provide the basis for inferring the nature of the interrelationships connecting the American Bottom to its hinterlands, which in turn will be utilized to draw some concluding inferences about Cahokia itself.

Culture Contact Situation I is recognized on the basis of the presence of a limited number of diagnostic American Bottom-derived or inspired traits within the context of an otherwise local cultural assemblage. As per our system definition above, Powell Plain and/or Ramey Incised pottery is always represented, but other traits like wall-trench houses, marine shell beads, and tri-notched projectile points might also occur. In all cases these presumably American Bottom-derived or inspired traits appear as minority items within an otherwise local assemblage, thus would normally be recognized as trait-unit intrusions in the terms of Willey et al. (1956). Examples of this culture contact situation described in this volume include Rench (McConaughy, Chapter 6), Cambria (Johnson, Chapter 14), and Mill Creek culture (Tiffany, Chapter 15). It is inferred that these sites were occupied by indigenous local peoples (i.e., no American Bottom peoples were permanently resident) who engaged in at least indirect, if not direct, exchange with the American Bottom.

Culture Contact Situation II is similar to No. I in that it is characterized by an admixture of nonlocal (i.e. American Bottom-derived or inspired) elements within a predominantly local (i.e., Late Woodland/Coles Creek) cultural context, but differs in the greater richness and completeness of the cultural inventory of Mississippian materials. This raises the possibility that a subset of the resident population could be of nonlocal, i.e., Mississippian, derivation. Three examples of this contact situation are described in this volume, the Yazoo Basin (Brain, Chapter 5), Shire (Claflin, Chapter 8) and Aztalan (Goldstein, Chapter 10). It is also possible that Rench should be considered under this contact situation instead of under No. I.

In the case of Aztalan the existence of a platform mound/plaza/specialized-mortuary precinct (in a region where no local antecedents are known) strongly suggests that a governing Mississippian elite, per-

haps of nonlocal origin, was resident at the site. By contrast, the evidence for American Bottom-derived or inspired traits in the Yazoo Basin is much more limited than at Aztalan. It consists mainly of imported ceramic vessels and/or local copies thereof. At least initially, there is no evidence of pronounced social or political transformation of the local culture. Similarly, although on a much smaller scale, the Shire site is characterized by a primarily mundane and secular context for American Bottom-related cultural materials. That a subset of the local, resident population of all of these sites was derived from the broad Cahokia world seems likely, although the alternative of intermittent culture contact, presumably for trade, that did not involve the protracted residence of nonlocal peoples cannot be totally discounted for the Yazoo Basin or Shire sites.

Culture Contact Situation III is similar to Numbers I and II in that it is characterized by the occurrence of a minority of American Bottom-derived or inspired traits within an otherwise preponderantly Late Woodland assemblage, but differs in that the Late Woodland culture involved has no known local antecedents. The best example of this contact situation is the Fred Edwards site described by Finney and Stoltman in Chapter 11. At Fred Edwards clearly nonlocal Mississippian materials occur within the context of a Late Woodland assemblage that also has no known local antecedents. We have inferred from these data that the Fred Edwards site represents a site-unit intrusion of Late Woodland peoples from northwestern Illinois or adjacent Iowa whose motivation was the direct procurement of local resources like galena and deer products for exchange in an American Bottom-centered exchange network. This contact situation is similar to No. I in that the Mississippian traits occur in low enough frequencies to suggest trait-unit intrusions, but differs in that the total site assemblage is suggestive of a site-unit intrusion. Unlike Contact Situation II, the inferred population movement involved Late Woodland, not Mississippian, peoples.

Culture Contact Situation IV differs from all the others in that it involves sites with virtually "pure" Middle Mississippian cultural assemblages that appear abruptly in regions that were formerly occupied by Late Woodland peoples. Examples of this contact situation discussed in this volume include Eveland in the Illinois Valley (Harn, Chapter 7) and Silvernale-Bryan-Energy Park (Gibbon and Dobbs, Chapter 12) and Diamond Bluff (Rodell, Chapter 13) in the Red Wing locality. Grit tempering of pottery as well as occasional other Late Woodland practices, like Effigy Mound construction at Diamond Bluff, occur in these assemblages, but always as decidedly minority elements. This suggests that the local Late Woodland traditions had been largely submerged or displaced by Middle Mississippian practices. From these data—especially the appearance of full cultural assemblages of generally non-local character in the absence of local antecedents—one could logically infer that a substantial influx of Mississippian peoples had occurred. This is certainly the view of Harn with respect to Eveland, a view shared by a number of other scholars (e.g. Conrad 1989, 1991; Emerson 1991; Griffin 1967; Wray 1952). The case for a migration-origin is as strong for the Silvernale phase as for Eveland on the grounds of the total absence of any known local antecedents. But, unlike Eveland, whose total assemblage closely resembles a potential external source area (i.e., the American Bottom), the Silvernale phase is so idiosyncratic, despite its undeniable Middle Mississippian caste, that it cannot be derived directly from any known source without some kind of intermediate, transformative steps that have yet to be documented archaeologically. In contrast to those who have taken the position that the Silvernale phase is to be attributed primarily to an influx of Middle Mississippian peoples (e.g., Griffin 1960; Emerson 1991), Gibbon and Dobbs postulate in Chapter 13 that the Silvernale phase arose as the result of the migration of a limited Middle Mississippian population segment and its subsequent interaction with an extant early Oneota population. In effect, then, they suggest that the Silvernale phase represents a case of Culture Contact Situation II as defined above, rather than Contact Situation IV. Their view rests heavily upon the fragile supposition that Oneota culture had already come into existence prior to A.D. 1000.

In contrast to the first four contact situations Culture Contact Situation V is defined on the basis of more tenuous lines of evidence for American Bottom-hinterland interaction, primarily stylistic copying of Powell/Ramey technology and iconography. In these sites true Powell Plain and Ramey Incised types are absent, but the presence of angular shoulders on some ceramic jars or of distinctive trailed scroll motifs, typically on non-Powell/Ramey or even on grit-tempered forms, reflect what can logically be interpreted as indirect cultural influences from American Bottom culture. The Cooke site, described by Markman in Chapter 9, represents the sole example of this culture contact type discussed in this volume. It seems likely that this and other Langford sites (e.g., Jeske 1990), along with such early Oneota sites as Carcajou Point (Hall 1962) and Bartron (Gibbon 1979), reflect processes of acculturation that occurred just beyond the active interface between an expanding American Bottom culture and its Late Woodland neighbors. It is also in this context that the earliest evidence of substantial maize cultivation appears in many parts of the upper Midwest, although the role of American Bottom cul-

ture in this is difficult to ascertain.

The foregoing discussion has described five kinds of culture contact situations, each of which provides the basis for inferring one or more distinctive processes of cultural interaction that linked the American Bottom to its hinterlands. Based upon this analysis, what inferences can now be drawn about Cahokia, the presumed center and primary energizing force underlying this network of inter-regional interaction?

From the perspective of the total system, Cahokia may be perceived as having had a direct or an indirect involvement in generating the observed inter-regional interaction. Direct involvement would have entailed decision making on the part of some residents of Cahokia to seek actively external resources, goods, services, or markets. Examples of such direct involvement in generating the interaction network would be the dispatching of settlers into the hinterlands to establish permanent colonies to control or engage in resource procurement, or to dispatch temporary procurement parties to known resource locations (e.g., chert outcrops or salt springs), or to dispatch traders on a regular basis into the hinterlands. On the other hand indirect involvement would entail processes that were not directly planned but which, nonetheless, had the effect of increasing cultural interaction between peoples of the American Bottom and its peripheries. Examples of such indirect involvement would be resource depletion/environmental degradation or socio-political conflict, both of which could have fostered emigration from the American Bottom. An additional form of indirect involvement would have been down-the-line exchange (Renfrew 1975) through which inter-cultural interaction could occur to the mutual benefit of all parties without any population movements, thus making centralized control difficult, if not impossible, to discern in the archaeological record.

A number of scholars have offered their views on the extent of the direct and indirect involvement of Cahokia in this interaction network based primarily upon their assessment of the nature of the Cahokia site. Those who stress the complexity of Cahokia, whether state or complex chiefdom, clearly perceive active, direct involvement on the part of the site's ruling elite in the procurement and distribution of nonlocal resources (e.g. Porter 1969; Gibbon 1974; Kelly 1991). The use of such terms as market, pochteca, extractive, and gateway center in such references unambiguously reflects the view that Cahokia was indeed an active player in the operation of this interaction network. By contrast, scholars who take a minimalist view of Cahokia's complexity in contrast to other Mississippian chiefdoms tend to perceive a more passive, indirect role for the site in the operation of the interaction network. For example, Milner (1990:27) feels that, "..it is quite unlikely. . that Cahokia was an expansionist, exploitive entity", while Emerson (1991:235) suggests that the migrants from the American Bottom were "refugees" rather than colonists, and Muller (1987:20) feels that, "Point-to-point exchange from neighbor to neighbor seems adequate to explain most, if not all, distributions of Mississippian exchange goods".

In conclusion I should like to employ the macro-scale perspective developed in this volume to focus upon the issue of Cahokia's direct versus indirect involvement in the operation of an inter-regional interaction network. If there was no direct involvement on the part of Cahokia's leadership in the procurement of non-local resources, virtually all of the archaeological evidence for cultural interaction within the network should be manifest either as down-the-line exchange or, if population movement was involved, as exchange with refugee settlements, as opposed to colonies, in the hinterlands. If the emigrants from the American Bottom were "losing or disgruntled elite groups removing themselves from the area controlled by Cahokia" (Emerson 1991:235), the persistence of close exchange relationships with the American Bottom makes no sense. From the evidence presented in this volume, it seems likely that a number of hinterland communities founded around immigrant populations—for example, Eveland, Shire, Aztalan, and Fred Edwards—are best perceived as active and willing participants in a Cahokia-centered exchange system. Considering the undeniable size and complexity of Cahokia at this time (the statehood issue aside), and the extensive amount of demonstrably exchanged goods documented archaeologically throughout the system, it is difficult to conceive of the site's elite as not being actively involved in orchestrating the procurement of these exotic resources. After all, the maintenance and validation of their exalted social positions almost certainly was heavily dependent upon their acquisition and control of the preciosities that were the symbols of their power (e.g., Perigrine 1991).

Two final points merit emphasis in the aftermath of this collection of papers. First, from a system-wide perspective, the nature of the materials exchanged should reflect profoundly upon the character of the system itself. Among the resources known to have been exchanged between Cahokia and its peripheries were the following: Powell Plain and Ramey Incised pottery, Mill Creek chert hoes, salt, galena, marine

shell beads and other items of personal adornment, copper, mica, and fireclay. Intensive studies of two of these commodities, salt and Mill Creek chert hoes, have each failed to uncover any clear-cut evidence of centralized control over their production or distribution (Muller 1984; Cobb 1989), thus calling into question the direct involvement of Cahokia's elite in the operation of an exchange system. But, if we adopt the distinction between subsistence goods and wealth proposed by Brumfiel and Earle (1987:4), it is immediately evident that salt and Mill Creek hoes must be considered the former (i.e., "food, drugs, and production-protection technology used to meet basic household needs") and not the latter (i.e., "primitive valuables used in display, ritual, and exchange"). By contrast, the remaining items on this most-exchanged list, with the possible exception of the ceramic vessels (but see Emerson 1989), are best characterized as wealth (I would also include the deer, elk, and bison products that have been postulated as exchange items by Johnson, Tiffany, and Finney and Stoltman in this volume). Under the supposition of a prestige-goods economy (Peregrine 1991), the direct involvement of a ruling elite in the procurement and distribution of such wealth items is not only expectable but probable. Accordingly, it seems eminently reasonable in light of the available system-wide evidence to postulate that Cahokia's elite during the A.D. 1000-1200 period were directly and actively involved in the procurement and distribution of wealth items, a) to validate their high status positions within Cahokia society, and b) to promote external alliances that could further enhance their positions of power (e.g., Brown et al. 1990). This observation alone certainly does not merit the elevation of Cahokia to statehood status, but it is inconsistent with the minimalist view of Cahokia as a " low-level chiefdom...at best" (Muller 1987:11).

Second, it is more than coincidence that a number of widely scattered communities that had apparently received immigrants from the broad Cahokia world during the time of the Stirling phase—for example, Shire, Aztalan, and all of the major Silvernale sites—were abandoned before the end of the Moorehead phase, i.e. during the period of Cahokia's decline. The synchroneity of the decline of Cahokia and the disappearance of a number of sites with which it was connected argues in support of the colonist/trader theory of settlement for portions of Cahokia's hinterlands rather than for the refuge theory.

References Cited

Brown, James A., Richard A. Kerber, and Howard D. Winters
  1990 Trade and the Evolution of Exchange Relations at the Beginning of the Mississippian Period. In *The Mississippian Emergence*, edited by Bruce D. Smith, pp. 251-280. Smithsonian Institution Press, Washington.

Brumfiel, Elizabeth M. and Timothy K. Earle
  1987 Specialization, Exchange, and Complex Societies: An Introduction. In *Specialization, Exchange, and Complex Societies*, edited by Elizabeth M. Brumfiel and Timothy K. Earle, pp. 1-9. Cambridge University Press, Cambridge.

Cobb, Charles R.
  1989 An Appraisal of the Role of Mill Creek Chert Hoes in Mississippian Exchange Systems. *Southeastern Archaeology* 8:79-92.

Conrad, Lawrence
  1989 The Southeastern Ceremonial Complex on the Northern Middle Mississippian Frontier: Late Prehistoric Politico-religious Systems in the Central Illinois River Valley. In *The Southeastern Ceremonial Complex: Artifacts and Analysis*, edited by Patricia Galloway, pp. 93-113. University of Nebraska Press, Lincoln.
  1991 The Middle Mississippian Cultures of the Central Illinois Valley. In *Cahokia and the Hinterlands: Middle Mississippian Cultures of the Midwest*, edited by Thomas E. Emerson and R. Barry Lewis, pp. 119-156. University of Illinois Press, Urbana.

Emerson, Thomas E.
  1989 Water, Serpents, and the Underworld: An Exploration into Cahokian Symbolism. In *The Southeastern Ceremonial Complex: Artifacts and Analysis*, edited by Patricia Galloway, pp. 45-92. University of Nebraska Press, Lincoln.
  1991 Some Perspectives on Cahokia and the Northern Mississippi Expansion. In *Cahokia and the Hinterlands: Middle Mississippian Cultures of the Midwest*, edited by Thomas E. Emerson and R. Barry Lewis, pp. 221-236. University of Illinois Press, Urbana.

Fowler, Melvin L.
  1989 The Cahokia Atlas, A Historical Atlas of Cahokia Archaeology. *Studies in Illinois Archaeology* 6. Illinois Historic Preservation Agency, Springfield.

Gibbon, Guy E.
  1974 A Model of Mississippian Development and Its Implications for the Red Wing Area. In Aspects of Upper Great Lakes Anthropology, edited by Elden Johnson, pp. 129-137. *Minnesota Prehistoric Archaeology Series* 11. Minnesota Historical Society, St. Paul.
  1979 The Mississipian Occupation of the Red Wing Area. *Minnesota Prehistoric Archaeology Series* 13. Minnesota Historical Society, St. Paul.

Griffin, James B.
  1960 A Hypothesis for the Prehistory of the Winnebago. In *Culture in History: Essays in Honor of Paul Radin*, edited by Stanley Diamond, pp. 809-865. Columbia University Press, New York.
  1967 Eastern North American Archaeology: A Summary. *Science* 156:175-191.

Hall, A. D. and R. E. Fagen
  1956 Definition of System. *General Systems* 1:18-29.

Hall, Robert L.
  1962 *The Archaeology of Carcajou Point*. 2 vols. University of Wisconsin Press, Madison.

Jeske, Robert J.
  1990 Langford Tradition Subsistence, Settlement, and Technology. *Midcontinental Journal of Archaeology* 15:221-249.

Kelly, John E.
  1991 Cahokia and Its Role as a Gateway Center in Interregional Exchange. In *Cahokia and the Hinterlands: Middle Mississippian Cultures of the Midwest*, edited by Thomas E. Emerson and R. Barry Lewis, pp. 61-80. University of Illinois Press, Urbana.

Milner, George R.
   1990 The Late Prehistoric Cahokia Cultural System of the Mississippi River Valley: Foundations, Florescence, and Fragmentation. *Journal of World Prehistory* 4:1-43.
Muller, Jon
   1984 Mississippian Specialization and Salt. *American Antiquity* 49:489-507.
   1987 Salt, Chert, and Shell: Mississippian Exchange and Economy. In *Specialization, Exchange, and Complex Societies*, edited by Elizabeth M. Brumfiel and Timothy K. Earle, pp. 10-21. Cambridge University Press, Cambridge.
Peregrine, Peter
   1991 Prehistoric Chiefdoms on the American Midcontinent: A World-System Based on Prestige Goods. In *Core/Periphery Relations in Precapitalist Worlds*, edited by Christopher Chase-Dunn and Thomas D. Hall, pp. 193-211. Westview Press, Boulder.
Porter, James W.
   1969 The Mitchell Site and Prehistoric Exchange Systems at Cahokia: A.D. 1000±300. In Explorations intor Cahokia Archaeology, edited Melvin L. Fowler, pp. 137-164. *Illinois Archaeological Survey Bulletin 7.*
Renfrew, Colin
   1975 Trade as Action at a Distance: Questions of Integration and Communication. In *Ancient Civilation and Trade*, edited by Jeremy A. Sabloff and C. C. Lamberg-Karlovsky, pp. 3-59. University of New Mexico Press, Albuquerque.
Stoltman, James B.
   1986 The Appearance of the Mississippian Cultural Tradition in the Upper Mississippi Valley. In *Prehistoric Mound Builders of the Mississippi Valley*, edited by James B. Stoltman, pp. 26-34. The Putnam Museum, Davenport.
Willey, Gordon R., Charles C. Di Peso, William Ritchie, Irving Rouse, John H. Rowe, and Donald W. Lathrap
   1956 An Archaeological Classification of Culture Contact Situations. In Seminars in Archaeology: 1955, edited by Robert Wauchope, pp. 1-30. *Memoirs fo the Society for American Archaeology* 11. Salt Lake City.
Wray, Donald E.
   1952 Archeology of the Illinois Valley: 1950. In *Archeology of Eastern United States*, edited by James B. Griffin, pp. 152-164. University of Chicago Press, Chicago.